AF765256

Routledge Handbook of Cultural and Creative Industries in Asia

Recent years have witnessed the remarkable development of the cultural and creative industries (CCIs) in Asia, from the global popularity of the Japanese games and anime industries, to Korea's film and pop music successes. While CCIs in these Asian cultural powerhouses aspire to become key players in the global cultural economy, Southeast Asian countries such as Malaysia and Thailand are eager to make a strong mark in the region's cultural landscape.

As the first handbook on CCIs in Asia, this book provides readers with a contextualized understanding of the conditions and operation of Asian CCIs. Both internationalizing and de-Westernizing our knowledge of CCIs, it offers a comprehensive contribution to the field from academics, practitioners, and activists alike. Covering 12 different societies in Asia from Japan and China to Thailand, Indonesia, and India, the themes include:

- State policy in shaping CCIs
- Cultural production inside and outside of institutional frameworks
- Circulation of CCI products and consumer culture
- Cultural activism and independent culture
- Cultural heritage as an industry.

Presenting a detailed set of case studies, this book will be an essential companion for researchers and students in the field of cultural policy, cultural and creative industries, media and cultural studies, and Asian studies in general.

Lorraine Lim was Lecturer in Arts Management at Birkbeck, University of London, UK. She co-edited *Cultural Policies in East Asia* (2014) and co-wrote a report for UNESCO on the impact of digitalization on culture in East Asia (2015).

Hye-Kyung Lee is Senior Lecturer at the Department of Culture, Media and Creative Industries at King's College London, UK. Her recent publications include *Cultural Policy in South Korea* (2018) and *Asian Cultural Flows* (2018).

Routledge Handbook of Cultural and Creative Industries in Asia

Edited by
Lorraine Lim and
Hye-Kyung Lee

Routledge
Taylor & Francis Group
LONDON AND NEW YORK

First published 2019
by Routledge

2 Park Square, Milton Park, Abingdon, Oxfordshire OX14 4RN
52 Vanderbilt Avenue, New York, NY 10017

Routledge is an imprint of the Taylor & Francis Group, an informa business

First issued in paperback 2020

Copyright © 2019 selection and editorial matter, Lorraine Lim and Hye-Kyung Lee; individual chapters, the contributors

The right of Lorraine Lim and Hye-Kyung Lee to be identified as the authors of the editorial material, and of the authors for their individual chapters, has been asserted in accordance with sections 77 and 78 of the Copyright, Designs and Patents Act 1988.

All rights reserved. No part of this book may be reprinted or reproduced or utilised in any form or by any electronic, mechanical, or other means, now known or hereafter invented, including photocopying and recording, or in any information storage or retrieval system, without permission in writing from the publishers.

Notice:
Product or corporate names may be trademarks or registered trademarks, and are used only for identification and explanation without intent to infringe.

British Library Cataloguing-in-Publication Data
A catalogue record for this book is available from the British Library

Library of Congress Cataloging-in-Publication Data
Names: Lim, Lorraine, 1980- editor. | Lee, Hye-Kyung, 1968- editor.
Title: Routledge handbook of cultural and creative in Asia /
edited by Lorraine Lim and Hye-Kyung Lee.
Description: New York : Routledge, 2019. | Includes bibliographical references and index.
Identifiers: LCCN 2018034978 | ISBN 9781138959927 (hardback) |
ISBN 9781315660509 (ebook) | ISBN 9781317337270 (epub) |
ISBN 9781317337263 (mobipocket encrypted)
Subjects: LCSH: Cultural industries—Asia.
Classification: LCC HD9999.C9473 A837 2019 | DDC 338.4095—dc23
LC record available at https://lccn.loc.gov/2018034978

ISBN: 978-1-138-95992-7 (hbk)
ISBN: 978-0-367-65965-3 (pbk)

Typeset in Bembo
by codeMantra

Contents

List of figures and tables

Figures

Tables

Preface

This book project was conceived by the late Lorraine Lim. Although both of us were interested in putting together a book on Asian cultural industries and policy, it was Lorraine who had the courage to transform such an idea into a concrete project and invited me as second editor. From drafting a book proposal, contacting authors to commissioning chapters, she worked hard with her usual acumen, efficiency, and cheerful attitude. Even during the difficult period when she was undergoing cancer treatments, she was reviewing chapters, insisting that spending some time on research would help her recovery. Sadly, she passed away in September 2017 at the age of only 37. It was early December 2017 when I resumed the project, asking all authors to send me their latest version of the chapters. This was followed by an intense process of review and revision as well as commissioning two new chapters. All authors were helpful and responsive and some of them even offered me editorial help. I appreciate not only their contributions but also their kind words and support. Georgina Bishop at Routledge has provided me with a lot of understanding throughout the process. Simone Wesner deserves special thanks for her friendship and encouragement, which I relied upon greatly. I am also grateful for Nobuko Kawashima's generous support and advice.

This handbook is dedicated to Lorraine Lim, who was a pioneer of research in Asian cultural policy and industries, and an inspiring person who was full of warmth, passion, and creative ideas.

Hye-Kyung Lee

Contributors

Chairin An is Assistant Professor of the Department of Cultural Content at Kyungnam University, South Korea. Her research interests are in creative labor, the cultural/creative production process, and organizational strategies for creative workers. She earned her PhD (in Creative Industries) from the University of Warwick. She is a former television program producer (YTN Media, Seoul) and she recently published *Creative Labour* (Communication Books) in Korean.

Sowparnika Balaswaminathan is a PhD candidate at the Department of Anthropology in the University of California, San Diego. She works with the sculptor community in Swamimalai, Tamilnadu that specializes in casting bronze sculptures that have religious, artistic, and archaeological values with grant support from several institutions including the India Foundation of Arts (with support from Bajaj Company). Sowparnika's research interests include museums, art and craft policy, religion, and political economy.

Thomas Barker is currently Associate Professor and Head of Film and Television at the University of Nottingham Malaysia. He has been a visiting scholar at the School of Theater, Film and Television at UCLA, Communications Study Centre at Universitas Indonesia, and at the College of Communication, National Chengchi University. He has published in *Asian Cinema*, *Cinema Poetica*, *TRANS*, and *The Jakarta Post*. His monograph *Going Mainstream: Indonesian Cinema after the New Order* is forthcoming.

Caroline Chapain is Lecturer in the Department of Management at the University of Birmingham, UK. She has been doing research and teaching at the University of Birmingham since 2005. Previously, she studied and worked in Canada for ten years. In particular, she worked for the Montreal Metropolitan Planning Organization from 2002 to 2005. She has expertise in local and regional economic development, particularly around the area of creative industries, creative and digital cities, economic restructuring and plant closures, transport planning, and public policies. In the last 12 years, she has been contributing to and leading on a variety of research projects on these topics for institutions such as Birmingham City Council, West Midlands in Europe, WSP, the UK Department for Transport, the UK national agency for innovation (NESTA), the Audit Commission, the British Council, the Economic Social Research Council, the Arts and Humanities Research council, and the European Commission.

Hsiao-Ling Chung is currently Associate Professor with the postgraduate Institute of Creative Industries Design, National Cheng Kung University, Taiwan. Dr. Chung completed her MA and PhD at Warwick University, UK, and her primary research interests lie in creating the critical dialogues between cultural creative industries policies, the cross-industry networking practices of creative talent, and CCIs' regional development in the contexts of cities and in Asia. Her recent works are published in the *International Journal of Cultural Policy*, *International Journal of Cultural and Creative Industries*, and *Cultural Policies in East Asia: Dynamics between the State, Arts and Creative Industries.*

Roberta Comunian is Reader in Creative Economy at the Department of Culture, Media and Creative Industries at King's College London, UK. She has recently researched the role of higher education in the creative economy and the career opportunities and patterns of creative graduates.

Dina Dellyana is a lecturer at the School of Business and Management, Institut Teknologi Bandung, Indonesia (SBM ITB). She studied Pharmacy at Padjadjaran University, took a Masters of Business Administration at Bandung Institute of Technology, and a doctoral degree in Science and Management (DSM-ITB). She enjoys participating in creative industries collaborative projects. Dina's research interests include business model innovation, SME development, business incubation and social media, and e-commerce for SMEs.

Catherine Earl, PhD, is a social anthropologist and policy analyst. Her research focuses on transformations of work and welfare, mobilities, and gender and social change. She has carried out ethnographic fieldwork in Ho Chi Minh City and the Mekong Delta since 2000. Her books include *Vietnam's New Middle Classes: Gender, Career, City* (2014) and *Mythbusting Vietnam: Facts, Fictions, Fantasies* (2018). Currently she is exploring mega-urban sociality, (in) civility and (im)mobility in public spaces on the Saigon Bus mass transit network.

Silvia Fok teaches at the General Education Centre, the Hong Kong Polytechnic University. She is the author of *Life and Death: Art and the Body in Contemporary China* (Bristol, 2013), *Performance Art in China: Site and the Body* (Taipei, 2010, in Chinese), and *The Stars Artists: Pioneers of Contemporary Chinese Art 1979–2000* (Taipei, 2007, in Chinese).

Xin Gu is a lecturer in the School of Media, Film and Journalism at Monash University, Australia. Xin has been prominent in the attempt to contextualize contemporary Western debates around cultural economy, creative cities, and cultural policy in the Chinese context. She is currently contracted by Routledge for a joint authored book, *Culture and Economy in the New Shanghai.*

Ruth Y. Y. Hung is Associate Professor of Comparative Literature in the English Department at Hong Kong Baptist University and Advisory Editor for *boundary 2: an international journal of literature and culture*, published by Duke University Press. Her research interests lie in the area of historical humanism, ranging from works to criticism to new and emerging forms of human sciences. Dr. Hung has lectured and published on modern and contemporary literatures and cultures. Her latest essays have appeared in *boundary 2, International Journal of Cultural Policy, Canadian Review of Comparative Literature,* and *Literature Compass.*

Kristina Karvelyte is Assistant Professor in the Department of Urban Planning and Disaster Management at Ming Chuan University, Taiwan. She holds a PhD from the School of Media and Communication, University of Leeds. Her research interests revolve around

Chinese cities, cultural policies in East Asia, culture-led urban development, large-scale cultural events, and cultural policy mobility/mutation. Kristina's current research is focused on examining the development and transformation of Taipei's cultural policy agenda.

Nobuko Kawashima is Professor at the Faculty of Economics, Doshisha University in Kyoto, Japan. Her research interests include cultural policy, cultural economics, and the creative/cultural industries. She is currently examining the Japanese government's policy of promoting Japanese popular culture abroad.

Yeran Kim is Professor in the School of Communications, Kwangwoon University, Seoul, South Korea. She has extensively published a number of papers and books, including 'Idol republic: global emergence of girl industries and commercialization of girl bodies', and *Faces of Word* and *Mobile, Girl@Digital Asia* (co-authored). Her current research focuses on the cultural intersection of affect, communication, and society in the contemporary social media ecology.

Novi Kurnia is a lecturer and researcher at the Department of Communication Science at Universitas Gadjah Mada, Indonesia. Kurnia finished her PhD study at Flinders University, South Australia, in 2014. Her thesis was about women film directors and their films in post-New Order Indonesia. Kurnia is also the founder and chair-person of IF!fest (Indonesian Film Festival) which was held in Adelaide in 2006, 2008, and 2009. She is also the organizer as well as jury member for several film festivals in her hometown, Yogyakarta. Her main interest is film, media, gender, and cultural studies. Her works have been published in national and international journals and books.

Hye-Kyung Lee is Senior Lecturer at the Department of Culture, Media and Creative Industries, King's College London, UK. Her publications include *Cultural Policies in East Asia* (2014), 'The challenges and opportunities for the diversity of cultural expressions in the digital era in East Asia' (UNESCO Bangkok Office 2015), *Cultural Policy in South Korea: Making a New Patron State* (Routledge 2018) and *Asian Cultural Flows: Cultural Policy, Creative Industries and Media Consumers* (2018).

Lee Yuen Beng is currently Chairperson of Postgraduate Studies and Senior Lecturer in the School of Communication, Universiti Sains Malaysia. He has published on Yasmin Ahmad and P. Ramlee as well as on gender, ethnicity, and horror in cinema, media studies, and creative industries in the *Asian Journal of Communication*, *Kajian Malaysia*, and the *Pertanika Journal of Social Sciences & Humanities*. He is also co-editor of the book *Media and Elections: Democratic Transition in Malaysia*. Lee is working on archiving dying trades in Malaysia through a series of short documentaries called *Adrian Lee's Reel Heritage Series*.

Thomas Evan Levy is Distinguished Professor of Anthropology and is the inaugural holder of the Norma Kershaw Chair in the Archaeology of Ancient Israel and Neighboring Lands at the University of California, San Diego, USA. A fellow of the American Academy of Arts and Sciences, Levy is a Levantine field archaeologist with interests in the role of technology, especially early mining and metallurgy, on social evolution from the beginnings of sedentism and the domestication of plants and animals in the Neolithic period to medieval Islamic times. Most of his fieldwork takes place in southern Jordan. Levy directs the cyber-archaeology laboratory at the Qualcomm Institute –California Institute of Telecommunications and Information Technology (Calit2) and Levantine Archaeology Laboratory on the main campus. Tom also conducts ethnoarchaeological research in India. Levy, his wife Alina Levy, and the Sthapathy traditional craftsmen from the village of Swamimalai co-authored the book *Masters of Fire – Hereditary Bronze Casters of South India* (Bochum: German Mining Museum 2008).

Pei-Ling Liao was the research fellow for the AHRC-funded creative cluster project Bristol and Bath by Design, at the University of the West of England, Bristol, UK. Her interests are cultural and creative clusters, cluster policy, and the cultural and creative industries value chain. She received her BS from Chinese Culture University (Taiwan) and her MURP from National Taipei University (Taiwan) before eventually studying for her doctorate at the University of Birmingham in 2007. In addition to her working experience, Dr. Liao was a town planner in both national and local government in Taiwan and an enthusiastic cultural and creative spatial study fan. She can be contacted at liaokatty@gmail.com.

Bjarke Liboriussen (PhD) is Assistant Professor in Digital and Creative Media at the University of Nottingham Ningbo China. His research follows two main strands: video games (including online gaming cultures and mobile gaming in China) and the creative industries (with special attention to the relationship between technology and creativity). His research has been published in journals such as *Convergence*, *Game Studies*, and *Games and Culture*.

Liew Kai Khiun is Assistant Professor at the Wee Kim Wee School of Communication and Information at the Nanyang Technological University, Singapore. His research covers the transnational circulation of popular culture and media between East and Southeast Asia as well as media cultures and heritage studies in Singapore. His works includes a monograph *Transnational Popular Culture and Memory in East and Southeast Asia* (2016). Kai Khiun teaches courses relating to media and communications, film and popular culture in the context of the Asia-Pacific region.

Lorraine Lim was Lecturer in Arts Management, Birkbeck, University of London, UK. Her research interests included creative cities, arts policy, creative industries, and cultural work. She edited a special issue on cultural policy in Asia for the *International Journal of Cultural Policy* (2012), co-edited *Cultural Policies in East Asia* (2014), and co-wrote a report for UNESCO on the impact of digitalization on culture in East Asia (2015). She passed away due to complications from cancer in September 2017.

Joaquin Lopez-Mugica is a lecturer of Spanish language and culture, and currently is Head of the Spanish Department at the University of Nottingham's China campus. He has recently completed his PhD thesis, which focuses on the intersections between representations of contemporary art and the modern Chinese city. He is a member of the Institute of Asia and Pacific Studies (IAPS) at the University of Nottingham China.

Chi Thong Ma is the national economics correspondent for the state broadcaster HTV in Ho Chi Minh City, Vietnam. He holds a Masters of Communication from RMIT University in Melbourne. He completed the Talkshow production short course conducted by Griffith Film School, TV News Production, and short courses on building the structure of news programs at Kantana Training Center, Thailand. He was the host and producer of *Guest of HTV* talk show, broadcast on HTV in 2011–12.

Maria Sharon Mapa Arriola has a Bachelor of Fine Arts degree from the University of the Philippines–Diliman and earned her Master of Arts in Art Theory and Criticism at the same university. Currently, she is a PhD candidate in the Philippine Studies Program at the Asian Center, University of the Philippines Diliman. Sharon has been in tertiary education for over 20 years. At present, she is Associate Dean of the School of Design and Arts–New Media Cluster of De La Salle-College of Saint Benilde.

Salfitrie Roos Maryunani is currently working towards her doctoral degree at Goldsmiths, University of London, UK. She obtained her MBA from the School of Business and Management (SBM), Bandung Institute of Technology (ITB), and a bachelors degree in Architecture Engineering from the National Institute of Technology (ITENAS), Bandung. As research interests go, she is primarily interested in the field of creative industries, particularly the development of creative cities and urban regeneration.

Christian Morgner is Lecturer in Communication and Culture at the University of Leicester, UK. His expertise spans the fields of urban studies, public and cultural policies, globalization studies, and creative industries. More recently he has published articles on art and urban space in Latin America, cultural policies, the global art world, and social theory. He has previously held positions and visiting fellowships at the University of Cambridge, Yale University, Hitotsubashi University (Tokyo) and the École des hautes études en sciences sociales (Paris). Currently, he works on projects about the creative industries in Tokyo, global cultural trends, and global cultural cities.

Justin O'Connor is Professor of Communications and Cultural Economy at Monash University, Australia, where he heads the research unit Culture Media Economy and is program leader for the Master of Cultural and Creative Industries. He is also Visiting Professor in the School of Media and Design, Shanghai Jiaotong University. He is part of the UNESCO 'Expert Facility', supporting the 2005 Convention on the Protection and Promotion of the Diversity of Cultural Expression, and a board member of Renew Australia. He has led several funded research projects in cultural policy and creative cities in Australia and China. He works closely with international and national cultural policy makers, and has published numerous writings on cultural economy, cultural policy, and creative urban policy in China.

Can-Seng Ooi is a sociologist and professor at the University of Tasmania, Australia. His research on Singapore's creative economy spans over two decades, with comparisons made to countries such as Denmark and China. Besides cultural policy and development, his creative industries research includes cultural tourism, heritage and nation building, and place branding.

Nissim Otmazgin is Director of the Institute for Asian and African Studies at The Hebrew University of Jerusalem, Israel and Research Affiliate at the Truman Research Institute for the Advancement of Peace. He is the author of *Regionalizing Culture: The Political Economy of Japanese Popular Culture in Asia* (2013) and (together with Michal Daliot-Bul) of *The Rise of the Anime Boom in the United States: Lessons for Global Creative Industries* (2017). His articles have appeared in *International Relations of the Asia Pacific, Pacific Affairs, Cross-Currents, Inter-Asia Cultural Studies, Contemporary Southeast Asia, Asia-Pacific Review, Media, Culture & Society, Journal of Comparative Policy Analysis, Asia-Pacific Journal: Japan Focus*, and *Contemporary Japan*.

Alongkorn Parivudhiphongs (PhD), aka AL, is a lecturer and researcher at the Department of Journalism and Informatics, Faculty of Communication Arts at Chulalongkorn University in Thailand. His research interests include journalism studies, infotainment, creative industries and digital economy, arts and cultural criticism. He is currently Assistant to the President of the university, responsible for social outreach and global engagement (2016–2020).

Phloeun Prim is Executive Director of Cambodian Living Arts (CLA). Phloeun was born in Cambodia during the genocide and raised in Canada. After returning to Cambodia he became part of the movement to use the arts for healing, social transformation, and economic development, first through a ten-year career at Artisans d'Angkor and more recently at CLA. While at CLA, he has overseen various strategic global programs, including Season of Cambodia festival in NYC in 2013, and more recently the development of the Arts for Transformation seminar course in partnership with NYU Abu Dhabi.

Frances Rudgard is Program Director of Cambodian Living Arts. Frances is originally from the UK and has been working in Cambodia since 2010. Having supported CLA through development and implementation of two strategic plans, Frances' main focus is now on developing regional networks and partnerships as CLA expands its activities within Asia.

Sonny Rustiadi is a member lecturer of the group Entrepreneurship and Technology Management Expertise at the School of Business and Management Institut Teknologi Bandung, Indonesia (SBM-ITB). He finished the doctoral program at Goldsmiths, University of London, UK, earned an MBA from SBM-ITB, Indonesia, and graduated from the Faculty of Economics, majoring in Accounting, at Parahyangan Catholic University, Indonesia. His research interests include entrepreneurship, creative industries, and business financing. Prior to joining SBM-ITB, Sonny worked in various companies including Arthur Andersen, PT. Belaputera Intiland, KPMG, and USAID. As a serial entrepreneur himself, Sonny has experience in various businesses including property management, retail telecommunication, fashion, education services, travel services, and interior design services.

D. A. E. Savitri Sastrawan, a Balinese nomad, is an arts and language freelancer. Her research interest is to explore the interdisciplinary possibilities in the arts and languages within global society and culture. This includes recollection of narrations in history, geography, and visual culture that existed within/about Bali and Indonesia.

Viriya Sawangchot is a cultural researcher based in Bangkok. In the 1990s, he was involved in music magazine and independent record label. He has taught in the cultural studies program at the Research Institute for Languages and Cultures of Asia in Mahidol University, Thailand, since 2009. He was an API fellow (2013–14) in the Asian Intellectual Program, Nippon Foundation, and conducted field research on creative cultural spaces in Osaka, Japan and Bandung, Indonesia. Currently, he runs an alternative cultural space called Non-Place in Nonthaburi, a suburb of Bangkok.

Aegyung Shim researches transnational aspects of South Korea's film, media, and entertainment industries. She is the co-author of *Korea's Occupied Cinemas, 1893–1948* (Routledge, 2011) and *The Changing Face of Korean Cinema, 1960–2015* (Routledge, 2016) — both with

Brian Yecies. She is also a past Korea Foundation Research Fellow and visiting scholar in the Institute for Social Transformation Research (ISTR) at the University of Wollongong, Australia.

Q. S. Tong is Professor of English at Sun Yat-sen University, China. He has published on issues of critical significance in comparative literary studies, with special attention to the historical interactions between China and the West. His current work focuses on the Chinese language reform movement in the early twentieth century and its social and political consequences. He is an editorial member of *boundary 2: an international journal of literature and culture* and *Journal of Asian Pacific Communication*.

Jason Vitorillo is Lecturer-in-Charge of the BA (Hons) Arts Management Program of LASALLE College of the Arts, Singapore. He holds an MA in Arts Administration from Teachers College, Columbia University, New York, USA. He was a recipient of the International Fellowships Program of the Ford Foundation in 2009.

Ken Wang (PhD) graduated from the Media, Communication and Sociology Department, University of Leicester, UK, in 2017. His research focuses on the local politics of creative industries policies in China and aims to advance the understanding of the development of Chinese creative industries policies through an analysis of municipal creative industries policies from different regions.

Andrew White is Professor of Creative Industries and Digital Media, and currently the Head of the School of International Communications, at the University of Nottingham's China campus. He is also Director of the AHRC Centre for Digital Copyright and IP Research in China. He has published his research in the form of journal articles, book chapters, newspaper articles, and a monograph with Palgrave Macmillan entitled *Digital Media and Society*; a Portuguese translation of this book, *Midia Digital e Sociedade*, was published in 2016.

Brian Yecies is Senior Lecturer in Communication and Media at the University of Wollongong, Australia, and a chief investigator on the Australian Research Council Discovery Projects: 'Mobile Webtoons: Creative Innovation in a New Digital Economy' (2018–20), and 'Digital China: from Cultural Presence to Innovative Nation' (2017–19). He and Aegyung Shim are the co-authors of *Korea's Occupied Cinemas, 1893–1948* (Routledge, 2011), *The Changing Face of Korean Cinema, 1960–2015* (Routledge, 2016), and *South Korea's Immersive Webtooniverse and the New Media Revolution* (forthcoming).

Yao Yiming was a student with the Masters in Mass Communication at the Wee Kim Wee School of Communication and Information at the Nanyang Technological University, Singapore. Her chapter is based partly on her course project on television cultures in Asia.

Introduction

Understanding of the cultural and creative industries in Asia

Hye-Kyung Lee

Why cultural and creative industries in Asia?

This handbook intends to provide readers with contextualized understanding of cultural and creative industries in Asia and present a groundwork that will serve as a key reference point for further scholarship in this area. It covers 12 different societies in Asia from Japan to India, whose political and economic circumstance vary: from mature democracies to a one-party regime and from highly advanced economies to those on a road to economic development. Yet, all of them are excellent sites where we can observe on-going, multivalent dynamics of the operation of cultural and creative industries and their development.

Authors of this book use 'cultural and creative industries' as a broad descriptive term to refer to cultural industries, arts, media, and heritage. 'Creative industries' is a globally popular but highly contested notion that entails notable commercial and economic imperatives. It is due to such imperatives that the notion aptly captures Asian societies' increasing stake in the culture–economy nexus and the emergence of a new generation of cultural policies that take cultural production, dissemination, and export as part of national economic strategy. Yet, the adjective 'cultural' is crucial: despite the argument that the above industries are now defined by their input (creativity), what truly distinguishes them from other industries and makes them socially significant is 'culture' as their distinct output. Hence, this book has chosen to adopt the term 'cultural and creative industries' (CCIs) and use it interchangeably with 'cultural industries' and 'creative industries'. After all, different Asian societies conceptualize cultural industries, arts, media, and heritage differently depending on the interplay between the local tradition of discoursing *culture*, the government's aspiration to develop new economy, and the influence of the 'creative industries' idea.

The CCIs in Asia have rapidly grown during the past two decades, and this is greatly attributable to the rising economic power of the region.[1] The success stories of Japanese games and anime industries, South Korea's film and pop music industries, and the Chinese TV and new media industries are no longer new. Meanwhile, Southeast Asian countries such as Indonesia, Malaysia, and Thailand are eager to make a stronger mark in the region's cultural landscape, perceiving the CCIs as a strategic sector where a significant economic leap may occur. Here, the increase in the region's cultural production capacity is worth noting.

For instance, feature film production in India (1,724 films), China (638), Japan (591), and South Korea (207) as of 2015 is comparable to that of the United States (738) and France (270) (UNESCO 2016: 9). The strengthened production capacity of Asian CCIs generates visible economic impacts such as their contribution to GDP, employment and export. At the same time, it helps to enrich culture in both 'dialogic' and 'museum' senses (Voon 2006). The thriving local CCIs provide more opportunities for members of society to 'speak' to each other and develop their identity and value as a community; they also offer cultural content such as distinct stories, themes, aesthetic expressions, styles, design, language, and music that reflect and are shaped by local contexts and ways of life. From this perspective, the rise of Asian CCIs means more diversity in global cultural economy in terms of 'who is speaking' and 'what is expressed and represented'.

This has been matched by the soaring consumption power of especially the emerging middle classes in the region who have nurtured transnational cultural appetites. While enjoying cultural and media products imported from outside Asia, these consumers show escalating desire for locally and regionally made cultural content (Kawashima and Lee 2018). It is within this context that China imports TV programmes mostly from Asia including Hong Kong and Taiwan (72 percent of the total import as of 2016).[2] Similarly, 58.5 percent of Japanese broadcasting content such as drama, animation, variety show, sports, and documentary are exported to Asian countries as of 2014 (KOCCA 2016: 8–9). As there is a surging volume and variety of appealing products from the region, cultural commodities originated from the existing global cultural centers such as the United States face tough competition. Although the United States is currently the world's biggest film market and enjoys a dominant position in other markets too, the circumstances could change in the future.

While protecting domestic producers and local cultural expressions is still an important agenda for many Asian countries, their CCIs actively seek ways to reach out to overseas audiences and secure a visible presence in the global cultural economy. A latest example is South Korean boy band BTS's topping of the Billboard 200 chart in March 2018 (BBC 2018), which indicates Korean cultural producers' 'soft' approach to global business: active pursuit of cultural hybridization, collaboration with talents, agencies, and platforms in global cultural centers, and direct engagement with overseas fans on social media. However, China seems to prefer a 'hard approach' – for example Dalian Wanda Group's buying up of cinema chains such as AMC (US), Hoyst (Australia), Odeon & UCI (Europe) as well as Legendary Pictures (US) – while also showing an interest in international co-production and knowledge transfer (BBC 2016; Financial Times 2017; see Yecies and Shim 2018 in this volume). This sometimes engenders anxiety and doubt in the receiving societies as capital power does not always produce soft power. Meanwhile, the global spread of Indian films might be another example to consider. The films form a distinct genre and are consumed by both Indian diasporic audiences and local audiences in many countries although it is not (yet) part of the mainstream cultural repertory. In short, the trajectories of Asian CCI's global move are not unitary and have triggered varied responses from non-Asian markets and audiences, from warm celebration of their distinct aesthetics to a feeling of discomfort caused by politically imbued concerns with the expanding hard power of China.

Creative industries discussion: where is Asia?

Asian CCIs have been widely commented on as part of the broader scholarly discussion of 'creative industries' (CIs), which is likely to attend to the genealogy of the creative industries idea, its meanings, economic impacts of these industries, and their mapping. Although the definition and boundary of CIs have not yet been settled, the available mappings and classifications indicate that the discussion in practice concerns arts, media, design, and cultural industries, or the broader cultural sector (Throsby 2008). While the ecology of CIs are frequently made sense of within the urban context ('creative city', 'creative cluster', and 'creative class'), more general accounts of the shape and operation of these industries appear to be a continuation of the existing understandings of cultural production, consumption, market, cultural policy, copyright, media convergence, and international trade of culture (e.g., Flew 2012).

When it comes to CCIs in Asia, the main theme in the existing literature is policy transfer and localization (Kong et al. 2006): 'diffusion and translation … adaptation and mutation of these policy "scripts" to adjust to local circumstances' (Flew 2010: 42). However, it should be noted that the discourse itself does not offer explicit policy scripts or a concrete logic of state intervention in CIs, leaving key areas for intervention and its main methods to be determined by local political and institutional factors. This explains why there is no coherent 'creative industries policy' in Australia, whose discourse of 'creative nation' in the mid-1990s inspired the UK cultural ministry's invention of 'creative industries' (The Australian 2018). Similarly, the development of creative industries policy in the UK has been quite slow, where the very idea of 'industrial policy' and 'state intervention' hardly gains currency.

The lively discussion on CCIs and active making of CCIs policy in Asia are frequently depicted as a consequence of the region's uptake of the Western idea of creative industries, and in fact this is a departure point for some chapters in this book. Yet, the unquestioned acceptance of this position is problematic because it is likely to assign one set of values (universality, theory, and policy invention) to British, Anglophone, and European contexts while associating Asia with the other set of values (particularity, empirical case, and policy mutation). Here, Asia is viewed as a place for empirical fieldwork rather than a core site for the production of theoretical knowledge (see Chen 2010: Chapter 5 for a broader critique of the uneven structure of knowledge production and the role of Asia in it). The consequence is that the dynamic growth of CCIs, the expansion of their markets, and related policy development in Asian societies during the past 20 years rarely feed into the theorization and conceptualization of CIs. The boom of Japan's cultural industries and their international success in the 1990s and South Korea's intense experience of 'inventing' cultural industries policy – rather than policy imitation – in the late 1990s and 2000s hardly informed the key understanding of CIs. Interestingly, these two countries did not subscribe to the idea of 'creative industries', preferring the term 'content industries', although the Japanese government has recently begun using the term 'creative industries'. The uneven structure of knowledge production poses a serious challenge to researchers working on CCIs in Asia: how can those 'national case studies' be transformed into theoretical knowledge?

One way to challenge the prevailing Anglo (UK)-centrism in the studies of creative industries would be to provincialize and localize the British and Anglophone experience of developing the industries and making relevant policies. At the same time, one can find some insights from the Asia-centric approach taken by cultural studies in Asia. When researching popular culture, cultural consumption and media flows in the region, the studies adopt an overall standpoint that can be summed up as 'Asia as method'. According to Kuan-Hsing Chen (2010: 212), this can be understood as 'a critical proposition to transform the existing knowledge structure and at the same time to transform ourselves'. He argues that by 'using the idea of Asia as an imaginary anchoring point, societies in Asia can become each other's points of references, so that the understanding of the self may be transformed, and subjectivity rebuilt'. The aspiration is to turn Asia into a site where cultural knowledge is generated, rather than a locality where theories that were produced in the West are imported, applied, and tested. This has resulted in the production of a rich volume of analysis of the conditions of regional cultural markets and consumers, cultural proximity/difference between Asian societies, the possibility of inter-cultural connection, and practices of transnational audiences in the region (e.g., Chua 2012; Chua and Iwabuchi 2008). The scholars intentionally find key references from Asian experiences, and their efforts to identify theoretically significant cultural consumption phenomena in the region have led to many writings focusing on the region-wide sharing of pop culture. Yet, they are concerned mainly with cultural consumption while paying little attention to the policy and economy of the region's CCIs, for instance, state policy, cultural and media production, and the actual operation of cultural businesses.

This handbook is a continuation and furtherance of the existing studies of CIs but, at the same time, tries to explore ways to incorporate Asian perspectives into the studies, regarding Asia as an important site for engendering key understanding of CCIs, which may involve questioning the existing assumptions. The book looks at five key areas that determine the dynamics of CCIs in Asia: state policy; culture of production and strategies of producers; circulation of CCIs' products and consumer culture; cultural activism and independent culture; and cultural heritage as an industry. Instead of highlighting policy transfer and mutation, the chapters endeavour to articulate the centrality of state policy, the importance of local contexts and institutions, cultural producers' strategies in and out of the given institutional framework, and participatory consumers and their impact on the CCIs. In addition, (geo) political and intra-regional environments, which are not much discussed in the existing West-centric literature, are taken seriously as a critical context for CCIs' development.

The centrality of state policy

Part I of this handbook points out the centrality of the state in conditioning political and social dynamics in many Asian societies. State policy – regulation and investment – is one of the most significant forces that impact the way Asian cultural and media products are made, disseminated, and consumed, thus shaping the ways in which these industries function. The more economic resources the countries have, the more active CCIs policy they can afford to make; so, it is not really surprising to see China, South Korea, Singapore, and Taiwan leading policy development in this area. While Japan, which is well known for its lack of interest in state cultural policy, has slowly joined the league, Southeast Asian countries demonstrate notable enthusiasm about CCIs' development as part of their national development strategy. While those societies with a strong tradition of cultural policy place 'cultural industries' (and the arts too) at the core of their CCIs policy, the latecomers are inclined to link the CCIs to economic upgrade and generation of tourism income.

We can notice gaps between countries in terms of state capacity in resource mobilization, policy implementation, and other activities required to achieve policy goals. Similarly, policy makers' views of the market are increasingly divergent: from the one seeing the state's 'push' (investment and support) as an essential condition for CCIs' development to the one calling for the active role of market forces. Another important factor to consider is state censorship and content regulation, which are still firmly put in place in a large part of the region although they constrain creativity and innovation, and thus could deter CCIs' growth.

In Chapter 1, Thomas Barker and Lee Yuen Beng critically examine the state-led development of CCIs policy in Malaysia and its embeddedness in the country's existing economic and innovation (ITC) policy. Being positioned as part of national strategy for economic catch-up, the policy has highlighted digital technologies and digital content, aspiring to transform Malaysia to the Southeast Asian hub of digital services. Yet, the top-down approach and cultural regulation by moral and religious norms are noted as obstacles to effective policy making. Chapter 2 by Alongkorn Parivudhiphongs looks into the substance and process of Thai CIs policy. Like the Malaysian case, we find the government's notable ambition for economic restructuring and regional (ASEAN) leadership in creative and digital economy. The policy is tightly bounded by local politics, institutions, and agendas such as 'sustainable economy', rural development, and SME support. The inclusive meaning of 'creative' and its overt economic concern explains why the policy eventually gave way to 'digital economy policy'. Importantly, the initial development of CIs policy in Thailand was the nation's response to the Asian financial crisis in 1997, which was also the case with South Korea where the sense of crisis facilitated a quick development of 'cultural industries' (later 'content industries') policy in the late 1990s. That is, contrasting the popular myth that the British creative industries idea motivated Thailand to develop CIs policy, the country borrowed the idea because it needed a new language that would capture its urgent task of economic restructuring.

In Chapter 3, Christian Morgner points out that the recent development of CIs policy in Japan was triggered by the overseas popularity of Japanese cultural products and fuelled by policy makers' belief in CIs' economic potential. In 2010, CIs gained official recognition with the foundation of the CIs Promotion Office under the Manufacturing Industries Bureau, the Ministry of Economy, Trade and Industry. In reality, however, the CIs policy is more about fusing nation branding ('Cool Japan') with the tourism and hospitality industry (food and beverages account for 70 percent of the total revenue of CIs). Apparently, the state's systematic support for cultural and media industries is still an alien idea in Japan.

Can-Seng Ooi and Roberta Comunian in Chapter 4 discuss the 'artpreneurial' ecosystem in Singapore by looking into education, social values and norms, policy environments, and market conditions. While seeing the rapid escalation of state investments in the arts, cultural infrastructure, and CIs, the authors point out the society's negative perception of doing arts as a profession, the exclusion of challenging artworks from state funding, the tendency of brain drain and the emerging need to support 'local' artists. Chapter 5 by Pei-Ling Liao and Caroline Chapain provides a detailed account of the development of CCIs cluster policy in Taiwan. Two different approaches to creative cluster are identified (a socio-culturally oriented, bottom-up approach and the application of industrial park policy), but both clusters struggled to develop due to the lack of consumers. The chapter argues that CCIs' growth requires mature market conditions such as increased disposable income and consumers' ability to appreciate creative products. From this perspective, the key role of a creative cluster would be to function as a platform where producers and consumers are directly engaged and put in a dialogue.

In Chapter 6, Ken Wang points that the majority of CCIs' funding in China comes from local governments. While all cities try to combine socialist management of culture with economic aspirations, local CCIs policies reflect and are tied to local contexts and conditions. For example, Harbin city's CCIs policy is closer to cultural policy with an emphasis on political and educational functions of culture while that in Guangzhou is visibly profit-oriented and market-centred. Beijing's CCIs investment emulates industry policy while being constrained by censorship and political considerations. Meanwhile, Kristina Karvelyte in Chapter 7 compares creative city policies in Shanghai, Hong Kong, and Taipei while commenting on their commonalities such as the increased economic instrumentalization of culture, rising public cultural spending, and policy makers' preference for 'fast policy'. Taipei takes more open and bottom-up approaches, however, not every stakeholder is included in policy discussion and cultural funding has strings attached. Meanwhile, Hong Kong and Shanghai's pursuit of international influence and success tends to disadvantage small creative organizations and unknown artists.

Producers and production

Part II of this handbook focuses on organizational, institutional, historical, national, and regional (geopolitical) contexts where autonomy of cultural producers are projected, internalized, and negotiated. Chapters in this part oppose the binary view that sets artistic autonomy against institutional and commercial constraints; rather, it is proposed that autonomy is contextually conditioned and, at the same time, conditions the contexts surrounding the CCIs. In Chapter 8, Chairin An discusses the paradoxical experience of creative workers who deal with various conflicts between organizational demands and individual creative ambitions. Examining the lived experiences of Korean television PDs (Producer Directors), the author argues that PDs patiently work with organizational and commercial imperatives for a long time in order to gain enough professional autonomy and thus secure bigger opportunities to express their creativity. In Chapter 9, Hsiao-Ling Chung points to the increasing audiovisual trade and talent exchange between Taiwan and China. Often, the cross-strait talent transfer raises concerns about 'brain drain' from Taiwan. However, Chung finds that their implications are much more complicated: via talent networks, Taiwanese creative workers find new opportunities, resources, and markets while continuously negotiating with commercialism and state control in China. Bjarke Liboriussen, Joaquin Lopez-Mugica, and Andrew White in Chapter 10 argue that creatives and artists in China develop their identity within the nation's 'literati' tradition. Looking at a group of Shanghai-based photographers, they find that such identification relates to philosophical discussions on the nature of Chinese creativity and China's place in the global knowledge economy. The photographers embody the intertwining of state-sanctioned attempts at exploiting China's history and traditional culture, critical resistance towards rampant modernization, and attempts at finding Chinese ways of 'becoming contemporary'. They are comfortable with such ambiguity, and thus offer an alternative philosophy to Western understandings of creative practice.

Chapter 11 by Nobuko Kawashima introduces a 'uniquely Japanese' institution of film financing: production consortium, a temporary committee among cultural businesses typically in film production, broadcasting, advertising, publishing, and merchandising. Each member of the consortium contributes to the production in return for the exploitation of the relevant right and fees from handling the business. This system effectively distributes risk and mobilizes the members' expertise. However, it is a closed system that does not help expand the financial base for film production beyond the usual member companies. It prefers films for entertainment with potential for ancillary businesses, leaving a large gap for independent film projects. In the next chapter, Justin O'Connor and Xin Gu point out that the existing policy transfer literature does not fully comprehend the deeper structural differences between China and the West. They witness the emergence of a unique logic of CCIs in Shanghai's M50, which began as a bottom-up creative cluster but increasingly became part of the city's strategy to become a global cultural city. The authors highlight not only large-scale cultural investments and active policy making in the city, which dwarfs that of most creative industry policies (in the West) but also specific socio-cultural roles played by these industries.

The next two chapters explore CCIs' development within regional as well as national contexts. In Chapter 13, Liew Kai Khiun and Yao Yiming investigate the co-production of historical fiction TV dramas between Singapore and China. The co-production was driven by Chinese television producers' interest in accessing expertise and talent in the Singaporean audiovisual industry, locations, and audiences, as well as their counterparts' keenness to tap into the huge China market. Yet, this trend waned at the turn of the 2000s, as the advanced Chinese television industry had little incentive to continue such co-productions, resulting in a televisual de-sinicization in Singapore. Brian Yecies and Aegyung Shim in Chapter 14 give a hands-on overview of the recent and on-going development of 'content industries' in South Korea. They comment on factors underpinning the Korean Wave (overseas popularity of Korean cultural commodities) such as entrepreneurial roles played by government policy and its agency KOCCA, the industries' increased capacity, their bold embrace of cultural hybridization and transcultural learning, and globalized marketing strategies. The authors stress potential regional synergies generated by Korean CCIs' capacity of knowledge transfer to Asia and China's ability to collaborate with Korean counterparts in artistic and financial terms.

Consumption and circulation

Part III of this handbook is themed with cultural consumers, consumption culture, and cultural circulation in the region. The emphasis is the embeddeness of cultural consumption in technological, social, and policy environments and, in turn, its engendering of new content and business model for CCIs and reshaping of the orientation of cultural companies. Cultural consumption today is highly transnationalized and consumers are open to appealing overseas products, especially from the region. Thus, without looking into consumption culture, media fandom and increasing transnational connections, the operation of CCIs in Asia cannot be fully understood.

In Chapter 15, Yeran Kim analyses the rise of *Mukbang* (real-time online broadcasting of people eating alone in front of camera) from a cultural studies perspective, focusing on the affective structure of Korea, in which the feelings of loneliness, solitariness, and isolation prevail within neoliberal and individualized social environments. She argues that *Mukbang* embodies the new political economic logic, in which the ambivalence of the active and passive acts of being watched eating is reformulated as a particular type of 'digital creative labour'. Kim introduces the term 'multisensorial capitalism' to capture the newly emerging nexus between the neoliberal capitalist economy, digital online network, DIY culture, and new cultural enterprises taking affect as a center of their business model. Ruth Y. Y. Hung and Q. S. Tong in Chapter 16, examine Chinese online users' active and satirical consumption of 'anti-Japanese war dramas'. Being produced in-between state policy and the market imperative, these dramas instigate popular nationalism in the viewers. While their exaggerated depiction of Chinese heroes become a subject of online parodies and satires, it seems unclear if active, playful consumption of this kind can lead to historically and politically conscious critique of state cultural policy and official historical narrative. Chapter 17 by Chi Thong Ma and Catherine Earl offers a rare opportunity for us to understand the recent transformation of the Vietnamese TV industry in line with the audience's increasing demand for popular programs. While the state broadcaster faces increasing competition from local television stations for market share, state influence on TV production and consumption is lessening. The authors highlight collaborations between the state broadcaster and private media companies, the popularity of reality shows, and the government's changing role. In short, television production, consumption, and regulation are transformed by marketization and the public's wider access to online media.

In Chapter 18, Nissim Otmazgin comments on the regional dissemination of Japanese popular culture in the 1990s and early 2000s, by concentrating on the innovativeness and newness of Japanese pop culture commodities, their regional fandom, and its implication for Japan's nation branding and economic policies. What is most interesting is the fact that the regional flow of Japanese pop culture affected local cultural production in Asian countries by providing local producers with new ideas, formats, and production strategies. For example, learning and borrowing from Japan used to be a key strategy of South Korean CCIs, which are now at the center of knowledge transfer among Asian CCIs. Finally, Chapter 19 by Silvia Fok traces the impact international art fairs have had in Hong Kong and the Asian region by focusing on Art Hong Kong (2008–12), Art Basel Hong Kong (2013–) and Art Central (2015–). Hong Kong's distinct position as the region's visual art center and its broader role with the global art world/market are also discussed. Finally, the chapter pays attention to the art fairs' influence on the local art scene and their potential contribution to the development of CCIs in Hong Kong, Macau, and mainland China.

Cultural activism, diversity, and independent culture

Although the boundary of creative industries is quite broad and inclusive, the basic emphasis of the existing literature is these industries' commercial potential. While the literature often points out gaps between expectation and reality, such as the lack of employment opportunities for creatives and exploitation of their free labor, the fundamental assumption is that CIs are a generator of wealth and a new engine for national economy. However, Part IV of this handbook problematizes the propensity to discuss CCIs from an economic and commercial framework, pointing out that their development is, in reality, indebted to thriving youth culture, subculture, and independent culture, and that there are varying ways for creatives to contribute to social movements and activism. In Chapter 20, Viriya Sawangchot discusses the development of indie music in Thailand, the process of which has been led by creative youngsters from the middle classes who pursue artistic ambition and DIY music making. Yet, the emergence and growth of indie music has been a complicated process where young artists are influenced by American and British music genres, negotiate with the existing institutions of the music industry such as mainstream labels and TV and radio music programs while exploring so-called 'non-institution' (flexible, project-based and collaboration-centred music making, distribution, and showcasing). Working both in and out of the mainstream music industry, these young musicians enrich pop music repertory, style, and genre in Thailand.

The next three chapters draw our attention to Indonesia, one of Asia's largest countries in terms of population. Chapter 21 by Novi Kurnia points out that, since the late 1990s, the Indonesian film industry has been diversified and decentralized with booming independent filmmaking in regions. One of the key contributors to this development is local film communities that are involved in film production, screening, festivals, and workshops. Looking into Cinema Lovers Community (CLC) Purbalingga, Kurnia shows how voluntary film communities play central roles in energizing the film industry in Indonesia. Meanwhile, Dina Dellyana and Sonny Rustiadi (Chapter 22) argue that the DIY approach to creative business is a key driving force of music and fashion industries in the city of Bandung, Indonesia. The chapter describes the motivation behind such an approach as well as its process across production, distribution, and promotion, where the two industries closely collaborate. It finds that the city's creative milieu and their connection to the prevailing youth culture gives rise to the DIY approach where young creatives balance artistic and economic imperatives with an accent on the former. Then, Sonny Rustiadi, D. A. E. Savitri Sastrawan, and

Salfitrie Roos Maryunani's Chapter 23 turns our attention to the contribution of creative practices to progressive politics and social movement, which hardly is a key concern of the exiting discussion of CIs. Two examples drawn from Bandung and Bali demonstrate how creative workers intervene in local politics via directly entering the governance system and actively partaking in social movements respectively.

In Chapter 24, Hye-Kyung Lee and Lorraine Lim examine the impacts of digitalization on the broader cultural sector in East Asian countries. The digitalization brings a wide range of noticeable opportunities for the diversity of cultural expressions by helping to generate new types of creative ideas and cultural forms, facilitating cheaper dissemination of cultural products, and increasing opportunities for collaboration and co-creation between cultural producers. Digitalization also gives rise to alternative spaces online that can play key roles in promoting the identities and agendas of marginalized groups. Yet, the authors find several challenges too: state censorship, digital divide, data gap, fierce competition in the attention economy, and the dual roles played by global online platforms in both promoting and limiting cultural diversity.

Heritage and the cultural market

In many Asian countries, traditional culture heavily shapes community identity and way of life. Heritage and traditional arts are usually seen as an object to be protected by the state but they are often explored and exploited in the context of tourism and trade, where their preservation and inheritance are conditioned by forces of entrepreneurship, marketization, and nation branding. In Chapter 25, Sowparnika Balaswaminathan and Thomas Evan Levy argue that the idea of 'craft' in India is entangled with nationalism and its revival/maintenance depends on the middle classes' consumption of handicrafts. Handloom textile is one of such examples. The media and public discourse of craft is informed by the contentious co-existence of neoliberal economic logic (economic values of handicrafts), Hindu nationalism (craft vs. Western ways of life), government promotion of the nation's craft, and the middle classes' cultural identification via craft consumption. The authors observe that the current anxiety that Indian consumers of handicrafts have about them are often anxieties about the current status of the nation and its future.

In Chapter 26, Frances Rudgard and Phloeun Prim present a case study of the activities of Cambodian Living Arts (CLA), a voluntary arts organization that has created work for young artists by launching a regular income-generating traditional performance. While demonstrating the nexus between cultural heritage and the market economy, the authors examine the dynamics of balancing the 'triple bottom line' of economic, social, and cultural return underpinning CLA's projects. Finally, Chapter 27 by Jason Vitorillo and Maria Sharon Mapa Arriola discuss the Philippine government's support for intangible heritage through the National Commission for Culture and the Arts (NCCA). One successful example is the Hudhud Schools of Living Traditions (HSLT) of the Ifugao indigenous community. The authors examine HSLT's framework, approaches, and systems. While looking into how the current cultural policy model responds to the needs of the communities, they also pose an alternative perspective based on collaboration between local communities and the government in shaping and articulating the policy.

Observing Asian societies' experiences, this handbook points out the critical roles played by the state, its orientation and capacity – discursive, financial, and administrative – in determining the nature of CCIs policy in line with the existing tradition of cultural policy and economic policy. Institutional, cultural, and technological environments as well as prevailing social norms, too, are part of the broader ecology of the CCIs and affect the subjectivity and professional identity of creative producers and their career trajectory, shaping cultural education and informing consumer tastes and capacity. Consumer creativity is played out in relation to political economy, and its implications are divergent: from boosting bottom-up independent culture, discursively subverting state ideology, both tackling and affirming dominant social discourses, and functioning as a new source of cultural commodity. This book has indicated that national political economy, embedded production, transnationalized media consumption, socially-specific consumer creativity, and DIY creative expressions circumventing resource shortage and diversifying national cultural repertoire, can be helpful frameworks for making sense of the CCIs and CCIs policy development in Asia. In addition, it calls for further discussion of the 'regional' approach to the understanding of Asian CCIs as the increasing transnational collaboration and competition, knowledge transfer, and cultural trades which take place within the rapidly shifting geopolitics, are a significant factor that conditions the operation of CCIs and their growth. Regional frameworks can also be instrumental in assisting scholars to identify significant cultural phenomena and reference points in the region and in seeking avenues to engender theoretical knowledge of CCIs out of national case studies.

Notes

1 Especially, the annual growth rate of developing countries in Asia is notably high, such as China (6.7 percent), India (7.1 percent), Indonesia (5.0 percent) and Vietnam (6.2 percent) (World Bank 2016). See https://data.worldbank.org/indicator/NY.GDP.MKTP.KD.ZG?locations=VN (accessed on 21 May 2018).

2 http://data.stats.gov.cn/easyquery.htm?cn=C01 (accessed on 21 May 2018). As of 2016, the import from Asia (1,510 million yuan) accounts nearly 72 percent of the total import of TV programs in China (2,099 million yuan).

References

The Australian (1 May 2018) Artistic creativity suffers without Australian cultural policy.

BBC News (12 July 2016) Odeon & UCI cinemas sold to China-owned firm.

BBC News (28 March 2018) BTS become first K-pop band to top US album charts.

Chen, K.-S. (2010) *Asia as Method: Towards Deimperialization.* Durham and London: Duke University Press.

Chua, B. H. (2012) *Structure, Audience and Soft Power in East Asian Pop Culture.* Hong Kong: Hong Kong University Press.

Chua, B. H. and Iwabuchi, K. (2008) *East Asian Pop Culture: Analysing the Korean Wave.* Hong Kong: Hong Kong University Press.

Financial Times (15 March 2017) Dalian Wanda is hitting Hollywood too hard.

Flew, T. (2012) *The Creative Industries: Culture and Policy.* London: Sage.

Kawashima, N. and Lee, H.-K. (2018 in press) *Asian Cultural Flows: Creative Industries, Cultural Policies, and Media Consumers.* New York: Springer.

KOCCA (2016) *Content Industry Trend of Japan.* Seoul: KOCCA.

Kong, L., Gibson, C. and Khoo, L. M. (2006) Knowledges of the creative economy: towards a relational geography of diffusion and adaptation in Asia. *Asia Pacific Viewpoint,* 47(2): 173–94.

Throsby, D. (2008) Modelling the cultural industries. *International Journal of Cultural Policy,* 14(3): 217–32.

UNESCO (2016) *Diversity and the film industry: an analysis of the 2014 UIS Survey on Feature Film Statistics.* Montreal: UNESCO Institute for Statistics.

Voon, T. (2006) State support for audiovisual products in the World Trade Organization: protectionism or cultural policy? *International Journal of Cultural Property,* 13: 129–60.

Part I
State policies

1

Creating within constraints

Creative industries policy in Malaysia

Thomas Barker and Lee Yuen Beng

Introduction

Malaysia has often been characterized as an illiberal or semi-authoritarian regime, in which civil liberties and forms of expression are curtailed and constrained (Yeoh 2010; Means 1996).[1] Control over speech is maintained through a political economy of media ownership linked to the ruling coalition (Nain 2002), legal mechanisms such as the Sedition Act, and the promotion of a top-down National Cultural Policy which is designed 'to create a stable and unified nation'.[2] These controls constrain forms of political and cultural expression, especially on 'sensitive' topics and content that is outside permissible limits or norms. In 2006, these tensions played out in the case of the documentary film *The Last Communist* by Amir Muhammad. Although the film passed censorship without cuts,[3] a concerted campaign by *Berita Harian* journalist Akmal Abdullah brought the film to the attention of the Ministry of Home Affairs which then decided to ban the film (McKay 2011). The film shows new film-making techniques and subject matter (Khoo 2011). But a film with 'communist' in the title was too provocative for what Benjamin McKay called 'current political anxieties' (2011: 54). The case of *The Last Communist* and others like it provoked informal and formal discussions within the arts and entertainment communities about the conditions under which culture can be made and consumed, suggesting that these are important questions for those involved in what we might otherwise call the creative industries.

It may seem a contradiction therefore that the Malaysian government has introduced and promoted the creative industries as a part of its policy agenda given that creativity invariably involves the creation or discussion of potentially contentious ideas and contrarian forms of cultural representation. Creative industries policy however seeks to depoliticize culture by downplaying the potentially political and radical elements of creativity to instead deploy the creative industries as a driver of economic growth, able to contribute to employment and national income. Like Singapore to the south, the promotion and fostering of the creative industries occurs under a contradictory set of circumstances: on the one hand the state wants to promote and develop the creative industries whilst on the other remaining highly sensitive to forms of speech and culture that go against prevailing norms (Chong 2011; Lee 2010). How this contradiction is managed if not resolved becomes an important topic of study telling us how the creative industries operate in countries without strong traditions of cultural and artistic autonomy and free speech.

It is within this contradictory space that this chapter considers the introduction of creative industries policy in Malaysia and the promotion of these industries. In 2009, the Malaysian government released a creative industries policy document called the Dasar Industri Kreatif Negara (DIKN, National Creative Industry Policy). It announced the government's intention to support the country's creative and cultural industries while bringing Malaysia into step with many other regional jurisdictions which have similarly pursued creative industries policies since the early 2000s. While the introduction of creative industries policy seems to represent a new development in how the Malaysian government approaches the creative work of its citizens, this chapter argues that because it involves an inherent tension between its economic and development ambitions with the realities of cultural and creative activity the outcomes do not live up to the hubris and rhetoric that has surrounded discussion of the creative industries. We consider therefore the ways in which these tensions have played out in policy terms since 2009 and the consequences this has for the creative industries, arts, and culture more broadly.

Regionally the creative industries have become a prominent sector of policy attention for governments seeking to develop forms of cultural production while achieving economic ambitions. In Malaysia, arts and media were managed and promoted under national development-orientated policies such as the National Culture Policy (1970) and agencies such as the National Film Development Corporation Malaysia (FINAS) established in 1981. Since the late 1990s, the global turn to 'creative industries' is also a neoliberal turn towards a market-orientated arts and culture policy (Flew and Cunningham 2010), superseding existing media, arts, and cultural policy introduced in an era of post-colonial nation building. Singapore introduced one of the first creative industries policies in the Southeast Asian region through its Renaissance City Plan of 2000 which aimed in part to 'unleash the economic potential of arts and cultural activities' (Kong 2009: 64). More recently, the Indonesian government established Bekraf (Badan Ekonomi Kreatif, Creative Economy Body) reporting directly to the President as an agency responsible for supporting and promoting Indonesia's creative industries especially film, animation, fashion, and the like. Malaysia's DIKN situates Malaysia within this regional and international move towards identifying, supporting, and promoting the domestic creative industries for internal and external markets.

There is substantial debate and slippage around the exact definition of creative industries (Banks and O'Connor 2009; Galloway and Dunlop 2007) and it is not our intention to reiterate that debate here. For our purposes, we can use the UNCTAD definition from their 2008 *Creative Economy Report* which defines the creative industries as:

> the cycles of creation, production and distribution of goods and services that use creativity and intellectual capital as primary inputs; constitute a set of knowledge-based activities, focused on but not limited to arts, potentially generating revenues from trade and intellectual property rights; comprise tangible products and intangible intellectual or artistic services with creative content, economic value and market objectives; are at the cross-road among the artisan, services and industrial sectors; and constitute a new dynamic sector in world trade.
>
> *(UNCTAD 2008: 13)*

Typically, the creative industries encompass film and television content, publishing, art, performance, theatre, advertising, computer programs, among others. These industries or sectors may be categorized into different groupings depending on the objectives of the defining body. Common to most definitions is the acknowledgment that the creative industries generate intellectual property based on the utilization of ideas or artistic skills. Creativity is also seen as an essential ingredient in the shift to post-industrial and knowledge economies where the manipulation of information, data, and ideas are said to drive economic growth. Many developed economies in the West see the creative industries as a panacea to economic stagnation and the decline in employment in traditional sectors of the economy such as manufacturing. Even though creative industries have often been promoted in contradistinction to low-skilled manufacturing, creative industries still involve many of the same challenges such as enterprise and labor management, state support, national culture policies, and education (Tschang 2009).

Arts and culture policy that developed in many European countries after World War II saw governments supporting and developing culture as a means of broadening access to traditional art forms to larger sections of the population and supporting cultural work (Crane 1992). Following the market-driven and deregulation turn of the 1980s, government support for the arts and culture came into question, especially since lofty ideals of public edification and state-supported art were seen as economically unsustainable or ideologically suspect. In the UK for example, this shift has been documented by Hesmondhalgh and Pratt (2005) who show how the shift has moved arts and culture policy away from the idea that it would develop cultural appreciation as a social good, to a much more economic emphasis on the potential contribution of creative industries to national income and employment. In the UK, the introduction of creative industries policy in the late 1990s through the DCMS (Department for Culture, Media and Sport) reflected this shift in thinking towards economic measures and was reflected in the export-orientated strategy of the 'Creative Britain' campaign. Despite the rhetoric around the creative industries and the hubris of its potential, problems have remained in defining the industries, and in subsequent policy formulation and implementation (Banks and O'Connor 2009: 366–367).

Malaysia's creative industries policy

Whereas developed countries have sought to promote the creative industries as a means of revitalizing economic activity following the decline in basic industry and manufacturing, Malaysia sees the creative industries as a way of becoming a developed nation. Because developed nations are seen to have a significant amount of their income derived from creative activity, Malaysia sees that to become a developed nation requires a similar-sized creative industries sector. Using the creative industries as a development pathway has been acknowledged by agencies such as UNCTAD, but arguably this link between the creative industries and becoming a developed nation has not been as clearly made as it has been in Malaysia. In the 1990s, Malaysia adopted a policy objective called Vision 2020 (Wawasan 2020) that aims for the country to be a high-income 'developed nation' by 2020 (usually measured as annual income of US $15,000/capita). In order to achieve this, Malaysia is seeking to transition away from its reliance on export-orientated manufacturing and resource extraction to a diversified economy with substantial service and knowledge sectors. When Prime Minister Najib Razak took office in March 2009 he reiterated his commitment to Vision 2020 by implementing the Economic Transformation Plan (ETP) under his office (PEMANDU).[4] The ETP is divided into 12 National Key Economic Areas (NKEA) which includes the creative industries.

Soon after Najib Razak became Prime Minister, Malaysia launched its own creative industries policy called the Dasar Industri Kreatif Negara (DIKN). Accompanying the policy was a MYR 200 million allocation to a Creative Industry Fund (CIF) as a 'catalyst for the development of creative industries activity'.[5] In its introduction, the DIKN is clearly positioned as part of the Vision 2020 strategy (KPKK 2009: ii), with the Minister of Information, Communication, and Culture noting in his forward that the 'creative industries represent an important source of economic growth and cultural proliferation for developed nations' (KPKK 2009: i).[6] Although the DIKN refers to creative industry policy from other countries including Australia, Great Britain, Singapore, and Hong Kong, it defines creative industries 'in the context of Malaysia' as:

> The mobilization and production of the abilities and talents of individuals or groups based on creativity, innovation and technology leading to the source of economic growth and high income to the country, with an emphasis on aspects of copyright and intellectual work in harmony with the culture and values of the various [racial] groups in Malaysia.
>
> *(KPKK 2009: 4)*[7]

As this definition suggests, as is also repeated throughout the DIKN document, much of the focus is on the potential economic contribution of the creative industries, especially in terms of national income and employment. As such, the economic benefits of the creative industries are seen as a means to achieve high-income status and to thereby help Malaysia fulfill its ambition of becoming a developed nation.

With such a significant emphasis on the economic contribution of the creative industries, little space is given to the meaning of culture or creativity in the DIKN. Reference is made to 'enhancing national culture' (*memartabatkan budaya bangsa*, KPKK 2009: 7) and the cultures of the 'various [racial] groups',[8] suggesting that culture is imagined as a manifestation of racially inflected cultural traditions and practices. This is in keeping with the dominant discourse in which culture is imagined as a static manifestation of one's race (or ethnicity) expressed through traditional art forms such as dance, dress, crafts, and largely fixed belief and value systems, and constituent of a greater national culture. This recalls how culture is defined in the National Culture Policy (1970) which was reiterated in April 2017 at the Culture Congress 2017 with specific links drawn to the role of the creative industries (Berita Harian 2017).[9] Material for the Congress asserts that the 'purpose of the creative industry is to radiate the values, image, and face of Malaysia' and that 'the mistake that is often made by art practitioners is only to think of creativity within the context of a single film, telemovie, or television series'. By asserting that creativity and the creative industries should fall into line with the state's normative definition of culture, there is little scope or recognition for communities or groups that manifest divergent or contrarian cultural forms. Other forms of culture can be delegitimized or considered outside the bounds of normative conceptualizations, thus making them prone to being denied support or recognition. This continues a top-down tradition of defining culture as a normative ideal in which the state is positioned as the arbiter or authority on cultural matters.

Accompanying the DIKN, the Creative Industry Fund (CIF) created under the auspices of the Prime Minister's Office (PEMANDU) was used to fund creative industries projects via loans (Kementerian Penerangan Komunikasi and Kebudayaan 2009: 3). The CIF targeted individuals and companies with a particular emphasis on supporting animation projects. When the fund was finished in 2013, it was revealed that 80 percent of the CIF was used for film and television projects, including MYR5 million (US $1.2 million) lent to production company Tanah Licin to part-finance their 2012 film *Hanyut* (*Astray*, dir. U-Wei

Haji Saari) (Mahpar 2010). Few other details about projects funded under the CIF are publically available, but in a frank admission in 2013, Fadhlullah Suhaimi Abdul Malek from PEMANDU described the CIF as 'a leaking bucket' because too many recipients had defaulted on repayments (The Malaysian Reserve 2013). In the case of *Hanyut*, the film ended up costing a total of MYR 18 million (US $4.5 million) to make and earned only MYR 76,486.25 at the local box office when it was released in 2016.[10] Although the higher budget is justified by *Hanyut* being a period drama, it cost more than ten times the average Malaysian film. It revealed not only poor financial oversight but began a pattern of the Malaysian government providing funding to individual projects rather than long-term investments in infrastructure for example by creating creative districts or education programs as other cities and countries have.

Despite the acknowledged problems with the CIF, it was nevertheless followed by the allocation of a further MYR 100 million (US $25 million) towards a Creative Industry Development Fund (CIDF). Directed by the Malaysian Multimedia and Communication Commission (MCMC), the fund specifically targeted television, mobile, and web content development. When the fund ended in 2014, 44 projects were funded of which 39 had launched (Malaysian Communications and Multimedia Commission 2014). Projects included the TV documentary *Lost over France: Malaysia's Unsung Hero* (2013, dir. Reza Zainal), produced by 3Line Media and broadcast on the History Channel Asia in 2013; and *Knowsy Nina wants to Know*, a cartoon series for four- to six-year-old children produced by Avant Garde Studios. CIDF also funded websites such as travel consultant website Islands of Malaysia (www.islands.com.my; www.myoutdoor.com); a handphone wallpaper site (www.wallpaper4share.com); and a website providing technological solutions for high-resolution panoramic photos (gigapan.com).[11] As with the CIF fund before it, much of the CIDF money went to funding specific products, broadening to include digital and online. Taking the websites as examples, not only is their 'creative' value questionable, but so is the selection process for these projects given that many of the websites no longer exist. Overall, this round of funding was poorly targeted with little thought given to sustainability, functionality, and value for money.

In 2012, another allocation of MYR 200 million (US $50 million) was announced but to be administered by a 'government investment arm' called MyCreative Ventures. In a tacit acknowledgement of the financial lapses with the CIF and CIDF, MyCreative Ventures is directed to make equity or debt investments into creative businesses of up to MYR 5 million at an interest rate of 6–8 percent. Financial management and repayment of loans are enhanced. Echoing the economic emphasis in the DIKN, MyCreative Ventures' stated missions are to create jobs, increase GDP, and 'elevate the status of Malaysia's creative industry via public awareness and social impact' (http://www.mycreative.com.my/about). Since it began in 2012, MyCreative Ventures has funded a broad range of businesses including companies working in fashion, education, art galleries, book publishing, performance, content creation, and video games. Stronger vetting of proposals comes at the cost of creating a new agency to administer the loans following a corporate structure and therefore separate to existing government ministries. MyCreative Ventures remains under the purview of PEMANDU and is populated by establishment and government figures with a board comprising Ahmad Farid Ridzuan from TV3, Tony Savarimuthu from brand consultancy Dentsu LHS, Mahyidin Mustakim former director general of FINAS, Farisha Pawan Teh COO of Primeworks Studios, film director Razak Mohaideen, and Wong Wen Miin from PEMANDU. While the financial accountability may have improved and with it the quality of businesses funded, MyCreative Ventures is much more visibly controlled by PEMANDU both institutionally and financially, raising questions about expanding role of the Minister of Finance (also the Prime Minister) in the Malaysian economy (Gomez et al. 2018) and the independence of the creative industries from government influence and ownership.

Alongside the funding and loans schemes, a number of new bodies have been established to assist in the implementation of creative industries policy and interface with practitioners. The Creative Content Industry Guild (CCIG) was established in 2011 under FINAS as an 'industry certification body' for creative content industry practitioners. According to the CCIG website, its membership now numbers over 6,400 people. This seems to mirror the suggestion in the DIKN for the establishment of an industry body to help regulate the creative industries, especially in terms of enforcing labor conditions and employment standards. CCIG only serves 'individuals involved directly or indirectly in the creative multimedia sector such as in TV, Film and Radio Production, Advertising, Animation, Digital Content and Music' and not theatre, performing arts, and dance. As a certification body, the CCIG duplicates the certification function of existing film and television industry associations such as the Malaysian Film Producers Association (PFM), Film Director's Association of Malaysia (FDAM), and Screenwriters Guild of Malaysia (SWAM). While these industry associations have been criticized for being inert and ineffective, the introduction of the CCIG did not reform or retire these existing associations, in effect requiring creative industries practitioners to now join two organizations in order to work. In 2016, members of some Associations publically criticized the CCIG for 'not doing anything to protect our welfare as scriptwriters' (The Daily Seni 2016), demanding that the CCIG be investigated by the Ministry.

Another body called the Creative Content Association of Malaysia (CCAM) was established in 2011 under the Economic Transformation Plan as an 'industry-led government funded association of the leading content creators in Malaysia'. Focusing on feature films, TV programs, and animation,[12] individuals and companies can become members of CCAM which was set up 'for the express purpose of promoting and exporting local content and creative services to overseas markets and international broadcasters'.[13] Its most prominent activities include the KL Converge digital economy symposium and digital content market in 2014, 2015, and 2016, and sponsoring a Malaysian film program at the Cambodian International Film Festival in 2015. Like MyCreative Ventures, CCAM comes under PEMANDU and shares its establishment character with CEO Mahyidin Mustakim former Director General of FINAS (2006–2011), assisted by a Council composed of Kamal Khalid (CEO, Media Prima Television Networks), Khairul Anwar Salleh (VP, Malay Language Business, Astro), Chin Yoke Kee (Film Point, advertising company), and See Chin Joo (digital animation company Inspidea Sdn Bhd). CCAM's Advisory Panel includes government bodies FINAS, RTM (Radio Televisyen Malaysia), MDEC, and the ETP. Although CCAM has industry representation, its organizational structure and leadership are still dominated by government agencies and ruling-party-linked companies.

New creative industries bodies are not only 'corporate' agencies established to manage these new policy areas, but the government retains a significant hand in their operation despite the rhetoric around the creative industries being market-orientated and populated by private enterprise. The central government retains control through funding and by populating the boards with establishment figures. Rather than being independent bodies located within the creative industries, they operate as extensions of the state designed to guide and direct the creative industries within the state's own conceptual and institutional purview. In particular, the creative industries have become a domain where the executive branch of the Malaysian government plays a lead role in allocating funding and guiding the policy directions through these new agencies (Gomez et al. 2018). Likewise, in the management of the creative industries new bodies duplicate many of the functions and roles of existing government agencies and ministries such as MCMC, FINAS, and MDEC, but are necessary because they bypass legacy institutions and ministries which remain burdened by civil service regulations and bureaucracy. It appears therefore that the creative industries have become even more regulated and subject to state interference through the creation of new oversight agencies and funding schemes.

The patterns of government participation in the creative industries echoes the model developed in the operation of the Multimedia Supercorridor (MSC) by the creation of the Multimedia Development Corporation (MDEC) in the 1990s. As Bunnell (2002) observed in the establishment of the MSC, although it was built on market-orientated neoliberal ambitions of foreign investment, deregulation, and private-sector-led development, the MSC retained a strong government hand through ownership, regulation, and a political regime unafraid to reintroduce restrictions if it was politically necessary or expedient. Bunnell (2002) notes that the establishment of MDEC to oversee the MSC as a private-sector entity and 'one-stop super shop' would assist foreign investors and companies from having to deal with multiple government agencies. Yet, in doing so, it expands the number of government agencies and obscures the fact that the MSC and MDEC 'have served to strengthen the direct authority of a re-scaled central state … and the upper executives in particular' (Bunnell 2002: 291).

The most significant infrastructural investment in the creative industries was the construction of the MYR 400 million (US $120 million) Pinewood-Iskandar Studios (PIMS) in Johor, by the government investment arm Khazanah Nasional. The official opening of the studio in June 2014 attracted much fanfare given that the studio was already producing the Netflix series *Marco Polo* (2014–2016). PIMS was said to 'place Iskandar Malaysia on the Creative Industries map and will link the creative hubs in both Kuala Lumpur and Singapore' (Khazanah Nasional 2009). In 2014 the Johor Tourism, Domestic Trade and Consumerism Committee Chairman claimed that PIMS would attract MYR 1.9 billion in investment and create 11,300 jobs between 2013 and 2020.[14] Yet, since *Marco Polo* was cancelled after its second season in 2016, PIMS has seen little activity and will not likely generate the income and employment that is hoped. Its problem has been market positioning and geographical location – too far away from Kuala Lumpur where most of the domestic production is centered, and too expensive for most regional productions to use. It speaks of larger issues in the creative industries policy of hubris and over-ambitious goals accompanied by poor planning and management.

To date, Malaysia's creative industries policy has been buoyed by announcements of co-productions, sales and distribution deals, and a growing regional reputation in digital content industries especially animation. Annual production figures in the film industry have also been increasing. Yet this has relied on significant state support leading some to question whether these industries are sustainable without government funding (Ch'ng 2015). While the creative industries are meant to be market-orientated, the government has continued to be heavily involved in the sector through funding schemes and through the operational hand of new agencies. As the next section argues, creative industries policy has also increasingly gravitated towards 'digital content' as a pragmatic drift with consequences for the scope and direction of creative industries as a whole in Malaysia.

Digital as creative

A broader trend that has become evident in Malaysian creative industries policy is the move away from traditional arts and towards 'digital content'. In the original DIKN document, the creative industries are divided into three categories – Multimedia, Fine Arts, and Heritage – but it has been the Multimedia category which has received the most attention and support. Activities in the Fine Arts and Heritage categories have received very little mention in funding or creative industries representation bodies since 2009. Instead most of the attention has been placed on activities in the Multimedia category including advertising, film and television, animation, and digital content. In part this is consistent with Oakley's (2009) observation that the arts have tended to 'disappear' from policy discussions in the UK as a discourse of 'innovation' has become dominant. Forms of traditional culture and arts are seen as 'heritage and educational' (Oakley 2009: 411) unlike 'novel and innovative' cultural products which employ new technologies such as digital content. In the case of Malaysia, traditional arts have been largely relegated to tourist displays and the few 'elite' cultural forms such as the Malaysian Symphony Orchestra survive through corporate backing. Neither have received attention in creative industries policy. Instead, new digital technologies and industries have been promoted since they are seen as innovative, entrepreneur-driven, technologically advanced, and more readily able to circulate in the global content economy, thereby generating income for Malaysia.

A preference for digital can in part be explained by the legacy government policies associated with the Multimedia Supercorridor (MSC) established in the early 1990s under the purview of MDEC. MSC was to be Malaysia's version of Silicon Valley and encompass an area from downtown Kuala Lumpur (KLCC Twin Towers) to the new airport in the south, incorporating the new administrative capital of Putrajaya and technology city of Cyberjaya. While it initially aimed to attract ICT and other technology companies, in the early 2000s, MDEC shifted emphasis to Creative Content and began giving 'MSC Status' to media, animation, and other digital and online companies. Although the MSC project has slowed in recent years and has required a geographical expansion beyond the original 'corridor' and a new focus on mobile applications, the MSC is still held up as a successful example of Malaysian innovation and investment. As Nicholas Garnham (2005) observes, creative industries policy is often derived from ICT policy which was ascendant in the 1990s as it was in Malaysia. ICT policy sought to develop information and communications technology as a growth area including internet infrastructure and computer software, which have become the technological and rhetorical backbone for new digital industries.

There has been a clear emphasis on digital media and digital content in post-DIKN creative industries schemes, events, and promotional material. Further investment schemes have tried to emulate the success of *Upin & Ipin*, an iconic Malaysian children's animation series made by local studio Les' Copaque Production and first launched in 2007. Although it is held up as an example of Malaysia's creative potential and niche opportunity, much of its success is due to the substantial backing and support Les' Copaque Production received from MDEC. A recent MYR 100 million Digital Content Fund (Dana Kandungan Digital) announced in the 2015 Federal Budget targets visual effects (VFX), computer animation, computer games, CGI, and more recently mobile applications. Other schemes focusing on digital content have operated under both MDEC and FINAS, including a special FINAS Special Effect Fund (Dana Kesan Khas – CGI) available to any film that included some amount of locally produced digital effects. Les' Copaque Production received MYR 1.4 million for their 2016 film *Upin & Ipin Jeng Jeng Jeng!* out of a total budget of MYR 4 million (Mazalan 2016). It is a continuation of trends already evident in earlier funding schemes and represents a narrowing of the creative industries vision laid out in the DIKN. With the almost complete disappearance of traditional arts and culture from consideration, digital is increasingly synonymous with creative.

While products such as *Upin & Ipin* allow Malaysian companies to generate original intellectual property that can circulate in the global digital economy, Malaysia is still seen as a low-wage, digital content factory for many larger companies based in countries such as Japan, the United States, and Australia. Malaysia has hoped to leverage this position in order to upskill its workforce and generate original intellectual property. One such case that exemplifies the dangers of this strategy was the opening of the Rhythm & Hues studio in Cyberjaya in 2009 under the MSC. Rhythm & Hues was at the time a California-based visual effects company with studios in Taiwan and Delhi where much of the labor-intensive work was completed. Employing 150 workers at its peak, the Cyberjaya studio worked on the visual effects for *The Life of Pi* (2012, dir. Ang Lee) a US $120 million Hollywood production, for which Rhythm & Hues won the Academy Award for Best Effects in 2013. However, in February 2013, just months before the award, Rhythm & Hues filed for Chapter 11 bankruptcy in the United States, laying off 250 staff, and threatening the viability of its global studios. During production for *The Life of Pi*, Rhythm & Hues' costs had risen substantially while their contracted payment from the production company remained fixed, effectively bankrupting the company (Variety 2013). Workers in the US staged protests and a documentary film was made about the episode, highlighting the cost pressures and business risks in creative industries. In Malaysia, the bankruptcy received scant media attention even though it was a cautionary tale about the risks of an ambitious global strategy in which Malaysia was positioned as a low-cost supplier of digital services to a company based overseas. The Malaysian office averted closure when the local CEO bought over the Cyberjaya studio, downsizing it and renaming the company Tau Films.

As former ICT policy backgrounds new creative industries policy, the result is a merging of creative industries with companies utilizing digital technology. Malaysia now boasts of companies and products including mobile games, educational software, animation, and visual effects. Malaysia is carving a niche for itself as a digital service center and digital leader in the Southeast Asian region, taking advantage of its good internet infrastructure, skilled and multilingual workforce, and global outlook. But it means that increasingly its creative industries policy is really a digital development agenda. It is not the whole range of creative activities that are targeted and developed by government policy, but rather a narrow set of digital content industries and functions. 'Digital content' has become a new focus area which is in effect an extension of previous ICT policy. Such activities are not by definition creative as much of the work is highly technical, requiring sophisticated computer design and coding skills, but the products they produce are categorized within the creative industries.

Constraining creativity

Missing from the DIKN, and especially in the 'Isu dan Cabaran' (Issues and Challenges) section, and in subsequent government circulars, is any mention of the conditions of creative and cultural production and especially artistic freedom. Isu dan Cabaran identifies support institutions, public awareness, intellectual property, human capital, technology, fund availability and management, marketing and promotion, infrastructure, research and development, and competitiveness as problems the creative industries in Malaysia face. All these problems are largely structural and institutional and require changes in the law, the establishment of new agencies, training programs, and audience development. Absent from the list is any mention of creative freedom or the cultural constraints that may inhibit creative work including forms of censorship whether from state agencies or from civil society. Not all creative and cultural activity can be reduced to its economic contribution, and much creative work cannot be measured solely on its economic merits. It stands to reason that only with a strong diversity of creative forms of expression can economically exploitative and viable ideas emerge and develop in conversation with or from arenas of creative expression that are political in nature.

Singapore faces a similar conundrum as it tries to develop the creative industries and creative work of its citizens on one hand, while limiting and constraining what can be said on the other. Filmmakers such as Tan Pin Pin, Roystan Tan, and Martyn See have found their work at various times subject to state interference or investigation for its alleged seditious, political, or dangerous content. When artists exist in such an environment, self-censorship and caution become the norm, as the state deploys forms of 'calibrated coercion' to manage contentious speech (George 2007). Contentious viewpoints cannot emerge and creativity that expresses desires and identities that are antithetical to the normative or acceptable categories are banned, censored, or discouraged. Singapore's strategy has been to attract large multinational media companies such as LucasFilm, HBO, and Disney to base their Asian headquarters in Singapore and take advantage of the supportive business environment of the city-state. However, it indicates that semi-authoritarian regimes struggle with creativity as both a threat and as an opportunity – often creating conditions that are conducive for neither, despite significant amounts of state support.

The lack of focus on creativity becomes relevant in the Malaysian context where illiberal politics and neoliberal economic themes run through the Malaysian political system. While the state has promoted an economically liberal creative industries policy through a state-supported free market, culturally the approach is much more illiberal and conservative. Ideas of freedom of expression are constrained by 'sensitivities' such as race and religion, and more recently charges such as sedition have been levelled at political activists, citizens posting on online services such as Facebook, and artists alike. Arguably, this accounts for the focus on digital content in Malaysia because it is less 'risky' compared to theatre and art for example which have traditionally been platforms for anti-establishment ideas. One of the clearest examples of this is the fact that the censorship board (Lembaga Penapisan Filem, LPF) is located under the Ministry of Home Affairs while FINAS, the national film development body, is located under the Ministry of Communication and Culture. This means that film content is seen as a national security concern and needs to be controlled according to political sensitivities. As a result, FINAS, which is meant to develop and promote the national film industry, has little influence over censorship decisions despite the fact that it is funding local productions, promoting them for export, and developing the local market. A number of examples highlight the contradictory space for arts and culture in Malaysia.

In a widely publicized case that attracted international media attention, Lena Hendry became the first Malaysian to be arrested and charged under the 2002 Censorship Act after she organized a closed screening of the British documentary film *No Fire Zone: The Killing Fields of Sri Lanka* (2013, dir. Callum Macrae) in 2013. As an activist addressing human rights issues, Hendry was using the documentary to discuss the situation in Sri Lanka. The screening came to the attention of the Sri Lankan embassy who protested to the Malaysian government, precipitating a raid on the screening venue and the arrest of Hendry. Many saw her case as selective prosecution, and Hendry proceeded to challenge the Censorship Act in the Supreme Court, arguing that the censorship law makes all films de facto illegal unless they have passed censorship thereby contravening her right to free speech as guaranteed in the Constitution. The appeal failed and in 2017 Lena Hendry was found guilty and fined MYR 10,000. Although many in the arts and film communities paid little attention to Hendry's case, primarily because she is an activist and not a filmmaker, her case nevertheless recalls Amir Muhammad's experience with *The Last Communist* a decade earlier, suggesting little has changed in the way that censorship is applied arbitrarily.

How political art is treated in contemporary Malaysia was evident in the removal of work called Sabah Tanah Air-Ku (Sabah My Homeland) from a small, Japan-Foundation-sponsored exhibition in Kuala Lumpur in February 2017. Sabah Tanah Air-Ku by the Sabah art collective called Pangrok Sulap depicts various forms of discontent in Sabah such as bad roads, land issues, illegal logging, exclusion, and political corruption. The piece was part of an exhibition of Southeast Asian and Japanese artists thinking about the future of Malaysia. Some confusion surrounded the removal of the artwork from the exhibition, but later news reports revealed that a member of the public – some sources suggested an art dealer – had written directly to the Prime Minister's office to complain. Playing safe, the Japan Foundation removed the artwork, issuing a brief explanation that said 'despite the earnest intentions of the artist there has been a misreading of the artwork' (Zurairi 2017). Members of the arts community were upset at both the complainant and the actions of the Japan Foundation. It shows the heightened fear in the broader arts community about possible censure and backlash from the state, the deference to the Prime Minister's office as arbiter of acceptability, and the skittish nature of cultural institutions.

Other cultural events have been cancelled without any overt political content. In April 2016, the fifth KL Urban Music and Art Festival was to be held at Sepang International Circuit, an hour's drive south of central Kuala Lumpur. Expecting an audience of up to 10,000 people, the festival would showcase local and international music acts. However, a month before the festival was to take place, Eddy Casmady, a local member of parliament from the ruling UMNO party, protested publically about the festival, claiming that it would 'undermine the morality of Malay youth'.[15] He accused the festival of promoting vice and immorality, posting a Photoshopped picture of two men kissing as part of his Facebook posting. A local Islamic NGO took up his crusade against the festival by lodging a police report which prompted the police to withdraw their permission for the event. Unable to respond to the attack and receiving no support from any of the creative industries agencies, the festival organizers moved the festival to another location accompanied by an announcement that they would no longer organize the festival in the future. What the whole episode showed was that a single vocal protest from a sitting parliamentarian, evoking Islam and the protection of public morality, could protest a music festival and face little resistance or public debate and questioning. This may have been seen as a moral victory for him and those that rallied to his cause and a way of raising his public profile and moral credentials, but it cast a shadow over the ability of local event organizers to stage events in the future (Azam 2016).

What these three recent episodes suggest is that it is hard to separate the creative industries as purely economic and apolitical activities from politically contentious forms of art and 'morally dubious' forms of entertainment. Despite the creative industries being a part of the government's stated agenda, it is still subordinate to political interests and if necessary, the whims of individual politicians. Long-established illiberal political traditions thus work to constrain the scope of permissible speech and the ability of proponents of creative industries to appeal for protection or consideration. Creativity therefore is expected to remain within certain limits – similar to Singapore in that certain issues, topics, and forms of expression remain off-limits. Creative work remains subject to both formal and informal censorship or can be prosecuted under existing laws such as sedition or blasphemy. This creates an environment of uncertainty and constraint for creative industries practitioners. This is not to say that it's impossible to work or that people are not producing critical work, but it requires creative producers to adopt a certain amount of self-control and self-censorship that others elsewhere may not have. It brings into question what is meant by 'creative' in the context of Malaysia's promotion of the creative industries. Creativity it seems must be well-behaved and allied to the state-driven project of national development.

Conclusion

Throughout this chapter we have argued that the promotion of the creative industries in Malaysia has not involved a reforming of either the existing state structures and its approach to culture nor a willingness to engage with the difficult issues of creative expression and contentious ideas. As Askerud argues, the shift to a knowledge economy and by extension creative industries involves the wholesale 'reorganization of society' (Askerud 2008: 252). In Malaysia's case, the creative industries are deployed as a means to further the developmental agenda of the Malaysia government towards its Vision 2020. It shares many similarities and continuities with the Multimedia Supercorridor project initiated in the 1990s. In that sense, the DIKN and subsequent creative industries schemes have only deepened the state's role and reach into the creative industries. It has not sought to fundamentally change or challenge existing paradigms of culture, or cultural hegemony, the education system, censorship, or the value of culture to the life and well-being of the citizenry. In the post-colonial developmental context, the motivations for developing the creative industries may be different to the underlying motivations in developed economies, but from the Malaysian case it seems that the results are largely the same. There is a tendency to instrumentalize the creative industries, and move away from traditional forms of culture, to embrace digital.

Notes

1 This chapter was written in 2017 before the historic May 2018 election in which the opposition, led by former Prime Minister Mahatir Mohammad, defeated the incumbent Najib Razak, which also ended 60 years of Barisan Nasional rule.
2 http://www.jkkn.gov.my/en/national-culture-policy
3 The Censorship Board sits under the Ministry of Home Affairs.
4 Note, this commitment to Vision 2020 has since been replaced with TN50, which shifts the end date to 2050.
5 'pemangkin kepada pembangunan aktiviti industri kreatif'. Source: 'Dasar Industri Kreatif', KKMM, http://www.kkmm.gov.my/index.php?option=com_content&view=articl&id=438&Itemid=135&lang=ms
6 Original reads: 'industri Kreatif merupakan salah satu sumber penting dalam pertumbuhan ekonomi dan percambahan budaya bagi negara-negara maju'.
7 Original reads: 'Penggemblengan dan penghasilan kebolehan dan bakat individu atau berkumpulan berasaskan kreativiti, inovasi dan teknologi yang menjurus kepada sumber kerberhasilan ekonomi dan pendapatan tinggi kepada negara dengan memberi penekanan kepada aspek karya dan hak cipta intelek selaras dengan budaya dan nilai-nilai murni kepelbagaian kaum di Malaysia' (DIKN, 4).
8 'pelbagaian kaum'
9 For the National Culture Policy see: http://www.jkkn.gov.my/en/national-culture-policy
10 FINAS, Tayangan Filem Ceraka, 2016, http://www.finas.gov.my/malaysian-box-office/
11 The website for Gigapan is owned by Carnegie Mellon University based in Portland, Oregon. It does not appear to have or have had any relationship with Malaysia.
12 http://www.creativecontent.my/controllers/public/faq/#15
13 http://www.creativecontent.my/controllers/public/background
14 http://www.thesundaily.my/news/1228870
15 'meruntuhkan akhlak anak muda melayu'. From his personal Facebook page: https://www.facebook.com/eddycasmady2015/photos/a.1619682591611443.1073741828.1619343928311976/1721232958123072/?type=3&theater.

References

Askerud, P. (2008). The creative industries: Asia-Pacific perspectives. In A. C. Reis (Ed.), *Creative economy : as a development strategy : a view of developing countires* (pp. 232–255). São Paulo: Itaú Cultural.

Azam, N. (2016, 3 31). *Dadah, arak: Polis batalkan konsert di Litar Sepang.* Retrieved 5 4, 2017, from MalaysiaKini: http://www.malaysiakini.com/hiburan/336018

Banks, M., & O'Connor, J. (2009). After the creative industries. *International Journal of Cultural Policy, 15*(4), 365–373.

Berita Harian. (2017, April 17). 11 Resolusi Kongres Budaya 2017. *Berita Harian*, p. 15.

Bunnell, T. (2002). Cities for Nations? Examining the City-Nation-State Relation in Information Age Malaysia. *International Journal of Urban and Regional Research, 26*(2), 284–298.

Ch'ng, C. C. (2015, April). *Does Malaysian's animation industry have a future?* Retrieved 05 04, 2017, from Penang Monthly: http://penangmonthly.com/article.aspx?pageid=4114&name=does_malaysias_animation_industry_have_a_future?

Chong, T. (2011). The Theatre and the State in Singapore: Orthodoxy and Resistance. Routledge.

Crane, D. (1992). *The Production of Culture Media and the Urban Arts* (2nd Edition ed.). Newbury Park: Sage Publications.

Flew, T., & Cunningham, S. (2010). Creative Industries after the First Decade of Debate. *The Information Society: An International Journal, 26*(2), 113–123.

Galloway, S., & Dunlop, S. (2007). A Critique of Definitions of the Cultural and Creative industries in Public Policy. *International Journal of Cultural Policy, 13*(1), 17–31. doi:10.1080/10286630701201657

Garnham, N. (2005). From cultural to creative industries. *International Journal of Cultural Policy, 11*(1), 15–29.

George, C. (2007). Consolidating authoritarian rule: calibrated coercion in Singapore. *The Pacific Review, 20*(2), 127–145.

Hesmondhalgh, D., & Pratt, A. C. (2005). Cultural industries and cultural policy. *International Journal of Cultural Policy, 11*(1), 1–13.

Kementerian Penerangan Komunikasi & Kebudayaan. (2009). Dasar Industri Kreatif Negara. Putrajaya: Kementerian Komunikasi dan Multimedia Malaysia.

Khazanah Nasional. (2009, 12 16). *Khazanah and Pinewood collaborate to develop a world class media production facility in Iskandar Malaysia.* Retrieved 5 1, 2017, from Khazanah Nasional: http://www.khazanah.com.my/khazanah/files/1c/1cecde9b-ef1b-4116-ae9c-c02b68a446df.pdf

Khoo, G. C. (2011). Through our own eyes: Independent documentary filmmaking in Malaysia. In S. G. Yeoh, *Media, Culture and Society in Malaysia* (pp. 137–159). Abingdon: Routledge.

Kong, L. (2009). Beyond Netowrks and Relations: Towards Rethinking Creative Cluster Theory. In L. Kong, & J. O'Connor (Eds.), *Creative Economies, Creative Cities: Asian-European Perspectives* (pp. 61–76). Dordrecht: Springer.

Lee, T. (2010). The Media, Cultural Control and Government in Singapore. Routledge.

Mahpar, H. (2010, July 31). Picture imperfect. *The Star.*

Malaysian Communications and Multimedia Commission. (2014). *Creative Industry Development Fund (CIDF-MCMC).* Retrieved December 3, 2016, from Malaysian Communications and Multimedia Commission: http://www.skmm.gov.my/Content-Development/Overview/Dana-Pembangunan-Industri-Kreatif-(DPIK-SKMM).aspx

Mazalan, R. (2016, June 1). *Filem baharu Upin & Ipin gabung animasi, watak hidup.* Retrieved 5 4, 2017, from Berita Harian: http://www.bharian.com.my/node/159801

McKay, B. (2011). Subtextual Controls: A Brief Guide ti the Culture of Censorship, Control and Regulation in the Origins of Cinema in Asia. In S. G. Yeoh, *Fringe Benefits: Essays and reflections on Maalysian Arts and Cinema* (pp. 49–74). Petaling Jaya: SIRD.

Means, G. P. (1996). Soft Authoritarianism in Malaysia and Singapore. *Journal of Democracy,* 7(4), 103–117.

Nain, Z. (2002). The structure of the media industry: implications for democracy. In B. T. Khoo, & F. K.-W. Loh (Eds.), *Democracy in Malaysia: Discourses and practices* (pp. 111–137). Richmond, Surrey: Curzon Press.

O'Connor, J. (2009). Creative industries: a new direction? *International Journal of Cultural Policy, 15*(4), 387–402.

Oakley, K. (2009). The disappearing arts: creativity and innovation after the creative industries. *International Journal of Cultural Policy, 15*(4), 403–413.

The Daily Seni. (2016, March 24). *Industry Associations deem CCIG 'Ineffective' and 'Confusing', Lobbies for FINAS to take Serious Action*. Retrieved 5 3, 2017, from Daily Seni: http://www.dailyseni.com/v4/industry-associations-deem-ccig-confusing-lobbies-for-finas-to-take-control/

The Malaysian Reserve. (2013, November 15). Creative industry can bloom, if they rise above grant-reliance. *The Malaysian Reserve*.

Tschang, T. (2009). Creative Industries Across Cultural Borders: The Case of Video Games in Asia. In L. Kong, & J. O'Connor (Eds.), *Creative Economies, Creative Cities: Asian-European Perspectives* (pp. 25–44). Dordrecht: Springer.

UNCTAD. (2008). Creative Economy Report 2008. New York.

Variety. (2013, 2 12). *Rhythm & Hues bankruptcy reveals vfx biz crisis*. Retrieved 5 2, 2017, from http://variety.com/2013/film/news/rhythm-hues-bankruptcy-reveals-vfx-biz-crisis-1118066108/

Yeoh, S. G. (2010). Introduction: Representation, cultural mediation, and Power in Malaysia. In S. G. Yeoh (Ed.), *Media, Culture and Society in Malaysia* (pp. 1–20). London: Routledge.

Zurairi, A. (2017, May 15). *Malay Mail Online*. Retrieved 5 4, 2017, from http://www.themalaymailonline.com/malaysia/article/japan-foundation-slammed-for-allowing-censorship-at-art-exhibition-video

2

Creative industries policy in Thailand

A story of rise and demise

Alongkorn Parivudhiphongs

Creative industries becoming a Thai policy agenda in the early 2000s

The gradual emergence of creative industries policy (CIP) on the Thai public policy agenda from the early 2000s needs to be understood in the context of a rapidly growing international debate about creative industries (CI), creative economy (CE) and CIP, dating back at least to the 1990s (Cunningham 2007, 2009a, 2009b; DCMS 1998, 2001; Flew 2012, 2013; Florida 2002, 2005; Hartley 2005; Hartley et al. 2013; Hesmondhalgh 2008, 2013; Hesmondhalgh and Pratt 2005; Howkins 2002; Keane 2007, 2009, 2013; Kong et al. 2006; Kong and O'Connor 2009; Lee 2010, 2014; Oakley 2004; O'Connor 2000, 2010; Pratt 2005, 2015; Pratt and Jeffcutt 2009; Throsby 2008). This debate was fuelled both by academic analyses and by contributions from practitioners, public agencies, and international organisations (UNCTAD, UNESCO, and WIPO). There was some confluence of academic and practitioner-led debate, with an emphasis on four, partly overlapping, areas of debate: (1) differing interpretations of key related concepts, such as creativity, CI, CE, CIP, or cultural policy; (2) the substance of CIP and related policies, its boundaries and its relationships with other policy domains; (3) the dynamics of policy making of CI as an international phenomenon driven by complex coalitions of national, international, and transnational actors and interests; and (4) the ideational or ideological underpinnings of CIP, especially the linkage between CIP and neoliberalism.

These debates also left their marks on policy development in Thailand. For example, Thai public policy makers paid attention to discussions about definitions and boundaries of CI sectors. They also reflected on the association and integration of CIP with existing policies, notably economic and cultural policies. The Thai experience, thus, underlines the power of CI and CIP as a 'travelling idea' (Hartley et al. 2013: 33; Prince 2010: 120; Wang 2004) that has influenced public policy making in both developed and developing countries around the world.

Of equal importance has been the emergence of CIP as an international – and regional – public policy phenomenon. Here, the Asian CIP experience is of most immediate relevance for the present discussion, both because it was closely monitored by Thai policy makers, but also because the CIP experience in some parts of Asia seems to show parallels with developments in Thailand, especially as regards the framing of CIP and its main thrust. In particular, it has been noted that in Asia the adoption of CIP is often justified with reference to the need to be able to compete in the global economy (Gibson and Kong 2005: 550). This can be seen in Singapore's strategy (Tan 2007); China's integration of CI in its cultural industries policy aimed at the promotion of creative cities, tourism and cultural products (Keane 2007, 2009, 2013; Wang 2004); or 'Create Hong Kong' for commercial and economic development (Hui 2003). In each case, blueprints of CIP from overseas have provided a framework. Yet, these countries have actively 'remade' CIP according to their regional and local aspirations. This observation also applies to Thailand, where, for example, Thai Food and Traditional Herbal Medicine were included among 15 CI sectors to be promoted (NESDB and TCDC 2009; The Secretariat of the Cabinet 2011) and where King Bhumibhol's concept of 'Sufficiency Economy' became inextricably linked to CIP.

While the outlines of an explicit CIP in Thailand only emerged from around 2007–2008 (see the following section), CI started to establish its presence in Thai policy making circles from the early 2000s. In 2000, the Ministry of Culture was resurrected, and an Agency for Information and Communication Technology was set up. Given CIP's close links to cultural policy and innovation policy, both were significant steps. Equally, the establishment of several knowledge-driven public agencies, including, in 2004, the Software Industry Promotion Agency (SIPA) and the Office of Knowledge Management and Development (OKMD) proved policy makers' growing receptiveness to CI-related debates, as did the setting up of the Thailand Creative and Design Centre (TCDC) under OKMD in 2005. These government agencies should later contribute to the development of an explicit CIP.

A fully-fledged Thai CIP? Ambitions and policy inclusivity

As in many parts of Asia, Thai policy makers sought inspiration from Western countries, especially the UK, and 'best practices' in the Asian region (NESDB and TCDC 2009: 45–56). But the main force propelling the emergence of CIP and, more generally, the search for 'a new economy' was economic conditions, as highlighted in Thai official reports, including *A preliminary report on Creative Economy* (NESDB and TCDC 2009) and the *Collection of Cabinet Resolutions on Creative Economy Policy* (The Secretariat of the Cabinet 2011).

In part, Thai policy makers, aware of the heavily export-dependent nature of the economy, were looking for ways to prevent the recurrence of major economic slumps, as experienced in the global crises of 1997 and, to a lesser extent, 2008. In part, continued political instability since the coup of 2006 also made the search for ways to stabilize the economy even more urgent (Oizumi 2013). The search for new paths in economic development took place against the backdrop of a rapidly changing regional environment, notably the growing challenge of the planned ASEAN economic integration from 2016; growing regional migration and illegal labor; and rising tensions over the use of energy resources (NESDB and TCDC 2009). As the main public economic policy agency put it, CIP began to be seen as device for 'a promising and sustainable economy' (ibid.: 8). Thus, from the outset, economic considerations were at the heart of CIP and provided the major driving force behind the rise of CIP in Thailand (NESDB and TCDC 2009; TCDC 2013, 2016).

Accordingly, from around 2008, key policy makers at the National Economic and Social Development Board (NESBD) and the Thai Ministry of Commerce, spurred by support from successive prime ministers, sought to move Thailand towards a 'creative nation'.

Between 2008 and 2012, under Prime Minister Abhisit, CI ideas fully blossomed into concrete government objectives, policy programmes, and detailed measures designed to promote CI and a 'creative economy' in Thailand. When it comes to including CI concepts in national economic policy, the Thai government tended to employ the term 'creative economy' to refer to the entire system of the creativity-driven economy, including promotion of CI sectors, ICT, R&D, and even the promotion of infrastructure. This provides evidence for a very encompassing definition for everything deemed 'creative' (Hartley et al. 2013: 55–58; Miller 2009: 88–99). However, CIP focused mainly on the selection of potential industries and businesses that were expected to form the main pillars of a creative economy.

From 2008, both CI and CE began to feature prominently on the official policy agenda and in official reports and proposals by national policy making agencies. To raise awareness of, and launch projects within, selected CI sectors, the Office of the Prime Minister released 11 missions and granted budgets for CI projects and undertook a 'Creative Thailand' campaign in 2010. As part of these efforts, it invited international CE/CI experts, such as John Howkins and John Hartley, to address the Thailand International Creative Economy Forum (TICEF) in 2010 and 2012 (Department of Intellectual Property – or DIP hereafter – 2010, 2012). The peak was reached when CIP was endorsed by both the Prime Minister and the NESDB as one of key missions set out in the 11th National Development Plan, covering 2012 to 2016. The plan identified 15 CI sectors that were seen to have considerable economic potential (see Table 2.1).

The emphasis on CI in the 11th National Development Plan (2012–2016), drafted under Prime Minister Abhisit Vejjajiva proved a high point in CIP ambitions. The final version of the Plan, covering 2012 to 2016, included 15 references to 'creative economy' and four to 'creative industries' (NESDB 2012). Clearly, CI and CE were expected to be the main focus of national economic development.

Table 2.1 Proposed classification of Thailand's creative industries

Classification	*Selection of Creative Industries*
Cultural heritage	Thai crafts
	Eco-tourism
	Thai food
	Traditional Thai medicines
Arts	Performing arts
	Visual arts
Media	Films and video
	Printing
	Broadcasting
	Music
Functional creation	Design
	Fashion
	Architecture
	Advertisement
	Software

Source: A Preliminary Report on Creative Economy (NESDB and TCDC 2009: 76)

Establishing substantive emphases

If we take a closer look at the substantive CIP emphases highlighted by the Abhisit government (2008–2011), three assumed particular importance. First, there was the thematic emphasis on intellectual property rights and protection. Second, the campaign 'Creative Thailand' emphasized themes such as creative cities, creative education, and creative labor. Third, there was an emphasis on 'Thailand as a Creative Hub for an ASEAN Creative Economy', aiming at a Thai leadership role in CE development in the region.

The link between CIP and intellectual property was strong in Thailand from the beginning, underpinned by the fact that Prime Minister Abhisit Vejjajiva and his government gave the Ministry of Commerce and its Department of Intellectual Property a leading role in CIP. CIP was, thus, closely tied to notions of value creation from intellectual property. In fact, under the lead of the Ministry of Commerce, Thailand's new economic model was seen to develop the creative economy and intellectual property rights (IPR) at the same time. This strong linkage was to some extent underpinned by economic statistics. Commissioned by the Fiscal Policy Research Institute (FPRI) in association with the Ministry of Finance, a study released in December 2009 by the Thailand-based, non-profit organization the Kenan Institute Asia showed that Thailand's creative industries contributed 1.067 trillion Bahts (£46.4 billion) in sales and more than 325 billion Bahts (£6.5 billion) in added value. These industries accounted for 9.5 percent of total Gross Domestic Product (GDP) with the value added amounting to 2.86 percent of GDP in 2008 (Kenan Institute Asia and Thailand's Fiscal Policy Institute 2009: 2–4). Thus, under the lead of the Deputy Minister of Commerce, Mr. Alongkorn Polabutr, IP protection was accorded a central place within CIP.

A second substantive emphasis was on 'Creative Thailand'. The government sought to generate income for local people from value-added traditional products and tourism, especially in 'creative towns' (DIP 2010, 2011) with a long history and culture; by recognizing local talents and their accomplishments; and by providing creative spaces for activities and exhibitions related to creativity. Several policies to develop CE not only responded to economic needs, but also to special demands from local communities with regard to education, cultural identity, social inequalities, and environmental concerns. Development of creative space would allow the emergence of creative cities. Thai policy makers saw that creative cities around the world were revitalized through cultural and social developments and they sought inspiration from these experiences.

The Office of Knowledge Management and Development (OKMD) was entrusted with carrying out five projects under the CE campaign. Under the 'Bangkok Creative City' scheme, these projects intended to encourage Bangkok residents to help turn the capital into a creative center for various areas, such as design, music, and food. In this way, Bangkok would be promoted as a liveable city and be made more attractive in terms of tourism and education. The establishment of the Thailand Creative and Design Centre (TCDC) for knowledge in design and the designation of a creative zone in Bangkok to serve as a center for both Thai and foreign artists were in line with this ambition. Policy makers also gave some consideration to developing Chiang Mai, Phuket, and Ayutthaya as creative cities, even though they were all already major international tourist destinations. One project under the Ministry of Commerce aimed to study and locate a prototype of a creative city in Thailand with a focus on culture and creative activities (The Secretariat of the Cabinet 2011: 18).

A further thematic emphasis in CIP was the effort to brand Thailand as a CE hub in Asia. On 26 February 2010, the Cabinet approved the Thailand International Creative Economy Forum (TICEF), which was to be co-organized with WIPO, UNDP, and UNCTAD.

Under the theme 'globaLOCALisation: local move, global success', which emphasized creative responses at the local level to globalization, the first TICEF was held in November 2010. It brought together approximately 1,000 creative professionals, entrepreneurs, and academics in creative sectors from over 50 countries (DIP 2010). Tellingly, the Forum also featured an exhibition 'Creative King' in honor of the creativity of King Bhumibhol and his royal projects.

The second TICEF, held in March 2012 under the theme 'Capturing Value through a Global Network', emphasized creativity and innovative responses of entrepreneurs and communities at the local level to global success. The parallel sessions included such themes as Creative Cities and Societies, Branding and Creative Design, Creative Content and Media, and Local Wisdom (DIP 2012).

At the first TICEF, Prime Minister Abhisit Vejjajiva announced that Thailand would seek to develop the concept of 'Creative ASEAN' in line with Thailand's own CIP. This and later similar statements were evidence of the recognition that the ASEAN community not only provided opportunities for the region to grow together, but also challenges owing to growing economic competition among its members.

The importance of antecedent policies

It is important to stress that the emergence of CIP in Thailand was, from the beginning, characterized by attempts to link existing policy traditions with a new orientation rather than efforts to mark a radical new departure and discontinuity. The key antecedent policy traditions that were linked to CIP included the Sufficiency Economy; Community-based Enterprises; and the Knowledge Economy.

The 11th NESDB plan (2011–2016) highlighted CE and CI as key elements of social and economic development. However, it was the King's philosophy *of Sufficiency Economy* that still took center stage, as it appeared 74 times against 15 and four explicit mentions of CE and CI, respectively. NESBD policy makers believed that the CI concept chimed well with the Sufficiency Economy, which had been a major point of reference for NESDB policies since the mid-2000s (NESDB and TCDC 2009: 135). The eco-friendly philosophy focused on living a moderate, self-dependent life without greed or overexploitation of natural resources. The NESDB (ibid.: 26–32) linked this concept to the fact that CI could decrease human reliance on, and excessive consumption of, natural resources. Therefore, it could be interpreted as being in line with Sufficiency Economy, which meant an economy based on human moderation.

The government sought to make it clear that CI was perfectly compatible, and to some extent, overlapping or even identical to concepts stressing sustainability and moderation. But this supposed harmony was not put to the test. The King's concept emphasized a moderate, self-dependent life without greed and embraced the idea of sustainable development. The NESDB included the royal philosophy in the 10th and 11th National Development Plan. CIP advocates, such as TCDC and the Ministry of Culture, also sometimes referred to the philosophy in their promotion schemes and activities.

The 10th NESDB Plan (2007–2011) also emphasized the importance of Sufficiency Economy in parallel with the encouragement of *community-based enterprises* for social and economic equality as well as promotion of new entrepreneurs, notably SMEs. SMEs and community-based enterprises were credited with a high potential to become the core components of CI sectors. Both were considered as a way to maximize human creativity in order to increase economic growth.

CIP also engaged with actors and interests related to *knowledge management*. The most important was the Thailand Creative and Design Centre (TCDC). As one of the key policy makers for CIP, it had a longer-standing interest in questions related to knowledge management. Established in 2005, this knowledge-driven center aimed to connect and promote interaction among creativity, skill, cultural assets, and business conducive to creating quality products and services that would met the global market demand. TCDC was seen as a major force in the CIP initiative, particularly with their background research on Thailand's Creative Economy in collaboration with NESDB (NESDB and TCDC 2009), which influenced the selection of 15 CI sectors. Besides, TCDC's mission in CIP development was to train creative talents for SMEs. The fact that TCDC had been a brainchild of the ousted Prime Minister Thaksin Shinawatra did not hamper its operation during the premiership of Abhisit Vejjajiva. In fact, the period witnessed TCDC push forward the development of creative economy to promote creative entrepreneurs.

CIP and policy inclusivity

At least four points relating to the substance of CIP from late 2008 to mid-2011 deserve highlighting. First, in Thailand, CIP clearly grew out of economic policy rather than cultural policy. The main thrust of the policy was to enhance economic competitiveness. The selection of core CI sectors and the thematic emphases that were discussed reflected policy makers' intention to play to existing strengths of the Thai economy rather than achieve any fundamental reorientation or aim at a paradigmatic shift. Thus, CIP was seen as giving a new impetus to economic policy, but it was not conceived of as a new distinct policy domain. In line with international experience, there was an acknowledgement that the commercialization of culture – notably cultural heritage – offered the prospect of some limited value added. But decisions on programmes and funding showed that CIP, in the government's understanding, was much less about commercializing cultural policy than giving greater emphasis to 'creativity' in economic policy.

Second, CIP in Thailand during the Abhisit premiership (2008–2011) was marked by what could be called 'conceptual inclusivity' of the idea of creative industries. Partly by design, and partly by default, CI and CE came to be more or less interchangeable in policy discussions and, perhaps more importantly, they were defined in only very loose terms. In fact, it could be argued that CI and CE as policy concepts did not achieve major directional influence in the sense of providing clear guidance for the identification of policy objectives, the definition of programmes, and the choice of policy instruments. Instead of encouraging clear choices in policy priorities, they served as inclusive reference points that allowed different actors to pursue their agendas without too much need for substantive policy co-ordination.

Third, this policy inclusivity also extended to the deliberate interweaving of antecedent economic development concepts with CI and CE. In particular, the government was at pains to stress the harmony between the King's concept of Sufficiency Economy and CI and CE, even though these concepts grew out of very different political, socio-economic, and cultural traditions.

A fourth important point relating to policy substance follows on from this deliberate linkage with pre-existing policies. While the Thai government, in line with international policy developments, did engage with the theme of the creative city, CIP was more intimately connected to rural development and to addressing urban–rural development disparities than having a strong metropolitan orientation, as in many other countries. In part, this orientation reflected long-standing emphases in Thai economic policy which has struggled with very significant regional imbalances in economic development; in part, the orientation was due to the linkage with the Sufficiency Economy which itself is very much focused on improving life for the many millions of Thais who live in underdeveloped rural areas. Moreover, to the extent that policy also encompassed the promotion of the economic potential of cultural heritage, such as traditional Thai crafts, they were also closely linked to rural development.

Reconfiguration and demise: politics overtakes policy

The ambitious CIP agenda of the Absihit government was fundamentally challenged by political change and instability. First, the newly elected government of Yingluck Shinawatra, which came into power after elections in July 2011, vowed to continue CI policy making, oversaw the arrival of a dedicated CIP agency – TCEA – and approved a specially allocated budget for CI development. Second, the unexpected military coup led by General Prayuth Chan-O-Cha in May 2014 caused the suspension of on-going CIP projects. This meant that CI policy making by TCEA was retarded and the special budget was put on hold. Finally, all CIP initiatives were officially revoked in November 2015. Instead, the military government announced the launch of the 'digital economy' as a new economic development model for Thailand, which, however, subsumed some CI sectors under its new umbrella.

CIP under the Yingluck government

Yingluck Sinawatra, sister of the exiled former Prime Minister Thaksin, came to power after the July 2011 elections, when the Abhisit government was roundly defeated. She had been publicly presented as leading the election campaign only six weeks before polling day. Her economic proposals championed CI and partly built on the policies of the previous government. Her Policy Statement of the Council of Ministers to the National Assembly on 23 August 2011 indicated that 'the structure of the Thai economy still relies heavily on exports and foreign investment, making it highly vulnerable to the uncertainty of the world economy' (Shinawatra 2011: 18). It emphasized economic restructuring policy as a key government priority and suggested continuity in the footsteps of Abhisit's government, which had faced similar economic conditions. Yingluck stressed that Thailand's economy since 2010 had only expanded at an annual average of 3.6 percent, which she considered lower than the national potential. One of her strategies was 'to develop goods and services for both domestic and global consumers by taking into account the concept of an innovation-driven, creative economy, and utilisation of local wisdom' (ibid.). This substantive emphasis seemed to bode well for the continuation of the CI agenda developed by the previous Abhisit government.

However, almost from the beginning, the new Yingluck government became mired in problems, including the two-month flooding disaster between December 2011 and January 2012, and growing political polarization nationwide. Yingluck's government had to confront heavy criticism for failing to turn its promised populist policies into action; it also faced allegations of widespread corruption. The beginning of the end of her political career started when her government announced an amnesty bill designed to grant a pardon to Yingluck's exiled brother, Thaksin. Eventually, a military coup took place in May 2014. It put an end to Yingluck's government and her policies, including her CIP initiatives.

If one tries to summarize the fate of CIP during this phase, a number of observations deserve highlighting. First, the status of CIP within the government's overall political agenda remained uncertain throughout. While there was a clear emphasis on the links between CI sectors and economic development, their expected economic contribution was never clearly spelled out and it remained unclear how CIP would be linked to other planks of economic policy. As a consequence, there was a discrepancy between the government's policy ambitions, as expressed in public statements, and operational action on the CI sectors.

As noted, the government established a Thailand Creative Economy Agency (TCEA) early on and its special status within the Office of the Prime Minister appeared to signal a high-level commitment to CIP. However, to the extent that concrete measures were debated at all, these focused on what appeared quite tenuous links between CI and the government's ambitious infrastructure projects. Thus, the Prime Minister herself assigned the TCEA to study how CI and CE could contribute to central planks of the government's agenda, notably the construction of a high-speed train system and SME support and development. The government also initiated the 'Thailand 2020: Connecting Thailand to the World' project that should promote the country's logistics system in order to become 'The Hub of Delivery'. CIs were here essentially referred to as part of a much more encompassing justification for the upgrading of the country's transport infrastructure. Their 'creative' dimension was exploited to justify the need for these projects and certain existing industries.

Second, the impression that CIP was little more than an 'add-on' was reinforced by the fact that the TCEA only had a small number of staff, unlikely to be able to develop and drive a major policy agenda. Moreover, TCEA was explicitly charged with a focus on promotion of CI-related businesses and industries through strategy development, but there was no organizational or policy link to wider macro-economic policy making. This impression was strongly reinforced by the drastic scaling down of the sectors that should be the focus of promotional activities.

Third, and following on from the previous point, there was an ideational narrowing in the sense that CI policy making became tightly focused on ideas stressing primarily the economic value creation aspects of CIs to the virtual exclusion of any other ambitions. Other economic aspects of CI, such as creative labor, education and training for human capital, and creativity management were hardly addressed and non-economic aspects of CIP were virtually abandoned.

Towards the demise of the CIP model

The coming into power of a military government spelled the demise of CI and CE as guiding concepts for economic policy. In the new Prime Minister's 23-page policy statement addressed to the National Legislative Assembly on 12 September 2014 (Chan-o-cha 2014: 11–18), the term 'creative economy' was mentioned only once, as a sub-item of the economic plan. The emphasis was now on the promotion of an agro-industrial and 'digital economy'. For instance, the agro-processing industry should be developed through greater attention to value chains and R&D; attention should be given to innovation development so as to improve 'value added for Thai food based on creativity and local wisdom'; and there should be more for industries driven by high technology and those fuelled by 'design and creativity'. Sub-item 6.18 of the policy statement called for greater support for the digital economy and its infrastructure in order to help 'all economic sectors' keep up with global trends and competition. This meant, in particular, producing and trading digital products, especially software, digital devices, and telecommunications. The use of digital systems to support the finance and service sectors – especially communication and entertainment – and to facilitate industrial products was seen as contributing to the 'development of a creative economy'.

It was not immediately clear whether this meant that CI and CE had been effectively abandoned in favor of a new focus on a digital economy, as the new government found CI ideas obsolete, or if, for political reasons, it did not want to associate its new policy with brainchild projects from the previous, conflicted governments. It was not until 24 November 2015 that the Cabinet of General Prayut Chan-O-Cha approved, in principle, the formal termination of CI and CE activities, resulting in the dissolution of the TCEA Office and related agencies and the cancellation of funding worth 596 million Bahts (UK £12 million), specifically for CI promotion. The termination was officially endorsed by a Royal Gazette of 13 January 2016. All remaining activities and projects related to CE were transferred to the Office of SME Promotion (Isaranews 2016).

The present article draws on research that covers the period between the early 2000s and mid-2016, when CIP policy-making had entered a period of hibernation. However, at the time of the final editing of the article in September 2018, the Office of the Prime Minister had once again been tasked to form a 'Policy Committee for Creative Economy Promotion' in order to formulate strategic policies for the development of the creative economy as part of a reform of economic structure in line with Digital Thailand and Thailand 4.0 as announced in the Royal Gazette, dated February 7, 2018 (TCDC 2018). Later, the Creative Economy Agency (Public Organization), aka CEA, was officially established by the Royal Gazette, dated August 13, 2018, to implement the promotion of CE. This suggests that notions of CE and CI, particularly for economic growth, is making a comeback in the policy-making field in Thailand.

Lessons from the Thai experience

From a comparative perspective, the Thai experience of the rise and demise of CIP holds important lessons in at least two respects. First, it underscores the substantive ambiguity and fluidity of CI and CIP. Second, it highlights how the policy making process shapes policy substance.

The search for policy substance: creative industries or creativity in industries?

When it comes to characterizing the CIP trajectory in Thailand, the overall story can be summarized as follows. Although there were repeated attempts at establishing CIP as a clearly circumscribed, distinct policy centered on the promotion of a selected number of sectors seen as being defined by their creativity, no solid agreement on what constituted the CI to be promoted emerged. Instead sectoral emphases shifted over time. Perhaps more importantly, the central tenets of CIP were never settled. As a result, there was little continuity not just in terms of sectors targeted, but also in terms of thematic emphases (such as 'creative cities' or IP protection); policy objectives (which targets should be achieved by when and at what cost); and in terms of policy instruments to be employed (e.g., the provision of information, subsidies, or instruments aimed at securing better access of local industries to national, regional, and global markets). In the Thai experience, the CI concept and related CIP initiatives were initially inspired by policy debates and policy experiences of some Western countries, the activities of international organizations engaged in promoting a CI agenda, and what was regarded as 'best practice' in some other Asian countries. These debates and policy initiatives were taken up very selectively by a range of public bodies, including the national policy planning office NESDB; ministries, notably the Ministry of Commerce and its IP Department; and some other public agencies. In the main, the different actors sought to align the concept of CI with their existing activities, so that CIP did not mean a major substantive reorientation of policy. To the extent that it promised the availability of additional sources of funding, CIP was taken up by a range of actors, including also the Ministry of Culture, and it provided welcome opportunities for the establishment of some new public bodies, without challenging the 'turf' of traditional players.

As part of this internalization of CI, the concept crept progressively into economic policy and, to a lesser extent, cultural policy; but it did not inspire a more far-reaching reorientation in either. Nor did CIP emerge as a distinct policy domain. Instead, it remained closely tied to the government's economic policy strategy. By the mid-2010s, CIP had largely lost any distinctiveness. It was, therefore, quite readily supplanted by a new digital economy strategy put forward by the new military government.

Several points noted in this brief summary account deserve further elaboration. First, as regards the framing of the policy challenge, during the phase from 2008, the policy challenge was defined primarily in terms of economic development. This understanding of CI and CIP was spurred by what were seen as long-term economic challenges to the Thai economy associated with the rise of new regional competitors and intensified competition driven by progressively integrating regional and global markets. Thus, CIP was first put on the agenda as a response to perceived economic risks and opportunities faced by Thailand. However, this economic framing quickly became complemented by references to non-economic concerns, centered on the notions of Thai-ness, nation, and national identity. The latter may be taken to indicate a strong link to themes traditionally associated with cultural policy. Yet, it is worth emphasizing that Thailand's successive National Economic and Social Development Plans produced by the NESDB underlined the linkage between economic development, social cohesion, and the integrity of the nation.

Second, when it comes to sectoral and thematic emphases of CIP, Thailand underwent a discussion process similar to that observed in other countries and the debate was initially very much influenced by international models and classifications. However, it soon became apparent that CIP in Thailand would be less about developing hitherto marginal or neglected sectors of the Thai economy. Rather, CIP would contribute to the further strengthening of those industries that have long been central pillars of the Thai economy, including agriculture and tourism. Hence, the emphasis was less on developing newly emergent creative sectors but rather on promoting and exploiting creativity in traditional core sectors.

Initially, CIP attempted to include all related sectors under one big umbrella, ostensibly in order to create an encompassing approach and engage a wide range of stakeholders, both within the executive machinery and in the economy and organized civil society. Accordingly, from a sectoral point of view, Thai CIP started out as inclusive, but with little substantive distinctiveness. This changed later, as the number of economic sectors to be addressed by CIP was drastically scaled back under the Shinawatra government.

When it comes to thematic emphases, one can identify a number of overarching themes, including 'creative Thailand' and 'creative ASEAN hub'; however, the linkage between these themes and concrete initiatives and measures remained tenuous. A further thematic emphasis referred to 'creative cities'. Here, Thailand referred to a broad international theme centered on creativity and urban and metropolitan development. But it is worth highlighting that this linkage between CI and a city focus was less prominent in Thailand than elsewhere. In Thailand, from the beginning, CIP was linked more closely to economic policy making in support of rural development and initiatives aimed at reducing spatial economic imbalances.

Third, unlike in some other countries, where CIP was presented as a major new departure in public policy, transcending traditional approaches to both economic and cultural policy, in Thailand, there was, from the beginning, a stress on policy continuity. CIP should build on traditional economic strengths and, critically, should not conflict with long-established fundamental ideas informing official policy planning, notably the Sufficiency Economy. Accordingly, CIP was not only oriented towards traditional mainstays of the Thai economy, but official documents also tended to discuss CI/CE in close association the Sufficiency Economy. This emphasis on continuity may have helped to build some initial support behind CIP or at least prevent early opposition; but it also meant that the transformative potential of CIP was bound to be limited.

Fourth, as regards concrete policy measures taken, we find a mix of organization, promotion, and regulation. A great deal of CIP was about creating an organizational framework for policy development and delivery. Several new committees for policy development were set up at the administrative level and a number of new promotional bodies were established. Importantly, promotional efforts were also largely the preserve of public bodies; there was little direct transfer of funds from the public to the private sectors. In other words, there was a strong orientation towards spending CIP funds within the public sector rather than channelling funding directly towards the private sector. This was one of the reasons why engagement with the private sector remained limited.

Next to organizational and promotional measures, regulation also played a role in Thai CIP. This observation applies, in particular, to the case of IP protection. The emphasis placed on IP, including initiatives to promote the creation of IP, its effective protection and commercial exploitation in part reflected the centrality that IP was accorded in international CIP debates. To some extent, Thai policy makers here followed international trends. But there were also two specific reasons behind the emphasis on IP. On the one hand, Thailand has long been seen as having ineffective enforcement mechanisms for the protection of intellectual property, especially in arts and entertainment. On the other, the Ministry of Commerce and, in particular, its Department of IP, were among the early champions of CIP. As a result, IP became an important component of CIP.

How the policy process mattered

As the preceding remarks already indicate, the development of policy substance – and the overall trajectory of Thai CIP – cannot be understood without paying attention to the policy process. Analyses of public policy making – rather than discussions of definitional and conceptual issues, analysis of policy substance, and policy critique – are quite rare in studies of both cultural policy and CIP. But, as the Thai case underlines, policy making matters.

The key reason why CIP failed to emerge as a distinctive policy in Thailand and did not take root lies in the interaction of institutional factors and diverging interests and ideas of public actors (political and administrative) and, to a much lesser extent, private actors (corporate and individual), which failed to crystallize into a reasonably coherent set of objectives and concrete policies.

First, there was considerable turmoil especially in the political institutions of the country, culminating in the effective suspension of the democratic institutions and their replacement by a military junta in 2015. Key parts of the constitutional framework were suspended. These upheavals were accompanied by several changes of government and high turnover at the level of political decision makers that made longer-term policy making very difficult. Moreover, turmoil drew away attention from ordinary policy making in those domains that were not seen to be directly related to security and law and order. There was not enough continuity at the level of institutions or key political actors to make it likely that innovative policies would be both formulated and implemented.

Second, political instability made it even more difficult to counter the effects of a deeply entrenched bureaucracy, which, in previous studies of the Thai socio-political system (Ockey 2004; Phongpaichit and Baker 2012; Liamputtong 2014) has tended to be seen as both powerful and hostile to innovation. Especially, strong bureaucratic defenders of traditional cultural policy, centered on protection and regulation, but with very limited ambitions in terms of promotion, continued to exert influence as did long-established policy ideas such as Sufficiency Economy favored by the royal household.

Third, the policy process was characterized by top-down CIP initiatives emanating from the Office of the Prime Minister and organizations closely linked to the center of government. If we focus on the evolving actor constellations and interests, it is clear that the decisive impetus for CIP initially emerged from the center, i.e. the Office of the Prime Minister and the NESDB. There was, in other words, a small team of senior politicians and bureaucrats who set the agenda and highlighted the economic potential of CIP. The emergence of a small team enjoying access to the Prime Minister helped to establish CI and CE rapidly on the agenda under the Abhisit government. But for the policy to succeed it would need to be able to mobilize both other parts of the government machinery – notably sectoral ministries and central agencies – and also the private sector. Both proved problematic. Instead, the top-down initiatives largely failed to diffuse throughout a highly fragmented bureaucracy, partly due to lack of knowledge and co-operation among other actors, partly due to a failure of the center to engage with sectoral actors and interests.

As regards relationships within the government machinery, the formulation and (partial) implementation of CIP created many inter-agency problems. Although the CIP initiative was endorsed by the Prime Minister and NESDB, and TCEA was supposed to be the key policy agency for its implementation, there were, by necessity, several other government bodies involved in CIP, notably when it came to moving from agenda-setting and decision-taking to actual implementation. The government's strategy relied on a setting up of several new small agencies and these new bodies had a clear self-interest in pushing the CI agenda. The Department of IP in the Ministry of Commerce was also among the early proponents of CIP, at least as far as it concerned intellectual property and copyright issues. But it proved much more difficult to convert other entrenched players, including the Ministry of Industry, the Ministry of Culture, and the Ministry of Tourism and Sports to the new agenda. As was to be expected, they were willing to engage with the CIP agenda only to the extent that it benefitted their own interests – notably in terms of funding – or at least did not appear to threaten them. In terms of policy making this meant that CIP was overly reliant on a push from the center of government, since none of the big players in charge of policy delivery had developed a major stake in the policy. When that push from the center faltered, with the resignation of Prime Minister Abhisit Vejjajiva, the small new CIP-related agencies that had been created were, in themselves, too weak to ensure the continuation of the policy. Moreover, there was an element of disenchantment. Thus, during 2010–2012, the government had sought to give a push with increasing budgets for CI projects, raising public awareness, and even a decision to add CI into national school curriculum. But beyond the setting up of new bodies, concrete measurable results were limited. Thus, goodwill was dissipated.

A similar pattern of a failure to widen the range of stakeholders in CIP is evident when it comes to the relations between government bodies and private sector and civil society organizations and interests. CI policy making cannot be described as a bottom-up process as there was very limited participation from stakeholders, especially entrepreneurs from selected CI. This lack of a systematic policy dialogue has been noted in other studies of the Thai political system (Feungchan 2006). There are at least three reasons for this: reluctance on the part of public bodies to recognize private sector organizations as legitimate participants in the process of formulating policy; organizational weakness on the part of private sector interest representatives and NGOs; and weariness to become involved with government bodies, which are seen as meddling rather than helping.

Fourth, much has been made by some authors of the role that international organizations and internationally recognized academics have played in spreading CI-related ideas and of their influence on policy making in different regions of the world. Thai CIP was conceptually influenced by DCMS in the UK and took inspiration from CI classifications by UNCTAD and IP and copyrights industries developed by WIPO. In a very selective manner, it also examined policy practices in Asian countries, such as the 'one village, one product' (OVOP) programme in Japan. Moreover, Thai policy makers sought to position Thailand as the hub of CI and CE within the ASEAN regional collaboration context. But although Thai policy makers engaged with Western CI experiences and also paid attention to developments in the regional neighborhood, the influence was indirect rather than direct. In other words, non-domestic actors did not themselves become major players in the Thai policy process, but provided ideational inspiration.

However, it is also noticeable that from the beginning 'imported' ideas were amalgamated with long-standing domestic guiding ideas, notably as regards policy justification and the choice of policy instruments. Thus, while there was a stress on linking CIP to economic development, as in the international debates, the early emphasis on the potential contribution of CIP to rural development and to addressing growing spatial disparities in economic development, although not unique, was an important feature of the Thai case. Moreover, economic justifications, although predominant, went hand in hand with references to ideas relating to national identity and Thai-ness. In this sense, Thai CIP justifications drew on ideas that are typically associated with cultural policy rather than economic development policy. Equally, instrumental ideas, relating to the choice of measures best suited to advancing CI and CE showed this tendency towards amalgamation with long-standing policy traditions. Thus, the creation of a range of public agencies charged with promoting diverse aspects of CIP was in line with a bureaucratic tradition that operates through the creation of public organizations, but puts little emphasis on policy instruments such as structured dialogue with affected interests and potential stakeholders or the direct channelling of funds to the private sector.

Concluding remarks: is CIP neoliberal?

The preceding section has sought to draw out how the study of the Thai CIP experience may contribute to a broader comparative agenda in the study of CIP, both in terms of the study of the substance of CIP and the process of policy making. There is, however, at least one further central point that deserves highlighting, although it has not been at the heart of the preceding analysis. 'Critical' issues have featured very prominently in the scholarly CI literature, with an emphasis on probing the ideological underpinnings of CIP. The dominant concern has been with the linkage between CIP and neoliberal policy agendas. This linkage has been made both in discussions of the Western, but also of the Asian experience (see Kong et al. 2006; Kong and O'Connor 2009; Lee and Lim 2014). As Flew (2012), for example, has noted

> arguments arising from the critical humanities in particular ... sees creative industries less as distinctive way of framing media and cultural policy questions, but instead as an ideological category. In particular, the turn to creative industries is seen as a concrete manifestation of neo-liberalism, understood as a global ideological project ... that has aimed

> to shift power and resources to corporations and wealthy elites ... A number of critical theorists have argued that media and cultural policy in the 1990s and 2000s has largely involved the implementation of neo-liberalism, often under the rubric of creative industries.
> *(ibid.: 176–177)*

Viewed against this background, the Thai case is notably for the absence of free-market rhetoric when it came to justifications for CIP. Instead of stressing the virtues of the free market and commercialization, justifications for CIP emphasized its benefits for development, its potential to help address economic inequality and imbalances, and sensitivity to social and economic needs outside the main urban centers. The Thai case, therefore, provides support for the view that CIP is open to alternative ideological underpinnings. This finding is in line with recent reviews of public policy for CIs (Bakhshi et al. 2015) that highlight that although economic rationales dominate in the justification of CIP, the substantive arguments for public intervention take on different forms depending on context.

A second point follows on from the previous observation, namely that economic interests are not necessarily the main drivers of CIP. One reading of the importance of non-economic considerations in CIP policy making stresses how public policy makers may act in a manner that is removed from narrow sectoral economic interests. Thus, Flew (2012: 182), e.g., raises the possibility of state actors pursuing innovative policy agendas that are not determined by corporate–cultural interests.

In a more critical reading, however, the interests of public policy makers, especially of bureaucratic actors, may come to outweigh the interests of those at whom public policies are ostensibly directed. Thus, CIP may come to be dominated by political-bureaucratic rather than economic interests. The Thai case provides evidence for a policy process that is centered on political-bureaucratic elites, with little systematic interaction with organized interests and civil society. Under these conditions, political power and bureaucratic self-interests may matter more than economic rationales.

References

In English

Bakhshi, H., Cunningham, S., and Mateos-Garcia, J. (2015) Public policy for creative industries. In Jones, C., Lorenzen, M. and Sapsed, J. (eds.), *The Oxford Handbook of Creative Industries*. Oxford: Oxford University Press.

Chan-o-cha, P. (2014) Policy Statement of the Council of Ministers delivered to the National Legislative Assembly Friday 12 September B.E. 2557 (2014) (accessed November 19, 2014: http://www.eppo.go.th/doc/gov-policy-2554-E.pdf).

Cunningham, S. (2007) Creative industries as policy and discourse outside the United Kingdom. *Global Media and Communication*, 3, 347–52.

Cunningham, S. (2009a) Creative industries as a globally contestable policy field. *Chinese Journal of Communication*, 2(1): 13–24.

Cunningham, S. (2009b) Trojan horse or Rorschach blot? Creative industries discourse around the world. *International Journal of Cultural Policy*, 15(4): 375–386.

Department of Culture, Media and Sport (1998) Creative Industries Mapping Document, London: DCMS (accessed May 12, 2012: https://www.gov.uk/government/publications/ creative-industries-mapping-documents-1998).

Department of Culture, Media and Sport (2001) Creative Industries Mapping Document 2010, London: DCMS (accessed May 12, 2012: https://www.gov.uk/government/publications/creative-industries-mapping-documents-2001).

Flew, T. (2012) The Creative Industries: Culture and Policy. Los Angeles, CA: Sage.

Flew, T. (2013) *Global Creative Industries*. Cambridge, UK: Polity.
Florida, R. (2002) The Rise of the Creative Class: And How It's Transforming Work, Leisure, Community and Everyday Life. New York: Basic Books.
Florida, R. (2005) *Cities and the Creative Class*. New York: Routledge.
Gibson, C. and Kong, L. (2005) Cultural economy: a critical review. *Progress in Human Geography*, 29(5): 541–61.
Hartley, J. (2005) *Creative Industries*. Oxford: Blackwell, pp 1–40.
Hartley, J., Potts, J., Flew, T., Cunningham, S., Keane, M. and Banks, J. (eds.) (2013) *Key Concepts in Creative Industries*. London: Sage.
Hesmondhalgh, D. (2008) Cultural and creative industries. In Bennett, T. and Flow, J. (eds.), *The Sage Handbook of Cultural Analysis*. London: Sage, pp. 552–69.
Hesmondhalgh, D. (2013) *The Cultural Industries*, 3rd edn. London: Sage.
Hesmondhalgh, D. and Pratt, A. C. (2005) Cultural industries and cultural policy. *International Journal of Cultural Policy*, 11(1), 1–13.
Howkins, J. (2002) The Creative Economy: How People Make Money from Ideas. UK: Penguin
Hui, D. (2003) *Baseline Study on Hong Kong's Creative Industries*. Hong Kong, China: Hong Kong Special Administrative Unit, Central Policy Unit.
Keane, M. (2007) Created in China: The Great New Leap Forward. London: Routledge.
Keane, M. (2009) Creative industries in China: four perspectives on social transformation. *International Journal of Cultural Policy*, 15(4): 431–43.
Keane, M. (2013) Creative Industries in China: Art, Design and Media. Cambridge: Polity.
Kenan Institute Asia and Thailand's Fiscal Policy Institute (2009) *Economic Contributions of Thailand's Creative Industries*, commissioned by Thailand's Ministry of Commerce. (accessed March 12, 2013: https://www.researchgate.net/publication/247157971_ECONOMIC_CONTRIBUTIONS_OF_THAILAND'S_CREATIVE_INDUSTRIES)
Kong, L. and O'Connor, J. (2009) Creative Economies, Creative Cities: Asian-European Perspectives. London, New York: Springer.
Kong, L., Gibson, C., Khoo, L. M., and Semple, A. L. (2006) Knowledges of the creative economy: towards a relational geography of diffusion and adaptation in Asia. *Asia Pacific Viewpoint*, 47(2), 173–94.
Lee, H. K. (2010) Problematising the creative industries discourse from a perspective of cultural market and creative labour. *Review of Cultural Economics*, 12(2): 3–21.
Lee, H. K. (2014) Politics of the creative industries discourse and its variants. *International Journal of Cultural Policy* (accessed January 12, 2015: http://www.tandfonline.com/doi/full/10.1080/10286632.2014.991783#.VzTChIR97rc)
Lee, H. K. and Lim, L. (eds.) (2014) Cultural Policies in East Asia: Dynamics between the State, Arts and Creative Industries. Basingstoke: Palgrave.
Liamputtong, P. (ed.) (2014) Contemporary Socio-Cultural and Political Perspectives in Thailand. Dordrecht: Springer.
Miller, T. (2009) From creative to cultural industries: not all industries are cultural, and no industries are creative. *Cultural Studies*, 23(1): 88–99.
NESDB (2012) The 11th National Economic and Social Development Plan (2012–2016) (accessed August 17, 2012: http://www.nesdb.go.th/nesdb_en/ewt_w3c/ewt_dl_link.php?filename=develop_issue&nid=3786).
Oakley, K. (2004) Not so cool Britannia: the role of the creative industries in economic development. *International Journal of Cultural Studies*, 7(1), 67–77.
Ockey, J. (2004) State, bureaucracy and polity in modern Thai politics. *Journal of Contemporary Asia*, 34(2), 143–62.
O'Connor, J. (2000) The definition of the 'cultural industries'. *The European Journal of Arts Education*, 2(3): 15–27.
O'Connor, J. (2010) *The Cultural and Creative Industries: A Literature Review*. Newcastle upon Tyne: Creativity, Culture and Education.
Oizumi, K. (2013) *Thailand Upholding a 'Creative Economy' – Concerns that Political Instability Will Be Heavy Weight*. Japan Centre for Economic Research 201, Asia Research Report, 47–60 (accessed May 2, 2013: https://www.jcer.or.jp/eng/pdf/2013asia_chapter4.pdf).
Phongpaichit, P. and Baker, C. (2012) Populist Challenge to the Establishment: Thaksin Shinawatra and the Transformation of Thai Politics. London: Routledge

Pratt, A. C. (2005) Cultural industries and public policy: An oxymoron? *International Journal of Cultural Policy*, 11(1): 31–44.

Pratt, A. C. (2015) Creative Industries and Development: Culture in Development, or the Cultures of Development? In: Jones, C., Lorenzen, M. and Sapsed, J. (eds.), *The Oxford Handbook of Creative Industries*. (pp. 503–515). Oxford: Oxford University Press.

Pratt, A. C. and Jeffcutt, P. (eds.) (2009) *Creativity, Innovation and the Cultural Economy*. London: Routledge.

Prince, R. (2010) Globalizing the creative industries concept: travelling policy and transnational policy communities. *The Journal of Arts Management, Law, and Society*, 40(2), 119–39.

Shinawatra, Y. (2011) Policy Statement of the Council of Ministers delivered to the National Assembly on Tuesday 23 August B.E. 2554 (2011) (accessed November 19, 2014: http://www.eppo.go.th/doc/gov-policy-2554-E.pdf).

Tan, K. P. (ed.) (2007) Renaissance Singapore? Economy, Culture, and Politics. Singapore: NUS Press.

Throsby, D. (2008) Modelling the cultural industries. *International Journal of Cultural Policy*, 14: 217–32.

Wang, J. (2004) The global reach of a new discourse: how far can 'creative industries' travel? *International Journal of Cultural Studies*, 7(1): 9–19.

In Thai

Department of Intellectual Property (DIP) (2010) *Mahakum Settakit Sangsun Nana Chart – Jak Moradok Tang Panya Su Khamsumret Radab Lok* (Thailand International Creative Economy Forum (TICEF): Globalization – Local Move, Global Success). Nonthaburi: DIP.

Department of Intellectual Property (DIP) (2011) Sarub Pon-ngan Samkan *Kong Krom Sabsin Tang Panya Mokarakhom* 2554 B.E. (Summary of DIP main tasks in January 2011) (accessed June 26, 2014: www.ipthailand.go.th/dmdocuments/jan.54.doc).

Department of Intellectual Property (DIP) (2012) *Mahakum Settakit Sangsun Nana Chart – Jak Nayobai Su Karn Klubkluen: Khunkha Jak Thongtin Su Sakon* (Thailand International Creative Economy Forum (TICEF): from policy to mobilisation: capturing local values, creating global impact). Nonthaburi: DIP

Feungchan, S. (2006) Praden Lae Panha Nayobai Satarana Nai Prathed Thai (Issues and problems with public policy making in Thailand) in *Public Policy and Planning, Unit 1–8*, Bangkok: Sukhothai Thammathirat Open University Press.

Isaranews (2016) *Yoklerk Kongtoon Settakit Sangsun Yang Pen Tangkan* (Officially Cancelled Creative Economy Fund), 14 January 2016 (accessed January 17, 2016: http://www.isranews.org/isra-news/item/44076-sss1).

National Economic and Social Development Board, and Thailand Creative and Design Centre (NESDB and TCDC) (2009) *Ran-ngan Karn Suksa Beugntong Settakit Sangsun* (A Preliminary Study on Creative Economy) (accessed December 15, 2015: http://www.nesdb.go.th/ewt_dl_link.php?nid=3788, 2011).

Secretariat of the Cabinet (2011) *Collection of Cabinet Resolutions on Creative Economy Policy*. Bangkok: Secretariat of the Cabinet.

Secretariat of the Cabinet (2018) *Royal Gazette, Decree on the establishment of Creative Economy Agency (Public Organization)*, dated August 13, 2018 (accessed September 18, 2018: http://www.ratchakitcha.soc.go.th/DATA/PDF/2561/A/059/27.PDF).

Thailand Creative and Design Centre (TCDC) (2018) *Royal Gazette, Order of the Office of the Prime Minister regarding Policy Committee for Creative Economy Promotion*, dated February 7, 2018 (accessed September 18, 2018: https://web.tcdc.or.th/upload/Rule.PDF).

Thailand Creative and Design Centre (TCDC) (2013) *Tummai Tong Settakit Sangsun (Why Creative Economy?)*. Bangkok: TCDC (accessed January 13, 2014: http://www.tcdc.or.th/creativethailand/book/19824).

Thailand Creative and Design Centre (TCDC) (2016) *Chub Krasae Settakit Sangsun (TCDC Outlook: Creative Economy Perspective)*, January–June 2016 (accessed April 12, 2016: http://www.tcdc.or.th/upload/downloads/ebook-TCDC-Outlook-vol1-th.pdf).

3

Governance and policy development of creative and cultural industries in Japan

Christian Morgner

The latest report from the United Nations Conference on Trade and Development (UNCTAD 2010: XXIII) indicates that exports of creative or cultural goods were worth US $592 million, which accounts for about 7 percent of world GDP. The global creative and cultural industries have shown considerable growth (nearly 15 percent) over the last ten years, even in the wake of the financial crisis in 2008. These developments reinforce the picture of the creative economy as a key driver of the world economy. In this global market, Japan is usually seen as a successful export economy and is among the top ten exporters of creative goods (UNCTAD 2010: 132). This international success is largely attributed to Japan's advances in new technologies, gaming, and anime (Hemmert and Oberländer 1998; Westlund and Caldoni-Lundberg 2007; Tschang 2009). In the global creative and cultural industries strongly influenced by US products, Japan's dominance in the global videogame, animation, and comics market can be seen as an exception. Videogaming was invented by Atari, but this market would not have become a global industry without companies like Nintendo and Sony. As demonstrated by Aoyama and Izushi (2003), this success can be attributed to the social and historical foundations of a creative imaginary of vibrant cartoons and animation films, in combination with a highly skilled and innovative consumer electronics industry.

Despite the configuration of the gaming industry within Japan, however, its artistic and creative potential is largely ignored. Although videogames play a significant role in the global cultural industry, they appear 'culturally odourless' (Iwabuchi 1998) in that they do not compete with cultural icons from the USA or *haute culture* products in film and the arts. Indeed, few studies or publications currently focus on the development of cultural and creative industries policy within Japan, and only a few government schemes foreground such policies. Recent publications in this area have focused mainly on China, South Korea, and Singapore or creative cities like Shanghai, Seoul, or Hong Kong (Hesmondhalgh 2002; Yusuf and Nabeshima 2005; Kong and O'Connor 2009; UNCTAD 2010; Howkins 2013; Flew 2013). Lee and Lim's (2014) publication on cultural policies and creative industries in East Asia also devoted most attention to China, South Korea, Singapore, and Taiwan, with only minor reference to Japan.

In focusing on cultural policy development at municipal and national levels within Japan and the rise of the creative industries, the present chapter looks at early-twentieth-century initiatives – in particular, those following the cultural restoration during the Meiji period. It is worth noting that terms such as *creative industries* and *creative economy* did not exist in Japan before the 1990s, although notions of culture and cultural identity were prevalent in governmental schemes and initiatives before that time. The chapter also includes a foray into Japan's cultural policies and industries during WWII and post-war developments until the late 1980s. However, the main focus is on more recent initiatives – especially government and policy-related initiatives – since the early 1990s, as Japanese policy makers became more engaged in debate on cultural policy and *content industries* (replaced in the late 1990s by the term *creative industries*). For instance, the foundation of the Creative Industries Promotion Office under the Manufacturing Industries Bureau at the Ministry of Economy, Trade and Industry in 2010 meant official recognition for the creative and cultural industries. This was an acknowledgement that Japan's cultural industries would play an important role in the government's New Growth Strategy under the unifying long-term theme of 'Cool Japan' (Cool Japan Advisory Council 2011).

Meiji restoration, cultural policies, and economic development

During the Meiji period (1868–1912), Japanese society went through an intense process of modernization. These fundamental changes affected the country's political, education, economic, and military structures and also had a lasting impact on Japan's cultural activities. Although the terms *cultural* or *creative industries* did not yet exist, many of the cultural and economic policies that emerged addressed areas such as art and design education, the formation of a film and recording industry, participation at international trade fairs and the promotion of cultural products overseas, especially in competition with China. The general framework underpinning these early polices was a modernization narrative known as Meiji ideology (Gluck 1985), driven by concerns such as rationalization, efficiency, and detraditionalization.

As in other countries (e.g., the USA, Holland and Britain), art education was introduced in primary and secondary schools in Japan at the end of the nineteenth century, emphasizing manual drawing, with clear intent to support industrial development. At that time, Western paintings were not recognized for their aesthetic pleasures but rather as 'a true representation of reality based in a spirit of rationalism' (Isozaki 1998: 23). In 1873, the first art school book was published, and art curricula were formulated (Okazaki 1985), and there were similar developments in tertiary education. The Technological Art School (Kobu Bijutsun Gakko) was founded in 1876, and art courses were subsequently offered at the newly formed Tokyo Academy of Art and at the Kyoto Higher Polytechnical School. The Japan Institute of Fine Arts (Nippon Bijitsu-in) was founded in 1898 (Kawakita 1976).

In combination with changes to the country's economic structure, these cultural developments also spurred Japan's early cinema and recording industry, and films have been produced in Japan since the late nineteenth century. Many of these early films were produced by networks of collaborators, but major studios like Nikkatsu, Shochiku, Teikine, and Toa Studios were founded soon after, and the first film magazines (such as *Katsudō shashinkai*, founded in 1909) began to emerge. These early silent films were not only popular in Japan, where they could compete with imports from Hollywood, but were also exported to other Asian countries. By the mid-1920s, the import of foreign films had declined to less than 30 percent as Japanese productions gained a market share of more than 70 percent (Raine 2014: 109).

Prior to the nineteenth century, Japan had no encompassing term or concept for music, and the Sino-Japanese compound *ongaku* referred more to orchestral sound. The emergence of 'Japanese music' was not driven by musicians but by educators, policy makers and intellectuals. As music became part of the early educational curricula, music schools such as the Tokyo Conservatory of Music (1907) were founded. This was followed by the emergence of music periodicals; the first music magazine (*Ongaku Zasshi*) was published in 1890 (see Mehl 2017). Many of the early writers in these magazines were employed at the Ministry of Education (Mori 1989). The first recordings of Japanese music using phonograph records (also known as 'Talking Machines') were conducted in 1902 by the American company Victor (Mason 1992). In the following year, a number of British and American companies visited Japan to produce a large number of records. They opened their first offices in 1907 in prestigious areas of Tokyo such as Ginza and Yokohama (Inoue 1977). Although the music industry took off rapidly and easily, Japanese policy in this area changed following the great earthquake in 1923, as the government focused on domestic production of certain goods to limit spending on imports. A new import law on luxury goods, which included films and records, came into force in 1924, and Japanese record companies were created in collaboration with British, American, and German companies, including Japan Columbia (1927), Japan Polydor (1927), and King Records (1930). As the main center of these cultural activities, Tokyo served as an inter-Asian hub for activities such as the import and localization of jazz into Asia, as well as the export of Japanese music to China and Taiwan (Miller 2006).

Japan's great tradition of craftsmanship in the areas of furniture, ceramics, and fashion (silk) generated international demand, and exotic and high-quality goods were exported to Europe and North America. The Japanese government (more than entrepreneurs) invested heavily in the modernization of these industries. As Ferguson (2004: 181) argued, these state-funded industries were afforded sufficient stability to produce these cultural goods efficiently. As well as being keen to encourage the production of these items, the Japanese government deployed a range of policies and measures to showcase them at home and abroad, notably through the international exhibitions and fairs that it organized or attended. One perennial Japanese national exhibition called *bunten* resembled the French Salon. The first was held in 1907 and attracted about 200,000 visitors – about one-eighth of the population of the metropolitan region of Tokyo (Omuka 2000). The Meiji government made it part of its political agenda not only to attend world fairs but also to manage and fund such expositions. The fairs provided a platform for presenting two images of Japan to the world: the strength to equal Western power, and a culturally unique and ancient nation that resisted Western influence (Christ 1996, 2000). While this careful planning and extensive use of government funds to highlight Japanese products (luxuries, arts, and design) was intended to boost international trade, these cultural events also served Japan's colonial policy (Park 2003). The twofold thrust of these cultural policies, showcasing Japan's superior skills and productiveness as well as the outstanding quality of Japanese culture, was particularly fierce in competing with China (Teow 1999).

Cultural policies as propaganda and post-war renewal

Japanese remission policies[1] in China did not differ greatly from those of their Western counterparts, which were driven by a mixture of pragmatic interests, ethnocentric rivalries, and idealism. However, as argued by Teow (1999: 197), their means and scope were quite different: 'Japan stood out as the only country that used its remission to institutionalize a cultural policy toward China'. In 1923, the Ministry of Finance in Tokyo established the China Cultural Affairs Bureau to enhance its cultural activities on the mainland. The rise of nationalism in Japan meant that the modernization project now became part of a culturally shaped agenda of colonization to integrate the colonies and occupied territories under the banner of the 'Greater East Asia Co-Prosperity Sphere'. In this environment, the cultural industries were principally used to 'protect' Asia from the influence of Western cultures. To this end, the Japanese copied the American model, using Hollywood actors to create propaganda films. Well-known artists, writers, film-makers, and musicians – the so-called *Bunkajin* or people of culture – travelled to the colonized territories and were involved in organizing a wider range of educational and cultural activities.

According to Kurasawa (1991), more than 20 films were produced and shown in Java between 1942 and 1945. Similarly, under the Japanese-led government in 1930s Manchuria (northern China), where a large number of Japanese films were exported, Japanese broadcasts were aired, art festivals were organized, and Japanese books and magazines were translated in large numbers (Suzuki 2005). Although these activities influenced cultural policies in these regions, they were largely considered a failure. The Japanese were ill-prepared, as they were largely unfamiliar with these nations' cultures, customs, and languages, and they often had to communicate with their Asian neighbors in English. Additionally, the US embargo prior to WWII and the large-scale industrialization during the war severely constrained Japan's cultural industries, for instance, materials for the production of films, musical instruments, and broadcasting equipment were scarce. Large parts of the film industry were shut down; modern music and dance, specifically jazz, had to go underground. This at least meant that some survived at a minor level to become influential in the post-war period.

Post-war modernization and rebuilding shifted Japan from a cultural policy-driven narrative to an economic version. The Japanese government considered cultural industries a risky investment, as nationalist cultural propaganda had harmed Japan's cultural standing in Asia. The government believed that the export of cultural products or ideas that had clear associations with contemporary Japan might hamper the formation of economic relationships with other countries. As a consequence, they did very little to support the commercial export of culture (Otmazgin 2012). This inactive position was further reinforced by American policies for rebuilding the country, which sought to neutralize political attempts to promote Japanese culture on the Asian continent. Cultural policies therefore had a strong inward focus and became an important element in the domestic rebuilding of the country but concentrated mainly on traditional arts (tea ceremonies, pottery, flower arrangements, and calligraphy). These policies were aimed not just at a cultural elite but at the entire Japanese population; the intention was that everyone should enjoy a healthy and culturally rich lifestyle at some minimum level (Watanabe 1999). Cultural diversity, access to cultural institutions, and financial support of non-profitable cultural industries became the main responsibility of the post-war Japanese government (Zemans 1999).

To support the traditional arts, the Agency for Cultural Affairs was separated from the Ministry of Education, Culture, Sports, Science and Technology in 1968 (see Figure 3.1) and became the main government driver of cultural policies within post-war Japan, consolidating the 'touchstone and desire of people throughout history to enjoy culture, participate in creation and find affirmation of humanity; the most fundamental and basic desire of human beings' (Watanabe 1999: 62). The extensions of Preservation of Cultural Properties Law (1975) formulated and implemented by the agency defined cultural activities in a very broad sense, beyond aesthetic activities, framing culture as an enhancement of life and society. In principle, it would seem reasonable to incorporate the creative industries in this formulation,

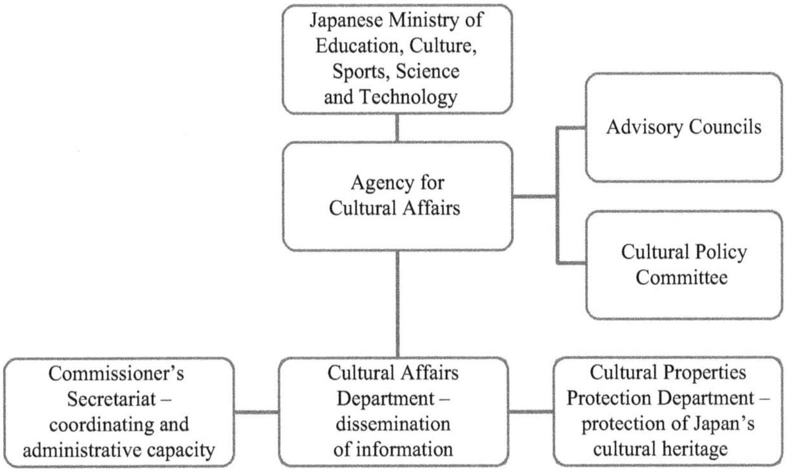

Figure 3.1 Organizational chart: Agency for Cultural Affairs (Source: Commissioner's Secretariat Agency for Cultural Affairs 2015: 1)[2]

but these were regarded as more viable and therefore received less support. Instead, the agency focused mainly on traditional art associations known as IEMOTO (tea ceremonies, pottery, flower arrangements, and calligraphy) or sought to legitimize the import of classical art forms from Europe (e.g., French and Italian paintings). During the 1970s and 1980s, public theatres (*Kokyo horu)* in particular received strong financial support from the government. This type of public spending was criticized in the Japanese media as 'box-building policies' (*Hakomono Gyosei*), referring to the many inefficient buildings financed through public spending (see Yamamoto 2005).

In addition to the Agency for Cultural Affairs, a number of initiatives were implemented at local level, including prefectural and municipal policies, promoting community development through culture. As one example, Yokohama's administration enacted a policy of 'culturalization'. In the 1960s, only a small number of prefectures had offices responsible for arts and culture, but since the 1990s, all prefectures have established such offices. The Japanese Arts Council was created in 1990, mainly to oversee arts funding. This agency is supported by a range of advisory councils and exerts considerable influence on the policy making process. Some cultural activities are spread across other ministries – for instance, art education is the responsibility of the Ministry of Education, and cultural exchange programmes are overseen by the Ministry of Foreign Affairs. For cultural industries, the focus on cultural preservation, heritage, and traditional arts inside Japan had two effects: the Japanese cultural market has remained self-sufficient for a long time (Kawasaki 1996), and cultural creativity and commodification were left entirely in the hands of the private sector.

The rise of 'Cool Japan'

The collapse of Japan's bubble economy in the late 1980s had a significant effect on the national cultural policy agenda and severely impacted the cultural and arts economy (Sugiyama 2006, Hiraki et al. 2009). Suddenly, Japan's industry that had traditionally focused on its domestic market needed to develop both a more international disposition and new industries that could drive future economic development. At this time, the Japanese government was coming to terms with a more ambitious cultural policy approach – notably, the term *cultural policy* itself was just beginning to enter the lexicon of Japanese arts administration and government policy (Wyszomirski 1998), appearing for the first time in a report for the Agency for Cultural Affairs in 1990. Japan's first official cultural policy plan was drafted in 1992 and led to the establishment of the Cultural Policy Office under the umbrella of the Agency for Cultural Affairs (see Figure 3.1). The Ministry of Education began to use the phrase '*cultural* policy' from 1993. The Japanese Arts Fund was set up to provide grants to kick-start creative projects, awarding more than 3,000 grants annually. This policy also referred to supporting wider creative activities and led to a range of new legislation that made it easier to establish creative spaces, especially art galleries and small-scale event venues, and creative spaces of this type increased substantially in number during the 1990s.

In 2003, a first attempt was made to copy classifications of creative industries developed in Australia and the UK (such as the UK Labour Party's use of 'Cool Britannia' in its 1997 election campaign) for secondary analysis of market data in Japan (Yoshimoto 2003). The most comprehensive report that used these classifications was actually published by a non-governmental research agency (NLI Research Institute) and aimed to demonstrate the capacity of the cultural industries in Japan and confirmed the need to develop categories to fit the Japanese market (Yoshimoto 2009). This initial analysis showed that total revenues in this market had almost doubled in the course of a decade. In 1989, creative industries in Japan had total revenues of about US $145 billion; by 1999, that figure had reached about US $280 billion. While considerably larger than UK figures at that time (about US $160 billion), this accounted for only a very small part of the Japanese economy as a whole. The report also demonstrated that Japan had the lowest overall employment rate in the creative industries as compared to Australia, UK, USA, Hong Kong, and Singapore. Additionally, the cultural goods produced and exported by Japan's creative industries were mostly games software (see Hanzawa 2004).

Unlike the UK, as reported by Yoshimoto (2003), Japan left the development of creative industries to private enterprises. However, noting the growing success of these companies, the Japanese government began to use the slogan 'Cool Japan' around 2005 for nation-branding projects (Valaskivi 2013). Finally, in 2010, the creative industries gained official recognition with the foundation of the Creative Industries Promotion Office under the Manufacturing Industries Bureau –not within the Agency for Cultural Affairs but under the auspices of the Ministry of Economy, Trade and Industry (see Figure 3.2). The new office favors the term *creative* or *content industries* rather than *cultural industries* (Hui 2007),[3] and adopting the 'Cool Japan' slogan was an acknowledgement that Japan's creative industries would play an important role in the government's 'New Growth Strategy' (Cool Japan Advisory Council 2011).

The 'Cool Japan' strategy is at its core a re-branding policy, presenting Japan not only as a manufacturing and tech-led nation but as a cultural and creative powerhouse. This mainly involves inter-ministerial activity to cultivate overseas markets, disseminating relevant information abroad by hosting international events. Formulated in the context of internationalization of the creative industries, the intention is to support Japanese industries entering new markets abroad. However, the approach has attracted considerable criticism (Daliot-Bul 2009; Morgner 2015), including the observation that the policy fails to define what is meant by *creative industry* and is based on questionable data and anecdotal evidence. According to the *Interim Report* (Creative Industries Internationalization Committee 2013: 2), 'There is no specific definition of "creative industries" in Japan'. A slightly modified version of this report, the 'Cool Japan Strategy', published by the Creative Industries Division of the Ministry of Economy, Trade and Industry (2012a, 2012b) listed the examples of fashion, food, animation, daily

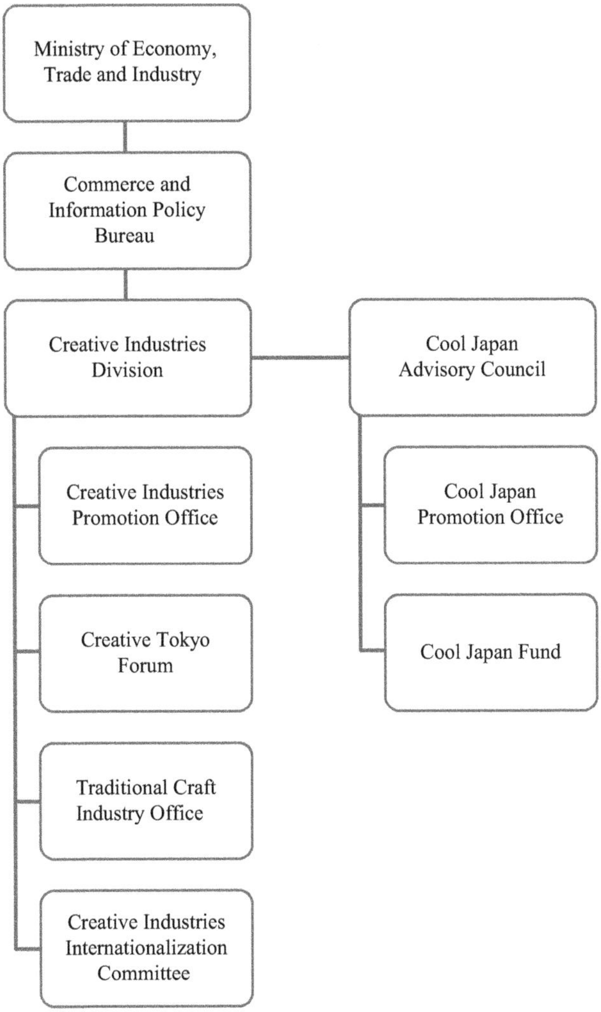

Figure 3.2 Organizational chart: Creative Industries Division (Source: Ministry of Economy, Trade and Industry; http://www.meti.go.jp/english/aboutmeti/data/aOrganizatione/index.html)[4]

goods, traditional craftwork of Japanese origin. A more recent version labelled the 'Cool Japan Initiative' (Creative Industries Division 2014) now includes tourism, advertising, music, and publishing, which are distinguished from traditional craft industries. These changing definitions make it difficult to assess the scale of the creative industries (Zuhdia, Prasetyob and Sianipara 2013). However, based on these examples, total domestic production in these sectors equals US $594 billion, with employment of approximately 5.9 million people.

As noted earlier, the 'Cool Japan' initiative is principally a re-branding strategy and is therefore intended to support Japan's economy as a whole rather than the creative industries alone. Most of the relevant policy documents stress that the spillover effects of this cultural re-branding will impact all industries. An often cited example is the game Pokémon; originally launched as videogame software, it has developed into a major media franchise, with a large number of associated products, including anime or movies, that are popular abroad as well as in Japan. This development impacted the videogame business in Japan as a whole, quadrupling overall sales from US $9 billion to almost US $37 billion. As one example, the Sanrio Company has become extremely successful in selling licences for its Hello Kitty products (rather than actual products) to businesses abroad. Other examples include the success of J-Pop and TV dramas overseas, which have impacted positively on Japan's image and contributed to an increase in tourism and interest in learning the Japanese language. This is acknowledged by the Creative Industries Internationalization Committee (2013: 3, my emphasis):

> Therefore, development of creative industries overseas can lead to significant ripple effects in both economic and non-economic effects, and greatly contribute to formulating and improving the *Japan brand* in the objectives.

Policy makers base this assumption on a range of 'evidence': (1) the creative branding of Japan by foreign countries; (2) the general popularity of Japanese cultural products; and (3) the small market share enjoyed by Japan in this global cultural economy (Creative Industries Division 2014; Creative Industries Division 2013a, 2013b).

1. The 'Cool Japan' initiative (Creative Industries Division 2014: 3) conducted a survey on the creative status of Japan, in which 36 percent of respondents judged Japan to be the most creative country. These results prompted policy makers to characterize Japan as 'the most creative country in the world' (Creative Industries Division 2014: 3).

   However, a closer look at these data reveals that this characterization as the world's most creative country relies on a highly selective comparison with certain Western countries. No other Asian countries were included in the survey, and Japan's self-assessment of its own creativity is among the lowest (26 percent).
2. The second source of evidence is largely anecdotal. Policy narratives have highlighted the international success of a few products, including Pokémon, Hello Kitty, and Japanese weekly manga. For instance, because the manga anthology *Shonen Jump* is enjoyed by a wide readership, including many Western countries, this is interpreted as a successful cultural export. In the same way, Japanese fashion and design are said to be in high demand at international fashion weeks and fairs (Sugiura 2008). This kind of anecdotal evidence prompted the American journalist Douglas McGray (2002) to coin the phrase 'Gross National Cool', which has since influenced the conception of 'Cool Japan' and the Japanese outlook on its own popular culture and creative industries (Fujita 2011;

Table 3.1 Comparative data on creative status

Creative status as seen from	*Japan*	*USA*	*Germany*	*France*	*UK*	*Others*
USA	34%	47%	5%	5%	1%	8%
France	37%	20%	8%	25%	5%	5%
UK	40%	10%	6%	3%	35%	6%
Germany	40%	15%	27%	7%	3%	8%
Japan	26%	39%	12%	16%	3%	4%

Source: Creative Industries Division 2014: 3

Mori 2011). However, these examples are based on a few exemplary cases, and the overall market size of these cultural products remains very small (Sugiura 2008).

3. The policy narratives in items (1) and (2) seek to legitimize the role of creative industry policies on the basis of already existing facts and figures and the current strength of this sector. This third item supports cultural policies by presenting a narrative of its future growth and possibilities, as in market reports reflecting the global scale of the creative industries, which is expected to double between 2009 and 2020 (A.T. Kearney market report, cited in Creative Industries Division 2014: 1). While growth in this market seems impressive and refers to future potential as a reason for supporting cultural industries, this relies on a different classification that includes food and beverages, which account for more than 70 percent of the total revenue of 'creative industries'. Other industries such as fashion are also likely to grow but they have a considerably smaller market share and are unlikely to attain the status of Japan's more traditional economic base in automobile or electronics.

The above assumptions have led Japanese policy makers to conclude that the country's creative industries can make a significant contribution to the Japanese economy if better integrated in the global market. Internationalization policy has sought to achieve this by creating a momentum for creative industries that would in turn reinforce the image of 'Cool Japan', principally by developing consistent communication channels and platforms with partners overseas and clustering small and medium companies in associations and consortia to lend them more weight and visibility abroad.

A first policy scheme proposes to educate overseas customers about the unique nature of Japanese products, linking this understanding to local profiles and enticing overseas customers to visit Japan and to experience the products directly. This policy is in principle an intercultural re-branding strategy to help foreign audiences to understand the cultural significance and attractiveness of products from Japan, linking sales and resources to local markets, and making Japan more attractive to foreign visitors and investment. This re-branding process attempts to create a Japanese brand that is more technical than content-driven – for instance, by subsidizing the subtitling of Japanese films, supporting large-scale festivals, and exploiting Japanese and overseas fan networks. With support from the Japan Brand Fund, the re-branding includes the development of international collaborations and of branches and operations abroad (Creative Industries Division 2013a), as well as large-scale events promoting fashion, design, or food.

The second policy scheme is much more local in focus and aims to build more capacity at urban level. This includes the Japanese Creative Cities Network; launched in 2005 in Osaka, this has been extended to a range of other cities that aspire to more creative status, including Yokohama, Kobe, Nagoya, and Kanazawa (Landry 2006). Some of these cities have also participated in international schemes, such as the UNESCO Creative Cities Network, UNESCO City of Design, and UNESCO City of Crafts and Folk Art. However, the Creative Tokyo project launched in 2011 remains the Japanese government's flagship project, with the slogan 'Tokyo will become the creative hub of Asia' (Creative Industries Division 2013b). This initiative adopts a non-interventionist approach, advancing internationalization of the Creative Tokyo brand by inviting leading talents from abroad, building links with other creative cities in Japan, and organizing art nights, festivals, and fashion weeks. As such, it does not really promote the creative industries already based in Tokyo, which account for 17.1 percent of Japan's creative establishments and 35.0 percent of creative employees (Yoshimoto 2009: 4).

'Cool Japan' was expected to gain momentum between 2010 and 2013. A number of new ministerial offices were created, and a number of policy initiatives were informed by the overarching idea. However, these policies were based on data that excluded other Asian countries (see Table 3.1), making the empirical evidence questionable or anecdotal. It should also be noted that categories and definitions of creative industries change over time, and none of these initiatives sought to develop a more profound understanding of this evolution or engaged in a more conceptual discussion of that term. With the exception of games, Japan's creative industries have largely declined in revenue terms in recent years (Kakiuchi and Takeuchi 2014). Additionally, the 'Cool Japan' strategy has encountered challenges in identifying measurable targets or units of assessment, and an increasing financial shortage has made it more difficult to fund large projects. As a result, the 'Cool Japan' initiative has waned, and early hopes for a quick r-branding to gain significantly improved access to the global market have not been fulfilled. As a consequence, important websites promoting projects have not been updated (Creative Tokyo was last updated in 2014), festivals have been discontinued, and some funding has been scrapped.[5] It should again be emphasized, however, that 'Cool Japan' is principally a re-branding policy to improve exports of cultural products, and neither the Japanese government nor any other municipal or governmental organization has developed a comprehensive policy targeting the internal composition of cultural and creative industry in Japan. In that light, it is perhaps unsurprising that Japan does not feature strongly in the recent commentary on the creative industries and receives little mention in the wider research.

Summary

Research on Japan's cultural and creative industries has focused primarily on the success, impact, and influence of these industries abroad, with particular emphasis on Japan's videogame and software industries at international level. However, little of the research to date has addressed related policy development within Japan. This chapter redirects attention to cultural policy development in Japan at municipal and national levels.

The early phase of Japanese modernization was driven by an ideology of cultural growth and improvement as Japan sought to join the league of global players by modernizing its economic, political and cultural structures. At that time, a range of new policies led to the formation of new educational organizations (schools and universities) teaching drawing, arts, and design. The Japanese government also invested heavily in key industries to develop new technologies while also promoting the country's craftsmanship and related cultural products at international fairs. A number of cultural policies were formulated to protect its cultural industries, notably film and music, but this changed somewhat with the rise of nationalism, as this ideology of Japanese modernization was forced on other countries in Asia. China was among the prime targets for this cultural transformation, and the arts and cultural industries formed part of an agenda to spread these ideas and to educate overseas audiences. Ultimately, however, most of these initiatives failed.

After WWII and the restructuring of Japan, the government planned to support the arts on a much broader scale providing access not only for cultural elites but for the whole population. Government initiatives sought to support arts and culture without interfering with the actual production or selection of cultural goods. A number of state-funded agencies were created for these purposes, but they mainly supported traditional arts and culture or were education-driven. This picture changed in the early 1990s, when Japanese policy makers discovered the potential of the cultural and creative industries. As part of this shift, a new strategy called 'Cool Japan' gained official recognition with the foundation of the Creative Industries Promotion Office under the Manufacturing Industries Bureau in 2010. The intention was that Japan's cultural industries would play an important role in the government's 'New Growth Strategy', overseen and managed by the Cool Japan Advisory Council. This re-branding strategy incorporates a range of policies to promote Japanese creative industries abroad or to enhance their status in other countries. This can be seen as a reversal of the earlier perspective, when the Japanese government was insufficiently active in this area. Despite all these new initiatives, the government did not intervene in the actual selection or promotion of particular cultural goods but focused mainly on ensuring a more concise narrative.

Some of the interviewees for this study (including local government policy makers and directors of creative industry festivals and creative companies) noted a lack of government urgency and knowledge and an unease about touching on arts and culture because of Japan's past. The lack of cultural clusters or concentrations of creative skills and knowledge in Japan's main urban centers means that this focus on enhanced presentation and representation seems inadequate to the needs of Japan's cultural industries (see Morgner 2014). Additionally, the main international market is for more traditional arts forms and cultural activities that are not integrated into the Cool Japan growth narrative. It seems that the lack of policies to strengthen the skills and infrastructure of Japan's creative industries may have undermined the 'Cool Japan' initiative, as the dispersed structure of the creative industries has been unable to support the narrative.

It seems clear that the difficulties described here are part of a larger historical entanglement of nationalism and cultural policies, hindering the development of cultural polices at municipal and national levels. As a consequence, there is no comprehensive strategy that supports the creative and cultural industries. More research is needed if these issues are to be addressed in a more profound way, offering more support for contemporary arts and creative activities. These industries' peripheral status and minor public support are important issues that need to be addressed more openly, as the cultural value of innovation, change, and deviance are not always cherished and promoted as a positive influence on society. In particular, the lack of a public forum and public debate to lend acceptance and legitimacy to these activities must be addressed more seriously and more openly by future policy initiatives.

Acknowledgment

I would like to thank Mariko Ikeda and the editors for their valuable comments and suggestions to improve this chapter.

Notes

1 Remission policies or procedures returned money to the country concerned. Most of the colonial superpowers had such remission policies in China, largely as political tools to control or influence the Chinese government without occupying the country.
2 This organizational chart represents a simplified version of the various branches of the Agency for Cultural Affairs. Only those branches and departments discussed in this chapter are included here; for a more detailed picture, see Commissioner's Secretariat Agency for Cultural Affairs (2015: 1).
3 Iwabuchi (2002) suggests that the terms *creative* or *content* reflect the government's preference for Otaku Bunka (Japan's geeky, but highly popular anime, manga and videogame subculture) rather than the more radical and alternative underground art scene. This image of Japan had already enjoyed some success abroad and could therefore be used as an international intermediary.

4 This organizational chart presents the various branches of the Ministry of Economy, Trade and Industry in simplified form. The focus is here on the Creative Industries Divisions and its subdivisions and advisory councils. For a more detailed description, see http://www.meti.go.jp/english/aboutmeti/data/aOrganizatione/index.html.

5 It seems that the government has not given up on this direction. The Olympic Games in 2020 will probably serve as a platform for Cool Japan, with a range of selected creative industries promoting this 'new' image. Prime Minister Shinzō Abe's appearance at the closing ceremony of the 2014 Olympic Games in Rio de Janeiro, dressed as Super Mario, offers a taste of what to expect.

References

Agency for Cultural Affairs (1990) *Wagakunino Bunkato Bunkagyosei* [*Cultural Policy in Japan: Current Situation and Future Question*], White paper, Tokyo.

Aoyama, Y. and Izushi, H. (2003) Hardware gimmick or cultural innovation? Technological, cultural, and social foundations of the Japanese video game industry. *Research Policy*, 32: 423–44.

Christ, C. (1996) Japan's seven acres: Politics and aesthetics at the 1904 Louisiana Purchase Exposition. *Gateway Heritage*, 17(2): 2–15.

Christ, C. (2000) The sole guardians of the art inheritance of Asia: Japan and China at the 1904 St. Louis World's Fair. *Positions: East Asia Cultures Critique*, 8(3): 675–709.

Commissioner's Secretariat Agency for Cultural Affairs (2015) *Policy of Cultural Affairs in Japan*. Tokyo: Agency for Cultural Affairs.

Cool Japan Advisory Council (2011) Creating a new Japan: Tying together 'culture and industry' and 'Japan and the world'. Available at: http://www.meti.go.jp/english/press/2011/pdf/0512_02b.pdf

Creative Industries Division (2012a) Cool Japan Strategy, January 2012. Available at: http://www.meti.go.jp/english/policy/mono_info_service/creative_industries/pdf/120116_01a.pdf

Creative Industries Division (2012b) Cool Japan Strategy, September 2012. Available at: http://www.meti.go.jp/english/policy/mono_info_service/creative_industries/pdf/121016_01a.pdf

Creative Industries Division (2013a) Cool Japan Initiative (Cool Japan Fund), November 2013. Available at: http://www.meti.go.jp/english/policy/mono_info_service/creative_industries/pdf/20131010_01a.pdf

Creative Industries Division (2013b) Promotion of the Cool Japan Strategy and the Creative Tokyo Project. Available at: http://www.meti.go.jp/english/policy/mono_info_service/creative_industries/pdf/121016_01b.pdf

Creative Industries Division (2014) Cool Japan Strategy, July 2014. Available at: http://www.meti.go.jp/policy/mono_info_service/mono/creative/file/1406CoolJapanInitiative.pdf

Creative Industries Internationalization Committee (2013) Interim report. Available at: http://www.meti.go.jp/english/press/2013/0621_01.html

Daliot-Bul, M. (2009) Japan brand strategy: The taming of 'Cool Japan' and the challenges of cultural planning in a postmodern age. *Social Science Japan Journal*, 12(2): 247–66.

Ferguson, N. (2004) *The Birth of the Modern World, 1780–1914*. Malden: Blackwell Publishing.

Flew, T. (2013). *Global Creative Industries*. Cambridge, UK: Polity.

Fujita, Y. (2011) Fabricating Japaneseness? The identity politics of young designers and artists in global cities. *International Journal of Japanese Sociology*, 20: 43–58.

Gluck, C. (1985) *Japan's Modern Myths: Ideology in the Late Meiji Period*. Princeton: Princeton University Press.

Hanzawa, S. (2004) The Japanese animation and home video game industries. *Japanese Journal of Human Geography*, 56(6): 29–43.

Hemmert, M. and Oberländer, C. (1998) (eds.) *Technology and Innovation in Japan: Policy and Management for the Twenty-First Century*. London: Routledge.

Hesmondhalgh, D. (2002) *The Cultural Industries*. Trowbridge: Sage Publications.

Hiraki, T., Ito, A., Spieth, D. A. and Takezawa, N. (2009) How did Japanese investments influence international art prices? *Journal of Financial and Quantitative Analysis*, 44(6): 1489–514.

Howkins, J. (2013) *The Creative Economy*. London: Penguin.

Hui, D. (2007) The creative industries and entrepreneurship in East and Southeast Asia. In C. Henry (ed.), *Entrepreneurship in the Creative Industries: An International Perspective*. Cheltenham: Edward Elgar Publishing, pp. 9–29.

Inoue, T. (1977) The recording industry in Japan. *JAES*, 25(10/11): 802–08.

Isozaki, Y. (1998) Artistic, cultural, and political structures determining the educational direction of the first Japanese schoolbook on art in 1981. In: K. Freedman and F. Hernández (eds.), *Curriculum, Culture, and Art Education: Comparative Perspectives*. Albany: State University of New York Press, pp. 13–29.

Iwabuchi, K. (1998) Marketing Japan: Japanese cultural presence under a global gaze. *Japanese Studies*, 28, 165–80.

Iwabuchi, K. (2002) 'Soft' nationalism and narcissism: Japanese popular culture goes global. *Asian Studies Review*, 26(4): 447–69.

Kakiuchi, E. and Takeuchi, K. (2014) Creative industries: Reality and potential in Japan. GRIPS Discussion Paper 14-04. Available at: http://www.grips.ac.jp/r-center/wp-content/uploads/14-04.pdf

Kawakita, M. (1976) Western influence on Japanese painting and sculpture. In: C.F. Yamada (ed.), *Dialogue in Art: Japan and the West*. Tokyo: Kodansha International, pp. 71–113.

Kawasaki, K. (1996) Art and cultural policy in Japan. In: R. Martorella (ed.), *Art and Business: An International Perspective on Sponsorship*. London: Praeger, pp. 195–201.

Kong, L. and O'Connor, J. (2009) *Creative Economies, Creative Cities: Asian-European Perspectives*. London: Springer.

Kurasawa, A. (1991) Films as propaganda media in Java under the Japanese, 1942–45. In: G.K. Goodman (ed.), *Japanese Cultural Policies in Southeast Asia during World War II*. New York: St. Martin's Press.

Landry, C. (2006) *The Art of City Making*. New York: Routledge.

Lee, H.-K. and Lim, L. (2014) *Cultural Policies in East Asia: Dynamics between the State, Arts and Creative Industries*. London: Palgrave Macmillan.

Mason, M. (1992) *American Multinationals and Japan: Political Economy of Japanese Capital Controls, 1899–1980*. Cambridge, MA: Harvard University Press.

McGray, D. (2002) Japan's Gross National Cool. *Foreign Policy*, 130: 44–54.

Mehl, M. (2017) Between the global, the national and the local in Japan: Two musical pioneers from Sendai. *Itinerario*, 41(2): 305–25.

Miller, K. H. (2006) Talking machine world: Selling the local in the global music industry, 1900–20. In: Hopkins, A. G. (ed.), *Global History: Interactions Between the Universal and the Local*. Houndmills: Palgrave MacMillan, pp. 160–90.

Morgner, C. (2014) World art cities: Theoretical considerations. Presentation at ISA World Congress of Sociology, Yokohama.

Morgner, C. (2015) An interim report compiled by the Creative Industries Internationalization Committee. *Cultural Trends*, 24(2): 194–96.

Mori, S. (1989) A historical survey of music periodicals in Japan: 1881–1920. *Fontes Artis Musicae*, 36(1): 44–50.

Mori, Y. (2011) The pitfall facing the Cool Japan project: The transnational development of the anime industry under the condition of post-Fordism. *International Journal of Japanese Sociology*, 20, 30–42.

Okazaki, A. (1985) American influence on the history of Japanese art education: The case of Akira Shirahama. In: B. Wilson and H. Hoffa (eds.), *The History of Art Education*. Proceedings from the Penn State Conference, Sine Locum, NAEA, pp. 59–66.

Omuka, T. (2000) The formation of the audiences for modern art in Japan. In E.K. Tipton and J. Clark (eds.), *Being Modern in Japan: Culture and Society from the 1910s to the 1930s*. Honolulu: University of Hawaii Press, pp. 50–60.

Otmazgin, N. (2012) Geopolitics and soft power: Japan's cultural policy and cultural diplomacy in Asia. *Asia-Pacific Review*, 19(1): 37–61.

Park, M. (2003) The directive functions of the Korean images in the colonial period (1910–1945): On Japanese painters' works in Kanten [in Japanese]. *Bigaku*, 54(1): 42–55.

Raine, M. (2014) Adaptation as 'transcultural mimesis' in Japanese cinema. In D. Miyao (ed.), *The Oxford Handbook of Japanese Cinema*. Oxford University Press, pp. 101–23.

Sugiura, T. (2008) Japan's creative industries: Culture as a source of soft power in the industrial sector. In Y. Watanbe and D.L. McConnell (eds.), *Soft Power Superpowers: Cultural and National Assets of Japan and the United States*. London: M. E. Sharpe, pp. 128–53.

Sugiyama, T. (2006) *Kuru Japan Sekai ga Kaitaguru Nihon* [*Cool Japan: The world wants to buy Japan*]. Tokyo: Shodensha.

Suzuki, S. (2005) *Nihon no Bunkanationalizumu* [*Japan's Cultural Nationalism*]. Tokyo: Heibonsha.

Teow, H. (1999) *Japanese Cultural Policy toward China, 1918–1931: A Comparative Perspective*. Cambridge: Harvard University Press.

Tschang T. (2009) Creative industries across cultural borders: The case of video games in Asia. In Kong, L. and O'Connor, J. (eds.), *Creative Economies, Creative Cities*. Dordrecht: Springer, pp. 25–42.

UNCTAD (2010) *Creative Economies Report*. Available at: http://unctad.org/en/Docs/ditctab20103_en.pdf

Valaskivi, K. (2013) A brand new future? Cool Japan and the social imaginary of the branded nation. *Japan Forum*, 25(4): 485–504.

Watanabe, M. (1999) Background on cultural policies and programs in Japan. In: Zemans, J. and Kleingartner, A. (eds.), *Comparing Cultural Policy: A study of Japan and the United States*. London: Altamira Press, pp. 61–112.

Westlund, H. and Caldoni-Lundberg, F. (2007) The creative class and social capital – Civil society, regional development and high-tech employment in Japan. CESIS Electronic Working Paper Series 112. Available at: https://static.sys.kth.se/itm/wp/cesis/cesiswp112.pdf

Wyszomirski, M. J. (1998) Comparing cultural policies in the United States and Japan: Preliminary observations. *Journal of Arts Management, Law, and Society*, 27(4): 265–81.

Yamamoto, A. (2005) The hakomono gyosei syndrome: Connecting culture with community development in Japan. Proceedings of Japan Anthropology Workshop, 16th Conference, University of Hong Kong, 17–21 March.

Yoshimoto, M. (2003) The status of creative industries in Japan and policy recommendations for their promotion, NLI Research Report. Retrieved from http://www.nli-research.co.jp/english/socioeconomics/2003/li031202.pdf

Yoshimoto, M. (2009) Creative industry trends – The creative industry profiles of Japan's ordinance-designated cities. NLI Research Report. Available at: http://www.nli-research.co.jp/english/socioeconomics/2009/li091015.pdf

Yusuf, S. and Nabeshima, K. (2005) Creative industries in East Asia. *Cities*, 22(2): 109–22.

Zemans, J. (1999) A comparative overview. In: J. Zemans and A. Kliengartner (eds.), *Comparing Cultural Policy: A study of Japan and the United States*. California: Altamira Press, pp. 1–60.

Zuhdia, U., Prasetyob, A. D., and Sianipara, C. P. M. (2013) Analyzing the dynamics of total output of Japanese creative industry sectors: An input–output approach. *Procedia Economics and Finance*, 5: 827–35.

4

The artrepreneurial ecosystem in Singapore

Enabling and inhibiting the creative economy

Can-Seng Ooi and Roberta Comunian

Introduction

One of the reasons why many artists remain poor is their 'denial of the economy' (Abbing 2002: 34). Abbing argues that the strong 'art-for-art-sake' value makes it difficult for them to address the commercial aspects of their works and their profession. Simply speaking, talking about money makes many artists uncomfortable (Ooi 2010a). On the other hand, artists around the world, including those in Singapore, are encouraged to be more entrepreneurial. Instead of taking a Kantian view of unadulterated art, artists should take on a more economic-oriented approach, as they address different aspects of their craft and profession. 'Artrepreneurs' see their art practice as business. Besides art making, they must also pay attention to promotion, marketing, pricing strategy, hiring a manager, engaging with art consultants and reviewers, canvassing art collectors, and devising internationalization strategies in making their art into a business enterprise (Becker 1984; Grenfell and Hardy 2007). They may also find ways to transfer their artistic skills into other industries. As an artistic entrepreneur or 'artrepreneur', the artist is more commercially pragmatic and business-like (Engelmann et al. 2012; Harvie 2015). Artistic integrity need not be sacrificed and business is often framed as part of art practice. As a result, artrepreneurs do not feel guilty having to engage in business, and are usually not dependent on public support.

Following this logic, there should then also be a conducive artistic entrepreneurial ecosystem or 'artrepreneurial ecosystem'. The idea of an entrepreneurial ecosystem is popular and has come to shape and define many creative and entrepreneurial districts, ranging from Silicon Valley in the USA to Zhongguancun in China (Isenberg 2010). While scholars argue about the effectiveness of such ecosystems, an ecosystem is generally defined as a 'diverse set of inter-dependent actors within a geographic region that influence the formation and eventual trajectory of the entire group of actors and potentially the economy as a whole' (Cohen 2006: 3–4). The interdependency and the interplay of various parties generate new business ventures. This view has come to dominate the development of the creative economy in many countries (Chapain et al. 2013). In such an environment, different creative domains are placed together in a place that has friendly regulations, quality higher learning institutions, easy access to creative workers, and access to the market (Comunian et al. 2010). Singapore is trying to create its artrepreneurial ecosystem, supported by cultural development policy, business regulations, educational institutions, an art market, and a receptive populace. The development of this ecosystem is part of the island-state's creative economy strategy.

The Singapore National Arts Council (NAC), in its aptly titled section of its *Annual Report 2014/15* 'Chapter III: Ecosystem', presents its perspective on creating the arts and culture ecosystem in Singapore (National Arts Council 2015: 45):

> We believe everyone can play a part in shaping Singapore into a distinctive global city for the arts. With more resources for the arts – from grants and partnerships to industry facilitation and arts housing, artists and arts groups can realize their ambitions and create excellent works of art that impact the communities and our nation.
>
> The Council requires a network of alliance to achieve its mission, and welcomes partnerships that will drive and build a sustainable arts future. With the unveiling of the $20million Cultural Diplomacy Fund by the Ministry of Culture, Community and Youth (MCCY), the National Arts Council has begun and will continue to raise the international presence of our arts and culture by seeking new markets, growing networks, and profiling the best of Singapore's artists.

The second paragraph of the quote demonstrates how the Singaporean authorities view art in the wider context of diplomacy, international business, and international exchange. This is an example of how cultural development and economic development are intertwined in the city-state. The entanglement of cultural policy and Singapore's economic development has received considerable research interest (Chang and Mahadevan 2014; Chang 2000; Chang and Lee 2003; Chong 2005; Kong et al. 2006; Lee 2004; Lim 2012; Ooi 2008, 2010b, 2011). Such studies often highlight the tacit aim of the Singaporean government in wanting to cultivate the creative capability of the population, and to introduce innovations and generate lucrative businesses. Such a goal requires the translation of creativity from the cultural creative industries to other industries (Trüby et al. 2008). For instance at the start of 2016, among other things, a new statutory board – SkillsFuture – was formed to inculcate in the population that education is a lifelong learning process with the aim of making the population more innovative and creative (Ho 2016; Seow 2016). Getting an education is to be seen as an ongoing marathon for the Singaporean worker and not merely a paper-chase at one's early stage of life. The worker needs to stay innovative and creative, and continuous training should help. Education is an integral part of developing and growing local creative economies and ecologies (Tan and Gopinathan 2000).

In this chapter we explore and unpack the different idiosyncratic dimensions of the artrepreneurial ecosystem in Singapore. It goes behind and beyond the official view of the arts ecosystem there. The chapter is structured in three parts. In the first part, we consider how this ecosystem was developed in Singapore following pressures from an intensification of a global discourse on the creative economy as well as from internal needs to re-define the cultural dimension of its economy. In the second part, we consider four pillars in the Singapore context that shape its artrepreneurial ecosystem, namely: the education system; the value and social norms of Singaporeans; the influence of broader policy and officials' understanding of creative expressions in a democracy; and finally the connection with internal and international markets (and competition). The final part draws conclusions and directions of future research in this fast-evolving topic.

The emergence of an artrepreneurial ecosystem: Cultural and creative industries in Singapore

After decades of fast economic growth since Singapore's independence in 1965, the role of the arts and culture was given a new perspective in 1989 (Advisory Council on Culture and the Arts 1989). In 2002, after various incarnations, Singapore's cultural development strategies were framed within the creative industries context (Economic Review Committee – Services Subcommittee Workgroup on Creative Industries 2002). This means that the arts and culture will play a bigger role in the growth and future of Singapore (Kong 2012; Lee 2004; Ooi 2011; Purushothaman 2016; K. P. Tan 2007; Wong et al. 2006). This bigger role is part of the strategy for the country to move away from its industrial economy to an innovation-led one. As part of the plan to generate prosperity through creativity and innovation, the arts and culture is core because it epitomizes creativity. For instance, in 2000, the then-Ministry of Information and the Arts envisaged Singapore as a 'Renaissance City' (Ministry of Information and the Arts 2000). The then-Deputy Prime Minister, now Prime Minister, stated in the same report that (Ministry of Information and the Arts 2000: 32–3):

> Creativity cannot be confined to a small elite group of Singaporeans ... In today's rapidly changing world, the whole workforce needs problem-solving skills, so that every worker can continuously add value through his [sic] efforts ... and the arts ... can be a dynamic means of facilitating creative abilities.

Over the years, numerous cultural institutions were created, including in the mid-1990s, the Singapore Art Museum, Asian Civilizations Museum, and the National Museum of Singapore. In 2015, the National Gallery was inaugurated. Esplanade – Theatres on the Bay, which opened in 2002, has become a lively arts venue and offers hundreds of free performances annually. There are now 172 art galleries and 183 performing arts venues in the city-state (National Arts Council 2015: 46). There are also cultural festivals, including the Singapore Biennale, Singapore Arts Festival, Singapore Writers Festival, and Singapore Film Festival. Recent trends include the increase in enrolment in tertiary arts courses from 3,793 in 2011 to 5,599 in 2014. In art philanthropy, private contributions climbed from S$26.6 million (US$20.5 million) in 2010 to S$53.8 million (US$41.4 million) in 2014 (National Arts Council 2015: 47–8). Flattering to the island-state, Singapore was lauded by the *South China Morning Post* as Hong Kong's main art hub competitor and is winning (Tsui 2016).

Arts and cultural development is now seen as part of the development of the creative economy. The tenuous relationship between cultural products, cultural policy, and creative economy has been discussed at length in some academic circles (Galloway and Dunlop 2007; Hesmondhalgh and Pratt 2005) and policy fora (Bakhshi et al. 2008). This questionable relationship is a reflection of entrenched traditional dichotomies and issues around work, consumption, and production in the creative and cultural industries, even though such dichotomies are questioned and intentionally broken down through policy attempts. While it is important to reflect on the historical development of Singapore to understand the current development of its artrepreneurial ecosystem, it is also important to consider the key dimensions that shape its current and recent development. In particular, and will be elaborated, we identify the following (Figure 4.1):

- *Education*: both in reference to development of arts in every student curricula, but also to its further specialization in higher education programmes;

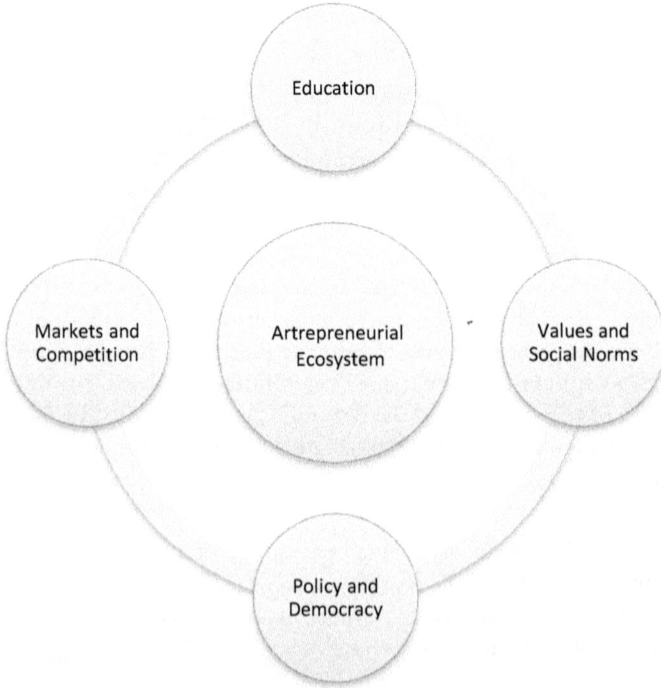

Figure 4.1 The four pillars of the artrepreneurial ecosystem

- *Values and social norms*: these shape the development of the ecosystem at various subtle levels, including influencing people's aspirations, anxieties and how they interact;
- *Policy and democracy*: the development of CCIs is shaped by direct policy interventions (especially in relation to cultural policy) as well as indirect ones. While democratic values are largely seen as necessary for the freedom of creative expressions, democratic creative expressions may challenge social and political status quos, and raise questions on policies;
- *Markets and competition*: the development of a cultural ecosystem also depends on its production (of ideas, objects, or events) meeting a demand, market, or audience. The balance between internal markers and broader international competition will also affect its development.

In the context of this book, these four pillars have probably larger application, in providing a framework to understand how creative ecosystems in different Asian contexts work and adapt. However, we believe these pillars might acquire different weight or significance in different economic and political contexts and therefore need to be understood in relation to local specificities.

Education

More commercial-oriented creative domains such as design and media tend to be identified as part of the creative industries plan (Council 2008; Economic Review Committee – Services Subcommittee Workgroup on Creative Industries 2002; Ministry of Information

2008). At the start of 2016, Singaporeans are again urged to be bold innovators, this time by the chairman of the Committee on the Future Economy, Liang Eng Hwa. To encourage this, the Singapore government is reorganizing the education system to promote lifelong learning, with the aim of producing more innovators and entrepreneurs (Lim 2016). The education system has a role to play in cultivating the young into an ambitious entrepreneurial class in the future. But the links between the arts and culture, creative education and a more innovative population run along a particular (flawed) logic in Singapore.

Being an entrepreneur entails being creative. Being innovative requires one to be creative. The education system should thus encourage creativity. And since the arts epitomize creativity, the arts should be encouraged and taught in school as they stimulate creativity and lay the foundation for future entrepreneurs and innovators. The centrality of the arts and culture in the creative economy is however challenged. Introducing creativity and the arts in schools does not necessarily lead to more entrepreneurial and innovative graduates, as we will discuss later. Many artists – albeit creative ones – are not entrepreneurial or economically successful. The term 'creativity' is ambiguous and vague, and creativity is not a single way of thinking, solving problems, or inventing ideas. The links between creative education, the arts and culture, and the creative economy have to be re-examined.

In the context of higher education and the creative economy, Comunian and Gilmore (2014) accentuate in their framework that there are three types of engagement and impact that wed creativity and industrial production. The first is linked to the simple presence of higher education in a specific local context and the 'estate value' it creates. In creative economy terms, this value is often translated into cultural productions. As Chatterton (2000) underlines, many city-universities have traditionally been well positioned in providing the city with cultural facilities (Ting 2014), such as art galleries and theatres, but more recently they have taken this role further by including a wider range of cultural facilities, such as media production facilities, recording studios, or rehearsal spaces. New 'creative hubs' developed by higher educational institutions seem to highlight the value of co-location and clustering that such learning and research organizations can play in the creative economy (AHRC 2011). Singapore is no different. The Prime Minister of Singapore has insisted that co-location of universities, dedicated research and development areas, creative districts, and start-up hubs have paid off in the city-state (Wong 2015). The National University of Singapore (NUS) has a music conservatory and an art museum, just a stone's throw from Singapore's innovation hub, LaunchPad@one-north. It remains unclear how such creative cultural amenities and creative industrial innovations interact. But the magazine, *The Economist*, stated that Block 71 at Ayer Rajah Crescent (as part of LaunchPad@one-north) hosts 'the world's most tightly packed entrepreneurial ecosystem, and a perfect place to study the lengths to which a government can go to support startup colonies' (The Economist, 2014).

Following from the first, the second type relates to the generation of 'creative knowledge'. Comunian and Gilmore (2014) highlight two dimensions of this creative knowledge. One closely relates to the idea of human capital, the other links to the idea of 'knowledge exchange'. In relation to the importance of human capital, Faggian and McCann (Faggian 2006: 497) argue that 'the primary role of the university system appears to be its role as a conduit for bringing potential high quality human capital into a region' and, therefore, having a highly skilled labor pool far outweighs the benefits generated by knowledge spillovers. This is also one of the arguments behind the popular 'creative class' theory (Florida 2006). The flow of creativity and cross-fertilization of ideas do happen but how that process can be managed and generate innovations quickly remain unclear. Regardless, the dialogic flow of creative knowledge and ideas is championed in all creative industries policies around the world, including Singapore (Ooi 2010b; Potts and Cunningham 2008). The earlier example of re-organizing Singapore's education system to produce a more innovative population is a case in mind.

The exchange of creative knowledge and ideas is not even and smooth. This is the third type of engagement between creativity and industrial production. The arguments that favor a role for higher education in the creative economy from a knowledge exchange perspective suggest that these institutions are expected to function as research and development laboratories (Cunningham et al. 2004) and be part of the broader innovation system (Bakhshi et al. 2008). This has become increasingly important in making the point that arts and humanities have a positive impact on society and provide good value for money. Some scholars see this focus on knowledge transfer and exchange as an imposition of a 'techno-economic' paradigm onto the arts (Bullen et al. 2004). Regardless, most higher education institutions have accepted this new perspective, thinking of it as an opportunity to add value to their work (Lindberg 2008; Powell 2007; Purushothaman 2016). Although the evidence gathered is mostly anecdotal, there is an increasing pressure to show the importance of these dynamics (Hughes et al. 2011). The exchange of knowledge between creativity and industry production is often asymmetrical. For example, it is easier for artists to emerge from non-art professions than for artists to become professionals that require technical and professional training. This means that the knowledge exchanges may not be balanced between different creative professions.

As expected, challenges remain in bringing education, the arts and culture into the industrial sector. Also from this perspective, the cultural creative industries are competing for creative individuals in other industries. Nevertheless, as highlighted by Comunian and Ooi (2016), Singapore shows a strong commitment to investing in its education infrastructure for its cultural creative economy push. This is reflected in the interest in careers in the arts as the prospects widen over the years with government funding for arts programmes and projects (Yang 2014). In particular:

- **New pre-tertiary specialized education:** In 2008, Singapore's School of the Arts (SOTA) became the first pre-tertiary level dedicated arts school in the city-state.
- **Funding and new status for existing providers**: Since 1999 the government raised the status of the two existing arts schools offering diploma courses (Lasalle College of Arts and the Nanyang Academy of Fine Arts (NAFA)) to be at the same level of funding as polytechnics, meaning that they are officially recognized and supported as tertiary education institutions.
- **New buildings and creative infrastructure at higher education level:** The Singapore University of Technology and Design was established in 2009. The Yong Siew Toh Conservatory of Music in NUS was established in 2001 as Singapore's first conservatory. The School of Art, Design and Media Building at Nanyang Technological University was completed in July 2006 at a cost of S$38 million (US$29 million). Following the Singapore government's plan and investment, Lasalle relocated in 2007 from the Goodman Road campus to the city area.
- **New partnership with international universities**: In September 2012 the Glasgow School of Art opened its first overseas campus, in partnership with the Singapore Institute of Technology. It delivers programmes in 'Communication Design' and 'Interior Design' (Glasgow School of Art Singapore 2018). In 2012, Lasalle and the Goldsmiths College of the University of London inked a five-year deal to offer 14 public-funded arts

degree courses. The Prime Minister of Singapore witnessed the event, demonstrating the government's seriousness in supporting quality arts education (Wong 2012).

- **New courses introduced by a variety of traditional and new providers**: New courses were introduced in 2000s, such as diplomas in arts management and theatre production design (NAFA) and more Master of Arts programmes and bachelor degree courses at Lasalle. Nanyang Polytechnic started offering a new diploma in motion graphics and broadcast design, and Temasek Polytechnic a new diploma in retail and hospitality design (Liaw 2007). Alongside the usual providers expanding their portfolios, new providers such as Hyper Island have been encouraged to provide new courses (Chew 2012).
- **Promotes an attitude towards learning and creativity:** The education system is still largely seen as unconducive for exploration and creativity. So yet again in new plans set up in 2016, the Singaporean government attempted to change people's attitude towards learning and creativity. Starting from primary school, children's educational progress will no longer be focused obsessively on academic results. The aim is to make learning more enjoyable. Pupils will be given more time to pursue a wider range of interests, 'sustain their curiosity, cultivate an innovative spirit and pursue a well-rounded education' (Philomin 2016). The love-for-learning approach is not new and has been advocated before. It is considered central in promoting the cultural creative industries.

In spite of these initiatives, there is resistance from employers, teachers, parents, and children, as the system aims to dilute the focus on examination results and career prospects. One big reason is that academic results remain the main quantifiable measure of a child's capability (Ng 2008; Ooi 2012). The concern for purpose and tangible results has even been expressed by faculty and students in the NUS-Yale Liberal Arts programme, which started in 2013 with the purpose of encouraging bold and open thinking (Liu and Lye 2016; Philomin 2015). Another issue facing Singapore, and other many newly democratized countries, is the freedom of expression that is often assumed and demanded in the creative economy. These two points will be discussed next.

Social values

While there are increasingly more positive stories of success about artists in the media, a career as a professional artist is still not considered stable and lucrative (Ooi 2012). Many artists we spoke to reveal their apprehension, and a professional visual artist, WB, gave advice for those who want to take that path: 'save up first'.[1] The sister of an established sculptor, who spoke anonymously, revealed that she wanted to be an artist too but having one member of her family (her older brother) as an artist is 'dangerous enough'. What she means by 'dangerous' is the high risk of not being able to sustain oneself economically as an artist. She is now an executive in a large multi-national, and has taken upon herself to support her brother in the future, if necessary. A full-time painter in Singapore, KJN, who graduated from a local art school, recalled that almost all his classmates have ambitions to be professional artists or want to work in the creative field after graduation. Five years after graduation, when we first met him, he estimated that only about 5 percent succeeded in that ambition in his class. In spite of the many professional artists in Singapore, these examples are views largely shared by artists, and show that a career in the arts is perceived as risky and not lucrative in Singapore. If one wants to be an entrepreneur who will make plenty of money, going into the arts is not the obvious option.

Resistance against art making often starts early in life. FST is a sculptor and also teaches in a local polytechnic in a design programme. During an interview in 2015, she recalls a recent encounter with a student's mother. One of her very talented students was punished by his mother because he was drawing human figures in his assignments, making his mother angry. The mother scolded her son and threw the pictures away. FST recollected:

> The mother thought her son was wasting time. 'What has design to do with drawing people?' The distraught student loves to draw and draws well since young, and his mother does not believe that all his drawings are part of the training and education, instead he is back to his old habit of pursuing a useless hobby.

As a result, FST met up with the mother to explain that drawing human figures is part of his design assignments. Among the artists, art teachers and ordinary Singaporeans we met, such a view is not the exception, even though few would admit that they would punish their own children for channelling much energy into drawing or doing art.

There is also a view that one can be an artist without formal training. Parents will want their children to have a strong professional foundation that would ensure the children's future financial stability. Their children can choose an art career later if they still desire and are 'everyday geniuses'. Everyday geniuses are individuals who are not formally trained but have become successful artists (Fine 2004). Such cases are however rare (Pralong et al. 2012). But for instance, in the 2015 UOB Painting of the Year award – the most prestigious painting prize in Singapore – Aaron Gan won the Gold Medal. Gan did not go to art school, and was running his own migration consultancy firm four years ago. He became a full-time professional artist because of his long-time personal ambition and interest. As a self-taught and naturally talented painter, he learned about the Singapore art world by reading up and talking to artists, curators, and reviewers. As an example of his enthusiasm, after meeting Ooi, Gan read Ooi's article on the emotional challenges in selling art in Singapore (Ooi 2010a), and showed great enthusiasm in knowing more and finding ways to navigate through the art world system. He asked for introductions to people in the art community and sought assistance, for instance, in getting an art historian to review and write a foreword for one of his catalogues. He is appreciative of Utterly Art, a gallery, for carrying his watercolor paintings. Gan is an artrepreneur. He is pro-active and the authorities want to see more cases like Gan. It also indicates that his lack of training in art career management can be compensated.

Failures to succeed in the arts can however be blamed on the artist. One artist recalled a question she was asked by an officer at the NAC: 'Why can't you be creative enough to make money?' During our interviews with creative educators, there was a clear acknowledgement that education should be relevant for the graduate's employment in the fledging creative economy. With the big investment that the government is making, some of the faculty and managers recognize the opportunities that the government initiatives would bring to their graduates. A university faculty member said: 'They're investing in infrastructure for which students, graduate students, will be needed to fill the posts that are opening'. There is a strong rhetoric of employability, and a belief that these graduates would be able 'to create their own jobs', another university faculty member said in another interview. Graduates are thus to be blamed themselves if they do not get into creative careers.

In other words, seeking a creative education is sometimes seen to be lesser than a science or technical one; it implies that one is not strong academically. If one is good academically, one can pursue one's creative dreams later by switching over. And if one is truly creative, one will find opportunities to be commercially viable. This creates fear and anxiety in people who choose the creative education path, which would affect the entrepreneurial spirit (Isenberg 2011).

Policy and democracy

The notion that democracy is necessary for the creative economy to flourish is questioned by the authorities in Singapore (Ooi 2010b). The Singaporean government asserts that every society is different, and Singapore must identify its own problems and find its own solutions. This is also the principle stance behind the city-state's cultural creative industry policy. This means that creative and artistic expressions can be controlled. For instance, for street performers, they need to audition and seek a license to perform at selected places. Their proceeds should also go to charity, so that artistic craft is not used as an excuse for begging in the streets (Othman 2009). In 2014, the Media Development Authority wanted to introduce a self-classification scheme to get arts groups to give age-appropriate ratings to their own works in line with the agency's classification code. More than 45 art groups rejected the scheme, knowing well that it is a programme that will lead to self-censorship, as arts groups take on responsibility to perform within the censorship guidelines or be punished if they classified their works wrongly. Consequently, the scheme was dropped because of the protests (C. Tan 2014). Award-winning film maker Tan Pin Pin's documentary *To Singapore, with Love* is banned in Singapore because it documents views of political dissidents who are in exile. The authorities found the film to 'contain untruths about history' even though it is critically acclaimed in international film festivals (D.M. Tan 2014). The Institute of Contemporary Arts (ICA) in Lasalle removed two objects from Loo Zihan's installation *Queer Objects: An Archive for the Future* in a gay-themed exhibition in 2016. Sex between men is a criminal offense in Singapore even though the law is not actively imposed. The two items were collected from the local annual pride event, Pink Dot. The exhibition catalogue however acknowledged that there were only 79 objects out of the 81 in the exhibition and the ICS director explained (Lee 2016):

> [The exhibition] is intended to be inclusive, particularly bearing in mind that we have young as well as mature students at Lasalle, many from different cultural and religious backgrounds.
>
> Ours is an open, highly visible gallery with a full glass facade. Due to the nature of two objects, which could potentially be considered offensive to some members of the public, we discussed with Wong Binghao [curator] and Loo Zihan, the artist, the possibility of removing the items, which were both sex toys. After our discussion, everyone agreed to exclude the items before the exhibition officially opened.

Censorship and creativity are seen to be incompatible notions (Chong 2012; Lee 2010; A. Tan 2007). Singaporean authorities have defined a 'balance' between the two (Ooi 2010b). They do not see a need for complete freedom of expression and total acceptance of diversity in nurturing the arts and culture. Even the Yale-NUS Liberal Arts programme has to be adapted to the 'Asian' context (Davie 2015; Liu and Lye 2016). In Singapore, a distinction is made between the creative process and the contents that come out of creative processes. The authorities encourage creative thinking but want people to steer away from publicizing certain views. All countries have laws that limit some form of expressions, for example, on pornography and hate-crimes. To the authorities in Singapore, lacking the freedom of expression in certain quarters such as expressions that disturb the multi-ethnic, multi-religious peace, as well as thoughts that challenge the authorities, does not mean that a city cannot become a creative arts hub. The arts and culture can still grow without having to delve into forbidden areas. Creative individuals are supposed to place their energy on being entrepreneurial and concentrate on economic development. So, the authorities also make an implicit distinction between economically valuable and economically less significant creativity. Former Prime Minister Goh Chok Tong revealingly mentioned that, 'It has not been proven that having more press freedom would result in a clean and efficient government or economic freedom and prosperity' (The Straits Times, 2005).

Furthermore, the Singaporean authorities take the view that although chaos and experiments are only expected in a creative ecosystem, the environment must also be stable and orderly enough to drive the creative industries in the desired direction. They have also accepted that creative spaces will sprout despite attempts at control. Creative and supposedly deviant expressions are largely tolerated as long as they are not attracting widespread attention and not threatening public peace. But as mentioned earlier the possibility of a clampdown has given rise to self-censorship and self-restraint. This is an effective form of policing without the need for active control.

Artists who want to express themselves in politically controversial ways will not get state support. These artists may still do their art but do not expect support for their enterprises from the state; it is not part of the art ecosystem that NAC will promote. Tellingly, in response to criticism that the Singaporean government has stifled artistic expressions that are socially controversial, the chief executive of the NAC, Kathy Lai, stated her organization's position (Lai 2015):

> These are taxpayers' monies and we, as custodians, need to balance rigorous processes with aesthetic sensibility to determine how they are to be utilised. We will have difficulty funding art with public funds if such works merely feed a desire for self-expression, without any consideration of their impact on the public and whether they truly enrich their lives.
>
> Those who advocate 'art for art's sake' and lament the arts are being 'instrumentalised' could reflect on whether it is such an ill if the arts are 'used' for the greater good of society.

The Singaporean artrepreneurial ecosystem has evolved into one with a purposeful logic. Artists' creative spirit is channelled through social, political, and also financial means. So besides the tendency towards self-restraint, the state-controlled media has presented some artists as trouble-makers and attention seekers. Anti-establishment art will not be sanctioned by the national art body. In the context of the arts and culture, many artists are economically viable only because of state support, for example receiving subsidies for art housing, grants for performances and exhibitions, invitations to overseas study trips and museum purchases. Receiving bad publicity may threaten future support from not only state agencies but also private ones. On the other hand, the high-handedness of the state has also inspired some artists in their works (Luger 2016; A. Tan 2007).

Markets and competition

There is a dilemma for the authorities as they try to lift the artistic standard in the country while many local artists feel that they are ignored and marginalized. An entrepreneurial ecosystem should welcome talents and competition. Best practices should be picked up and introduced into the local system. The many international collaborations in Singapore's creative higher education apparently indicate that the authorities want to introduce quality creative education but also embrace foreign approaches. More importantly, in the case of partnership with international universities, all involved (Singaporeans and internationals) are keen to point out that there is a degree of reciprocity, which goes beyond the formal degree validation processes which international institutions offer to local institutions. 'It is a two-way partnership, it's not a one-way partnership, it's not just a validation relationship but really looking at what kind of opportunities are there for both sides to learn and create new knowledge, create new transnational relationships', posited an interviewed teacher from the School of the Arts or SOTA. However, from a broader higher education policy perspective, there is a recognition of some dependency created, as a higher education policy maker we interviewed spelt out:

> The advantages, you actually quickly have quality programme that is certified by a good university overseas and you have then good capability transfer from these institutions. With the capability transfer the disadvantage is that you are a price taker, and as a price taker you are more subjected to the terms that you would not like, so it is not ideal in the long run to sustain a model fully on partnerships.

Besides adopting foreign higher education into the Singaporean system, Singapore wants to attract local and foreign creatives. In fact, the country has suffered from a drain of artists. There are many examples of Singaporean artists leaving the country because of its artistic limitations. For instance, a Canada-based Singaporean sculptor was a recipient of the highest arts accolades in the city-state, the Cultural Medallion in 2014. Similarly, Boey Kim Cheng, a poet, left Singapore for Australia after winning the NAC's 1996 Young Artist Award in 1997. Conceptual artist Lim Tzay Chuen represented Singapore in the 2005 Venice Biennale, and his controversial work of moving the tourist icon of Singapore, the Merlion, to Venice was eventually disallowed on the official ground of costs; he is now based in Beijing. Han Kee Juan, Director of the Washington School of Ballet, left Singapore for the Australian Ballet School in Melbourne in 1976 when he found opportunities lacking in Singapore and has thus not pursued a career in his home country (Tan 2009).

On the other hand, the authorities welcome foreign creative and productive talents to the city-state. The influx of foreigners (not just foreign artists) is a political issue for many Singaporeans. The 2011 elections saw the People's Action Party losing ground, and the public discourse took on a populist and xenophobic turn (Tan and Lee 2011). Policies are still in place to attract productive and innovative workers for the sake of the country but at a more measured manner. For instance after the year-long celebrations of Singapore's 50th jubilee in 2015, the authorities revealed plans to 'future-proof' the city-state. They have committed a record sum of S$19 billion to Research and Development (Chang and Hio 2016). Much of the research money will go to solving challenges the country faces, such as water purification, cyber security, and handling emerging infectious diseases (Lin 2016). The chief of the Singapore National Research Foundation – the organization handling this pool of research grants – Low Teck Seng, revealed that his organization has more than 60 fellows, and to make Singapore into a top research hub it has to 'cream off the best in the world' (Lin 2016).

A similar argument is put forward by Comunian (2011) looking at the regeneration of Newcastle–Gateshead. While local policy ultimately aims to grow local creative economies, they often have to consider supporting a form of parochialism while taking the opportunity to support international artists. The balancing act of valuing local culture while trying to emerge as an international cultural player (Comunian and Ooi 2016) remains a challenge in

Singapore. So in this context, many attention-grabbing sculptures in public places are not local. Instead expensive Dalis, Boteros, and Lichtensteins are used to brighten up the concrete jungle in the financial and shopping districts. Local artists interviewed complain that public funding for the arts often go to foreign artists and art businesses. It is at times perceived that support for international artists hinders the local artrepreneur. As a representative of the arts community, nominated Member of Parliament then, Audrey Wong, voiced this concern in response to the increased arts funding in the 2011 Singapore government budget (Yen 2011): 'There is a concern that the additional funding will go towards international events like the recently concluded art fair, Art Stage, or attracting foreign productions to our shores.'

The Singapore artrepreneurial ecosystem is not isolated from the island's shores. Singapore is a very cosmopolitan and international city. The argument is to what extent the authorities should shield local artists from international competition.

Conclusions

The chapter has highlighted that the growth and support towards cultural and creative production in East Asia – and specifically Singapore – needs to be connected with multiple aspects defining its ecosystem. In particular, we identify four pillars: the education system, the value and social norms of the place, the influence of broader policy, and the Singaporean authorities' definition of democracy, and finally the connection with internal and international markets (and competition). In the case of Singapore we detailed the often divided perspective of a global city that aims to move forward supporting new creative educational opportunities and new markets, but that is still anchored in established social norms and a narrow definition of freedom of expression. While the will and policy interventions might allow Singapore to emerge in the international arena of creative and cultural production, the opportunity to embrace creativity fully rests in promoting a broader understanding of the value of culture and of the need for artistic freedom to support creativity. In the context of this book, which explores a range of national and cultural contexts in East Asia, we believe that a better understanding of the role of these four pillars can provide an increased understanding of the creative and cultural industries. This could help in providing a framework to understand how creative ecosystems in different Asian contexts might work, evolve, and adapt under increased pressures not only from policy but also from changing social values. Nevertheless these pillars would acquire different weight or significance in different economic and political contexts and therefore need to be examined in relation to local specificities.

Note

1 The two authors have immersed themselves into the Singapore art world. Between them, in-depth interviews were conducted since 2007. Artists of various disciplines, policy makers, art school teachers, and other relevant stakeholders were approached. Besides formal interviews, other data sources are used in this study, including informal discussions, documents, news stories, and participant observations.

References

Abbing, H. (2002) *Why are Artists Poor? The Exceptional Economy of the Arts.* Amsterdam: Amsterdam Universtiy Press.

Advisory Council on Culture and the Arts (1989) *Report of the Advisory Council on Culture and the Arts.* Singapore: Singapore National Printers, Singapore. Retrieved from http://openlibrary.org/books/OL2015500M/Report_of_the_Advisory_Council_on_Culture_and_the_Arts.

AHRC (2011) AHRC announces £16m boost for Arts and Humanities researchers and the UK Creative Economy. Swindon.
Bakhshi, H., McVittie, E., and Simmie, J. (2008) Creating innovation: Do the creative industries support innovation in the wider economy? London.
Becker, H. S. (1984) *Art Worlds*. Berkeley: University of California Press.
Bullen, E., Robb, S., and Kenway, J. (2004) "Creative Destruction": knowledge economy policy and the future of the arts and humanities in the academy. *Journal of Education Policy*, 19, 3–22.
Chang, A.-L. and Hio, L. (2016) Singapore commits record $19b to R&D. *The Straits Times*. Retrieved from str.sg/ZHfQ
Chang, S. and Mahadevan, R. (2014) Fad, fetish or fixture: contingent valuation of performing and visual arts festivals in Singapore. *International Journal of Cultural Policy*, 20(3), 318–40. https://doi.org/10.1080/10286632.2013.817396
Chang, T. C. (2000) Renaissance revisited: Singapore as a "Global City for the Arts." *International Journal of Urban and Regional Research*.
Chang, T. C. and Lee, W. K. (2003) Renaissance City Singapore: a study of arts spaces. *Area*. Retrieved from isi:000183813200002
Chapain, C., Clifton, N., and Comunian, R. (2013) Understanding creative regions: bridging the gap between global discourses and regional and national contexts. *Regional Studies*, *47*, 131–34.
Chatterton, P. (2000) The cultural role of universities in the community: revisiting the university - community debate. *Environment and Planning A*, 32(1), 165–81. https://doi.org/10.1068/a3243
Chew, M. (2012) Swedish digital media school opens branch here. *The Straits Times*.
Chong, T. (2005) Singapore's cultural policy and its consequences. *Critical Asian Studies*, 37(4), 553–68. https://doi.org/10.1080/14672710500348455
Chong, T. (2012) The Theatre and the State in Singapore: Orthodoxy and Resistance. London: Routledge.
Cohen, B. (2006) Sustainable valley entrepreneurial ecosystems. *Business Strategy and the Environment*, 15(1), 1–14. https://doi.org/10.1002/bse.428
Comunian, R. (2011) Rethinking the creative city: the role of complexity, networks and interactions in the urban creative economy. *Urban Studies*, 48(6), 1157–79. https://doi.org/10.1177/0042098010370626
Comunian, R. and Gilmore, A. (2014) From knowledge sharing to co-creation: paths and spaces for engagement between higher education and the creative and cultural industries. In A. Schramme, R. Kooyman, and G. Hagoort (eds.), *Beyond Frames Dynamics between the Creative Industries, Knowledge Institutions and the Urban Context* (pp. 174–85). Delft: Eburon Academic Press.
Comunian, R. and Ooi, C.-S. (2016) Global aspirations and local talent: the development of creative higher education in Singapore. *International Journal of Cultural Policy*, 22(1), 58–79.
Comunian, R., Chapain, C., and Clifton, N. (Eds) (2010) Location, location, location: exploring the complex relationship between creative industries and place. *Creative Industries Journal*, 3(1), 5–10. https://doi.org/10.1386/cij.3.1.5_2
Council, N. A. (2008) *Renaissance City Plan III: Arts Development Plan*. Singapore: National Arts Council.
Cunningham, S., Cutler, T., Hearn, G., Ryan, M., and Keane, M. (2004) An innovation agenda for the Creative Industries: Where is the R&D? *Media International Australia Incorporating Culture and Policy*, 112(1), 174–85. https://doi.org/10.1177/1329878X0411200114
Davie, S. (2015) Yale-NUS "has to adapt liberal arts model to Asia." *The Straits Times*. Retrieved from http://news.asiaone.com/news/education/yale-nus-has-adapt-liberal-arts-model-asia
Economic Review Committee – Services Subcommittee Workgroup on Creative Industries (2002) *Creative Industries Development Strategy: Propelling Singapore's Creative Economy*. Singapore: ERC.
Engelmann, M., Grünewald, L., and Heinrich, J. (2012) The new artrepreneur – how artists can thrive on a networked music business. *International Journal of Music Business Research*, 1(2), 31–45.
Faggian, A. (2006) Human capital flows and regional knowledge assets: a simultaneous equation approach. *Oxford Economic Papers*, 58(3), 475–500. https://doi.org/10.1093/oep/gpl010
Fine, G. A. (2004) Everyday Genius: Self-Taught Art and the Culture of Authenticity. Chicago: University of Chicago Press.
Florida, R. (2006) Regions and universities together can foster a creative economy. *Chronicle of Higher Education*, 53(4), B6. Retrieved from http://creativeclass.com/rfcgdb/articles/Regions and Universities Together Can Foster - Chron of Higher Ed.pdf

Galloway, S. and Dunlop, S. (2007) A critique of definitions of the cultural and creative industries in pubic policy. *International Journal of Cultural Policy*, 13(1), 17–31. https://doi.org/10.1080/10286630701201657
Glasgow School of Art Singapore (2018) Programme Overview. http://www.gsa.ac.uk/study/gsofa-singapore/programmes/
Grenfell, M. and Hardy, C. (2007) *Art Rules: Pierre Bourdieu and the Visual Arts*. Oxford: Berg.
Harvie, J. (2015) Funding, philanthropy, structural inequality and decline in England's theatre ecology. *Cultural Trends*, 24(1), 56–61. https://doi.org/10.1080/09548963.2014.1000586
Hesmondhalgh, D. and Pratt, A. C. (2005) Cultural industries and cultural policy. *International Journal of Cultural Policy*. Retrieved from http://www.informaworld.com/10.1080/10286630500067598
Ho, O. (2016) SkillsFuture under MOE to "integrate education, training." *The Straits Times*. Retrieved from str.sg/ZHjg
Hughes, A., Kitson, M., Probert, J., Bullock, A., and Milner, I. (2011) *Hidden Connections: Knowledge Exchange between the Arts and Humanities and the Private, Public and Third Sectors*. London: Arts and Humanities Research Council.
Isenberg, D. J. (2010) How to start an entrpreneurial revolution. *Harvard Business Review*, 88(6), 40–50.
Isenberg, D. J. (2011) Entrepreneurs and the cult of failure. *Harvard Business Review*, 89(4), 36.
Kong, L. (2012) Ambitions of a global city: arts, culture and creative economy in "post-crisis" Singapore. *International Journal of Cultural Policy*, 18(1), 279–94. https://doi.org/10.1080/10286632.2011.639876
Kong, L., Gibson, C., Khoo, L.-M., and Semple, A.-L. (2006) Knowledges of the creative economy: towards a relational geography of diffusion and adaptation in Asia. *Asia Pacific Viewpoint*, 47(2), 173–94. https://doi.org/10.1111/j.1467-8373.2006.00313.x
Lai, K. (2015, November 7) The tough balancing act of arts funding. *The Straits Times*. Retrieved from str.sg/ZEWG
Lee, J. X. (2016) Sex objects removed from art show. *The Straits Times*. Retrieved from str.sg/ZCiL
Lee, T. (2004) Creative shifts and directions. *International Journal of Cultural Policy*. Retrieved from http://www.informaworld.com/10.1080/1028663042000312525
Lee, T. (2010) The Media, Cultural Control and Government in Singapore. London: Routledge.
Liaw, W.-C. (2007) New poly courses zoom in on creativity and hospitality. *The Straits Times*. Retrieved from http://www.timesdirectories.com/Singlenews.aspx?DirID=101&rec_code=50660
Lim, J. (2016) Singaporeans urged to be bold innovators. *The Straits Times*. Retrieved from str.sg/Zjgj
Lim, L. (2012) Constructing habitus: promoting an international arts trend at the Singapore Arts Festival. *International Journal of Cultural Policy*, 18(February), 1–15. https://doi.org/10.1080/10286632.2011.651131
Lin, Y. (2016) More public money will go to projects that improve Singaporean lives, says NRF. *The Straits Times*. Retrieved from str.sg/ZHfm
Lindberg, M. E. (2008) Higher education-to-work transitions in the knowledge society: the initial transition and positional competition point of view. *Higher Education in Europe*, 33(4), 375–85. https://doi.org/10.1080/03797720802522577
Liu, P. and Lye, C. (2016) Liberal arts for Asians. *Interventions*, 1–15. https://doi.org/10.1080/1369801X.2015.1126194
Luger, J. (2016) Singaporean "spaces of hope?" *City*, 1–18. https://doi.org/10.1080/13604813.2015.1090187
Ministry of Information, C. and the A. (MICA) (2008) Resonance: A MICA newsletter. Singapore: MICA.
Ministry of Information and the Arts (2000) *Renaissance City Report: Culture and the Arts in Renaissance Singapore*. Singapore: MITA. Retrieved from http://www.mica.gov.sg/renaissance/FinalRen.pdf
National Arts Council (2015) *National Art Council Annual Report FY 2014/15*. Singapore. Retrieved from https://www.nac.gov.sg/naccorp/naccorp/media-resources/annual-reports/annual-report-2014-2015.html
Ng, J. (2008, December 10) Young talents shun careers in the arts. *The Straits Times*.
Ooi, C.-S. (2008) Reimagining Singapore as a creative nation: The politics of place branding. *Place Branding and Public Diplomacy*, 4, 287–302
Ooi, C.-S. (2010a) Cacophony of voices and emotions: dialogic of buying and selling art. *Culture Unbound*, 2, 347–64.
Ooi, C.-S. (2010b) Political pragmatism and the creative economy: Singapore as a City for the Arts. *International Journal of Cultural Policy*, 16(4), 403–17. https://doi.org/10.1080/10286630903118071

Ooi, C.-S. (2011) Subjugated in the creative industries: The fine arts in Singapore. *Culture Unbound, 3*, 119–37. Retrieved from http://www.cultureunbound.ep.liu.se/v3/a11/cu11v3a11.pdf
Ooi, C.-S. (2012) Education and becoming an artist: experiences from Singapore. In C. Mathieu (Ed.), *Careers in Creaive Industries* (pp. 254–69). New York: Routlege.
Othman, D. (2009) Busking rules will not stifle vibrant streetscape. *The Straits Times.*
Philomin, L. E. (2015) Yale-NUS courses "do not match" students' academic expectations. *Today.* Retrieved from http://www.todayonline.com/singapore/yale-nus-courses-do-not-match-students-academic-expectations
Philomin, L. E. (2016) More time for students to pursue broader range of interests: MOE. *Today.* Retrieved from http://www.todayonline.com/singapore/more-time-students-pursue-broader-range-interests-moe
Potts, J. and Cunningham, S. (2008) Four models of the creative industries. *International Journal of Cultural Policy.* Retrieved from http://www.informaworld.com/10.1080/10286630802281780
Powell, J. (2007) Creative universities and their creative city-regions. *Industry and Higher Education*, 21(5), 323–35. https://doi.org/10.5367/000000007782311867
Pralong, J., Gombault, A., Liot, F., Agard, J.-Y., and Morel, C. (2012) Unpacking unsuccess: socio-cognitive barriers to object career success for French outsider artists. In C. Mathieu (Ed.), *Careers in Creaive Industries* (pp. 237–53). London: Routledge.
Purushothaman, V. (2016) Cultural policy, creative economy and arts higher education in renaissance Singapore. In R. Comunian and A. Gilmore (Eds), *Higher Education and the Creative Economy: Beyond the Campus* (pp. 201–20). London: Routledge.
Seow, J. (2016) New statutory boards to focus on skills, employment. *The Straits Times.* Retrieved from str.sg/ZHbR
Tan, A. (2007) Theatre and cultures: Globalizing strategies. In K.P. Tan (Ed.) (pp. 185–200). Singapore: NUS Press.
Tan, C. (2014, August 23) Proposal for self-classification dropped by MDA. *The Straits Times.*
Tan, D. M. (2014) Film on exiles, *To Singapore, With Love*, has four screenings at arts festival in London. *The Straits Times.*
Tan, J. and Gopinathan, S. (2000) Education reform in Singapore: towards greater creativity and innovation. *NIRA Review*, 7, 5–10.
Tan, K. P. (2007) In renaissance Singapore. (K.P. Tan, Ed.). Singapore: NUS Press.
Tan, K. Y. L. and Lee, T. (2011) *Voting in Change: Politics of Singapore's 2011 General Election.* (K. Y. L. Tan and T. Lee, eds.). Singapore: Ethos Books.
Tan, T. (2009) The one that went away. *The Straits Times.*
The Economist (2014) All together now. *The Economist.* Retrieved from http://www.economist.com/news/special-report/21593582-what-entrepreneurial-ecosystems-need-flourish-all-together-now
The Straits Times (2005, November 1) Singapore ranked No. 140? Why SM isn't worried. *The Straits Times.*
Ting, L. (2014) Campuses get creative. *The Straits Times.*
Trüby, J., Rammer, C., and Müller, K. (2008) *The Role of Creative Industris in Industrial Innovation* (Vol. 08–109). ZEW, Center for European Economic Research.
Tsui, E. (2016) Singapore turning into arts hub while Hong Kong still stuck in mud. *South China Morning Post.* Retrieved from http://www.scmp.com/lifestyle/arts-entertainment/article/1909286/singapore-turning-arts-hub-while-hong-kong-still-stuck
Wong, C. Y. L., Millar, C. C. J. M., and Ju Choi, C. (2006) Singapore in transition: from technology to culture hub. *Journal of Knowledge Management*, 10(5), 79–91. https://doi.org/10.1108/13673270610691198
Wong, R. (2012) Lasalle-Goldsmiths tie-up another boost for the arts. *My Paper.* Retrieved from http://news.asiaone.com/News/Latest+News/Singapore/Story/A1Story20120301-330944.html
Wong, S. Y. (2015) Investment in R&D has paid off: PM Lee. *The Straits Times.*
Yang, C. (2014, September 26) Careers in the arts sector drawing the young. *The Straits Times.*
Yen, F. (2011) Budget for the arts should fund local talents. *The Straits Times.*

5

Challenges in developing the cultural and creative industries (CCIs) of Taiwan

The issue of local context in cluster policy

Pei-Ling Liao and Caroline Chapain

Introduction

In researching the cultural and creative cluster and its policy, the most frequently asked question is why some cities can successfully develop it but others cannot (Moss 2002; Montgomery 2003, 2004; Kong 2005, 2007; Pratt 2009). Current research findings and policy makers understand that there is a significant impact of local cultural, social, and economic contexts on policy implementation and function (Scott 1996, 2004, 2006; Montgomery 1995, 2003, 2004, 2005; Martin and Sunley 2002; Mommaas 2004; Kong 2000, 2005, 2007, 2012; O'Connor 2007; Pratt 2008; Evans 2009; Keane 2009; Storper 2013). In many East Asian cities, the economy has always been the policy priority. However, without serious consideration and planning in relation to local contexts, an application of the cluster model to the cultural and creative industries (CCIs) has proven difficult to implement (Kong 2005; Kong et al. 2006; Kong 2007; Chou 2012; Keane 2009).

The development of policy for CCI clusters in Taiwan is grouped into two policy initiatives: (1) cultural and social initiatives which include supporting and promoting art and cultural assets, traditional techniques (in craft, for example), tourism and post-industrial spatial preservation for the betterment of society; and (2) the economic initiative focused on promoting industries such as digital, information communication and technology (ICT) and creative industries to facilitate economic revitalization of Taiwan (Kong et.al. 2006; Kong 2000, 2005; Yue 2006; Keane 2009). This shows that, within Taiwan's context, the term CCIs inherently covers art, culture, society, communities, consumption, and markets (Kong 2000; Chang 2000; Yim 2002; Kong et al. 2006; Chou 2012).

In the mid-1990s, the Taiwanese government adopted the term 'cultural industries' as part of its social and cultural spatial planning initiatives,[1] which were based on similar initiatives from Japan. Meanwhile, it was also pursuing the 'creative economy', with an emphasis on the well-established ICT industries, through economic initiatives such as cluster policies. It should be also noted that Taiwan has a close relationship with surrounding countries such as Hong Kong, Singapore, Japan, and South Korea and hence its public policy thus tends to draw on policies from them. In the past three decades, Taiwan, like some of its neighbors, has put in place various CCI cluster policies.

This chapter adopts a longitudinal approach to examine how changes in Taiwan's local contexts have affected the development of these policies and their trajectories. It examines two cases using primary and secondary data such as policy documents, archives, statistical data, and interviews of policy makers, cluster management agents/companies, artists, and academics. The documents and data gathered cover the period 1990 to 2011 and 47 interviews were conducted, including 30 interviews at the two case study sites, two interviews with NGOs that support the development of the CCIs and 15 interviews from the related public sectors (the Department of Urban Development and the Department of Cultural Affairs of the Taipei City Government, the Council of Cultural Affairs, the Ministries of Economic Affairs and the Industrial Development Bureau, and the Council for Economic Planning And Development of the Executive Yuan) in 2007, 2009, 2010, and 2011.

Developing cultural and creative cluster policy in Taiwan

The development of Taiwanese cultural and creative cluster policy is closely related to the changes in its economic structure and urban development. It was also consistently revised in order to cope with the rapid changes occurring due to globalization. Looking at the following two cases, we will demonstrate how policy initiatives and governance approach were modified over time and how social and cultural values influenced these policies.

The first case is Hua-Shan Cultural and Creative Park. It was a formerly disused piece of state-owned land after a winery (brewery) that occupied the land moved out of Taipei City in 1987. In 1993, the Taipei City government approved a planning application that aimed to convert its zoning from residential, commercial, railway, and road usage to a government office zone (Taipei City Government 1993[2]). However, without a physical construction plan, this space was left unused for ten years, until 1997 when some artists and creative workers started to use the space for art and cultural activities and events. Between 1999 and 2002, the public and private sectors were trying to agree on the best way to manage the park. During this period, the Association of Culture Environment Reform Taiwan, as a representative of the Council of Cultural Affairs, a government body, managed Hua-Shan. In 2003 and 2004, L'Orangerie International Art Consultant (Co.), a private art and exhibition consultancy company, started operating the park. This changed in 2007 when the Council of Cultural Affairs signed a contract with another private enterprise – the Taiwan Cultural-Creative Development (Co.)[3] – to operate and manage the park. The trajectory of this cluster demonstrates how a creative cluster can develop from bottom-up and non-profit initiatives – here artists and creative workers initially – and can then be run by private companies with regards to management and operation. However, due to the government intervention in the park's land-use through its planning permission, including spatial usage and zoning, a potential contradiction and conflict has been visible between public interests, commercial profits, and industrial incubation/development.

The second is Nan-Kang Software Industrial Park, an urban regeneration project located in Taipei City. Driven by economic purposes, it was aimed at industrial transformation. This top-down cluster policy in line with the traditional cluster approach has been managed by a real estate development company[4] and has been a key hub for creative industries such as digital industries, game and design industries. Both of these case studies will show how local contexts affect CCI cluster development and what function and role clusters may play in supporting CCIs. In order to examine this, it is first necessary to look into how CCI cluster policies have developed in Taiwan as well as what kind of changes the governance of these clusters has undergone. It will then be possible to see how socio-cultural contexts have affected CCI cluster development. In the following sections, we will discuss the major findings of the two case studies.

The trajectory of CCI cluster policy development

CCI cluster policy has been formulated by combining the agendas of CCI development and economic/urban development together. While economic initiatives aimed at revitalizing the economy and supporting industrial transformation, social and cultural initiatives were intended to facilitate community cohesion and rebuilding of local identity in rural areas and urban areas in decline. Over time, CCI cluster policy was adjusted, modified, and reconciled to cope with rapid social and cultural changes.

The term CCIs was first mentioned in the policy document '*The six years plan of national construction*' published in 1991. This document described how the government would like to support industrial transformation centered on knowledge-based industries. It implied that the creative industries such as design, digital, software, and games industries should be supported at a national policy level. Thus, the economically initiated cluster policy in the early 1990s, which focused on knowledge-based industries, was the same cluster approach that was used to build up industrial parks/districts for manufacturing, export-trade and ICTs in the 1980s (i.e. the Hsinchu Science Parks[5]) (Chung 2012). This is the case for Nan-Kang Software Industrial Park.

The social/cultural initiative cluster policy was a strategy used to cope with urban issues, such as a declining population, a lack of job opportunities, and unused spaces. This policy was learnt from Japan's experiences, where the local communities and the government tried to revitalize declining rural and suburban areas by using cultural assets, skills, and products, creating new job opportunities and building local consensus (Hwang and Miyazaki 1996: 977). In 1995, the Council of Cultural Affairs (CCA) in Taiwan launched the *Total Community Design* policy with the slogan, 'Culture Industrialization and Industry Culturalization' and the notion of 'Cultural Industry'. It aimed to revitalize the economy in rural areas and towns by using local cultural assets for community formation and social cohesion (Chung 2012: 341–2). Industrial transformation left many factories and warehouses unused, which provided the best space for conducting those approaches. Those unused spaces usually also have historical and cultural significance for a place. This policy was named '社區(Community) 總體(Comprehensive) 營造(Construction)' – ('Community Renaissance') (Lin and Hsing 2009; Kong et al. 2006), and presented the three main themes of a cultural cluster. The community here refers to the residential unit, such as neighbourhood or township. These communities suffered from the growth of the urban area, population migration, and lack of job opportunities resulting in their decline. The Taiwanese government was inspired by Japan, and believed that a holistic plan that 'comprehensively' takes into account the localized factors and unique landscape, cultural assets, and skills would play an important role in counteracting post-industrialization and globalization processes. The result of these actions and plans should positively regenerate the local area through a phenomenon of 'renaissance' (Hwang and Miyazaki 1996; Lin and Hsing 2009; Kong et al. 2006).

Taiwanese policy makers have believed that CCIs should be able to create the best economic profit by using a cluster approach. The policy discourses such as creativity city, creative economy, and creative class (Porter 1998; Landry 2000; Florida 2002) imply that a spatial cluster would contribute to attracting talent, re-imaging and branding a city, and promoting and incubating CCIs. As such the cluster policy would not only function for developing CCIs but also for delivering various policy purposes. These two cluster policies with a focus on CCIs were highlighted in the national development policy, *Challenge 2008*, in 2002. This document officially included artistic and aesthetic creation in the list of a knowledge-based economy as a main strategy. In line with this, Hua-Shan Art and Cultural District was assigned as the first official cluster policy in the 'Five wineries-breweries reuse plan'[6] (Cultural Policy White Paper) of the *Cultural and Creative Industry Development Plan* (Taiwan Government Executive Yuan 2002). This policy had the objective of revitalizing the economy and developing CCIs at a national level. In *Challenge 2008*, the sub-projects 'Industrial Value Heightening Plan' and the 'International Innovation and R&D Base Plan'[7] (Taiwan Government Executive Yuan 2002) designated Nan-Kang Software Industries Park as a place to facilitate the creative industries such as design, software, and digital-based industries.

The purpose of announcing the CCI cluster projects at a national policy level was to show that the government was capable and interested in enlarging the market value of the CCIs and to introduce CCI workers and their products to the general market, as well as attracting talent and also indicating to other countries in the region a desire to facilitate cooperation and competition. Additionally, the government had attempted to test to what extent that cluster approach could function for CCIs. The cluster policy approach was reiterated in the '*The white paper on cultural policy*' (CCA 2004). In 2009, the policy document *Creative Taiwan* focused spaces and commercial incentives, and based on this policy, the government endeavored to further promote CCIs and advocate for their economic effect. This document highlighted the importance of CCI clusters, but also pointed out an important issue – a lack of legislation to underpin CCI development. Subsequently, 2010 saw the announcement of the 'Law for [Act of] the Development of the Cultural and Creative Industries (LDCC)'. This law formalized the definition of the CCIs and also classified the types of industries included.[8] In addition, it clarified the roles, rights, and responsibilities held by different levels of government and relevant departments in the central government and also introduced tax deductions and other incentives. This means that since 2010, CCI cluster policies have had firmer support from the government.

In the transition and development of CCI cluster policies, however, the two chosen cases reveal three key challenges affecting the cluster policy implementation and development: firstly, tensions between different aims pursued by public and private sectors respectively; the impact of various approaches to CCIs; and challenges coming from the local contexts. The following sections will discuss and analyse how these issues have influenced the development of these two CCI clusters.

Different aims pursued by public and private sectors

The 'Taiwan miracle' (see Kong et al. 2006: 184) perfectly demonstrates how successfully the cluster approach functions for economic development. Before martial law ended, Taiwanese economic development and related policy were planned and controlled by the government. In 1987, Taiwan formally became a democratic country, and the market economy started to affect policy formulation and implementation. As opposed to a government-led economy, the free market is harder to predict and measure the potential outcome of government policy. This is more so with CCI policy as the end-user determines the final value for the CCI product and their demand, which is difficult to predict, will guide the CCI market

(Pratt 2004; Hartley 2004). According to experience of manufacturing and high-technology cluster policies, offering comparable policy incentives (tax deductions, land acquisition and rental deductions) was deemed a priority and the best approach. Yet, our two cases revealed a completely different story: the failure of the policy focused on producers. Nan-Kang Software Industries Park struggled and was delayed by an insufficient number of companies moving into the park and/or their closure, caused by an immature consumption market for CCI products in the 1990s. This resulted in a lack of demand for space.

In contrast, at this stage, Hua-Shan Cultural and Creative Park was operated by a private company while there was a lack of appropriate public legislation to offer policy incentives such as tax exemptions and subsidies or regulation with regards to the management and operation of the park. In this circumstance, as this park was operated by a private 'company', more interest was paid to increase commercial profits and attract investment through an entrepreneurial approach.[9] This worried the artists, cultural workers, studios, and small companies who worked there (United Daily News 2003).[10] They argued that management by a private enterprise meant high rent and commercial orientation which would potentially eliminate the existing artistic and cultural atmosphere. To address this concern, policy makers set up a rent cap and a minimum amount of space that had to be used for CCI incubation as part of the agreement with the enterprise which was awarded the management contract of the park. This initiative helped to balance the economic objectives of the cluster as well as the cultural and creative actors' expectations. However, without a clear understanding of the creative labor market and the nature of CCIs (Caves 2000) and of the conflicts between a commercial company running a place for profit and an industry requiring massive incubation support, despite the imposed cap the allowed increase in rental price became unaffordable for the nascent small cultural and creative businesses within the park.

Practically, the existence of public and private contractual relationships helped compensate the public sector's weaknesses in terms of business operation and management as well as reducing public spending on the park development and construction. In addition, management by a private company provided a better intermediation between the CCI products and their potential markets. Finally, it should be noted that between public sectors, between the public and private sectors, and even between the private sectors (SMEs, individual workers, and entrepreneurs) there are conflicts. This means that CCI cluster policies need to be consistently modified and adjusted. Participants have different aims and are consistently reconciled by adopting various governance approaches. The public sectors all agree that the entrepreneurial approach in which an enterprise operates and manages a CCI cluster would be the best option. This approach basically ensures that clusters can support themselves financially and then will be able to sustain the development of CCIs, via offering cheaper rent and providing dedicated production spaces, without seeking subsidies from the public sector. This is why the entrepreneurial approach has been widely adopted as the main policy strategy (Mommaas 2004; Evans 2005; Capik 2007; Kong 2007). This approach is expected to give clusters better accessibility to the potential customer/client, which strengthens branding and marketing of the CCIs.

Impact of various approaches to governance

Before 2012, multiple policy actors including the Ministry of Economic Affairs, Ministry of the Interior, Ministry of Education, Council of Cultural Affairs and Council for Economic Planning and Development were in charge of CCI clusters and related policies (CCA 2009). Basically the main policy relating to cultural policy was formulated by the Council for Cultural Affairs (CCA, the predecessor of the Ministry of Culture), but the creative industries, including the digital, design, film, and games industries, were under the purview of the Ministry of Economic Affairs. Such a division caused notable difficulties:

> some departments such as the Council of Cultural Affairs are only involved in policy formulation and not in policy execution. It means that they may be good at policy research and formulation but have no idea how to drive industry development in practice. On the other hand, departments such as the Industrial Bureau of Ministry of Economic Affairs, may know how to drive industrial development, but are less clear in identifying the differences between the CCIs and general industries. For example, they seem to misunderstand the concepts and definitions of the CCIs and their development approach shouldn't be the same approach as that for developing manufacturing or ICTs.
>
> *(An NGO worker 2009)*

However, without legislative support, the CCI development and cluster policy formulation were mainly led by the economic departments, especially the Ministry of Economy; the Council of the Cultural Affairs was just for providing policy consultation. This economy-oriented government structure basically has difficulty in understanding the essential conditions that are required for the CCIs to develop and grow. Then, a restructure of the governance system took place with the Ministry of Culture being established in 2012, replacing the Council of Cultural Affairs. The new ministry started to take responsibility for CCI policy formulation, which was underpinned by specific legislation – 'Law for [Act of] the Development of the Cultural and Creative Industries (LDCC) (2012) – offering a clear definition of the CCIs as well as clarifying the division of labor among government ministries in terms of developing CCIs as well as offering guidelines to local government on how they could support the sector'.[11]

However, it was quickly revealed that the development of CCIs depends on the demands and preferences of the consumer market. To be financially successful, CCI workers need to compete for consumers whose tastes ultimately decide the economic value of CCI products. This is different from the circumstances of mass manufacturing industries that was the focus of cluster policy traditionally. Most importantly, the economic value of CCI products is difficult to measure without knowing the final purchase price, which has to be accepted by both producer and consumer. This reveals a challenge for cluster policy, particularly because the cultural and creative workers may not only be focused on a monetary value, but also on obtaining someone's appreciation and understanding of their 'product'. Thus, applying traditional cluster policy to CCIs may help their development through commercialization and enhanced accessibility to the potential market, but can conflict with the culture of art for art's sake prevailing in these industries. The two case studies reveal that so far such conflict may have resulted in CCI workers becoming disengaged from the cluster.

Both CCI clusters struggled at the early stage of policy implementation. So, policy makers tried different models of cluster governance to balance commercial profits, policy purposes, and the cultural and creative workers' interests, notably by putting in place a dedicated professional private company (a consultation agency combining three companies from hospitality, publishing, and hotel industries) to govern each cluster. The professional agency took the initiative in terms of spatial operation and management. This operational model was to ensure that the demands and the needs for both industry and market would be satisfied.

But the problem was that the CCI cluster policy was adopted while industrial transformation was on-going and before its market and consumption demand emerged. This explains why the policy faced difficulties in making social, cultural, and economic conditions more facilitative to the growth of CCIs.

> This is about social atmosphere, an enthusiasm for a rapid wave of fashion and design products, or maybe you call it cultural industries. Taiwan has had less than 100 years to accumulate its own culture and history, if you only count contemporary Taiwan … In theory, cultural and historical assets which have only existed for 20, 30 or 40 years could be considered to be 'historical site'. When you look at the Western cities, those local indigenous and historical heritages are normally over one hundred years old. This affects how our consumers look at 'cultural production', whereby the culture and arts have less value now as compared to fashion or pop brands.
>
> *(An NGO worker 2009)*

> The effort put in by government concerns education, aesthetics and values cultivation. This requires a long-term effort and a certain amount of input from the public sector. When the consumers have enough sense and art and culture and ability to appreciate them, the consumption market will grow and increase spontaneously, thus driving the creative workers and creativity,
>
> *(An academic 2009)*

The existing research finds that the consumer and consumption market dramatically affect the development of the CCIs, and this awareness should inform the orientation of CCI incubation (Storper 2013; Throsby 2010; Pratt 2008, 2009; Hartley 2004, 2008; Towse 2002; Caves 2000). The Taiwanese government's use of public–private partnership and entrepreneurial governance approach is meant to help CCIs to access the market. However, this policy still face difficulties when the socio-cultural factors such as cultural education, consumption capability, and consumer taste are not mature. These factors affect the economic values of CCIs through end-user accumulation and shaping their cultural preferences.

Challenges from the local contexts

When the CCIs and CCI clusters were first introduced by the government in the 1990s, the above-mentioned factors were yet to develop. CCIs have culture and creativity at their core, and culture and creativity are rooted in the social-cultural contexts which affect consumers' art and aesthetic appreciation and their social values which directly relate to how CCIs are valued. Indeed, the existing research reveals that CCI cluster policies in East Asian countries have been influenced by socio-cultural contexts of a given country, such as history, institutional factors, customs, social values, and the education system (see Kong 2007;[12] Keane 2009;[13] Evans 2009; Hartley 2008, 2004; Scott 2006; Flew 2002).

1. The impact of education

In Taiwan, the ethos of Confucianism influences social and cultural customs and values. It influences consumer behavior and the market of CCIs by affecting how arts, cultural, and creative products are valued (Zhong 2010; Lin and Hsing 2009). Taiwan's history as a former colony, along with its being a multicultural society, encourages people in Taiwan to display great openness towards foreign CCI products and their over-valuation compared to local ones. In an interview,[14] a CCI worker stated:

> In Taiwan, the customer is still willing to pay a higher price for an international brand than for a local brand. A 'brand' means a lot to the customers and becomes important

> in developing the consumption market here. This impacts how much you want to pay, which indicates the size of the local market and types of CCIs product that will be accepted in this market.
>
> *(A CCI worker 2010)*

This results in the local brand being under-estimated and often being lower priced, so that local cultural and creative workers struggle to develop a proper market while local talents often migrate to the countries nearby (Liao 2014).

In general, under the influence of Confucianism, the art and cultural disciplines such as performing arts, visual art, and design are marginalized in the education system. Education is focused on those subjects and skills that make one employable and allow one to earn a good salary and hence live a better life. Maths, science, finance, economics, and business are always prioritized. This leads to a very critical challenge for CCI development: talent shortage (Yeoh 2005; Scott 2006, 2004; Keane 2009).

Without the support of the education system and a change in social expectations, the CCI labor market has been limited in term of quality, capacity, quantity, and salary level. Potential talents and workers are not able and willing to remain in the industries:

> Under the influence of education system and social institutions in Taiwan, doing arts and culture is not considered as professional career by people who work in a bank or have a 'proper' occupation. The students who graduate from a good university have more interest in working for companies like ICTs in TSMC (Taiwan Semiconductor Manufacturing Company Limited) and HTC (High Tech Computer Corporation). In contrast, those with lesser academic achievements at a college or technologically-focused university become the main workforce for games, design and/or animation industries. It does not mean they are not good talent, but we do need some management talent ... The low salary[15] has caused a brain drain. This is an issue that the public sector should deal with.
>
> *(A CEO 2009)*

The case studies reveal that CCI workers are well aware of the unequal distribution of fame and financial gains (i.e., the winner takes all) and are concerned about how long it would take for them to be established in their field. Normally, students who study arts and creativity-related disciplines have to decide to either stay in these industries in the long term in order to achieve their career goals, or choose a non-CCI career for a more stable life. Accordingly, CCI workers expect the government to devise policy measures to support them during the long period of their 'development' before success is attained. This has been recognized as a critical agenda for CCI policy in Taiwan.

2. *The impact of the value chain*

Although the idea of CCIs arrived in Taiwan in the 1990s, the economic conditions were not yet mature enough to underpin CCIs. In the early 1990s, Taiwanese GDP was still below 10,000 USD.[16] Without enough money to spend, the demand for cultural and creative consumption is reserved and restrained. When the market is immature, the development of CCIs is limited, no matter what the policy implemented to support the CCIs. This explains why CCI cluster policy was difficult to implement in Taiwan in the first two decades.

In the mid-2000s, GDP grew dramatically to reach over 20,000 USD in 2011, which directly affected households' disposable income and, therefore, their demand for CCI products. This shifting economic and social environment allowed the cultural and creative cluster initiatives to advance. In addition, the growth of the internet and digital technology at the beginning of the 2000s provided more opportunities for CCIs to be valued, sold, and evaluated (Hartley 2004) and to more easily access and understand the market (Flew 2010). This change enabled CCIs to become more competitive and develop more direct relationships with their consumers, who take increasingly active roles.

> This differentiates the CCIs clusters with traditional cluster. We would argue that within the Taiwanese context, CCIs clusters' function and role are more about providing a place where cultural producers and consumers are able to communicate each other. Many consumers just 'look' at my products. When they actually start to consider buying it, they may ask: what is its function? How is it used? Is that expensive? And then decide: oh, I was just interested. Although they may not actually buy the product, their interest and questions show respect to me and my product. This could influence other customers and this kind of interaction and appreciation of arts and CCIs products take time to happen and pretty much rely on the literary and aesthetic education.
>
> *(A CCI worker 2009)*

> Currently, the CCIs cluster is still acting as a space for 'merchandising' and selling, but what we want to do is to tell the consumer the meaning and story behind our product, something I usually do here.
>
> *(An artist 2010)*

In a way, the CCI cluster plays a similar function and role as social media and other intermediators, which increase the frequency of information and knowledge exchanges between users (consumers) and producers (creators). As such, the cluster plays the role of gatekeeper or platform, where CCI workers can access and understand their consumers and markets.

Discussion and conclusion

The discussion in this chapter provides a different way of looking at CCI cluster policy in Taiwan. The policy has faced three important problems/issues: first, using an industrial cluster approach to CCI clusters; second, the unsupportive local social-cultural contexts; third, the impact of overall economic conditions on the development of CCIs.

The interview results revealed clear evidence that using an entrepreneurial approach, within the framework of public and private partnership, can be appropriate when the local consumer market is not yet ready to support the CCIs. But there also exists other reasons for taking such an approach.

> Developing a cluster put too much financial pressure on the public sector. We (public sector) believe that the private sector knows the consumption market better and could operate the park financially efficiently. Basically, those businesses know what the cluster needs and how to make the cluster profitable. This will be a positive influence on the development of the CCIs and promote the cluster too. In other words, the private sector

> (those businesses) know better than the public sector how to run a 'profit-oriented' business. No matter whether you like it or not, the cluster does need to make profit in order to survive.
>
> *(A public sector worker 2009)*

> For the Council of Cultural Affairs, it is difficult to support an industry when there is not enough market to underpin its development. This is the situation for CCIs. Developing CCI clusters would be a dream job for us, but the current policy maker (meaning the Ministry of Economic Affairs) wants to develop the CCI cluster by using the same approach used to develop Hsinchu Science Park. It aims to drive CCI clusters through CCI events and activities etc.
>
> *(A CCA officer 2009)*

However, some concerns have been raised such as the rise in rental price and the issue of balancing art/creativity and commercial purposes. From the CCI workers' point of view, the cluster did provide them with a place to access their market and to interact with customers, but this was limited depending on the management contract in place with the existing operating company.

> The rental is too high now after having successfully hosted several events. When there are events or exhibitions here, the income from the visitors could support the rent. But, we will need to be invited for those occasions by the cluster's operator, we could not afford to rent a place here monthly.
>
> *(A CCI worker 2009)*

This research shows that by an entrepreneurial approach, the clusters do provide a very limited amount of support to the cultural and creative actors in terms of production. However, they help cultural and creative producers in terms of branding and developing consumer markets. In line with this, policy makers should be aware that there is tension between achieving policy objectives and commercial objectives. The current public–private partnership approach has highlighted a need for further discussion on the best way to support CCI clusters. The policy maker may need a governance approach that can flexibly adjust to better manage the clusters to reflect and deliver public interests (the interests of consumers, companies, cultural and creative workers, and local communities). Secondly, the roles of the 'cluster' (space) are important not only in terms of production, distribution, governance, competitiveness, or branding but also because it provides a direct path from consumer to product.

> Cultural and Creative Industries Park does contribute to the CCI development. However, it is just a basic requirement, only focusing on the cluster is not enough to ensure the development of the CCIs. A space like Hua-Shan, without customers and visitors, is nothing.
>
> *(A CCI worker/art agency 2009)*

This leads back to the wider value of the CCIs rather than only the production values. Indeed, the weakness in accessing the market is one of the biggest challenges for CCI development. The cultural and creative clusters have become a platform that provides better opportunities for matching consumers and producers. This also highlights another potential function of a cluster: to nurture aesthetic appreciation in consumers in their daily life.

While public investment systems was mentioned as a critical issue during interviews, the bureaucratic system has little understanding of the CCI market. As the majority of the workers are still looking for public support, the public sector may need to understand that to financially assist CCI incubation and development requires a structured incubation plan. Interviews with policy makers have revealed that to efficiently develop CCIs and achieve policy purposes, they should only support those CCIs which have succeeded in the market.

> Current criteria for evaluating the effect of public funds and subsidies on CCIs are based on the examination of the market. The problem is, if the companies could pass the market examination, they would not need policy funds urgently.
>
> *(A CEO 2009)*

This issue is also mentioned in the literature by Garnham (2005: 28):

> Yet the problem here is that quality and excellence are open to the market test of consumer preference and access is, by definition, not a problem, since a successful creative industry has solved the access problem through the market. If it is successful, why does it need public support? If it is unsuccessful, why does it merit public support?

It is also important to notice that CCI cluster policy has been used by policy makers (usually the ruling party) to address political purposes by showing a successful delivery of highly visible CCI cluster initiatives as an clear image of their achievement towards the next election[17] (Kong 2000; Cho 2007). Martin and Sunley (2003) pointed out why cluster initiatives are often being used for political purposes: 'we should expect the cluster idea to act as an umbrella brand for many different things. The core meaning of clusters lies more in this image than in a coherent and carefully defined set of ideas'. In Taiwan, the *image* of a CCI cluster has helped policy makers obtain attention from the public for election purposes. CCI clusters can be also expected to deliver a prompt policy achievement in two to four years and have thus become the most visible and effective national policy strategy for winning the 'election' (Cho 2007; Chung 2012).

> You will discover a horrible truth when government is involved in the cluster's governance by following the concepts of traditional cluster … The concepts adopted for Science Park such as a wall, a management center or a regulation will be used for CCIs. What is the function and effect of the cluster for CCIs? It is for election. The politician needs quick effects/results for election. That is completely wrong.
>
> *(An officer at Artist and Arts Foundation 2009)*

This makes CCI clusters one of the most popular policies, especially when it can be seen to achieve various goals from urban regeneration, branding, industrial promotion to tourism development, cultural industrial development, and economic revitalization (Pratt 2005, 2009; Cho 2007; Chou 2012; Chung 2012).

Looking at cities in Eastern Asia, the majority of challenges in CCI cluster policy implementation comes from a lack of consideration of how clusters should be formed during the policy formulation process and how the commercialization of the cluster affects CCI development and its dynamics (Yang et al. 2015; Kong 2012; Lu et al. 2011; O'Connor and Gu 2010; Evans 2009; Hutton 2003). Most of these challenges can be explained by the state of the local contexts, including the lack of engagement of local communities, the disconnection between the cluster operation and cultural and creative actors, and an insufficient consumer market to underpin the long-term sustainability (Kong 2009, 2007, 2012; Pratt 2009; Evans 2009; Chou 2012; Chung 2012). These factors are all directly impacted by a lack of understanding and under-developed consumption, where education, social values, and customs play a critical role in the ecosystem of the CCIs. The potential of cluster exists beyond its support for production and is found in its intermediary roles linking the cultural and creative workers, the market, and the consumer. Thus, we suggest policy makers recognize that the cluster could be considered a complex 'platform' to increase the possibility of market access and also to enlighten the consumer in still-developing local contexts.

Table 5.1 The development of CCI cluster policies

Years	*Policy*	*Content*	*Effect and purpose*
1990–95	Comprehensive communality Buildings	The cultural industry was introduced through the concept of 'cultural industrialization, industries culturalization', in which the 'Total Community Design' was taken as the main approach to develop the cultural industries.	The term 'cultural industries' was introduced officially in Taiwan.
1991	The six-year plan of national construction	It was a comprehensive policy agenda, which set up a wider range of policy strategy by using 'knowledge-intensive industries' including the digital industries, design industry, telecommunication and microprocessor industries for economic purposes.	This policy was basically aimed at facilitating the CCIs by taking the traditional manufacturing industry with the economic initiative policy proposed.
2002	'Challenge 2008: National Development Plan'	Included the 'Ten Key Individual Plans',[1] in which the Cultural and Creative Industries Development Plan (Hua-Shan CCIs Park) and International Innovation and R&D Base Plan (Nan-Kang Software Industries Park) are related to CCI development.	The economic contribution of creative industries was considered together with the concerns with cultural industries under this policy. Apart from this, the economic initiative that focused on the local communities was extended to cover the city's economic challenges and the issue of urban redevelopment.
2004	The white paper on cultural policy	Three volumes: Current Status and Important Trends, Policies and Policy Implementation, and Vision and Challenges: continuing the 'community buildings' concepts, the idea of *culture and creative parks* were mentioned. Five old wine factories and warehouse were assigned to be these parks.	A policy guideline for cultural policy, and CCI clusters were highlighted and became important in CCI policies.

(Continued)

Years	*Policy*	*Content*	*Effect and purpose*
2009	Creative Taiwan (2009–13)	Two plans, first set of the plan was an environment preparation plan that sought to: • Strengthen multiple investment and award subsidies • Improve business counselling and promote cross-sector integration and R&D • Promote market flow for brands in Taiwan and develop domestic and overseas markets • Increase HR training and matching mechanism • Improve cluster effects Second set of plan: The industrial flagship plan	Creative Taiwan set out an objective to turn Taiwan into 'an Asia-Pacific confluence of CCIs' and develop the mainland Chinese and international markets.
2010	Act of the Development of CCIs	Definition of the CCIs and the classification of CCIs	Direct CCI cluster development in response to the increasing importance of CCIs and the integration of the Cultural Affairs Council into the Ministry of Culture. This restructuring of the government organization has relocated the various culture-related administrations/departments from other departments (such as Tourism and Communication, Industrial Development and Business, Education and even Business and Foreign Trade departments) into the Ministry of Culture. This ensures that the Ministry of Culture has full jurisdiction over cultural policies and their formulation.

NOTE:

1 The ten key plans : e-Generation Manpower Cultivation Plan; Cultural and Creative Industry Development Plan; International Innovation and R&D Base Plan;_Industrial Value Heightening Plan; Doubling Tourist Arrivals Plan; e-Taiwan Construction Plan; Operations Headquarters Development Plan; Island-wide Trunk Transportation Construction Plan; Water and Green Construction Plan; New-Home Community Development Plan.

Table 5.2 The changes in policy rationales, governance approach, and impacts of local contexts

		1995 — *2000*	*(2002)* — *2005*	*(2007)* — *2010*
Hua-Shan Cultural and Creative Park	Governance	Private initiative Economic purpose predomination Historical building reuse National level governance	Public intervention – negotiation Private initiative dismissed	Public and private collaborative partnership Toward commercial and business
	Local contexts	Economic structure – manufacturing to service industries Production focus – ICTs, manufacturing Education (labour, employment, consumption, cultural appreciation) Values on CCIs	Missing role of local government Values on CCIs production Market emerging	Entrepreneurial-led initiative Emerging of local market and consumption
NanKang Software Industrial Park	Governance	Planned economy policy Economic initiatives (top down) Under-development CCIs Planning approach National-level government predominance Public and private cooperation – management and operation	Local coordination (planning, traffic plan) Market economy	
	Local context	Values (Cultural and Creative Industries) cultural production Education (arts preference, appreciation) (consumer market) Market (local market) Industrial network/basis	(After 2005) Consumer/user Internet International market	

Notes

1 In 1994, the term 'Cultural Industry' first emerged under the label 'Culture Industrialization, Industries Culturalization', initiated by the Council of Cultural Affairs (CCA). This term drew attention to ways to rehabilitate the decline of local communities by using their indigenous cultural and social content and incorporate them within local spatial plans. These policies were inspired by the 'Total Community Design' initiatives implemented in Japan (Hwang and Miyazaki 1996). The Total Community Design initiatives were based on an approach centered around the 'Cultural Industry' and aiming 'to redevelop a local community as a unit by using their indigenous assets, skills or capital from in particular traditional culture and historical materials' (Hwang and Miyazaki 1996: 977). It was interpreted in many different English terms (such as 'Community Renaissance'), but basically the sense of the translation is similar to using the Chinese characteristics of '社區 (community), 總體 (comprehensive), 營造(construction)' (Liao 2014: 149)

2 Taipei city urban planning Instructions (No. 82024841), 15 April, 1993, (http://www.budwebgis.tcg.gov.tw/twobook/pdf/P082010.pdf, accessed September 7, 2009).

3 This enterprise was established by three companies: a publishing house, a design company, and a hotel company (Hua-Shan CCIs Park website, accessed September 22, 2009).

4 In 2012, Nan-Kang Software Industrial Park contained 351 companies, 18,860 employees, and averaged profits of around 1,999 hundred million NTD (6.66 billion USD) (per business unit annual revenue) (Taipei Economic Quarterly 2012). This park houses high-tech and ICT-based industries including companies such as Microsoft, HP, IBM, Sony, HSBC, SIMENSE, NEC, Infineon Technologies, Pericom, Philip, AMD, DynaComware, InterServ, Wave splitter, EPCOS, AVNET and FUJITSU. (http://data.taipei/opendata/datalist/publicationMeta/download;jsessionid=BF45423A51F82F9DD5A1D20F11482375?id=e4a2e6b9–90c9-4d4e-a2ea-5f75843e812a&rid=ca3da5f6-4fe3–4248-b6de-4167cb041815)

5 This economic-driven cluster has had a significant contribution on economic development by applying the industrial cluster for manufacturing and ICTs in Taiwan from the 1960s–1990s (see Chou 2012; Kong, O'Conner et al. 2009).

6 The five wineries-breweries reuse plan includes Taipei (Hua-Shan),Taichung, Hualien, Chiayi, and Tainan (http://reading.udn.com/act/2016creativepark/p002.html, first accessed November 11, 2008).

7 Challenge 2008 – National Development Plan (http://www.ndi.org.tw/ndied/cive01p1.htm, first accessed May 2, 2009).

8 See 'Article 3', the definition of the 'Cultural and Creative Industries': https://mocfile.moc.gov.tw/mochistory/ccaImages/laws/247/1-0-5.pdf (first accessed December 22, 2011).

9 Mommaas (2004), in the discussion on the strategy of operating and managing the CCI clusters, mentioned: 'Together, these considerations produced an atmosphere throughout the entire field of the arts and culture in favor of a more "entrepreneurial" approach. The subsidy regime had to be reorganised in order to stimulate, instead of stifle, the circulation of artistic qualities. In addition, more attention, money and space were needed for new media formats, for the cultural activities of younger generations of ethnic minorities, and for bringing cultural activities outside the conventional walls of vested art institutions. To free that money, and to increase its public reach, vested subsidised companies and institutions like museums and theatres were forced to increase their income from entrance fees' (p. 519). The entrepreneurial approach here referred to is the development strategy in which the cluster's operation and management is focused on how to increase income and attract the market and customers, and by doing so, it ensures a certain extent of financial sustainability to carry on supporting CCIs and developing the cluster.

10 United Daily News, 09.01.2003. Hua-Shan special district is formally named the Taipei wine factory and listed city-own heritage 〈華山特區 正名台北酒廠 列入古蹟, sheet 18 United Daily News, 17 Nov. 2003, The last night of the art organization in Hua-shan (藝協最後一夜 華山演至天明一不捨原創風 畢業這晚 發起土狗幫和創藝聯盟 監督未來), sheet 12A.

11 This law has formalized the definition of the CCIs and their industrial classification. Article 3 defines the CCIs and classifies them into 16 industries (see Table 6.5). Compared to previous policy documents, Article 3 added to and justified the classification of CCIs. Two new industry categories were added: '15: Popular music and cultural content industry' and '16: Other industries as designated by the central Competent Authority'. In the classification, the LDCC adjusts the original 'Design' sector (used in the classification from the 'Challenge 2008: National Development Plan' document) into 'Product design industry' and 'Visual communication design industry'.

Furthermore, it adjusts 'Digital Entertainment' to 'Digital content industry' which covers a wider range of relevant industries in order to gain better economic achievement.

In addition, the LDCC gave clearer roles to national and local governments in supporting the development of CCIs by stipulating the specific duties of various public sector organizations in Article 12. Through this law, MOC becomes the main national organization to conduct CCI policy. However, Article 25 of the law specifies that public sector organizations need to involve themselves in CCI cluster development processes and sort out inter-departmental policy integration as well as collaborate with the private sector.

Finally, the LDCC also provided guidelines on how local government could support CCI policies through subsidizing CCI workers, management of the clusters, organization of cultural events and the mapping of local CCIs. Based on this law, it gives local government administrative power to create CCI clusters and to adopt cluster policies at local level. Thus, the cluster has been considered an effective strategy by local policy makers for election purposes. Cultural activities, entertainment, and media events which tend to produce significant economic effect are selected in priority by the policy makers when conducting CCI cluster policies (Liao 2014: 158).

12 Hong-Kong West Kowloon Cultural District

13 Cultural and Creative District/Park at Beijing

14 This includes 45 interviews with representatives from the public sector (including planning, industrial development, tourism, and the cultural sectors, both local and national governments; CCI workers (handcraft, game designer, industrial designer, fashion designer, film maker) and the private sector (including the management company and exhibition company). Within-case and cross-case analyses are used to decrypt the data gathered in this research.

15 The average salary for undergraduate students from design and game-related subjects is roughly 800 to 1000 USD per month; for Master degree level it is around 800 to 1200 USD.

16 See http://statdb.dgbas.gov.tw/pxweb/dialog/statfile9L.asp

17 This is also the reason why cluster has been considered the most beneficial policy strategy in eastern Asia: what it can bring and contribute to winning the election as the best election manifesto (Kong 2000).

References

Capik, P. (2007) BOOK REVIEW: Asheim, B., Cooke, P. and Martin, R. (2006) (eds.), Clusters and regional development: critical reflections and explorations. *Regions Magazine,* 266(1): 26–7.

Caves, R. E. (2000) *Creative Industries: Contracts between Art and Commerce.* Cambridge, London: Harvard University Press.

Chang, T. C. (2000) Renaissance revisited: Singapore as a 'Global City for the Arts'. *International Journal of Urban and Regional Research,* 24: 818–31.

Cho, M. (2007) Construction of Hong-dae Cultural District: Cultural Place, Cultural Policy and Cultural Politics. Doctoral dissertation, Bielefeld University.

Chou, T.-L. (2012) Creative space, cultural industry clusters, and participation of the state in Beijing. *Eurasian Geography and Economics,* 53(2): 197–215.

Chung, H. (2012) Rebooting the dragon at the crossroads? Divergence or convergence of cultural policy in Taiwan. *International Journal of Cultural Policy,* 18(4): 37–41.

Council for Cultural Affairs (CCA) (2004) The white paper on cultural policy, executive Yuan, Taiwan, R.O.C [online]. Available from: http://english.cca.gov.tw/ct.asp?xItem=12192&ctNode=4063 [accessed September 19, 2012].

Council of Cultural Affairs (CCA) (2009) Creative Taiwan – CCIs development project-action plan [online]. Available from: http://www.cci.org.tw/cci/upload/law/ 20100604104150–8dd3d038610f19c0bd08739c496f4052.pdf [accessed November 17, 2011].

Evans, G. (2005) Measure for measure: Evaluating the evidence of culture's contribution to regeneration. *Urban Studies,* 42(5/6): 959–83.

Evans, G. L. (2009) From cultural quarters to creative clusters: Creative spaces in the new city economy. In Legner, M. (Ed.), *The Sustainability and Development of Cultural Quarters: International Perspectives.* Stockholm: Institute of Urban History, pp. 32–59.

Taiwan Government Executive Yuan (2002) *Challenge 2008: Six-Year National Development Plan* [online]. Available from: http://www.gio.gov.tw/taiwan-website/4-oa/20020521/2002052101.html [accessed May 2010].

Flew, T. (2002) Beyond ad hocery: Defining creative industries. In *Proceedings Cultural Sites, Cultural Theory, Cultural Policy, The Second International Conference on Cultural Policy Research*, Wellington, New Zealand, January 23–26. Available from: http://eprints.qut.edu.au/archive/00000256 [accessed May 2010].

Flew, T. (2010) Toward a cultural economic geography of creative industries and urban development: Introduction to the Special Issue on creative industries and urban development. *The Information Society*, 26(2): 85–91.

Florida, R. (2002) *The Rise of the Creative Class*. New York: Basic Books.

Garnham, N. (2005) From cultural to creative industries. *International Journal of Cultural Policy*, 11(1): 15–29.

Hartley, J. (2004) The 'value chain of meaning' and the new economy. *International Journal of Cultural Studies*, 7(1): 129–41

Hartley, J. (2008) From the consciousness industry to creative industries: Consumer-created content, social network markets and the growth of knowledge. In Holt, J. and Perren, A. (eds.), *Media Industries: History, Theory and Methods*. Oxford: Blackwell, pp. 231–44.

Hutton, T. (2003) Service industries, globalization, and urban restructuring within the Asia-Pacific: New development trajectories and planning responses. *Progress in Planning*, 61(1):1–74.

Hwang, S. H. and Miyazaki, M. (1996) Total community design as a culture rehabilitation in Taiwan: Methodology on activation regional community (1) [in Japanese]. *Bulletin of Japanese Society for Science of Design*, 43(1): 97–106.

Keane, M. (2009) The capital complex: Beijing's new creative clusters. In Kong, L. and O'Connor, J. (eds.), *Creative Economies, Creative Cities: Asian-European Perspective*. London: Springer. pp. 77–95.

Kong, L. (2000) Culture, economy, policy: Trends and developments. *Geoforum*, 31(4): 385–90.

Kong, L. (2005) The sociality of cultural industries. *International Journal of Cultural Policy*, 11(1): 61–76.

Kong, L., Gibson, C., Khoo, L.-M. et al. (2006) Knowledges of the creative economy: Towards a relational geography of diffusion and adaptation in Asia. *Asia Pacific Viewpoint*, 47(2): 173-194

Kong, L. (2007) Cultural icons and urban development in Asia: Economic imperative, national identity, and global city status. *Political Geography*, 26(4): 383–404.

Kong, L. (2009) Beyond networks and relations: Towards rethinking creative cluster theory, In Kong, L., and O'Connor, J. (eds.), *Creative Economies, Creative Cities: Asian-European Perspective*. London: Springer, pp. 61–76.

Kong, L. (2012) Improbable art: The creative economy and sustainable cluster development in a Hong Kong industrial district. *Eurasian Geography and Economics*, 53(2): 182–96.

Kong, L., Gibson, C., Khoo, L.-M. et al. (2006) Knowledges of the creative economy: Towards a relational geography of diffusion and adaptation in Asia. *Asia Pacific Viewpoint*, 47(2): 173–94.

Landry, C. (2000) *The Creative City: A Toolkit for Urban Innovators*. London: Earthscan Publications.

Liao, P. (2014) The Adaptation of the Cultural and Creative Industries Cluster Policy in Eastern Asian Cities: The Case Studies in Taiwan. Doctoral dissertation, University of Birmingham.

Lin, C.-Y. and Hsing, W. C. (2009) Culture-led urban regeneration and community mobilisation: The case of the Taipei Bao-an Temple Area, Taiwan. *Urban Studies*, 46(7): 1317–42.

Lu, J., Milano, P., and Indaco, D. (2011) Creative industry in Hong Kong. Available from: http://www.innovhub-ssi.it/c/document_library/get_file?uuid=8b875c19-26e1-44d5-9dbc-38bed90082c0&groupId=11636 [accessed 2016].

Martin, R. and Sunley, P. (2003) Deconstructing clusters: Chaotic concept or policy panacea? *Journal of Economic Geography*, 3(1): 5–35

Mommaas, H. (2004) Cultural clusters and the post-industrial city: Towards the remapping of urban cultural policy. *Urban Studies*, 41(3): 507–32.

Montgomery, J. (1995) The story of Temple Bar: Creating Dublin's cultural quarter. *Planning, Practice and Research*, 10(2): 135–71.

Montgomery, J. (2003) Cultural quarters as mechanisms for urban regeneration, part 1: Conceptualising cultural quarters. *Planning Practice and Research*, 18(4): 293–306.

Montgomery, J. (2004) Cultural quarters as mechanisms for urban regeneration, part 2: A review of four cultural quarters in the UK, Ireland and Australia. *Planning Practice and Research*, 19(1): 3–31.

Montgomery, J. (2005) Beware 'the creative class'. Creativity and wealth creation revisited. *Local Economy*, 20(4): 337–43.

Moss, L. (2002) Sheffield's cultural industries quarter 20 years on: What can be learned from a pioneering example? *International Journal of Cultural Policy*, 8(2): 211–19.

O'Connor, J. (2007) The Cultural and Creative Industries: A Review of the Literature. London: Creative Partnerships.
O'Connor, J. and Gu, X. (2010) Developing a creative cluster in a postindustrial city: CIDS and Manchester. *The Information Society*, 26(2): 124–36.
Porter, M. E. (1998) *On competition*. Boston, MA: Harvard Business School Publishing.
Pratt, A. C. (2004) Creative clusters: Towards the governance of the creative industries production system? *Media International Australia,* 112: 50–66.
Pratt, A. C. (2005) Cultural industries and public policy: An oxymoron? *International Journal of Cultural Policy,* 11(1), 31–44.
Pratt, A. C. (2008) Cultural commodity chains, cultural clusters, or cultural production chains? *Growth and Change,* 39(1): 95–103.
Pratt, A. C. (2009) Urban regeneration: From the arts 'feel good' factor to the cultural economy: A case study of Hoxton, London. *Urban Studies,* 46(5-6): 1041–61.
Scott, A. J. (1996) The craft, fashion, and cultural-products industries of Los Angeles: Competitive dynamics and policy dilemmas in a multisectoral image-producing complex. *Annals of the Association of American Geographers,* 86: 306–23.
Scott, A. J. (2004) Cultural-products industries and urban economic development: Prospects for growth and market contestation in global context. *Urban Affairs Review,* 39: 461–90.
Scott, A. J. (2006) Creative cities: Conceptual issues and policy questions. *Journal of Urban Affairs,* 28(1): 1–17.
Storper, M. (2013) Keys to the City: How Economics, Institutions, Social Interaction, and Politics Shape Development. Princeton: Princeton University Press.
Throsby, D. (2010) *The Economics of Cultural Policy.* Cambridge: Cambridge University Press.
Towse, R. (2002) *Copyright in the Cultural Industries.* Cheltenham: Edward Elgar Publishing.
United Daily News (09.01.2003) Hua-Shan special district is formally named the Taipei wine factory and listed city-own heritage.
Yang, Z., Hao, P. and Cai, J. (2015) Economic clusters: A bridge between economic and spatial policies in the case of Beijing. *Cities,* 42: 171–85.
Yeoh, B. (2005) The global cultural city? Spatial imagineering and politics in the (multi)cultural marketplaces of South-east Asia. *Urban Studies,* 42(5): 945–58.
Yim, H. (2002) Cultural identity and cultural policy in South Korea. *International Journal of Cultural Policy,* 8(1): 37–48.
Yue, A. (2006) Cultural governance and creative industries in Singapore. *International Journal of Cultural Policy,* 12(1):17–33.
Zhong, S. (2010) Industrial Restructuring and the Formation of Creative Industry Clusters: The Case of Shanghai's Inner City. Doctoral dissertation, University of British Columbia.

6

Creative industries with Chinese characteristics

A comparative analysis of public funding for culture in three Chinese cities

Ken Wang

Introduction

It is well known that China imported the policy discourse of creative industries from the UK and has established Cultural and Creative Industries (CCI)[1] policies since the 2000s (Flew and Cunningham 2010). While the creative industries policy in the UK and the broader Western context is often regarded as a neoliberal cultural policy, there is a wider debate about whether China has also chosen the neoliberal route (Harvey 2005; Arrighi 2007; Nonini 2008). Neoliberalism may be one aspect of Chinese CCI policies, but authoritarian control, local autonomy,[2] and an uneven development of CCI between various regions may also have characterized Chinese CCI policies, thus rendering them different from their British or Western counterparts. Several current studies criticize the impact of authoritarian control on cultural creation in China (Wang 2004; Ren and Sun 2011; Keane 2013). However, they have not considered the influence of local autonomy and regional inequality. This paper thus aims to advance the understanding of Chinese CCI policies through focusing on the municipal policies of different regions.

Case studies of municipal CCI policies in Beijing, Harbin, and Guangzhou will help us to better comprehend 'the Chinese context' for developing CCI. Despite the discrepancy between strategies adopted by the municipal governments from these different Chinese cities, they are all increasingly adopting neoliberal elements, implying that Chinese CCI policy is a complex amalgamation of neoliberal and state-driven approaches to culture and creativity.

The Chinese context for developing creative industries

The Chinese state has gradually promoted the commercialization of culture under state control since the 1980s. Before the 1980s, the central government controlled cultural production and promoted culture as a political and educational tool to secure the leadership of the Chinese Communist Party and to pursue socialist civilization (White and Xu 2012). Although during the 1980s and 1990s, the state began to recognize the economic value of cultural products and allowed private enterprises to conduct cultural production (Flew 2012), the State Administration for Radio, Film and Television (SARFT) and the State Press and Publication Administration (SPPA) were established for the regulation and licensing of the production of audiovisual and print media (Keane 2013). In addition, the government announced 'Seven Forbidden Content Categories' for media production[3] (Zhao 2008: 66). In the 2000s, the state began to officially use the term 'Cultural Industries'[4] in policy documents such as the *Tenth Five Year (2001–05) Plan for the Development of National Economy and Society* (State Council 2001) and promoted a reform of the 'cultural system' (wenhua tizhi). The reform transformed cultural institutions (wenhua shiye danwei) that had functioned as public cultural service providers into commercial cultural enterprises (Tang 2009). It is 'best illustrated by a widening of commercial forms of management and financing' in the cultural sector (Keane 2013: 13). However, authoritarian control still has influence on cultural production. As Ong (2006) argues, 'pro-market policies are interwoven with a socialist state and private enterprises flourish alongside repressive laws' (6).

Besides state control, local autonomy and regional inequality should not be ignored. With regards to local autonomy, Keane and Zhao (2014) note that national cultural policies only play a guiding role, and 'much policy is deliberately vague and open to interpretations' (157). O'Connor and Gu (2012) further argue that 'city policy-makers are much more directly involved in detailed operational decisions "on the ground" and – in contrast to the more "abstract universal" interventions at national level – stand directly to benefit, to suffer, from their consequences' (289). Therefore, national policies are not specific enough and leave local policy makers to interpret and implement policies independently, leading to a certain degree of diversity in local practices. Not only have the terms 'creative industries', 'cultural and creative industries' and 'cultural industries' been used unsystematically by various cities (Zhang and Kloudova 2011), but several cities also have their own definition and classification of local cultural or creative industries.[5] Moreover, 89.47 percent of the public funding source supporting CCI comes from local finance rather than the central government (Liu et al. 2014: 59), and local governments exclusively decide on the use of local public funding. Finally, different Chinese cities have failed to exert the same extent of censorship on cultural production. Zhao (2008) points out that 'the party-state's post-1989 disciplinary power has become much more dispersed, localized and internalized by each level of the propaganda hierarchy' (33).

Regional inequality is another important characteristic for the Chinese context. Since the 1980s, cities in the southern coastal area have been encouraged by the central government to develop a market economy and invite foreign investment (Fan 1997). Huang et al. (2003), however, argue that 'the central government's promises of opening up in all directions and favoring the development of interior regions, by and large, fell on deaf ears throughout most of the 1990s' (274). With regional development priorities, cities along the southern coast are more open and have greater financial revenue as well as economic strength than the cities of the northern inland. Fan (1997) debates that 'Deng's uneven development policy has led to a widening development gap between the coastal areas and the interior' (620). Peng (2000) adds that parallel to the fully emphasized promotion of private enterprises and market in the south, the remaining shadow of planned economy and government interventions still influenced the north. With regards to the cultural sector, the southern coastal cities consistently developed faster than cities in other areas. In addition, the formation of the Chinese cultural market originated in the south and subsequently spread across the whole country (Keane 2000). National policies provide the general direction for the development of the whole country. However, with local autonomy and a stark contrast between the north and south of China, the specificity of municipal CCI policies from different regions is significant for a full understanding of the development of CCI policies in China.

The use of public funding in three selected cities

The development of CCI is dependent upon support and guidance through cultural policy (Oakley 2004), which is defined as the 'sum of government activities in relation to culture, or what governments choose to do or not to do in relation to culture' (Bell and Oakley 2014: 46). In the selection of case studies for the analysis of Chinese municipal CCI policies and their focus on the use of public funding, two factors were considered: (1) case studies are chosen from both the north and south of China because of their discrepancy in promoting the market economy; (2) the selected cities are either municipalities directly under the central government (including Beijing, Shanghai, Tianjin, and Chongqing) or provincial capital cities. This contributed to an increased availability of policy documents as opposed to other prefecture cities. As a result, Guangzhou, Harbin, and Beijing were selected. Guangzhou as an important southern coastal port and provincial capital in particular has been more advanced in promoting the development of cultural market and cultural system reform than other Chinese cities (Zhang 2012). The northernmost inland provincial capital city, Harbin, has fallen behind national CCI policies and the gap is constantly widening. Beijing was selected as it is the nation's capital. For each city, the study triangulated relevant CCI policy documents[6] and interviews with policy makers[7] to provide a multi-dimensional analysis of CCI policies at the municipal level.

The analysis of this chapter covers the period from 2006 to 2013. It focuses on the use of public cultural funding on CCI promotion in each city and aims to explore the extent of differences in the cities' cultural policies in terms of their accommodation of commercialism and encouragement of the use of non-public financial sources for cultural organizations and activities that were previously publicly funded. The results will feed into the analysis of neoliberal tendencies in local cultural policies.

Beijing

The municipal government of Beijing has displayed an increasingly commercially and digitally oriented trend in supporting local CCI since 2006. It is an important precondition that no content or products oppose the Party or the government, have negative attitudes towards national heroes, or distort history and guide citizens to harm society. They need to pass government censorship before circulating in the market (Beijing Development and Reform Commission 2006). When Beijing municipal government began to establish CCI policies in 2006, the *Policies for the Promotion of Beijing's Cultural and Creative Industries* stressed the use of public funding in two directions: (1) infrastructure[8] for cultural and creative clusters, and (2) support for products or projects that pass government censorship, have proprietary intellectual property rights, and have reached at least 20 percent of their completion. Enterprises applying for the fund need to have run for more than two years[9] (Beijing Municipal Financial Bureau 2007; Interviewee 4 2014). Moreover, the CCI policy further required potential applicants to demonstrate that their projects or products can generate economic benefits as well as contribute to retail and export (Beijing Municipal Bureau of Finance 2009; Beijing Municipal Bureau of Finance 2012). The municipal government focused particularly on supporting burgeoning industries (including digital television, mobile multimedia, internet and software development) and key software creative clusters (for example, the Zhong Guancun software independent innovation zone) in order to expand the market demand for high-tech products and facilitate economic growth (ibid.).

As policy makers never established an evaluation system to judge the cultural value of cultural products, measurable commercial outcomes have increasingly become the dominant factor when supporting culture. Policy maker 6 from the Development and Reform Commission explained the rationale behind the use of funding:

> We always think about whether we need to question the municipal government's use of public funding for cultural industries because … it will disturb the market order. There are already 50,000 cultural enterprises in Beijing …Which one should get the money…?
> *(Interviewee 6 2014)*

The development of Beijing municipal cultural policies shows that the use of public funding for CCI is increasingly governed by monetary valuation, which exemplifies the argument of Keane and Zhang (2008) that CCI became an economic driver, and cultural policy is increasingly used as an economic policy. Admittedly, the aesthetic quality of culture is unquantifiable (Gray 2009; O'Brien 2014). However, the foundation of cultural policy is to promote culture independently of commercial profit (Mulcahy 2006), and cultural policy makers are responsible for the support of non-profitable cultural products of high aesthetic quality. The development of Beijing municipal policies, however, shows that policy makers neglected the evaluation of the aesthetic quality of cultural products in favor of a commercially oriented use of government funding, which marginalizes the unquantifiable nature of culture.

In addition, since 2006, the municipal government has aimed to decrease financial support for previously publicly funded cultural enterprises and improve their efficiency in attracting private capital. Particularly, in 2009, the government began to use 100 million yuan (USD 15.24 million) from public funding as a Leading Fund (yindao zijin) to leverage non-public capital to support cultural enterprises (Creative Industry Leading Group 2009). The Leading Fund purchased shares of venture capital companies, which required them to invest at least twice the contribution of the Leading Fund. After a determined period the municipal government withdrew from the Leading Fund. As a result, the funding recipients have since been invested in solely by the venture capital companies (ibid.). The Leading Fund has gradually expanded its remit to various kinds of cultural and creative investment foundations, loan and bonding companies that are established by private capital. In 2012 alone, the municipal government successfully used 900 million yuan (USD 137.16 million) of public funding to leverage a 20,000 million yuan (USD 3,048 million) investment to support 338 projects in CCI (Interviewee 3 2014). Policy maker 3 explained the trend of using local public funding: 'Since the use of the Leading Fund in 2009, we have aimed to transfer the direct subsidy on culture to a more marketization way' (Interviewee 3 2014).

The city's CCI policies also stressed that '(the municipal government) will require both the government and the market to provide public cultural products and services' (General Office of the People's Government in Beijing 2011). Between 2006 and 2013, the development of policies shows that the role of the municipal government gradually changed from simply being a sponsor for cultural enterprises to a facilitator linking culture and market. However, the Beijing municipal government has not encouraged the entry of non-public capital in all cultural enterprises. Current political news websites and newspapers are still maintained under government control. As the political center, Beijing also exerted more control on the entry of non-public capital than national regulations. The latter limited the investment of foreign capital to television and movie productions in the form of joint capital, with the state holding more than 51 percent of the shares (National Ministry of Culture 2009). Meanwhile Beijing municipal policies added that private and foreign capital is only allowed to enter the broadcasting and television advertising companies accounting for less than 49 percent of the shares (Beijing Development and Reform Commission 2006). During the selected period, municipal policy makers in Beijing simultaneously promoted economic growth and authoritarian control, following the argument of Tong and Hung (2012: 273) that 'what we see here is the concurrent operation of the cultural market and the state'. Ren and Sun (2012) highlight that the municipal government is involved in the conflicting roles of maintaining state control and promoting the marketization of culture at the same time. Beijing municipal policy makers are thus not only adopting a neoliberal but also an authoritarian approach to culture.

Harbin

As one of the important industrial bases of China, Harbin focused primarily on heavy manufacturing, raw material, and mineral industries but downplayed the development of a cultural market prior to 2005[10] (Guan and Li 2007). Since 2005, Harbin started to pay increasing attention to local cultural development. In addition, the city was among the first to follow a planned economy, but the last to shift to a market economy[11] (ibid.). The pre-existing ideas of planned economy, which focused on supporting public cultural institutions rather than market competition, thus had greater influence on Harbin (Liu 2010). Authoritarian control is of additional importance. Unlike Beijing, Harbin municipal policies have not provided extra guidance (other than national policies) for an increased creation of cultural products around patriotic and rural themes as well as those for young people (General Office of the People's Government in Beijing 2011). Policy maker 6 from the Cultural Press and Publication Bureau stated that the municipal government also aimed to provide more guidance for cultural production than national regulations. However, 'we do not have enough funding to support good creations, and cultural producers have to think about the commercial profit first in order to survive' (Interviewee 16 2014). Given the influential factors above, Harbin municipal policy makers started later and moved more slowly to promote the commercialization of culture (which has passed municipal government censorship).

Between 2006 and 2008, the municipal government used public funding in three main directions: (1) products that embody Harbin's characteristics and are competitive in the cultural market; (2) covering the expenditure of public-owned cultural institutions (including art performance troupes, newspapers as well as broadcasting and television), upgrading equipment of printing and publishing enterprises, and the maintenance of cinemas; (3) subsidies for scientific and educational films, children's films, and academic works that are advocated by the municipal government and the Party (Harbin Municipal People's Government's 2007). The commercial profit of cultural products was not the prime focus, and Interviewee 15 further explained that: 'Our city has funding for commercial cultural enterprises ... It depends because we do not have an evaluation system to help us to decide which enterprise should get the funding that time' (Interviewee 15 2014).

Between 2008 and 2010, in response to the national policy *Opinions about Promoting the Development of Animation Industries (State Council No. 20)*,[12] which emphasized the importance of financial and institutional support for the development of animation and software industries (State Council 2006), Harbin municipal government added public funding to promote these. However, influenced by the remainder of planned economy, municipal policy makers did not specifically consider the commercial return that public funding can bring. The municipal government required zero registered assets, a subsidy for electricity fees, and purchased cloud computing software and a three-dimensional printer worth several million yuan for the small and medium enterprises (SMEs) in the cluster.[13] A policy maker from the Institute of Technology and Information Commission stated that 'during that time they [the animation industries] were not afraid of losing money, and the municipal government was supporting them' (Interviewee 14 2014).

Between 2006 and 2010, Harbin's cultural consumption increased in the areas of computer software, television and broadcasting programs, animation products, and tourism, and in 2010, the per capita GDP reached USD 5,583 (Harbin Municipal People's Government General Office 2011). Policy maker 20 from the Publicity Department explained that consumption within the entire society upgraded from the basic living level to the cultural level (Interviewee 20 2014). Under these circumstances, the Harbin municipal government has, since 2011, sought to strengthen local cultural industries and increase the commercial output of cultural industries by 25 percent annually (Harbin Municipal People's Government General Office 2011). Correspondingly, the municipal government and policy makers began to explicitly underscore commercial profit and the high economic benefit of burgeoning industries. The *Policy about the Implementation of Support for the Development of Non-public Owned Cultural Enterprises* stated that 'the proportion of the public funding will be increased on promising projects or products that are produced by non-public cultural enterprises' (ibid.). Though policies did not provide an evaluation system to judge which culture was more promising, policy makers explicitly highlighted the commercial-related factors: 'The projects' and enterprises' contribution to increase tax revenue and raise financial revenue will also be considered' (Interviewee 20 2014).

In 2013, policy makers continued to stress commerciality and profitability. More public funding was added in the form of a Leading Fund (yindao zijin) (Harbin Municipal Financial Bureau 2013), which focused on enterprises of both cultural and technological elements and a broader market (Interviewee 20 2014). Policy makers were digitally oriented and the funded enterprises originated mainly from burgeoning industries including the production of animation videos, software development, cloud computing, and new media (Interviewee 12 2014).

Furthermore, Harbin municipal government only slowly promoted the privatization of culture. Specifically, between 2006 and 2010, municipal policies encouraged private and foreign capital to support culture without publishing specific strategies to embrace non-public capital. On the other hand, the policies sought to ensure 'the obvious advantage of state cultural capital' (Harbin Municipal People's Government's 2007). Policy makers emphasized public funding over the importance of market investment in supporting culture, however, Policy maker 17 from the local Financial Bureau stated that 'the amount of funding is too small to drive the development of cultural enterprises. It is the biggest bottleneck for developing cultural industries in our city' (Interviewee 17 2014).

In 2011, given the increase of cultural consumption, municipal policy makers aimed to equally increase the commercial output of cultural industries. Correspondingly, the municipal government no longer emphasized the advantage of state capital and began to promote the role of the market instead. The *Policy about the Outline of Harbin's Cultural Development Plan* stated that the municipal government would 'follow the market economy regulations and give full play to the basic role of market forces in allocating resources' (Harbin Municipal People's Government's General Office 2011). The municipal government announced a lowering of barriers and simplification of the process for the entry of non-public capital (ibid.). In addition, public funding was no longer simply used to subsidize cultural enterprises but to leverage market investment. In 2013 alone, the municipal government successfully used 40 million yuan (USD 6.12 million) as a pledge for 40 cultural enterprises to receive market investment, amounting to 164.75 million yuan (USD 24.62 million) (Yin 2014). Harbin implemented measures to facilitate the entry of non-public capital later, albeit slower than Beijing and Guangzhou, and the domination of institutional culture has also been gradually weakened. Until 2012, the industrial value of non-public cultural enterprises added up to

70.87 percent of both public and non-public cultural enterprises (Wang 2012). The number of public enterprises simultaneously decreased from 3,897 in 2007 to 900 in 2012 (Statistics Bureau 2014). The quantity and benefit of non-public cultural enterprises have surpassed that of public ones. Policy makers increasingly decreased the power of public-owned culture and mobilized greater non-public capital to support culture. However, it is characteristic for Harbin that the municipal government did not decrease the amount of public funding in promoting the privatization of culture. All three selected cities have encouraged the entry of non-public capital to support culture; however, Figure 6.1 demonstrates that not all of them have decreased public funding.

Hesmondhalgh et al. (2015) argue that: 'It is certainly true that the practices of neo-liberalisation (as opposed to the theory of neo-liberalism) extend far beyond questions of public expenditure'. However, with more non-public capital entering the cultural field, the government should be able to save more costs. Connell et al. (2009) note: 'The expansion of market relations allows, in theory, a lower level of public spending' (333). In Harbin, however, the municipal policies aimed to increase public funding instead of decreasing it. The *Outline of Harbin's Cultural Development Plan (Harbin No. 7)* explained that 'on the basis of the 40 million yuan (USD 6.096 million) Special Fund for Promoting Cultural Development (xuanchuan wenhua fazhan zhuanxiang zijin), (the municipal government) aims to increase the amount alongside the increase of financial revenue' (Harbin Municipal People's Government's General Office 2011).

The majority of public funding has been used as Leading Fund. Moreover, funds supporting cultural enterprises transformed from previously public-funded cultural institutions have not been decreased (Interviewee 15 2014). In addition, funding for performing art troupes remains stable, because these are still required for charity shows for communities, universities, and welfare institutions (Harbin Municipal People's Government's General Office 2011). Interviewee 15 (2014) states that 'the municipal government will continue to support these troupes through fiscal subsidies. The amount of subsidy will not decrease, and the strategies will not change'. Beijing and Guangzhou have not specifically emphasized this point. Besides this, Harbin municipal policies also highlighted welfare support for private cultural businesses: 'The municipal government will not collect business, urban construction and additional education tax for individual households who carry out cultural business

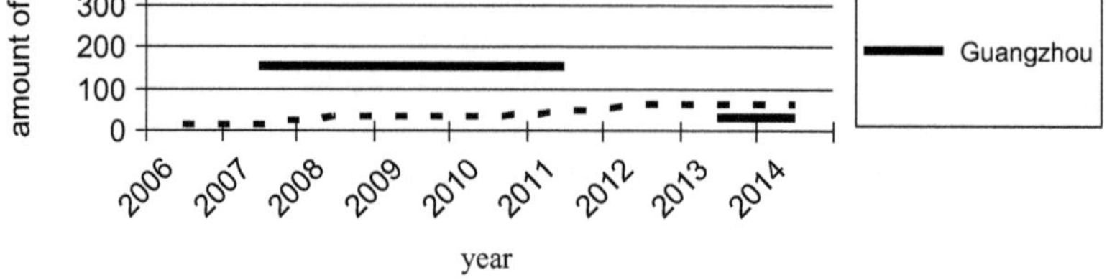

Figure 6.1 The amount of government funding between 2006 and 2013[14] (Source: Data was obtained from relevant municipal policies between 2006 and 2013)

with revenue less than 5000 yuan (USD 762) per month in urban areas' (Harbin Municipal People's Government's General Office 2011).

Guangzhou

As the city of the southern coast that moved first in promoting market economy, Guangzhou is more commercially and digitally oriented in the use of public funding than the other two cities and continues to embrace non-public capital to support culture. Between 2007 and 2011, municipal policies focused particularly on the funding of animation and software industries to improve Guangzhou's competitiveness and to create further wealth (Guangzhou Municipal People's Government 2006). According to the *Policies about Supporting the Development of Software and Animation Industries*, the allocation of public funding hinged on the amount of investment and commercial outcomes of animation enterprises. This implies that only those enterprises that invested more than ten million yuan (USD 1.53 million) for over five years are entitled to 5 percent of their total investment in funding, and the maximum amount of funding for each enterprise cannot exceed 3 million yuan (USD 0.46 million). The policy maker from the Publicity Department explained further preconditions for funding: 'We need to consider the continuity of the project and whether we can see the result of the investment in a short time' (Interviewee 28 2014).

In 2013, the municipal government placed further emphasis on the use of public funding for the integration of culture and technology in the emerging development zone LuoGang (Cultural Bureau of Guangzhou Emerging Development Zone 2013). One policy maker from the Cultural, Broadcasting and Television, Press and Publication Bureau stated that the municipal government is still in the process of developing a concrete plan on how to use the funding. Two elements, however, have already emerged: (1) cultural products that contain high technology like animation and software, and (2) those rendering increased commercial returns (Interviewee 23 2014). The policy maker explicitly emphasized that 'the profit should be the aim and should be considered when investing in cultural industries … All strategies should be useful in helping to drive the development of the cultural industries and make more money' (Interviewee 23 2014).

Commercial profit has been the key element of Guangzhou municipal policies in allocating public funding, and culture has been treated as an economic resource, which is invested in in order to gain greater commercial profit (Yu'dice 2003). Although Guangzhou's cultural production is also under authoritarian control by the municipal government, their regulations are less strict than national regulations on cultural production. As stated by Policy maker 25, Macao Asia satellite television, CETV, and Star TV, all of which are not broadcasted in Beijing and the inland, could be directly watched by Guangzhou's audiences (Interviewee 25 2014).

Compared to Harbin, Guangzhou has chosen a different approach towards funding CCI, focusing on an efficiency of public funding by decreasing public funding with the aim of promoting the privatization of culture. Although Guangzhou continues to rank among the first three Chinese cities with regards to its financial revenue (Zhang 2011), it has not provided more public funding for culture than other cities. One policy maker from the Financial Bureau even stated that Guangzhou's spending on culture occupied just 1 percent of the entire government expenditure, which is the minimum amount required by the state (Interviewee 27 2014). A policy maker from the Cultural, Broadcasting and Television, Press and Publication Bureau explained that 'the funding will break the balance of the market, and cause unequal competitions between cultural enterprises … Guangzhou actually aims to leave the market more free space to develop' (Interviewee 25 2014). Policy maker 28 from the local Publicity Department continued: 'The issues related to the market should be decided by the market itself' (Interviewee 28 2014).

On this basis, the municipal government aimed to bring more non-public investment into the cultural market as highlighted by a policy maker from the Publicity Department: 'We aim to establish a marketization, diversification and open industrial mechanism … if the state has not clearly rejected the entry of certain capital in a certain field, we all welcome [them to come into the cultural field]' (Interviewee 26 2014).

Since 2003, Guangzhou CCI policies have emphasized the gradual decrease of state capital by the municipal government and their aim to bring in further private capital to support cultural enterprises (Guangzhou Municipal People's Government 2003). The policy maker continued that cultural enterprises in Guangzhou could obtain investment from various resources including private foundations[15] rather than simply public funding (Interviewee 27 2014). These foundations attract much non-public capital and have various investment directions. The Guangzhou Cultural Art Development Foundation supports the development of cultural and art institutions; the Guangzhou Overseas Chinese Cultural Development Foundation promotes primarily traditional Chinese culture among the Chinese expatriate communities and the Revitalization of the Cantonese Opera Foundation raised 1 to 3 million yuan (USD 0.15–0.46 million) annually for supporting the creation of Cantonese Opera (Interviewee 27 2014). The municipal government continues to push further previously publicly funded culture to the market, and embrace greater private capital to support it. The trend follows Hesmondhalgh's (2007) argument that 'strong traditions of public ownership and regulation … were … severely limited during the neoliberal turn' (135).

As Guangzhou moved faster than other cities in promoting the market economy, it exerted less control and censorship on cultural production than national regulations, and placed greater emphasis on the commercialization and marketization of culture. Still, Guangzhou municipal policies are also characterized as a hybrid of neoliberalism and authoritarianism.

Discussion and conclusion

O'Connor and Oakley (2015) argue that culture is an economy that is different from other industries because it contains intrinsic benefits that should not be ignored or marginalized. These benefits include individual and collective meaning making, autonomous expression, citizenship, and aesthetic pleasure. O'Connor (2016) continues that

> the various practices of arts and culture give texture and shape to our collective and individual lives, and how we relate to the world around us. We cannot allow these to be overruled by abstract machine of market efficiency and return of investment.
>
> *(O'Connor 2016: 31)*

The chapter criticizes the excessive commercialization of culture in the selected cities. If they continue to follow the current trend of developing local culture, they might face the danger of eroding the distinctiveness of culture. CCI policies, however, do not necessarily have to retreat to the pure art form, as cultural and economic value are both indispensable for these industries (Banks 2015). The challenges for the selected cities, however, are to seek the balance of cultural and economy priorities within the cultural and creative industries, not leaving cultural production governed solely by commercial considerations.

The present study of the use of public funding for culture in three Chinese cities demonstrated that municipal policy makers from different regions have discrepant thoughts and approaches when promoting local CCI. Despite these discrepancies, their municipal policies are all increasingly influenced by neoliberalism but remain tied to authoritarianism to different extents. Harvey's (2005) understanding of 'neoliberalism with Chinese characteristics' implies that policy makers increasingly adopt neoliberal elements under authoritarian control. However, his analysis simply follows the Western model and studies neoliberalism in China as a monolithic entity. This approach cannot reflect that the unevenness of the trend of cultural neoliberalization and its interaction with authoritarian governance across different regions. My research thus concludes that Chinese CCI policies cannot be simply described with ready-made terms such as 'neoliberalism' or even 'neoliberalism with Chinese characteristics'. On the contrary, Chinese municipal CCI policies are generally characterized as a hybrid of neoliberalism and authoritarianism, influenced by the pre-existing idea of planned economy and the consideration of welfare provision to different extents, and are inflected by local history and circumstances. Specifically, influenced by its previous focus on manufacturing industries and the remaining vestige of planned economy, the northern inland city of Harbin moved more slowly than the southern coastal cities in promoting marketization and commercialization of culture and paid greater attention to the welfare support of culture. Beijing as the seat of the central government focused more on authoritarian control. Guangzhou, the southern coastal port city, has more opportunities to communicate with the capitalist places of Hong Kong and Macao, and is thus more heavily influenced by the capitalist system and more market-oriented in promoting the commercialization of culture.

Chin (2011) argues that 'policy making is not a static but an ongoing and continuous process' (194). Policies keep being updated at different times. Thus, it is impossible to cover all periods within this policy study. However, influenced by the authoritarian context and local autonomy as well as regional inequality, Chinese creative industries policies are no simple duplication of British creative industries policies. As argued by Jana Modronova (2012), 'the only apparent characteristics of the China model that authors seem to agree on, is its propensity for continuous experimentation and learning, expressed in the Chinese saying "crossing the river by touching the stones"' (1).

Appendix

Table 6.1 Summary of the amount of government funding of the three case studies between 2006 and 2013

	Amount of funding for culture in each city (million yuan)		
Year	*Harbin*	*Beijing*	*Guangzhou*
2006	10	667	
2007	10	667	150
2008	27	667	150
2009	27	500	150
2010	27	500	150
2011	40	500	150
2012	60	900	
2013	60	900	30
2014	60	900	30

Notes

1 'Creative industries', 'cultural industries' and 'cultural and creative industries' have been used unsystematically in different cities. Beijing municipal policies used both 'cultural and creative industries' and 'cultural industries', Harbin and Guangzhou municipal policies referred to 'cultural industries'. This paper uses the term 'cultural and creative industries' for the analyses of all the three cities.

2 Local autonomy is defined as 'a mechanism or device to allow local people, ethnic or other groups claiming a distinct identity to exercise direct control at their own will over affairs of special concern to them' (Ghai 2000: 8). Wei (2009) demonstrates that Chinese local autonomies are divided into four types, including ordinary local governments such as the three cities selected for this research, governments of special economic zones, self-governments of ethnic autonomous areas, and governments of special administrative regions (for example, Hong Kong). However, the promotion of local autonomy does not imply less authority exercised by the central government, and 'by and large, the PRC is still a very centralized unitary state' (ibid., 586). Wei (2009) further summarizes that the local government's responsibilities mainly cover 'the examination and approval of projects and issuing of licenses to newly established firms; delivery of goods and materials; resource allocation; investment with self-financing; use of foreign investment; delegation of control of State-owned Enterprises; autonomy to set prices of commodity; and profit sharing with central government' (585).

3 The seven forbidden categories include content 'harmful to national unity, sovereignty, and territorial integrity, harmful to national security, honor and interest, inciting national division and damaging national unity, disclosing state secrets, slandering and libel, promotion of obscenity, superstition, and violence, and other content prohibited by laws and administrative orders' (Zhao 2008: 66).

4 'Cultural industries' were defined as 'business industries that produce cultural products and provide cultural services' (National Ministry of Culture 2003). The sectors include 'performance, film, recording and video industry, cultural entertainment industries, cultural tourism, internet, books, newspaper and journals, cultural relics and works of art and artistic education' (ibid.).

5 Beijing and Guangzhou have their own definition and classification of CCI.

6 Bell and Oakley (2014) summarize two categories of cultural policies: the 'regulations of culture', including policies of 'censorship, protection (from market forces), ownership (for example, of the press)' (47), and the 'support or promotion of culture' including 'patronage, state funding for culture' (ibid.). The two categories are intertwined. For this research, I selected policy documents from 2006 to 2013 which attend to policies of the two categories.

7 This research is partially based on interviews with policy makers who are engaged in making CCI policies in the three selected cities. Cultural and creative industries are related to many aspects in the society and CCI policies are never made by one department in the municipal government. Generally, the local Publicity Department plays the main role in the policy making process. They organize officials from the Financial, and the Cultural Bureau, the Institute of Technology and the Information, as well as Development and Reform Commission to form a temporary policy making group. This group is responsible for establishing CCI policies based on previous investigation and discussion. The interviewees are members of the policy making groups in the selected cities. In order to protect the interviewees, the policy makers' names are not revealed, instead, they are numbered according to the order they accepted interviews (Beijing: Interviewees 1–10; Harbin: Interviewees 11–21; Guangzhou: Interviewees 22–30).

8 Including electricity, utilities, water, heating, communication, and the construction of primary roads (Beijing Municipal Financial Bureau 2007).

9 For example, the drama 'The Clown Emily (xiaochou aimeili)', produced by the private-owned media company Happy Twist, was granted 2 million yuan (USD 3.048 million) of special funds because (1) its content had passed government censorship, (2) there was no dispute concerning its intellectual property, and (3) the company had a steady business income for more than two years. In addition, the drama has been performed more than hundred times and earned 12 million yuan (USD 1.8288 million) commercial profit (Li 2009).

10 Between 1958 and 1977, the cities in north-eastern China played important roles in contributing to the economic development of the whole country (Guan and Li 2007). However, since 1978, China began to transform its industrial structure and placed more emphasis on the information industries. As a result, the north-eastern cities began to lose their advantages and gradually fell behind the southern coastal cities. In 2004, the central government put forward 'zhenxing dongbei' (revitalise

north-eastern China), which encouraged Harbin and other important north-eastern cities to transform their industrial structure (Peng 2000).

11 The northern inland cities have more natural resources (coal, wood, and petroleum) than the coastal cities of the south. Therefore, the central government identified the former as the national industrial base establishing a planned economy system in these cities in 1953. The southern coastal cities gradually followed (Guan and Li 2007). Here, the central government first promoted market economy in 1978 in order to lower the risk of damaging the development of an industrial base in the north (ibid.).

12 Since the 1990s, the development of animation industries in China has increasingly fallen far behind the growing market demand (State Council 2006). In 2004, the total output of cartoons in China added up to 29,000 minutes while the market demanded 268,000 minutes (Xue 2010: 245). Sixty percent of the Chinese animation market are Japanese cartoons (Gu 2005). As animation products have a profound influence on young people, in 2006 the central state issued the *Opinions about Promoting the Development of Animation Industries (State Council No. 20)* in order to improve the competitiveness of Chinese animation industries and cultural security.

13 Generally, if entrepreneurs want to found and register a company, they are required to prove to the local Industrial and Commerce Bureau that they have already owned assets of at least 30,000 yuan (USD 4.572,000). As part of the cluster, however, entrepreneurs are not bound to these requirements (Interviewee 6, 2014). Moreover, the municipal government also subsidized the electronic fees of enterprises in the cluster. Thus, they only need to pay less than 10 yuan per hour instead of the usual several hundred yuan per hour (ibid.).

14 The private foundations in this paper refer to legal entities that have been established by individuals for objectives such as philanthropy.

15 Data was obtained from relevant municipal policies between 2006 and 2013.

References

Arrighi, G. (2007) *Adam Smith in Beijing: Lineages of the twenty-first century*. London: Verso.

Banks, M. (2015) Valuing cultural industries. In: O'Connor, J. and Oakley, K. (eds.), *The Routledge Companion to the Cultural Industries*. London: Routledge, pp. 35–45.

Beijing Development and Reform Commission (2006) *Beijing shi wenhua chaungyi chanye touzi zhidao mulu (Investment guidance category of Beijing cultural and creative industries)*. Beijing: Development and Reform Commission.

Beijing Municipal Financial Bureau (2007) *Wenhua chuangxin fazhan zhuangxiang zijin guanli shiyong banfa (The administrative measures about the special fund on the development of cultural and creative industries)*. Available from: http://zhengwu.beijing.gov.cn/gzdt/gggs/t1242470.htm [accessed March 24, 2014].

Beijing Municipal Bureau of Finance (2009) *Guanyu jinorng cujin shoudu wenhua chuangyi chanye fazhan de yijian (Policies about how to promote the development of cultural and creative industries in capital city through finance)* (No. 144). Beijing: General Office of the Beijing Municipal People's Government.

Beijing Municipal Bureau of Finance (2012) *Beijing shi wenhua chuangxin fazhan zhuanxiang zijin guanli banfa (The administrative measures of the special fund on the development of Beijing's cultural innovation)*. Beijing: Beijing Municipal Bureau of Finance.

Chin, Y. C. (2011) Policy process, policy learning, and the role of the provincial media in China. *Media, Culture & Society*, 33(2): 193–210.

Connell, R., Fawcett, B., and Meagher, G. (2009) Neoliberalism, new public management and the human service professions. *Journal of Sociology*, 45(4): 331–8.

Creative Industry Leading Group (2009) *Beijing shi wenhua chuangyi chanye chuangye touzi jijin guanli banfa (Measures for managing the venture capital leading funds in Beijing cultural and creative industries)* (No. 7). Beijing: Creative Industry Leading Group.

Cultural Bureau of Guangzhou Emerging Development Zone (2013) Zhuanxiang zijin shiyong jihua *(Policies about the use of special fund)*. Guangzhou: LuoGang Cultural Bureau.

Fan, C. (1997) *Uneven Development and Beyond: Regional Development Theory in Post-Mao China*. Oxford: Blackwell Publishers.

Flew, T. (2012) *The Creative Industries: Culture and Policy*. London: Sage.

Flew, T. and Cunningham, S. (2010) Creative industries after the first decade. *The Information Society: An International Journal*, 26(2): 113–23.

General Office of the People's Government in Beijing (2011) *Beijing shi shierwu shiqi renwen Beijing fazhan jianshe guihua (Plan for the development and construction of humanities Beijing in the 12th five year period.*Beijing: General Office of the People's Government.

Ghai, Y. (ed.) (2000) *Autonomy and Ethnicity, Negotiating Competing Claims in Multi-Ethnic States*. Cambridge: Cambridge University Press.

Gray, C. (2009) Managing cultural policy: pitfalls and prospects. *Public Administration*, 87(3): 574–85.

Gu, L. M. (2005) Riben katong zhanling quanqiu dongman bantu de 60% (Japanese cartoon occupied 60% of the world's cartoon market). Available from: http://finance.sina.com.cn/roll/20050726/0206228645.shtml [accessed July 13, 2018].

Guan, J. and Li, Q. J. (2007) Dongbei lao gongye jidi de wenhua zhuanxing yu fazhan (Cultural transfer and develop northeast old industrial base). *The Border Economy and Culture*, 43: 5–8.

Guangzhou Municipal People's Government (2003) *Guanyu Guangzhou shi jiakuai wenhua shiye fazhan ruogan zhengce de yijian (Suggestions about the policies on quickening the development of Guangzhou cultural institutions)* (No. 12). Guangzhou: Municipal People's Government.

Guangzhou Municipal People's Government (2006) *Guangzho guanyu fuchi dongman chanye fazhan de yijian (The policies about supporting the development of software and animation industries)* (No. 44). Guangzhou: Municipal People's Government

Harbin Municipal Financial Bureau (2013) *Haerbin shi wenhua chanye yindao zijin butie zijin shishi xize (Measures for using the cultural industries leading funds in Harbin).* Harbin: Municipal Financial Bureau.

Harbin Municipal People's Government (2007) *Guanyu wenhua tizhi gaige he wenhua chanye de ruogan zhengce (Some policies about supporting the development of cultural industries and cultural reform system).* Harbin: General Office of the Harbin Municipal People's Government.

Harbin Municipal People's Government's General Office (2011) *Guanyu fuchi fei gongyouzhi wenhua qiye fazhan de shishi yijian (The policies about implementation of supporting the development of non-public owned cultural enterprises)* (No. 8). Harbin: General Office of the Harbin Municipal People's Government.

Harvey, D. (2005) *A Brief History of Neoliberalism*. Oxford: Oxford University Press.

Hesmondhalgh, D. (2007) *The Cultural Industries*, 2nd edition. London: Sage.

Hesmondhalgh, D., Nisbett, M., Oakley, K., and Lee, D. (2015) *Culture, Economy and Politics: The Case of New Labour.* New York: Palgrave Macmillan.

Huang, J., Kuo, C. and Kao, A. (2003) The inequality of regional economic development in China between 1991 and 2001. *Journal of Chinese Economic and Business Studies*, 1(3): 273–85.

Keane, M. (2000) Cultural policy in China: Emerging research agendas. *International Journal of Cultural Policy*, 6(2): 243–58.

Keane, M. (2013) *Creative Industries in China: Art, Design and Media*. Cambridge: Polity Press.

Keane, M. and Zhang, W. H. (2008) Cultural creative industries or creative (cultural) industries? In Hu, H.L. (ed.), *China's Cultural Industries Forum*. Shanghai People's Publishing.

Keane, M. and Zhao, E. J. (2014) The reform of the cultural system: Culture, creativity and innovation in China. In Lee, H. and Lim, L. (eds.), *Cultural Policies in East Asia: Dynamics between the State Arts and Creative Industries.* Hampshire, UK: Palgrave Macmillan, pp. 155–73.

Li, L. Q. (2009) *Zhongguo wenhua chanye fazhan de caizheng yu jinrong zhengce yanjiu (Study of the financial policy for Chinese cultural industries).* Beijing: Chinese Financing Press.

Liu, W. (2010) Several problems of the policies concerning Harbin's cultural development. *The Journal of Harbin Committee School of the CCP*, 6 (72): 89–91.

Liu, D. L., Lin, L., Wen, Z. K., Ding, W. C., and Zeng, J. (2014) The present situation and development trend of China's cultural industry investment. In Zhang, X. M., Wang, J. X. and Zhang, J. G. (eds.), *Blue Book of China's Culture*. Beijing: Social Science Academic Press, pp. 41–65.

Modronova, J. (2012) *Rethinking Neoliberal Processes in the Case of China*. Available from: https://thesis.eur.nl/pub/13208/Jana%20Mudronova_RP%20final%20full%20 draft _1507.pdf [accessed April 24, 2016].

Mulcahy, K. (2006) Cultural policy: Definitions and theoretical approaches. *The Journal of Arts Management, Law, and Society*, 35(4): 319–30.

National Ministry of Culture (2003) Guanyu zhichi he cujin wenhua chanye fazhan de ruogan yijian (Views on supporting and promoting cultural industries). Available from: http://www.chinaculture.org*/gb/cn_law/2004–06/28/content_49710.htm [accessed May 30, 2011].*

National Ministry of Culture (2009) *Wenhua chanye touzi zhidao (Investment guidance of the cultural industries).* Available from: http://www.bjci.gov.cn/287/2009/09/18/14117039.htm [accessed June 7, 2014]

Nonini, D. (2008) Is China becoming neoliberal? *Critique of Anthropology*, 28(2): 145–76.
Oakley, K. (2004) Not so cool Britannia: The role of the creative industries in economic development. *International Journal of Cultural Studies*, 7(1): 67–77.
O'Brien, D. (2014) *Cultural Policy: Management, Value and Modernity in the Creative Industries*. New York: Routledge.
O'Connor, J. (2016) After the creative industries: Why we need a cultural economy. *Platform Papers*, 47: 1–60.
O'Connor, J. and Gu, X. (2012) Shanghai: images of modernity. In Ansheier, H. and Isar, Y.R. (eds.), *Cities, Cultural Policy and Governance*. London: Sage, pp. 288–300.
O'Connor, J. and Oakley, K. (eds.) (2015) *The Routledge Companion to the Cultural Industries*. London: Routledge.
Ong, A. H. (2006) *Neoliberalism as Exception: Mutations in Citizenship and Sovereignty*. US Durham, NC: Duke University Press.
Peng, C. F. (2000) Which aspect on earth makes northern people inferior to southern people – the analyses of the notion difference between southern people and northern people. *Review of the Market Economy*, 5: 4–7.
Ren, X. F. and Sun, M. (2012) Artistic urbanization: Creative industries and creative control in Beijing. *International Journal of Urban and Regional Research*, 36(3): 504–21.
State Council (2001) *Wenhua chanye fazhan shiwu guihua (The tenth five-year plan of cultural industries development)*. Beijing: State Council.
State Council (2006) *Guanyu woguo dongman chanye fazhan de ruogan yijian (Opinions about promoting development of animation industries)* (No. 32). Available from: http://www.cnki.com.cn/Article/CJFDTotal-JLZB200611005.htm [accessed January 26, 2015].
Statistic Bureau (2014) *Analyses of development of Harbin cultural industries*. Available from: http://www.hlj.stats.gov.cn/tjfx/dstjfx/201410/t20141023_29483.htm [accessed June 20, 2015].
Tang, W. (2009) *Wenhua tizhi gaige (Cultural system reform)*. Available from: http://news.xinhuanet.com/ziliao/2009-09/30/content_12133893.htm [accessed September 18, 2013].
Tong, Q. S. and Hung, R. Y. Y. (2012) Cultural policy between the state and the market: Regulation, creativity and contraction. *International Journal of Cultural Policy*, 18(3): 265–78.
Wang, J. (2004) The global reach of a new discourse: How far can 'creative industries' travel? *International Journal of Cultural Studies*, 7(1): 9–19.
Wei, D. (2009) Local autonomy in the context of Chinese political modernization. In Oliveira, J.C. and Cardinal, P. (eds.), *One Country, Two Systems, Three Legal Orders – Perspectives of Evolution*. Berlin Heidelberg: Springer-Verlag, pp. 583–90.
White, A. and Xu, S. J. (2012) A critique of China's cultural policy and the development of its cultural and creative industries: the case of Shanghai. *Cultural Trends*, 21(3): 249–57.
Wang, Z. (2012) *Harbin Aims to Establish Venture Capital Fund for Cultural Industries*. Available from: http://www.smehrb.gov.cn/html/zwpd/zxyw/2012/0815/32938.html [accessed June 26, 2015].
Xue, X. D. (2010) The development strategy of the Chinese cartoon industry under the impact of Japanese anime. *International Conference on Network and Finance Development*, 245–48.
Yin, Z. F. (2014) The famous cultural city strategies quicken the development of cultural industries in Harbin. *Harbin Daily*, 6 March. Available from: http://www.citure.net/info/201436/201436140504.shtml [accessed July 3, 2014].
Yu'dice, G. (2003) *The Expediency of Culture: Uses of Culture in the Global Era*. Durham and London: Duke University Press.
Zhang, J. C. (ed.) (2011) *Chinese Creative Industries Report (2011)*. Beijing: China Economic Publishing House.
Zhang, J. C. (ed.) (2012) *Chinese Creative Industries Report (2012)*. Beijing: China Economic Publishing House.
Zhang, J. P. and Kloudova, J. (2011) Factors which influence the growth of creative industries: Cross-section analysis in China. *Creative and Knowledge Society*, 1(1): 5–19.
Zhao, Y. Z. (2008) *Communication in China: Political Economy, Power and Conflict*. Plymouth: Rowman & Littlefield.

7

Probing the cultural turn in Shanghai, Hong Kong, and Taipei

The moments of triumph and despair

Kristina Karvelyte

Introduction

A few decades ago, the arts sector in most countries used to receive far less attention than other areas of the public sector and was generally considered to have 'a minor status within the political system' (Gray 2002: 78). In the Global North, things started to change in the early 1980s, when cultural and artistic practices became increasingly noticed, widely promoted, and subsequently, placed within the center of policy debate, particularly in the context of urban and regional policies. For most urban policy makers, culture and the arts coupled with the broad notion of 'creativity' gained appeal as a potential solution to their problems, promising to fill the gap left by the decline or relocation of traditional manufacturing industries, to boost consumer-oriented economic growth, to push the revitalization of urban spaces, and to enhance the image and economic competitiveness of the city in the global marketplace (Harvey 1989a; Zukin 1991; Grodach and Silver 2013).

A widening use of symbolic and aesthetic practices in urban and regional development policies is commonly referred to as a 'cultural turn' (Zukin 1995; Gibson and Klocker 2005; Pratt 2009). The cultural turn in urban development can be broadly characterized by the widening scope of the instrumentalization of culture, where particular focus rests on those cultural policy strategies that are seen as 'useful' to the city's promotion, regeneration, and economic growth (Evans 2009; Grodach and Silver 2013; Bell and Oakley 2015). Typically, these strategies revolve around the building of new cultural landmarks and cultural/creative districts, the hosting of cultural events, the facilitation of various cultural projects and activities, the development of the cultural and creative industries and, more generally, the making of the so-called 'creative city' (Landry and Bianchini 1995; Florida 2002).

For their allegedly wide-ranging contributions to the city's economy, promotion, and general quality of life, these cultural policy strategies have been increasingly used and praised by urban policy makers across the world, including those in East Asia (see Yeoh 2005; Kong et al. 2006; Kim 2017). This trend prompted the emergence of a new body of research that interrogates the adoption of 'imported' urban cultural policies in East Asian cities (see, for example, J. Wang 2004; Yeoh 2005; Kong et al. 2006; O'Connor and Gu 2006; Hutton 2012; Lee and Lim 2014; Kim 2017; Wang et al. 2015). However, to date there is still an evident lack of comparative, multisite studies on this subject. This chapter marks one of the first attempts to fill this gap. It addresses some general patterns of the cultural turn in Shanghai, Hong Kong, and Taipei as part of probing the influence and implications of 'imported' cultural policy initiatives on the cultural landscape of Chinese cities.

In this context, the term 'Chinese' represents cultural and ethnic ties that are shared among cities situated in the territories of mainland China, Taiwan, and Hong Kong. According to Tu (1991), altogether these territories form a symbolic universe that he refers to as 'Cultural China'. A common ethnicity, language, and similar world-views reduce the possibility of cultural differences potentially affecting the results of this research. Although Taiwan, Hong Kong, and mainland China share strong cultural and economic ties, there are some significant differences in their political systems and historical backgrounds. As a result, all three cities have developed different urban identities and adopted distinct approaches to governance models of cultural policy. It is these notable differences among the three cities that make these three cases 'meaningfully contrasting' (Bryman 2008: 58). As a result, their comparative study provides a better understanding of the varying effects and depths of the cultural turn in Chinese cities.

For this study, data were obtained from document analysis and semi-structured elite interviews carried out between July 2014 and January 2015.[1] A range of policy documents, including city government reports, annual policy addresses, policy guidelines and research papers were selected for the analysis. A total of 32 interviews were conducted with local policy makers, policy advisors, academics, and industry professionals working in the fields of design, film, and performing arts.

The study findings revealed four general patterns that underpin the cultural turn in Taipei, Shanghai, and Hong Kong. These patterns, which are closely interwoven with each other, include: increased economic instrumentalization of culture; rising public spending on culture and the arts; growing involvement of local policy makers in the cultural sector; and the emergence of new cultural policy strategies and 'quick fixes' designed to push the cultural turn of the cities. In this chapter, drawing on selected examples from Hong Kong, Taipei, and Shanghai, I highlight some of the ways in which these patterns have (re)shaped the cultural trajectories of these three cities, bringing both new tensions and new opportunities to local policy makers, artists, and practitioners.

Pattern I: Increasing economic instrumentalization of culture

Culture-led urban development is commonly linked with growing inter-urban competition for investment, a skilled workforce, and other means of capital accumulation. This competition increased due to a number of interconnected trends and developments, including: the emergence of cities as global players in their own right; deindustrialization followed by the rise of service industries; the globalizing capitalist economy; pervasive economic uncertainty; and uneven spatial development (Harvey 1989a; Brenner and Theodore 2002; Pacione 2009; Peck 2011). According to Harvey (1989a), inter-urban competition leads to the proliferation of various short-term 'civic boosterism' practices aimed at producing 'all sorts of lures to bring capital into town' (11). The increasing use of culture and the arts in urban regeneration and economic development policies is an instructive example of 'civic boosterism' in action.

A growing attachment of culture to market-oriented economic growth has been one of the points of concern among critics of the cultural turn (Zukin 1991; McGuigan 2004; Gray 2007). As Zukin (2001) rightly observes, until the 1980s culture was viewed as 'a by-product of wealth', whereas today it is seen predominantly as 'a generator of wealth' (n.p.). In effect, all traditional cultural policy themes and goals, such as artistic excellence, cultural diversity or arts education 'have been remade and reprioritised alongside urban economic revitalisation objectives' (Grodach and Silver 2013: 2). As with cities in the Global North, local policy makers in East Asia now also often use and promote Western formats of urban cultural policies as a means of shifting from industrial to service economies, attracting foreign investment, skilled workers and tourists, and, more generally, as tools for enhancing the comparative advantage of cities (Yeoh 2005; Kong 2007; Lee and Lim 2014; Kim 2017). Although all of these objectives repeatedly surfaced during my analysis of local policy documents in Shanghai, Hong Kong, and Taipei, the central goals attached to the cultural turn – as market-oriented policy strategy – seem to vary from city to city.

In Shanghai, the adoption of the cultural turn is particularly closely linked with inter-urban competition for foreign investment. Since the early 1990s, in light of economic decentralization, Shanghai has sought to attract more foreign capital, and subsequently, to strengthen its position at home and on the global stage. In order to achieve these goals, the Shanghai Municipal People's Government (SMPG) adopted a series of 'civic boosterism' strategies that were 'in line with international practice' (Wu 2000: 1365). These strategies included generous investments in local infrastructure, amenities, and city branding campaigns (Zou 1996; Wu 2000). It was in this context that culture has been first recognized as a means to generate an economic impact and it was also in this context that Shanghai launched what O'Connor and Gu (2006) called 'the most ambitious creative industries programme [in China]' (281). By the end of 2010, there were 15 cultural quarters and 80 creative clusters established in Shanghai (SMPG 2011b). In the Twelfth Five-Year Plan, a series of additional 'creativity fixes' (Peck 2007), including the promotion and development of cultural facilities, creative environments, and events, were introduced as important strategies for making the city more competitive and more attractive for businesses and tourists (SMPG 2011a).

In Taipei's policy discourse, the adoption of 'imported' cultural policies has been commonly described (and justified) as a tool for dealing with deindustrialization and inter-urban competition. In the six-year national development plan *Challenge 2008 (Tiaozhan 2008)* the cultural and creative industries were included among ten key development areas that had to be addressed in order to strengthen the economic competitiveness of Taiwan. In *Challenge 2008* these key development areas were seen as new forms of production models, 'more suited to the "post-Fordist" age' (trans. from Chinese, Executive Yuan 2002: 37).

In the Hong Kong Special Administrative Region (HKSAR), culture – as an economic measure – has been discussed primarily in relation to the city's tourism industry. Tourism accounts for 5 percent of the total GDP and is considered one of the four pillar industries of Hong Kong (CSD 2013). Despite its rapid development in the 1980s, Hong Kong's economy experienced a significant decline in the late 1990s, after the Asian financial crisis hit the city in 1997 (Song et al. 2003). In this context, the cultural sector was seen as a means of economic rejuvenation. The link between tourism and culture was clearly established in the *1998 Policy Address* that referred to the need for a more strategic use of cultural practices for the promotion of Hong Kong as a tourist destination (HKSAR Government 1998, par. 46). Since the 2000s the scope of instrumental roles attached to culture and the arts in Hong Kong has increasingly broadened due to growing territorial competition and capital/labor mobility.

It should be acknowledged, however, that in all three cities economic considerations have never been the *only* driving force behind the cultural turn. While an in-depth discussion of other motives behind the adoption of imported cultural policies is beyond the scope of this chapter, it is worth noting that none of these cities have experienced the same extent of deindustrialization as their counterparts in Europe or North America (see J. H. Wang 2004; Gu 2012; Lee et al. 2013). In addition, and perhaps more importantly, in all three cities, the state remains at the center of all developments, which means that urban cultural policy strategies are largely shaped by national interests and ambitions (see Kong 2007; Lee and Lim 2014; Kim 2017).[2]

Considering that there might be other factors driving the cultural turn in cities, it is perhaps not surprising that of the three given cities, only in Hong Kong does the value of culture seem to be assessed primarily in economic terms. Here the HKSAR government has been focused on capital accumulation and growth since the British settlement in the 1830s. Subsequently, the government has always been reluctant to support those public sectors that have been considered a poor fit to its market-driven policy agenda. Until the mid-1990s, culture and the arts – as non-trade related public services – were largely neglected in terms of public funding and infrastructure (Ooi 1995). Due to limited and fragmented public support for the arts, commercially unviable projects had few opportunities to emerge and sustain themselves (see Ooi 1995).

It seems that the cultural turn has pushed the economic instrumentalization of culture in Hong Kong even further. As Ho (2017) observes, since the late 1990s the cultural policy framework of Hong Kong 'has shifted from checks-and-balances towards centralised market orientation' (57). This shift reflected the HKSAR government's attempts to differentiate Hong Kong from other Chinese cities, to strengthen its competitiveness in the region, and to revive its tourism industry and the economy more generally (see Lui 2008; Chu 2012; Ho 2017).

Under British colonial rule, the funding and regulation of the city's cultural policies was divided between three major institutions: the Recreation and Culture Branch under the Government Secretariat; and two independently elected organizations – the Urban and Regional Councils. In 2000, for the first time in Hong Kong's history, the cultural administration functions were brought under the jurisdiction of one agency, a newly established Leisure and Cultural Services Department (LCSD). The centralization of decision-making power in the areas of culture and the arts has been intertwined with neoliberal urban restructuring strategies, and used, somewhat paradoxically, 'to "outsource" governance' (Purcell 2009: 145; see also Ho 2017).

The corporatization of some major cultural groups in Hong Kong (such as the Hong Kong International Film Festival, Hong Kong Repertory Theatre, Hong Kong Dance Company, and the Hong Kong Chinese Orchestra), which followed soon after the re-organization, exemplifies this point. Although today these cultural organizations still receive regular public subsidies from the government, they are now forced to operate as commercial enterprises and have little room to accommodate experimental art or other creative but potentially unprofitable projects. Ultimately, this hinders the cultural growth and development of the city, and imposes a certain degree of pressure on local cultural practitioners and artists, who are increasingly finding themselves caught in a tug of war between artistic expression and commercial appeal (Lee et al. 2013).

For instance, the Hong Kong International Film Festival (HKIFF), which was long considered a 'niche' event, is under increasing pressure to be 'culturally entertaining' (Wong 2011: 218; see also Cheung 2016). As one respondent from the HKIFF explained:

> We depend a lot on good box office returns. The revenues from the box office comprise a very important part of our annual operating budget, because the government subsidies are simply not enough. We must ensure [good] box office [results] at any cost. ... Our

> survival depends a lot on the local audience who buy tickets. … That's why we have different kinds of films to satisfy different tastes.
>
> *(Practitioner B, Hong Kong, 2014)*

In order to 'satisfy different tastes', since the 2000s, the Festival has introduced a number of new 'highlights' to its program, including the Asian Film Award, the Young Cinema Competition, and the Short Film Competition.

It is important to acknowledge that the HKIFF could be considered as having a privileged status in Hong Kong, because contrary to many other cultural organizations it still receives regular support from the government. Given an economic landscape in which supposedly privileged cultural groups face increasing pressure to sustain themselves, those cultural groups that are less likely to be funded on a regular basis withstand even more competition when fighting for one-off grants from the Hong Kong Arts Development Council (HKADC), let alone everyday operational costs. This again shows that there is little interest within the government in protecting commercially unviable and more vulnerable groups that are increasingly threatened by local, regional, and global competition. Somewhat ironically, this situation occurs in the wake of increased public spending on culture and the arts, discussed in the next section of this chapter.

Pattern II: Increased public spending on culture and the arts

Since the early 2000s, public expenditure for culture has been notably raised in all three cities. Shanghai's public spending on culture has experienced a particularly sharp rise over the last decade or so. In 2017, the city is set to spend around 5.4 billion yuan (€702 million) on culture and the arts (SMPG 2017).[3] This amount is up by more than twofold compared with 1.9 billion yuan (€248.3 million) in 2009 (SMPG 2010). Over the last 15 years Taipei's public spending on culture has also risen twofold, from NT$3.1 billion (€95 million) in 2001 to NT$6.1 billion (€183 million) in 2016 (DBAS 2017). Hong Kong's expenditure for culture and the arts has increased by around 83 percent from HK$2.3 billion (€254 million) in 2000 to HK$4.2 billion (€464 million) in 2016 (HKSAR Government 2017).

However, this surge in public funding seems to benefit primarily *selected* or 'privileged' cultural groups. Study findings reveal that world-renowned artists and commercially appealing projects tend to get more support from local governments, whereas projects of smaller scale and impact often remain neglected (see also Lee et al. 2013). All three cities exhibit this tendency to varying degrees of intensity. However, when we look at Shanghai we see a most instructive and potentially alarming phenomenon. Although over the last decade culture-led development of the city has been widely publicized and supported, the government's commitment to the actual cultural 'turn' still remains to be seen.

Contrary to other global cities in Europe and North America, Shanghai is a *state-centered* global city (Hill and Kim 2000). This means that it is primarily the interests of the state, or rather those of the Chinese Communist Party (CCP), that guide the cultural policies of the city. Over the past few decades, these interests have revolved not only around China's economic performance, but also around its growing ambition for broader global influence and leadership (Wang and Zheng 2008; Wang 2011). As stated in the *Outline of the Cultural Development during the National Eleventh Five-Year Plan Period (2006–2010)*:

> In order to win in the global competition, it is not enough to enhance the nation's economic, technological and military strength. It is also necessary to increase its cultural

> strength. To obtain the leading position and to seize the initiative in the global competition, we must … [therefore] rapidly develop public cultural institutions [*wenhua shiye*] and cultural industries [*wenhua chanye*], to cultivate the vitality of our nation, to strengthen national cohesion, and to increase national creativity.
>
> *(Trans. from Chinese, State Council 2006: 4)*

The pursuit of this 'cultural strength' was the primary driver behind the adoption of the cultural turn in Shanghai. In the Twelfth Five-Year Plan, where the city unveiled its ambition to turn Shanghai into an 'international cultural metropolis' (*Guoji wenhua da dushi*), the need for strengthening the 'overall' international influence and the cultural soft power of the city was named as one of the major reasons behind this aspiration (SMPG 2011a).

Consequently, as my research findings reveal, the primary, if not exclusive, focus of the city authorities lies in supporting either large-scale cultural projects that can generate coverage in the international media or those cultural initiatives that have already achieved international recognition. In other words, it is the international impact that matters most for cultural policies in Shanghai. This ties in with the narrative of 'international influence' (*guoji yingxiangli*) that underpins Chinese soft power policy discourse (Wang 2011). During my interviews, several respondents from the industry and academia have noted that the government always opts for the 'best', 'the greatest', 'world-class' performers:

> Normally, a Chinese understanding of a large, mega cultural event [is that the event] should be the best of the best,
>
> *(Practitioner D, Shanghai, 2014)*

> This is so important for Shanghai to make a statement. The outer appearance, the surface is very important to Shanghai. … [For this reason], the number of performances … and the number of high-level artists … is [particularly] important.
>
> *(Practitioner C, Shanghai, 2014)*

The CCP's infatuation with 'the best' and 'the greatest' affects more vulnerable groups, such as small-scale cultural organizations, community arts projects, and young artists. Given that most of them cannot deliver an immediate international impact, they remain largely neglected and receive very limited (if any) support from the government.

It is also worth noting that in order to gain access to public funds, the work of local artists is not only expected to meet 'world-class' standards, but also to maintain specific Chinese characteristics, which ultimately also serve to enhance the global appeal and international impact of local cultural production. According to de Kloet (2010), it is namely the global demand for ethnic differences in the arts world that is currently 'haunting Chinese artists with the spectre of Chineseness' (446). A comment from one of my respondents who works for the China Shanghai International Arts Festival (SIAF) seems to support this claim:

> Currently, the major challenge for the SIAF is to showcase those Chinese works that could interact with the world and that could reach the world. This is very important. Chinese elements need to be expressed using the world's language.
>
> *(Trans. from Chinese, Practitioner E, Shanghai, 2015)*

What is more, in China all artistic work must also comply with strict censorship laws. In other words, Chinese artists and performers are expected to be creative while being restricted, and internationally appealing while maintaining their 'Chineseness'. Naturally, many local artists find it quite challenging to meet all these demands and expectations and, as a result, are unable to secure public funding.

A vast majority of Shanghai citizens also have little to gain from rising public spending on culture and the arts. The SMPG shows little concern for investing in arts education and involvement of the local community in the arts, because 'local influence' (*difang yingxiangli*) is deemed to provide little value for the 'internationalization' of the city. In accord with this argument, a number of industry professionals in Shanghai indicated that audience development has never been a top priority for local policy makers and complained about the lack of government interest in outreach programs and other projects related to community engagement and participation (see also Huang 2015). There also seems to be little effort in granting easier access for the public. At the time of writing, the tickets to most shows in the SIAF started at 80 yuan (€10) and went up to 1,880 yuan (€245). In Shanghai, where a current minimum wage is merely 2,190 yuan (€286) per month, a vast majority of people simply cannot afford these prices. As a result, these events are accessible mainly for local elites rather than all members of the public. In this context, the cultural turn in Shanghai emerges as merely a bouquet of 'carnival masks' (Harvey 1989b) used to conceal rather than to address the social problems and inequalities of the city.

Pattern III: Growing involvement of the government

The rise in public expenditure on culture in Shanghai, Hong Kong, and Taipei indicates the growing interest of the local governments in the cultural affairs of their cities.

One notable outcome of this trend is the emergence of a more productive and intense dialogue between politicians and industry professionals. My interviews with the design industry professionals in Taipei and Hong Kong show that in recent years they have been provided with more opportunities to voice their ideas and concerns and, in turn, feel more involved in the decision-making process. Moreover, they feel that they have been able to change policy makers' views on the value of design. As one respondent from the Taiwan Design Centre describes:

> We have assisted some officials in the government. They attended some classes where we introduced them to the notion of 'design thinking'. This has prompted the officials to launch new projects that involve various design companies and associations. … Before people from the design industry … had very few opportunities to work with the government.
>
> *(Trans. from Chinese, Practitioner C, Taipei, 2014)*

The emergence of two-way discussions indicate some important and potentially positive shifts in the cultural policy-making process. However, in light of the economic instrumentalization of culture, we should also ask who benefits and who loses from these discussions. My study findings indicate that local policy makers are neither interested nor capable of hearing what *all* industries and *all* cultural groups have to say. There is always a select group of industry professionals, often representing major cultural organizations, that seems to be shaping the agendas of the emerging dialogue. One academic from Taipei described this selective group as 'cultural elites':

> [Within this group] everyone knows each other. … They share funding, they share resources, they share information. … This so-called 'cultural elite' gets lots of benefits from the government.
>
> *(Advisor/Academic A, Taipei, 2015)*

This finding is in accord with earlier observations that the expanding number of policy actors involved in cultural policy making does not necessarily mean that this process is becoming 'more democratic' (Bell and Oakley 2015: 20). All major decisions concerning culture and the arts are still made by the elites and for the benefit of elites, although in a more contested environment (Bennett 1998; Grodach and Silver 2013).

The growing public spending on culture not only points to rising interest in culture and the arts within the local governments of Shanghai, Hong Kong, and Taipei, but also manifests their right to intervene, either directly or indirectly. There are several different ways in which this intervention occurs.

Firstly, the decisions that governments make about what (or whom) to support and to what extent, guide and shape the direction of the cultural turn. The case of the Hong Kong Year of Design 2012 (HKYD 2012) exemplifies this argument. The HKYD 2012 was aimed at the promotion and facilitation of the design industry in the city. The event comprised various activities, exhibitions, and fairs taking place throughout the year, and was fully funded by the government.[4] Generally the HKSAR government tends to provide only partial financial support for events in the city, thus the provision of full funding for this particular event clearly was a strategic policy choice. As explained by one of the organizers of the event, the HKYD 2012 was in line with 'the government's commitment to the development of the design industry' in Hong Kong (Practitioner C, Hong Kong, 2014). Indeed, since the late 1990s, the design industry, along with a long-established film industry, has occupied a central position in Hong Kong's creative industries' development agenda (HKADC 2006).

Moreover, government funding *per se* often comes with strings attached. My study findings show that there are certain requirements or expectations that cultural groups and organizations in all three cities need to meet in order to secure regular inflows of funding, such as generating wide-reaching and positive publicity, contributing to the city's economic development, and ensuring international impact.

In some cases, these expectations can become so deeply embedded in the knowledge of local artists and cultural organizations that they are simply accepted as good practice. The case study of Taipei exemplifies this point.

In Taipei, all major cultural organizations are granted a great degree of autonomy. They usually receive their funding through a semi-public body – the Taipei Culture Foundation – and are not officially bound to follow the preferences of the government. Nevertheless, a closer look at the work of local artists and practitioners reveals that their decisions still appear to be largely guided by the government's aspirations. My interviewee, who is a senior staff member of the Taipei Arts Festival, inadvertently admitted that the government's expectations for the stronger presence of local artists do shape and influence the program of events:

> The Department of Cultural Affairs only provides us with general directions. For instance, they may say that they hope we could increase the number of local audiences, that we should include more young local talents in our program, or that we should support local performing arts groups. ... These are some of the major directions. Thus, they do not really intervene in our work. ... But we have to be able to explain how we help local arts groups, and what our contribution is to the field of performing arts in Taiwan.
>
> *(Trans. from Chinese, Practitioner A, Taipei, 2014)*

In a similar, but more explicit manner, the government's aspirations for the 'internationalization' (*guojihua*) of Taipei, which somewhat echoes the narrative of 'international impact' in Shanghai, also exerts influence on the cultural sector. The aspirations are either directly or indirectly passed on to the individual artists and performers, which in turn inevitably affects the direction and focus of their work. During my interviews with local cultural practitioners in Taipei, the government's narrative of 'internationalization' has been often adopted to rationalize the value of their projects:

> [Referring to the Taipei Arts Festival:] In recent years we have been facilitating cooperation with a vast number of foreign artists. We mediate between foreign and Taiwanese cultural groups and invite them to create together. ... Our festival might not be able to generate profits, but we can achieve other goals. ... The number of international exchanges ... is also one our achievements.
>
> *(Trans. from Chinese, Practitioner A, Taipei, 2014)*

> This year, for the first time we signed the contract with Filmscope. So the Taipei Film Festival is now part of film festivals network. ... We are more *guojihua* [international] now.
>
> *(Practitioner B, Taipei, 2014)*

In a similar vein, the narrative of the 'creative economy' has been used by the design industry in Hong Kong to strengthen their case for funding:

> The funding from the government to us is quite substantive. But we have to deliver. Impact is very important. ... [Hong Kong] used the HKDY 2012 to tell the world ... that we care about design. ... We are sending the world a message that we cherish the creative economy.
>
> *(Practitioner C, Hong Kong, 2014)*

These examples show that industry practitioners often speak the language of policy makers (see also Nisbett 2013). In addition, and perhaps more importantly, they also indicate that by being an increasingly important source of funding, the government undoubtedly exerts a certain degree of influence on the local cultural arena.

Pattern IV: Fast policies call for fast solutions

As explained earlier, the cultural turn in urban development is manifested through a vast number of cultural policies and policy programs, including the development and promotion of the cultural and creative industries, the adoption of the creative city policy narratives, the building of cultural landmarks, and the launch of new cultural events. Essentially, all of these policies are 'fast policies' (Peck and Theodore 2015) in a sense that their adoption process typically takes place in a short period of time, 'often overriding traditional and more circumspect policy processes' (Prince 2012: 192). This means that they are often adopted without proper assessment and preparation (Peck and Theodore 2012). Drawing on Taipei's case, Wang (2010) refers to this tendency as *nalai zhuyi* ('borrowism'), arguing that local policy makers often overlook the need for careful evaluation of the actual benefits and values (if any) that these policies could bring to the city (see also Chiu and Lin 2014).

Imported urban cultural policies can also be seen as 'fast policies' with regards to their promise of imminent results. The expanding number of cultural events, landmarks, and venues, the facilitation of local talents, and the development of cultural and creative industries are claimed to enrich, stimulate, and reinvigorate the city and its cultural life (see Landry 2000; Florida 2002). However, it appears that the road towards this immediate cultural 'renaissance' is often not as easy and clear-cut, because imported cultural policies are often unable to yield any effective solutions for already existing deficiencies. In fact, my research revealed that they instead tend to impose an additional set of demands and pressures on the local cultural arena because as 'fast policies' they call for fast results. Amid accelerated cultural development, these demands can become somewhat disruptive in effectively addressing difficult issues. In effect, cities are often inclined to apply 'quick fixes' that only treat the symptoms, but not the real problem.

Take, for example, the development of a local talent base in Shanghai and Hong Kong. In Shanghai, this process has been relentlessly obstructed by severe restraints on artistic expression and highly centralized decision-making powers (see Tong 1994; Shan 2014). In Hong Kong, where the government has shown little interest in supporting commercially unviable projects, the development of emerging artists was restricted by financial constraints (see Ooi 1995; Ho 2017). Study data suggests that, while the cultural turn in urban development has undoubtedly exposed this problem, it placed the central focus on facilitation of those artists who are capable of meeting the desired 'international' standards, rather than on supporting local artists at large. Moreover, to compensate for the shortage of local talents who meet 'world-class' standards both cities seem to take a faster (though less beneficial) route: they employ foreign artists. For instance, at the Shanghai International Contemporary Theatre Festival (also known as ACT), foreign production typically accounts for around 70 to 90 percent of the festival's program (ACT 2014).

The adoption of the cultural turn has also unveiled the need for facilitation of cultural consumption. Culture-led urban development is essentially consumption-centric – it relies heavily on people who are willing and able to consume cultural goods and services (Pratt 2011). The advocates of the 'creative city' policy script seem to assume that the demand for cultural products is already there (see Landry 2000; Florida 2002). Nevertheless, the findings of this study suggest that in many cases the demand for cultural consumers needs to be created.

The case of the design industry accurately exemplifies this point. In the last decade, the design industry has experienced a rapid growth, occupying one of the leading positions among the cultural and creative industries not only in Taiwan, China, and Hong Kong, but also in Singapore, South Korea, and Japan (Kong et al. 2006; Kim 2017). According to Evans (2009), the placement of non-cultural sectors, such as design or tourism, at the center of the cultural turn represents 'a reversal of the relationship which traditionally located the arts at the core' (1008). This 'reversal' requires the subsequent reversal of interest among the public towards design products and services. People not only need to be convinced about the 'usefulness' of design, but also need to be willing (and able) to pay for its products.

Study findings indicate that in order to ensure a successful leap forward for the design industry, all cities have invested and continue to invest a lot of time, effort, and money in developing, or rather *constructing*, a demand for design products. In this context, large-scale design events, such as the World Design Capital Taipei 2016, Design Week in Shanghai, and the HKDY 2012 serve as educational-manipulative platforms for promotion of the design industry. As stated in the Hong Kong Design Centre's (HKDC) annual report, one of the key purposes of the event was to 'engage the entire community in realising the vision of "A City Driven by Design"' (HKDC 2014: 74). During my interview with the senior organizer of the event this objective was repeatedly outlined. At some point it started to sound more like an attempt to indoctrinate rather than to educate the public:

> Our role is to inject the creative mind-set, design mindfulness into the community. … Of course, it takes time to get design deep tucked into people's mind-set, but that's why we have to continue to do it, to advocate, to educate, to communicate.
>
> *(Practitioner C, Hong Kong, 2014)*

In a similar vein, several respondents in Taipei have also noted that large-scale design events are aimed at manifesting the importance of design in people's lives. According to the representative from the Taiwan Design Centre, such events enable people to see that 'design can truly change the city' (trans. from Chinese, Practitioner C, Taipei, 2014).

Clearly, the creation of demand cannot rely solely on events and outreach programs. This is a very long and challenging process that may require reforms in educational and other public policy sectors, provided the government is willing to go all the way. Thus, the emergence of the discussion regarding arts education in the midst of the cultural turn is perhaps not coincidental.

The need for audience development and arts education was repeatedly underlined during the interviews with government officials and industry professionals in all three cities. It is worth noting, however, that my respondents in Taipei demonstrated considerably less concern about these issues than those in Shanghai and Hong Kong. A possible explanation for this might be the central government's commitment to sustained support for culture and education, which dates back long before the emergence of the idea of the cultural turn (see Chu and Lin 2001). This support, which has proved to be highly controversial and politically motivated (see Chun 1994; Chu and Lin 2001), seems to have paved a way for the emergence of a relatively large and diverse group of arts consumers in Taiwan.

Unlike Taipei, Shanghai has historically shown little interest in cultivating local audiences, because, as noted earlier, 'local influence' is still of little importance for the authorities. As a result, borrowing from Abbas' (2000) reflections on Shanghai, 'what we find here is an example of transnationalism without a corresponding transnational subject' (783). In Shanghai, a large number of event tickets never reach the box office, but according to my respondents, are instead given out to government agencies and government-affiliated sponsors (see also Ma 2012). Many respondents also indicated that the audience in China often lacks understanding of how to behave in a theatre and how to show respect to artists as well as other audience members. Ticket give-away practices further contribute to this problem. As one respondent recalls:

> I have seen performances where the audience came with lunch packages and started chatting, having snacks, and [so on]. This means they got the ticket as a gift, they did not value it.
>
> *(Practitioner C, Shanghai, 2014)*

In this case, the ticket give-away practice is a symptom rather than a cause of the problem. By giving away a large number of tickets to sponsors and government officials, which helps to maintain high attendance rates, Shanghai applies a quick-fix approach to address the issue of audience building.

A closer look at Hong Kong's response to a very similar problem reveals a completely different approach. The cultural turn of Hong Kong has been largely underpinned by an expanding number of cultural activities, events, and arts venues. This includes Hong Kong's most ambitious (and most controversial) cultural project to date – the building of the 40-hectare West Kowloon Cultural District.[5] The upsurge in cultural infrastructure prompted an unforeseen realization that supply may exceed demand. Unlike Shanghai, the HKSAR government responded with a long-term strategy. As one senior government official from the LCSD explains:

> There are a lot of requests from the arts sector that if you build those halls, when you need talents to go in, you need audiences to go in … so government is injecting a lot

> of money in building up audiences, in training up audiences, talents, also training arts personnel.
>
> *(Official D, Hong Kong, 2014)*

Indeed, since 2000, the HKSAR government has been actively involved in supporting various outreach programs and activities. In 2014, the LCSD's Audience Building Office (est. in 2000) held a total of 1,067 arts education and audience-building activities (LCSD 2015). This is a 47 percent increase since 2002 (LCSD 2003).[6]

In addition, the government has also changed its approach to arts education. Those of my interviewees who voiced their concern about the lack of interest within the local community in the arts commonly blamed it on Hong Kong's education system. Although the city prides itself on having one of the most highly educated populations in the world (Pearson 2014), for many years arts education was largely absent from Hong Kong's public schools. In 2000, following the publication of the policy consultation document *Learning to Learn – The Way Forward in Curriculum*, the HKSAR's Curriculum Development Council (CDC) adopted a new curriculum framework for elementary and high school education, which addressed arts as one of the key learning areas. In order to nurture 'creativity, openness, flexibility and aesthetic sensitivity' (CDC 2000: 56) among students, the scope of arts education in schools has been expanded from music and visual arts to media arts, dance, and drama. Altogether these measures indicate a long-term commitment of the HKSAR government to audience building and arts education.

The increasing interest in audience and talent facilitation in Hong Kong, where local government historically showed little interest in arts education, was one of the most interesting and unanticipated findings of my research. It reveals that globalizing cultural policies can indeed bring about some positive changes in local cultural policy making.

Conclusion

The main intention of this chapter was to expose some of the ways in which imported cultural policies are transforming the cultural landscapes of Shanghai, Hong Kong, and Taipei. Each and every one of these ways, which I chose to call 'patterns', have been observed with varying degrees of intensity in all three cities. The four general patterns of the cultural turn I have witnessed include: increased economic instrumentalization of culture; rising public spending on culture and the arts; growing involvement of local policy makers in the cultural sector; and the emergence of new cultural policy strategies and 'quick fixes' designed to push the cultural turn of the cities. Through these patterns I have explored different tensions and opportunities that the adoption of the cultural turn has brought to local policy makers, artists, and practitioners in Chinese cities.

In the wake of the cultural turn, all three cities have started to show more interest in culture as an economic engine. The establishment of the link between culture and the economy has marked an important shift in the ways local policy makers address and deal with urban cultural policy. On the one hand, local governments now are more rigorous, more ambitious, and more generous in terms of arts funding and support. On the other hand, they are more selective, more controlling, and more protective of their agenda, which leaves little room for those forms of arts that lack elements of spectacle, international impact, or commercial appeal. In other words, there is increasingly more emphasis placed on culture as 'display' practices as opposed to cultural policy 'proper' in cities (see McGuigan 2004).

However, it seems that like any other 'neoliberal experiments' (Brenner and Theodore 2002), the cultural turn in Chinese cities does not necessarily deliver the intended or promoted results. Here I defer to my interviewee from Shanghai, who rightly observed that turning the city into a finance and business center is often much easier than making it into a cultural center:

> You need to spend much more time, a lot more years on culture. In addition, its development is also strongly linked with the place *per se*: has it any traditions of its own? Has it any [cultural] resources? Cultural growth [of the city] ties in with many different things.
> *(Trans. from Chinese, Practitioner A, Shanghai, 2014)*

In a similar vein, Ponzini (2012) comments that cultural and reputational capitals are based on long-term accumulation and 'it might be difficult to alter these despite massive investments in cultural and specialized services' (106). Indeed, the success or failure of the cultural turn not only depends on solid investments in cultural infrastructure and amenities, but also largely relies on the inherited cultural landscape of the given city, including both its virtues and deficiencies. Neither cultural events nor cultural landmarks will be able to deliver on the image of a 'culturally vibrant city' if the cultural ecosystem of the city is not robust. As shown in this study, while the adoption of 'fast' cultural policies may expose the existing problems, it is unlikely to provide effective solutions, because it takes years of commitment and coordinated efforts to earn symbolic capital for the place. Nevertheless, most cities often choose to neglect this important aspect before throwing themselves into zero-sum competition for 'up for grabs' titles of 'international cultural metropolis', 'cultural city', or 'creative city'.

While shedding some light on the moments of triumph and despair of the cultural turn in Chinese cities, this chapter neither provided, nor intended to provide, an in-depth assessment of *all* opportunities, challenges, and implications posed by the cultural turn. This points to the need for more comparative studies on the ramifications of the cultural turn in East Asia. A future study investigating the reception of imported cultural policies within the local communities of Shanghai, Hong Kong, and Taipei would be particularly useful in refining the findings of this research.

Notes

1 The study reported in this chapter is part of a broader PhD project (2017) that looked at the use of large-scale cultural events in Shanghai, Hong Kong, and Taipei as part of the reworking of the 'creative city' policy discourse in East Asia.
2 I talk more about other rationales underpinning the cultural turn in Shanghai and Hong Kong elsewhere (see Karvelyte 2017).
3 All values provided regarding public expenditure for culture and the arts in Taipei, Shanghai, and Hong Kong do not include public spending on sports.
4 The HKYD 2012 has received around €1 million (HK$8.9 million) from the government (HKDC 2014).
5 For detailed discussion regarding the West Kowloon Cultural District project in Hong Kong see Lui (2008) and Kong et al. (2015).
6 In 2002, the Audience Building Office hosted a total of 724 arts education and audience building activities (LCSD 2003).

References

Abbas, A. (2000) Cosmopolitan de-scriptions: Shanghai and Hong Kong. *Public Culture*, 12(3): 769–86.
ACT (2014) *About Us*. [Online]. Available at: http://www.actfest.com/aboutus1_en.html [accessed September 25, 2017].

Bell, D. and Oakley, K. (2015) *Cultural Policy*. London: Routledge.
Bennett, T. (1998) *Culture: A Reformer's Science*. London: Sage.
Brenner, N. and Theodore, N. (2002) Cities and the geographies of 'actually existing neoliberalism'. *Antipode*, 34(3): 349–79.
Bryman, A. (2008) *Social Research Methods*, 3rd edn. New York: Oxford University Press.
Census and Statistics Department (CSD) (2013) *The Four Key Industries and Other Selected Industries*. [Online]. Available at: http://www.censtatd.gov.hk/ [accessed October 9, 2017].
Cheung, R. (2016) Ever-changing readjustments: the political economy of the Hong Kong International Film Festival (HKIFF). *New Review of Film and Television Studies*, 14(1): 59–75.
Chiu, S. and Lin, W. (2014) Jiangou chuangyi chengshi: Taibei shi zai zhengce lunshu shang de misi yu xianzhi (Building a creative city: some myths and limitations of the policy discourse in Taipei City). *Dili Xuebao*, 72(1): 57–84.
Chu, S. (2012) Brand Hong Kong: Asia's World City as method? In Chan, K. (ed.), *Hybrid Hong Kong*. Oxon: Routledge, pp. 95–107.
Chu, Y. and Lin, J. (2001) Political development in 20th-century Taiwan: state-building, regime transformation and the construction of national identity. *China Quarterly*, 165(1): 102–29.
Chun, A. (1994) From nationalism to nationalizing: cultural imagination and state formation in post-war Taiwan. *Australian Journal of Chinese Affairs*, 31: 49–69.
Curriculum Development Council (CDC) (2000) *Learning to Learn – the Way Forward in Curriculum*. [Online]. Available at: http://www.edb.gov.hk/en/curriculum-development/ [accessed October 17, 2017].
Department of Budget, Accounting and Statistics (DBAS) (2017) *Taibei shi difang song yusuan* (Taipei City General Budget). [Online]. Available at: http://dbas.gov.taipei/ [accessed May 21, 2017].
Evans, G. (2009) Creative cities, creative spaces and urban policy. *Urban Studies*, 46(5/6): 1003–40.
Executive Yuan (2002) *Tiaozhan 2008: guojia fazhan zhongdian jihua (2002–2007)* (Challenge 2008: National Development Plan (2002–2007)). Taipei: Executive Yuan.
Florida, R. (2002) *The Rise of the Creative Class: And How It's Transforming Work, Leisure, Community and Everyday Life*. New York: Basic Books.
Gibson, C. and Klocker, N. (2005) The 'cultural turn' in Australian regional economic development discourse: neoliberalising creativity? *Geographical Research*, 43(1): 93–102.
Gray, C. (2007) Commodification and instrumentality in cultural policy. *International Journal of Cultural Policy*, 13(2): 203–15.
Gray, C. (2002) Local government and the arts. *Local Government Studies*, 28(1): 77–90.
Grodach, C. and Silver, D. (eds.) (2013) *The Politics of Urban Cultural Policy: Global Perspectives*. Oxon: Routledge.
Gu, X. (2012) The art of re-industrialisation in Shanghai. *Culture Unbound*, 4(1): 193–211.
Harvey, D. (1989a) From managerialism to entrepreneurialism: the transformation in urban governance in late capitalism. *Geografiska Annaler B*, 71(1): 3–17.
Harvey, D. (1989b) *The Urban Experience*. Baltimore, MD: Johns Hopkins University Press.
Hill, R. C. and Kim, J. W. (2000) Global cities and developmental states: New York, Tokyo and Seoul. *Urban Studies*, 37(12): 2167–95.
HKSAR Government (2017) *Previous Budgets*. [Online]. Available at: http://www.budget.gov.hk/2017/eng/previous.html [accessed May 21, 2017].
HKSAR Government (1998) *The 1998 Policy Address*. Hong Kong: HKSAR Government.
Ho, L. (2017) From 'no cultural policy' to 'centralised market orientation': the political economy of Hong Kong cultural policy (1997–2015). *Global Media and China*, 2(1): 57–73.
Hong Kong Arts Development Council (HKADC) (2006) *A Decade of Arts Development in Hong Kong*, Hong Kong: Hong Kong Arts Development Council.
Hong Kong Design Centre (HKDC) (2014) *A City Driven by Design. 2012–2013 Annual Report*. Hong Kong: HKDC.
Huang, C. (2015) Guancha zhongguo: shanghai guoji yishujie de ling yi ge jiaodu (Observing China: another view of the Shanghai International Art Festival). *Shanghai Yishujia*, 22(6): 10–11.
Hutton, T. A. (2012) The cultural turn and urban development in Asia. In Daniels, P. W., Ho, K. C. and Hutton, T. A. (eds.), *New Economic Spaces in Asian Cities: From Industrial Restructuring to the Cultural Turn*. Oxon: Routledge, pp. 31–50.
Karvelyte, K. (2017) From arts desert to global cultural metropolis: the (re)branding of Shanghai and Hong Kong. In Durrer, V., Miller, T. and O'Brien, D. (eds.), *The Routledge Handbook of Global Cultural Policy*. Oxon: Routledge, pp. 247–64.

Kim, C. (2017) Locating creative city policy in East Asia: neoliberalism, developmental state and assemblage of East Asian cities. *International Journal of Cultural Policy*, 23(3): 312–30.
de Kloet, J. (2010) Created in China and Pak Sheung Chuen's tactics of the mundane. *Social Semiotics*, 20(4): 441–55.
Kong, L. (2007) Cultural icons and urban development in Asia: economic imperative, national identity, and global city status. *Political Geography*, 26(4): 383–404.
Kong, L., Ching, C. and Chou, T. (2015) *Arts, Culture and the Making of Global Cities: Creating New Urban Landscapes in Asia*. Cheltenham: Edward Elgar Publishing.
Kong, L., Gibson, C., Khoo, L. M. and Semple, A.L. (2006) Knowledges of the creative economy: towards a relational geography of diffusion and adaptation in Asia. *Asia Pacific Viewpoint*, 47(2): 173–94.
Landry, C. (2000) *The Creative City: A Toolkit for Urban Innovators*. London: Earthscan.
Landry, C. and Bianchini, F. (1995) *The Creative City*. London: Demos.
Leisure and Cultural Services Department (LCSD) (2003) *Annual Report 2002*. [Online]. Available at: http://www.lcsd.gov.hk/dept/annual2002/en/main.php [accessed October 30, 2017].
Leisure and Cultural Services Department (LCSD) (2015) *Annual Report 2014–2015* [Online]. Available at: http://www.lcsd.gov.hk/ [accessed October 30, 2017].
Lee, E., Chan, E., Chan, J., Cheung, P., Lam, W. F. and Lam, W. (2013) *Public Policymaking in Hong Kong: Civic Engagement and State–Society Relations in a Semi-Democracy*. New York: Routledge.
Lee, H. K. and Lim, L. (eds.) (2014) *Cultural Policies in East Asia: Dynamics between the State, Arts and Creative Industries*. London: Palgrave Macmillan.
Lui, T. (2008) City-branding without content: Hong Kong's aborted West Kowloon mega-project, 1998–2006. *International Development Planning Review*, 30(3): 215–26.
Ma, R. (2012) Celebrating the international, disremembering Shanghai: the curious case of the Shanghai International Film Festival. *Culture Unbound*, 4(1): 147–68.
McGuigan, J. (2004) *Rethinking Cultural Policy*. Maidenhead: Open University.
Nisbett, M. (2013) New perspectives on instrumentalism: an empirical study of cultural diplomacy. *International Journal of Cultural Policy*, 19(5): 557–75.
O'Connor, J. and Gu, X. (2006) A new modernity?: The arrival of 'creative industries' in China. *International Journal of Cultural Studies*, 9(3): 271–83.
Ooi, V. (1995) The best cultural policy is no cultural policy: cultural policy in Hong Kong. *International Journal of Cultural Policy*, 1(2): 273–87.
Pacione, M. (2009) *Urban Geography: A Global Perspective*, 3rd edn. Oxon: Routledge.
Pearson (2014) *Index: Which Countries Have the Best Schools*. [Online]. Available at: http://thelearningcurve.pearson.com/index/index-ranking [accessed October 17, 2017].
Peck, J. (2011) Creative moments: working culture through municipal socialism and neoliberal urbanism. In McCann, E. and Ward, K. (eds.), *Mobile Urbanism: Cities and Policymaking in the Global Age*. Minneapolis, MN: University of Minnesota Press, pp. 41–70.
Peck, J. (2007) The creativity fix. *Fronesis* [Online], 24. Available at: http://www.eurozine.com/pdf/2007-06-28-peck-en.pdf [accessed March 9, 2017].
Peck, J. and Theodore, N. (2015) *Fast Policy: Experimental Statecraft at the Thresholds of Neoliberalism*. Minneapolis, MN: University of Minnesota Press.
Peck, J. and Theodore, N. (2012) Follow the policy: a distended case approach. *Environment and Planning A*, 44(1): 21–30.
Ponzini, D. (2012) Competing cities and spectacularizing urban landscapes. In Anheier, H.K. and Isar, Y.R. (eds.), *Cultures and Globalization: Cities, Cultural Policy and Governance*. London: Sage, pp. 99–110.
Pratt, A. C. (2009) Policy transfer and the field of the cultural and creative industries: what can be learned from Europe? In Kong, L. and O'Connor, J. (eds.) *Creative Economies, Creative Cities: Asian-European Perspectives*. London: Springer, pp. 9–23.
Pratt, A. C. (2011) The cultural contradictions of the creative city. *City, Culture and Society*, 2(3): 123–30.
Prince, R. (2012) Policy transfer, consultants and the geographies of governance. *Progress in Human Geography*, 36(2): 188–203.
Purcell, M. (2009) Resisting neoliberalization: communicative planning or counter-hegemonic movements? *Planning Theory*, 8(2): 140–65.
Shan, S. (2014) Chinese cultural policy and the cultural industries. *City, Culture and Society*, 5(3): 115–21.

Shanghai Municipal People's Government (SMPG) (2010) *Guanyu shanghai shi 2009 nian yusuan zhixing qingkuang he 2010 nian yusuan shibenji yiban gonggong yusuan caoan de baogao* (A Report on the Shanghai City's 2009 Budget Implementation and the 2010 Public Budget Draft). [Online]. Available at: http://www.mof.gov.cn/zhuantihuigu/10nianyusuanbaogao/yusuanbaogaohuibian10/ [accessed May 21, 2017].

Shanghai Municipal People's Government (SMPG) (2017) *Shanghai shi 2017 nian shibenji yiban gonggong yusuan zhichu yusuan biao* (The Shanghai City (Municipal Level) General Public Expenditure Budget Sheet for 2017). [Online]. Available at: https://www.czj.sh.gov.cn/zss/zt/ysbgjd_9587/ysbgjd2017n/czysb/ [accessed May 21, 2017].

Shanghai Municipal People's Government (SMPG) (2011a) *Shanghai shi guomin jingji he shehui fazhan di shierge wunian guihua gangyao* (An Outline of the Shanghai's Twelfth Five-Year Plan for National Economic and Social Development). Shanghai: SMPG.

Shanghai Municipal People's Government (SMPG) (2011b) *Shanghai shi wenhua chuangyi chanye fazhan 'shierwu' guihua* (The 12th Five-Year Plan for the Development of Shanghai's Cultural and Creative Industries). Shanghai: SMPG.

Song, H., Wong, K. and Chon, K. (2003) Modelling and forecasting the demand for Hong Kong tourism. *International Journal of Hospitality Management*, 22(4): 435–51.

State Council (2006) *Guojia 'shi yi wu' shiqi wenhua fazhan guihua gangyao* (The Outline of the Cultural Reform and Development during the Period of the National Twelfth Five-Year Plan). Beijing: State Council.

Tong, Q. (1994) Power, ideology and economy: cultural policy in China. *European Journal of Cultural Policy*, 1(1): 109–20.

Tu, W. (1991) Cultural China: the periphery as the center. *Daedalus*, 120(2): 1–32.

Wang, G. and Zheng, Y. (eds.) (2008) *China and the New International Order.* Oxon: Routledge.

Wang, J. (ed.) (2011) *Soft Power in China: Public Diplomacy Through Communication.* New York: Palgrave Macmillan.

Wang, J. (2004) The global reach of a new discourse: how far can 'creative industries' travel? *International Journal of Cultural Studies*, 7(1): 9–19.

Wang, J., Oakes, T. and Yang, Y. (eds.) (2015) *Making Cultural Cities in Asia: Mobility, Assemblage, and the Politics of Aspirational Urbanism.* London: Routledge.

Wang, J. H. (2010) Wenhua/chuangyi chanye, chuangyi jieji/chengshi lunzhe de pipan xing jianshi (A critical view on the discourses of the cultural and creative industries, the creative class and the creative city). *Si yu Yan*, 48(1): 131–90.

Wang, J. H. (2004) World city formation, geopolitics and local political process: Taipei's ambiguous development. *International Journal of Urban and Regional Research*, 28(2): 384–400.

Wong, C. (2011) *Film Festivals: Culture, People, and Power on the Global Screen.* London: Rutgers University Press.

Wu, F. (2000) The global and local dimensions of place-making: remaking Shanghai as a world city. *Urban Studies*, 37(8): 1359–77.

Yeoh, B. (2005) The global cultural city? Spatial imagineering and politics in the (multi)cultural marketplaces of South-East Asia. *Urban Studies*, 42(5): 945–58.

Zou, D. (1996) The open door policy and urban development in China. *Habitat International*, 20(4): 525–9.

Zukin, S. (1991) *Landscapes of Power: From Detroit to Disney World.* Berkeley, CA: University of California Press.

Zukin, S. (1995) *The Cultures of Cities.* Oxford: Blackwell.

Zukin, S. (2001) Whose culture? Whose city? The paradoxical growth of a culture capital. [Online]. Available at: http://www.cpu.gov.hk/en/events_conferences_seminars/conference_20010731.html [accessed March 27, 2017].

Part II

Producers and production

8

The negotiated creative autonomy in the organization-based TV labor market

Chairin An

Historically, most cultural theorists and cultural sociologists have assumed that the power of the market decreases the level of creative autonomy available to creative workers during the cultural production process. In describing the 'culture industry', Adorno and Horkheimer (1992) presumed that the commercialization of the cultural industry would bring about standardization of cultural products because creative workers would be forced to follow market demands and trends to ensure commercial success. Meanwhile, Bourdieu (1993) made the distinction between two types of cultural production and contended that the 'field of restricted production' creates 'pure' cultural products and producers are able to enjoy a high level of autonomy; in contrast, producers involved in the 'field of large-scale production' are unable to maintain their own principles during the production process. Similarly, DiMaggio (1977) assumed that large media conglomerates tend to produce standardized products lacking in creativity, while relatively small cultural companies produce more innovative outcomes. If such a perceived dichotomy between the arts and commerce is accepted, some may argue that discussing the autonomy of creative laborers in the context of the largely commercialized environment is an unworthy pursuit as the conclusion must be obvious: that is, there is no such thing as creative autonomy in this context.

However, it may be too simplistic to assume that contemporary creative workers are entirely subordinated to industrial pressure, or that they completely eschew the economic success of the industry primarily based on principles of artistic ambition (Banks 2007; Oakley 2009). Above all, in the contemporary cultural/creative industries, the tension between creativity and commerce can be considered to enhance rather than diminish levels of creativity and innovation. Commercial and cultural/creative values are not necessarily polarized, and creative workers are supposed to naturally co-consider both values of their products during the production process.

To discuss the issues of creative autonomy in the contemporary cultural/creative production process, the environment and working conditions should also be considered. In recent studies on the creative labor market, many have focused on changing recruitment trends, which have shifted away from long-term employment at a single organization toward short-term, project-based contracts. Indeed, in Western television labor markets, for example the UK or US, the career trajectories of media laborers are increasingly dependent on project-based employment, and the career development process has already become highly individualized (Stoyanova and Grugulis 2012). Some have used the concept of 'boundaryless careers' to describe the individualized career development process in the media labor market (Arthur 2008; Eikhof et al. 2012), in which laborers must assertively monetize their own abilities independent of a stable organizational status. McRobbie (2002a) also contended that the commercialization and individualization of cultural work would bring a 'decline in creativity' (524). While many have stressed the negative effects of project-based and short-term employment in the undoubtedly commercialized cultural/creative industries, such as insecurity and casualization of creative laborers (Ross 2009; Stoyanova and Grugulis 2012; Davenport 2006), the significant discussion on the appropriate organizational relationship for creative laborers has been somewhat overlooked. Indeed, creative laborers are still related to an organization to a certain degree, either as a freelance worker or a part-time contract laborer, and managing organizational relationships is one of the most essential capacities that they should have in order to continue their career in a stable manner within the media industries. Undoubtedly, media organizations in this context would follow market principles. Considering this, an important question regarding the matter of creative autonomy remains: to what extent can creative laborers follow their own creative ambition under commercialized organizational circumstances?

This chapter will focus on presenting the paradoxical experience of creative laborers within the organization-based working environment, in which they face conflict between organizational demands and their individual creative ambitions. To examine the lived-experiences of creative laborers in the organization-based work environment that primarily follows market principles, the South Korean (hereafter Korean) light-entertainment television industry was selected to be an appropriate field.[1] In particular, the case of a television PD (Producer-Director)[2] – a core creative role in Korean entertainment TV program production – was considered, because the individual career development process of a PD in this field is still fundamentally dependent upon organizational status.[3] Based on my own empirical research with Korean entertainment television PDs, I suggest in this chapter that we need to consider the multiple identities of creative workers to understand the specificity of creative labor and their pursuit of creative autonomy. My study shows that PDs come to formulate two prominent social identities alongside their own individual identity; specifically, an organizational identity and a professional identity.[4] Since each identity naturally respectively reflects individual creative ambitions, organizational needs, and the professional standards of a given organization-based program, PDs experience differing but concurrent desires during the creative production process. As a result, PDs bring to bear a variety of values in their program production process (including personal, cultural, organizational, and market values) and thereby negotiate a level of creative autonomy within the commercialized organizational environment.

By linking such a complex negotiation process of the level of creative autonomy to the notion of multiple identities of creative workers, the chapter argues that creative laborers are able to actualize their own creative ambitions to a certain degree, and this ultimately enables them to bring a variety of values to their programs and their organizations. I believe this approach towards creative laborers will allow us to understand the specificity of cultural/creative work from a new angle, by revealing the dilemmas and ironies that creative laborers experience due to the complex environmental relationships within the contemporary cultural/creative industries.

Historical background

The organization-based labor market of the PD position is built on the particular historical background of the Korean television industry; specifically the launch of the state-run broadcaster in Korea (KBS-TV),[5] which was the direct consequence of decisions taken by the military government. Although many have suggested that the abbreviation 'PD' stands for various combinations of words (for example, Planning Director, Program Director, Producing Director and Producer-Director) (Cho et al. 2000; Lee 1993), it seems most convincing that the term PD was first created during the improvised launch process of KBS-TV (Baek et al. 2008), which has been the foundation of today's organization-based production system and PD career path. In September 1961, the military government announced its plan to launch state-run TV broadcasting, and scouted Chang-Bong Choi[6] to become the leader of the founding team of KBS-TV. Choi selected the launch team from his previous colleagues at HLKZ-TV (the first private broadcaster in Korea), most of whom were Directors. Meanwhile, the government also recruited new employees to become assistants to the Directors and their official position was 'Producers' (Baek et al. 2008). In the American television production system, Producers are in overall charge of both pre-production and production, drawing on their own individual networks and specialized experiences. As such, expecting new recruits to function as Producers was, in many ways, doomed from the outset. According to Jeong-Tae Hwang, who was a KBS-TV Director from HLKZ-TV, new employees could not sufficiently learn what the role of Producer entailed due to a lack of human resource support and training (Baek et al. 2008: 217). Unexpectedly, however, in February 1962 and shortly after the launch of KBS-TV, the government reformed the organization by firing all specialists originally hired from the private sector in order to both structure the organization as a government agency and to keep the production process under control. New Producers were therefore required to take up the Directors' responsibilities and the roles of Producer and Director were naturally merged. Throughout this process, the majority of tasks were merged around the Director's role (as opposed to that of the Producer) due to the perception that Directors were more influential (Baek et al. 2008), and this process has been the foundation upon which today's organization-based production system and PD career path has been built.

Throughout Korean broadcasting history, the creative role of PDs was historically significant as they naturally balanced various tensions and dilemmas from the outset; namely, the needs of government with the needs of the audience. As described above, the complex role of PD itself was initially constructed by reflecting the paradoxical working environment within the state-run broadcaster: Producers, who were newly recruited and submissive to Directors, were suddenly transformed into fully autonomous agents by governmental order and took the role of both Producer and Director. As a result, today's PD role has come to deal with not only personal creative ambition, but also with the originality, quality, and marketability of a television program.

The organization-based professionalization process of the PD position

The distinctive correlations between broadcasting organizations and PDs could be identified by observing the particular professionalization process of the PD role. During the organization-based professionalization process, PDs learn not only to accumulate necessary specialized knowledge and skills, but also to construct their peer network and professional contacts – one of the most essential assets in the career development of a PD. Since broadcasting organizations offer the opportunity for proper professional training and involvement with an experienced and established group of colleagues, entering into an established television organization is an indispensable condition for PDs to become sufficiently professionalized in the labor market. Thus, throughout the program production process, PDs need to manage complex and paradoxical relationships with their broadcasting organization; in particular, with regard to their level of creative autonomy, PDs experience constant negotiation between their own desires (both present desires and future aspirations) and the needs of the organization.

1. The organization-based recruitment process of PDs

The production system of the Korean television industry has largely been developed through the experience of KBS-TV, which initially set up an integrated factory-style production process. Traditionally, being a PD in the Korean television industry meant that the candidate has an elitist educational background. The recruitment process for the PD position was similar to that of the general recruitment process for a civil servant. In the past, most PD expectants applying to the few established terrestrial broadcasters were required to have a university degree, and according to a study by Lee (1993), who observed the entry-level education of PDs in the three major terrestrial broadcasters (KBS, MBC and SBS), more than half of the PDs were graduates from Seoul National University, which is the nation's top school. Although educational requirements have eased following the recent expansion of the television labor market, it remains true that almost all established broadcasters implicitly require a Bachelor's degree to be held by those hoping to work as a full-time PD. Furthermore, those without prior work experience who wish to work as a full-time PD must pass an official entry examination, meaning that prospective PDs are only really able to begin developing their PD career once they have entered into an organization. Even in the case of part-time employed PDs and freelancers, to begin their PD careers, they more or less need to belong to a broadcasting organization as the television program production process is typically overseen by a systemized television organization.

2. The organization-based training process of a PD

The emergence of an organizational identity (during the AD to ordinary PD stages)

Typically, having entered into a broadcasting organization, new recruits go on to become an Assistant Director (AD).[7] As is often the case in any occupation, great perseverance is needed to become established as an autonomous creative worker. Although each PD's experience of both job security and the crafting process varies, all PDs experience long-term on-the-job training as an AD. Regardless of where they are employed, individuals are trained in the skills of a PD through an apprenticeship-like training system (known in Korea as *Doje*) during their time as an AD. During the on-the-job training of *Doje*, an immediate superior (usually a PD) is assigned to a new recruit and he or she takes responsibility for the AD's learning.[8] At this stage, new recruits learn not only the basic skills of editing, directing, casting, and communication, but also absorb much implicit knowledge: for example, the vocabulary, tacit rules, and norms of the given organization. In an environment that is strictly controlled by their superiors, the new recruits become familiarized with the particular culture of the firm. The period during which an individual will serve as an AD varies according to the different genres and organizations. The majority of my interviewees observed that about eight years of training is needed to become established as a Main PD in the light-entertainment genre; as a Main PD an individual is believed to have sufficient experience and specialized knowledge to run a single program production as a team leader. To understand the typical career trajectory of a PD in Korea, an outline of this trajectory, from the beginning stage through to the stage of maintaining, is presented in Figure 8.1.

In any form of broadcasting organization, the life of an AD is characterized by an extremely heavy workload and poor working conditions. All interviewees expressed their experiences in the AD period as 'challenging', but at the same time also very 'enjoyable'. Interviewees shared that at first they were disillusioned when they realized they did not have sufficient skills or knowledge to immediately create an influential program, and discovered that their initial role in the organization was more similar to that of an errand boy/girl. It seemed that the experience of working as an AD did not align to interviewees' initial expectations of the job or their ideals about becoming a PD. It was not the heavy workload that disappointed them because that was their expectation of the PD role, but they became disillusioned when they realized they would have little opportunity to make something 'real', an experience that would have allowed them to actualize their own creative ambitions through the creation of a program (Interviewees SL, EK, and JL).

Such disappointments may be the reason why so many interviewees remember their first editing experience so favorably (for most, their first opportunity to edit something 'real' was when they were asked to make a short trailer for a program, normally around 30 seconds long) (Interviewees JL, SL, EK, YP, EH, and HS). In addition, PDs also shared that they experienced true happiness when they first saw the video they had edited on air, and at such a point, PDs began to identify themselves with this work: the tendency to describe a program (or short trailer) as 'mine' was observed in every interview. Even by editing a short video clip, interviewees had naturally expressed their own tastes and creative ambitions: thus, showing the videos they had made to others caused them to feel almost 'naked' as the video was based on 'my' thoughts (Interviewee EH). Many interviewees stated that the 'enjoyable' part of AD life was primarily based on such creative production processes, even if their tasks were relatively small compared to those of senior PDs (Interviewees SL, JL, HS, YP, and YJ). While attempting to express their creative ambition through a short video clip, ADs become very sensitive to the reactions of viewers and their feedback, as they wish to receive confirmation from people around them that their own way of making a video is accepted within the organization and the professional field. In this process, they naturally learn the shared aesthetic criteria of producing a program within the organization.

Figure 8.1 Typical process in becoming a Main PD

By identifying what is the 'right' way to deliver a message via video content, they begin to internalize a certain standard of program making. Yet this should not be interpreted as the disappearance of their personal creative ambitions and idealism; rather, this tendency appears to be a starting point from which PDs learn how to balance their own individual creative ambitions with organizational demands. For instance, to reach the ultimate goal of creating something 'real' – that is, producing their own program as a Main PD – ADs frequently need to put aside their own views and follow the shared criteria of program production within their organization. As such, from this stage, PDs begin to formulate their organizational identity alongside their own creative ambitions.

After a long period of training, ADs are at some point given the opportunity to become an Ordinary PD.[9] At this stage, individuals begin to have much greater responsibility in the program production process. However, since Ordinary PDs are not yet perceived as qualified to carry program production from the incubation stage through to post-production as a leader of a single production team, PDs at this stage typically support the program production process of their senior (Main PD) as a 'Second' or 'Third' PD. During this period, PDs prepare their own debut as a Main PD. Thus, it could be said that Ordinary PDs are still in on-the-job training, and every single task is perceived as a kind of test preparing them to debut as a Main PD in the future. Thus, individuals must behave in accordance with the shared standard to reach their ideal of making 'my' program.

PDs at both AD and Ordinary PD stages do not merely absorb the creative styles of their superiors or organizational preferences; by watching and following shared aesthetic standards, they come to develop their own creative ambitions within a realistic frame of reference. In other words, PDs come to learn how to imbue their preferences and tastes within the shared standards of television program production. Indeed, most interviewees admitted that ADs and Ordinary PDs implicitly develop their own imagination as they support the performance of their seniors (Interviewees SL, HS, JL, WL, YP, HJ, and JP). From this perspective, it seems that PDs at these two early career stages start to experience the emergence of an organizational identity by balancing the rules of the organization with their individual creative ambitions and their own idealism. Although the level of creative autonomy at these two stages is somewhat limited, for PDs this training period is perceived as a kind of rite of passage to acquire sufficient negotiating authority with organizations in their future career. In this sense, the period of working as an AD and Ordinary PD could be characterized as the socialization process of a PD as an employed creative laborer. Over time, trainees both develop their creative ambitions and learn how to actualize these ideas with a shared language. While keeping and developing their 'enjoyment' derived from involvement in the creative production process, PDs at early career stages come to learn the existing rules and norms of their organizations.

Using van Zoonen's model of organizational identity (1998: 137), the emerging organizational identity of a PD as an employed creative laborer is illustrated in Figure 8.2. PDs who initially have certain idealistic notions expressed as 'I', as an organizational member gradually come to have a perception of 'us'. However, as seen in the figure, organizational identity is inherently fluid based on negotiations between the given structures and the subjectivity of an individual PD. The organizational identity of a PD sits between individual creative ambitions and organizational power and standards. Thus, this form of organizational identity is subject to change based on changes in either organizational circumstances or personal situations. As we shall see, at the Main PD stage both structures and subjectivity change with the emergence of another identity (that of the professional identity), and this leads to changes in the process of negotiating the PD's level of creative autonomy.

Figure 8.2 The construction process of the Organizational Identity of a PD

Emergence of a professional identity (during the main PD stage)

As an individual's career develops, an Ordinary PD becomes a Main PD with his or her own program production. In the Korean language, an individual's debut as a Main PD is known as 'Ip-bong' (입봉).[10] This could be understood as a sort of ritual that celebrates the end of the training period. Typically, senior PDs or managers in an organization confirm whether an Ordinary PD or AD has enough knowledge and experience to produce a single program with the full authority of a Main PD. According to interviewees, it tends to take much longer to become a Main PD in a large company due to a congestion of personnel.

Once established as a Main PD, PDs come to have relatively high levels of discretionary authority as professionals and take full responsibility for the results of program production. Although most PDs are employees within a larger organization, as a Main PD they are in many ways relatively free from supervision and the constraints of the organization, being given responsibility to lead their production teams as qualified professionals. Most interviewees believed that those who have debuted as a Main PD become trusted professionals who are expected to have sufficient knowledge and skills to make any style of program at the required level of quality and popularity.

From this stage, the gaps between individual PDs become larger and peers are perceived not only as colleagues but also as competitors. Indeed, since success (or otherwise) of their programs will be attached to their professional reputation, PDs need to imbue their name with excellence and uniqueness in the minds of both their employers and their audiences. From this stage, PDs begin to formulate their professional identity and start to acquire greater negotiating power for higher levels of creative autonomy. Typically, a PD's professional capacity is assessed by viewer ratings; thus, Main PDs sometimes willingly set aside their own tastes and preferences to achieve higher ratings and thereby to construct a certain degree of trust between themselves and the organization. This behavior not only occurs in the early days as a Main PD, but from time to time, PDs again attempt to build such trust to broaden the range of opportunities available to them. Some may interpret this phenomenon as a subordinate individual creative worker who cannot resist the given organizational structure, but many of my interviewees described such moments as another rite of passage to achieve a higher level of creative autonomy as a professional.

The majority of interviewees stated that they have a kind of dream proposal, which they wish to produce if external conditions are propitious to them (Interviewees JP, JL, SL, WL, BM, SP, EK, HWS, and TM). For PDs, being granted the creative freedom to make a program they liked was perceived as a great reward. To achieve such a reward, paradoxically, they did not hesitate to make a program for the organization, even if this program did not entirely fit with their own creative ambitions (Interviewees BM, HJ, and JL). At moments such as this, the individual's organizational identity becomes the most salient, but again, this does not mean that their individual and professional identities have been entirely subsumed. Rather, this could be interpreted as strategic career management. If PDs can successfully manage their careers, the possibility of maintaining a higher level of creative autonomy increases.

It is true that PDs who began their career in one of the few relatively stable organizations in the Korean television industry will have experienced more advantageous conditions from the outset; however, the power of an organization alone does not guarantee that a well-qualified professional PD will automatically become an established Main PD. Indeed, almost half of the interviewees who began their careers as freelancers or part-time employed PDs within small production companies are now working as Main PDs in established broadcasters (Interviewees WL, JP, EH, YP, JL, TM, and HWS). The majority of interviewees emphasized the importance of continually maintaining their individual creative ambitions, as this was the primary driving force that enabled them to endure the intensive training process and to continually develop their own style and creative capacity (Interviewees WL, SL, JJ, YJ, BM, HJ, HS, and SP). Likewise, reaching the final stage of career development as a Main PD does not mean that the ability to create new and valuable programs is unconditionally guaranteed. It is now that the real competition as a content creator begins and Main PDs should endlessly endeavor to produce not only creative but also popular programs to both enhance their own reputation and benefit the organization as a whole.

Three Different Identities of a Main PD and the Resultant Negotiated Creative Autonomy

Thus it appears that a Main PD has three differing but concurrent identities: a *creative self* who continually seeks to realize their creative ambitions, an *employed creative laborer* who successfully negotiates between their ideals and the existing organizational power, and a *creative professional* who seeks to both develop their own reputation and defend their discretionary rights over the production process by demonstrating their professional capacity.

Negotiation between these identities occurs frequently for Main PDs and numerous instances were described by my interviewees. One example is the issue of ratings, for which it appeared that PDs had multi-faceted, sometimes conflicting, desires born out of each identity (see Figure 8.3).

> First, PDs appeared to derive their own personal satisfaction as a creative self from ratings. Viewer ratings are the primary source by which the audiences' reactions can be identified and feedback on a program obtained. As a creative self, just like any other cultural producer, PDs naturally desire to reach the largest audience possible by sharing their creative world and personal perspective. However, to catch the audience's eye, PDs inevitably compromise as they feel there is a need to follow certain trends and formulas to achieve higher ratings.

Second, by increasing the viewing figures, PDs wish to increase the level of creative autonomy they are given during the program production process. If the viewership of a program is high, PDs enjoy a considerable level of autonomy in the organization. However, to reach this point, PDs must make numerous compromises, acquiesce to a variety of

Figure 8.3 Three different desires in regard to ratings

organizational interventions, and must negotiate with their managers and seniors until they are able to demonstrate their capacity for achieving good viewership ratings. In other words, to achieve creative autonomy in an organization, PDs must first paradoxically 'give up' much of their autonomy during the production process.

Finally, PDs also bear ratings in mind when considering the development of their career over the longer term. The development of a PD's career typically takes many years, and with the recent increase in the level of mobility in the PD labor market, building a good reputation by making a popular program has become more important. Presumably, in the later phase of their career, most PDs also wish for their own styles and preferences to become a trend, just as a few star PDs have become a brand themselves. High audience figures are obviously critical to the formation of such outcomes.

To become an independent creative laborer in the future, which is promising but uncertain, PDs actively negotiate the level of autonomy in their work. However, considering the very nature of a cultural product, which is largely uncertain and unpredictable, even if a PD achieves a great level of creative autonomy by bringing in higher ratings, the temporary agreement of the level of creative autonomy is inevitably very weak: such a temporary agreement could be withdrawn at any time because a 'currently popular program may fail tomorrow' (Interviewee BM).

On examining previous studies of 'precarious' creative labor, some may argue that the decision of a PD to compromise himself or herself to the industrial and market structures for the promise of greater creative autonomy in the future is nothing but the subordinated attitude of a vulnerable creative laborer within the commercialized market (for example, Ross 2009; Ursell 2000; McRobbie 2002a, 2002b). It was however also clear in my interviews that the creative value of the broadcasting industry is largely dependent on the individual creative capacity of PDs. At least, when it comes to television program production, how the results of sophisticated market research and trend analysis would be applied to the actual creative production process is still largely dependent on the creative capacity of individual PDs, which cannot easily be replaced. Well-established PDs not only bring newness and

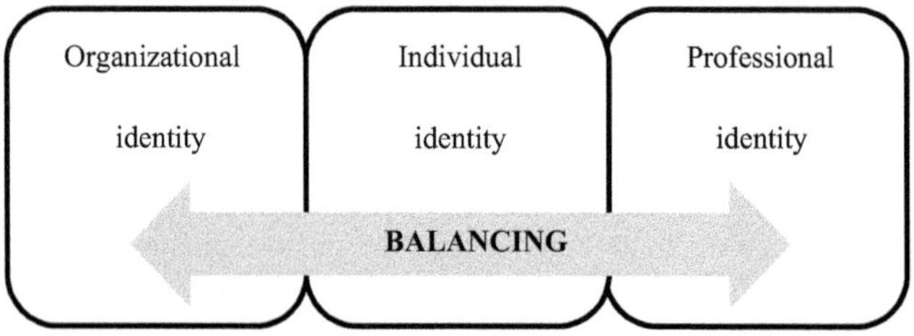

Figure 8.4 The three identities of a PD

value to the market, but also have the ability to properly negotiate and balance the needs and demands of both the market and the organization. Such an ability to negotiate and balance is possible due to the strength of their own intrinsic motivation, their own personal desire to achieve higher ratings, and their wish to become established in the market as a creative laborer.

The interrelationships between the three selves (creative self, employed creative laborer, and creative professional) are always subject to change according to structural and subjective factors. Thus, a PD's multiple identities are not fixed but are inherently fluid. To achieve a satisfactory level of creative autonomy, PDs learn to balance various environmental factors with their three different identities (see Figure 8.4), and in the process, the subjective individual who attempts to maintain their own creative ambitions holds the helm.

The important role of individual identity in the negotiation process of creative autonomy

> During the negotiation process of creative autonomy, a PD's basic desire to produce something creative based on their own creative ambition remains constant throughout the career development process. Figure 8.5 presents the formulation process of the multiple identities of PDs and the negotiation process between the three different identities with differing levels of creative autonomy.

As a PD's career develops, their own standards of creativity shift, change, and develop to reflect various organizational and industrial criteria and norms. Nonetheless, interviewees clearly articulated how their individual desire as a creative self played a key role during the process of negotiating their creative autonomy.

Of course, the negotiation process and its results varied according to each interviewee's personality and their situation. While some PDs took a firm stand against organizational interventions and were demanding in protecting their own criteria regarding the creative value of television programs (Interviewees HJ and BM), several other interviewees admitted that they sometimes 'gave up' their preferences to not only attain a higher level of market value (viewership), but also to maintain their stable organizational status and to ensure their long-term career as a professional (Interviewees JL, JP, and TM). Even in the case of those PDs who temporarily renounced their creative ambition however, it was clearly observed that PDs tried their best to protect the core creative value of the program based on their own individual standards. It could therefore be said that the assertive negotiation of the level of creative autonomy became possible because of a PD's determination to

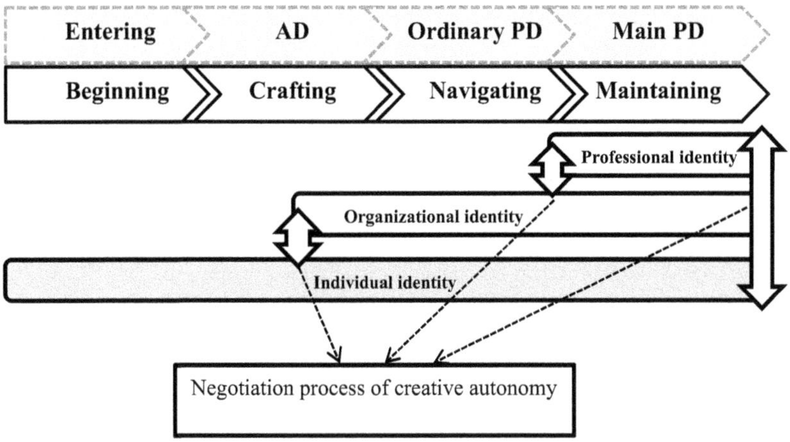

Figure 8.5 The foundational role of individual identity in the negotiation of creative autonomy[11]

actualize their own creative ambitions. Interviews also revealed that it was this distinctive tendency among PDs that was the core driver of creativity in a highly commercialized television industry:

> Basically, PDs follow something enjoyable to them. I don't think James Cameron initially designed the concept of *Avatar* to make a fortune. Probably, the starting point of *Avatar* production would have been like … 'This should be interesting'. It is the basic mind-set of creative workers who make video content – we start to think something new when it seems enjoyable to us.
>
> *(Interviewee WL)*

Discussion

My interviews have revealed that creative workers do not exclusively seek their own creative ambitions; in fact, the PDs I interviewed were not dramatically different from the ordinary workers of any occupational field who wish to make a living from their work in an organization. Alongside their creative ambitions as a creative self, interviewees presented a high level of interest in maintaining a good level of economic stability by attaining a stable organizational status. When considering the long term, PDs also desired to shape a more positive professional career path by managing their reputation and networks. Overall, the most distinctive characteristic of PDs as creative laborers was the persistence with which they sought individual satisfaction from the creative production process throughout their career trajectories based on their individual identity as a creative self. This becomes the core foundation for explaining why we need to consider the importance of providing a good level of creative autonomy to creative laborers for the sustainable development of organizations and the industry as a whole.

These findings are dissimilar to common assumptions that have denied the possibility for creative autonomy to exist within the commercialized cultural/creative industries. Although the market circumstances of the entertainment television industry are undoubtedly efficiency-led, interviews revealed that creative workers were continually seeking to broaden the scope in which they were able to express their own creative ambitions through their programs. Rather than being 'tendentially eliminated' over time (Adorno 1991), the form of creative autonomy held by individual creative workers has come to have a more complex and multi-layered structure within the commercialized creative industries. Some may argue that this concept of negotiated creative autonomy and its emphasis on the key role of the individual identity of creative laborers may reinforce one of the well-known tendencies of creative organizations, which tend to let creative workers take full responsibility for the production process and its result, without offering an appropriate level of protection to the workers when innovations fail (Ross 2009; Gill and Pratt 2008). However, I believe that my approach rather provides a firm reason to guarantee a good level of creative autonomy to laborers, as it shows the irreplaceable value of individual creative workers.

From my own research, it appeared that the external working conditions and atmosphere, which are intentionally designed to motivate creative laborers to work more passionately, are not enough to compel creative workers to continue in a demanding creative career (as I myself have experienced), and I have sought to understand what motivates television PDs who maintain such an existence. The enjoyment of creative workers in the creative production process cannot be deliberately shaped or educated externally, through factors such as organizational standards or norms. The majority of interviewees observed that their 'seemingly insane' choice to continue the PD career is possible because of their innate tendency to enjoy producing something interesting for themselves and audiences (Interviewees OJ, YJ, WL, HS, JL, YP, BM, and JP). Although in some ways, I am arguing that the ability to enjoy the creative production process is innate and rooted in an individual's personality, not deliberately shaped or managed by structure or external pressures, this is however distinct from the myth of creative genius as the ability to enjoy the process does not guarantee the quality of the work.

Of course, creative laborers' individual identities are surely affected by the commercial market environment and organizational pressures, and the level of creative autonomy could be largely limited. But the individual identity of creative workers as a creative self still produces the core creative value of the industry, and their strong tendency to actualize their own creative ambitions becomes the essential grounds to bring innovation to the market. Such intrinsically motivated workforces, which have also been professionalized with specialized knowledge, skills, and networks, cannot easily be replaced with marketing strategies or risk-averse management logic, and this irreplaceable value of individual creative workers becomes one of the core assets of the contemporary creative industries. This leads us to the need to combine the ideals of individual creative workers with the overall aims of creative organizations. To do so, cultural and media firms need to understand the certain tendencies creative workers have, naturally developing their multiple identities and endeavoring to satisfy their core desire to bring creativity to the industry, by negotiating their level of creative autonomy.

Throughout this chapter, I have observed the need to understand creative laborers as a group of people who desire not only to maintain their own creative ambitions but who also care about their organizational status and professional careers. To do this, I introduced a new conceptual framework of creative autonomy with the idea of multiple identities of creative workers, and attempted to analyze the compound attitudes of creative laborers, who desire not only to actualize personal creative ambition but also to maintain a good level of economic stability and a professional career for the longer term. I believe this approach allows us to better understand the intricately twisted and complex relationship between commerce and creativity throughout the creative laborer process. Such a recognition leads us to rethink the need to develop an appropriate organizational management strategy that understands the importance of providing a proper level of creative autonomy to creative laborers, to enable them to assertively bring core creative values to the organization.

Acknowledgments

I would like to thank Chris Bilton for his review and encouragement with this chapter.

Notes

1 This chapter is drawn from my PhD dissertation, entitled 'The multiple identities of creative labourers and negotiated creative autonomy: An empirical research with light-entertainment television PDs in South Korea' (An 2016).

2 The position of PD, which is a central role in the television production process, is known to exist only in South Korea. Among South Korean PDs, the term 'PD' is considered to be rather ambiguous and many use the term interchangeably with that of 'Producer'. Previous studies share the perspective that the abbreviation PD stands for a variety of word combinations, including: Planning Director; Program Director; Producing Director; or Producer-Director. Among these, Producer-Director is thought to be the optimal understanding of the role as a PD both produces and directs a program. The particular historical background will be described in the next section.

3 Due to the tendency for Korean entertainment programs to still be produced primarily within an in-house production system, most PDs who wish to establish their career need to belong to a stable broadcasting organization, at least until they have become sufficiently professionalized.

4 For this research, I conducted semi-structured and in-depth interviews with 16 PDs (Main PDs) currently working in the Korean entertainment TV industry. They were working in the light-entertainment genre, across various types of broadcasting organizations (including terrestrial broadcasters, cable broadcasting companies, and production companies) and employment types (full-time, part-time, and freelance). To closely observe the lived experiences of creative autonomy within the organization-based working environment, the specific career stage of Main PD, which plays a core role during the program production process in the Korean television industry, was carefully selected (the average career length was 14.4 years).

5 In 1973, KBS-TV became the public broadcasting organization, KBS, due to an amendment of Broadcast Law.

6 Chang-Bong Choi was a media professional who had both studied the media industries and experienced US television production. According to an interview with Choi, although he insisted that at least one year would be needed to create a new TV broadcasting station, the military government offered him only three months (Baek et al. 2008). The improvised launch of KBS-TV was barely completed on 25 December 1961 and a foreign film was the first program to be aired as no original content had yet been created. See Yu et al. (2007).

7 The term AD is, in some ways, inappropriate because an AD supports a PD throughout the whole production process. It may be more logical to use the terms 'APD' or 'AP' ('Assistant PD'), but the term AD can be interpreted to have come about in an atmosphere in which the role of Director is believed to be more influential than that of a Producer.

8 The *Doje* (도제) system is similar to that of the training process in the US film industry for project-based production teams, which offers small tasks to trainees and allows them to learn by watching their seniors in action (see Defillippi and Arthur 1998).

9 The length of training period as both AD and Ordinary PD varies according to each organizational circumstances. The majority of my interviewees confirmed that it takes approximately five to eight years to become a Main PD in the light-entertainment genre.

10 PDs who started their career as freelancers tend to have a somewhat different understanding of the debut; however the term 'debut' or 'Ip-bong' here refers to the time when a PD produces a program as the first Main PD and handles the program production from idea incubation to post-production stage.

11 In this figure, the starting point of the organizational identity is at the middle of the crafting stage. This reflects the specificity of the organizational identity construction process, which is not automatically constructed by entering into an organization, but is gradually formulated by experiencing and understanding various organizational norms, rules, and standards.

References

Adorno, T. W. (1991) *The Culture Industry: Selected Essays on Mass Culture.* London: Routledge.

Adorno, T. W. and Horkheimer, M. (1992) *Dialectic of Enlightenment.* London: Verso.

Arthur, M. B. (2008) Examining contemporary careers: A call for interdisciplinary inquiry. *Human Relations,* 61: 163–86.

Baek, M., Kang, K. and Lee, S. (2008) Seoul television (KBS-TV) ui chogi bangsong jojig munhwa hyeongseong (The Birth of a State-run Broadcasting Station in Korea Focusing on the Formation of Early Organizational Culture of KBS-TV). *Hangug Bangsonghagbo,* 22: 189–229.

Banks, M. (2007) *The Politics of Cultural Work.* Basingstoke: Palgrave Macmillan.

Bourdieu, P. (1993) *The Field of Cultural Production: Essays on Art and Literature,* New York: Columbia University Press.

Cho, J., Shin, Y. and Cho, D. (2000) *PD ga sseuneun PD lon (The Theory of PD System).* Seoul: Danagihoeg.

Davenport, J. (2006) UK film companies: Project-based organizations lacking entrepreneurship and innovativeness? *Creativity and Innovation Management,* 15: 250–57.

Defillippi, R. J. and Arthur, M. B. (1998) Paradox in project-based enterprise: The case of film making. *California Management Review,* 40.

Dimaggio, P. (1977) Market structure, the creative process, and popular culture: Toward an organizational reinterpretation of mass-culture theory. *The Journal of Popular Culture,* 11**:** 436–52.

Eikhof, D. R., Haunschild, A. and Schöler, F. (2012) Behind the scenes of boudarylessness: Careers in German theatre. In: Mathieu, C. (ed.), *Careers in Creative Industries.* New York: Routledge.

Gill, R. and Pratt, A. (2008) In the social factory? Immaterial labour, precariousness and cultural work. *Theory, Culture & Society,* 25: 1–30.

Lee, E. (1993) Hangug bangsong peulodyuseo nodongsijang-ui guseongjeog teugseong-e gwanhan yeongu (The Study of the Compositional Factors of the Labour Market of the Korean Broadcasting Producers). Masters Thesis, Seogang University.

Mcrobbie, A. (2002a) Clubs to companies: Notes on the decline of political culture in speeded up creative worlds. *Cultural Studies,* 16: 516–31.

Mcrobbie, A. (2002b) From Holloway to Hollywood: Happiness at Work in the New Cultural Economy? In*:* Du Gay, P. and Pryke, M. (eds.), *Cultural Economy: Cultural Analysis and Commercial Life.* London; Thousand Oaks, CA: Sage.

Oakley, K. (2009) From Bohemia to Britart – art students over 50 years. *Cultural Trends,* 18: 281–94.

Ross, A. (2009) *Nice Work If You Can Get It: Life and Labor in Precarious Time.,* New York; London: New York University Press.

Stoyanova, D. and Grugulis, I. (2012) Tournament careers: Working in UK television. In: Mathieu, C. (ed.), *Careers in Creative Industries.* New York: Routledge.

Ursell, G. (2000) Television production: Issues of exploitation, commodification and subjectivity in UK television labour markets. *Media, Culture & Society,* 22: 805–25.

Van Zoonen, L. (1998) A professional, unreliable, heroic marionette (M/F: Structure, agency and subjectivity in contemporary journalisms. *European Journal of Cultural Studies,* 1: 123–43.

Yu, S.-Y., Park, Y.-G. and Lee, S.-G. (2007) *Hangug-ui midieo sahoemunhwasa (The Sociocultural History of the Korean Media).* Seoul: Hangug-eonlonjaedan.

9

Brain drain or brain gain?

Examining the talent networks in audiovisual coproduction between Taiwan and China

Hsiao-Ling Chung

Creative migrants and the talent flow

According to theories on the creative economy (Howkins 2001) and creative class (Florida 2005, 2002), talent-driven economy thrives on the prospect that the cultural and creative input of those that are highly skilled and idea-driven competitively yield economic output. In particular, individualized motivations, largely project-based ad hoc working patterns, informal hiring, and non-linear career progression of the talented make the creative industries different to other sectors and have led to a new way of organizing business (Oakley 2006). Also, creative processes require diverse individuals to interact with each other and with the wider social and cultural context to generate and exchange ideas (Bilton and Cummings 2014). The intangible influence of talent is not determined quantitatively (Hesmondhalgh and Baker 2011; Pratt 2008; Shearmur 2007), and depends on a clustering infrastructure that brings it together (Turok 2003). Correspondingly, it is found that the motivation and mobility of 'cultural talent' to migrate is driven by the expectations of the talent for better economic and career possibilities, access to larger markets, interaction with other producers of culture, and entrepreneurial pursuits for international reputation (Solimano 2008).

Insofar as each talent is seen as a mobile vessel of cultural influence through creative interaction, it is suggested that the phenomenon of 'creative migration', especially how cross-border talent collaborations may further enrich the tacit knowledge of creative individuals who were involved in the process, deserves more understanding (Hansen 2009; Carr et al. 2005). Such talent collaboration and migration would ideally contribute to a healthy knowledge flow and cultural stimulation, as the phenomenon of brain drain has been a key feature of the global cultural industries. However, with economically valuable individuals clustering in more promising countries or regions, this phenomenon could be critiqued from the perspective of the imbalance of intangible resources, skills, and knowledge between talent sending and receiving societies (Zweig 2006; Kuznetsov and Sabel 2006). Yet, the case of Taiwan demonstrates that such 'creative migration' might promote cultural diversity and exchanges, creating a counter-siphon effect called *brain gain* (Carr et al. 2005).

A recent milestone in the cross-strait *brain drain* history between Taiwan and China occurred in 2001, when China entered the World Trade Organization (WTO), which led to rapid economic reforms and urbanization, resulting in a large market and talent demand from businesses in China (Zweig 2006; Leng 2002). In particular, as Zweig (2006) has noted, aside from developing infrastructure and industries, China, in its national plans, also endeavored to reverse the talent outflow, for example, the global trend stretching from the 1960s to the 1990s, when more technical and creative personnel chose to migrate to North American and European countries; in response, the number of returnees increased sharply since approximately 2000, with an increasing number of talented people abroad returning/moving to China, and China being the current talent hotspot in Asia. These were also the peak years for Taiwanese talents to establish themselves in the Chinese audiovisual sector, starting with collaborations with the Hong Kong film industry, and leading on to Chinese TV and film industries over the said decade (Ku 2011; Liu 2007).

Looking at the present Taiwanese cultural and creative industries (CCI) development, the current trends show a talent inclination towards China, which has caused increasing anxiety in the cultural sector in Taiwan, as the former culture minister Lung Ying-tai warned publicly that 'our CCI talent are "hooked away" by China!'.[1] However, it would be insufficient to see the current tendency of talent migrating as simply a brain drain, or as an ongoing physical loss of talented individuals to China. Rather, the notion of 'creative talent flow' is more adequate to explain the dynamics of the cultural and creative exchange between talents from both sides, which contributes to the further development of talent and their cultural and professional knowledge.

This chapter firstly provides a background to such a flow to show the wider economic-political-cultural complexity that Taiwanese talents need to absorb when they make the crossing; and secondly, instead of China-focused market research, the study discusses the context of Taiwan, whose position in the existing discussion is rather marginalized and less explored. Emphasis is given to understanding the why and how of these moves, in order to draw out implications for future policy development.

The political-economic-cultural setting

Taiwan is an island state, with a multicultural society influenced by both Western and Asian cultures and civilizations. Taiwan experienced the presence of the Dutch and Spanish during the 17th century, followed by the Japanese colonization from 1895 to 1945. Later, 'mainlanders' arrived in Taiwan from all parts of China at the end of the Chinese Civil War in 1949. This has provided Taiwan, the Formosa Island, with a rich, diverse cultural heritage deeply rooted in Chinese culture. Of its current 23 million people, more than 18 million are 'native' Taiwanese, that is, descendants of the Chinese who migrated from the southern provinces of China during the 18th and 19th centuries. Taiwan's population also contains about half a million indigenous residents, believed to be of Malayo-Polynesian origin.[2]

The cross-strait talent network (CSTN) in this study refers to talent exchange and collaboration in the audiovisual sector under the evolving cross-strait relationship (CSR) between Taiwan and China, separated by the Taiwan Strait in the west Pacific Ocean. This separation has been characterized by political tensions after the Chinese Civil War. Following the end of the civil war in 1949, the Republic of China (ROC) government, under the Chinese Nationalist Party (Kuomintang or KMT) withdrew to Taiwan, and a period of Martial Law followed until 1987. During these four decades, Taiwan saw major political, social, cultural, and industrial progress.

Politically speaking, since 1949 maintaining the status quo of bilateral and international relations has been a challenge for Taiwan. Retrospectively, the CSR can be said to have opened up when the KMT government lifted Martial Law and began to allow its citizens to visit relatives in China in 1987. This was regarded as a policy based on humanitarian considerations, and it subsequently further expanded into cross-strait trading (West 1993), culminating with the '92 Consensus'. During the cross-strait meeting in 1992, a consensus as the basis for peaceful CSR development was reached on routine affairs, to the effect that 'both sides of the Taiwan Straits adhere to the one-China principle with respective interpretations'.[3]

Yet important political changes have taken place in the context of Taiwan since the year 2000, as the new pro-Taiwan independence Democratic Progressive Party (DPP) took up government for the first time in Taiwan's history. The DPP's relatively confrontational stance towards the CSR, pushing the 'one country on each side' doctrine as it did, resulted in increased CSR tension, and led to Taiwan being marginalized internationally (Lin 2008). Since the KMT's regaining of power in 2008, the government has re-opened CSR negotiations with China according to the principle of 'putting Taiwan first for the benefit of the people', resulting in today's modes of exchange.

Economically speaking, Taiwanese industries have experienced sharp growth since the 1990s with the opening of cross-strait trading. This political and economic progress has been accompanied by a cultural and democratization process in Taiwan, with public debates increasingly involving issues such as Chinese tradition and modernity, multicultural and democratic society and, most importantly, the nature of 'Taiwanese identity' (Wang 2004; Hsiau 2000). As a result, it may be said that by the end of the 1990s, policies in Taiwan largely responded to the voice of Taiwanese consciousness, the needs of social integration and, more significantly, economic transformation.

However, an increasing number of businesses relocating to China placed economic pressure on Taiwan, in that it led to declining job opportunities in the island (Day and Yao 2004). These developments occurred at a time when Taiwan gradually was starting to lose its economic advantages in the manufacturing and high-tech sectors, both globally and regionally, especially in addressing the growing competition from China, when Taiwan gained formal entrance into the WTO in 2002 (Rigger 2013). Consequently, the Taiwanese government introduced 'Challenge 2008 – National Development Plan' (Executive Yuan (Cabinet) Taiwan 2002), a six-year policy guideline to create new national competitive advantages. Substantial investments were made that aimed to turn Taiwan into a 'Green Silicon Island', that is, a clean, high-tech, and innovative island-state. Significantly, among the ten major development plans of the policy guideline, the CCI were for the first time included in the national development agenda, and have since then been regarded as the new engine for Taiwan's future development. Wide-ranging strategies have been taken to increase so-called *soft power*, to present Taiwan on the global stage through its strengths and talent in the arts, design, culinary skills, fashion, tourism, and so on. Analysts believe that these efforts are also aimed at distinguishing Taiwan from China by establishing its own cultural brand and identity (Wang and Lu 2008).

However, due to a relatively small domestic market, foreign trade remains crucial to Taiwan. In fact, China is now Taiwan's most important trading partner – Taiwan's largest export destination and second largest source of imports – representing over 21 percent of total trade, up from 7 percent in 2002 (Meltzer 2014). Furthermore, in order to boost cross-strait economic integration, the most significant trade agreement, Economic Cooperation Framework Agreement (ECFA), was signed in 2010 (Cross-strait Economic Cooperation Committee Taiwan (2010). The agreement was regarded by the WTO Director-General as notable not only because it would considerably improve CSR and help to integrate Taiwan further into the world economy,[4] but because it was taken as a major cultural achievement, as CSR would witness more progress if both sides increased cultural exchange and cooperation.[5] Since then, CSR has been improving dramatically, culminating in a historical dialogue between the leaders of China and Taiwan on November 7, 2015 in Singapore, the very first meeting between leaders from both sides since the Chinese Civil War ended in 1949. While it may be seen on the one hand that China recognizes the need for a new approach in its relations to Taiwan, in times of global and local economic turmoil, Taiwan also needs to adopt a prudent approach to advance its interests.

Culturally speaking, the issue between Taiwan and China is more complex, despite the two sharing ethnic and cultural backgrounds (Hughes 1997; Tu 1996). While cross-strait CCI collaboration is encouraged as a gateway to advance the regional and global markets for Chinese-speaking cultural products, it has caused certain concerns for practitioners, scholars, and authorities alike on issues ranging from talented Taiwanese migrating to China to CCI production practices that often lead to the dilemma of having to choose between 'either' embracing Chinese values 'or' preserving Taiwanese culture (Zhao and Yan 2012). Other issues include ECFA follow-up consultations on CCI development in Taiwan addressing topics such as IPR protection agreements, to safeguard the interests of Taiwanese talent and firms (Mainland Affairs Council Taiwan 2011).

According to the official 'White Papers on SMEs in Taiwan' (Ministry of Economic Affairs 2015), and the 'Media Reform: Objectives and Strategy' documents,[6] the Taiwanese government is using market competition, rather than state intervention, as its governing principle in its industrial developments, while encouraging businesses to maintain self-discipline, that is, the ability to be self-motivated and expand while staying on track with the overall development goals of the government, suggesting a low degree of government control. Conversely, the authorities in China have sought to develop CCI strategically through their 11th, 12th and 13th 'National Five Year Development Plans' (2005–2020), to transform China from 'the big nation of people to the great nation of talents' by measures such as encouraging its CCI enterprises to operate cross-regionally and offering incentives to overseas talents, especially those from Taiwan who share Chinese cultural and linguistic backgrounds (Tan 2015; Feng 2014; Fang 2014).

Overall, as the series of 'Cross-strait CCI City Competitiveness Reports' (Asian-Pacific Cultural Creative Industries Association 2015) indicate, Taiwan currently enjoys advantages in its soft power, while China has long-term strengths in capital mobilization, market size, and centralized policy strategy; however, both sides face issues of international competition and demand for talent. The intricate political-economic-cultural interrelationship serves as a backdrop to the increasing CSTN. Rather than focusing on regulations concerning cross-strait audiovisual coproduction, the following section reviews the recent Taiwanese policies related to the notion of talent, talent development, and exchange practices.

'Personnel' exchange in the Motion Picture Act

On the subject of talent exchange, there are strict limitations in terms of quotas for personnel exchange in film industry policies and laws in Taiwan. The Motion Picture Act of Taiwan came into effect in 1983 and included 52 articles regarding content regulation, production, and distribution. With respect to foreign talent exchange and personnel hiring, the Film Law Enforcement Bylaws, first enacted in 1984, state that the hiring of foreign personnel requires equal entry conditions as for Taiwanese personnel. During the mid-1990s, the number of talent exchanges began to increase, particularly due to the regulation of the Operational

Direction of Mass Media Business Conducting News Coverage and Production in Mainland China, introduced in 1992 (Government Information Office 1992), which stipulated the coproduction quota for mainland Chinese members to 'no more than 1/3 of the total number of personnel and staff' within the entire Taiwanese-based production team.

In fact, it is found that a general notion of 'talent' in screen industries has been conceptualized by the Taiwanese authorities as 'personnel' of specialized knowledge for technical expertise and industrial know-how (Council of Cultural Affairs (CCA) 2009b, 2004). As cross-strait trade began to increase during the 1990s, the Taiwanese government further enacted three sets of laws to define the conditions and regulations concerning cross-strait talent exchange and franchise trading and broadcasting scenarios: (1) The Licensing Law for Chinese Audiovisual and Publication to be Imported or Broadcasted in Taiwan (1993); (2) The Execution Principles for Chinese Filmmaking Personnel to Participate in Taiwanese Domestic Movie Production (2009); and (3) The Hour Regulation of Chinese Audiovisual Program to be Broadcasted in Taiwan (2011). The Execution Principles set a strict quota (33 percent) for Chinese personnel on Taiwanese-based coproduction projects, which applied to actors, directors, and producers, as well as arts and technical departments. While the Taiwanese government acknowledged that talent exchange, both on and off screen personnel exchange, in the Pan-Chinese region through coproduction is an inevitable trend (Ministry of Culture 2013), it was yet to recognize the significance of the intangible and tacit potential through talent exchange via coproductions (Wei 2005).

'Talent' exchange in cultural and creative industries policies

The concept of 'talent' started to be acknowledged and broadened when Taiwan joined the global CCI trend from the late 1990s. There has been consistency throughout the government's discourse and measures in terms of how talent can be 'trained' into becoming 'specialists' through technical-oriented and market-geared curricula. More specifically the 'talent' of these individuals is seen as acquired knowledge that can be reproduced from training courses implemented in the higher education system (Yang and Huang 2011). Meanwhile, 'talent' is also perceived as unique individuals originating and nourished within a unique cultural environment, who then draw on their personal experience as inspiration for creative, culture-based productions and help define culture through delivering a 'cultural image' (CCA 2009a, 2004). A similar focus on the 'creative' can also be identified in *Creative Taiwan* (2009), the first ministry-level Action Plan to promote CCI. It set out its objective to transform Taiwan into 'an Asia-Pacific confluence of cultural and creative industries' and has specified the importance of formulating a government-sponsored networking platform and database for matchmaking talents such as actors and screenplay writers with the widening regional market.

With regard to talent exchange, the White Paper in 2004 started to emphasize the significance of transforming the CSR into a positive drive to allow the domestic CCI to reach a bigger market (CCA 2004). Various subsidy programs have therefore been introduced to encourage cross-strait talent exchange, as it is essentially the 'exchange of culture'. However, an economic-oriented perspective on the value of talent prevails in recurring statements, through the uses of phrases and words such as 'of high potential' and 'profitable'. Throughout the *Creative Taiwan* plan, CCI were also seen as a new economic system, based heavily on individual talent and their cultural backgrounds. The audiovisual industry, in particular, was designated as one of the 'flagship industries' to drive a culture-based new economy. In sum, both the *White Paper* and *Creative Taiwan* envisioned regional and global talent exchange through audiovisual coproduction as the potential gateway to bring the waning Taiwanese film industry into a 'renaissance'. By comparing the DPP-formulated *Challenge 2008* (2002) with the KMT-formulated *Creative Taiwan* (2009), a distinctive paradigm shift with regards to China and its CCI market potential to Taiwan can be seen, that is, a change from 'potential competitor' to 'cooperative partners'. Apparently, the Taiwanese authorities needed to recognize that the practice of talent collaboration is an inevitable trend.

In this sense, it is important to look into the latest Cultural Ministry's CCI development guideline, 'Production Commercialization Value: Construction and Innovation of CCI Value Chain Program' (2013–2016) (Ministry of Culture 2013a). While its 'Talent Cultivation and Training' sub-plan is acknowledged as a response strategy to China's aggressive actions in attracting Taiwanese talent, the program as a whole is limited and limiting in that it still emphasizes the development of skills training, certification systems, marketing competence, and brokering talent through international exchange and business courses. As such, a training-based focus may be seen as the government's effort to create an enabling environment and policy framework that is suitable to the dynamic and diverse nature of skill development; however, the potential and need to cultivate and nurture talent through existing and increasing talent collaborations is overlooked.

'Service providers' in the Economic Cooperation Framework Agreement

The groundbreaking Economic Cooperation Framework Agreement (ECFA), which took effect in 2011, is regarded as a milestone in cross-strait service industries development and in steering the Taiwanese market into the pan-Chinese region. As seen from its preamble, ECFA is valid 'across the Taiwan Strait, adhering to the principles of equality, reciprocity and progressiveness and with a view to strengthening cross-strait trade and economic relations'. Articles in the agreement include film and television broadcasts as one of the service-based industries. Based on this context, however, the documentation has not specified the types of talent exchange, except for mentioning cross-strait audiovisual coproduction. Regardless of its deficiency in addressing detailed regulations on exchange, the trade agreement – in regards to the relationships and roles of service providers and receivers – implies how cross-strait talent exchange is becoming a common practice within the audiovisual sector. For example, in Article 5, the '"service provider" refers to any individual from either Taiwan or China who provides service'. In addition to highlighting the importance of refocusing and redefining 'talents' from a professional service-based perspective, the agreement may be regarded as an instance of the Taiwanese government encouraging local talent to provide their skills as a form of professional service in cross-strait trading.

The task of the above review was to demonstrate, firstly, that evolving conditions relating to policy, economy, and culture have triggered the transformation of Taiwan's economy, and hence the cross-strait talent exchange mode involved has moved from a one-way exchange to a two-way collaboration. From personnel, talent to service provider, and talent development, the cross-strait context remains the subject of on-going change. Yet the apparent talent flow is often viewed more pessimistically, with Taiwan's tacit resources being 'drained' to China (Jen 2015; Tsen 2012), and the roles played by talent in such a flow have been taken for granted within a market-oriented policy and phenomenon.

Therefore, given the issues of Taiwanese talent development and how the greater Chinese market provides wider prospects, an understanding of how the talents themselves perceive the CSTN is needed. In particular, it will be helpful to closely look at how 'producers' – who are the organizing and 'behind the scene' talents – perceive their roles within the network. This

Table 9.1 List of interviewed producers

No.	*Interviewed producers/ title*	*Working experience*
1	Film producer/Production director	20
2	Film producer/Self-employed/Funder of audiovisual production studio	6
3	Film producer/Chairperson of film production/distribution company	30
4	TV/Film producer/Freelance	22
5	TV/Film producer/Freelance	25
6	TV/Film producer/Managing director of audiovisual production studio	15
7	TV Producer/Senior artists' agent	10
8	TV Producer/President of multimedia production association	15
9	TV/Film producer/Production executive	4
10	TV/Film producer/Chairperson of media corporation group	38

is because they play key roles in the upstream production sector where the economic potential and cultural value of the content is determined. This qualitative empirical research involved ten face-to-face, semi-structured in-depth interviews carried out during the period from February to July 2014, with Taiwanese film/TV producers whose average industry experience was 18.4 years. They were in charge of official approved coproductions between 2011 and 2014.

By drawing out the implications of the CSTN in coproduction practice, this following section aim to build on the above findings from three major issues: (1) To examine the current brain drain or brain gain with regard to talent network practices; (2) To look more closely at the cultural-commercial spectrum in the talent network; and (3) To highlight the implications for talent development in the converging Chinese and Asian regional market.

Producers' perception of the talent network in cross-strait coproductions

Producers' mediating and moderating roles for network and talent development

Firstly, the producers' open, yet mixed feelings towards the talent network can be said to reflect the increasingly market and commercial-driven CSTN, yet the producers' central concerns are still fundamentally about producing cultural and creative content, and to a larger extent 'independent' production, that is to produce the film with their own means and not being controlled by the majors or investors, which can be seen from the following extracts:

> The talent network depends very much on producers' personal connections, bringing a proposal and visiting all sorts of different people, trade fairs … China is too big and competitive; you need some local informants to get to meet with the distributors or investors, just to try to get the production funded.
>
> *(Interview 6)*

> The approval system in China is a huge challenge for Taiwanese producers' communication ability, now we can only work on a single production proposal at a time, one-off, and trading on my social network, we are not yet able to establish any long-term strategic partnership, so I just need to explore all possible routes when we are planning.
>
> *(Interview 1)*

It has also become obvious that the Taiwanese side is largely undercapitalized, and in need of market and Chinese investment, and it is therefore found that the producers play a role as a 'creative, culture and commercial gatekeeper' for incoming resources. This is seen in the comments from a senior female TV producer who has been living in Beijing for more than eight years, who commented on how she perceived her role in the CSTN:

> After these years living and working there, I can operate things in all their complexity with ease now, because I am a weaver in China. (with gestures) The web extends outward with complicated layers upon layers, and all the nodes represent different connections … Besides, apart from knowing who, knowing who has what is more critical! Now I can drink massive amounts, because I have to know their bargaining power, and this will influence my decision, especially on whether we could achieve consensus on topic and content.
>
> *(Interview 7)*
>
> The 'routes', 'connections' and 'layers' all underline the complexity involved in the network. However, looking at the individual level, the fact that the talent is growing into and with the network is considered by most interviewed producers to be beneficial, as their individual learning and growth is embedded within the market growth. Both young and senior film/TV producers also reflected thus, in a rather sentimental tone:
>
> We did look around for possible Chinese partners through all kinds of our connections, but some were just too arrogant … But as one of the younger generation film producers in Taiwan, I know it is the trend and reality, I am very clear that I need to join the trend and learn all those things, the fact is Taiwan is too small, we need to reach out.
>
> *(Interview 2)*
>
> I have worked in Taiwan for film and TV productions for more than 25 years, and I just found that my job is now shifting from being art-oriented to business-oriented. I worked so hard in the past only to satisfy what directors wanted, but now I have to control the budget seriously in order to cope with the complicated coproduction practices … The learning environment in China is much better!
>
> *(Interview 5)*

In addition, vivid examples are given by a senior female producer, who sees her own career growth as a direct result of cross-strait coproduction, and a senior producer, who shared his talent incubation plan:

> I started out as an actress's agent; pure and simple. My role has changed substantially because I am now a producer who can work with stakeholders in China and then connect and contribute back to Taiwan! I would like my own career portfolio to be developed further by helping other Taiwanese talents achieve their goals!
>
> *(Interview 7)*
>
> It's an interesting and challenging time for talent, as we are trying to bring the right talents for the right productions, and all kinds of opportunities have become possible, so we are now investing in pitch training and how to develop their original ideas and

> story-telling ... It's about being able to recognize our Taiwanese talent and then actually being able to do something with it!
>
> *(Interview 10)*

Indeed, the fact that the talents contribute to and grow with the network as the producers see their roles expand during the process directly highlights the issues regarding their development and future strategies.

Creative first, commercial second, and culture-centered production

Secondly, it is found that the influx of network resources is introduced alongside the network development with discernible tensions and pressures on producers. Hence, it is notable that the reflexivity of producers' cultural identity also reveals that the CSTN development evolves with their personal inner-level awareness, struggles and professional growth.

> It is about helping each other, but I have to say, Taiwanese talents are losing our creative advantages quickly, as the quality of the talent pool in China has improved dramatically, we need to have more of a sense of crisis.
>
> *(Interview 4)*

> We approached some private investors in China, but it is *not* [emphasis mine] about whether we need to do something for them in order to get their funding, we are very clear about our bottom-line! I need to make sure that the director or scriptwriter is ok with those things that may affect their original ideas.
>
> *(Interview 5)*

> Now many first-tier actors, scriptwriters, directors or production managers want to work on coproduction in order to make their way into China, but it is hard ... I spend a lot of time taking care of their over-expectations and frustration, because I would need to tell them that you can try your home-grown ideas, but be aware that the Chinese side may not want that.
>
> *(Interview 1)*

The awareness of the 'bottom-line', 'director's view', 'frustration' and 'homegrown' ideas, all indicate that the talent network, for the producer, involves balancing two opposites: commercial calculations and creative aspiration. Yet while the 'creative first, commercial second' accounts for more than their 'choice', this principle is no easy task, as can be seen below:

> If there are any concerns about getting into the CSTN network, it would be that I am afraid I might lose my own identity as a Taiwanese and independent producer, yet it is a long way to get to know about China and to find someone with a cultural sense and mutual understanding that I could truly work with.
>
> *(Interview 4)*

The above quotation shows that the 'localized ways' of doing 'business' underlie the pressing need to connect to the local culture in China, reflecting one of the prominent issues shared among the interviewees: Taiwanese talents now need to interact with the Chinese market in a steady and in-depth manner, so as to establish the necessary trust bonds with stakeholders.

But it may be seen that cultural exchange has proven to be more profound. The interviewees shared a prominent point, namely that in order to consolidate the 'localization' and 'relationships', the starting point has to be from culture, which is peoples' cultural exchange from both sides.

> Both sides have to promote cultural exchange, and film and TV coproduction is simply one of the many ways. Current coproduction is not the real cultural exchange, and it is more or less only revisions of scripts because of China's approval system … so intensive communication is greatly needed during the entire process.
>
> *(Interview 3)*

Brain gain through cultural and professional exchange

Thirdly, a self-learning curve can be found with the interviewees who further stressed the importance of the 'cultural' and 'localized' ways of interacting with the Chinese public and stakeholders, so as to carry out coproduction as a 'business', which might be taken as a strategic approach towards cross-strait coproduction.

> We now need to look at each coproduction project in a much broader way … I think the Taiwan brand is always there, but it's just been culturally emphasized more with our exchange increasing, now the producers should think that each coproduction is about building sub-brands, that is, each coproduction has to have a recognized Taiwanese cultural value that is absorbed into more and more levels of the network and into the people in China, to promote real cultural exchange from both sides.
>
> *(Interview 7)*

> It looks like Taiwan talents are now being recruited by China passively, but in reality I found that we are proactively establishing Taiwan's cultural brand through the Chinese market, and the truth is, the more interactions we have with them, the more we know ourselves.
>
> *(Interview 10)*

> We are working 'with' them, not working 'for' them! Through coproduction with them, we understand our cultural differences so as to really understand the cultural features of ourselves.
>
> *(Interview 6)*

Indeed, at the production level, it is evident that while networks emerge, producers and other talent might benefit from, and contribute to, the cultural vision of content-making and 'knowing ourselves' by working 'with' the Chinese counterparts, which is also illustrated below:

> The audiovisual industry needs creativity and ideas, which means attracting talents from diverse backgrounds. Such talent-based CCI infrastructure and process comes directly and naturally from what we mean by cultural content making … both on-screen and behind-the-scenes talent should see the greater Chinese market rather positively and objectively, because then we have more resources to invest in our own talent.
>
> *(Interview 10)*

Towards a bigger picture for talent development

Finally, when asked about their expectations in terms of prospects for talent development under the evolving regional market, most interviewed producers immediately commented and stressed that a broader vision on the CSTN upfront is needed. Production-led talent networking is the most fundamental infrastructure for triggering a broader economic return for cultural production and talent development, and such a consensus may be illustrated by the following extracts:

> With partners from both sides on board, we are becoming more appealing to other talents, be they Taiwanese or Chinese, actors, stylists, or cinematographers; and more importantly, we can draw more market attention ... we need a bigger audience for our work.
>
> *(Interview 2)*

> Looking back on the collaboration process, we Taiwanese should learn how to share resources, and not just keeping or hiding things for ourselves ... We need to make the pie bigger by sharing know-how and connections, be they local, regional, and more importantly international.
>
> *(Interview 8)*

> It's about our mentality ... instead of worrying about whether or how to enter the China market, it is critical to aim higher with a bigger picture and think about how Taiwanese talents' strength could go global, and then to try to mobilize the resources from China ... we should take their resources to prepare our talent in Taiwan. This gives a more diverse cultural soil for Taiwanese talents to grow, to learn, and to reflect on their own ability and identity; they need those to go further.
>
> *(Interview 10)*

Overall, empirical findings are characterized by three prominent points, as follows: (1) the producers' attitudes toward the talent network are very straightforward and open in that they all highlighted the unstoppable trends with CSTN despite the complicated cross-strait relationship, yet mixed feelings abound in terms of the ensuing trade-offs; (2) the purpose of coproduction fundamentally concerns fulfilling their creative aspirations, yet the fact of having to 'choose' between their own artistic pursuits and Chinese investors' preferences highlights issues concerning the cultural identity and values upheld by the producers; (3) while the producers' own self-driven entrepreneurship guides other Taiwanese talent through these constraints, the producers' somehow transformational experiences demonstrate that the talent's learning in the process results in the talent involved being able to be aware of and express their identity and grow.

Network characteristics and implications

The case of CSTN shows that such a network opens up challenges to individuals, as well as demands for personal and professional growth. CSTN practices have helped to create exchange and learning dynamics across the strait, and within and across talents, allowing Taiwanese talents to exploit a broader range of possibilities for future growth. While the current CSTN dynamics appears to be somewhat random, three prominent networking characteristics may be identified which emerge alongside some noticeable developmental implications for future prospects.

Entrepreneurial and individualised network

The self-driven entrepreneurial nature and actions of producers contribute to a dynamic, yet disconnected talent network. This shows that networks are driven by producers' entrepreneurial actions, which have consequences for the CSTN as a whole. Self-driven practices can be seen as the most important initial condition of the cross-strait and cross-culture networking dynamics, in the sense that these practices might guide the talents' enduring motivations and persistence through their personal or professional dilemmas. While the study shows that Taiwanese talents are capable of organizing and adapting themselves to the increasing network complexity in the regional market, due to the rather disorganised networking, the picture of how far the individualized and micro-level interactions and exchanges within the cross-strait regional system start to fall into patterns of a bigger picture still remains elusive.

The elusiveness of such networking reinforces the fact that the personal and emotional needs of these talents are increasingly neglected underneath the surface of the autonomous problem-solving process, and suggests that such networking is becoming even more demanding, which underlines the significance of the roles played by the behind-the-scenes producers who facilitate and filter the multi-directional sources for creativity from inception, which is essential in content production. Accordingly, the producers are as important as the 'creatives', and their impacts on bridging the culture, creativity, and commerce should be appropriately understood in terms of their internal logic driven by a mixed ecology of creative aspirations, choices, motives, practicality, and tensions.

Networking dependent on personal relationship

Personal networks have become a double-edged advantage in terms of maintaining a long-term and strategic network. It has become evident that such networks provide a basis for producers to grow the CSTN. It also shows that these social agents or informants from either side are only randomly brought into the network. Such findings indicate that the way in which the talent forms the network tend to be rather arbitrary.

In addition, it may be seen that the CSTN formation is the result of a combination of several different factors such as funding requirements, market demands, creative aspirations, and more importantly cultural compromises. Yet as has been shown, on the one hand, localized ways of networking have become crucial in substantiating the network and the individual talents within; on the other hand, the talent is being shaped and adapted in a cross-cultural way, and the cultural consensus and trust between them, as well as competition and collaboration, are becoming the building blocks of the network infrastructure. In other words, it is also important for cultural policy makers to understand that efforts in developing Taiwanese CCI talent are not just about proving technical, marketing, or managerial training; they are about providing opportunities and environments for personal interactions, and more profoundly, about cultivating the cultural literacy of the Taiwanese talent.

The platform needed for talent networking

The project-based, one-off nature of CSTN remains apparent, and this has resulted in the needed supporting system behind the talent being neglected. As suggested, the identification of the CSTN pattern has been a tricky task due to producers' largely self-driven practices and lack of long-term strategic partnerships and sharing of platforms among other local producers or agents, revealing problems concerning the prevalent one-off project-based network. As the findings show, with individual talent's growth, strategic planning with the CSTN in fact becomes desirable to accommodate the talent's professional development. Firstly, there is a need for a platform that is capable of building on the accumulation of the talent's collaboration experiences and resources. Secondly, it is suggested that the network needs to encompass individual self-transformational experiences, as the networks revolve around individual talent's learning, which is the most noticeable characteristic of the network phenomenon.

To conclude, this study contributes to knowledge in the field in that real CSTN practices and dynamics in the recent brain drain phenomena in Taiwan have been investigated in empirical terms. The Taiwanese case shows that talents are deeply embedded in, and evolve with idea-driven yet culture-sensitive CCI productions in the broader Chinese context. The network issues identified center firstly on the fact that creative talent should not be taken for granted as free agents for cultural exchange or tradable service providers for economic development, and should be positioned at the core of CCI development, as they contribute to building the infrastructures needed for the regional network. Secondly, the ongoing talent network shows that Taiwanese talents should take a broader view of the CSTN, seeing China as presenting an opportunity to work with a creative pool of greater diversity, complexity, and commercial practices. In particular, the flow of Taiwanese talent to China should not be considered simply as brain drain, but as brain gain in the long run, as the nourishment of culture, expertise, identity recognition, and professional practices will benefit talent's accumulation of knowledge in regional CCI development.

Finally, as the CSTN is still emerging and evolving with the changing cross-strait relationship, it is worth observing its development in a broader context. It would be instructive to further investigate how the CSTN in CCI impacts upon other sectors and regional partnerships. It is also critical for future research to explore the role of intermediaries within such networks, as this study has indicated, but has not discussed in depth. Overall, understanding the reconfiguration of brain drain or brain gain is not about simply mapping content output as a result of networking and collaboration. Rather, it requires policy makers and practitioners to go beyond looking at the cross-strait relationship as a matter of balancing cultural or identity tensions between 'Taiwanese' and 'Chinese', to considering the nature of such CCI talent networks and tracking the growth and transformation of talents while they are pursuing their creative aspirations beyond geographical boundaries.

Acknowledgment

This chapter is partially based on Dr. Hsiao-Ling Chung's National Science Council (Ministry of Science and Technology)-funded research project: *Mapping the Talent Networks: The Cross-strait Audiovisual Content Collaboration between Taiwan and China* (NSC 102–2410-H-006–109).

Notes

1 Lung Ying-tai: CCI talent are hook away by China. Available at: http://www.chinatimes.com/newspapers/20130914000947-260115, *China Times* [online] September 14, 2013 [accessed June 15, 2015].

2 Taiwan History- An Overview. On-line Library of Formosan Association for Public Affairs (FAPA), Washington, US. Available from: http://www.fapa.org/generalinfo/Taiwan's_history.htm [accessed March 15, 2015].

3 The 1992 Consensus: Ensuring Cross-strait Peace and Prosperity, Office of the President of the Republic of China. Available at: http://english.president.gov.tw/Default.aspx?tabid=1124&itemid=34645&rmid=3048 [accessed June 9, 2015].
4 Statement from the World Trade Organization (WTO) Director-General Pascal Lam. In an interview with Taiwan's Central News Agency. Available at: http://taiwanreview.nat.gov.tw/ct.asp?xItem=114129&CtNode=1337&mp=1/ [accessed Feb 2, 2014].
5 Beijing mayor stresses ECFA's role in Cross-Strait cultural exchange. Available at: http://news.xinhuanet.com/english/china/2012-02/19/c_122721360.htm/ [accessed March 3, 2012].
6 *Taiwan's Media Reform: Objectives and Strategy.* Available at: http://www.taiwan.gov.tw/ct.asp?mp=999&xItem=13786&ctNode=1940/ [accessed March 19, 2014].

References

Asian-Pacific Cultural Creative Industries Association (2015) *Cross-strait Cultural and Creative Industries City Competitiveness Reports.* Taipei: Asian-Pacific Cultural Creative Industries Association.

Bilton, C. and Cummings, S. (2014) *Handbook of Management and Creativity*, 1st edn. Chichester: Edward Elgar

Carr, S. C., Inkson, K, and Thorn, K. (2005) From global careers to talent flow: reinterpreting 'brain drain'. *Journal of World Business*, 40(4): 386–98.

Council for Cultural Affairs Taiwan (CCA) (2004) *The White Paper on Cultural Policy.* Executive Yuan, Taiwan. Available at: http://english.cca.gov.tw/ct.asp?xItem=12192&ctNode=4063/ [accessed January 19, 2014].

Council for Cultural Affairs Taiwan (CCA) (2009a) Creative Taiwan – Cultural and Creative Industries Development Project – Action Plan. Available at: http://www.cci.org.tw/cci/upload/law/20100604104150-8dd3d038610f19c0bd08739c496f4052.pdf/ [accessed February 19, 2015].

Council of Cultural Affairs Taiwan (2009b) *The Motion Picture Act.* Available at: http://law.moj.gov.tw/LawClass/LawAll.aspx?PCode=P0040002/ [accessed May 24, 2014].

Cross-strait Economic Cooperation Committee Taiwan (2010) *Cross-Straits Economic Cooperation Framework Agreement.* Available at: http://www.ecfa.org.tw/ [accessed May 24, 2014].

Day, D. C. and Yao, A. (2004) Taiwan's National Identity and Political Integration across the Taiwan Strait. Paper presented at the conference 'Regional Integration, State-Building and Conflict Settlement in Europe and Asia', Oct. 11–12, 2004.

Executive Yuan (Cabinet) Taiwan (2002) *Challenge 2008: Six-Year National Development Plan.* Available at: http://www.gio.gov.tw/taiwan-website/4-oa/20020521/2002052101.html/ [accessed March 12, 2014].

Fang, C. (2014) Issues for cultural industries development in the 13th Five Year Plan. Smart Culture. Available at: http://tccanet.org.tw/article-619.html#.VNr92PmUclR/ [accessed March 18, 2015].

Feng, H. C. (2014) Cultural and creative industries: the economic engine for the next two decades. La Vie, (126): 106–8.

Florida, R. (2002) The economic geography of talent. *Annals of the Association of American Geographers*, 9(7): 743–55.

Florida, R. (2005) *The Flight of the Creative Class: The New Global Competition for Talent.* New York: HarperBusiness, HarperCollins.

Government Information Office (GIO), The Executive Yuan Taiwan (1992) *Operational Direction of Mass Media Business Conducting News Coverage and Production in Mainland China.* http://db.lawbank.com.tw/FSYS/FSYSLST.aspx?no=Q003 [accessed August 10, 2015].

Hansen, H. K. (2009) Migration of the creative class: evidence from Sweden. *Journal of Economic Geography*, 9(2): 191–206.

Hesmondhalgh, D. and Baker, S. (2011) *Creative Labor.* Abingdon and New York: Routledge.

Howkins, J. (2001) *The Creative Economy: How People Make Money from Ideas.* London: Allen Lane.

Hsiau, A. C. (2000) *Contemporary Taiwanese Cultural Nationalism.* New York: Routledge.

Hughes, C. (1997) *Taiwan and Chinese Nationalism: National Identity and Status in International Society.* London and New York: Routledge.

Jen, L. Y. (2015) *Exploring Taiwan Brain Drain Phenomenon – The Factors Analysis of Employees' Job Hopping Overseas Tendency in Taiwan.* Masters Thesis, National Chiao-Tung University, Taiwan.

Ku, S. L. (2011) *A Study on Opportunities and Difficulties of Film Co-production between Taiwan and China: Funds, Human Resources, and Market.* Masters Thesis, Shin-Hsin University, Taiwan.
Kuznetsov, Y. and Sabel, C. (2006) *Global Mobility of Talent from a Perspective of New Industrial Policy*, Research Paper No. 2006/144, UNU-WIDER. Available at: http://info.worldbank.org/etools/docs/library/201210/Search_Networks_final1.pdf/ [accessed August 19, 2014].
Leng, T. K. (2002) Economic globalization and it talent flows across the Taiwan Strait: the Taipei/Shanghai/Silicon Valley triangle. *Asian Survey*, 42(2): 230–50.
Lin, C. Y. (2008) *Re-establishment of Taiwan's Diplomacy and National Defense.* Paper presented in Institution of European and American Studies, Academia Sinica. Available at: http://www.mac.gov.tw/public/Attachment/052715311034.pdf/ [accessed June 18, 2014].
Liu Xiancheng (2007) The trend of cross-border interaction in the film industry in the Asian-Pacific Chinese region, *Movie Appreciation* 133:39–49.
Mainland Affairs Council Taiwan (2011) Mainland China Policy and Works. https://www.mac.gov.tw/News_Content.aspx?n=9223A12B5B31CB37&sms=35FA2C4073CF4DFB&s=-405B2DE84910291E [accessed September 12, 2015].
Meltzer, L. (2014) *Taiwan's Economic Opportunities and Challenges and the Importance of the Trans-Pacific Partnership.* Brookings Institution, Center for East Asia Policy Studies, East Asia Policy Paper, no. 2, January 2014. Available at: http://www.brookings.edu/~/media/research/files/papers/2013/09/30-taiwan-trans-pacific-partnership-meltzer/taiwan-trans-pacific-partnershipmeltzer-012014.pdf/ [accessed June 1, 2015].
Ministry of Culture Taiwan (2013a) *Production Commercialization Value: Construction and Innovation of CCI Value Chain Program (2013–2016).* Available at: http://www.ey.gov.tw/Upload/RelFile/26/698429/102000024963AB1020424.pdf/ [accessed June 18, 2015].
Ministry of Culture Taiwan (2013b) *Taiwan Audiovisual Industry in the Global Competition: Strategy and Policy.* Availableat:http://www.bamid.gov.tw/BAMID/Code/NewListContent47.aspx?id=64c780e9-1c93-4d64-a0c2-44920773d01e. [accessed May 2, 2014].
Ministry of Economic Affairs Taiwan (2015) White paper on SMEs. Available at: http://www.moeasmea.gov.tw/lp.asp?ctNode=307&CtUnit=36&BaseDSD=7&mp=2/ [accessed December 20, 2015]
Oakley, K. (2006) Include us out – Economic development and social policy in the creative industries. *Cultural Trends*, 15(4): 255–73.
Pratt, A. C. (2008) Creative cities: the cultural industries and the creative class. *Geografiskaannaler: Series B – Human Geography*, 90(2): 107–17.
Rigger, S. (2013) *Why Taiwan Matters: Small Island, Global Powerhouse.* Lanham, MD: Rowman & Littlefield.
Shearmur, R. (2007) The new knowledge aristocracy: a few thoughts on the creative class, mobility and urban growth. *Work Organization, Labor and Globalization*, 1(1): 31–47.
Solimano, A. (2008) The international mobility of talent and economic development: an overview of selected issues. In A. Solimano (ed.), *The International Mobility of Talent: Types, Causes and Development Impact.* Oxford: Oxford University Press, pp. 21–43.
Tan, C. Y. (2015) *Expectation for Cross-strait Economic Cooperation.* National Policy Research Foundation. Available at: http://www.npf.org.tw/1/15045/ [accessed May 20, 2015]
Tsen, C. M. (2012) *Brain Drain and Its Challenge to Brain Crisis in Taiwan.* Masters Thesis, National Cheng Chi University. Available at: http://nccur.lib.nccu.edu.tw/handle/140.119/57077 [accessed May 20, 2013].
Tu, W. M. (1996) Cultural identity and the politics of recognition in contemporary Taiwan. *China Quarterly*, (148): 1115–40.
Turok, I. (2003) Cities, clusters and creative industries: the case of film and television in Scotland. *European Planning Studies*, 11(5): 549–65.
Wang, H. Y. and Lu, Y. C. (2008) The conception of soft power and its policy implications: a comparative study of China and Taiwan. *Journal of Contemporary China*, 17(56): 425–47.
Wang, L. J. (2004) Multiculturalism in Taiwan: Contradictions and challenges in cultural policy. *International Journal of Cultural Policy*, 10(3): 301–18.
Wei, D. (2005) An exit or abyss? The challenges and opportunities of Taiwanese film coproductions. Available at: http://www.taiwancinema.com/ct_52452_332/ [accessed March 31, 2014].
West, L. A. (1993) *Reform of China's Foreign Trade System and Prospects for Freer Trade.* Center for International Research, U.S. Bureau of the Census.

Yang, Y. C. and Huang, W. Y. (2011) *Observations of the Predicaments of Training Creative Specialists in Taiwan's Cultural and Creative Industry – From the Aspect of Cultural Policy*. Available at: http://ir.lib.ksu.edu.tw/handle/987654321/13797/ [accessed May 24, 2014].

Zhao, Y. and Yan, R. T. (2012) The unresolved issues of cross-strait film and television cooperation after the adoption of the ECFA–National Policy Research Foundation Review No. 099-086. Available at: http://www.npf.org.tw/post/1/8165 [accessed June 11, 2015].

Zweig, D. (2006) Competing for talent: China's strategies to reverse the brain drain. *International Labor Review*, 145(1–2): 65–89.

10

Contemporary Chinese creatives as literati

Bjarke Liboriussen, Joaquin Lopez-Mugica, and Andrew White

Introduction

The importation of the creative industries[1] policy and discourse in China in the early twenty-first century has both reinforced the government's desire to encourage more innovation and amplified existing tensions over differing conceptions of creativity. Along with China's entry into the World Trade Organization (WTO) in 2001, the adoption of policies to develop the creative industries has bolstered the nation's rapid modernization program. Producers of creative content in China have found themselves having to navigate difficult domestic and international policy domains, where restrictions on content and pressure to project a certain image of China at home have been complicated by a need to produce content which appeals to highly commercial global markets. As this chapter will demonstrate, attempts to resolve this tension have engendered a creative industries policy approach significantly different not only from other continents, but from the rest of Asia too. It is against this background we conducted interviews to explore how and why some of today's Chinese artists choose to identify themselves as 'literati'. The literati's 'purist' view of art opens up a space for critical reflection, from the perspective of the Chinese creative producer, on China's integration into global creative industries discourse and policy making.

We begin the chapter with an overview of the complex historical background for some contemporary artists' self-identification as literati. We then engage with the interview material, highlighting how contemporary Chinese creatives navigate an increasingly globalized intellectual and artistic landscape. Finally, we reassess the role of the Chinese artist as literati by framing the figure within constantly developing creative industries policy and discourse.

Historical background

The traditional Chinese view of artists as literati stems from longstanding, interconnected notions of literacy, education, and civilization. It is tempting to begin with the characteristics of Chinese language when tracing the roots of the literati tradition. Fluency in Mandarin Chinese has never been a guarantee for successful verbal communication with the Chinese, since several of the dialects and vernaculars have so little in common with standard Mandarin (*putonghua*).

The written language, however, carries meaning rather than sound, allowing communication across otherwise impregnable linguistic barriers. Since the written language has stayed essentially the same for more than 2000 years, '[t]he literate have thus always shared a common culture, uniting past and present through the educated people of all periods' (Rawson 2007b: 20).

Confucianism elevated writing to the status of one of the 'six arts' (Lee 1947: 489–90) and deepened a respect for literacy and education already present in Chinese culture (Xia 2014: 45). Writing grew into an art form, calligraphy: a mode of expression thought to convey not only the meaning of the written word but also the writer's personality. Farrer places the emergence of calligraphy somewhere in the Six Dynasties period (265–589) and lists a number of necessary conditions for this development:

> First, there had to be readily discernible difference between the best and worst examples. The craft had to be accorded esteem over and above its usefulness for communicating ideas or facts. Its practitioners also had to be highly regarded, and finally a canon had to be established so that each new generation had a starting point from which to develop and judge their own skills.
>
> *(Farrer 2007: 92–3)*

Calligraphy was practiced and developed by literati, or 'scholar-officials' as they are sometimes called (Farrer 2007: 93). In keeping with Confucian thought, recruitment to this elite group gradually became institutionalized with a formal examination system. This move from aristocracy to meritocracy culminated during the Tang dynasty (618–906) (Weber 1946: 424) with everyone who wanted to become 'members of the central and local bureaucracies' having to prove themselves in examinations that tested 'their knowledge of the great writings of literature and philosophy of the past' (Rawson 2007b: 21). From then on, China was essentially ruled through institutionalized meritocracy, at least in principle. Merit was measured in knowledge of officially sanctioned intellectual achievements of the past,[2] and (through calligraphy) expression of such knowledge had an artful dimension. The governing class of literati did not only find themselves on top of 'an intellectual hierarchy through which the more educated ruled the less educated and the literate ruled the illiterate' (Lee 1947: 491), they also took responsibility for passing wisdom and beauty on from generation to generation.

Another characteristic of the literati, a certain aloofness, comes to light by turning our attention from calligraphy to the closely related art form of painting. Early Chinese painting took several forms and served various functions but 'all of the most highly respected latter Chinese painting evolved directly from calligraphy' (Farrer 2007: 102). In the eleventh century, 'a general theory of painting was created which elaborated for the first time a distinction between amateur "scholars" and professional "artisan" painters' (Clunas 2009: 141). Su Shi (1037–1101) was the main theorist responsible for this conceptual development. Su listed a number of key characteristics of what he was the first to call 'scholar's painting': 'the relationship between such painting and the élite art of poetic composition, the disinterestedness of the true scholar-painter, who will never work for financial reward, and the superiority of spontaneous creation over laborious technique' (Clunas 2009: 142).

Later, during the Ming dynasty (1368–1644), what is today known as 'literati painting' '[emerged] as a distinct category' (Rawson 2007a: 355), and the notion of the artist as a scholarly-minded amateur was applied within all categories of the arts. By the eighteenth and nineteenth centuries, this artist persona had developed into a dominant ideal

(Clunas 2009: 165),[3] an ideal artist who might very well exhibit an intellectualist 'attitude of contempt and disgust toward military valor and physical work' (Lee 1947: 490) as well as the 'traditional Chinese literati disdain for commerce' (Chen 2010: 38).

What effects did the upheavals of the late nineteenth and twentieth centuries have on the notion of artists as literati? Chen insists that the literati ideal withstood 'the modernization project that accompanied the Western imperialist invasion' (Chen 2010: 265). Although 'reform-minded Han literati were forced to adopt notions such as tolerance and equality', adoption of such notions merely touched the surface of a deeply ingrained – and, in Chen's analysis, deeply 'racist' – logic (Chen 2010: 265) that secured Han superiority. The literati might in their meritocratic way be telling you, from their vantage point at the top of the hierarchy, that you have not made it because you have not worked hard enough (Chen 2010: 265–6).

Also Gong (2012: 27) comments on the strength of traditional literati thinking and its deep Confucian roots. Noting a general shift from 'culturalism' to 'economism' in Chinese society, Gong (2012: 29) describes how a 1980s period of 'cultural confidence of intellectuals' has been followed by a period of marginalization triggered not only by the events of 1989 but also by 'the lure of materialism [which is] irresistible, even to the most high-minded intellectuals'. That is not to say, however, that all '[c]ontemporary Chinese writers, filmmakers, and intellectuals' with 'a sense of social and cultural responsibility' (Gong 2012: 31) need to shy away from consumerist contemporary society. Gong suggests a more complicated model at odds with the traditional dichotomy of economy and culture, and offers the author Yu Qiuyu (born 1946) as an example:

> In this postsocialist period when anti-intellectual commercialization is rampant, [Yu] embodies such elitist concepts as culture, tradition, and intellectual. Yet he himself is being commercialized and mediatized and becomes an intellectual celebrity precisely due to his well-packaged elitism.
>
> *(Gong 2012: 56)*

Indeed, it could be argued that cultural intervention must take place 'when economic development has become the predominant, single significant theme of contemporary Chinese society' (Gong 2012: 31). To some extent, Gong's argument resonates with the idea that the development of the creative industries in China holds potential for broader societal change (see, for example, Keane 2013: 38).

Ofoto

If today's Chinese artists refer to themselves as 'literati', they are, then, making claims to a complex and richly historically resonant position in Chinese society. Our case study of the contemporary literati relies on semi-structured interviews of photographers and curators, some of whom are associated with the Ofoto art gallery in M50, Moganshan Lu, one of Shanghai's many so-called 'creative clusters'. The interviews were conducted in English in Shanghai between 2013 and 2016. We do not necessarily find it useful to label all the artists interviewed as literati but respond, rather, to the need to rethink the fundamental meanings of the term in the contemporary art scene of China

One of us is part of a larger research project involving several case studies of contemporary art practice in China. For the purpose of this chapter, Ofoto was selected from this larger set of cases through 'elite-sampling' (Bennett and Elman 2006), and supplementary interviews were then conducted with key respondents. The Ofoto respondents were singled out by virtue of their knowledge of the literati topic as well as their strong personal sense of Chinese identity, qualities confirmed by their Shanghai photographer peers. The literati position is, as suggested in the previous section, rooted in both Confucianist and Daoist moral virtues as opposed to market-oriented professionalism and the Communist Party's cultural and ideological control of the arts. The case study elaborates on this ambiguous position of the literati in being critical of both the instrumentalism of the Western concept of creativity and the Chinese state restrictions on cultural content, while themselves adopting a position that many would view as similarly restrictive in its cultural conservatism.

The literati's ambiguous position

Delving into the literati sensibility of some of Ofoto's artists can enable one to develop a better understanding of the complex interplay of different artistic outlooks as they pertain in contemporary China. Luo Yongjing (born 1966) has attempted to capture this as: 'to be literati is the one who is "smart" for the arts and literature, well-educated and most of all choosing to be ignorant about the trend and market' (interview with Luo, September 21, 2015). Luo thus offers the literati role as an alternative to the logic of the propaganda or commodity system and also suggests that being a contemporary literati entails engagement with the literati as a historical figure. This engagement with the literati past is carried out both by individuals and through collective collaboration in Ofoto. Engagement with the literati past can sometimes be associated with cultural essentialism and neoconservative pride (Barme 1995). In this sense, and as stated above, while being a contemporary literati challenges both China's ruling ideology and global capitalist discourses on the creative industries, the literati position is deeply conservative. This is an ambiguity which will be explored in more detail below.

After more than a decade promoting photographic work in Shanghai, Ofoto founder and art director Yu Huang stresses the importance of the curators and their contribution to the artists' vision in contemporary art. This collaboration between curators and artists in Ofoto includes discourses that can be seen as part of artistic practice itself and also the creation of texts that inform and actively engage with a broad audience who are not always familiar with the artistic works, as Huang illustrates:

> We are just interested in good works in which the identity of the artists can easily be read in their images. Their message-making or their use of aesthetics devices are of vital importance in our selections. We believe that Ofoto started a platform of more pluralistic ideas in Chinese contemporary photography. Chinese traditional aesthetics and Western modes of expression can be explored.
>
> *(Interview with Huang, September 22, 2015)*

In this quotation, Huang points to a space for comparative thinking that challenges the country's cultural policies which decry critical attempts to historicize the present (Wang 2004). Huang's curatorial position and traditional selection relies on both art history and locally based conditions, with artists and curators in Ofoto using a complex interplay of memory and contemporary 'anxiety' (of which more later) to revisit the past. Luo and Huang both also stress the importance of aesthetic autonomy and artists' strong Chinese subjectivities in their ways of excavating the Chinese past, which goes against the anti-traditional and collective iconography of the Socialist Realism period. Luo detaches himself from external social reality, when he acknowledges that 'the trend is more political, commercial, industrial and superficial. Ofoto is trying to stay away from this. It is working with the creative artists based on his individual vision, no matter if he is literati or possesses a Chinese style' (interview with Luo, September 21, 2015). In this sense, we see in Luo's call for a cultural memory derived partly from home-grown aesthetics and ethical meanings his eagerness to re-fashion both the past and present of Chinese artistic formations in Ofoto.

This is at odds with the government's cultural agenda, which is more prone to accept nostalgic 'consumable' products than 'historicised' artworks (Dai and Chen 1997). The curatorial role in China started with the internationalization of Chinese contemporary art at the brink of the second millennium (Zhang 2003). Ofoto has looked for ways of strengthening the exchanges between artists and curators. The curatorial can be seen to aid the artistic community in China by introducing independent strategies and practices that differ from those of the Chinese Ministry of Culture. Ofoto's curatorial approach also evades the dominant aesthetic of the transnational art-gallery system as much as possible in order to support an environment of multiple spatial and temporal conditions for diverse audiences' reception of art, where located discursive contexts and narratives are also taken into consideration (Gladston 2016). The ultimate goal, according to another Ofoto photographer, Zhu Hao (born 1969), is to foster a multiplicity of artistic expressions and interactions to enrich the gallery experience as much as possible:

> In one of my group exhibitions named 'Misinterpretation' (2009), an important number of Chinese styles and motifs were closely working together, where it was possible to find sameness and differences, which somewhat tells what Ofoto is about. I do not think Chinese contemporary artists can return to the same type of creation as the literati, but in many of their visions of the urban landscapes, such as *Feng Shui* [it literally means 'Wind Water'] skyscrapers can be visually registered as mountains, and cars which are running through roads can be visualised as rivers. So as the Song literati [960–1279], we could also find both aloofness and worldliness in today's cities.
>
> *(Interview with Hao, June 22, 2016)*

This dynamism between artist and curator can be found throughout Luo's artistic work, which draws inspiration from his own Chinese identity in order to relate to the socio-political context of late socialist China. Luo uses mainly photography to unravel the hidden beauties of Chinese daily life. His photographic approach is not conceptual, as Huang asserts: 'Luo has the camera in his eye, a third eye, and from there, he creates his own poetic worlds while pointing at some objects' (interview with Huang, September 22, 2015). The focus on the inner poetic qualities rather than on external reality can be interpreted as the result of a social and cultural environment that suppresses the expression of feelings and affection among artists. His visual exploration not only focuses on history and photography as narrative but also on local motifs and modes of remembering in the context of Chinese modernity. Furthermore, Luo also aesthetically explores political imagination in Confucian terms, in which the individual and the country interact with each other.[4] Added to this is Luo's assertion that to share memories is an effective means of developing creativity, a further indication of how artistic critique in China often tends to mine traditional cultural resources.

Gao (2011: 115) also suggests that this historical or philosophical subjectivity can be connected with Chinese historical or literary forms to return to 'cultural nationalism and fundamentalism' as an 'identified memory'. However, this return to the nativist China or the so-called *bentu* is also arguably akin to what Gao (2011: 110) considers an 'unidentified memory' that can emerge with its engagement with the contemporary art market. For Gao (2011: 115), Chinese contemporary art is conceived by its indigenous cultural forms and styles as a mixture of local *bentu* and liberal Westernized 'global *bentu*'. These contradictory behaviors both manifest latent rigid and more fluid etiquettes to retrieve the past and unfold counter-narratives of Chinese modernity. Adopting a subtly different position on the concept of *bentu*, Luo (interview, September 21, 2015) proposes that this has been rooted in Confucian and Daoist impulses, as an emancipatory vision uncontaminated by either Western liberalism or Chinese socialism.

Ofoto's organizational culture

An important aspect of the Chinese creative industries is the way in which the government directs activity towards officially designated clusters. While these types of clusters and artistic quarters are also prominent in Western cities, in China they are more usually linked to the wider government-driven program of the industrialization of culture:

> The idea that industrial models can be applied to cultural production recalls the kind of thinking that prevailed in the *tiyong* era of the nineteenth century. The transformation of science parks into creative incubators and the gentrification of disused industrial space is evidence of this mentality. There is a tendency on the part of many officials, supported by developers, to argue that the construction of cultural parks will attract 'talent'. In a nation where talent was traditionally identified from above: through the imperial examination process prior to 1911 and by the ability to integrate Marxist principles into artwork under revolutionary socialism, the idea that creativity emerges from the grassroots is somewhat foreign.
>
> *(Keane 2011: 29–30)*

Providing incentives for creative workers to work within these clusters was a means by which the Chinese government could continue to exert a measure of control on content in an environment where direct control of cultural institutions was being loosened as a result of marketization in the 1980s and 1990s (White and Xu 2012: 250).

While this appears at first sight as an approach specifically associated with the Communist Party's way of dealing with the complexities of its opening up policy, the cluster model can be seen as in some way reflective of traditional ways of working in China. This can be illustrated in the example of Ofoto, whose organizational system accords with a traditional Chinese detachment from politics and commerce historically embodied, for example, in the Southern literati[5] during the Song Dynasty (960–1279). Ofoto is particularly keen to encourage discussions about conceptions of aesthetics and culture in China, as Huang explains:

> Ofoto cultural workers are people who are enthusiastic about what they and we do. Our backroom, it is a special area for our tea practices, our tables and chairs full of food in lunch times represent our sharing spaces, in which we talk about culture and aesthetic ideas on photography or calligraphy. We try to spend as much time as possible together, and the level of trust and loyalty that we have achieved is rewarding for me and the other cultural workers.
>
> *(Interview with Huang, September 22, 2015)*

For Huang, these discussions impact on the working practices of the literati, where work time becomes a cyclical reenactment of the past to create an organizational culture resistant to Westernized forms of market-oriented professionalism. Huang goes on to claim that:

> Despite the fact that the cultural industries are a Western concept, in Ofoto we have adopted the needs to our own ways of doing things. For example, the idea of horizontal forms of work can also be translated into our creative infrastructure which connects curatorial professionals and artists to collaborate and spend as much time as possible together at work, but also during our 'tea time'. Most of the cultural workers in Ofoto have been in Ofoto for more than a decade, I think, this form of collaboration that can be very Chinese, works for us.
>
> *(Interview with Huang, September 22, 2015)*

Although, the Shanghainese freelance photographer Ni Weihua (born 1968) does not extrapolate Ofoto's horizontal and collaborative relationships in other artist studios or clusters, he does however claim that:

> Ofoto is unique in its manner of reinforcing the humanist values of Chinese traditional art and culture, in the sense that it attempts to know its own boundaries. Thus, it opens up the possibility to produce new innovative forms and languages. Like Ofoto, many other art galleries are examples of harmony in Chinese art management. Art directors, curators and artists know where the vertical hierarchies are, but in their day-to-day basis those links can become horizontal and flexible. There is a kind of formal and informal culture that is respected by Chinese creative workers.
>
> *(Interview with Ni, May 20, 2016)*

Clusters in mainland China are thus organized in a more systematic way than the bottom-up ideal (not always realized) which predominates in the US and UK, from where the cluster model originates. Nonetheless, clusters not only subvert Western ideas of market-oriented professionalism but also enable local experimentation to flourish in ways that confound narratives of the party-state using these organizational forms to impose uniformity on the cultural sector (White and Xu 2012: 253–4).

The significance of 'generational' knowledge

An aspect of the contemporary artistic scene in China where organization and forms of knowledge intersect is in 'generational' knowledge. For Luo, old and new skills and techniques, whether drawn from Chinese or Western traditions or innovations, are necessary and vital conditions for good artwork:

> We try mainly to find young and new artists instead of the established ones. Artists are different from one another. Only we choose for Ofoto the artists who care a lot about Chinese culture and the literati spirit. They can be old like me or young as Yang Yongliang [born 1980, an artist famous in China for his digital landscape compositions]. A good artist should be aware of all kinds of technologies, old or new and choose to use the ones that best express his ideas. Our selection of artwork is very simple: good or bad.
>
> *(Interview with Luo, September 21, 2015)*

The labelling of an artist born in 1980 as 'young' is significant in the Chinese context where public discourse around the social and cultural effects of the country's rapid economic changes often take generational difference as its starting point. As the first generation to grow up in the 'new China' of material wealth, the so-called *balinghou* generation (literally eight-zero-after, that is, those born 1980–89) is both envied and chastised by older generations for embodying a new attitude of carefree consumerism (Liboriussen 2016). In some parts of the Chinese creative industries, *balinghou* (as well as younger) creative workers are expected to be expert users of the digital tools and technologies seen as emblematic of their generation (Liboriussen 2015). In the above quotation, Luo refuses this generational logic by insisting that the practitioner's choice of tools (of 'technologies, old or new') transcends it – yet he also insists that the artists with whom he associates himself should somehow connect themselves with the past, that they should 'care a lot about Chinese culture and the literati spirit' (interview with Luo, September 21, 2015). In this sense, the young artist Yang Yongliang (born 1980) emphasizes that the work of the literati creator can be continued in the present, and be actualized with digital technologies:

> When I was a child, I learned Chinese traditional painting and calligraphy for about ten years. Later on, I studied visual communication at the University, where I began to touch digital photography and multimedia technology, and all types of softwares. Even if I was deeply influenced by Chinese traditional culture such as *Shanshui* painting, a form of Chinese landscape painting, technology helped me to revive this conventional vision. My digital techniques allowed me to transfer the old Chinese *Shanshui* landscape into the rapid and derelict urban changes of Shanghai and connect it to contemporary society.
>
> *(Interview with Yang, July 19, 2016)*

Part of this literati spirit is artistic assessment that ignores the commodity values of the market and instead embraces the aspects of the literati class which encounter truth virtues between modernity and tradition in which the diversification and professionalization of the production and distribution of art may come to terms with a critical literati and elitist-intellectual management position.

Luo also acts as an official-scholar whose public position, as Professor of Photography at the Shanghai Institute of Design, could be said to establish parallels with the interventionist critical spirit of official-literati. This hegemonic visual array responds to a:

> [post-]socialist realism [which] was so reified as to become the classicism of Chinese culture for decades. In its official dogmatism and formulaic emotion, it abandoned realism's original edginess, earthiness, and engagement with socio-historical reality. It forgot the lived experience for ordinary people on the ground.
>
> *(Wang 2008: 498)*

Luo's literati position mediates between intervention (Confucianism) and non-intervention (Daoism) (Ortis 2011: 4). Luo seems to situate himself closer to the non-interventionist humanistic side of the literati, when he says 'it is the attitude towards life that counts. It does not matter if you make a living with art or other professions; neither are you rich nor poor' (interview with Luo, June 21, 2016). Luo's invisible world could be seen through his compositional sophistication and his search for harmony and interaction between perfection and less perfect qualities of everyday life:

> The core of literati in an art piece is something invisible. It is in the artist's blood. It is like a taste in a dish, the poetic in the words or the melody in a song. You can sense but you cannot see, you can feel but you can't tell.
>
> *(Interview with Luo, September 21, 2015)*

This citation may acknowledge the importance of the literati's conception of creativity having a mystique that cannot be comprehended by the layperson, a deliberate distancing of the literati from the social while providing a means by which the official ideology of art and culture can be challenged. This mode of thought fits with the original conceptualization of creativity – as a gift bestowed to geniuses – in the Western tradition (McIntyre 2012) but jars with more recent developments of the concept. The dominant view among Western researchers today is that although the cultural impact of their work might obviously differ, the artist's and the layperson's creativity are the same in terms of underlying psychological mechanisms (for example, Csikszentmihalyi 1996; Boden 2004). This conceptualization of creativity fits into political discourses that encourage a shift towards a more 'creative' economy as well as discourses that encourage creativity as a goal of education for the benefit of the individual learner in terms of both employability and personal fulfilment. Informed by the literati ideal, however, the Ofoto respondents' view of creativity as something in 'the artist's blood' resolutely insists on an elitist link between creativity and professional practice, as well as a clear separation of professional and non-professional practices.

The literati and the Chinese creative industries

Having heard from the artists themselves, we now reassess the role of the Chinese artist as literati in light of the 'creative industries' discourse and policy, which for the past decade has attempted to reshape the place of art and artists in Chinese society. In order to perform this reassessment efficiently, we return once more to the historical background, picking up from the foundation of the People's Republic in 1949.

The most striking features of the literati are its self-understanding as an elite caste of artists as well as its disdain for commerce. The post-1949 period has thus been a challenging time for Chinese artists of this ilk. From 1949 to the beginnings of the so-called reform and opening-up period in 1978, artists were forced to shed their hitherto elite status as they were co-opted into the state system to produce social-realist art. While there was a short period from around 1978 to 1989[6] where artists could experiment freely largely outside both the political system and global markets, since the early 1990s artists have been constrained both by domestic restrictions on 'political' content and the pressure to compete in commercial environments where rising property prices and withdrawal of state subsidies have made their working lives more precarious. Wang (2012: 223) alludes to the existential crisis that this has induced in many artists in his suggestion that the Chinese art world is in a perpetual state of 'anxiety'.

In this century, this sense of anxiety has been amplified by China's enthusiastic adoption of global discourses and associated policies on the creative industries. This not only is an affront to the literati's notions of commerce-free art, but also challenges its authority as arbiter of artistic value. For, more so than the adoption of other economic policies from overseas, the importation of Western ideas about creativity and the creative industries has caused profound disruption in China's view of itself, exposing contradictions that the state appears unable to resolve. Chinese officials were not naïve about the likely effects of this profound policy shift, which explains why they initially rejected the term 'creativity' (Keane 2011: 1). But concerns that China needed to 'catch up' to the more creative economies and the fact that the country has a large cultural deficit – a sense of inadequacy exacerbated by the success of Japan and Korea in the creative industries – led to the acceptance that creativity should be encouraged in the Chinese economy (Keane 2011).

The Chinese government's conception of creativity is, however, radically different from the way in which the term is understood in the Western world, from where it originated. It is less associated with the notion of individual genius and more with collective forms of creativity, especially where this relates to government policies on innovation and creative clusters. While it is true to say that the Romantic idea of individual genius upon which the discourse of creativity is based is challenged in the West, it still remains the guiding philosophy of the creative industries in that part of the world (Pang 2012: 50). It is also linked to a particularly Western understanding of modernity, which in the UK, where the term 'creative industries' was first used as basis of policy support for the industries so described, is associated with the idea of post-industrialism (Keane 2011: 19). This is an attractive idea for Chinese policy makers, particularly in the way in which it underscores their efforts to improve soft power through city branding strategies. Art places a key role in that and, notwithstanding some of our own arguments about the critical role of the literati in the development of the Chinese creative industries, it is claimed that many artists are comfortable in contributing to the branding of the city (Pang 2012: 138, 157).

It might be argued that a pragmatic capture of the term 'creative industries' would enable Chinese policy makers to pursue other goals which are more suitable for China's stage of development. This can be seen in relation to the eliding of creativity with innovation in the eyes of Chinese scholars and policy makers, with influential Chinese Academy of Social Sciences (CASS) Professor Zhang identifying the synergies between the development of what are usually termed in China as the cultural industries with the development of a national innovation system (Flew 2012: 49); this is part of a wider official program to make China an 'innovative nation' by 2020 (Keane 2011: 1).

All this need not be threatening to Chinese artists, because after all there is no reason why encouraging greater innovation in industry is necessarily incompatible with promoting creativity in the arts. However, partly for censorious reasons but also because of its concern about China's significant trade deficit in cultural products, Chinese policy makers view culture as a resource that can be monetized rather than a means by which artists will exercise their free expression. This means that Chinese artists are subject to the same commercial pressures as their counterparts in the Western world without having similar degrees of latitude to those who want to shun commercialism and offer critiques of the societies in which they live. Nonetheless, as demonstrated above, the literati caste of artists has carved out a space for critique, even if it is an ambiguous form of critique. And while some scholars are skeptical about contemporary Chinese artists' capacity for and willingness to critique (Pang 2012: 157; Wang 2012: 227), Cheung's (2014: 226) study of 12 contemporary Chinese artists identifies criticism of government restrictions as well as of China's enthusiastic embrace of modernity. That many of these critical works of art use traditional Chinese motifs to emphasize their points about the social cost of China's rapid modernization (Cheung 2014: 239) is a further indication that the official discourse of cultural and creative industries in the arts has been unable to prevent the literati tradition from becoming a rallying point for those who seek an alternative vision of how creativity might function in China.

But, as if to illustrate the ambiguity inherent in the literati's seeming oscillation between critique and conservatism, the policy framework for the Chinese creative industries is based on modes of production which are similar to those in the literati tradition. In order for the concept of creativity to be accepted in China it had to be conceptualized as a collective rather than individual form. The manifestation of this thinking was the creative cluster (*chuangyi jijuqu*), an industrial form which proliferates in many Chinese cities. As we have seen earlier with the observations of how the literati caste reproduced itself through the imperial examination system and how they are keeping their collective knowledge alive through the type of interactions which are taking place in shared spaces such as Ofoto, the Chinese cluster model could have been designed with these artists in mind. The earlier mentioned notion of the literati passing their knowledge down through succeeding generations is similar to the idea of Marshall ([1920] 1997), the late-nineteenth- and early-twentieth-century economist who, in his studies of the building up of generational knowledge in industrial sectors of northern England, provided the inspiration for the Western model of the creative cluster. In this sense, these modern-day industrial cluster models could be said to be China's way of adapting creative industries policy to something compatible with its own philosophical tradition, a tradition in which the literati play a prominent role.

Conclusion

Historically steeped in Confucian, meritocratic values, and Daoist ideals of reclusiveness, the literati artist is a quintessentially Chinese figure. In our Ofoto case study, interviewees demonstrated one way of reconciling this complex figure of the past with a contemporary need for innovation in both artistic and organizational aspects as a means of becoming a successful member of what is today labelled 'the creative industries'. By aligning themselves with the literati position, as they themselves interpreted it, the interviewees discovered new possibilities of balancing the commercial with the aesthetic and critical. That balancing act allowed them to carve out their own spaces for both individual and collaborative practices and thinking somewhat beyond the demands of both the global marketplace and the political restrictions of the one-party state. The collaborative aspect of their practices and thinking are perhaps the most striking, as it reaffirms a special Chinese collectivist understanding of creativity while providing a potential space for artists for social critique. The creative cluster is the most visible and most frequently used official tool for driving the Chinese creative industries forward. To see the notion of the literati resurface in the midst of China's creative industries boom, and to see it resurface within an institution that is so central to official creative industries policies, is a thought-provoking and timely reminder that no matter how Western the idea of creativity is, China has the capacity to both integrate and transform international impulses. Moving forward, scholarly attention to the implementation and impact of creative industries policy in China needs to pay attention to how such policy developments are not merely applied to China but also trigger complex cultural reactions within the country, as exemplified by the resurfacing and reinterpretation of the literati role.

Notes

1 We use the term the 'creative industries' here because it is the most common way of referring to them internationally. However, as we will explain later, sensitivity to the word 'creative' in China means that these same industries are often referred to as the 'cultural and creative industries' in that country (Gu 2014: 177–81; Keane and Zhao 2014: 156, 164–5) or, as some of our interviewees expressed it, the 'cultural industries'. We have mainly used the creative industries in this chapter but occasionally use the other terms where appropriate.
2 The canon consisted of key Confucian, Daoist, and Buddhists texts (Farrer 2007: 95).

3 Dong Qichang's art-theoretical intervention towards the end of the Ming period was a decisive moment in the development of the ideal of the scholar-painter. Dong grounded his theory in Chan Buddhism and associated literati painting with the so-called Southern school (Clunas 2009: 161).
4 Like the Northern literati, where court art scholars were more concerned with changing the social order of the country during the Yuan dynasty (1271–1368) (Li 1999).
5 Southern school poetic literati exiled in order to indulge their poetic aesthetics in remote zones (Li 1999).
6 With the exception of the Anti-Spiritual Pollution Campaign (1982–5), which brought restrictions to Westernized modernist and individualist values (Larson 1989).

References

Barme, G. R. (1995) To screw foreigners is patriotic: China's avant-garde nationalist. *The China Journal*, 34: 209–34.
Bennett, A. and Elman, C. (2006) Qualitative research: recent developments in case study methods. *Annual Review of Political Science*, 9: 455–76.
Boden, M. A. (2004) *The Creative Mind: Myths and Mechanisms*. Abingdon: Routledge.
Chen, K.-H. (2010) *Asia as Method: Toward Deimperialization*. Durham, NC: Duke University Press.
Cheung, M. (2014) Contemporary Chinese art and the dream of glocalisation. *Social Semiotics*, 24(2): 225–42.
Clunas, C. (2009) *Art in China*. Oxford: Oxford University Press.
Csikszentmihalyi, M. (1996) *Creativity: Flow and the Psychology of Discovery and Invention*. New York: Harper Perennial.
Dai, J. and Chen, J. T. H. (1997) Imagined nostalgia. *Boundary*, 24(3): 143–61.
Farrer, A. (2007) Calligraphy and painting in official life. In Rawson, J. (ed.), *The British Museum Book of Chinese Art*. London: The British Museum Press, pp. 84–133.
Flew, T. (2012) *The Creative Industries: Culture and Policy*. Los Angeles: Sage.
Gao, S. (2011) *A New Thoughtfulness in Contemporary China: Critical Voices in Art and Aesthetics*. Bielefeld: transcript Verlag.
Gladston, P. (2016) *Deconstructing Contemporary Chinese Art: Selected Critical Writings and Conversations, 2007–2014*. Berlin: Springer.
Gong, H. (2012) *Uneven Modernity: Literature, Film, and Intellectual Discourse in Postsocialist China*. Honolulu: University of Hawai'i Press.
Gu, X. (2014) Creative industries, creative clusters and cultural policy in Shanghai. In Lee, H.-K. and Lim, L. (eds.), *Cultural Policies in East Asia: Dynamics between the State, Arts and Creative Industries*. New York: Palgrave Macmillan, pp. 174–92.
Keane, M. (2011) *China's New Creative Clusters: Governance, Human Capital and Investment*. London: Routledge.
Keane, M. (2013) *Creative Industries in China: Art, Design and Media*. Cambridge: Polity Press.
Keane, M. and Zhao, E. J. (2014) The reform of the cultural system: culture, creativity and innovation in China. In Lee, H.-K. and Lim, L. (eds.), *Cultural Policies in East Asia: Dynamics between the State, Arts and Creative Industries*. New York: Palgrave Macmillan, pp. 155–73.
Larson, W. (1989) Realism, modernism, and the anti-"Spiritual Pollution" campaign in China'. *Modern China*, 15(1): 37–71.
Lee, S.-C. (1947) Intelligentsia of China. *American Journal of Sociology*, 52: 489–97.
Li, Z. (1999) *The Path of Beauty: A Study of Chinese Aesthetics*, trans. L. Gong. Beijing: Morning Glory Publishers.
Liboriussen, B. (2015) (Digital) tools as professional and generational identity badges in the Chinese creative industries. *Convergence*, 21(4): 423–36.
Liboriussen, B. (2016) Balinghou and qilinghou: generational difference and creativity. In Keane, M. (ed.), *Handbook of Cultural Industries in China*. Cheltenham: Edward Elgar, pp. 64–79.
Marshall, A. ([1920] 1997) *Principles of Economics*, 8th edition. Amherst: Prometheus Books.
McIntyre, P. (2012) *Creativity and Cultural Production: Issues for Media Practice*. Houndmills: Palgrave Macmillan.
Ortis, J. (2011) The art of being: a study of the relationship between Daoism and art. *Journal of Undergraduate Research at Minnesota State University, Mankato*, 11: 1–14.

Pang, L. (2012) *Creativity and its Discontents: China's Creative Industries and Intellectual Property Rights Offenses*. Durham, NC: Duke University Press.

Rawson, J. (2007a) Glossaries. In Rawson, J. (ed.), *The British Museum Book of Chinese Art*. London: The British Museum Press, pp. 347–70.

Rawson, J. (2007b) Introduction. In Rawson, J. (ed.), *The British Museum Book of Chinese Art*. London: The British Museum Press, pp. 13–43.

Wang, B. (2004) *Illuminations from the Past: Trauma, Memory, and History in Modern China*. Stanford: Stanford University Press.

Wang, B. (2008) In search of real-life images in China: realism in the age of spectacle. *Journal of Contemporary China*, 17(56): 497–512.

Wang, C. (2012) The art of anxiety: China's social transformation and the uncertain reception of Chinese contemporary art. *Journal of Visual Art Practice*, 11(2–3): 222–9.

Weber, M. (1946) The Chinese literati. Trans, H. H. Gerth and C. W. Mills. In Gerth, H. H. and Mills, C. W. (eds.), *From Max Weber: Essays in Sociology*. New York: Oxford University Press, pp. 416–44.

White, A. and Xu, S. (2012) A critique of China's cultural policy and the development of its cultural and creative industries: the case of Shanghai. *Cultural Trends*, 21(3): 249–57.

Xia, G. (2014) China as a 'civilization-state': a historical and comparative interpretation. *Procedia – Social and Behavioral Sciences*, 140: 43–7.

Zhang, Q. (2003) Chinese curators: directed but lacking a path. Trans. P. Bloom. In Li, A. (ed.), *Critics' Criticisms and Self-Criticisms*. Shanghai: Shanghai Bookstore Publishing House, pp. 198–204.

11

The production consortium system in Japanese film financing

Nobuko Kawashima

Introduction

A major economic feature of all the creative and cultural industries is their riskiness. Typically, the initial cost of making the content is large whereas the marginal cost of reproducing a unit of copy is minimal. When the product is popular among a large number of consumers, investment is recouped and beyond that threshold what comes in is net profits. However, as the economist Caves (2002) has extensively argued, 'nobody knows' is the character of these industries; consumers have diverse interests and tastes, which are hard to predict and can change over time. Producers of the cultural and creative industries need to invest in production under such uncertain demands. Among all the creative industries, film is an exemplar. It is exceptionally expensive to make, whereas consumers buy cinema tickets without really knowing what to expect as the values of the film in question are revealed only when it is watched.

Financing production is of prime importance for films in particular, as the size of the budget effectively determines the genre and the target market. Large budget movies are for a global audience with non-culturally specific content like action, whereas small budget movies may be social or human dramas for specific audiences or niche markets. While films nowadays can be produced on shoestring budgets with the use of the latest technology, films that aim to hit the box office need gigantic budgets. Hollywood blockbusters are typically made with budgets ranging from USD 100 to 200 million or even more with the heavy use of computer graphics and other technologies for spectacular effects.

To raise funds for a film project has thus constantly been a major issue for films of all kinds and for the industry internationally. To deal with this issue, film producers most typically try to secure distribution channels at the project development stage. Hollywood majors possess international distribution networks as well as subsidiaries and companies connected by the same capital for exploiting film properties by selling the rights to television networks, DVD companies, video-on-demand operators, merchandisers and so on, all of which may lead to high rates of financial success in the medium to long term. Projects that have successfully secured contracts with Hollywood majors, thus, can obtain basic funds supplemented by other loans (called gap financing) but will transfer all the rights to the majors upon delivery.

Independent film producers outside this system raise funds by pre-sale to distributors and broadcasters.

In some countries, films may be financed by public funds. In Europe, for example, such funding is extensive because film is considered to be part of the national culture that needs protection by the state. In other countries, particularly in Asia, film production may be publicly supported based on the national economic policy of promoting content production as it is considered a key to the broader policy of promoting an ICT- and IP-driven economy.

In Japan, neither a strong distribution sector with an international reach nor ample public funding for film production exists. Nevertheless, Japan is among the top countries with large numbers of annually locally produced films that take more than half the share of the domestic market. A distinctive feature of the film market in Japan is that box office hits have been dominated by local films rather than Hollywood blockbusters in the last ten years (Tables 11.1 to 11.3). This chapter focuses on one major factor that has led to such a strength in the industry, namely, the 'production consortium' system for film production.[1] Its details will be discussed later, but for the time being a production consortium can be understood as a loose bundle of companies, including a major studio, an advertising company, a television broadcaster, a publisher and some others, each of which contributes to the production budget in return for access to the exploitation of the film's copyright and ancillary rights. Prior to the prevalence of this financing scheme, major studios basically had to finance production on their own. With new players from other industrial sectors coming into the film business, however, budgets as well as distribution channels and windows have expanded, which rescued the industry from the decline of the 1970s and 1980s. This method of film financing, perhaps unique to Japan, is now established as mainstream for major movie projects. It works as a strong financial infrastructure for the industry, but has a number of problems and issues.

Table 11.1 Share of national films in the market in 2015 (%)

North America	*India*	*South Korea*	*China*	*Japan*	*France*	*UK*
88.8	85.0	52.2	61.6	55.4	35.5	44.5

Source: Data compiled from FOCUS 2016, European Audiovisual Observatory

Table 11.2 Japanese film market, 1955–95

Year	*Number of local films released*	*Number of foreign films released*	*Total admissions (thousands)*	*Share of local films (%)*
1955	423	193	858,912	65.8
1960	547	216	1,014,364	78.3
1965	487	264	372,676	66.7
1970	423	236	254,799	59.4
1975	333	225	174,020	44.4
1980	320	209	164,422	55.0
1985	319	284	155,130	50.9
1990	239	465	148,000	41.4
1995	289	321	157,885	37.0

Source: Data compiled from Motion Picture Producers Association of Japan (Eiren) website

Table 11.3 Japanese film market, 2000–15

Year	*Number of local films released*	*Number of foreign films released*	*Total admissions (thousands)*	*Share of local films (%)*
2000	282	362	135,390	31.8
2001	281	349	163,280	39.0
2002	293	347	160,767	27.1
2003	287	335	162,347	33.0
2004	310	339	170,092	37.5
2005	355	375	160,453	41.3
2006	417	404	164,585	53.2
2007	407	403	163,193	47.7
2008	418	388	160,491	59.5
2009	448	314	182,297	56.9
2010	409	308	174,358	53.6
2011	441	358	144,726	54.9
2012	554	429	155,159	65.7
2013	591	526	155,888	60.6
2014	615	569	161,116	58.3
2015	581	555	166,630	55.4
2016	610	539	180,189	63.1
2017	594	593	174,483	54.9

Source: Data compiled from Motion Picture Producers Association of Japan (Eiren) website

This chapter will firstly describe the background to its development and give details of this unusual system of film financing. It will then critically assess its impact on the film industry of Japan today and its future development.

In the following, factual information has primarily been obtained from industry-related websites and literature. Attendance at various seminars over the years for industry professionals in film, often organized by UNIJAPAN (a semi-public organization that hosts the annual Tokyo International Film Festival and promotes Japanese films abroad), has informed my research. For inside information on the actual practice of production consortia (discussed below), personal interviews with industry figures including a Japanese film studies professor and two producers of a major anime production company in Tokyo were undertaken specifically for the purpose of preparing this chapter.

The film economy of Japan, 1955–2016

The Japanese film industry is one of the oldest in the world, and during the 1920s and the 1930s was on a par with the American and European movie industries in size, experiencing the first 'Golden Age'. Based on the so-called studio system, whereby major directors, scriptwriters, and actors would exclusively work for the companies to which they were contracted, the major studios continuously supplied large numbers of films.

However, the film industry of Japan, like those in the US and Europe, rapidly declined within a decade after the Second World War in the face of the development of television broadcasts and increased leisure options for the public. The year 1958 marked the apex of admissions reaching 1.1 billion, meaning average admission per person was 13.4 times per year for the whole population (Motion Picture Producers Association of Japan, n.d.). Since then, admissions have constantly declined to the order of 150 million towards the 1980s and 1990s, the majority of which were taken by foreign films. Only the Japanese majors, a few in number, vertically integrated with distributors and theatre chains were the players in film business in this period. As a whole, films were cheaply produced in a narrow range of genres including Yakuza movies (stories of mafias) and soft pornography to cater to limited audiences. Theatres looked outdated, unfashionable, and dirty to the general public, not a fun place to visit for entertainment and leisure.

A major change occurred in the early 1980s with the advent of television broadcasters starting to invest in this area. Japan has had a strong television industry, comprising five national networks of terrestrial broadcasting along with the public broadcaster NHK with two channels. Private broadcasters' total revenue has been about 2.5 trillion yen[2] in recent years (22.7 billion USD), mostly from advertising. In the post-war economic development from the 1960s to the 1980s television advertising was very active in stimulating consumer demand. Among the broadcasters, competition to attract viewers was intense, which then raised the price of advertising, but as an industry to which entry is limited the business of commercial broadcasting has stayed relatively safe and lucrative for all the stations.

Broadcasters however try to develop and invest in new areas in small ways from time to time, and involvement with film making, though it may not look that far from their core business of providing audio-visual content to the masses, was such a venture. It was motivated by the escalating price of broadcasting licence fees of movies at that time. One early example was set by Fuji Television, which invested in *Nankyoku Monogatari* (1983) produced by Kadokawa Publishing House, a major media-entertainment conglomerate with its roots in publishing. The film was a mega-hit, earning 5.9 billion yen (53.4 million USD, calculated by the method then adopted, namely, by distribution revenue as opposed to by box office revenue).[3] The total budget for the film is said to have been 2.5 billion yen or so (22.7 million USD), large by the standard of the time, of which the amount invested by Fuji Television is unknown, but apparently the station's involvement in the project was substantial.

Stimulated by the success of this particular film, other stations jumped on the bandwagon. At this point, however, television stations and Kadokawa mentioned above were, other than the major studios, the sole investors in film projects. The escalating cost of film production and the demand for risk distribution started to require more investors. The production consortium system thus emerged in the 1980s, particularly for animation films. With live action films, too, a major landmark was made by Fuji Television, when it released *Odoru Daisosasen* (*Bayside Shakedown*) in 1998 as a sequel to the TV series of the same title aired in early 1997. Unlike the above example of *Nankyoku Monogatari*, where Fuji TV did not own the original source, the Bayside project tried to cash in on the success of the drama televised by Fuji by extending the story and hiring the same cast, director, and staff. The box office revenue for this movie was more than 10.1 billion yen (USD 101 million),[4] one of the highest grossing films of all time in the Japanese market, including Japanese and non-Japanese films (except animations). The *Bayside Shakedown* franchise had three subsequent films released in 2003, 2010, and 2012, as well as spin-off movies focusing on some of the protagonists in the series, each of which was a box office success. The franchise has included extended versions of the television series for broadcasting, music CDs of soundtracks, small programs for mobile phones, novelized works and accompanying booklets, as well as a theatre play. The 'production consortium' system, the very focus of this chapter, was employed for funding this film, and it is around this time that the system became the norm and significantly boosted the industry.

Film finance

The previous section has discussed the rise of the production consortium system as a major form of film funding in Japan since the late 1990s. In order to better understand the distinctiveness of this system, it would be useful to explain other mainstream methods of film financing more widely seen in other countries. The following mostly draws on Wasko (2003), Finney (2015), Moore (2011), and Erickson et al. (2010).

There is a variety of financial sources that film producers may be able to tap into. Not all of them are available in one country and each film project is made by a different combination. It is possible to divide the sources into two groups, according to whether they are involved in the production and distribution chain of film properties or not. The group that is embedded in the value chain includes film and VoD/DVD distributors and sales agents, broadcasters, video-on-demand and subscription VoD operators (such as Netflix). These stakeholders need films for their core businesses and may pay specified amounts in order to obtain rights (for home video, theatre distribution, broadcasting, etc.) even before the film is shot or at least commit themselves and make actual payment upon delivery of the films. In most countries, funds are raised by such pre-sales to these stakeholders.

The other group is outside the value chain and invests in film projects in order to make profits. So-called angels[5] and other investors are included in this group, who may provide funds on loan or as equity. This source is significant where these people exist, but that is only in a few countries where the film business is exceptionally large, such as the US and India. More conventional stakeholders in this group are financial institutions such as banks, who might grant credit to film projects. It must be noted however that banks of this kind rarely exist outside southern California where film is a major economic sector and banks are used to lending money to film projects.

Specialist banks of this kind are not only in constant business with major studios who possess large assets, but also deal with independent producers as well. In lending money to independent projects, banks may analyse the plans by paying attention to the major talents involved, such as the cast and the director, as well as the film script. They like to ensure that the project in question has secured contract with one of the major Hollywood distributors so that wide distribution of the film and 'exploitation of the film property' (meaning Hollywood majors taking full advantage of commercial opportunities in DVD production, online distribution, broadcasting, and merchandising) are guaranteed. A letter of such guarantee issued by a major is very significant as it is a sure sign of financial security that the studio will pay the producer a specified amount of money upon delivery of the film, out of which the bank will be repaid ahead of others. To further enhance the security of bank loans, professional services are highly developed in southern California in law and accounting. Of particular importance are insurance companies that issue 'completion bonds'[6] as insurance against the non-completion of film production. With complex webs of contracts that define the rules and order of repayment, banks are able to grant credit to film projects. As mentioned above, such a highly developed system and the large number of business experts for film are rarely found outside Hollywood, which gives rise to the need for other revenue sources. Public money plays a role here.

Public funding for film may well be for cultural reasons of the protection and enhancement of national cinema but also to promote an industrial sector whose strategic importance is acknowledged by the state. Thus, there may be a selection of grant applications on the basis of cultural and artistic merit, but there may also be 'automatic' support that provides funds for film projects, repayable if they turn out to be a commercial success (which, however,) rarely happens, effectively making the payment grant-in-aid. Another source of public support that is increasingly significant and almost unmissable for film production is available from a large number of countries and state governments of the US and Canada in their hope to attract location shooting. Large-scale productions are particularly welcome as they create local employment for audio-visual workers and contribute to the local economy. Tax rebates, special grants, free services for location searches, and introduction to local service providers are provided to incentivize film producers to come and stay in the area for film shooting and post-production. In fact, the provision of such tax incentives to attract foreign productions has almost become an international competition (Elmer and Gasher 2005).

The above has listed possible sources of funds for film production, but most of these are unavailable in Japan. First, bank loans to film projects are almost non-existent, unless the producer puts forward his own house as collateral. Projects may raise funds by the pre-sale of rights, but this is under-developed as the majors have until recently been vertically integrated. With the decline in the financial strength of the majors, distributors and others in the value chain are even more inactive in financing. Finally, public funding for film is almost non-existent in Japan. Japanese cultural policy is very small scale anyway – funding for the arts and culture is largely left to market mechanisms while funds available from national and local governments are allocated to maintain museums and theatres and to preserve cultural heritage. To discuss Japanese cultural policy at length is beyond the scope of this chapter and interested readers are referred to Kobayashi (2014), Kawashima (2014) and Otmazgin (2012). Just to give a sense of the scale of Japanese cultural policy, expenditure by the Agency for Cultural Affairs (ACA), a central department for cultural policy within the Ministry of Education, Science and Technology, is about 0.1 per cent of total public expenditure, whereas its French and South Korean counterparts account for over 1 per cent. Within the small budget of ACA of 104 billion yen (2016, 943 million USD), only 1.85 per cent, or 1.9 billion yen (17 million USD), is related to film and media arts (meaning digitally created graphics and moving images of an artistic nature). Recently other ministries of central government have started to provide funds to support the export of film, which however is very limited in terms of size and purpose (Kawashima 2016). This support is mainly for boosting exports, not towards production in the first place.

Without any established source of funding except for majors' self-finance, the Japanese film business shrank and stagnated from the 1960s to the 1980s until other entertainment businesses, such as publishing houses and television stations, came to be involved.

Production consortia

With the successful examples shown by Fuji TV explained above, not only television companies but also those in the film value chain, and most importantly big businesses in other industrial sectors, have become interested in investing in films. The spread of multiplexes around the country that has helped revitalize cinema has also been a contributing factor to this phenomenon. The development of multiplexes was initiated by the American major Warner when it opened the first one in Japan in 1993 and disturbed the conventional configuration of the majors and their affiliates. Cinema-going has started to become popular again. Against such a background, the production consortium system emerged and by now has become standard. We now turn to describe what this is.

A typical production consortium includes a major trading company, an advertising agency, a television network, a video company, a publishing house, a merchandiser, a music label, and a film major. No two competitors in the same industrial sector customarily join a consortium. Members are only loosely tied by contract as a temporary partnership to co-own properties and make decisions unanimously, but do not form a formal company like the Limited Liability Company (LLC), a standard legal entity set up for specific film production in the US, and its variations around the world.

Each member has a particular stake in the film project in addition to the purely financial return obtained if the movie turns out to be a hit. For example, Mitsui and Mitsubishi, two giant Japanese trading companies who have invested in satellite and cable broadcasting and their own channels dedicated to films, obviously want to get involved in premium content production. They have also invested in convenience store chains, where movies, animation in particular, may be promoted with piles of tie-in products like food and other daily items whose packages feature movie characters. Such campaigns create 'event movies' and attract the attention of consumers and stimulate spending in the stores. A publishing house may be involved as the provider of the source material for movies and can expect an increase in the sale of comic books if the films are hits. Movies financed in this way, animation in particular, tend to generate merchandising opportunities for toys and other items that can sell very well, so the participation of a merchandiser is predictable. An advertising agency will take account of all the advertising and promotional activities.

It must be noted however that a toy company, for example, does not monopolize the merchandising rights as all the rights collectively remain the property of the partnership. The profit from merchandising thus will be returned to the whole consortium and distributed among the members as previously agreed, normally according to the proportion of the investment. The toy company however will receive fees for the transaction in addition to the share, which are said to be a very significant motivator for participation. Other members from different business categories join for the same reason.

There are two players that should not be missed in a production consortium with unique interests and roles to play: a film studio and a television station. The studios have long experience in the film business and good access to distribution channels to theatres nationwide. As has been mentioned, television stations play a key role here as they often have the rights to the source material (i.e. TV dramas) and experience in the making of audio-visual products for mass entertainment. The possession of the means of free advertisement is unique to them and of utmost importance to the consortium. When films in which the stations have invested are due to be released or just prior to that, major members of the cast appear on television shows to talk about the work and encourage viewers to come to cinemas. In this way the chances of recouping the investment may well become higher and DVDs of the original drama may sell well, leading to another sequel on television. Each of the four national broadcasters (apart from the public broadcaster NHK) invest in about ten projects of this kind per year, amounting to the majority of movies distributed by the three majors. Such synergy effects are expected by all the members.

Assessment of the production consortium system

It is undeniable that the system of the production consortium has rescued the film industry from its decline of the 1970s and 1980s by expanding the funding base and by incorporating the style of 'light' popular entertainment learned from television. The expansion of exploitation opportunities for film properties, although other investors will gain the relevant rights, has helped create event movies similar to Hollywood blockbusters, thereby pushing the place of film into the mainstream, consumerist media culture (Kawashima 2014). Such cross-fertilization potential is particularly noteworthy for films made through this system involving stakeholders from diverse industries. In that sense, the production consortium system may in effect work for the production of entertainment content across the industries of film, anime, manga, music, and games.

However, there have been some deficits caused by the reliance on this system. One obvious consequence has been the dominance of adaptations of TV dramas at the top of the box office, possibly undermining the ability of film makers to make films for the big screen in the long run. Similarly, it is possible to foresee a weakened ability to develop films within the studios and the continued absence of that ability within production companies, as the properties always come from elsewhere and the majors only respond to them. For consumers, only entertaining, easy-to-understand movies of live action and animation, which production consortia tend to prefer as safe bets, dominate the cinema scene, whereas artistic films and non-Japanese films are finding it increasingly difficult to have any chance of wide release. Independent distributors who buy quality works from abroad are disappearing as their business is particularly volatile and independent art house cinemas are also closing down.

This state of film culture is a concern for film policy as a cultural policy, as one of its major goals is to make a range of works available and accessible to the public. The film policy of any country (except the US) has traditionally been concerned with the protection of national cinema (against the inflow of Hollywood movies) since the early twentieth century. Today, as film policy admits to the fact that extremely commercial films (from Hollywood) satisfy a certain consumer demand, 'protectionism' has been replaced with the goal of 'diversity' to support non-Hollywood (including national) works (see, for example, the website of the British Film Institute and CNC 2016: 199).[7] That is, policy aims to promote films from a wide range of themes, genres, and scales to cater for diverse consumer tastes so that a rich audio-visual culture is nurtured in the country.[8] ACA's film policy in Japan, although limited in budget, mentions the importance of a variety of Japanese films (ACA, website),[9] and the Ministry of Economy, Trade and Industry (METI), the lead ministry for entertainment industries for economic policy, also seems to be concerned about the lack of quality 'middle-range' films – those between 10 and 50 in the box office ranking and earning between 1 and 5 billion yen, which are not for niche film aficionados but can attract a substantial audience base (METI 2009: 35–6). The current production consortium system does not address this segment.

The second issue raised by the spread of the production consortium system is that the financial base for films is, in effect, restricted and no longer has the prospect of expansion. Consortium members are from a very small pool of large established firms, totalling 40 or so at most (Wakabayashi et al. 2015), that specialize in the respective businesses. As has been mentioned, member companies are mostly interested in receiving their fees by dealing with specific exploitation activities and the synergy effects generated by the film that benefit their *respective businesses*. In fact, according to my informants, they are not keeping their eye on the overall financial achievement of the film, even whether it recouped or not. They may well be interested in the success of the project, but only to the extent that it affects the kind of profit most relevant to their core business. Reports on certain areas such as theatrical release and video rentals may be circulated among the members from time to time, but it is said that most do not bother to look at them. Furthermore, the leading company of a consortium is only the administrator, and is not required by law or custom to produce accounting reports to the members. It is thus difficult to know, for outsiders as well as for the members, precisely how much a film has made in total via theatrical release, broadcasting, home video rentals, merchandising, and so on against the investment made. The individuals in charge of film projects from the member companies are, after all, salaried employees and the performance of the film projects does not significantly influence their careers. They only want to report to their bosses that the companies' core businesses benefited from participation, i.e. an increase in the sale of the comic book title in the case of a publishing house and more advertising contracts in the case of an ad agency. However, they have little interest in other kinds of profits generated by the film project and the long-term performance of the whole process. In short, no one takes care to exploit the film property to the maximum and keep the financial picture of the project visible. Investors from outside the usual circle of membership, such as overseas investors, financial institutions, and individuals, would need a transparent accounting system and good governance for internal control, but in the current form, consortia are not required to have these in place. As far as current members are concerned, they are satisfied with the present system that lacks transparency, despite their unlimited liabilities for the projects, because it is simple and time-effective and they acknowledge each other as respectable, reliable, and safe partners.

The third problem about the production consortium system is the lack of leadership within a consortium, with no one in a position to make important decisions; it is merely a union of companies that get together for a specific film project in which the members need to reach unanimous agreement on major issues. Export is a typical problem, as the local counterpart would demand all rights (i.e. to theatre release, broadcasting, online distribution, etc.), but the members have different degrees of business interest in export. If some are reluctant or opposed, negotiation does not move forward and the potential buyer from abroad would lose interest by the time a decision is arrived at. The absence of a central power within the consortium prevents quick decision-making for business deals, sometimes critical in creative control as well. This deficiency prevents international co-production from development. Japan as a country has no international treaty with foreign countries for film co-production (except one with Canada, which is dormant) and provides no tax incentives for foreign productions shooting in Japan or for investment in film production. China and South Korea are quickly developing a close relationship with regard to film and other content production and enhancing their presence in the Asian region (Yecies 2016) together, while Japan is staying aloof when in fact its domestic market is going to shrink due to the ageing population.

Also worrisome is that projects go ahead when companies expected to become members are convinced of the economic potential by seeing the presence of a television network and the proven record of the source material to be recycled in the project. The members have little experience of or interest in judging the cultural or even economic value of the proposed film *on the basis of the story*, skipping the most important part of film development. In the long term and taken together, these tendencies might lead to film makers losing their edge in terms of their capability to make quality films.

Conclusion

This chapter has described the production consortium system that is a mainstream form of financing film production, particularly for large-scale projects of entertainment value, in Japan. Prior to the emergence of this, films were solely financed by the Japanese majors, none of whom, however, had the capacity to revitalize the film industry and the cinema scene that had declined between the 1960s and the early 1980s. With the participation of television networks in the consortia, several dozen films (including animation) are produced in Japan, taking a large share of the domestic market. What is distinctive about these consortia is the usual presence of publishing houses, trading companies, advertising agencies, and merchandisers whose main businesses are outside the creation of audio-visual products. By spreading the risk inherent in the film business, the consortia system has expanded the financial base for film production in Japan. The role played by television networks is of crucial importance for public relations as well as in providing source material that has a proven record of market success.

Despite these contributions to the revival of the industry and advantages of the system, however, this chapter has pointed out the system's deficiencies and problems. One major inherent problem is the system's exclusiveness. The lack of transparency and accountability, which is tolerated among current players, would not induce those from outside to invest. The lack of interest shown by existing members in the overall financial performance of the film through theatrical release and the exploitation of all the rights does not help, either, to expand the current structure. A very large number of independent film projects do not, despite the international reputation enjoyed by their directors for quality films, benefit from the closed system as it is only concerned with commercial gain from participation. Middle-range films that can attract a substantial base of audiences, probably the middle-aged, are not made in the current system and this audience remains unsatisfied with what is available. This is also true in the US where movie-watching is essentially seen as a teenage pastime, where the under-served demand of the middle-aged for genres other than sci-fi/adventure/action was confirmed by such hits as *Lincoln* (2012), *The Best Exotic Marigold Hotel* (2011) and its sequel (2015) (GEM Standard 2015). Younger generations tend to spend more time in media consumption with their portable devices and might soon isolate themselves from cinemas. Thus, one can argue that what is important for film culture and the economic vitality of the industry is a diversity of offerings, which, however, is decreasing in Japan. Despite the numbers of local films produced and their share of the domestic market, which may suggest the strength of the industry, in fact it is doubtful that this current position will be sustainable in the years to come.

Notes

1 The term 'production committee' as an English translation seems to appear more often, but 'production consortium' more appropriately expresses what the entity entails and will be used throughout this chapter.
2 Throughout the chapter, US dollar equivalents are given for reference purposes, calculated at the rate of 110 yen to a dollar.
3 The website of the Motion Picture Producers Association of Japan provides information. http://www.eiren.org/toukei/1983.html (in Japanese, accessed February 22, 2017).
4 The website of the Motion Picture Producers Association of Japan. http://www.eiren.org/toukei/1998.html (in Japanese, accessed February 22, 2017).
5 Angel investors are 'individuals who invest in project on a one-off basis rather than as part of an overall strategy, and have low overheads and tend to trust their own judgement and instincts on an investment' (Finney 2015: 250). They also 'want upside and involvement and link to creative element and lifestyle' (Finney 2015: 84).
6 A completion bond is 'a contractual commitment issued by a Completion Guarantor agreeing to either (a) complete and deliver a picture on time or (b) repay the bank if timely delivery is not achieved' (Moore 2011: 5), for which a fee as a percentage (from 2 per cent to 5 per cent) of the production cost (the combined above-the-line and below-the-line costs, often excluding costs relating to acquisition of rights and payments to lead actors) is charged.
7 http://www.bfi.org.uk/supporting-uk-film (BFI, accessed June 10, 2017).
8 To enhance the economic vitality of the industry is another aim of film policy (e.g. see CNC 2016: 199). Financial and managerial strength is a prerequisite for a vibrant film scene, and this in turn serves cultural purposes, too.
9 http://www.bunka.go.jp/seisaku/bunkashingikai/seisaku/08/shingikeikahokoku22/03_9.html (in Japanese, accessed June 11, 2017).

References

Caves, R. E. (2002) *Creative Industries: Contracts between Art and Commerce*. Cambridge, MA: Harvard University Press.
Centre national du cinéma et de l'image animée (CNC) (2016) *Results 2016*. Paris: CNC.
Elmer, G. and Gasher, M. (eds.) (2005) *Contracting Out Hollywood*. Lanham, MD: Rowman & Littlefield.
Erickson, G., Tulchin, H. and Halloran, M. (2010) *The Independent Film Producer's Survival Guide*, 3rd edn. New York: Shirmer Trade Books.
Finney, A. with Trianna, E. (2015) *The International Film Business*, 2nd edn. London: Routledge.
GEM Standard (2015/07/10) *Mitasarete inai kankyokuso toshiteno chukonen* (The Middle-aged Audiences Under-satisfied), http://column.gempartners.com/?p=11506 (webpage in Japanese, accessed June 10, 2017).
Kawashima, N. (2016) Film policy in Japan – an isolated species on the verge of extinction? *International Journal of Cultural Policy*, 22(5): 787–804.
Kawashima, N. (2014) The film industry in Japan – prospering without active support from the state? In Lee, H.-K. and Lim, L. (eds.), *Cultural Policies in East Asia*. London: Palgrave Macmillan.
Kobayashi, M. (2014) The paradigm shift in local cultural policy in Japan. In Lee, H.-K. and Lim, L. (eds.), *Cultural Policies in East Asia*. London: Palgrave Macmillan.
METI (2009) *Eiga sangyo bijinesu moderu kenkyukai houkousho* (Report on the research group on the business model of the film industry) (in Japanese). Tokyo: METI.
Moore, S. (2011) The Biz, the Basic Business, Legal and Financial Aspects of the Film Industry, 4th edn. Los Angeles: Silman-James Press.
Motion Picture Producers Association of Japan (website) http://www.eiren.org/statistics_e/index.html (accessed February 22, 2017).
Otmazgin, N. (2012) Geopolitics and soft power: Japan's cultural policy and cultural diplomacy in Asia. *Asia-Pacific Review*, 19(1): 37–61.
Wakabayashi, N., Yamashita, M., Yamada, J., and Noguchi, H. (2015) Gyoshutekina kigyoukan nettowaku ga hatten saseta jissenkyodotai (Collaborative entities for practice developed by dense inter-firm networks) (in Japanese). *Soshiki kagaku* (Journal of Organization Studies) 28(4): 21–34.
Wasko, J. (2003) *How Hollywood Works*. London: Sage.
Yecies, B. (2016) The Chinese-Korean co-production pact: collaborative encounters and the accelerating expansion of Chinese cinema. *International Journal of Cultural Policy*, 22(5): 770–86.

12

Creative milieu in China – 'disjuncture' in the global cultural economy

Justin O'Connor and Xin Gu

Introduction

In this chapter we examine the idea of the 'creative cluster', one of China's key policy models for promoting both the creative city and cultural-creative industries. We do so with a particular focus on Shanghai, and on a well-known art cluster in that city, M50. While the Chinese creative cluster could be presented in fairly instrumental 'policy transfer' terms, it came as part of a wider 'creativity' agenda closely linked to a normative account of the relationship between liberal democratic governance and a new round of creativity-led innovation. More particularly, it comes associated with notions of the 'creative milieu' that have rarely taken hold in Chinese creative clusters. M50, however, is one case where we can clearly identify such a milieu. Our account here charts the trajectory of M50 from bottom-up organic cluster to one closely integrated into Shanghai's culture-creative industry system. However, we want to avoid the standard characterization of a top-down, state-led use and abuse of creativity for the purpose of real estate development or gentrification (though this is often the case) and suggest other dynamics at work.

Many of the claims around creative industries and creative cities in the West were founded on a need to find replacement jobs in a post-industrial economy and to re-think the function of the city as a competitive global entity. The competitive advantage of the West was now to be found in its ability to create ideas and innovate rather than manufacture things. The UK government launched its rebranding of the cultural sector as 'creative industries' in 1998 with a claim that this would see Britain become the 'creative workshop of the world', in an *aufhebung* of its glorious industrial past (DCMS 1998). The rise of the 'knowledge economy' in the form of (mostly) US-based media technology companies, the increasing reach of IP generation and exploitation after WTO, and the powerfully affective images of start-ups and young entrepreneurs emerging in the seemingly autonomous new space of the internet, reframed 'creativity' as a crucial economic resource – one the West was best suited to exploit (Hutton 2007; O'Connor 2011).

Creativity thus came with a bundle of values and normative claims about the requisite socio-economic and political frameworks which were very difficult to ignore. Creativity demanded new kinds of cities (or at least, zones therein) which encouraged creative milieus, new kinds of industrial organization (SME ecosystems), and new kinds of subjects able to autonomously create and innovate. That bundle included three key figures. First, is that of the autonomous artist which animates the imaginary around the new creative subject and the kind of entrepreneurship to which this (ideally) gives rise. Second, is the 'creative milieu', a semi-autonomous network embedded in particular urban places and through which new ideas emerge, circulate, mutate, and accelerate. Third, is the SME economy which operates in a zone between the firm (internal, hierarchy) and the social (external, network), between competition and collaboration, between the market and 'civil society', and which is held to operate as a kind of 'ecosystem' which is not amenable to top-down state planning or corporate control.

These three figures are closely connected within the creativity agenda, and though they each have different genealogies, they share a common root in a liberal-democratic/enlightenment narrative that is not easily adaptable by the Chinese state (O'Connor 2011). We are not, in stating this, returning to an essentialism against which China's 'divergence' can be measured; or rather, in charting this divergence we are not thereby making a (usually negative) normative judgement. China's policy makers are very aware of the implications of the creativity agenda for their own political regime, wary of connections between creativity and 'democracy', just as openness to trade in cultural goods and services brought concerns with 'cultural security' (Garner 2015). This is frequently characterized as hypocritical instrumentalism – the Chinese government wants creativity effects but without the 'dangerous' (i.e. democratic) consequences that come with it (Keane 2013). We want to suspend such a judgement for a moment and look at other factors.

China's policy shift from cultural industries (*wenhua chanye*) – a term it had adopted in a positive manner in 1998 – to creative industries (*chuangyi chanye*) can be understood in the context of that deepening and acceleration of China's post-1978 reforms – from *gaige kaifang* (reform and opening) to *gaige chuangxin* (reform and innovation) – in which new kinds of producing and consuming subjects would be required (O'Connor and Gu 2006; Pang 2012). 'Creativity' is seen to provide a key element necessary for a next stage of economic development in which a certain kind of innovation and new forms of symbolic consumption would be central. As has been well-documented, the Chinese state has had some difficulties in accepting the term 'creative' as opposed to 'cultural' industries (Hui 2006; Keane 2007). The Chinese word for creativity (*chuangyi*) arrived via Hong Kong where the UK neologism was first translated, and it relates specifically to artistic rather than technical innovation (*chuangxin*) (Hui 2006). As in the West this art-derived form of creativity was now to be distributed across a wider section of the population and animate a proliferating sector of new 'creative' industries. Creativity in this sense, however, was not something that the Chinese state could easily divest from its cultural policy connotations, an area strictly supervised by the government since 1949.

Despite its instrumentalization as a new economic agenda, the Chinese state saw 'creativity' as directly pertaining to those issues of art and culture that had long been the strict province of the Culture (or Propaganda) ministry. The national government attempted to separate creative from cultural industries, allocating the former to the economic agenda and the latter to the cultural (and thus under the control of the Culture ministry). This led to some rather arbitrary taxonomies in which, contrary to UK and EU usages, the term 'creative industries' was expanded to include many non-cultural activities (business consulting, R&D) as well as activities such as hairdressing (Keane 2007). The key distinction was about 'safe' rather than 'sensitive' content rather than state versus market per se; both the cultural and creative industries were to be subject to market disciplines (Garner 2015). The ambiguity between 'cultural' and 'creative' marked cluster policy, which in Shanghai was also divided into cultural/creative, with the economic and propaganda (or publicity) departments overseeing their respective entities (Luan et al. 2016). One way of managing this, following well-worn practice of regional testing (Zhang and Peck 2014), was for the national government to allow Shanghai to push ahead with the creative industries agenda, in a wait-and-see policy. The high levels of cross-over and ambiguity between cultural and creative industries eventually resulted in a composite term, the cultural-creative industries (Chen 2012).

Creative clusters

In 2005 the Shanghai municipal government adopted the term 'creative industries' and positioned the 'creative cluster' as the main mechanism whereby these industries might be developed as a part of a global city (Chen 2012; Keane 2013; O'Connor and Gu 2014). The rapid proliferation of these clusters in Shanghai – where the number reached almost 200 at one point – and elsewhere across China has been well documented (Zheng 2010, 2011; Zheng and Chan 2013). Equally well documented, especially in Shanghai, has been the ways in which these clusters performed more as real-estate mechanisms than as dynamic nodes in a creative ecosystem. From the perspective of Shanghai as a whole, it has also been suggested that these do very little to promote the overall creative economy of the city, other than perhaps as image capital (fashion shots, art openings, young creatives taking coffee and so on) (O'Connor and Gu 2014, 2016).

Here, seemingly, is an example of failed policy transfer: relentless reduction of cultural or creative objectives to the imperatives of government-sponsored real-estate development and urban branding ultimately not delivering those outcomes for which the creative cluster was originally intended. The Shanghai government itself has struggled to define to itself what the real purpose of clusters is – real estate, lifestyle branding, or cultural content production (Luan et al. 2016). We might also see this as a process of adaptation, where policy transfer is more volatile and the 'assemblage' thereby created much more provisional and fluid (Oakes and Wang 2016). This 'policy mobilities' approach does cast light on cluster policies in China (O'Connor and Gu 2016), but we would suggest that the mutation of a cluster such as M50 responds much more to a deeper, structural difference between China and its Western policy sources than this literature often allows.

On the face of it the idea of the creative cluster involved a set of straightforwardly instrumental benefits which, while requiring some local adoption, could be outlined in the language of business development.[1] In practice this pragmatic, instrumental policy recipe bore little relation to what actually happened in these clusters or how local Chinese policy makers conceived of their purpose. There was a clear attraction to the idea of these clusters and the image of Western-inspired modernization they brought with them, but the operationalization of that idea in the Chinese context resulted in a very different configuration whose interest for us goes beyond the invocation of 'hybridization' or 'indigenization' (Appadurai 1990).

The idea of creative clusters has a complex provenance (see Granovetter 1985; Scott 2000; cf. O' Connor 2004; O'Connor and Gu 2010; Peck 2002). Its most immediate origin lay with Michael Porter's (Porter 1998, 2000) papers which were usually cited along with the idea. But specifically 'creative' clusters also drew on Charles Landry's work which positioned the cultural dimension as primary (Landry 2000). A city's vibrant culture was an index of its wider creative potential, one that could be used to signal to footloose capital and draw global talent to the cultural 'brand' of a city. Culture was also to provide new sources of employment and competitiveness, as it moved closer to economic centre stage. Cities could only deliver this, Landry argued, if they adopted the more 'holistic' non-linear, non-instrumental approach associated with art. The 'creative city' thesis thus connected urban embeddedness, networked interdependency, and the knowledge economy with that other trope of the 'elective affinity' between art, artists, and the city that could be traced back through the metropolitan avant-gardes and modernisms of the pre-and inter-war periods, with their privileged 'villages' and 'quarters', through to *La Vie Bohème* of Baudelaire and others stretching back to the early nineteenth century. Sharon Zukin's work (1989) would facilitate this connection when she explicitly charted the emergence of an 'artists zone' in SoHo, showed how artists had been drawn to this part of the city and had been, ultimately, allowed to thrive by the planners. Her book, however, was mainly intended to show how this was a precursor to a new form of gentrification based less on physical destruction than cultural 're-landscaping'. The urban milieu she evoked, under the synecdoche of 'loft living', has since been rolled out by urban authorities in flagrant contradiction of her critical intent.

This urban milieu has been explored extensively, and from multiple perspectives (see Lloyd 2006; Currid 2008) of which we would elaborate on two particular elements that have emerged with reference to the cultural context in China. The first is how this milieu allows for the kinds of labour available – a combination of paid (usually low-skilled) and unpaid (usually art-related) – in which creative careers can take their first steps. While economically marginal activities, they allow the building up of 'symbolic' or reputational capital which allows them (or some of them) to eventually move on. This pattern of working also evokes images of an artistic 'autonomy' closely related to the notion of the bourgeois public sphere that emerged between the sixteenth and eighteenth centuries in Europe and America. Classically, of course, bohemia was vehemently opposed to the bourgeois commercial mainstream; but as with other cultural figures, in the 1990s the 'creativity' agenda set out to recoup that autonomous opposition as a capacity to be nurtured in the name of 'wild' innovation. This agenda was a deepening of that form of liberal governance (in Foucault's (2007) sense) that worked with and utilized, rather than trying to directly control and restrict, the autonomous individual. This deepening has been represented as a new 'creative' capitalism (Boltanski and Chiapello 2005; McRobbie 2015). Such a deep-seated shift to a new creative capitalism building on the innovation effects of autonomous, even fissiparous individuals, was not one readily transferable to China!

One further crucial element needs identifying – crucial because it was this that allowed these notions of the creative city to enter China in a usable package. The specific idea of the creative cluster grew out of four distinct elements. First, was artist-run spaces that took off from the late 1970s. Second, were areas of urban regeneration, often around heritage or waterfront areas, which included leisure, specialist retail, and animation programmes, often including small-scale workspace aimed at 'creative' professionals (designers, architects). Third, the growth of 'arts precincts' with a high number of subsidized institutions, also including office and production facilities for the creative sector. Fourth, the restauration of old industrial buildings, often as part of a wider area's regeneration, for the use of art and cultural/creative industries.

Thus the technocratic-sounding list of expected benefits flowing from the creative cluster policy model was clearly much more than that. They imply a benign combination of creative(s) autonomy and an urban milieu that nurtures and connects that creativity to the wider cultural economy of a city, itself structured around a highly networked open ecosystem of SMEs. Creative clusters are thus seen as longer-term investments, and the returns as part of a common good ('positive externality') not solely recouped by the cluster management itself – hence the presence of public money in many creative clusters. Moreover, though many of the cultural externalities are seen as economic (nurturing the context for further creative innovation), they are also seen as valuable in themselves, adding to the public good of city life. Creative clusters then depend on shared visions (imaginaries), expectations, and values that are often implicit but very real nonetheless.

Thus the cultural dimension can often take precedence over their purported economic outcomes – sometimes explicitly. Even when framed as part of a wider economic strategy they are often defended against more aggressive gentrification and make an attempt to ensure (or 'curate') common cultural values in their tenants/suppliers/audiences, often as part of the 'feel', the shared symbolic capital of the place. Indeed, eeconomic relationships within creative clusters are ambiguous, where cultural and non-cultural entrepreneurship have to negotiate different approaches to profit and business ethics generally (O'Connor 2004).

The reduction of creative clusters in Shanghai to real-estate machines requiring immediate and high returns for investors, can be seen as a refusal of the local state to pursue anything other than short-term financial gain. Alongside this, is a sense that creative autonomy is neither expected nor respected in these clusters. No wonder then that many commentators (including us, O'Connor and Gu 2014) see them as failures.

M50 as an 'authentic' cluster

M50's emergence stands apart from the more general process of the policy transfer of creative cluster into the Chinese context. This transfer has been overwhelmingly instrumental, in two ways. First, local policy makers and urban planners in Chinese cities bought into the economic functionality of clustering theory with very little awareness of the kind of socio-cultural contexts in which these economic functions were supposed to be embedded, or the wider values they articulated. To local governments it seemed like a fairly straightforward policy transfer, creative clusters mapping neatly onto the industrial, science and technology bases and parks that characterized China's developmental state approach.

Second, the motivations and expectations at local district level (the level determining land use) were characterized by rather mundane concerns. The pressures on local government to generate income from their control over land use, as well as to show how they were promoting the creative industries, combined to make creative clusters a relatively low-cost option for generating new tax revenue through using industrial land for commercial purposes; re-using old industrial buildings with minimal refurbishment (Zheng 2010, 2011; Zheng and Chan 2013); and attempting to recoup and control any innovation effects by having direct oversight over the activities of the tenant companies. The main lines of criticism have been that the real-estate functions have trumped other creativity effects. Developers have misunderstood the needs of the creative sector; have gone for tenants able to pay higher rents; promoted consumption (cafes) and exhibition/retail rather than production; and even if they did manage to attract creatives these were isolated or uncoupled from the surrounding urban context (by walls and less physical kinds of exclusion) (O'Connor and Gu 2014). Shanghai government, at both municipal and district levels, certainly bought into these pragmatic and instrumental objectives (see Gu 2014 for the history and rationales behind the development of M50).

For Chinese policy makers, creative industries and creative cities were seen as a ramping up of the cultural industries sector in the wake of digital innovation, copyright industries, and high-end real estate driven by creative business services. While this is clearly 'instrumental' (just as it is in the West) it involves less a refusal of 'creative autonomy' but continues (from the point of view of the party-state) an older idea of mobilizing artists in the service of national advancement. Even this cursory glance would show how the idea of the creative urban milieu, and the autonomy of creatives, would have a very different valiancy in China.

Similar things could be said about the SME economy, though the issues here have a somewhat different provenance. Clearly, the rise of small businesses and entrepreneurs was central to the post-1978 reforms, and promoted by Deng in the face of strong opposition from within the party establishment. However – though we can only state this here – the green light to Shanghai could be seen to mark a shift in power towards a state-sponsored and top-down development that side-lined these small businesses in favor of the privatized SOEs and the local states that had interests in them. Huang's (2008) account of Shanghai is convincing: the post-1992 municipal government sought to stimulate urban development through large-scale state investment (financed by land sales) and foreign direct investment in ways that marginalized the small business sector. The dominance of state-backed (often former) SOEs and their *guanxi* networks is prevalent in Shanghai, and even more so in the cultural industries sector. In this sense creative clusters can be seen as one way of promoting the kinds of micro-businesses associated with creative innovation while keeping control – not just ideologically but in terms of the kinds of innovation effects they might introduce.

Coming back to the scale of the creative cluster, and in particular those that are aimed at the artist, then, we would first have to understand the kinds of attachment or identification – that 'elective affinity' – between artists/creatives and their immediate urban environment. After that we can look at how the governance of these spaces acknowledge and/or utilize that affinity and consequently the voice of artists within them. By 2005 both creatives and governments/developers agreed on the desirability of re-using old buildings, and mostly on the appropriate 'low-intervention' aesthetic to be found in the West (though it is now ubiquitous) (Gu 2012). The frictions emerged around how artists wanted to operationalize in order to create a space in which they would wish to work – a question that might be couched as professional recognition rather than 'autonomy'.

How then do management and artists relate to each other in Chinese creative clusters? To what extent do artists co-identify with a cultural space embodying certain values? How are they using the power of their 'professional expertise' to preserve the spaces for artistic use? Do they have power to exclude what they consider to be poor-quality artists or non-cultural businesses, or to ensure non-cultural businesses work within the cultural value system of the cluster? Who actually exercises such power and how?

Art spaces and identities

The first group of artists moved into M50 in 1999. The artists who moved in used to be affiliated with public institutions – working as university lecturers or as salaried artists in professional associations, artist workgroups (*danwei*), or SOEs. When they were pushed out of the state system during the privatizations of the 1980s, financial necessity saw them seek out affordable working spaces, and led them to empty factories. The attraction of industrial warehouses for artists was new to government officials, as the manager of M50, recalled:

> When some artists first approached us about renting our factory warehouses, we don't know whether it is legal. We try to keep a low profile. We don't know how much we should charge for rent because there is no comparison … Some of the contracts are just verbal agreements with the understanding that they have to move out if there is trouble … It was totally ad-hoc, in many ways secretive.
>
> *(Interview with author, January 17, 2010)*

The uncertain official status of many of the art clusters before 2005 – in Shanghai and China generally – was advantageous to artists in terms of keeping the rent below the threshold of commercial rents. Commercial rent was still about 30 times more than the average rent of a creative cluster within the inner-city zone (with a few notable exceptions) at the end of 2012.

The potential of old factories to act as a collective space for artists – rather than simply being cheap – was not widely acknowledged within the art community for some time. Artists in M50 worked within their studios most of the time and did not actively seeking connections with others. As one of the first artists moving into M50, Han Yuqi recalled:

> When my friends asked me to move here, I was very critical at first. Artists don't need to work from the same place. We don't really collaborate – how can you paint together with one another? It is an absurd idea. When I got here, there were already some artists here, but we don't really talk to one another.
>
> *(Interview with author, March 24, 2010)*

At first then, these artists, long used to a clear institutional affiliation, did not register the new spaces as anything other than answering a purely material necessity. Increasingly, however, the idea of a collective art space, in a location that somehow resonated with an emergent 'artistic persona', began to grow. For many artists, these scruffy, unconventional, urban-edge sites were a good fit with the emergent, 'cutting-edge' identity of Chinese contemporary art. Chinese contemporary artists began to understand their potential role in the re-articulation of these urban spaces just as their Western counterparts had a decade earlier. They also shared a recognition of how their artistic *habitus* needed to be in dialogue with their creative works – that one fed the other – and this in turn impacted upon the symbolic value of their immediate urban environment and its synergies with this work and persona.

After the privatization of the cultural sector in the 1990s, artists not only found their income threatened but the ending of their institutional affiliation also meant that a key source of their social identity as artists disappeared. There were few social spaces available outside such institutions in which an 'artistic' identity might be created. The limited de-politicization in the 1980s saw many artists and intellectuals seek a more symmetrical relationship to the party-state, in which their specific expertise might be recognized. This de-politicization, sometimes presented as a liberation from politics (Smith 2008), was also experienced as marginalization (something similar happened in post-Soviet Russia), with Western notions of 'autonomy' lacking the kind of historical precedent or institutional framework that would compensate for this. The growing success of contemporary Chinese art internationally and the arrival of this art world in China itself had a profound impact on local artists. It represented a space in which de-institutionalized artists might both make money and find a position they could inhabit. They began to adapt to the artistic persona as figured within this global discourse. Sometimes their products seemed an opportunistic exploitation of their unexpected global popularity – the growing cliché of iconoclastic/ironic uses of Maoist and other communist symbols, for example. But what was also being learned was the idea of aesthetic self-determination and how this was to be built into careers. The artistic persona and the kinds of artistic career strategies needed to access the global cultural markets became central to much of what M50 came to be about.

Han Yuqi was one of the key members of the *Preserve M50 Committee*, set up in 2002, composed of artists, urban planners, writers, and historians. Her two books – the *Seine of the East* (Han 2004) and the *Sound of the River* (Han 2006) – articulated convincingly a case among policy makers for warehouse preservation through the lens of her artistic sensibility.

Her books were subsequently promoted by senior urban planners and policy makers in Shanghai. Ironically, one of the key arguments that Han put forward – to view these places as new kinds of cultural infrastructure for Shanghai – has driven the process of urban gentrification in ways that artists did not then anticipate, though it is since very familiar. Her books, echoing the work of urban conservationists in re-positioning New York lofts as desirable historical and aesthetic objects, opened up industrial Shanghai to the art-led 'regeneration' of industrial spaces in Shanghai. Han's evocation of Shanghai's industrial tradition articulates the 'authenticity' of industrial warehouses as a highly local nostalgia. Her urgent call for preservation in the face of imminent demolition helped position an aestheticized artistic lifestyle as an important aspect of a reinvigorated Shanghai, within which artists would have a key role to play. Because of these arguments made by the local arts community, clusters began to adopt a preservation ethos in industrial heritage sites. Warehouse and factories that would have been demolished were carefully preserved and given new life as creative clusters. The role the arts communities played in the development of this new cultural landscape allowed urban planners to make spatially concrete the emergent governmental narrative connecting Shanghai's glorious past with its future as a global metropolis. In the years leading up to 2005 and for a few years afterwards many artists and architectural historians were invited to give advice and to mentor cluster development projects. Many district governments would give free land to art communities in the hope of nourishing the local creative identity, as did SOEs. Thus in 2011 Shanghai Phoenix Textile Manufacturing Factory, also owned by Shanghaitex, was re-designated as *Taopu* Art, in association with *Shanghart* and M50. Providing free or low-rent spaces for art studios and galleries, the aim was to revitalize its adjacent area.

Some of the key amenities in clusters were initially developed by artists and demonstrate some key prototypes of creative clusters. The first café in M50 was established by artists in its early days. Their purpose was not profit but rather to provide a suitable space within which Western curators and collectors could meet. As one of the first artist tenants in M50 recalled:

> We needed a place to see collectors and curators, most of whom are Westerners, [thus it became] a café. We wanted to keep them here so they got to see the studios and the way we work, feel that art pulses here. Most of the cafés in Shanghai at the time were not very atmospheric. So we decided to do it ourselves.
>
> *(Interview with author, March 29, 2010)*

The initial low financial stakes involved in M50 encouraged artists' clustering and interaction. It was particular attractive to those who were just starting out. There were many experimental art forms in M50 providing a fertile ground for new talent to get feedback from their peers. Han recalled the intensity of art exhibitions in M50 when she first moved in:

> There was always something going on here. For artists, you could just put up an exhibition in your own studio. And everyone that matters would come and see the show. And everything you needed to see was here too … Not just local Shanghai artists but people from all over China. You don't have that in Arts Colleges where most of us came from.
>
> *(Interview with author, March 24, 2010)*

Shanghai Visual Arts College established its *99 Space* within M50 in order to enhance its students' exposure to the art world. A lecturer from Shanghai Visual Arts College directing the art space suggested that it was beneficial for arts graduates to have a close encounter with the 'industry':

> They get to meet other creatives here but more importantly for them, they get to see how the industry operates, like the galleries, curators and learn how to put up an exhibition.
>
> *(Interview with author, January 15, 2010)*

M50's experimental exhibition space and gallery spaces were crucial for young artists who could not afford to display their works in the city's more established art galleries. And most importantly, these gallery spaces were becoming part of the global art trade with Western curators and collectors flocking to the site looking for emerging young talent. *Shanghart* was the most important gallery internationally collecting Chinese contemporary art. Its original exhibition and warehouse space, operating within M50 since 2004, saw Lorenz Helbling developing close collaboration with artists within M50 and promoting them to the outside world. *Shanghart* has since become one of the most highly rated Chinese contemporary art galleries and Lorenz Helbling one of the most influential persons in the Chinese art scene. One artist described M50's global appeal in early 2005:

> You could not have found a place that attracted that many Laowai (foreigners) in Shanghai. We don't know why they came, or what they did here. They seemed to know their way around without us providing any information, they knew when an exhibition was on, and by whom. And they just chatted with the artists in their studios ... We had a few foreign artists renting studios here too.
>
> *(Interview with author, January 13, 2010)*

Those artists within M50 were better positioned to pick up the most recent global cultural trends. In return, these global trends – and the trade that went with these – began to influence the constitution of the broader art scene in the city. The identity of being an internationally connected artist based on values such as 'cutting edge', 'anti-authoritarian' and 'individualism' was translated widely into local arts practices.

Governance

As M50 began to grow in reputation artists became aware of their weight within the decision-making process in the old factory. Initially a marginal group, brought in while the management sought out 'proper' light-industrial tenants, artists and their requirements were given more attention by the management as they gained in profile. Some of these artists began to develop into the kind of cultural intermediary figure noted in Western culture-led renewal projects. They were able to articulate the needs of artists in the language of the cluster management, finding ways in which the former could help achieve, and perhaps appropriately modify, the goals of the latter. M50 had a particularly sympathetic manager; in most Shanghai clusters this was somewhat limited. However, as the local state got more involved in this high-profile cluster, the professional expertise of artists and their aspirations to collectively sustain shared cultural values had decreasing traction in M50.

M50 is governed by Shanghai Textile Development Corporation, a state-owned enterprise (SOE). It had to convert to other business activities as manufacturing declined and moved its operations to cheaper locations in the west and northwest of China. Shanghaitex was a key actor promoting creative clusters in Shanghai from the very beginning (Gu 2014).

Its good connections with district governments gave it an influential voice in the making of local cultural policies, which privileged SOE domination of cluster development over private enterprises. This had wider implications for the development of clusters in Shanghai, as they increasingly spoke to the ambition of local governments. One of the key differences between local government clusters and private ones is that the former are not expected to be big money spinners *in themselves*. In many ways, clusters are branding exercises – developing landmarks to pave the way for other commercial developments that would draw on the symbolic capital that accrued to adjacent sites. Although it may seem that the artists' efforts in preserving M50 were successful, the demolition and redevelopment of the area surrounding M50 has never stopped.[2] However, the distinctive role of SOEs extended beyond this strategic 'gentrification'; their financial ability to play a longer game not only allowed clusters like M50 to mature, but they also facilitated the linkage of these clusters to the strategic cultural-creative industries ambitious of Shanghai.

The clusters set up by SOEs had two key advantages. They had less financial burden – they did not pay rent on their buildings – and thus did not need to pass this on to creative tenants; and it was often in the SOE's interests to take a more strategic view, raising the profile of the local arts community (and their own relationship to it) and linking the local scene to broader opportunities both locally and nationally. In effect SOEs could play a long game, and as such they could often do more to sustain the creative scene through their non-market (or at least long-term strategic) behavior. Rents in most SOE-managed creative clusters were significantly lower than those where SOEs were not acting as the management companies. Shanghaitex seems to have taken a conscious decision to preserve a unified identity of the arts community within clusters, as it tried to link to municipal and national-level policy ambitions for the promotion of creative industries. M50's manager insisted that he would maintain the level of cheap rents to those artists who have made M50 what it is now and support young and emerging artists who are in need of studio spaces. Since 2007, M50 has hosted its annual *Young Artist Awards* in order to nurture creative talents by providing free studio spaces for winning artists. These measures have been important in contributing to its artistic identity by excluding high-street brands and commercial amenities that aren't consistent with the cluster ethos of M50.

M50 is still considered an exceptional case, mainly because the manager's commitment to the arts community increased as his knowledge of the sector grew. The long-term manager of M50, Jing Weidong, had not only responded positively to the first approaches from artists but increasingly identified himself with the local arts community.[3] He even shared concerns with artists over the progressive gentrification taking place in the adjacent area and argued for a preservation plan for M50. He recalled how he turned down the offer by the urban planning office to provide a bus route for easy access to M50 by tourists:

> M50 is not any tourist spot. We don't want to attract crowds; we want to preserve the artistic atmosphere here. We want artists to be able to work here without being disturbed. They need a peaceful environment, not a busy market.
>
> *(Interview with author, January 17, 2010)*

It may be argued that M50 was only possible because of the shared values and understanding between the artists and cluster manager. It is also true that SOEs are able to plough profits back into these refurbished factories because they have a legal social responsibility to provide employment opportunities for redundant workers and other welfare provisions. Jing claimed that M50 was never meant to turn profit:

> It's always been about better than nothing. We were a rundown factory living on government subsidy with hundreds of redundant workers attached. A creative cluster showed a route out of this abyss. We can restore the factory, pay for workers by re-employing them as cleaners and security workers. And we have an identity in Shanghai, when one mentions art venues, we are definitely no.1 on the list.
>
> *(Interview with author, January 17, 2010)*

Nevertheless, things started to change when M50 acquired a global recognition as the place to be for contemporary Chinese art in the city. More overtly commercial galleries moved into M50, representing successful artists or intermediaries with strong links to the local state. M50 is now an increasingly exclusive art-market cluster linked to some well-connected artists and patrons, with little involvement of the artist community. The only way of becoming part of it is to pay the high rent. Artists in the cluster stopped actively promoting the development of the wider art scene. A clear gap began to open between the cluster as showcase and business centre and as a node in the wider art scene. The two were no longer perceived as mutually beneficial, as the success of those in M50 became uncoupled not only from those still trying to make it, and who found it increasingly exclusionary and 'official', but also from any role as a site of peer group validation, involving the accumulation of reputational capital and the formation of the artistic persona as in the classic creative milieu described above.

Rents became too high for some just starting out and the overrepresentation of commercial art galleries turned a coveted art production space into a space of exhibition and consumption. The symbolic gain from M50 thus became increasingly focused on well-established artists and galleries. As it became more institutionalized, new arrivals came who were not committed to a shared artistic vision and this further disrupted the scene in significant ways.

> There are all kinds of art now here. Some are really bad, landscape, portraits etc. M50 became a retail market for people want to sell art directly to the public ... They saw foreigners buying Mao's laughing statue, now you see them everywhere ... terrible. As a result, we can't bring serious collectors out here anymore, they will be shocked and will be disgusted by what they saw. Quite a lot of people moved out to avoid this.
>
> *(Interview with author, June 28, 2015)*

Many art studios relocated, their place taken by commercial art galleries. Looking over the transformation of M50 over the last decade, Han Yuqi observed a significant change of atmosphere in M50.

> Artists used to visit each other's studio and comment on their works and share ideas. Now it's like a market full of tourists, so we just lock ourselves inside so uninvited tourists won't bother us.
>
> *(Interview with author, May 20, 2012)*

The management seemed no longer as keen to balance these functions, as the role of M50 within the newly global city and as national showcase took pre-eminence. This in turn testified to the growing institutionalization of the contemporary art scene, with well-known and well-connected artists now separating themselves from those without this state-sponsored symbolic capital. M50's institutional prestige allowed certain artists and art world intermediaries to develop strong *guanxi* connections with the local state, and this in turn changed the function of M50.

Conclusion

What conclusions can we take from the above? Is the story of Shanghai creative clusters one of policy imitation, real-estate profits, and short-term return on investment? In large part, yes. M50, along with some of the other art clusters such as *Tianzifang*, represents a somewhat different case. It had elements of that 'organic' development associated with artist 'quarters' or 'villages' in the West, and it acted as a space of learning and exchange for artists and intermediaries, along with managers and policy makers who we can associate with the 'creative milieu'. What we, and others, have also charted is the growing commercialization of these art clusters (and resulting 'gentrification' of the adjacent areas), a process driven by local state agents and often, well-connected artist-entrepreneurs. It would thus be straightforward to describe this as a kind of 'authoritarian' state-driven neoliberalism, a variant on that process of arts-led urban gentrification so well documented in academic literature. But we wanted to end by taking a line not in direct contradiction to this but suggesting another perspective.

We might suggest that the increasing commercialization of M50 relates less to the need to secure increasing returns, either directly from its tenants or through development effects on adjacent areas. Though both these play a role, the emphasis on large, internationally known artists and galleries is also a result of the Shanghai municipal government taking contemporary Chinese art more seriously. It may be less concerned now with the nurturing of an artistic milieu, or the cluster as a learning zone for emergent artists (functions it had more or less observed from a distance) than with how to 'scale up' the production of internationally recognized contemporary Chinese art. M50 has to be seen not just as a lucrative real-estate development – in terms of scale it really is a small player on this field – but also as a key part of a wider infrastructure for contemporary art assembled over the last decade by the Shanghai government such as the development of the Rockbund Museum along Yuanmingyuan Road behind the Bund; the re-use of Shanghai Expo sites as huge contemporary art galleries; the growth of large-scale public and private galleries along the West Bund, including an art 'free trade zone'; the usual slew of biennales and art prizes: all these represent an attempt by Shanghai to compete with New York, London, Paris, Tokyo, and so on. This represents a kind of return to the historic role of Shanghai as a cultural industries capital, a privileged site for the production and consumption of culture, linked, then as now, not just to commercial gain but as part of an ideological project, this time 'soft power' rather than national revolution (Garner 2015).

These global ambitions, and the massive soft and hard infrastructural investments they entail, are as determinant here as are arts-inflected 'growth coalitions' (Zhong 2015: 6). There are some real issues to be explored around the impact of this huge systemic planning on creative clusters, even those with the financial and *guanxi* clout of M50. The ways in which the grassroots or 'non-elite' art scene is progressively disempowered may have some effect on the longer-term viability of M50, but, like 798 in Beijing, it continues to represent an important entrepôt for the international art world. Perhaps M50's absorption into this international circuit has more effect on the viability and internal coherence of the non-elite art scenes increasingly excluded from it. Set against this, however, Shanghai's massive strategic investment in visual art – part and parcel of a similar investment in the cultural creative industries writ large – is something currently absent from most Western countries. Most of these remain committed in principle to investment in the arts, despite swinging cuts in many places. Many governments, especially in Europe, remain committed to promoting the 'creative industries', and yet actual levels of investment in these sectors is frequently less than the arts themselves. There is a sense that underneath the celebratory rhetoric of creativity, the investment and the policy tools required to put this into effect are simply not there. The default cultural policy is to facilitate and oversee the commercial media sector, picking up the tab (to a lesser and lesser extent) for the 'market failure' of the arts.

China does take the cultural creative industries seriously, and has allocated the funds and established the policy mechanisms to follow through. As the Blue Books published by the Shanghai Academy of Social Science illustrate, Shanghai takes their economic impact very seriously, while currently in the West such impact barely registers in public policy. Shanghai's strategy certainly took policy ideas and models from Western practice – and in the early days this could look pretty gauche. But it is now adapting these ideas and models to its particular context in a way that becomes increasingly distinct from that of the West. Its organizing dynamics can no longer be captured in a dialectic of top down/bottom up, or of the liberation of cultural SMEs from the shackles of the state, as 'creativity' rips through the Chinese social and political system (Keane 2013). We suggest there is a need to take a look at what the Chinese state is doing in this space from a different perspective – an attempt we make elsewhere (O'Connor and Gu forthcoming).

China generally has sought to operationalize the creativity agenda, well aware of the ideological incompatibilities (notably the link made between creativity, autonomous subjects, and liberal democracy) this frequently involves. We certainly do not seek to evade the normative judgement these call for – just to withhold such until we are clear as to what is at stake. For beneath the rather brittle and defensive cultural statements and the increasing restrictions on cultural expressions under Xi Jinping's regime, there is a view of the contemporary role of cultural production and cultural policy that cannot be dismissed as simply the control of the party-state (though it is that too).

If the Chinese government assigns to the (somewhat arbitrarily defined) creative industries a purely commercial value, it retains a control over the cultural industries as part of its cultural system – though that does not prevent a powerful commercial logic running through these too. The investment in the art infrastructure clearly brings a range of commercial benefits, from real estate to city branding, but it is also part of 'soft power' – China's reputational reach as an emergent global hegemon. As such, investment in creative arts and design programmes are growing, with universities being pushed by central government to make these more vocational. There is also an increased legitimation of 'art' as a career, with students choosing more of these kinds of programmes year on year – including overseas.[4] As we suggested, it is this kind of systemic investment for long-term strategic purposes, as much as real-estate development, that has increased the institutionalization, commercialization, and institutionalization of the art clusters.

What is less clear is how the system of cultural production relates to the overall objectives of the Chinese state, its concern to secure the values of 'socialism with Chinese characteristics', and more generally, how notions of individual citizenship and collective belonging are to be secured within the cultural production system. The ways in which mass cultural production enhanced or undermined the public sphere, not simply as part of the liberal democratic system as with Habermas (1989), but that 'social horizon of experience' through which we make sense of our lives together (Hansen 1991; Negt and Kluge 1993) – this question had been at the very root of the re-invention of the 'cultural industries' as an entity to be positively engaged with in the early 1970s (Oakley and O'Connor 2015). What was at stake was not the economic impact of this sector but its role in progressive social change. This is now less of a question for public policy in the West, as many governments have abdicated responsibility for the mass production of culture to the commercial sector, now global but as US-dominated as ever. That the system of cultural production might be considered from the point of view of how it enhances, or otherwise, our collective social experience, is a concern that has disappeared below the horizon of the Western polity since the 1980s. The consequences of this are just becoming apparent, in the bitter re-assertion of local collectivities 'abandoned' by globalization and its elites. Speculatively, we can end by saying that China might not have the answers we are looking for, but its questions as to how to create a system of cultural production that also functions as an integral part of a cohesive social system might one day have to become ours again.

Notes

1 In 2009, we began an Australian Research Council funded project LP0991136 *Soft Infrastructure, New Media and Creative Clusters: Developing Capacity in China and Australia*, with Queensland University Technology, Creative 100, Qingdao, and Shanghai Jiaotong University. Cluster benefits were listed as: the transfer of tacit knowledge through informal learning; the efficient sourcing of skills and information; competition/collaboration between complementary business producing learning and efficiency effects; the development of inter-cluster trading, networking and joint projects; the delivery of common services – from utilities to business support, training and industry events; facilitating targeted application of industry development policies; cross-subsidy or government support allowing cheaper rents or other benefits for small companies and entrepreneurs; inspiration by proximity; common branding and identification; the contribution to and benefit from a nearby 'innovative urban milieu'.

2 The rubbish dump has been tidied up and converted in part into a furniture shop to be suitably situated in a cultural complex. The large site of the Flour Mill, which began to be excavated back in 2010, is still under development. No one knows exactly what will become of it. Artists in M50 suspect that it will become a high-end shopping cum leisure entertainment site – it's not hard to understand the model based on the success of Tianzifang. More commercial galleries and souvenir shops have moved in, extending the M50's 'cultural' influence beyond the original boundaries of the factory to include the adjacent residential zones (many of which are still waiting to be demolished).

3 Jing Weidong had been manager since the early 1990s, and continues in this role.

4 The authors are involved in an Australian Research Council (DP150101477 –*Working the Field*) project looking at early career trajectories among artists in Shanghai.

References

Appadurai, A. (1990) Disjuncture and difference in the global cultural economy. *Theory Culture and Society,* 7: 295–310.

Boltanski, L. and Chiapello, E. (2005) *The New Spirit of Capitalism.* London: Verso.

Chen, Y. (2012) Making Shanghai a creative city: exploring the creative cluster strategy from a Chinese perspective. In van Geenhuizen, M. and Nijkamp, P. (eds.), *Creative Knowledge Cities: Myths, Visions and Realities.* Cheltenham: Edward Elgar.

Currid, E. (2008) *The Warhol Economy: How Fashion, Art, and Music Drive New York City.* Princeton, NJ: Princeton University Press.

DCMS (1998) *Creative Industries Mapping Document.* London: DCMS.

Foucault, M. (2007) *Security, Territory, Population: Lectures at the College de France 1977–78.* London: Palgrave Macmillan.

Garner, B. (2015) The new Cultural Revolution: Chinese cultural policy reform and the UNESCO Convention on Cultural Diversity. *The Political Economy of Communication,* 3:1: 57–82.

Granovetter, M. (1985) Economic action and social structure: the problem of embeddedness. *American Journal of Sociology,* 91: 481–510.

Gu, X. (2012) The art of re-industrialisation in Shanghai. *Culture Unbound*, 4: 193–211.

Gu, X. (2014) Creative industries, creative clusters and cultural policy in Shanghai. In Lee, H.-K. and Lim, L. (eds.), *Cultural Policies in East Asia: Dynamics between the State, Arts and Creative Industries.* London: Palgrave Macmillan, pp. 174–92.

Habermas, J. (1989) *The Structural Transformation of the Public Sphere*. Cambridge, MA: MIT Press.
Han, Y. (2004) *Seine of the East*. Shanghai: Guji Publishing.
Han, Y. (2006) *Sound of the River*. Shanghai: Guji Publishing.
Hansen, M. (1991) *Babel and Babylon. Spectatorship in American Silent Film*. Cambridge, MA: Harvard University Press.
Huang, Y. (2008) *Capitalism with Chinese Characteristics. Entrepreneurship and the State*. Cambridge, MA: Cambridge University Press.
Hui, D. (2006) From cultural to creative industries: strategies for Chaoyang District, Beijing. *International Journal of Cultural Studies*, 9(3): 317–31.
Hutton, W. (2007) *The Writing on the Wall: China and the West in the 21st Century*. London: Little Brown.
Keane, M. (2007) *Created in China: The Great New Leap Forward*. London: Routledge.
Keane, M. (2013) *Creative industries in China*. Cambridge and Maldon: Polity Press.
Landry, C. (2000) *The Creative City*. London: Comedia.
Lloyd, R. (2006) *Neo-Bohemia: Art and Commerce in the Postindustrial City*. London: Routledge.
Luan, F., He, Y. and Wang, H. (2016) The types of evolution and locational characteristics of Shanghai creative industry districts development. In Rong, Y. M. and Hua, J. (eds.), *The Blue Book Series on Shanghai Cultural Development: Annual Report on Cultural Industry Development of Shanghai*. Shanghai Academy of Social Science Press. [In Chinese]
McRobbie, A. (2015) *Be Creative: Making a Living in the New Culture Industries*. London: Polity.
Negt, O. and Kluge, A. (1993) *Public Sphere and Experience: Towards an Analysis of the Bourgeois and Proletarian Public Sphere*. Minneapolis, MN: University of Minnesota Press.
Oakes, T. and Wang, J. (2016) Introduction. In Oakes, T., Wang, J. and Yang, Y. (eds.), *Making Cultural Cities in Asia: Mobility, Assemblage, and the Politics of Aspirational Urbanism*. London: Routledge, pp. 1–14.
Oakley, K. and O'Connor, J. (2015) Cultural industries: an introduction. In Oakley, K. and O'Connor, J. (eds.), *The Routledge Companion to the Cultural Industries*. London: Routledge. pp. 1–32.
O'Connor, J. (2004) 'A special kind of city knowledge': innovative clusters, tacit knowledge and the 'creative city'. *Media International Australia*, 112: 131–49.
O'Connor, J. (2011) Economic development, enlightenment and creative transformation: creative industries in the New China. *Economiaz*, 79: 108–25.
O'Connor, J. and Gu, X. (2006) A new modernity? The arrival of 'creative industries' in China. *International Journal of Cultural Studies*, 9: 271.
O'Connor, J. and Gu, X. (2010) Developing a creative cluster in a post-industrial City: CIDS and Manchester. *The Information Society*, 26(2): 124–36.
O'Connor, J. and Gu, X. (2014) Creative industry clusters in Shanghai: a success story? *International Journal of Cultural Policy*, 20(1): 1–20.
O'Connor, J. and Gu, X. (2016) Creative clusters in Shanghai: transnational intermediaries and the creative economy. In Oakes, T., Wang, J. and Yang, Y. (eds.), *Making Cultural Cities in Asia: Mobility, Assemblage, and the Politics of Aspirational Urbanism*. London: Routledge, pp. 21–35.
O'Connor, J. and Gu, X. (forthcoming) *Cultural Economy in the New Shanghai*. London: Routledge.
Pang, L. (2012) *Creativity and its Discontents: China's Creative Industries and Intellectual Property Rights Offences*. Durham, NC: Duke University Press, p. 8.
Peck, J. (2002) Political economies of scale: fast policy, interscalar relations, and neoliberal workfare. *Economic Geography*, 78: 331–60.
Porter, M. E. (1998) Clusters and the new economics of competitiveness. *Harvard Business Review*, December: 77–90.
Porter, M. E. (2000) Location, competition and economic development: local clusters in a global economy. *Economic Development Quarterly*, 14(1): 15–34.
Scott, A. J. (2000) *The Cultural Economy of Cities: Essays on the Geography of Image-Producing Industries*. London, Thousand Oaks, CA: Sage.
Smith, K. (2008) *Nine Lives: The Birth of the Avant-Garde Art in New China*. Hong Kong: Timezone8.
Zhang, J. and Peck, J. (2014) Variegated capitalism, Chinese style: regional models, multi-scalar constructions. *Regional Studies*, 50(1): 1–27.
Zheng, J. (2010) The 'entreprenuerial state' in 'creative industry cluster' development in Shanghai. *Journal of Urban Affairs*, 32(2), 143–70.
Zheng, J. (2011) 'Creative industry clusters' and the 'entrepreneurial city' of Shanghai. *Urban Studies*, 48(16): 3561–82.

Zheng, J. and Chan, R. (2013) A property-led approach to cluster development: 'creative industry clusters' and creative industry networks in Shanghai. *Town Planning Review*, 84(5): 606–32.
Zhong, S. (2015) Artists and Shanghai's culture-led urban regeneration. *Cities*, http://dx.doi.org/10.1016/j.cities.2015.09.002
Zukin, S. (1989) *Loft Living: Culture and Capital in Urban Change*. New Brunswick, NJ: Rutgers University Press.

13

Having played with swords

Trajectories of Singapore-China co-productions of historical fiction television dramas

Liew Kai Khiun and Yao Yiming

Introduction: Journey East

Between 1998 and 2000, the television drama adaptation of the Chinese folk mythology, *Legends of the Eight Immortals* (东游记), was screened to audiences across Chinese-speaking countries from China to Singapore (Teo 1999). The eight characters featured in the Taoist-themed narrative of the journey to immortality are not only worshipped in Chinese folk religion, but have also inspired literary as well as film and television adaptations (Seal and White 2016: 144–5). Although listed as a Television Corporation of Singapore (now Mediacorp) production, this serial was a transnational Singapore, China, and Taiwan co-production. The series' co-production companies included China's Sichuan TV Drama Production Center, and Jiangsu World Film and Television Production Center. Filmed in Singapore, Malaysia, and China, and fronted by then Taiwanese celebrity Steve Ma Jintao, the cast included both Singaporean and Chinese actors (*The New Paper* 1998: 19). The production's continued popularity on social media 20 years after its screening shows that *Legends of the Eight Immortals* remains etched in transnational television's collective memories. However, in light of the increasing independence of China's television industry as well as its improved production standards, casting, and distribution over the years, such co-production arrangements now seem to be a thing of the past.

Through the case study of co-produced historical fiction drama adaptations of folklores and Wuxia martial arts novels set in pre-modern historical contexts, this chapter explores the trajectory of Singapore–China television collaborations. In mapping out the changing stages of such collaborations from their beginnings in the 1980s to the remaining trickle in the past decade, we discuss both the nature and strategies of the co-production as part of the formation of the more transnational 'pop culture China' that Singapore has been instrumental in weaving together. Issues related to Singapore's role in the acculturalization or televisual Sinicization will be highlighted, as the republic's mainly ethnic Chinese society became acquainted with the alien narrative of Chinese historical fiction. The city-state might have used the growing Chinese market and television industry to platform its historical fiction dramas as exports and co-productions in the 1990s. However, these co-productions decreased significantly a decade later due to the now mature domestic Chinese media producing its own drama serials. This has led to the televisual de-culturalization of Singapore, whereby her actors are compelled to play more local and contemporary roles, and forgo the costume-wearing and swordplay roles formerly exported to a larger regional stage.

Co-producing pop culture China

Characterized by a mixed television menu of domestic, regional, and Western content on local television networks, and the ease of domestic circulation through portable media, Asia's television landscape has been relatively transnational in nature. Despite the Sinophobic climate arising from the Cold War geo-political divisions between Mao's China and its non-Communist neighbouring countries, Chinese language television dramas continued to be diffused regionally from Hong Kong and Taiwan (known collectively as 'Gangtai') to Southeast Asian countries. Audiences in China likewise quietly watched Gangtai productions through transmissions of Hong Kong television networks from neighbouring Guangdong province or illegal pirated portable media from the late 1970s to the early 1990s.

On the one hand, modern and urbane lifestyles in contemporary crime, romance, and teenage 'idol' dramas appealed to telemodernities (Lewis et al. 2016) in audiences from developing societies in the 1980s. On the other, the seemingly politically odourless and decontextualized genre of historical fiction drama adaptations of Chinese mythological folklore, historical epics, and martial arts Wuxia narratives characterized transnational television distribution. As these texts stem from the classical and vernacular cultural memories of Chinese literary and folk traditions rather than ethno-political ideologies from contemporary nation-states, they are de-centered along the more fluid and hybridized Sinophone cultural landscape to Sinitic communities with flexible citizenship (Chan and Fung 2011; Shih 2011; Feeley 2012; Yue and Khoo 2014). Television adaptations of these dense literary texts and amorphous oral traditions were instrumental in including these Sinitic communities and the broadcasting stations co-producing these historical fictional television dramas as part of the transnational televisual Sinophone audience.

Hence, the overseas Chinese media was initially vital to a re-emergent post-Mao China navigating the mediascapes of international capitalism after decades of isolation. Decades of neo-realist Soviet-Maoist political aesthetics of the People's Republic of China (PRC) had discouraged the narratives of romance and action, and regarded the folklore and Wuxia genres as feudal and superstitious. The Chinese appetite for these genres was fed by Gangtai television productions prior to their revival by the China television industry. The revival, marked by CCTV's 1986 production of *Journey to the West* (西游记), was well-received by both China and overseas Chinese audiences, resulting in China-based television companies reaching out to counterparts in Hong Kong, Taiwan, and Singapore for co-productions.

Scholars have widely discussed the factors for transnational television co-productions. The global burgeoning of de-regulated commercial television stations and their respective audiences have led to a universal search for a greater volume of content to fill the airspace in the region and more intensive transnational co-productions (Jin 2007; Zhu 2008). For the Chinese television industries led by the highly interventionist central government (Zhang 2011), co-production initiatives served the multiple purposes of cultural diplomacy, appropriating creative production techniques, and incorporating overseas Chinese celebrities into domestic television productions (de Burgh et al. 2012). Thus, China's television companies reached out to counterparts in Singapore, Hong Kong, and Taiwan, collectively known as Xingangtai (新港台). Xingangtai denotes the nodes of transnational Sinophone mediascapes or 'pop culture China' (Chua 2001). Collaborations were sought with Xingangtai media companies because China believed its common ethno-cultural heritage with these localities would help overcome ideological differences and enable its productions to reconnect with the global mainstream. Drawn by the promise of the potentially large Chinese market, Xingangtai broadcasting stations were keen to invest in these prospective collaborations and broaden their 'cultural-linguistic market base' (Straubhaar 2007: 167–77). The larger market base, greater audience numbers, extensive funding, enlarged talent pool, and additional filming locations have collectively moulded close to three decades of China-Xingangtai co-produced television dramas, and resulted in the evolution of a more cosmopolitan and transnational cultural China.

Historical fictional dramas pioneered some of the earlier co-productions. This genre, known also as 'ancient costume' or guzhuang (古装) dramas, comprised television adaptations of historical events and biopics, historical fantasy, Chinese literary classics, Chinese religious folklore or Shenhua (神话), and Wuxia (武侠) martial arts novels by Louis Cha (查良鏞) under his penname Jin Yong (金庸). Historical events and biopics tend to follow historical personalities such as emperors, generals, queens, and concubines; they are often based on historiographical narratives rather than dramatic fiction. Notable examples of recent historical biopics are the China Central Television's (CCTV) trilogy on Qing Dynasty emperors: *Kangxi Dynasty* (康熙王朝) in 1999, *Yongzheng Dynasty* (雍正王朝) in 2001, and *Qianlong Dynasty* (乾隆皇帝) in 2003. Historical biopics on emperors and their courts or 'palace dramas' are subject to the Chinese state's authoritarian revisionist historiographical interpretations (Zhu 2005, 2008). More severe in tone, these productions focus on the political debates, intrigues, and manoeuvres in court affairs. Fictionalized narratives using actual historical personalities as references tend to be more romantic, as seen in the 1998 Taiwan-based *My Fair Princess* (还珠格格) about a feisty princess in Emperor Qianlong's court, and Hunan Broadcasting System's 2011 time travel drama *Scarlet Heart* (步步惊心) about a contemporary working woman mysterious teleported into the Qing court with rivalling princes. Unlike the severity of palace dramas made in China, fictionalized historical fantasies like *My Fair Princess* and *Scarlet Heart* were transnational co-productions fronted by Hong Kong and Taiwanese celebrities. Historical fantasy dramas contrasted with the more masculine formal politics of historical biopics, as they are centered along more feminine themes of romance and folklores.

Television adaptations of Chinese literary classics include *Romance of the Three Kingdoms* (三国演义), *Dream of the Red Chamber* (红楼梦), *Journey to the West* (西游记), and *Water Margin* (水浒传). As Chinese audiences are largely familiar with these texts, adaptations have been popularly produced in China, Hong Kong, and Taiwan. Except for some playful themes in *Journey to the West* (where the Monkey God and his companions accompany Buddhist pilgrim Xuanzhang to India), the themes in the Chinese literary classics are often more intricate and severe. Faithful television adaptations of these classics often have high production costs, owing to the large number of episodes.

Fantasy, magic, spirituality, martial arts and pugilism are found in the semi-fictitious martial arts world of the Jianghu (江湖) portrayed in historical, Shenhua, and Wuxia dramas. Here, characters exist simultaneously in the imaginary worlds of the supernatural 'Three Realms' (三曹) of Heaven, Earth and Hell in folk cosmology, and the righteous knight errantry in the more anarchic world of the 'Jianghu'. Contrasting with the legally defined physical locale like the Three Realms, the Jianghu exists more as an imagined community, and is a projection of abstractness and ungraspable emotions (Wu 2012: 65). *Liaozhai* (聊斋), the *Legend of the Eight Immortals*, and stories on the deifications of vernacular Taoist saints and Bodhisattvas are among the more common television adaptations of folklore. Jianghu-themed television productions are usually adaptations of Jin Yong's novels. His *Condor Heroes* (射雕英雄传) series has been the most enduringly popular. From its first adaptation by Hong Kong's Television Broadcasts Limited (TVB) in the 1970s, *Condor Heroes* has been frequently remade by various Chinese-language television stations in Hong Kong, China, Taiwan, and Singapore. Set in the Song and Qing Dynasties, Jin Yong's narratives popularized historical fictions further by combining the modern notions of individual romance, identity, and belonging with traditional chivalry and fantastic martial arts skills.

Within the Wuxia genre is the figure of the Xianxia (仙侠) or 'Heavenly swordsman'. Endowed with supernatural godlike powers, the Xianxia saves humanity from dramatic apocalyptic situations in fictitious environments in pre-modern China. *The Gods and Demons of Zu Mountain* (蜀山剑侠传), written by Huan Zhu Lou Zhu (还珠楼主) in the 1930s, is one of the most familiar Xianxia television adaptations. It has been adapted for television on many occasions, most notably by Hong Kong's TVB in 1990 and Jiangsu Station in 2015.

The final leg of the imaginative timeline of historical fiction dramas stretches from China's Republican era to the end of the Second Sino-Japanese War in 1945, and generally excludes sensitivities vis-à-vis the geo-political tensions in the founding myths between the nationalist Kuomintang and the Chinese Communist Party. The most prominent Republican era or Mingguo (民国) drama was *The Bund* (上海滩), produced by Hong Kong's TVB in 1980, and featuring a chaotic mix of mobsters, warlords, and colonial interests in the chaotic but cosmopolitan treaty port of 1930s Shanghai.

Even though implicit analogies to contemporary politics may be drawn from various historical fiction dramas, the collaborative production and distribution of television historical fiction tend to be both historically and politically decontextualized from contemporary politics, and distant from the founding myths of current nation-states. As Singapore's co-productions with Chinese historical fiction television dramas will reveal, the production and distribution of such content within the transnational televisual Sinophone is culturally more porous and diffused.

Tropical Tang Dynasty: making historical fiction dramas for the People's Republic

Home to both transnational Chinese film businesses like Shaw Brothers and Cathay Organization from the 1920s, colonial Singapore was no stranger to the fluid networks of regional entertainment (Chan and Yung 2003; Chung 2007). Their influence, however, waned under the interventionistic People's Action Party (PAP) government that was keener on industrialization than leisure. In contrast, transnational networks manifested differently for television productions. Television in Singapore started officially in 1963, with its curatorial directions mirroring the postcolonial city-state of prescribed multiculturalism and programming patterned along the official classifications of the republic's ethno-linguistic demography. With its separation from the Federation of Malaysia after a brief merger in 1963–5, the ethnic Chinese population became the numerical majority, making up 75 percent of a then total of 3 million people. However, the television stations and programming of the sole national broadcaster, Radio and Television Singapore (RTS), subsequently renamed Singapore Broadcasting Corporation (SBC), were divided along the English, Malay, Tamil, and Chinese languages. Although SBC started with educational and cultural programming, its gradual corporatization resulted in the production of local television dramas in the late 1970s (Koh 1990: 725–35; Tay 2015). Chinese language station, Channel 8, led the direction for local television dramas, as it was backed by firm commercial sponsorship and a large ethnic Chinese audience base.

Up to the early 1980s, Singapore was an asymmetrical recipient of television dramas (including historical fiction) from Hong Kong and Taiwan within the larger televisual Sinophone landscape. The situation changed upon the state's realization of the need for more local content, particularly with the government's restriction of media in regional Chinese languages such as Hokkien (Taiwanese productions) and Cantonese (Hong Kong productions). Due to ongoing Cold War divisions and China's infant television industry, the choices for Mandarin/Putonghua programmes were limited. Thus, SBC was compelled to produce its own television dramas. Historical fiction was among SBC's earlier productions, as attested by 1985 time travel drama *Men from the Past* (大侠吴三奇) featuring medieval Chinese pugilists in modern Singapore, and 1986 drama *Men of Valour* (盜日英雄传) featuring General Yue Fei and his men defending the Song Dynasty against Jin invaders (Leong 1985). To a certain degree, these drama productions were made possible through the engagement of Hong Kong's technical expertise as well as martial arts choreographers. These early transnational incorporations laid the groundwork for the subsequent larger-scale co-productions with China.

The opportunity to collaborate with China came with SBC's 1983 drama, *The Awakening* (乌锁南洋), now considered the flagship of Singapore television. Guangdong Television Station reportedly bought the rights to screen *The Awakening* for about USD 1,000 per episode for all 27 episodes, thereby signalling the PRC's open-door policy and desire to learn from Singapore (Leong 1985). Although based on the Chinese coolie migrant experience in colonial Singapore rather than pre-modern history, the drama serial gained popularity in China, paving the way for more Singapore-made Chinese-language productions. In total, Singapore exported 26 drama series to China in the 1980s and 22 in the 1990s (Huang and Zhao 2016: 241). While these dramas were most likely not co-productions, Chinese bloggers' online televisual reminiscences show that Singapore-produced 1988 Hong Kong TVB historical fiction like the *Two Most Honourable Knights* (绝代双骄) starring then Singapore-based Hugo Ng, and 1993 Singapore-made *The Great Conspiracy* (莲花争霸) were popular with audiences in China in the late 1980s and 1990s. The popularity of these fast-paced and imaginative Singaporean and Hong Kong productions coincided with the PRC's period of cultural trade deficit, created by its Soviet-inspired neo-realist and ideologically driven television productions (Xu 2015).

The search for co-producers in the historical fiction or 'period drama' genre came after the screenings of *The Awakening* in Guangzhou and Shanghai. Preparations for collaborative historical fiction dramas commenced after Singapore reportedly agreed to provide technical expertise and scriptwriters in return for a wider pool of actors and martial arts practitioners as well as filming locations in China (Hie 1985: 8). By the 1990s, such co-productions became common in the larger televisual Sinophone landscape. The establishment of a filming city and theme park in Singapore, Tang Dynasty Village (modelled after Hong Kong's Song Dynasty Village), anticipated this trend, as it sought to create an imagined medieval Chinese metropolis in the equatorial modern city-state (Tan 2017).

The authors built upon Zhang Zi Xuan's 2012 compilation of Singapore–China television co-productions to create the table listing all such drama series (1994–2009) in Table 13.1 (see Appendix). While discussions on co-produced drama series with China launched Singapore–China television co-productions, the concept was only actualized nearly a decade later in the mid-1990s. We have verified the various production companies against the end credits in the productions, and reproduced the English titles and Romanized Chinese names of the artistes as provided by Mediacorp. Our table also includes several co-productions with the short-lived Singapore Press Holdings (SPH) Mediaworks terrestrial television station that were omitted from Zhang's 2012 study. Between Mediaworks' formation in 2001 and merger with Mediacorp at the end of 2004, it and Tangren Media co-produced several historical fiction dramas, most notably *Romance of the Book and Sword* (书剑恩仇录) in 2002.

The production houses and companies with which Mediacorp and Mediaworks have worked were mostly based in provinces keen for tie-ups as well as inter-provincial collaborations with external bodies for capital, talent, and expertise. Some prominent television stations like Jiangsu TV and Hunan TV started out with such co-productions, and remain actively engaged in incorporating the wider transnational Chinese talent base into their dramas. Over time, media organizations like Tangren Media have also branched out into more trans-local and transnational collaborations. Established in Shanghai in 1998, the Tianjin-based joint-venture company was active in drama tie-ups with Mediacorp and Mediaworks.

In addition to *Romance of the Book and Sword*, its other noteworthy co-productions with Singapore are *A Chinese Paladin* (仙剑奇侠传) in 2004 and *Strange Tales of Liaozhai II* (聊斋奇女子) in 2008. These co-productions also gave Singaporean artistes like Chen Tianwen, Li Nanxing, Christopher Lee, and Fann Wong access to the significantly larger stage in China, transforming them from local artistes to regional celebrities like their counterparts in Hong Kong and Taiwan. The next section will outline these historical fiction television dramas' cultures of co-productions so as to elucidate their growth and decline.

Locations, languages, actions: co-production televisual cultures

It would be premature to assume that Singapore's ethnic Chinese majority automatically connected the city-state to the broader East Asian Sinitic communities, particularly in the co-production of historical fiction dramas. Released in 1994, *Silk and Romance* (情丝万缕) was the first Singapore–China co-production. However, this collaboration was only possible after Singapore television had spent nearly a decade developing the necessary technical and cultural expertise, and after these drama productions had achieved popular recognition. Thus, appreciation of the dynamics of these wider transnational collaborations comes in two stages: co-option of then trendier Hong Kong martial arts filmmaking and storytelling, followed by co-productions with Chinese counterparts keen to evolve their production aesthetics.

To compete with Hong Kong television imports in the 1970s to 1980s, SBC's Channel 8 started to engage and co-opt the expertise of HongKongers in its local television productions. Several outstanding Hong Kong personalities in historical fiction dramas came to Singapore. For example, Jiang Long (江龙), known for his involvement in martial arts films, eventually headed the production unit of Channel 8 (*The Straits Times* 1986: 4). Influenced by Wuxia swordplay and Bruce Lee's cinematic martial arts choreographies in the Shaw Brothers films of the 1960s, Hong Kong's television stations brought the historical fiction genre to the small screens of the living room. Attributable to the aesthetics formed from the fast pace of living in the congested urban metropolis, Hong Kong's martial arts choreography is characterized by action, movement, and violence (Teo 2010; Yip 2014). In the production stage, wirework and trampolines are often used to allow performers to take flight and flips, thereby creating the superhuman dexterities of the screen pugilists. Such movements are further accelerated and detailed through post-production editing where short average shot lengths of camera zooms are intertwined with intermittent undercranking (slow motion) to emphasize climaxes of fight scenes (Hunt 2003: 159; Gravestock 2006). The rapidity of movement in these dramas, complemented by the emphasis on shorter and less scripted dialogues as well as a mixture of contemporarized soundtracks and theme songs, were adopted by Singapore television (Koh 1989: 4). These cinematic stylizations were alien to the Singapore television culture formed by the postcolonial PAP government's focus on education rather than entertainment.

Accounts of SBC's earlier challenges in making historical fiction dramas included the production crew's lack of relevant expertise, the material inadequacies of wardrobe and props, and the actors' bodily discomfort as they were swathed in thick costumes in Singapore's equatorial heat (Leong 1981: 9; *The Straits Times* 1986: 4; Teo 1999: 2). Actors unaccustomed to the archaic and formal Chinese dialogue in these historical fiction dramas were also faced with language proficiency challenges. This issue was due to successive generations of Singaporean artistes schooled in the English language that is lingua franca as well as the language of administration and business in the republic. Criticisms on the lack of scenic authenticity in the location shoots set in easily recognizable public parks like the Chinese Garden and the Singapore Botanical Gardens gave rise to public doubts on these dramas' ability to appeal to a contemporary Singaporean audience through narratives set in an imaginary China. Despite the production crew's efforts to avoid filming the contemporary urban environment, the impossibility of excluding the lush greenery of Singapore's landscape resulted in audiences complaining about the 'coconut trees' in period dramas (Tan 1986: 4). As the producer Jiang Long noted, there were no significant 'mountains, streams and lakes' in Singapore for these productions (Yam 1990: 7). Consequently, locally made historical fiction dramas had lower viewership than both their contemporary counterparts and Hong Kong imports (ibid.).

The tide turned when both the production crew and actors grew acquainted with the format of historical fiction productions. The availability of more customized filming spaces such as Tang Dynasty Village and SBC's new film location outlet in Tuas (a remote western part of Singapore) helped to improve the mise-en-scène of these dramas. A refreshing change came in 1991 when historical fiction dramas went to Anhui and Xiamei in China for some of their location shoots (Guan 1993: 12). Relocating filming locations to China in the 1990s reduced the Xingangtai broadcasting stations' production costs as it negated the necessity of constructing artificial sets, and it provided audiences with the spatial authenticity of a 'real China' as well as the 'actual' sites where the events on screen supposedly took place (Chua 2012: 19). Location shoots for the first Singapore–China co-produced drama, *Silk and Romance*, took place in the historical city of Suzhou in Jiangsu province with the local knowledge provided by Jiangsu Broadcasting Corporation. Subsequently, Hengdian World Studio in Donyang City, Zhejiang, became the most popular filming site for scenes relating to palaces and courts as well as medieval streets. Nonetheless, logistical reasons meant that some location shoots continued to take place at 'Chinese'-looking sites in Singapore, which Singaporean audiences would have been quick to recognize.

The talent base for these productions was also gradually expanded to include artistes, directors, technical crews, and special effects teams from different regions. Table 13.1 in the Appendix to this chapter shows the mix of Singapore, Hong Kong, Taiwan, and Chinese actors as the main cast in each drama, enabling audiences in the region to concurrently identify with familiar faces and be exposed to other local actors. This publicity was especially critical to Singaporean artistes like Fann Wong, Chen Tianwei, and Christopher Lee, whose exposure would have otherwise been limited to Singapore.

Aside from the cast and mise-en-scène, Singapore–China historical fiction co-productions of the 1990s were also marked by differing television formats and voice dubbings. Firstly, Singapore used the B/G Phase Alternating Lines (PAL) Colour Encoding System, whereas China used PAL D. Audiences familiar with these dramas would have been able to distinguish the place of production from the screen resolutions of their television sets. The more obvious difference was in the area of dubbing. To compensate for the actors' poorer grasp of the standard of Chinese language needed in these historical fiction dramas, Mediacorp consistently engaged its voice dubbing team, namely Zheng Bingtai (郑炳泰), Li Yamei (李雅梅), Lin Decheng (林德成), and Xie Xiecheng (谢协成), whose voices were probably as recognizable as the faces of the cast in these co-produced dramas. However, the Singaporean production crew and their Chinese counterparts were reportedly able to communicate well with each other backstage as they had Mandarin/Putonghua in common (Guan 1993: 12). While Singapore's predominantly ethnic Chinese society may be familiar with Chinese historical fables and folk mythologies, the sense of Chineseness imbibed through collective cultural memories does not correlate automatically with the ability to make such television productions or connect with larger Sinitic communities.

Location shoots, costumes, and dubbing were Singaporean productions' deliberately conscious acculturalization with the imaginations of Chinese historical myths as well as its repackaging as modern television dramas with Hong Kong-styled cinematic aesthetics and martial arts choreographies. In this manner, Singapore took a critical step nearly a decade ahead of China, and was subsequently able to learn the ropes of such productions. Thus, Singapore was able to be a meaningful co-producer to aspiring Chinese television stations in the 1990s. At the height of such co-productions, the dramas were made at an estimated cost of SGD 7 million (USD 4 million) in the 1990s (*The Straits Times* 2003: 19). Each episode of the *Legend of the Eight Immortals* amounted to about SGD 100,000 (USD 60,000), twice the budget for an entire contemporary local drama serial (Teo 1999). Despite Chinese television stations' eagerness to co-produce dramas with Singapore in the 1990s and early 2000s, China has now superseded Singapore television production's expertise, talent, and resources. As China is now fully capable of producing its own high-quality historical fiction dramas, Singapore–China co-productions came to an end. Without the large Chinese market, Singapore may end up being televisually de-Sinicized, losing the knowledge of the past three decades in producing imaginary Chinas on the small screen.

Back to Nanyang: ebbing of historical fictional and televisual de-Sinicization

There has been a dearth of Singapore-produced Chinese historical fictions for about a decade, as Mediacorp content is presently focused on the local 'heartland'. In spite of several public announcements of 'Memorandums of Understanding' and contracts, co-productions of historical fiction dramas with China have seemingly come to an end. Mediacorp's current lack of interest in this genre and China's disinterest in co-productions with Singapore are attributable to the maturation of the Chinese media industry and competing historical fiction content from South Korea on Sinophone television.

In the early 1980s, China wanted to learn from the international media industry, particularly from the overseas Chinese societies of Hong Kong, Taiwan, and Singapore. Three decades later, at the turn of the twenty-first century, China's media industry has grown in confidence as investments, productions, domestic audiences expanded significantly. The 1980s state restrictions on the 'feudal' themes of Wuxia and folklore were also relaxed. Like CCTV's trilogy on the Qing Dynasty emperors, certain historical biopics were even endorsed by the national leadership. While the Chinese historical fiction narratives were culturally malleable to different overseas Chinese communities, the regional popularity of Korean historical fiction led the Chinese state to exert greater control on the historiographical trajectories of its own dramas, especially in the dramaturgical treatment of state power, territorial integrity, and social order.

Korean historical fiction dramas were welcomed initially in China, but the Chinese authorities were soon disturbed by the anti-Han nationalistic undertones that they perceived in these productions. *Jumong*, produced by Munhwa Broadcasting Corporation (MBC) in 2008, was hugely popular in Korea and around the world. The Chinese government, however, banned it for making Korean claims on Chinese territory (Eng 2011). The feared overreliance on foreign television dramas provided the impetus for the Chinese state to actively boost local productions. Thus, filming theme parks like the complex in Hengdian were established with the exact replica of Beijing's Forbidden Palace, and the scale of production of Chinese historical dramas increased. This momentum was enlarged by the burgeoning pool of domestic artistes and crew, supported by the growing numbers of regional television stations. As China's speed of economic growth has surpassed the Asian dragons of the 1980s like Hong Kong and Singapore, it no longer needed sources of external capital in co-productions.

At the same time, Korean television dramas, including historical fiction, came into the limelight in the early 2000s and gained rapid popularity in the Chinese television market that had been dominated by Taiwanese and Hong Kong productions for decades. The visibly heavy investment in Korean television historical fiction such as *Dae Jang Guem* and *Queen Seondoek* resulted in these dramas gaining broader mainstream followings in the region. Collectively, historical fiction dramas from China and South Korea have significantly eclipsed their Xingangtai counterparts. As there is little point in competing against big-budget and large-scale historical fiction productions, Xingangtai television stations are less focused on the genre. Consequently, the regional stage for both the artistes and technical crews in Chinese historical fiction has shrunk. While it was common for Taiwanese, Hong Kong, and Singaporean artistes to front the lead roles in co-produced historical fiction a decade ago, the same could not be said for the younger generation of Xingangtai actors in China today. These trends collectively represent a televisual de-Sinicization, as China takes the lion's share of Chinese historical fiction production, and peripherizes Hong Kong, Taiwan, and Singapore from one crucial component of the televisual Sinophone.

Once envisioned as a movie town and bustling theme park, Tang Dynasty Village became increasingly irrelevant as more television and film productions shifted to China in the 1990s. The final blow came with the Asian financial crisis in 1997, which forced its operations to cease. Left abandoned for close to a decade without any relevance, Tang Dynasty Village was finally demolished in 2008 (Tan 2017). Given the ongoing trends in China, it is likely that Chinese historical fiction dramas in Singapore will follow the path of this theme park.

Conclusion: limited period

The case study of Singapore–China co-production of historical fiction television dramas illustrates the need to examine television cultures at both the national and transnational levels. In some respect, these narrative fantasies probably appealed to Chinese audiences worldwide because they were derived from Chinese literary classics, historical fables and folklore, and contemporary fictions of the past. Singapore television recognized this appeal and explored this genre in two ways: creating local productions to compete with imported Hong Kong dramas in the 1970s–1980s, and expanding its audience reach into China's burgeoning television industry a decade later. These two stages can be characterized as televisual acculturalization and Sinicization, as Singaporean producers struggled to acquaint themselves with the knowledge of making such Chinese historical fictions in contemporary Singapore.

To produce these dramas, they first engaged and co-opted Hong Kong expertise, while expanding the infrastructure of filming locations and studios in Singapore. Despite public reservations that such investment did not translate into high viewership, Singapore television persisted in historical fiction and began to explore filming sites in China. Secondly, they co-produced historical fiction dramas with upcoming provincial Chinese broadcasting stations in order to expand the talent base, filming locations, expertise, and networks for Singapore television. This resulted in more elaborately staged productions and significantly more viewers, which in turn transformed local Singaporean actors into regional celebrities.

After almost 30 serials spanning over a decade, the momentum for these co-productions dropped as Singapore's relevance dwindled vis-à-vis China's developing media industry and its ability to independently make such historical fiction dramas. Without this platform, the new generation of Singaporean actors has fewer opportunities for the swordplay that transformed their predecessors into transnational celebrities. As Mediacorp becomes televisually de-Sinicized from the Sinophone of Chinese historical fiction and Singapore television is peripherized in the televisual Jianghu, it is evident that the trajectory of co-productions is not necessarily linear and convergent.

References

de Burgh, H., Zeng R. and Chen S. (2012) Chinese television 'internationalization' and the search for creativity. *Creative Industries Journal*, 4(2): 137–54.

Chan, J. and Fung, A. (2011) Structural hybridization of film and television production in Hong Kong. *Visual Anthropology*, 24(3): 77–89.

Chan, K. B. and Yung, S. S. (2005) Chinese entertainment, ethnicity, and pleasure. *Visual Anthropology*, 18(2–3): 103–42.

Chua, B. H. (2001) Pop culture China. *Singapore Journal of Tropical Geography*, 22(2): 113–21.

Chua, B. H. (2012) The regionalization of television and China. *Chinese Journal of Communication*, 5(1): 16–23.

Chung, S. P. Y. (2007) Moguls of the Chinese cinema: the story of the Shaw Brothers in Shanghai, Hong Kong and Singapore. *Modern Asian Studies*, 41(4): 665–80.

Eng, R. (2011) China–Korea culture wars and national myths: TV dramas as battleground. *The Asia-Pacific Journal*, 9(13): 1–25.

Feeley, J. (2012) Transnational spectres and regional spectators: flexible citizenship in new Chinese horror cinema. *Journal of Chinese Cinemas*, 6(1): 41–64.

Gravestock, P. (2006, 1 June) The real and the fantastic in the Wuxia Pian. *Metro Magazine* (148): 106–10.
Guan, L. (18.04.1993) Roughing it out in China. *The Straits Times*, p. 4.
Hie, H. C. (1985, 2 June) SBC and China to make period dramas together. *Singapore Monitor*, p. 8.
Huang, Y. J. and Zhao L. M. (2016) Singapore's media image in China. In Zheng, Y. and Lye, L. F. (eds.), *Singapore–China Relations: 50 Years*, Singapore: World Scientific, pp. 227–50.
Hunt, L. (2003) Kung Fu cult masters: stardom, performance and 'authenticity' in Hong Kong martial arts films. In Jancovich, M., Reboll, A. R., Stringer, J., and Willis, A. (eds.), *Defining Cult Movies: The Cultural Politics of Oppositional Taste*. Manchester: Manchester University Press, pp. 157–71.
Jin, D. Y. (2007) Transformation of the world television system under neoliberal globalization, 1983–2003. *Television and New Media*, 8(3): 179–96.
Koh, S. T. (1989, 20 October) Contemporary dialogue in period dramas. *The Straits Times*, p. 4.
Koh, T. A. (1990) Culture and the arts. In Sandhu, K. S. and Wheatley, P. (eds.), *Management of Success: The Moulding of Modern Singapore*. Singapore: Institute of Southeast Asian Studies, pp. 710–48.
Leong, W. K. (1981, 18 December) Hongkong and Taiwanese directors offer to help SBC. *The Straits Times*, p. 9.
Leong, W. K. (1985, 13 March) SBC drama serial being shown in China. *Straits Times*, p. 40.
Lewis, T., Martin, F. and Sun W. (2016) *Telemodernities: Television and Transforming Lives in Asia*. Durham, NC: Duke University Press.
Seal, G. and White, K. (2016) *Folk Heroes and Heroines around the World*, 2nd edn. Santa Barbara, CA: ABC-CLIO.
Shih, S. M. (2011) The concept of the Sinophone. *PMLA*, 126(3): 709–18.
Straubhaar, J. (2007) *World Television: From Global to Local*. California, London, New Delhi and Singapore: Sage.
Tan, E. (2017) *State of Buildings*. [online] Tang Dynasty Village. Available at https://stateofbuildings.sg/places/tang-dynasty-city (accessed March 5, 2018).
Tan, J. (1986, 27 April) Should SBC play with swords? *The Straits Times*, p. 4.
Tay, J. (2015) Dramatizing the nation: television, history and the construction of Singaporean identity. In Tay, J. and Turner, G. (eds.), *Television Histories in Asia: Issues and Contexts*. London and New York: Routledge, pp. 92–111.
Teo, P. L. (1999, 8 February) TV serials dressed to kill. *The Straits Times*, p. 2.
Teo, S. (2010) The aesthetics of mythical violence in Hong Kong action films. *New Cinemas: Journal of Contemporary Film*, 8(3): 155–67.
The New Paper (1998, 23 November) This Immortal has no time to love, p. 19.
The Straits Times (1986, 16 February) Hongkong veteran takes over reins at drama unit, p. 4.
The Straits Times (2003, 19 January) Why make Wuxia TV shows? p. 10.
Wu, H. Y. W. (2012) A journey across rivers and lakes: a look at the untranslatable Jianghu in Chinese culture and literature. [online] *452°F: Electronic Journal of Theory of Literature and Comparative Literature*, (7): 58–71. Available at http://www.452f.com/pdf/numero07/07_452f-mono-helena-yuen-wai-orgnl.pdf (accessed April 4, 2018).
Xu, M. (2015) Chinese TV dramas in the regional market: aspiring to be a cultural actor? *Telematics and Informatics*, 32(1): 98–107.
Yam, N. (1990, 8 August) Limited period. *The Straits Times*, p. 4.
Yip, M.-F. (2014) In the realm of senses: sensory realism, speed and Hong Kong martial arts cinema. *Cinema Journal*, 53(4): 76–97.
Yue, A. and Khoo, O. (eds.) (2014) *Framing Sinophone Cinemas*. London: Palgrave Macmillan.
Zhang, H. (2011) The globalization of Chinese television: the role of the party state. *The International Communication Gazette*, 73(7): 573–94.
Zhang, Z. X. (2012) 中国大陆与新加坡电视剧合拍研究 (Study on the TV dramas co-produced by Mainland China and Singapore). *Contemporary Communication*, 2(187): 101–05.
Zhu, Y. (2005) Yongzheng Dynasty and Chinese primetime television. *Cinema Journal*, 44(4): 3–17.
Zhu, Y. (2008) Transnational circulation of Chinese television drama. *Global Media and Communication*, 4(1): 59–80.

Appendix

Table 13.1 Singapore–China co-productions of historical fiction dramas

S/N	*Drama title* 电视剧名	*Premiere* 首播时间 *(in Singapore)*	*Production house/producer* 拍摄公司/出品公司	*Main cast (by country and region)* 主演
1	*Silk and Romance* 情丝万缕 (Wuxia)	1994	• Mediacorp • Jiangsu Broadcasting Corporation (China)	Pan Lingling (Singapore) Chen Tianwen (Singapore) Chen Chuanzhi (Singapore)
2	*Ghost Catcher* 天师钟馗 (Folklore)	1995	• China Television Company Limited (Taiwan) • Mediacorp	Jin Chaoqun (Taiwan) Fan Hongxuan (China) Chen Tianwen (Singapore)
3	*Legend of the White Hair Bride* 白发魔女传 (Wuxia/Xianxia)	1996	• Mediacorp • Shanghai Oriental Television (China)	Huang Biren (Singapore) Lina Ng (Singapore) Ann Kok (Singapore)
4	*Sword and Honour* 铁血男儿 (Fictionalized narrative)	1997	• Mediacorp • Shanghai Paradise Film and Television Group (China)	Cao Guohui (Singapore) Cheng Jianhui (Singapore) Chen Tianwen (Singapore)
5	*The Royal Monk I* 真命小和尚 (Fictionalized narrative)	1997	• Mediacorp • Ningbo Television Production Center (China)	Jun Cao (China) Chen Tianwen (Singapore) Sun Shaobin (Singapore)
6	*The Royal Monk II* 真命小和尚2 (Fictionalized narrative)	1997	• Mediacorp • Shanghai Paradise Film and Television Group (China)	Jun Cao (China) Chen Tianwen (Singapore) Sun Shaobin (Singapore)
7	*Legend of the Crow* 乌丫传说 (Folklore)	1998	• Mediacorp • Shanghai Paradise Film and Television Group (China)	Jiang Cen (Singapore) Hong Zhaorong (Singapore) Chen Chuanzhi (Singapore)
8	*The Legends of the Eight Immortals* 东游记 (Folklore)	1998	• Mediacorp • Sichuan Television Production Center (China) • Jiangsu Tiandi Film and Television Production Center (China)	Steve Ma (Taiwan) Phyllis Quek (Singapore) Jacelyn Tay (Singapore) Jerry Chang (Singapore) Yvonne Lim (Singapore)

9	*Legends of Nezha* 莲花童子哪吒 (Folklore)	1999	• Mediacorp • Shanghai Paradise Film and Television Group (China)	Cao Jun (China) Lo Haiqiong (China) Xui Sushan (Singapore) Cheng Jianhui (Singapore) He Yongfang (Singapore)
10	*Master Swordsman Lu Xiaofeng I* 陆小凤传奇之决战前后 (Wuxia)	2000	• Mediacorp • Children's Film Studio (China) • Golden Throat Holdings Group Company Limited (China) • Zhejiang Asian Television Cultural Transmission Company Limited (China) • Beijing Jinyingma Media Company Limited (China) • Sichuan Eying Video and Advertisement Company Limited (China) • Wenhua Production Company Limited (Taiwan)	Jimmy Lin (Taiwan) Christopher Lee (Singapore) Tao Hong (China) Theresa Lee (Hong Kong)
11	*Master Swordsman Lu Xiaofeng II* 陆小凤传奇之凤舞九天 (Wuxia)	2001	**Producer:** Mediacorp **Production houses:** • Children's Film Studio (China) • Golden Throat Holdings Group Company Limited (China) • Zhejiang Asian Television Cultural Transmission Company Limited (China) • Sichuan Eying Video and Advertisement Company Limited (China)	Yiu Wai Suen (Taiwan) Christopher Lee (Singapore) Gigi Lai (Hong Kong) Yvonne Lim (Singapore)
12	*Madam White Snake* 白蛇新传 (Folklore)	2001	• Mediacorp • Young Pei-pei's Workshop (Taiwan)	Fann Wong (Singapore) Christopher Lee (Singapore) Crystal Chang (Taiwan) Vincent Chiao (Taiwan)
13	*Romance of the Book & Sword* 书剑恩仇录 (Wuxia)	2002	• SPH Mediaworks • Tangren Media Company Limited (China) • China Television Company Limited (Taiwan)	Vincent Zhao (China) Kym Ng (Singapore) Esther Kwan (Hong Kong)

(Continued)

S/N	Drama title 电视剧名	Premiere 首播时间 (in Singapore)	Production house/producer 拍摄公司/出品公司	Main cast (by country and region) 主演
14	*Moon Fairy* 奔月 (Folklore)	2003	• Mediacorp • Shenzhen Broadcasting Corporation (China) • Shanghai Media Group (China) • Jiangsu Broadcasting Corporation (China) • Hubei Economic Channel (China) • Hangzhou South Lake Pearl Channel (China) **Production houses:** • Beijing Film Art Advertising Agency (China) • Beijing Tongyin Media Cultural Transmission Company Limited (China • Hunan Xiaoxiang Film Production Studio (China)	Fann Wong (Singapore) Christopher Lee (Singapore) Yue Wu (China) Kai Lian (Taiwan)
15	*Happy and Lucky* 吉祥如意 (Fictionalized narrative)	2003	• SPH Mediaworks • Tangren Media Co Ltd	Dicky Cheung (Hong Kong) Esther Kwan (Hong Kong) Guo Liang (Singapore)
16	*A Chinese Paladin* 仙剑奇侠传 (Xianxia)	2004	• SPH Mediaworks • Tangren Media Company Limited (China)	Hu Ge (China) Bryan Wong (Singapore) Guo Liang (Singapore)
17	*My Fair Lady* 我爱钟无艳 (Fictionalized narrative)	2005	• Hubei Economic Channel (China) • Hangzhou South Lake Pearl Channel (China) • Jilin Broadcasting Corporation (China) • Guangdong Broadcasting Corporation (China) **Production houses:** • Mediacorp • Shenzhen Film Production Studio (China) • Yiwenyuan Studio Company Limited (China) • Shenzhen Today Video Media Company Limited (China) • Beijing Pioneer Film Art Investment Company Limited (China)	Fann Wong (Singapore) Gallen Lo (Hong Kong) Kam Kong Tsui (Hong Kong) Yvonne Lim (Singapore)

18	*The Palm of Ru Lai* 如来神掌 (Wuxia)	2005	• Young Pei-pei's Workshop (Taiwan) • Jiuzhou Audio-Video Publishing House (China) • Xian Xinyi Film and Television Culture Investment Company Limited (China) **Production house:** • Mediacorp	Julian Cheung (Hong Kong) Athena Chu (Hong Kong) Christopher Lee (Singapore)
19	*The Dragon Heroes* 赤子乘龙 (Wuxia)	2005	• Mediacorp • Shanghai Film Group Corporation (China) • Shanghai Shangyin Digital Transmission Company Limited (China) • Shanghai Shangyin Digital Production Company Limited (China)	Ren Quan (China) Li Xiaolu (China) Christopher Lee (Singapore)
20	*The Lucky Stars* 福禄寿三星报喜 (Fictionalized narrative)	2005	• Xiaoxiang Film Group (China) • Beijing Tianzhong Film (China) • Beijing Alliance Film Investment Company Limited (China) • Nanjin Audio Flim and Television Company (China) • Guangzhou Broadcasting Corporation (China) • Jiangsu Star Culture Investment Company Limited (China) • Nanjing Broadcasting Group Co. Ltd (China) **Production Houses:** • Mediacorp • Shanghai Film Group Corporation (China) • Shanghai Shangyin Digital Transmission Company Limited (China) • Shanghai Shangyin Digital Production Company Limited (China)	Bobby Au-yeung (Hong Kong) Fann Wong (Singapore) Christopher Lee (Singapore) Zheng Xu (China)
21	*The Little Fairy* 天外飞仙 (Folklore)	2005	**Producers:** • Mediacorp • Xian Tailun Film and Television Culture Company Limited (China) **Production houses:** • Tangren Media Company Limited (China) • Mediacorp	Ge Hu (China) Lin Yicheng (Taiwan) Phyllis Quek (Singapore) Chen Xiu Li (Malaysia) TAE (Thailand)

(*Continued*)

S/N	*Drama title* 电视剧名	*Premiere* 首播时间 *(in Singapore)*	*Production house/producer* 拍摄公司/出品公司	*Main cast (by country and region)* 主演
22	*The Lotus Lantern* 宝莲灯 (Fictionalized narrative)	2005	• China International Television Company (China) • Beijing Tianxinxing Film and Television Culture Company (China) • Guangzhou Dong Hexing Film Video Company (China)	Jun Cao (China) Vincent Chiao (Taiwan) Yvonne Lim (Singapore)
23	*The Strange Tales of Liaozhai* 新聊斋志异 (Literary classic/Folklore)	2005	• Shanghai Film and Television Company Limited (China) **Production houses:** • Yunnan Broadcasting Corporation (China) • SPH Mediaworks	Ke Hu (China) Liqun Li (Taiwan) Wang Lujiang (Singapore)
24	*Fairy of the Chalice* 夜光神杯 (Folklore)	2006	• Huhan Liujin Culture Media Company Limited (China) • Zhejiang Haofengjing Film and Television Entertainment Company Limited (China) • Hubei Xinlian Industrial Development Company Limited • Shanghai Youdu Broadband Science Company Limited • Mediacorp	Roger Kwok (Hong Kong) Zhang Ting (Taiwan) Liu Tao (China) Christopher Lee (Singapore) Yvonne Lim (Singapore)
25	*Magical Hands* 猜心妙手 (Fictionalized narrative)	2006	• Beijing Taihe Film and Television Investment Company Limited • Shanghai Film Group Corporation(China) • Beijing Huakuntianyin Film and Television Culture Development Company Limited (China) • Phoenix Film and Television Company Limited (China) • Shanxi Broadcasting Corporation (China) • Guangzhou Broadcasting Corporation (China) • Mediacorp	Jacky Wu (Taiwan) Pu Miao (China) Fann Wong (Singapore)
26	*The Strange Tales of Liaozhai II* 聊斋奇女子 (Literary classic/Folklore)	2008	• Tangren Media Company Limited (China) • Mediacorp	Nicky Wu (Taiwan) Fann Wong (Singapore) Daniel Chan(Hong Kong) Ying Qu (China)

27	*The Shaolin Warriors* 少林僧兵 (Wuxia)	2009	• Shenguang Communication Company Limited (China) • Shenzhen Media Group (China) • Mediacorp • Guangdong Xinghe Communication Company Limited (China) • Beijing Huakun Longsheng Culture Communication Company Limited (China) • Shenbing Tianjiang Communication Organization (China) **Production houses:** • Shaolin Temple Culture Broadcasting (Dengfeng) Limited (China) • China Television Media Limited (China) • Beijing Yibo Film Production Limited (China)	Sammo Hung (Hong Kong) Li Man (China) Christopher Lee (Singapore)
28	*The Scarlet Kid* 红孩儿 (Folklore)	2009	• Mediacorp • Guangdong Guangya Film and Television Transmission Company Limited (China) • Beijing Datang Huihuang Film Investment Company Limited (China) • Huishi (Hainan) Company Limited (China) • Beijing Qisizhengwei Networking Technology Company Limited (China) • Beijing Lanxingyue Film and Television Planning Company Limited (China) • Beijing Chaoxuan Culture Communication Company Limited (China) • Jiangxi Broadcasting Corporation (China) • Hunan TV (China)	Ding Yujia (China) Vincent Chiao (Taiwan) Yip Tung (Taiwan) Phyllis Quek (Singapore)
28	*The Lotus Lantern Fable* 宝莲灯前传 (Fictionalized narrative)	2009	• China Television Production Center (China) • Beijing Songlian International Film and Television Cultural Media Company Limited (China) • Beijing Galaxy Film and Television Cultural Transmission Company Limited (China) • Mediacorp	Vincent Chiao (Taiwan) Xiaoqin Liu (China) Yang Zhou (China) Yvonne Lim (Singapore)

14

South Korea's creative industry markets

Looking beyond 2020 to a rising creative economy

Brian Yecies and Aegyung Shim

Introduction

Since the election of President Kim Dae-jung's government, the transnational dissemination of Korean popular culture, aka the 'Korean Wave' (or *Hallyu* in Korean), has gradually transformed Korea from an Asian backwater into a vibrant, trend-setting, ultra-modern and super-wired society. Through the application and development of 'soft power', there has been a transnational ebb and flow of Korean cultural content into the People's Republic of China (hereafter China), Taiwan, Vietnam, and Japan, among other countries. This expansion of the Korean Wave has invigorated Korea's key creative industries – including film, television, drama, food, fashion, gaming, and its popular music industry (K-pop).

Underpinning the power and vitality of the Korean Wave is Korea's advanced technological infrastructure, which President Kim's administration accelerated with its *Cyber Korea 21* policy. Korea's vision statement for leading the country into the next century as a superpower in terms of information communication technologies (hereafter ICT), this document was intended as a blueprint for building a public infrastructure that would make Koreans the most wired and computer-savvy nation in the world. The factors that have specifically favoured Korea are the innovation of a truly state-of-the-art next-generation mobile telecommunications and internet backbone, and the subsequent development and dissemination of revolutionary 'smart phones' as well as Digital Multimedia Broadcasting hardware/devices/services in the mid-2000s. In turn, the rapid transnational take-up of K-pop at home and abroad – along with gaming, a key component of '*Hallyu* 2.0' (Lee and Nornes 2015) – has propelled Korea's music and other creative industries well beyond the traditional production, distribution, and consumption channels dominated by major international industry leaders.

Many scholars and savvy media audiences know that South Korean cinema is one of the most innovative national cinemas in the world, and a key energizer of what the Korean government calls 'global *Hallyu*'. Since the unexpected success of the blockbuster action–drama *Shiri* (1999), which outsold Hollywood's mega-blockbuster *Titanic* (1997) at the Korean box office, an army of creative practitioners and firms has transformed Korea's global media and digital culture industries and attracted a following among local and international audiences.

Their efforts have produced accessible content with a Korean inflection, thus opening new spaces for Korean cultural expression – voices silenced by decades of military dictatorship (1961–88), three years of US Army occupation (1945–48), and 35 years of Japanese colonial rule (1910–45).

However, unlike Korean cinema's prominent position on the contemporary world cinema stage, but equally as powerful in scope, the Korea Creative Content Agency (hereafter KOCCA) is a little-known organization that has been supporting the globalization of Korea's creative industries by pursuing a strategy of 'going out' and selling the nation's cultural products since its creation in 2001. Today, KOCCA, as well as the dominating CJ Group conglomerate (*chaebol* in Korean) and a range of other firms are promoting Korea's creative industries as part of a global economic and cultural marketing strategy that has seen successful expansion into China, the world's largest market. China is the 'new wild frontier' where Korean film and digital media companies are heading in droves to exploit new opportunities (see Yecies 2016). In turn, Chinese media practitioners and firms have been leveraging the export-oriented expertise for which Korean cinema and *Hallyu* in general has become celebrated around the globe. In early 2018, CJ Group announced that it would expand its cultural and e-commerce enterprises into a multi-billion income generator by 2021, via a merger between its CJ E&M – Korea's biggest entertainment and media group, and CJ O Shopping – the *chaebol*'s home shopping and e-commerce arm (Frater 2018). Once completed, this move will place CJ Group high among the top global companies seeking to increase significant growth and targeted sales in the creative industries well into the 2020s. The rise of the Chinese market, as well as other Asian markets such as Indonesia, Malaysia, Thailand, Turkey, and Vietnam, holds the key not only to KOCCA and CJ Global's achievement of sustained economic and cultural success, but also to that of Korea as a nation.

To present some new insights to the volume's readers, this chapter provides historical and policy information on the pillars of South Korea's creative industries. It specifically explores key developments in the gaming, animation and cartoons, webtoons, and popular music (aka K-pop) sectors. The authors begin with an overview of the Korea Creative Content Agency, South Korea's primary government agency that facilitates the development of creative and cultural contents in domestic and international markets, and then cover each of the abovementioned areas in some detail. It is hoped that this chapter will offer a deeper understanding of some of the vital activities that are impacting on the future shape and scope of Korea's growing creative industries. This is a dynamic arena that now features innovation hubs, start-up accelerators, and co-working spaces as part of Korea's larger creative and digital economy.

Cultural policy shift and the new 'global *Hallyu*' leader: Korea Creative Content Agency

Between the 1960s and 1980s cultural products such as feature films, television programs, and radio broadcasts in South Korea (hereafter Korea) were utilized by Korea's military governments to advocate national policies and to promote recurring pro-government messages, as well as themes of hard work and loyalty to the nation. However since the military era began to end in 1988, the Roh Tae-woo (1988–93), Kim Young-sam (1993–98), and subsequent Kim Dae-jung (1998–2003) governments began paying more attention to new trends in the 'information-driven society' and 'knowledge-based economy'. Under Kim Dea-jung in particular, cultural products were viewed as a kind of national treasure worth protecting and supporting, especially those with commercial viability and economic value

(Yim 2002; Otmazgin 2011; Kwon and Kim 2014). All of Korea's major family-run conglomerates (*chaebol* in Korean), as well as other minor industry players, began to explore never-before-seen globalization strategies and simultaneously became increasingly aware of international cultural products and markets. In response to this expanding view of the world in a post-military government society, Korea's creative industries – primarily film, music, and gaming, received escalating monetary support from the government, which in turn, assisted the larger and more general task of stimulating the economy. The nation was truly in the midst of a major paradigm shift in which creative and cultural contents had both economic *and* cultural value. In short, the Korean government saw the promulgation of proactive cultural policy as a key mechanism for not only supporting but also encouraging the creative industries, which soon became known as key components of *Hallyu*.

A major turning point occurred in early 1999 when President Kim Dae-jung's administration innovated the stratagem of 'support without intervention' at the core of its Framework Act on the Promotion of Cultural Industries, which also launched the Culture Industry Promotion Fund. From this point, the Korean government allocated 1 percent of the nation's entire budget to the cultural industries in order to promote and expand Korean cultural products internationally. An additional complementary benefit was the creation of an increasing number of creative and cultural industry departments across the nation's universities. Almost overnight, the Ministry of Culture and Tourism (MCT; now called the Ministry of Culture, Sports and Tourism: MCST) acquired the means to advance and popularize, that is, promote the production of Korean creative and cultural content at home and abroad. Facilitating the translation of this content into multiple languages eventually became part of the production and promotion mix. The subsequent massive rise of *Hallyu* after 2000 is discussed in detail elsewhere.[1] Suffice it to say that Korea's creative industries made a global splash, thanks in part to proactive government policy support. KOCCA is now the backbone to this support framework. It is the government agency that oversees the development and expansion of Korea's creative industries on both domestic and international fronts. It was created in 2001, however it was transformed radically in 2009 when it incorporated other quasi-government sub-agencies in this area (Korea Broadcasting Institute, Korea Game Industry Agency, and Korea IT Industry Promotion Agency) and expanded its capacity. Although KOCCA's remit includes some film, the bulk of film industry promotion, support, education, and training remains under the *tutelage of the* government-supported, self-administered *Korean Film Council (hereafter KOFIC).*

KOCCA provides financial, educational, and business networking support surrounding the production, marketing, and promotion of creative and cultural content, as well as the global development and expansion of human and cultural technology implementation across each of these sectors. Presently, it operates eight global outposts: China (Beijing – since 2001, and Shenzhen – since December 2017), Japan (Tokyo, since 2001), United States (Los Angeles, since 2004), United Kingdom (London, since 2004), and its newest offices in Brazil (São Paulo, since mid-2016), Indonesia (Jakarta, since late 2016) and the United Arab Emirates (Abu Dhabi, since March 2016). Each branch pursues the organization's abovementioned chief functions. Given this chronology, Asia was (and still is) KOCCA's primary target market with the US and UK a close second.

Representatives in each of KOCCA's international offices attempt to promote the contents produced by Korean animation, character licensing, music, mobile media, and feature/short films to local companies and practitioners. They facilitate local networking opportunities and gather information on government policy, distribution channels, technological developments, legal requirements, and employment trends, as well as support promotion, marketing, co-production, and distribution opportunities for Korean cultural producers and their content throughout different markets. They also host a range of conferences, showcases, and seminars in industry trade shows and other cultural events. In this way, KOCCA attempts to remain at the forefront of global *Hallyu*, and its outpost officers are faced with assisting the Korean government and Korea's creative industry workers with predictions of future policy and market trends. Each of KOCCA's localized websites feature details and the latest news regarding trends in K-dramas, television broadcasting formats, K-pop, mobile gaming, webtoons and films, as well as creative industry events such as the November 2017 Korea Brand & Entertainment Expo (KBEE) in Vietnam co-organized by the Ministry of Culture, Sports and Tourism and the Ministry of Trade, Industry and Energy, KOCCA, and Korea Trade-Investment Promotion Agency (KOTRA).

Korea's broadcasting industry

Even before the Korean Wave's onset in the early 2000s, television broadcasting has played an important role in the CCI mix. Presently, there are four free-to-air channels in Korea: Educational Broadcasting System (EBS); Korean Broadcasting System (KBS); Munhwa Broadcasting Corporation (MBC); and Seoul Broadcasting System (SBS). Both EBS and KBS are 'public broadcasters'. KBS is the longest running broadcaster, beginning as a radio broadcaster in 1927 during the Japanese colonial period. It acquired its first television station in 1961 after Park Chung Hee staged a military coup that led to decades of authoritarian rule. KBS transitioned from a government to a public broadcaster in 1973, however, it operates as a public corporation under the influence of the government. Beginning in 1990, Korea's Broadcasting Act mandated that an overwhelming majority (80 percent) of all television programs needed to be of domestic origin. This was the beginning of a new era of protecting the local market from foreign content from the US and other places – produced with higher production values – that had the potential to attract Korean audiences away from domestic content (Kwak 2012). This type of domestic quota system still exists today.

A major turning point for Korea's free-to-air television broadcasters occurred in 2005 after Digital Multimedia Broadcasting (DMB) was released as a next generation network – accessible on one of the many state-of-the-art mobile devices that average Koreans were using. DMB, a digital radio transmission system for distributing television, radio, and data (i.e. multimedia) content to mobile phones, laptops, and automobile navigation devices, began to draw global attention because its entire ecosystem was totally dominated by Korean players and domestic content. Foreign – primarily giant US – media and telecommunications firms had no access to Korea's DMB airwaves because of the different spectrum frequencies in play. Thus, domestic content producers had free reign to broadcast 'Korean-wave' content, which by now was captivating domestic audiences with their high production values, dynamic genres, and star-driven stories. Eventually the absence of subscription fees, as well as competing IPTV platforms, services, and mobile apps began to erode the market strength of DMB, and presently the system is struggling to remain alive. Nevertheless, its story speaks volumes about the Korean IT, ICT, and creative industries' ability to compete against outside players. Among the top Korean variety and drama television programs that have fuelled the Korean Wave across DMB (and traditional broadcasting) channels are: *Jewel in the Palace*, *Winter Sonata*, *Autumn in My Heart*, *My Love from the Star* and *Running Man*. New web-based dramas – netcast by Naver and/or Daum, Korea's two giant internet portals – including *Love Detective Sherlock K* and *Prince's Prince* are now contributing to the continuation of Korean Wave's popularity via new platforms and devices, which have some of the highest consumer penetration rates in the world.[2] In short, advances across Korea's traditional and next-generation broadcasting industry have enabled it to become one of the global leaders in the production of domestic creative and cultural contents, which in turn, have fueled the innovation in mobile and consumer digital technologies and practices, digital mobile television broadcasting, online gaming, and social networking platforms, as well as the deployment of high-speed internet infrastructure.

Increasingly since 2012, Chinese broadcasting firms have developed strong relationships with Korean broadcasters. They have been actively purchasing Korean television formats since 2012, including *I Am a Singer* (2012, Hunan TV), *Running Man* (2014, Zhejiang TV), *Dad! Where Are We Going?* (2013, Hunan TV), *We Got Married* (2015, Jiangsu TV), *Real Men* (2014, Hunan TV), *Grandpa Over Flowers* (2014, Hunan TV), *Infinite Challenge* (2015, CCTV), and *Abnormal Summit* (2015, Jiangsu TV). The localized Chinese versions of these programs are usually co-produced with Korean producers and crew members, who guide the Chinese broadcasters to create content for local audiences. *The Greatest Love* produced by Korean television director Kim Young-hee and broadcast by Hunan TV, is a massive hit in China. Highlights include the release of Korean–Chinese web drama – *Dream Knight* – by JYP Entertainment (Korean) and Youku Tudou, and the Korean–Chinese web drama *Dr. Mo Clinic.* More recently, *Running Man*'s long-time program director Im Hyung Taek, left the series to produce the show's Chinese version: *Hurry Up, Brother,* and MBC announced plans to assist with a Chinese remake of its popular drama *She Was Pretty.* Collaborating in these ways clearly demonstrates the momentum behind China and Korea's synergistic internationalization strategies.

The K-pop factory

In recent years, Korean popular music has become the most visible and far-reaching creative industry vehicle for advancing the Korean Wave, and thus Korea's soft-power. K-pop is a type of contemporary music performed (and consumed) by teens and twenty-somethings across a variety of genres. According to foreign critics, the trend-setting and dazzlingly choreographed K-pop idol stars are younger, more animated, better dressed, better looking – achieved in part through plastic surgery – and more able to carry catchy tunes than singers from other countries. Korean groups that have made particularly big waves abroad include boy bands DBSK (aka TVSQ), Big Bang, 2AM, 2PM, Infinite, SHINee and EXO, and girl groups Girls' Generation, 2NE1, Wonder Girls, KARA, Miss A, After School and f(x). The meteoric rise to fame of these acts astounded *Time* magazine, which in its March 7, 2012 issue labeled K-pop as 'South Korea's Greatest Export.'

Entrepreneur Lee Soo-man (who formed SM Entertainment in 1989) is one of the primary producers behind a variety of idol groups, heralding K-pop's international surge to fame in the 2000s. SM Entertainment became the leader of the 'Big Three' of the Korean music industry (followed by YG Entertainment and JYP Entertainment), pioneering the industrialization of K-pop and its star-cloning processes. Between the mid- to late 1990s and the mid-2000s, SM Entertainment's primary target market for its K-pop acts has been Asia. For example, Kwon Boa (commonly known as BoA, the 'Queen of K-pop') enjoyed notable success in Japan, the second biggest national music market outside of the US. Her promotion outside of Korea resulted from SM Entertainment's identification of Japan as an enormously lucrative market, 20 times the size of the Korean market. The multi-language and multi-country marketing strategy used to promote BoA outside of Korea has become the model that SM Entertainment uses for other artists such as TVXQ, Super Junior, Girls' Generation, and EXO.

Since 2006 SM Entertainment has been recruiting acts from outside of Korea to join its pool of domestic talent. This novel global audition process resulted in the recruitment of singer-vocalists Henry from Super Junior-M, along with f(x)'s Amber and EXO's Chris – all three were to become key members of their respective K-pop acts. From this point, every act managed by SM Entertainment included at least one member drawn from outside of Korea – now a distinctive feature of the company's global strategy. Today, SM Global Auditions are held in 18 cities across seven countries, including China, Japan, the US, Canada, Indonesia, Thailand and, of course, Korea.

Today, SM Entertainment is the biggest music company in Korea – in part due to its pioneering and strong ties with mega video-sharing social networking service YouTube, which offers fans a dynamic range of music videos in various formats and language versions, as well as artist greetings, news, segments of live performances, and teaser videos before a new act/group is officially released. SM Entertainment's strategy of using YouTube as its primary distribution channel affords the K-pop industry a direct route to global exposure, bypassing major international music labels such as Universal Music Group, Sony Music Entertainment, and Warner Music Group – aka the 'big three' major international record labels. As a new media platform, YouTube provides affordable and unlimited access to visual content that transcends the promotional materials available to fans from K-pop company websites.

By the end of 2013, the nine-member Korean girl group, Girls' Generation, shocked the global music industry by winning the video of the year award for *I Got a Boy* at the YouTube Music Awards, beating favorites such as Lady Gaga, One Direction, and Miley Cyrus. Additionally, SM Entertainment received a YouTube Partner Gold Play award for its SMTown channel, a plaudit earned for achieving 1 million or more subscribers. The award testifies to SM Entertainment's dual strategy of internationalization and maintaining a heavy online presence. To date, K-pop video clips on YouTube have been viewed more than 7 billion times in over 230 countries. KOCCA's sponsorship of K-Pop Night Out events at leading festivals and trade shows, such as Seoul International Music Fair (aka MU:CON), South by Southwest (SXSW in Austin, Texas), Canadian Music Week (Toronto), Music Matters (Singapore), and Marché International du Disque et de l'Edition Musicale (MIDEM in Cannes, France), has been a productive tool for introducing new acts to global audiences and for strengthening bi-lateral friendships between Korea and other nations, including China.

As far back as 2008, the K-pop music scene in China has been fueled by a series of important and gradually increasing number of collaborations. In 2008, Super Junior-M (M stands for Mandarin) made its debut with its first hit single and music video of *U*. In 2010, Wonder Girls entered the Chinese market by releasing a Chinese version of their single, *Nobody, Tell Me* and *So Hot*. In 2012, EXO-M (M stands for Mandarin) expanded Korea–China K-pop encounters by releasing a Chinese version of *What is Love,* and in 2014 Chinese cinema legend Jackie Chan broke into the Korean music scene by creating the hip-hop boy idol group JJCC under the Jackie Chan Group Korea label. More recently, YG Entertainment – one of the 'big three' Korean music industry firms – has entered an unprecedented era of expansion with direct investment from China: Tencent invested 30 million USD, while Weiying Technology invested 55 million USD, making YG Entertainment the largest global K-pop company of its kind (*China Daily* 2016). Tencent's role here must be accentuated because it is one of China's largest and most powerful multinational conglomerates with a range of subsidiaries across the creative industries, as well as internet-related platforms, including mobile gaming and Artificial Intelligence (AI) technology. Even Gangnam-style star PSY is staging a comeback, but in China rather than Korea. PSY is participating as a mentor in the Chinese variety show *Heroes of Remix*, which connects singers and DJs, and showcases live Chinese electronic dance music. Numerous other well-known Korean idol groups with Chinese members include (or have included): Super Junior-M (Han Geng and Zhou Mi); EXO and EXO-M (Kris, Luhan, Tao, and Lay); Miss A (Fei, Jia); and f(x) (Victoria).

In 2018, and probably well into the 2020s, we are witnessing an increasing two-way flow between Korean and Chinese popular music acts and management companies. Thus, K-pop is a pillar engine driving the transformation of the Korean (and Chinese) creative industries, earning the sobriquet 'new *Hallyu*' (*shinhallyu* in Korean) and writing a vibrant new chapter into the Korean Wave story – all the while keeping Korea at the forefront of the global music industry.

The national sport of gaming, or 'e-sport'

Korea is known as one of Asia's largest gaming hubs, where online and mobile gaming is a big part of the nation's social environment and governing policies, and where professional gamers have a celebrity status (Feijoo et al. 2012; Fung and Ho 2016). Playing video games as well as watching people playing video games in *PC bangs* (Korea's internet cafes), large sports stadiums, and on gaming-dedicated television channels (e.g. OnGamenet-OGN; MBCGame) has been a common practice for years. Since 2004, the Korean government has also sponsored various awards to encourage the growth of the domestic gaming industry, including recognition for 'Best Games of the Month', 'Korea Game Grand Awards', and 'Best Game Scenario Commission Competition'.

The basic history of Korea's gaming industry dates back to 1996 when Kim Young-sam's government jump-started this sector by promulgating the Sound Records, Video Products and Game Software Act. This Act expanded the manufacture of sound records and video products, eventually leading to their protection under increased freedom of speech and press by subsequent decrees made by the Constitutional Court. Within three years, the game industry was recognized as a genuine cultural industry in its own right. In 1999, during the same year the Kim Dae-jung government launched its *Cyber Korea 21* vision statement, outlining Korea's aspirations to become the most wired nation and ICT-savvy society in the world, the quasi-government Korean Gaming Development and Promotion Institute was established (renamed Korea Game Industry Agency in 2002). Certainly, online gaming was part of Korea's 'knowledge-based economy'– as if it was as important and as popular as World Cup soccer (Jin 2010). In fact, to increase its global competitiveness, the Gaming Development and Promotion Institute opened a branch in Japan, about two years before KOCCA opened its outpost there.

As *Hallyu* was beginning to make a mark in global markets around 2000, so too was the Korean gaming industry. Specifically, the Ministry of Culture, Sports and Tourism supported the Korea e-Sports Association, which managed the complex job of broadcasting e-sports, organized ongoing events, regulating worker/programmer employment conditions, facilitating venture capital investment, and promoting game playing to the public at large. The World Cyber Games (WCG) competitive e-sports event (sponsored by Samsung Electronics and Microsoft) was launched in 2001, and China has hosted the finals three times: Chengdu in 2009, and Kunshan, Suzhou in 2012 and again in 2013.[3] By 2003, Korea Game Industry Agency had operationalized all aspects of the gaming industry, including the ratings of games, training certification standards, and support of gaming education courses at universities and other vocational academies across Korea (Park et al. 2014). Finally, in 2009, Korea Game Industry Agency became a sub-organization of KOCCA, and the gaming industry now benefits from synergies created across the KOCCA ecosystem, including the global activities and momentum generated via its eight international offices. Some of the top Korean mobile/social media (and online) game developers include: Com2Us (*Summoners War*); Netmarble Games (*MARVEL Future Fight, Raven/EvilBane*); WeMade Entertainment (*CandyPang, The Legend of Mir, Counter-Strike, StarCraft: Brood War* and *Warcraft III*); Gamevil (*Darkness Reborn*); Nexon (*DomiNations*); NHN PixelCube (*Wooparoo Mountain*); and NFLY Studio (*Infinite Stairs*). Supporting the advancement of mobile and social gaming, and facilitating internationalization strategies remain a key part of the creative industries and a national priority of the Korean government, which now has an eye on innovations in virtual reality, augmented reality, and artificial intelligence software and hardware applications. Clearly, translation support will continue to be a key strategy for localizing Korean games and apps in multiple international markets.

According to the 2016 *White Paper on Korean Games*, the Korean game market increased by 7.5 percent in 2015, demonstrating a noticeable change from 2014, and pushing the sector to a new historical peak (KOCCA 2017a). In 2015, online games accounted for 49.2 percent of the market, followed by mobile games increasing steadily from 29.2 percent (in 2014) to 32.5 percent and PC rooms with 15.5 percent. These three categories account for 97.2 percent of the total gaming industry, which accounts for the largest proportion of Korea's creative industry exports – currently exceeding 6.31 billion USD (Yoon 2017).

China is now Korea's largest export market for online games, and thus a key partner for assisting in the internationalization of Korea's gaming industry. However, Korea's market penetration rate in China has begun to decrease due to a combination of factors. First, the acquisition of foreign games by Chinese firms has created a significant boost. For example, in 2014, Korean game developer Actoz Soft was sold to China's online game developer Shanda Games. Until this sale, Shanda had licensed the Korean game *Legend of Mir* from Actoz Soft, giving the Korean company unprecedented access to the Chinese market. Ironically, the fortune that Shanda made from this deal was large enough to enable Shanda to become a public company on the NASDAQ exchange, and in turn it purchased Actoz Soft in full (So and Westland 2010). Second, and probably resultant of the first factor, China's home-grown gaming industry has begun to rise; a lion's share of the World's best gamers are now from China. Other joint investments from major Chinese players continue to bind the Korean and Chinese markets together. In 2014, Tencent invested around 20 million USD in PATI Games, a Korean mobile game developer, making Tencent the second largest shareholder in PATI Games (KOCCA 2014). Tencent also purchased nearly one-third of Korea's CJ Games Corporation for 500 million USD, and invested 530 billion KRW in Netmarble Games, and 130 billion KRW in 4:33 Creative Lab (Shu 2014). In 2016, Chinese company Ourpalm acquired a significant stake in Webzen, the video game developing arm of NHN Entertainment – a major Korean internet and entertainment company (Lee 2016). Finally, in February 2018, Tencent purchased a large stake in Shanda Games, and in turn, Shanda Games (via its Korean subsidiary Actoz Soft) invested about 10 million USD in Korea's major online gaming company, Kakao Games (Lee 2018; Shi and Han 2018). Plainly, these types of acquisitions are further expanding Tencent and China's online and mobile platform pipelines of content for the booming global games and larger creative industry market. In short, the collaborative ventures and internationalization strategies examined here present Korean players with many challenges, such as the sharing of trade secrets and intellectual property, and retaining local and global audiences. However, this 'double-edged sword' may be a small price to pay given that the rapid expansion of China's mobile gaming and media sectors only show signs of accelerating.

Currently, KOCCA's movements in Abu Dhabi, UAE are telling of its latest tilt toward new creative industry opportunities in the Middle East, where K-dramas have been popular for some time. In late 2014, when one of the authors visited Dubai, posters of the romantic comic-historical-fantasy *Rooftop Prince* (2012) were featured prominently on billboards throughout the Digital Media City there, and electronic shops in the massive Dubai Mall displayed PSY Gangnam-style music videos on televisions and projectors as part of their sales promotion campaigns. In 2016, KOCCA and the Abu Dhabi Media Zone Authority signed a historic Memorandum of Understanding, strengthening industry and collegial ties between Korea and the Middle East. According to the agreement, KOCCA will provide a range of vocational training programs run by Korean creative experts, as well as a series of business-matching initiatives for SME creative economy start-ups, while opening new doors for Korean producers of creative and cultural content. In so doing, KOCCA and the Korean government now have their eyes on the larger market opportunities in the UAE, which has strong inroads to Saudi Arabia, where King Salman bin Abdulaziz Al Saud's recently published *Saudi Vision 2030* outlines an unprecedented plan for nurturing the cultural and entertainment industries, and a much larger aim of transforming Saudi Arabia into a strategic hub bridging Asia, Europe, and Africa.[4] Korea and its creative industries – as well as their Chinese partners – now have the chance to contribute directly to this 'Middle Eastern dream'.

Korean animation and cartoon industry and a new era of digital *Hallyu*

Finally, the most exciting and dynamic part of the creative industries in Korea, and the apparent leader of the next generation of *Hallyu*, or what we are calling 'm-*Hallyu*' (mobile *Hallyu*), can be seen rising from the animation and cartoon sectors. Specifically, online and mobile webtoons are becoming the most visible and profitable aspect of the Korean Wave in an evolving digital media environment. What follows is a brief historical overview of webtoon's predecessors and their rise and fall, and rise again to fame.

Korea has a long, active and colorful history of comic book and animation culture that symbolizes the underlying creativity of serialized webtoons and the nation. A meander through the Korea Manhwa Museum in Bucheon, a permanent home for one of the largest collections of comic and webtoon culture in Korea, offers visitors an overview of this conventional history today. The very first images were wood-block printed cartoons on paper. During its earliest years, comics primarily appeared in newspapers, which flourished in the modernized newspaper industry during the Japanese colonial period (1910–45) – at least until 1937, when Japan's total war effort forced Koreans and all aspects of Korean society to focus on the military agenda. After gaining independence in August 1945, comics experienced an enthusiastic revival, with satirical political cartoons and children's educational comics gaining wide appeal. As one can imagine, the eruption of the Korean War in mid-1950 impacted on the commercial production of comics, but a small number of titles (with a small number of pages) were published in Busan and Daegu. Continuing around the Korea Manhwa Museum, one learns that in the late 1950s, comics began to regain their popularity and a number of comic cafes (predecessors of the *PC bang*) emerged, where guests could read and/or borrow a variety of popular titles. Many drama-style titles were localized versions of or at least inspired by Japanese manga. Throughout the 1960s, Hapdong became one of the top publishers of comics, and its monopoly of the industry, plus censorship under the Park Chung Hee government significantly reduced the creative potential of the field by hindering smaller publishers and local artists. At this time, at least according to the conventional record, comics were seen by the government as 'hazardous' materials that negatively interfered with youth education and corrupted young minds.

A turning point for comic books occurred during the 1970s after Korean society began to experience rapid industrialization, and pop magazines featuring different comic genres (children's, sports, romance, and adult erotica) began attracting wider readership. The 1980s represents a 'golden-age' of comics in Korea due to the economic growth resulting from these genres – in spite of the difficult social conditions experienced during strict military governments. But, similar to a small number of films that contained democratization themes, comics with social commentaries began to connect with local readers. After Korea experienced democratization in the 1990s, print manwha became a staple among other forms of popular culture, and the industry began to experience a significant *renaissance*. Between 2013 and 2014, manwha's value as pillar in the creative industries increased after a small number of magazine titles were registered as national 'cultural assets'.[5]

Animations in Korea also have a lengthy history, albeit shorter than comic books, dating back to the 1960s. The best known animation made after Liberation is *The Ant and the Grasshopper* (1961) (Kim 2006). Based on its success, the Park Chunk Hee military government soon began using animated films as tools for disseminating government ideology and educating the public. In 1966, Park's Ministry of Public Information mandated that between approximately 30 percent to 50 percent of all animations on television, which was now becoming more popular in Korea and also inundated with US content, must be of domestic origin (Yim 2002). The industry was immediately invigorated. A technological breakthrough occurred a year later with the production of Korea's first color feature film animation, *Hong Gil-dong* (1967). Subsequent animations featured revolutionary heroes, the best known of which is *Robot Taekwon V* (1976), which inspired numerous sequels, and an English-dubbed version that was released on VHS in 1986 in the US (as *Voltar the Invincible).* Similar to comic books, the aesthetics in many animations released during this period, including *Robot Taekwon V,* were influenced by Japanese popular animation.

Throughout the mid-to-late 1980s (and up until the mid-2000s), Korean studios and animators primarily completed original equipment manufacturing (OEM) work for the US and Japanese animation industries. Encouraged by the Korean government, this type of activity benefited the overall interests of national economic development (Jin 2016). Korean-American Nelson Shin's AKOM Production Co. worked on *The Simpsons* television series, while others assisted with Fox Network's *X-Men,* Warner Bros. Animation and Steven Spielberg's Amblin Entertainment's jointly produced *Tiny Toon Adventures* and *Animaniacs* series. Around this time, Korean animation factories were conducing about half of the world's outsourced animation jobs. To increase their profit margins, some South Korean studios sub-subcontracted their OEM work to animation studios in North Korea, such as Scientific Educational Korea (SEK Studio), known for its work on the animated fantasy *Empress Chung.*

After 1993, an increasing number of independent filmmakers began creating animations on their own without government support or interference, or commercial pressures. Trendsetters outside of the commercial film industry enjoyed limited success at the box office. Then in 1995, Kim Young-sam's Ministry of Culture and Tourism began to recognize the commercial value of the creative and cultural industries, and it revealed new strategies for subsidizing and promoting the animation industry. One of the first events to benefit from this new higher status was the inaugural Seoul International Cartoon and Animation Festival (SICAF), which still runs strong in 2018 as one of the top global events of its kind. The launch of the first Bucheon International Animation Festival (BIAF), one of the few festivals in Asia that cater exclusively to students, followed in 1999.

Another decisive moment occurred in 2003 with the first broadcast of the children's animated series *Pororo* on EBS, and the subsequent development of its character-driven one-source-multi-use (OSMU) licensed product line, including pencil cases, notebooks, backpacks, and action figures. OSMU refers to the production and promotion strategy that spins off a variety of products and tie-in campaigns from a single creative source or program. *Pororo* has been syndicated and licensed to broadcasters in over 100 countries across the globe, making the series one of the most popular Korean children's animations. Today, the OSMU integrated marketing strategy is one of KOCCA and MCST's chief mantras because of the increased potential for animation projects to globalize their characters via a full range of merchandise – items which Asia's growing middle class is gobbling up with its new-found disposable income. A range of vocational animation studios and educational and training centers established in 2009 by KOCCA and the Seoul city government, are attempting to build upon *Pororo*'s success by nurturing the next generation of animators.

Unexpectedly, or simply because of this government attention on animation, commercial players have become motivated to join the crowd. One feature-length animation in particular that has made waves at home and in China is Myung Film's *Leafie, a Hen into the Wild* (2011), which broke the previous attendance records set by *Hong Gil-dong* (1967) (Elley 2011; Hoad 2013). *Leafie*, which Myung Film made in collaboration with Korean media giant Lotte Entertainment (investor and distributor), was Myung Film's first feature-length animation. It achieved unprecedented box office results for a film of its kind, primarily because of its high production values and outstanding story line. *Leafie* is one of only a handful of feature films officially exported to China and was Korea's first feature-length animation to play on China's growing number of multiplex screens. *Leafie* received international acclaim after winning the Best Sitges Family Film Diploma at the 2011 Sitges Film Festival in Spain, and Best Animated Feature Film at the 2011 Asia Pacific Film Award in Australia. Predictably, following the success of *Leafie*, MCST announced increased funding support for the animation industry, especially for family animations that could also reach wider audiences in international markets – in similar ways to Disney films. After 2013, domestic animation projects now had access to a never-before-seen amount of support funding. In 2015, the Korean government pledged to invest approximately 350 million USD in the animation and character industries to assist with overseas market expansion, especially in China (KOCCA 2017c).

Since 2002, Korean animations have had a noticeably increasing presence in China. For example, in 2002 *Space Hip Hop Duck* (2002) was released as the first official co-produced television animation, and then in 2007 *Little Wizard Tao* (2007) was co-produced between Korea's G&G Entertainment and China's Motion Magic Digital Entertainment. Five years later, the television animation series and feature film *Crucuru and Friends* (2012) was created by Korea's Ffango Entertainment and China Film Group. And, in 2015 the first Korean Chinese Animation Co-production Forum was held in Seoul, hosted by the Korean Film Council and China's Film Bureau of State Administration of Press, Publication, Radio, Film and TV. Currently in 2018, *Big Fish & Beognia* is being produced in collaboration with Beijing's B&T Studio and Korean animation house Studio Mir, and industry representatives on both sides have establish the Global Animation Partners, as a joint venture with eight South Korean and 19 Chinese animation firms. Three South Korea animations: *Flying Superboard, Asianosauru*, and *Capsule Boy*, have been selected for the first joint investment projects. Korean–Chinese media encounters are only becoming stronger.

At the time of writing in 2018, the largest expanding part of Korean animation and the creative industries more widely is in webtoons. The top seven commercial platforms/sites in Korea that provide distribution access to webtoons are: NAVER LINE webtoon, Daum webtoon, Nate webtoon, Tstore webtoon, T tale, Lezhin Comics, and Olleh Market, and there are more than 25 other smaller channels too. Korea Manhwa Contents Agency (KOMACON), formerly known as Bucheon Cartoon Information Center, has played a central role in developing the industry at large and negotiating with these commercial platforms on behalf of webtoon artists. KOMACON continues to expand and connect manhwa with all of KOCCA's umbrella cultural and IT sectors, as well as film, animation, TV dramas, and games. Today, despite the historical 'lowbrow' status and censorship of print manhwa in Korea (and probably elsewhere around the globe), the comic artform is now being pushed into uncharted mobile media territory, thus evolving into a unique literary and aesthetic genre of its own. Webtoons are now seen by leaders in Korea's creative industries as the ideal core content for a OSMU strategy. In the past, Korean children's animation characters such as *Pororo* – as a brand – have been a hit in Korea, largely due to the faithful following of the OSMU model. However, webtoons are breaking new ground in this arena.

According to representatives at KOMACON, one in three people in Korea reads webtoons on a smart device each week, and many are paying subscription fees to do so (KOCCA 2015). This steady high volume of consumption is keeping webtoon artists busy to the point where an established webtoon artist is earning about 5,000 USD per serialized issue. Over a one-year period, this salary is equivalent to approximately six times the amount that a film screenwriter usually makes. Today, over 5,000 artists are working in the field, and over 6,000 issues have been published via webtoon platforms in Korea. The statistics are even larger when including translated versions for international markets such as the US, Australia, Japan, China, UAE – to name only a few, where Korean webtoons are growing in popularity on a daily basis. Especially in China, local media groups have begun to purchase the rights to certain webtoons in order to create their own television dramas and films. In late 2015, Naver sold *Gigi Goegoe* to a Chinese filmmaker, and in early 2016 – prior to the so-called THAAD missile crisis that curtailed a large percentage of collaborative Korea–China ventures, Kakao-Daum, Korea's most popular mobile SNS (Kakao Talk), entered a joint venture with the Chinese Huace Group, to release the following Korean webtoons to China's expanding mobile media market: *Girl in the Mirror, The Helping Breakup Ghost, Just One Shot* and *Cashero.* Other print and digital comics that have become the basis of Chinese feature films and television shows include *Tazza: The High Rollers* (2006) and *With God* (2017); and television dramas include *Full House* (2004), *Flower Boy Next Door* (2013), and *Misaeng* (2014). In this way, content flowing from Korea's creative industries is continuing to make fresh inroads into China's emerging creative industries, while also pushing Korea's creative and cultural industries into the next decade and beyond.

Conclusion: expanding Korean–Chinese creative industries encounters

Across the global creative industries, '*Hallyu*' and 'Korean Wave' are both buzzwords and expressions of Korea's soft power that encapsulate the astounding success currently enjoyed by Korean cultural content, in terms of both production and export values. Despite creative input from a variety of international contributors, the meteoric rise of Korean cinema, K-pop, and now webtoons was not anticipated by most global media industry players. In addition, by circumventing the barriers to entry (and costs) associated with traditional media production and distribution channels dominated by a few major global players, successfully exploiting the promotional space offered by YouTube, and a variety of other mobile media platforms, and also being an early adopter of this new commercial phenomenon, Korea's creative industries have become world leaders in an intensely competitive field.

On a practical and economic level, KOCCA is assisting Korean companies and practitioners with marrying their production experience and advanced technical skills with China and other countries' local distribution networks and manufacturing base to create products with transnational appeal. In China's case, given that the local market has further ground to offer foreign content, co-producing with a Korean partner and/or licensing Korean content are effective ways forward. To achieve these outcomes, cultural businesses as well as policy makers such as KOCCA are attempting to follow various localization strategies, that is, Koreans are becoming 'cultural chameleons'. Meanwhile, KOCCA outposts in the US, Japan, China, Indonesia, Brazil, the UK, and UAE are showing that catering for unique local market needs is important for further developing the spread and promotion of Korean media and popular culture. As these cases show, and especially in China, Korea is expanding its soft power while enabling international and Chinese cultural producers to develop soft power of their own, creating new pathways for media collaboration and offering new insights about 'soft power competition' in the region.

Ironically, while Korean firms and practitioners are increasing their cultural presence in China, they probably still warrant greater attention in the region – for the ways in which Korean creativity is contributing to innovation in China and assisting China's cultural exports, thereby enhancing Chinese soft power. China is now working to export its culture with the aim of enhancing its own soft power and creating a positive image on the world stage (Keane et al. 2018). As the present authors see it, Korea's success with *Hallyu*, which returned substantial economic benefits in a short period through the export of cultural products, is being scrutinized by China for its own commercial and political ends.

As a result of these developments, *Hallyu* has taken on a new meaning: the spread of Korea's creative industries is no longer a one-way street, and multi-directional cultural flows are developing through collaboration between Korea and other countries in which KOCCA outposts are operating. We may speak of the emergence of an 'Asian Wave', of which *Hallyu* has up until now been the driving force. Yet, with the growing popularity of K-pop and webtoons in particular in regions as diverse as Asia, Europe, the US, and South America, regional 'tagging' of Korea's popular cultural products may no longer be necessary, because what is important for both content creators and consumers is not where things are produced, but for whom they are intended.

Today, international media collaborations and joint ventures are enabling Chinese and other international producers to make bigger and more technically savvy feature films and to utilize other digital media content that transcend the types of productions made under local industry and regulatory conditions. On top of this, genre choices and mobile media cultures are changing and expanding across Asia – thanks in part to the technical expertise and creative nous of the Korean creative industry firms and practitioners that have been working in Asia and/or with Asian partners during the past decade. In these ways, Asia's creative industries more broadly are beginning to show an increasing ability to compete with better-funded US media content and also the novel genres for which Korean cultural content is known. At the same time, Asian companies are benefiting progressively from their investments in the Korean and US markets.

Heading into the 2020s, the situation looks like a positive scenario for the creative industries across Asia. This especially holds true in China, with the promise of the Chinese government's Internet Plus strategy that was released in March 2015. This is a major initiative which aims to integrate mobile internet, cloud computing, big data, the Internet of Things, and Artificial Intelligence (AI) with modern manufacturing, and to encourage the healthy development of e-commerce, industrial networks, and internet banking across international markets. Korean practitioners may hold one of the keys to achieving the 'Internet Plus dream' – for both China and the region. As this chapter shows, Koreans have contributed to the expansion of Chinese traditional and new media in terms of the refinement of genres, themes, and story lines, as well as technical skills, and Chinese media companies have enabled Korean creative industry workers to increasingly internationalize their approaches to overseas markets. In 1996, the Constitutional Court in Korea deemed that the censorship of films and other audio-visual products was illegal. In this new creative and digital economy, which now includes small-to-medium start-up enterprises, as well as ICT, science and technology research and development, and the deployment of superfast broadband infrastructure, Korea's global experience and success with its own brand of style and technical prowess is proving instrumental in developing a collaborative relationship with Asia and its expanding creative industries.

Notes

1 Chua and Iwabuchi 2008; Kim 2011; Yecies and Shim 2011; Kim 2013; Hong 2014; Kwon and Kim 2014; and Yecies and Shim 2016.
2 See OECD broadband statistics update available at: http://www.oecd.org/sti/broadband/broadband-statistics-update.htm. Accessed May 1, 2018.
3 See: http://www.wcg.com/us/#history.
4 An English-language version of *Saudi Vision 2030* is available at: http://vision2030.gov.sa/en.
5 For other aspects of this history, see: KOCCA 2017b and Yamanaka 2013.

References

China Daily (2016, May 31) S Korea music giant attracts Chinese investors. Available at: http://www.china.org.cn/arts/2016-05/31/content_38568881.htm (accessed May 1, 2018).

Chua, B. H. and Iwabuchi, K. (eds.) (2008) *East Asian Pop Culture: Analysing the Korean Wave.* Hong Kong: Hong Kong University Press.

Elley, D. (2011, December 28) *Leafie. Film Business Asia.* Available at: http://www.filmbiz.asia/reviews/leafie (accessed June 12, 2015).

Feijoo, C., Gómez-Barroso, J. A. and Ramos, S. (2012) Mobile gaming: Industry challenges and policy implications. *Telecommunications Policy*, 36(3): 212–21.

Frater, P. (2018, January 18) Korea's CJ orders up merger of media and shopping units. *Variety.com.* Available at: http://variety.com/2018/biz/asia/korea-media-giant-to-emerge-from-cj-em-merger-with-shopping-business-1202668041/ (accessed May 1, 2018).

Fung, A. and Ho, V. (2016) Game industries in Asia: Towards an Asian formation of game culture. In Hjorth, L. and Khoo, O. (eds.), *Routledge Handbook of New Media in Asia.* London and New York: Routledge, pp. 337–90.

Hoad, P. (2013, January 23) South Korean animation: is the underdog finally having its day?' *The Guardian.* Available at: https://www.theguardian.com/film/filmblog/2013/jan/22/south-korean-animation-king-pigs (accessed May 1, 2018).

Hong, E. Y. (2014) *The Birth of Korean Cool: How One Nation is Conquering the World through Pop Culture.* New York: Picador.

Jin, D. Y. (2010) *Korea's Online Gaming Empire.* Cambridge, MA: MIT Press.

Jin, D. Y. (2016) Hybrid local animation's global appeal. In *New Korean Wave: Transnational Cultural Power in the Age of Social Media.* Chicago: University of Illinois Press, pp. 91–110.

Keane, M., Yecies, B. and Flew, T. (eds.) (2018) *Willing Collaborators: Foreign Partners in Chinese Media.* London: Rowman & Littlefield.

Kim, J. (2006) Critique of the new historical landscape of South Korean animation. *Animation: An Interdisciplinary Journal*, 1(1): 61–8.

Kim, K. (2011) *Virtual Hallyu: Korean Cinema of the Global Era.* London: Duke University Press.

Kim, Y. (ed.) (2013) *The Korean Wave: Korean Media Go Global.* London and New York: Routledge.

Korean Creative Content Agency (KOCCA) (2014, November 19) $19.7M in Korea's PATI Games Available at: http://www.koccaeurope.com/2014/11/tencent-invests-19-7m-in-koreas-pati-games/ (accessed May 1, 2018).

Korean Creative Content Agency (KOCCA) (2015, January 21) Korea cartoon & webtoon market trend. Available at: http://www.koccaeurope.com/2015/01/info-graphics-korea-cartoonwebtoon-market-trend/ (accessed May 1, 2018).

Korean Creative Content Agency (KOCCA) (2017a) 2016 Whitepaper on Korean Games. Seoul: Korea Creative Content Agency. Available at: http://www.gamehub.or.kr/gamehubnew/databbs/FileDown.do?atchFileId=FILE_000000000237483&fileSn=1&bbsId=B0000146 (accessed May 1, 2018).

Korean Creative Content Agency (KOCCA) (2017b) 2016 Manhwa saneop baekseo (2016 Graphic Novel Industry White Paper). Seoul: KOCCA Industry Support Department.

Korean Creative Content Agency (KOCCA) (2017c) Aenimeisyeon saneopbaekseo (2016 Animation Industry White Paper). Seoul: KOCCA Industry Support Department.

Kwak, K. (2012) *Media and Democratic Transition in South Korea*. London and New York: Routledge.

Kwon, S. and Kim, J. (2014) The cultural industry policies of the Korean government and the Korean Wave. *International Journal of Cultural Policy*, 20(4): 244–439.

Lee, A. (2018, February 7) Former Chinese online games market leader gets investment from Tencent. *South China Morning Post*. Available at: http://www.scmp.com/tech/apps-gaming/article/2132432/former-chinese-online-games-market-leader-gets-investment-tencent (accessed May 1, 2018).

Lee, C. (2016, March 10) Chinese investment, double-edge sword for S. Korean gamemakers. *Yonhap News Agency*. Available at: http://english.yonhapnews.co.kr/national/2016/03/10/7/0301000000AEN20160310003951320F.html (accessed May 1, 2018).

Lee, S. and Nornes, A. (eds.) (2015) *Hallyu 2.0: The Korean Wave in the Age of Social Media*. Ann Arbor, MI: University of Michigan Press.

Otmazgin, N. (2011) A tail that wags the dog? Cultural industry and cultural policy in Japan and South Korea. *Journal of Comparative Policy Analysis: Research and Practice*, 13(3): 307–25.

Park, G., Kim, M., Oh, I. and Kang, S. (2014) The success story of the cultural industry in Korea: The case of the game industry. Seoul: Ministry of Strategy and Finance, Republic of Korea.

Shi, R. and Han, W. (2018, April 3) Shanda invests $9.4 million in Kakao Games. *CaixinGlobal.com*. Available at: https://www.caixinglobal.com/2018-04-03/shanda-invests-94-billion-in-kakao-games-101229789.html (accessed May 1, 2018).

Shu, C. (2014, March 24) Tencent acquires 28% stake in South Korea's CJ Games for $500M. *TechCrunch.com*. Available at: https://techcrunch.com/2014/03/26/tencent-cjgames/ (accessed May 1, 2018).

So, S. and Westland, J. (2010) *Red Wired: China's Internet Revolution*. London: Marshall Cavendish.

Yamanaka, C. (2013) Manhwa in Korea: (Re-)Nationalizing comics culture. In J. Berndt and Kümmerling-Meibauer, B. (eds.), *Manga's Cultural Crossroads*. New York: Routledge, pp. 85–99.

Yecies B. (2016) The Chinese–Korean Co-Production Pact: Collaborative encounters and the accelerating expansion of Chinese cinema. *The International Journal of Cultural Policy*, 22(5): 770–86.

Yecies, B. and Shim, A. (2011) Contemporary Korean cinema: Challenges and the transformation of 'Planet Hallyuwood'. *Acta Koreana*, 14(1): 1–15.

Yecies, B. and Shim, A. (2016) *The Changing Face of Korean Cinema, 1960–2015*. Routledge Asia's Transformations series. New York: Routledge.

Yim, H. (2002) Cultural identity and cultural policy in South Korea. *International Journal of Cultural Policy*, 8(1): 37–48.

Yoon, Y. (2017, September 7) Korea's content exports show annual growth of 8% on average. *BusinessKorea*. Available at: http://www.businesskorea.co.kr/news/articleView.html?idxno=19232 (accessed May 1, 2018).

Part III
Consumption and circulation

15

Sell your loneliness

Mukbang culture and multisensorial capitalism in South Korea

Yeran Kim

Introduction

The dramatic expansion and penetration of social media into each and every part of life has made it possible for anyone who so desires to make the self publicly visible. Innumerable images of the private self have saturated the public space across virtual and actual worlds. In forming great imagery-spaces, 'being watched' as well as presenting the self has become a significant kind of 'work' in the mediated life world (Andrejevic 2003). The visual features and social implications of the 'publicly private self' (Papacharissi 2010), prosperous through social networking such as YouTube, are worth noting in the exploration of the cultural and political meanings of the self and the relations of the private and the public, which seem to have made a radical shift with the expansion of digital network societies. Individual communicative actions of interactivity and interpassivity (Kim, Y. 2015; Zizek 1999) are intertwined in the transformation of the sensorial, affective, and cognitive topology of the private and the public.

Moreover, the role of media technology and its socio-economic logic of operation are critical in the account of repositioning the self in relation to the social. In the so-called age of social media, personal data is intended to be blatantly and effectively converted to economic, social, cultural, and political values (Couldry and van Dijck 2015). This is fundamentally related to the role that media technologies play in cultural industries in the current context of 'communicative capitalism', in which human discursive activities are reduced to the means of creating social and economic surplus values (Dean 2009; 2010). One's sense, affect, cognition, social relations, and psychic and physical activities, all of which are constitutive of the human subject, are aggregated and transformed into economic values in the current neoliberal regime governing life and death (Foucault, 2008).

A specific case that I would like to draw attention to is the cultural boom of eating shows, or *Mukbang* in Korean. From television broadcasting to the internet and social media, a variety of visual materials presenting food, eating, and cooking have become dramatically popular over the past few years in South Korea. While star chefs and entertainers are dominant in the arena of mass media, the internet is populated with the subcultural practices of *Mukbang*. The personal broadcasting of *Mukbang* on the internet is vigorous among young people in their twenties. They are keen to participate in the cult rituals of broadcasting the self-image of eating in public. Most join the *Mukbang* culture by watching video clips while the more active and ambitious voluntarily produce and circulate *Mukbang* video clips themselves. The private self who is eating in one's own room is revealed to anonymous voyeuristic gazes, while gluttony, pleasure, and social desire are intermingled in such virtual scenes. The culture of *Mukbang* also suggests a meaningful aspect of the affective structure of Korea in which the feelings of loneliness, solitariness, and isolation are pervasive as social individualization and fragmentation have deepened. *Mukbang* expresses and also spreads such social affects, which are shared among young people in their virtual intimacy in the digital and networked mediation.

The second aspect is concerned with the political economic logic embedded in *Mukbang*. The ambivalence of the active and passive acts of being watched eating is reformulated as a particular type of 'digital creative labour' (Kim, Y. 2016). *Mukbang* is operable just in the digital economy of attention (Goldhaber 1997), through which the performer anticipates obtaining not only social attention or fame but also economic profit from the audiences' payment of cybermoney. There are terms and conditions that have been established on the division of profit between producers and the internet platform companies in the market of User Created Content (UCC). In the case of Afreeca TV, for instance, a BJ, meaning a broadcasting jockey, has 60 per cent and the platform company has 40 per cent of the total profit created from cybermoney called Star Balloons, which is paid by the audience members of the show on Afreeca TV. The monetization of eating, which has been considered as one of the most natural and instinctive behaviours of all beings, necessary for survival, is transformed into a kind of digital and creative labour, as well as a commodity.

Finally, I conclude my paper by suggesting the use of the term 'multisensorial capitalism' as a way to address the merits and limitations of previous terms, in order to better articulate the current actual forms of living and working in the intersection of neoliberalism, post-capitalism, and digital technology networks – for example, the notion of biocapitalism, as proposed by Morini and Fumagalli (2010), where more weight is put on labour than on consumption. Consequently, the reality, in which the distinction between labour and consumption is blurred, is insufficiently explained, such that even members of the audience of the mass media themselves are commodified in the course of media consumption (Smythe 1981). Another term, communicative capitalism, coined by Jodi Dean (2009, 2010), is featured mostly in a discursive aspect. Thus, the actuality in which the material and immaterial, and the corporeal and discursive are increasingly integrated into the process of (de)subjectivation in the present capitalist and network society, has not been seriously considered.

In comparison, my proposed concept, multisensorial capitalism, is intended to focus on the element of *sensation* in the everyday practice of digital networked communication. This is not least because the actuality needs to be explained, in which both the material and the immaterial, the physical and the linguistic, the body and mind, labour and leisure, and production and consumption, are intertwined in the generation of surplus values in the digitalized life-world. The interrelated, simultaneous deployment of heterogeneous realms, which have been traditionally considered as separate or opposite to one another, is now seen as being coexistent, and mutually formative and strengthening. In the novel form of the mixed operation of production *and* consumption, one's affect, sense, body, action, intelligence, cognition, social relations, and psychic and physical activity for living, or one's subjectivity in its totality, are motivated, invested, celebrated, and exploited in multisensorial capitalism as, I would argue, this is increasingly becoming the core of cultural and creative industries.

The transmediated development of *Mukbang* in South Korea

An anonymous internet user in 2009 showed one person eating alone – this started the movement *of Mukbang* in South Korea (Hong and Park 2016); however, it was thanks to television broadcasting showing several eating and cooking programmes, famously called *Mukbang,* that eating and cooking shows have become dramatically popular over the last couple of years. While the word *Mukbang* had remained unknown to most people except some peculiar appreciators of cyber subculture, the adoption by television broadcasting channels of *Mukbang* has brought it into huge popularity, enabling it to become one of the most mainstream types of media content in Korea as of 2015.

The Korean history of *Mukbang* on television broadcasting and film started with the male film star Ha Jungwoo, known by the nickname the 'legend of *Mukbang*' among audiences (Lee 2015). His style of eating, which is characterized by a good appetite and an abundant scale of consumption, easily caught the attention of large audiences. Then the trend of *Mukbang* massively and quickly moved and extended across different social groups. Female stars and children, who conventionally should desire a small amount of food in Korea, have rushed to join in the performance of *Mukbang*, many of them immediately achieving great popularity. Woonho, an eight-year-old boy who appeared in a reality programme as the son of TV entertainer, is an example. He has become a lovable celebrity with his performance of eating a great amount of Chinese noodles 'like a storm' (Lee 2015).

Since *Mukbang* has achieved great success, several broadcasting companies have become very busy producing and delivering various formats of *Mukbang* to the extent that the term 'the era of *Mukbang*' has become a colloquial expression. The portion of *Mukbang* on the internet has steeply increased to the extent that 10–15 per cent of all programmes broadcast on Afreeca TV end up on *Mukbang* (Hong and Park 2016). In terms of TV broadcasting, *Mukbang* has become one of the most popular genres as of 2015, with its popularity gradually increasing since 2010, when Ha Jung Woo became famous as a *Mukbang* actor. *Mukbang* reached its culmination in that year, in terms of both quantitative and qualitative aspects. *Mukbang* is distinguished from conventional food programmes: with respect to the latter, approximately 15 programmes (1990–2010) were generally informative and educational, normally targeted at housewives, whereas the former, approximately 24 programmes (2010–16) were almost entirely entertainment oriented, based on popular gastronomic culture and featuring male celebrities (Hong and Park 2016). The media platforms on which they appear are also diversified as real-time shows on television are continuously available on VOD services via the internet. The idealistic discourse of the chef, in a foreign language unfamiliar to most Korean people, has become quickly habituated within people's fantasy. The type of young, handsome male chefs, who are said to have been educated and trained in famous cooking schools such as *Cordon Bleu* and fine restaurants in Europe and the USA, and who are running trendy restaurants in Seoul, have suddenly appeared on many televized food programmes, while a generous middle-aged-man-type like Baek Jong Won has also become a great celebrity with his simple, feisty, and frank style of cooking and eating. The guests appearing in these television programmes are mainly male celebrities who are ignorant of cookery, so they are supposed to learn gradually how to cook while observing and appreciating the star chefs' wonderful dishes. A series of such programmes are called *Cookbang* (i.e., Cooking Broadcasting) or *Mukbang*, depending on where the emphasis is put between cooking and eating. Diverse modes of application of *Cookbang* and *Mukbang* have been cultivated, one example of which is combining the narratives of travelling, cooking, and eating. In this type of programme, handsome male entertainers and celebrities very often appear as amateur chefs, who soon turn out to be good cooks, seen staying in villages, beach towns, or farming areas, and cooking with local produce and serving their friends.

Interestingly and also problematically, all these cooking and eating television programmes are male dominated. The male monopoly has influenced a change in the social representation of cookery culture, which has hitherto been defined as a female responsibility in the traditionally patriarchal order of South Korea. The trend of male-dominated food programmes on television may be explained from several interrelated perspectives. One is that the gender division of labour, in which men are in charge of social activity and economic production and women in charge of reproductive labour in the private sector, may be seen to be transformed in male-centered *Mukbang*. However, more critically, this apparent sweeping aside of gender roles may also mean that women are becoming more and more invisible in public spaces. This is because the work of cooking, which has been traditionally defined as a female chore, taken for granted and concealed in the private kitchen, is now a spectacle portrayed by men and glamorized as a highly fashionable profession in the media. In contrast to the spectacular visualization of the male cook in the media, Korea is one of the countries in which the economic and social gap between men and women is immense. According to OECD research (OECD 2014a), the gender wage gap between men and women in Korea is the largest of all OECD countries with women earning 62.6 per cent of men's salary. Whereas many OECD member countries have seen the gap narrow, Korea is the exception with the degree of the gap not much narrowing in the last ten years (Kim; G. 2017; Kim, S. 2014; OECD 2014b). The degree of male engagement in unpaid household work is the lowest out of OECD countries as well, with Korean men reported to spend only 45 minutes on housework per day (Lim 2017). Despite such a disastrous social reality of gender disparity, men's gesture of cooking in the media has brought them a great deal of fame and popularity. The discordance between reality and the media representation is striking enough that a neology of *Yosiknam* ('Sexy Cooking Man' in Korean) has become a common maxim in popular imagination, which celebrates a new type of masculinity perfectly possessed with superb economic and cultural capital.

Against the background of the prosperity of the male chef on television, the cyber subcultural scene on the internet has been seen to develop a rather different style of *Mukbang* and this is the very point I would like to focus on in the following pages. In particular, the questions of gender and sexuality, and the meaning of eating as a particular form of digital creative labour are discussed.

The social and affective context of *Mukbang*

The genesis of *Mukbang* on the internet is not clear, but it is supposed that *Mukbang* started on Afreeca TV in 2009 by an anonymous internet user (Lee 2015). The massive success of *Mukbang* on television has in reverse greatly influenced the internet boom of *Mukbang*. People, particularly from younger generations, have developed a strong interest in *Mukbang* not only in watching the video clips but also in performing and exhibiting video clips of *Mukbang* of themselves in their everyday life.

The most famous platform for *Mukbang* in Korea is Afreeca TV on the internet, which is also very often linked with YouTube. Afreeca TV is a well-known website for personal broadcasting, having quickly emerged as one of the main sites for cyber-based cultural practices encompassing online games, sports, beauty and lifestyle, short films, drama, and performance arts in Korea. The neology of BJ, an acronym for Broadcasting Jockey that refers to the person who produces and broadcasts his/her own video clips, has also become familiar within Afreeca TV. The action of exhibiting self on social media like Afreeca TV is not limited to cultural practice but is also deeply embedded in the complexity of economic structures interwoven with digital, consumerist, and communicative capitalist forces. With this in mind, those engaged in the cultural networks of production, distribution, and consumption of user-created contents are, with some degree of variation, depending on his/her own choice of position, oscillating between cultural authenticity and economic profit, tending to be involved in the commercial order consisting of sponsorship, advertisement, and self-branding.

The expansive popularization from mass media to the internet and social media suggests a significant shift in the formation of sociality in the practice of *Mukbang*. The agency performing and broadcasting *Mukbang* is shifting from celebrities to ordinary young people. This change does not simply mean an increase in the number of participants in the culture of *Mukbang*. More significantly, the habituation of *Mukbang* in everyday life implies that *Mukbang* has been constructed as a social reservoir and circuit in which the young people's psychical reality, including various threads of anticipation, anxiety, desire, and fantasy, are stimulated and intermingled.

Afreeca TV is a Korean-styled virtual network platform similar to YouTube, on which ordinary individuals can produce and circulate their own created video clips and run personal broadcasting. While the initial trial of *Mukbang* did not draw much attention from internet users, the act of eating is seen to have already been growing enormously as a cultural form in diverse ways. Food has already developed as a popular topic on the internet and social media worldwide. Particularly in Western advanced capitalist societies, several social and cultural factors combined in the development of food practice on the internet: the expansion of food industries, the increase in the concerns around health and body, the habituation of individualistic urban lifestyles, consumerist desire for gourmet culture, and the rising avarice for excessive imagery of food like foodporn and 'gastronomic voyeurism' (Vincent 2014) in the media-saturated popular culture (Rousseau 2012). Additionally, digital network ecology has invigorated the narcissistic desire for not simply consuming food but more expansively exhibiting the self-image of enjoying a gorgeous gourmet culture, and the ambition for achieving fame in the ubiquitous voyeuristic structure of gazing into others' daily lives.

Equally significant to the postmodern influence of Western food culture is another important factor involved in the growth of *Mukbang* on the internet in Korea, which is also specific to the social condition of contemporary Asia. It is said that *Mukbang* originated and became popular in the early 2000s in Japan (Hong and Park 2016). Japanese society was struggling with economic decline during that period, accompanied with social instability which is often symbolized by a shrinking of the middle class, precarization among the young generation, a lowering birthrate, and the tendency towards an aging society. It was in this context that the younger generation in Japan – the *Satori* generation, which has been increasingly squeezed by social and economic hardship and has lost hope for the future – became indulgent with an individualistic and solitary lifestyle (Houruichi 2015; Haworth 2013; Kim, H. 2015). They are described as having a lack of optimism, ambition, and desire for real life in the present and the future, in contrast with the conventional model of the urban, affluent nuclear family's lifestyle complete with a secure job, a lovable family, and a safe and pleasant house, car, and leisure. Partly due to shifting social structures (objective factor) and partly due to voluntary choice (subjective factor), Japanese young people have separated themselves from the ideal image of the middle class in advanced society, and instead have placed themselves in the cozy cocoon of living alone (Houruichi 2015).

The Japanese subculture of indulgence in solitary life with the signifier of living alone has made an implicit but significant impact in the shaping of young people's lifestyle in

South Korea. Korea is seen to have followed a path similar to Japan, which is described as a symptom of the post-capitalist and neoliberal restructuring of society. A considerable number of social statistics have evinced the symptom, marked by a steep increase in the number of one-person households (some 25 per cent out of all households), high competition in education and employment, and an increase in unemployment (Woo and Park 2007). The scale of desperation among highly educated young people or NEET (Not in Education, Employment, or Training) is serious to the extent that according to the National Assembly Research Service in Korea, the rate of self-identified NEETs among young people aged under 29 and with a university/college degree is 24.4 per cent, recorded as the third highest country among OECD countries in 2015, following Greece (39.2 per cent) and Turkey (24.5 per cent) (Jhoo 2015). The word 'survivalism' (Kim, H. 2015) has become naturalized to the young people's experiential lifeworld, while the reality of life is often compared to the 'hunger games'. In addition, subcultural items as well as mainstream media products from Japan have been enthusiastically adopted by Korean young people who see the commonness of lived reality between both societies. Cultural items such as Japanese cartoons and movies have attracted Korean young people, in which the *Satori* generation's novel lifestyles are characterized as a calm, simple and yet solitary life away from social conflicts and frictions. The practice of young, precarious, and solitary life forms in the *Sampo (3-Po)* generation, a Korean term for the Satori generation, means 'giving up' three basic elements for living such as courtship, marriage, and childbirth. While the list of what has been 'given up' has been continuously extended with the addition of other elements like housing, jobs, cars, and even human relations and so on, the N-Po (giving up everything) generation has finally and sadly come into being. In an ironic expression, young people's lives are seen to be reduced to the act of satisfying the self by cooking and eating alone.

It is not new that the internet has become a virtual – but affectively realistic – site in which young people's hardship, cynicism, and humour have creatively but sarcastically mushroomed in Korea. In the last few years, they have referred to themselves with the self-styled *Ying-eh*. *Ying-eh* literally refers to 'surplus' in economic terms but has a social implication, meaning a "useless residual". While calling themselves *Ying-eh*, young people like to express their frustration and pessimism in terms such as "We have become nothing", or "Maybe we cannot make it" (Kim, S. 2011). The collective feeling configured in *Ying-eh* is not limited to personal lamentation or blame but is also an expression of political critique of the social and economic contradictions and disparities which have actually caused them to feel useless in the world. A variety of cultural content has been produced, revealing the feeling of *Ying-eh*, in the forms of webtoons (internet cartoons), video clips, music, light literature and so on. These materials highlight the young people's reluctance and/or inability to become engaged in strenuous competition to achieve success, combined with other capitalist elements of life such as getting jobs, accumulating wealth, starting a family, and advancing in their career.

Mukbang is an interesting cultural invention among Korean young people who have come to be socially so placed but who also have willingly created an extremely solitary lifestyle. Considering that living alone is related to eating alone, some people living alone like having meals together with the virtual image of someone personally unknown to them appearing on the computer monitor in *Mukbang*. The act of eating alone in the actual world but eating together with a virtual connection may have several connotations in terms of the reality the contemporary younger generation has confronted, such as a socio-economic structure of precarity, refuting the Asian tradition of a large family life, domestication within the post-capitalist reinforcement of individualism, and cyber-subcultural practices of sharing pleasure. The contradictory interweaving of the emptiness of actual life and excessiveness of virtual mediation, and actual loneliness and virtual togetherness have brought numerous young people in the state of *Mukbang*, as one of the few happy, cosy, and accessible spaces available to them.

It is hardly surprising that *Mukbang* on the internet has massively grown for it appears to be close to young people's everyday life of eating alone. Furthermore, *Mukbang* plays a role in offering a substitutive satisfaction in the way in which a performer seems to eat not only various kinds but also enormous amounts of food. Considering that numerous prohibitive and disciplinary norms are required in members of society, the exploration of unlimited appetite in *Mukbang* simultaneously stimulates and comforts people's unresolved desire for emancipation from the many social rules. Specific to South Korea, where the social pressure to manage the body to be beautiful and slim with a diet of eating little has become an invisible rule for women and gradually men as well, watching someone massively eating is an effective method to indirectly liberate oneself from psychological and physical repression. *Mukbang* has also played a role as a collective fantasy reservoir. While the rates of marriage and birth have become seriously lower in Korea, much like in Japan,[1] food avarice represented in *Mukbang* is considered ambiguously mixed with sexual desire. It is argued that single men and women, who are living unmarried and without partners or relationships, are seen to prefer to satisfy their reduced sexual desire with an excessive appetite for food in substitution (Jung, H. 2015).

In short, *Mukbang* is both the reality and fantasy of Korean society, encompassing young people's need, desire, anxiety, and pleasure, and is excessively produced and consumed behind the hyper-glamorous neoliberal vision of an ever-innovative world. In addition to this side of the social affective structure of *Mukbang*, it is also crucial to note the cultural industrial forces monetizing *Mukbang*, particularly in the economic context of users' participatory culture on the internet. This problem is concerned with the cultural industrial logic, in which the individual natural behavior of eating is reduced to an economic activity of labour.

Mukbang as a gendered cultural form

While the popularity of *Mukbang* is continuously growing across various media, "female BJ *Mukbang*" has been set up as a particular genre. The female BJ genre has established itself as a singular genre due to its gender specificity. Closely related to the patriarchal socio-cultural order, female BJ configures a rising idol but also represents a well-domesticated and commodified subject to male audiences who economically dominate her by viewing and buying her labour of eating. Some female BJs have become celebrities, and a particular categorization to assess *Mukbang* BJs and make star BJs is often shared among internet users. A blogger, for instance, summarizes the qualifications of great female BJs: a suitable volume of eating noise (not too loud and not too quiet), a great amount of food consumption and, in terms of appearance, a diverse range of expectations from a pretty and slim girl to that of a wild and fat tomboy.[2]

The pretty and slim girl archetype is represented by BJ Shoogi. Her persona is that of a charming and cute little girl similar to characters in Japanese manga. Nevertheless, her appetite is massive enough to surprise internet users, with many of them becoming enthusiastic fans. She runs her own broadcasting channel on the Afreeca TV site and her video clips of *Mukbang* are easily available on YouTube. Opposite the pretty girl, another type of female BJ of *Mukbang*, characterized as a 'butch' girl, is represented by Wangjoo. She is aggressive, chubby, and robust and her language is crude and rough.

The cultural and economic features of *Mukbang* may be analysed from the perspective of novel popular cultural aesthetics. Firstly, from an aesthetic perspective, the characteristics of female *Mukbang* consist of multi-sensorial elements, principally because the genre is inseparable from the human multi-sensorial act of eating. The peculiarity of *Mukbang* lies in the exaggerated sensoria of voracity. For instance, various senses are stimulated in the performance of *Mukbang*, such as eating sounds, endless talking, wild gestures, and offering foods to the audience from the hands, big and crude utensils, quick and incessant gluttony, and rich and spicy foods. All of these elements seem to express the BJ's valour, bravery, and even imprudence, authenticated as a virtue of *Mukbang*. This virtue of *Mukbang* dissents from the social norm of a 'good girl', the definition of which conventionally includes moderation, carefulness, and sophistication.

Secondly, in political and economic terms, *Mukbang* is part of digital capitalism, recognized by commercial apparatuses that are associated with the material structure of the participatory culture of *Mukbang*. Diverse sorts of sponsorship, advertisement, and fan gifts of cybermoney (which is convertible to real money) in the form of Star Balloons called *Byulpoongsun*, are incorporated in the broadcasting of video clips of *Mukbang* on the internet. It also animates gastronomic consumerism, as BJs are always expected to play the role of giving audiences fresh and rich information about restaurants and culinary trends. They are not only continuously eating, but also restlessly chatting with the audience about the different tastes of foods as well as trivial life stories and current affairs. As a result of their hard work in their performances of eagerly eating and talking about foods, some BJs have built up a global fandom. Open and yet intimate communications conducted in the form of real-time chat is intrinsic to the shaping of the relationships between BJs and fans.

In *Mukbang*, the actions of eating and talking are accordingly transformed to service labour in the logic of supply and demand in mediation with cybermoney. Intriguingly, it has become a convention that a BJ will say, "Thank you. I will eat well" from time to time during the show and particularly when audiences pay cybermoney in real time. At the same time, doing *Mukbang* is emotional labour (Hochschild 1983), for as time goes on, the pleasure of eating, which is obvious at the beginning of the show, turns into the masochistic pain of eating. Most foods used in *Mukbang* are exceptionally spicy, rich, and heavy and some BJs are seen to feel pain in eating more. Nevertheless, as a kind of sacred mission, the BJ, with a reluctant and yet determined face, keeps eating with the final goal of finishing the meal.

Audiences' responses are also notable in the running of *Mukbang* according to the logic of the digital cultural industry. Many audiences easily throw questions and enjoy chatting on the internet and a large fan base is sometimes formed by subscription to the home pages of a particular BJ on Afreeca TV. A considerable part of a BJ's income comes from fans' payment of Star Balloons, the equivalent of cybermoney, during the broadcasting of *Mukbang* and it is often reported that certain famous *Mukbang* BJs earn several hundred thousand dollars in US money (Jung 2015). A male fantasy operates in providing strong support for female *Mukbang* BJs, as revealed in a fan's confession on her homepage, 'My ideal female type has been changed (from a modest girl) to a woman eating well, thanks to you'.

The work of eating as digital creative labour

I have suggested the concept of 'digital creative labour' elsewhere to account for the novel form of economic subjectivity and ethics of labour which have emerged in the neoliberal and post-capitalist regime of culture and economy in mediation with digital media technology. I am defining this term as follows:

> Digital creative labour contains the three layers of labour: values of digital labour (participation, voluntarism and sharing); the norms of creative labour (creativity, passion and autonomy); and the neoliberal logic (freedom, innovation and competition).

> These layers are not exclusive but, in reality, overlap with one another in enhancing the synergistic impact on the subject formation of a young economic man. The converged normalisation of the technological, cultural and economic values are internalised and embodied at every moment of the subject's practices of labour. Thereby, the binaries, such as freedom and subordination, emotion and will, cultural creativity and economic rationality, which have been typically considered separate or even opposites, are smoothly articulated into the labourer's life.
>
> *(Kim, Y. 2016)*

Various concepts from affective labour, emotional labour, immaterial labour to living labour, have pinpointed a similar tendency in which the mode of labour has been radically transformed in the post-capitalist era (Hardt and Negri 2004; Lazzarato 1996). For instance, Morini and Fumagalli (2010) coin the terms 'biocapitalism' and 'biolabour' in which the whole aspects of life are 'put to work' for the objective of the maximization of economic values. According to the authors, the nature of biocapitalism is explained as the blurring, mixing, and intersection between the elements that have been conventionally considered to be divided in the industrial capitalist order. Thus, both the material and immaterial elements of human subjects such as relational, emotional, and cognitive faculties are captured in work; the system of production is configured in the network-structure which is engineered with linguistic, communicative, and transport technologies. 'Life is put to work' and the role of living and working relations is directly incorporated within the productive activity; human resources are at the core of the new organizational culture of enterprises. Here, the intellectual and relational resources of the human subject are converted to exchange value, which is governed by the grammar of money. Thus, what is exchanged in the labour market of biocapitalism is subjectivity itself, encompassing its experiential, relational, creative dimensions. And the 'potentiality' of the human's life is entirely exploited and commercialized. Morini and Fumagalli (2010) also theorize that labour in biocapitalism in the form of biolabour. 'Biolabour' is explained in four categories: relational labour, linguistic and cognitive labour, symbolic labour, and corporeal and sensorial labour. Morini and Fumagalli thus recapitulate that biolabour takes a form of the ensemble of the vital cerebral–physical faculties of humans (Morini and Fumagalli 2010).

My idea of digital creative labour may fall in a particular mode of biolabour, but with an emphasis on the digital network ecology and the novel form of labour emerging in cultural and creative industry. This is at least because in the participatory network culture *and* economy, it is conspicuous that the conventional divisions are blurred between economy and culture, work and leisure, production and consumption, work and play, compulsion and voluntariness, and obligation and pleasure. In such a massively conjunctive, complicated, and concatenated 'bio-medial-affective communicability' (Munster 2013: 119), virtually all elements constitutive of human subjectivity, such as affect, emotion, cognition, knowledge, values, communication, motorial sense, corporeal movement, social relations and activities, all of which form 'life itself', are absorbed in the logic of the commercialization of life.

In accepting such a macro level of theorizing the contemporary modes of labour, I also want to focus on the area of digital media industries, where the forces of digitalization and creative industries converge on a grand scale. Korea has dramatically developed its digital technology industries since the late 1990s to recover from the economic recession. At the same time, creative industry emerged as a major field in the national economy, especially in relation to the context in which the Korean Wave became widely recognized as an important cultural and economic agenda (Jin and Yoon 2014; Shim 2006). Digital creative labour, again in the Korean context, is a particular mode of labour which has emerged through the convergence between digital technologies. This particular mode of creative labour is embedded in specific work ethics, such as individualistic freedom, autonomy, and competition for success or at least survival in the vortex of economization of each and every part of social culture.

In seeing *Mukbang* as a representative form of digital creative labour, the practice of digital creative labour is formative of the creation of a particular culture of production and work ethics as follows (Kim, Y. 2016). Firstly, in the perspective of the political economy, digital creative labour is ambivalent in that its spirit of freedom and autonomy is subject to capitalist power relations. It appears as a 'playground' submerged in the context of digital capitalism (Scholz 2012). Here, the economic rationality oflabour and hedonistic consumerism are easily articulated in the formation of the ethics of work. The human subject happily and willingly commodifies his/her own labour, gradually evolving as human capital. Secondly, within a cultural aspect, digital creative labour is associated with the capitalization of human communication. With a certain degree of individual variation, digital creative workers try to display the most desirable images of the self, through incessant and minute processes of monitoring, designing, and presenting their emotions, language, behaviour, time, and space on the various sites operated across multiple social media networks. The endeavour is also required to create good social relations and broaden networks. Thirdly, regarding the ethics of work, digital creative labour overlaps the elements that are typically assumed to be oppositional to each other, such as emotion/reason, passion/interest, and cultural creativity/economic rationality. The seemingly conflicting elements of alienation/exploitation, and freedom/subordination are furthermore entwined to be interlocked in the normalization of a self-precarized ethics of labour (Lorey 2015). Fourthly, while it is dominated by the ideologies of freedom and autonomy, the irony is that the reality of digital creative labour is inherently subsumed under the power of control. At the same time, the instability and precarity structured in the neoliberal regime becomes deeply and firmly entrenched in the terrain of digital creative labour. From Deleuze's perspective, 'control' is the mechanism of the numerical modulation of code. Much like 'surfing', control operates in an open environment onto the 'dividuals', which are in the incessant modulation and mutation, existing in the mode of masses, samples, data, markets, or banks (Deleuze 1995). Multiple forces of control, from self-discipline to corporate surveillance and popular synopticon, converge on digital creative workers throughout their body, emotions, rationality, will, and desire. In short, digital creative labour refers to a culture of labour that is, under the herald of the neoliberal ideology of autonomy, the heterogeneous affective and material constituents of individualism and pragmatism. The cultural ethics of creativity, freedom and cooperation are reformulated in the post-capitalist economic values of innovation, entrepreneurialism, and the maximization of profit.

The combinative work of eating and being observed in *Mukbang* is based on relations between the BJ and the audience, which engender a control system operated through the 'attention economy' (Goldhaber 1997) over the BJ as an eating machine. This continues by means of the BJ's constant chat and offering of information and knowledge of foods and restaurants or trivial human interests as well as eating, with every action of her performance being productive of the imagery and language of corporeal desire for food and sexuality. The orgy, in intensive circulation between the pole of prodigality and pleasure and that of surveillance and pain, excessively stimulates a multi-sensory experience and promotes the fantasy of eating.

Mukbang in multisensorial capitalism

In conclusion, within the social context, cultural and aesthetic features and politico-economic structure of *Mukbang*, I suggest the concept of 'multi-sensorial capitalism', highlighting its conjunction and disjunctions of corporeal, visceral, sexual, and affective elements both of production and consumption, work and play, and labour (digital creative labour included) and leisure.

Four points are made on multi-sensorial capitalism. Firstly, the creature's multiple senses and behaviours, such as eating, are transformed to a particular kind of labour of being watched to eat at the same time as various corporeal, sensorial, affective, cognitive, and social propensity and capabilities are amplified, reformulated and reorganized as human resources for doing work. Secondly, related to the first, the divisions made in modernity, such as production and consumption, pain and pleasure, obligation and freedom, subjection and autonomy, social obligation and subject desire, and economic rationality and voluntary creativity, blur and overlap. Thirdly, the peculiar popularity of cultural commodities, such as *Mukbang,* suggests that the social structure of affect in the current neoliberal society becomes the object of consumption such as the commodification of human affects, relations and experiences. Fourthly, the expanding digital practices of production and consumption to social critique, social and psychical elements such as loneliness, psychological and material lack and difficulty, social insecurity, economic precariousness coupled with the competitive ambition for success are interwoven in the multisensorial and capitalist practice of *Mukbang.* Last but not least, the human affect, sense, and behavior, and social relations situated in people's everyday life are monetized for the purpose of the creation of surplus values in the structure of digital capitalism. Here is not only the active expansion and strengthening of human networks – as very often highlighted in entrepreneurial discourses – but, more significantly, even the *lack* of networks expressed in living and eating alone and the shared effects of loneliness are utilized as useful commercial items. Thus, multi-sensorial capitalism renders the spectacularization of a deteriorated landscape highlighting a precarious life-world and the fetishization of the lonely self.

Notes

1 Total fertility rate of South Korea was 1.26 in 2016, with which South Korea is reported to be the lowest country in terms of TFR among the OECD countries.
2 http://blog.naver.com/roeli/220262139422 (accessed August 7, 2016).

References

Andrejevic, M. (2003) *Reality TV: The Work of Being Watched.* Lanham, MD: Rowman & Littlefield Publishers.

Couldry, N. and van Dijck, J. (2015) Researching social media as if the social mattered. *Social Media+Society,* July–December, 1–7.

Dean, J. (2009) *Democracy and Other Neoliberal Fantasies: Communicative Capitalism and Left Politics.* Durham, NC and London: Duke University Press.

Dean, J. (2010) *Blog Theory: Feedback and Capture in the Circuits of Drive.* Cambridge: Polity.

Deleuze, G. (1995) Postscript on Control Societies. In *Negotiations.* New York: Columbia University Press, pp. 177–82.

Foucault, M. (2008) *The Birth of Biopolitics: Lectures at the Collège De France 1978–1979,* (Graham Burchell, trans.). New York: Palgrave Macmillan.

Goldhaber, M. (1997) The attention economy and the net. *First Monday,* 2, 4–7.

Hardt, M. and Negri, A. (2004) *Multitude: War and Democracy in the Age of Empire.* New York: Penguin.

Haworth, A. (2013) Why have young people in Japan stopped having sex? *The Observer.* Available at http://www.theguardian.com/world/2013/oct/20/young-people-japan-stopped-having-sex (accessed December 31, 2015).

Hochschild, A. (1983) *The Managed Heart: Commercialization of Human Feeling.* Oakland, CA: University of California.

Hong, S. and Park, S. (2016) Emergence of internet Mukbang (foodcasting) and its hegemonic process in media culture (Korean). *Media & Society*, 24(1), 105–50.

Houruichi, N. (古市憲壽) (2014) *Desperate Country, Happy Youths* (translated in Korean). Seoul: Min En Sa.

Jhoo, D. (2015) Korea shows 3rd-highest NEET rate in OECD. *The Korea Times*. Available at: http://www.koreatimes.co.kr/www/news/nation/2015/12/116_194122.html (accessed December 31, 2015).

Jin, D. and Yoon, K. (2014) The social mediascape of transnational Korean pop culture: *Hallyu 2.0* as spreadable media practice. *New Media and Society*, October (online first).

Jung, H. (2015) Expression of giving up middle-class dream through appetite. *Sin Dong Ah*. http://news.donga.com/List/3/all/20150419/70785884/1 (accessed December 31, 2015).

Kim, G. (2017) The income gap between men and women in Korea is largest among OECD. https://news.joins.com/article/21724441 (accessed September 16, 2018).

Kim, H. (2015) Survival, survivalism, young generation from the viewpoint of the sociology of the heart. *Korean Sociology*, 49(1), 179–211.

Kim, S. (2011) Structure of feeling in webtoons – from *Ying-uh* to *Byungmat*. *Trans-Humanities*, 4(2), 101–23.

Kim, S. (2014) The income gap between men and women in Korea is largest among OECD countries for 13 years. http://www.hani.co.kr/arti/economy/economy_general/649792.html (accessed September 16, 2018).

Kim, Y. (2015) Globalization of the privatized self-image: the reaction video and its attention economy on YouTube. In Hjorth, L. and Khoo, O. (eds.), *Routledge Handbook of New Media in Asia*. London and New York: Routledge, pp. 333–42.

Kim, Y. (2016) A portrait of the creative worker as a young economic man: digital creative labour in South Korea. In Iwabuchi, K., Khoo, O. and Black, D. (eds.), *Asian Cultural and Media Studies Now*. Lanham, MD: Rowman & Littlefield, pp. 175–89.

Lazzarato, M. (1996) Immaterial labour. In Hardt, M. and Virno, P. (eds.), *Radical Thought in Italy: A Potential Politics*. Minneapolis: University of Minnesota, pp. 133–47.

Lee, S. (2015) Do you know the first Korean *Mukbang*? Hankook-ilbo. Available at: http://www.hankookilbo.com/v/46f6ed0fa3e14bd8920443a542920e4d (accessed December 31, 2015).

Lim, J. (2017) '45 minutes a day'. Korean men do housework the least among OECD countries. https://news.joins.com/article/21722217 (accessed September 16, 2018).

Lorey, I. (2015) *State of Insecurity: Government of the Precarious*. London: Verso.

Morini, C. and Fumagalli, A. (2010) Life put to work. *Ephemera: Theory and Politics in Organization*, 10(3/4): 234–52.

Munster, A. (2013) *An Aesthesia of Networks: Conjunctive Experience in Art and Technology*. Cambridge and London: MIT Press.

Organization for Economic Co-operation and Development (OECD) (2014a) Gender wage gap. Available at: http://www.oecd.org/gender/data/genderwagegap.htm (accessed December 31, 2015).

Organization for Economic Co-operation and Development (OECD) (2014b) *Balancing Paid Work, Unpaid Work and Leisure*. Available at: http://www.oecd.org/gender/data/balancingpaidworkunpaidworkandleisure.htm (accessed December 31, 2015).

Papacharissi, Z. (2010) *A Private Sphere: Democracy in a Digital Age*. Cambridge: Polity.

Rousseau, S. (2012) *Food and Social Media*. Plythmouth: AltaMira Press.

Shim, D. (2006) Hybridity and the rise of Korean popular culture in Asia. *Media, Culture and Society*, 28(1), 25–44

Scholz, T. (2012) *Digital Labor: The Internet as Playground and Factory*. New York: Routledge.

Smythe, D. W. (1981) On the audience commodity and its work. In *Dependency Road: Communications, Capitalism, Consciousness, and Canada*. Norwood, NJ: Ablex, pp. 22–51.

Vincent, J. (2014) Gastronomic voyeurism: The South Korean trend that means you'll never eat alone. *Independent* (28 January 2014). http://www.independent.co.uk/life-style/gadgets-and-tech/gastronomic-voyeurism-the-south-korean-trend-that-means-youll-never-eat-alone-9090847.html (accessed August 14, 2016).

Woo, S. and Park, G. (2007) 88-*Man-won Genereation – Economics of Hope in the Era of Frustration*. Seoul: Radian.

Zizek, S. (1999) 'The interpassive subject'. Available at: http://www.egs.edu/faculty/slavoj-zizek/articles/the-interpassive-subject/ (accessed July 27, 2014).

16

Classic or farce?

Making a spectacle of the 'anti-Japan drama', 2000–15

Ruth Y. Y. Hung and Q. S. Tong

The success of contemporary Chinese popular culture, especially television dramas set against the background of the Sino-Japanese War in the 1930s and early 1940s, is inseparable from the so-called 'anti-Japan serials' 抗日剧, a category of historical dramas that the State Administration of Radio, Film, and Television (hereafter SARFT) promotes as a major 'theme drama' 主旋律电视剧. This chapter concerns itself with the category of 'anti-Japan serials' from their emergence as a group of 'theme dramas' at the turn of the twenty-first century to their entrance into a production boom in 2010, as marked by the nation-wide broadcast of *Snow Leopard* 雪豹.[1] The last few years have witnessed the genre's mutation both qualitatively and quantitatively. Since 2010, the 'anti-Japan serials' have evolved from a narrative art through the market economy into what netizens have come to call *leiju* 雷剧 or *shenju* 神剧 – literally, 'thunderous serials' or 'super serials' that verge on the farcical, in some cases the mere ludicrous.

This paper establishes that in these 'anti-Japan serials'' we have a situation in which popular media and state media engage with each other in a complex relationship of distrust and collaboration. We subject the serials to critical attention not just because they have become monstrously vulgar, absurd, farcical, or buffoonish, but, more importantly, because we feel obliged to establish from this form of 'theme dramas' a case representative of contemporary cultural industry. We argue that such a case, unique as it is, has constantly been defining the current socio-political culture of the People's Republic of China (PRC). For one thing, around 2013, both SARFT and consumers of pop dramas began to condemn the set of 'super serials' via their own designated channels and with contradictory intentions and purposes, aiming sometimes to rectify buffoonish representations of the past and other times to challenge the government's valorization of the war itself. Yet, whether it is the authorities seeking to limit the extent of popular entertainment in its cultural industry or audiences struggling to show that the 'super serials' are altogether an insult to their intelligence, the 'anti-Japan dramas' as a whole thrive on the business of whole-nation entertainment *and* state propaganda. Has the Chinese television 'industry', which is secured by a vertically integrated system, now given in entirely to the market economy following the loss of authorial control over the processes of mass production, distribution, and consumption?[2] Has the state-market now finally entered into the era of popular entertainment and financial success in a way that would fundamentally alter the former equipoise of power between the state and the market? Historically, 'anti-Japan' narratives, the production of which is evidence of the authorial government as the compass and yardstick in the industry, had moments of political and ideological success, as seen in the 'Red Classic' movies 红色经典 of the 1950s and 60s[3] and even as pop serials in the post-Deng PRC. Contemporarily, as mass cultural products with propaganda purposes, they have succeeded in directing popular criticism toward the official stories of Japanese predation. They have also served to redirect potential domestic dissatisfaction away from the party-state and towards its remembered and contemporary enemies. Somewhat more subtly, as they enter into post-WTO China's (television) economy, these historical narratives, now in their latest form of *shenju* 神剧, also enter into the age of mass production, multi-media entertainment, and popular pleasure. In so doing, they follow a profit-driven and profit-driving formula, creating not only a political common-sense but also, even if inadvertently, a platform in which political desires and domestic dissatisfactions disperse in a manner that will, ultimately, both falsify *and* satisfy the Chinese Communist Party's (CCP) claim for itself as the guardian of 'China' and its way forward.

Production and criticism

On April 10, 2013, in its current-affairs series *News 1+1,* the state-broadcaster China Central TV (CCTV) presented a program entitled, 'Could "Anti-Japan Serials" be Staged as Such?'[4] In a disdainful tone, CCTV reprimanded the ailments plaguing the genre: far-flung interpretations of history, excessive and perverted presentation of sexual violence, melodramatic dialogues, hyperbolic celebration of 'anti-Japan idols', fatuous plots, and floppy narrative logic. Indeed, examples of 'super' elements in the current wave of 'anti-Japan dramas' abound. Here, a bare-handed Chinese soldier tears a Japanese enemy in half; there, a battalion commander downs Japanese planes with hand grenades; down the road, a People's Liberation Army icon stops a moving train by flying up a bike.

The adjectival compound 'super serials', as translated from the Chinese noun *shenju* 神剧, denotes a sense of excess and the supernatural in the everyday experience of television and entertainment consumption. The adjective *shen* 神 and its counterpart in our context, *lei* 雷, literally mean 'God' and 'thunder' respectively. These supernatural forces, which are in effect technological excess, create the desire for, and enable the consumption of, features of mass entertainment in contradiction to state-governed historical narratives: clichés, sex, violence, special effects, martial arts chivalry, comic-book type superheroes, and idol pop stars. The employment of mass-entertainment features in the production of 'serious historical drama' not only results in a boom in the amount of crude production and advertising, especially onscreen product placement, but it also changes the art form, which now contains characteristics from such drama types as 'costume drama', 'youth romance', 'action drama', 'fantasy drama', 'martial arts legend', and 'spy thriller'.[5]

That mass entertainment and profit-making are a central part of the stock-in-trade of these popular serials is indisputable. What *is* disputed, however, is how the popularity of these crudely produced spectacles can ever be sustained. On the one hand, 'Mr. Shao', a buyer in the industry, said in an interview with *Jiefang Daily* in April 2013, 'We select our purchases in accordance with ratings based on market surveys. The ratings of anti-Japan serials are really not bad.'[6] On the other hand, as the former CCTV director Xia Jun posted on *Sina Weibo* in early 2013 his exasperated comments on 'anti-Japan dramas' – 'What's up with China's TV industry? Take a look around Hengdian [a major Chinese television studio] and you'll see 40–50 casts and crews fighting [Japanese] "devils." Where's the creativity?'

(Nasr 2013), these statements were reposted 10,000 times and generated over 2,600 comments, with most of the respondents emphatically sharing Xia's anxiety. Elsewhere, at the National Committee of the People's Political Consultation Conference (CPPCC) held in March 2013 in Beijing, internationally acclaimed actor Chen Daoming, member of CPPCC and winner of several grand national prizes, explicitly rejected the 'super serials': 'They are horseplay. ... They not only turn history into amusements, but are outright distorting the past.'[7] Chen's professional training, credentials, and acting career should lead the public at large to associate him with a more orthodox position on the CCP's role in the Sino-Japanese War. Yet, among those who align with Chen's position on *shenju* are also dwellers and participants of unofficial public forums; they have often been the source of some of the most critical and subversive comments on the party-state and on the contemporary socio-political scene.[8] They include bloggers, microbloggers, and participants of community-based web forums (known as bulletin board systems, BBS, or *luntan* 论坛 in Chinese).

Indeed, despite the fact that the public has frequently subjected CCTV to criticism and satire in recent years,[9] the orthodox position on the dramas has found counterparts of sorts in contemporary audiences, especially, but not exclusively, from individuals who have grown up with the 'Red Classics'. In Fall 2012, *NetEase, one of the largest multi-platform internet service companies,* published a promotional article about 'five novel measures' that TV drama directors employ to reinvent the 'anti-Japan theme serials' from ideological straitjackets into hit television shows, underscoring the fault lines of the 'super serials' (Xiao Ni 2012). The article received more than a thousand posts, with most of them being one-sidedly negative about the measures, not to mention *shenju* themselves. One commenter laments the implications of the seeming national obsession with demonizing Japan: 'I boycott this type of shows as a rule. They just make me feel ashamed. It is an ill-fated nation which portrays its modern history in this manner' (Xiao Ni 2012). Interestingly, commentators who reprimand *shenju* do not dismiss the 'theme dramas' as a whole. Instead, they recommend for each other classic examples of the category: 'One should watch instead *My Chief and My Regiment* 《我的团长我的团》(2009). It is the kind of "anti-Japan drama" that has really shown the national spirit seventy years ago' (Xiao Ni 2012). The next commenter in line writes, 'The classic example *par excellence* ... is *The Line* 《生死线》(2008)' (Xiao Ni 2012).

Consumption

Curiously, whether orthodox representatives or random netizens, critics of *shenju* have come to denounce the programs for reasons that precisely give rise to the proliferation of the 'theme dramas'. If the SARFT devised the category of 'anti-Japan dramas' as one important 'theme serial' in the first place, it was to guarantee its own control over the historical narrative of the war. And it is likewise to guarantee the monopoly of such a cultural production as the anti-Japan serials that their audiences, whose imagination and taste are at once empowered and domesticated by the market economy, have come to shun and reject. In other words, state control, by its own account, has merely achieved in words to rescue these 'historical dramas' from becoming a malleable visual commodity. In reality, it releases the narratives into the market – which appropriates them for creating new special effects, fusion genres, or idiosyncratic characters, and in so doing risks committing to the market of mass entertainment a little more than it would like. Meanwhile, audiences find that state censorship has never produced anything but rules, conventions, prototypes, and even terror. In confronting a state-orchestrated art form that dictates a national historical event which, nonetheless, induces popular nationalism, some audiences are trapped into tolerating a situation in which censorship makes a virtue of its vice. Precisely, these audiences comply with the simplification and vulgarization of a narrative art in a particular sense, subsequently but unwittingly 'permitting' themselves of the mass consumption of state propaganda as a whole.

Such is the central paradox of the state–market cultural economy in the PRC of the twenty-first century. In analyzing the stakeholders of this market of 'anti-Japan serials', blogger Jia Ye explains:

> One wonders if anti-Japan super serials have so outrageously defied rules and overwhelmed the audiences, why there should still be a market for them. This is a seriously mistaken expectation. Such a market is not only in existence but also big; the serials do enjoy steady ratings. With regard to this, I have first-hand experience. My father-in-law, well into his eighties, is a military man who has come out of the Civil War and the Korean War. As soon as he finishes his meal, he would stay by the television for the 'super serials.' He does this every day, missing not a single episode. In effect, the audiences are mostly elderly people who are relatively less educated. This group of people have neither high cultural taste nor good critical judgment. They also lack confidence, and need thus 'enemies' who are extremely retarded to satisfy their pride. The only criterion [they hold on to] is that China finally would defeat Japan.
>
> *(Jia Ye 2015)*

On the one side, we find those who invoke the dictum that dramas about the Sino-Japanese War should respect the historical national sentiment. Taking the 'cathartic value' of this category of television shows for granted, these audiences assume that historical dramas must be subject to validation by the genre's traditional appeals to 'national consciousness'. By national consciousness, they refer to such sentiments as 'anti-imperial nationalism' that the CCP first nurtured in the public at the height of Japanese imperialism in 1937 (see Hu 2003). This group of audiences accepts the political morality of patriotism and the party-state's discourse of national unity and national liberation, even while recognizing that the idea of threats to the 'nation' is anachronistic and that it is mostly a *post facto* reconstruction of contemporary politics.[10] These audiences' 'respect for history', if any, is not committed to how a historically verifiable representation of Sino-Japanese relations produces the pathos it desires to represent; instead, they are concerned with establishing the appropriate discursive ambience in which that pathos could be displayed and purged. Importantly, these audiences – whom we call veteran-minded commemorators – anchor their appeal to the genre not on grounds of historical authenticity, but on their experience of some crudely mediated sentiments of 'national consciousness'.

Alongside the veteran-minded commemorators are those who reject what the commemorators take for granted, that is, an uncritical acceptance of the CCP as an effective force of resistance in the Sino-Japanese War. These audiences are 'cynics' in the way they disregard altogether the historical value of the 'anti-Japan serials', which, for them, are always by default a sort of state propaganda. This attitude of reception is critically informed but imaginatively unproductive. These audiences know well that historical dramas are generally packaged in an ideologically-preset illocution, that as 'theme dramas' they are staged in accordance with the state's rhetoric of nationalism. Their criticism, however, passes over the problematics of the cultural and public value of *shenju*, focusing instead on the dramas' lack of technical and entertainment sophistication. One online commenter wrote, '[Super] anti-Japan serials are the fakest! They rape the intellect of viewers!' (Xiao Ni 2012). Another simply stated, 'Mere bullshit. A heap of cultural rubbish put together by "pop idols" and "counterfeits." Myths that would only poison later generations. … It gives me headache as soon as I see the plastic sockets in *Hengdian* [World Studios]. Could they be more fake?' (Xiao Ni 2012).

In addition, the nonchalant attitude towards the political motivations of the 'theme serials' as a whole feeds a reading of *shenju* as illustrative of the bankruptcy of the official ideology. In actuality, these 'audiences' express their criticism in the form of a kind of vengeful joy: internet spoofing. The Chinese term for 'spoofing' is *e'gao* 恶搞 – 'the practice of technology-enabled, multimedia online parody and digital communication among Chinese Internet users'.[11] In the context of *shenju*, it refers to the practice of seeking fun and laughter out of the historical mistakes and/or outright production slips found in *shenju*. Their enjoyment of the serials corresponds to the number of comments, posts, and reposts that their own spoof of a particular scene in the drama is able to attract and produce.[12] Before they are critics, these spoofers are satirists – playful 'copycats' of artistic glitches, in and through whom the outright vulgarity and buffoonery of the 'anti-Japan dramas' reach yet another level. In other words, the spoofers grow to dislike the 'super serials' so much that they turn to virtual reality and cynicism. What they resent in artistic, historical, and ideological terms, they embrace in some sort of fanatically silly pranks. Shaftesbury once remarked in his 1711 essay 'The Freedom of Wit and Humor' that

> the natural free spirits of ingenious men, if imprisoned or controlled, will find out other ways of motion to relieve themselves in their constraint; and whether it be in burlesque, mimicry or buffoonery, they will be glad at any rate to vent themselves, and be revenged on their constrainers. … 'Tis the persecuting spirit has raised the bantering one: and want of liberty may account for … the corruption … of pleasantry and humor.
>
> *(Shaftesbury 2001: 71–2)*

Following on from Shaftesbury, we seek to point out that the spoofs of 'super serials' contain an incoherent mix of intentions and callings – ideological, socio-political, statist, and/or dissenting – and that they, at their best, may become a productive 'site of negotiation' for the political culture of the PRC. Although the spoofers seem to be contradictory in their action, 'criticizing' the 'super serials' as though they have any aesthetic value, much of the time they see vulgarity and buffoonery as the political equivalent of public criticism, and the purpose of critical engagement is simply the deepening and continuation of *shenju*'s rhetorical vice. Yet, we must assess how much the spoofers' 'corrupt humor' has really guided cultural taste or oriented and disciplined popular political energies. In the opinion of those in the field, *shenju* soldiers on with nothing but critique in the form of perverse humor to guide it. 'The ratings of *shenju* are not bad, especially after they become a topic of public critique. Many people will want to watch them, if only watching them means criticizing them. For the serials, [criticism] is better than no ratings.'[13] As the era of 'anti-Japan dramas' wears on, 'crudely produced' *shenju* has now gained an 'afterlife' thanks to 'rounds of internet spoofing. … Public snigger and clamor make *shenju* ever more popular. Under the effect of "finding pleasure in bad taste," *shenju*'s ratings and click-through rate surge, motivating some profit-driven producers and television stations to "fight" for market share' (Liu Yang 2015). Thus, both *shenju* and *e'gao* contribute to ratings. Now, as one internet commenter concludes, 'As long as ratings are high, who [among directors] is going to care about creativity?' (Nasr 2013).

State contribution

So far, we have attributed the popularity of 'anti-Japan' *shenju* to the Chinese television economy, consumer desires and tastes, and the various levels of popular spoofs. We have tried to account for the phenomenon that has resulted in these serials enjoying huge market success and popular ratings despite severe criticism. Considering the unique circumstances of the PRC, the relationship between audience responses and producer considerations could never be straightforward; it must thread its way through state planning and censorship. Therefore, before honing into the more general question about the constitutional tendencies of the contemporary Chinese cultural market, in which the 'anti-Japan serials' occupy a dominant share, we must point to the state's contribution, both directly and indirectly, to this 'market'. For one thing, since the mid-2000s, SARFT, in tightening control over nearly every format and topic of television dramas, has turned 'anti-Japan serials' into one of a few 'safe' categories that the market can still produce without risking censorship.[14] In return, television producers capitalize on this 'gap' in the state's cultural policies even if their ultimate purpose is to capture the market.

Regarding the government's role in cultural production, directors know that domestic and international politics routinely comes into play and that the state-market is responsive to its demands. For guarantee of broadcast and profit, they must come to terms with the state's political needs that inflect its cultural policies. Over the decade, as a result of the Jiang Zemin government's moderate approach to Sino-Japanese relations,[15] producers had relatively greater leeway to transform the 'Red Classics' by outgrowing traditional strategies of representation and commercializing the art form. Directors and producers have even begun to anticipate guidelines from the SARFT and direct them to their own course and benefit – a procedure that virtually assures them a monopoly over the medium. As mentioned at the beginning of this essay, this period of market success of 'anti-Japan dramas' began in 2001 and underwent a marked change as the form entered the era of mass entertainment at the end of the decade. This timeline indicates just how the industry at the start of the twenty-first century corresponds directly to popular anti-Japan nationalist sentiments and to the SARFT's guidelines, which, in turn, correlate with a *reciprocal* relationship between Chinese public sentiments and the PRC's approach towards Japan. The timeline therefore reflects two sets of facts.

First, audiences having consumed for a decade the 'theme dramas' could intelligently engage the historical content. Over the decade, therefore, directors needed to address competition from other 'theme serials' as they had to increasingly appease some well-informed audiences. They had to meet both economic and ideological demands: to produce profits and to translate the cultural policy into a narrative art. Indeed, examples of quality 'anti-Japan serials' in the decade abound. Unlike the 'Red Classics', producers of 'anti-Japan serials' began with a conscientious effort to complicate the official cultural policy, thus indulging themselves and their audiences in the representation of various hitherto suppressed ideological consciousness and political experience. They were not content with, for example, the characterization of flat wartime heroes or flat villains descended or adapted from propagandist 'Red Classics'. Commercial serials like Gao Xixi's *History's Skyline*《历史的天空》(2004) and Jiang Qitao's *The Road*《人间正道是沧桑》(2009), in spite of their status as officially sanctioned dramas first released by CCTV in celebration of the CCP's leadership in the Sino-Japanese War, go so far as to show ideological differences most poignantly and from an emphatic perspective. In both dramas, the directors are not content with having communist prototypes as protagonists presiding over screen space and time. Rather, they want to highlight historical accidents and opportunities as an essential part of the nation's political fate and ideological choice. Therefore, when these two dramas need to confront issues of ideological differences and faith, they tend to translate them – what used to be a life-and-death matter during the Civil War period and the Cultural Revolution (1966–76) – into well-contained conflicts between family members and sympathetic friends, and sometimes even into tormented feelings between lovers. In *The Road*, Yang Tinghe, head of the family, expresses the ideological difference that splits the early Republic in allegorical and familial terms: 'I have two sons. One sells shoes, the other umbrellas. Which should I look forward to? rainy days? or sunny ones?'[16]

Both Zhao Baogang and Wang Ying's *Nighttime Harbin* 《夜幕下的哈尔滨》(2008) and An Jian's *Aunt Duohe*《小姨多鹤》(2009) are excellent examples of 'anti-Japan serials' invested in the portrayal of Japanese humanism. In *Nighttime Harbin,* this includes bringing to the domestic screens an important character hitherto dismissed in this type of story: the Japanese pacifist Yuichi Ichiro, son of a sinologist who goes to the wartime Republic in pursuit of his ill-fated love for a Chinese woman. *Aunt Duohe* eulogizes the love, sacrifice, and humanity of the Japanese woman Duohe 多鹤. Duohe, abandoned and considered a 'waste' in the wake of the Japanese retreat from Manchuria, is the story's heroine who spends the most important years of her womanhood in the early years of the People's Republic. The serial explores the texture of Japanese subjectivity and femininity by concentrating on the vicissitudes in the psychological development of Duohe.

What is remarkable in these 'anti-Japan serials' of the 2000s is that, unlike the 'Red Classics' or the latest 'super serials', the main characters give blood and voice to identities and subjectivities usually suppressed in the CCP's official account of the Chinese Revolution. These characters add a new historical dimension to orthodox literature about the Sino-Japanese War and contribute both to the genre's achievements in finding for humanity a broader definition and to the trend of popular nationalism. While maintaining the integrity of Chinese national consciousness and the realism of Chinese people's sufferings in the 'War of Resistance against Japan', these serials create new points of entry in narrating the war and do so, remarkably, in their role as triumphant products of state-propaganda and state-market combined. The four serials briefly discussed above are prize-winning dramas; *History's Skyline* and *The Road*, notably, won the prestigious 'Flying Apsaras Award' 飞天奖, the longest running television award first presented by the Ministry of Culture and later taken over by SARFT and the Motion Picture and Arts Committee 电视艺术委员会. Through this generation of 'anti-Japan dramas', directors assert their place in the television market, in which new spectacles and technologies of representing the war could be tested.

Second, and in relation to the first, the history of the 'anti-Japan dramas', from their inception to their production boom since the late 2000s, corresponds well to the Chinese people's 'anti-Japanese nationalism', which, in turn, has shaped the policy options – political, foreign, and cultural – available to the Beijing government regarding Japan. During the years between 2001 and 2006 when Junichiro Koizumi was the Japanese Prime Minister, a series of events took place to escalate popular anti-Japanese sentiments into full-scale national protests. Among them the following stand out: the Japanese history textbook controversy in the spring of 2001 and again in 2005; recurrent controversies over the ownership of the Diaoyu/Senkaku Islands that conjured up the 2003 territorial dispute; and Koizumi's repeated visits to the Yasukuni Shrine. All these events would only be topped in 2005, the year in which large-scale nationalist protests against Japan becoming a permanent member of the UN Security Council (UNSC) were staged in major cities. Significantly, despite popular nationalism at the start of the 2000s, the government, possibly out of fear for 'any nationalist backlash both from within and outside the Party', *waited* till the spring of 2005 when it too needed to undermine Japan's bid for a permanent seat on UNSC by creating 'openings for ... public mobilization'.[17] In other words, if 'anti-Japan dramas' were a product of popular nationalism well monitored by the authorities in the first half of the 2000s, those after 2005 benefit increasingly from a crude nationalism that the government in effect cultivates via the policy of tolerance if not tacit consent. This now popular *and* populist nationalism against

Japan, once unleashed in the mass entertainment market, easily becomes fuel for the firing of *shenju*. As Ian Johnson, the *New Yorker* journalist, reports after visiting the *Hengdian* World Studios, China's 'new site of resistance against Japan', in 2013:[18]

> Superhuman powers … figure prominently in Hengdian productions. Such stories defy the Communist Party's official championing of science, but the censors let them pass, because they reflect a larger Chinese belief in the supernatural and allow filmmakers to demonstrate the superiority of China's cultural tradition. One of my favorite productions in this genre is "The Anti-Japanese Magical Knight," a 2010 story about a six-man team of martial artists who appear to defeat the Imperial Japanese Army single-handedly. In the goriest scene, one of the stars bursts into a Japanese fortress and punches a soldier with such force that his fist penetrates the man's torso, causing him to split down the middle as if he were a block of wood; guts and blood spew like water from a hose. In other scenes, heroes fly or dodge bullets fired at point-blank range – they have the kind of Gumby-style elasticity that allows them to do extreme back bends. I watch it in the same campy spirit in which I watch "Airplane!," but its tone is resolutely serious. Indeed, the six knights are meant to symbolize the way that the Chinese used ancient tradition to trump Japan's modern military. Crude nationalism has long been a feature of Chinese productions. [O]ne Chinese soldier is to be shown dying for every Japanese who dies. That could prove to be a bonanza for the extras: one estimate suggested that, last year, seven hundred million Japanese died in Chinese films.
>
> *(Johnson 2013)*

This description of the actual 'site' of 'anti-Japan' narratives makes it plain that the sheer spectacularity of a sort of 'Chinese' physical might could take the fancy of post-2005 Chinese audiences, and illustrates too the general public's adulatory, unsophisticated attitude to traditionalism. In this sense, the state propaganda machine is presented more than ever before with the opportunity to entertain a mix of audience tastes, and thereby an occasion when an unusually wide spread of audience groups could be counted on. Indeed, as the cultural policies continue to thematize 'anti-Japanese narratives', it is a good indication that despite the trend to develop the genre into 'super serials', SARFT is not inclined to close down the business. First of all, the contents of these 'super serials' are nationalistic even if they are at once products and targets of lampoon. Passing them through censorship, knowing the inverse yet popular elements in these dramas would come to offset the seriousness of a historical genre must be unutterably difficult. Yet in the end, quantity more than quality counts in the age of mass entertainment and multi-platform media. The production and reception of *shenju* surged at a time when the state authorities attempt to achieve a national voice and consciousness that would entice its subjects. There is a distortion of history, to be sure, but perhaps not a distortion of state intent. After all, in many cases, the audience and netizens have demonstrated in their varied response that they are neither hesitant about making recourse to their Chinese identity nor torn between amusement and disenchantment in their consumption of 'crude nationalism'. It is left again to the state and the market to negotiate and redress the historical balance.

Conclusion

A strange case of the television market phenomenon, the 'anti-Japan serials' have generated a media event representative of the cultural industry in the PRC. It also marks the twenty-first century as a time in the history of the Chinese television economy that witnesses the irreversible loss of a concentrated ownership over both the content of mass entertainment and audience reception. Meanwhile, although SARFT often attempts to gain and maintain control over the cultural industry, it has its share in making and corrupting the entertainment market. For one thing, the Xi Jinping's model of authoritarianism owes it to itself to catch up with the demands of the highly competitive mass entertainment economy; it is remarkably resilient when confronted. In the case of the 'anti-Japan serials', two factors have contributed towards the maintenance of state authority: first, it tolerates an unintended cultural phenomenon and takes the opportunity to domesticate a wide and presumably light-minded public; second, it demonstrates a recursive sensitivity to the nature of *authorship* in the twenty-first century. Who is plotting these serials and, ultimately, who should be responsible for this trend of turning the memory and representation of Japanese invasion of China, one of the most important episodes in the history of the Second World War, into skittish, carnivalesque media events? Is it the party-state? The television market economy? Or the entertainment-seeking audiences? It is here, where SARFT, while in no whit displaced in ultimate authority, develops an effective art of governmentality by refraining from its past role of gauging a singular source of authority.

Contradictory as the party-state and the audiences may be in their response to the 'theme serials', the fact remains that their conflict of interest helps transform the Chinese cultural industry into a joint state-market enterprise in which non-serious amusement and popular pleasure become serious contenders to replace ideological and propagandistic arts. While Chinese television serials have indeed compromised the state for the market economy in the last few years, thus facilitating a louder fanfare of critical voices and frequently creating media events that ignite socio-political and public contests, the 'anti-Japan serials' neither owe their popularity entirely to online viral nor direct public criticism for a more constructive discourse of political imagination. The success of the serials, 'classical' or 'super', suggests not only that mass culture and socialist propaganda find their mutual friend in popular pleasure but also that escapists of ideological indoctrination are, quite simply, the illusionary skeptic. The private imagination, the lonesome wit of individual audiences and spoofers, do not drive public criticisms, and media virals are just as self-consumptive and politically ineffective as *shenju*.

Notes

1 At the time of its first release in 2010, *Snow Leopard*, notably casting the 26-year-old idol star Wen Zhang文章as the protagonist, remained in the lists of Top Ten and Top Thirty across more than 26 major cities and was arguably the 'single serial that hits half of China'. Already, critics found *Snow Leopard* symptomatic of *shenju*'s emphasis on developing visual spectacles and larger-than-life super-heroes, and of the genre's full entrance into the era of mass amusement (see Han 2013: 45).

2 We have shown elsewhere that in the PRC, the state comprehends and builds the cultural industry in collaboration and negotiation with the entertainment market. See Tong and Hung (2014).

3 The 'Red Classics' are arguably the earlier form of the 'anti-Japan serials' before the pop dramas themselves mutate and burgeon into some grossly hilarious *shenju*. In the 1950s and especially during the 'Cultural Revolution', the PRC halted formal education and promoted a series of Red Classics – propagandistic movies that depict the Eighth Route Army in the North and the New Fourth Army in the South effectively and successfully resisting the Japanese invasion. Examples of these movies are: *Guerrillas on the Plain*《平原游击队》(1955), *Railway Guerrilla*《铁道游击队》(1956), *Tunnel Warfare*《地道战》(1965), and *Little Soldier Zhang Ga*《小兵張嘎》(1965).

4 CCTV (2013). See also *Tianjin City Post (2015).*

5 According to the count of production application, in the first four months alone of 2015, figures show that 'anti-Japan dramas' occupy 20.7 percent of the whole PRC's serial-drama market, in which 'contemporary history' and 'contemporary legend' occupy over 40 percent of the application. See SARFT public announcement at http://dsj. sarft. gov. cn/tims/site/views/applications. shanty? appName=note.

6 *Jiefang Daily* (2013).
7 *Sina News* (2013).
8 For an up-to-date, comparative, and balanced evaluation of how the culture of blogging and interactive online platforms in general provides 'unprecedented opportunities for netizens to both engage in national-level debate' (Leibold 1024).
9 One recent example of the CCTV failing to lead public discussion to its intended outcome has to do with the incident of 'Dongguan anti-prostitution crackdown' in early 2014. During the event, the CCTV acting as the PRC's official media exposed the sex trade in Dongguan, thinking obviously that the topic is safe for public discussion and intending to use the program to kick off a series of public attacks against prostitution. Contrary to CCTV's expectations, netizens began posting threads to 'stand by' the Dongguanians on social media platforms such as Weibo and Weixin (WeChat), detonating what China Change calls 'a powder keg' against the propaganda machine. See Jia Jia (2014).
10 See Perry Link for an account of the historical development of anti-Japan sentiment in the PRC and how the twists and turns of such a development are inseparable from the multi-level purposes of 'the regime' and 'the people at the top in China ... who are used to maintaining a smooth façade' (Link 2012).
11 According to the *Encyclopedia of Humor Studies*, *e'gao* employs such techniques as 'photoshopping still pictures and remixing [found] meaning? footage from movies and television programmes to lip-synching popular songs'. Historically, the practice 'first appeared in early 2000 but did not become nationally popular until the mid-2000s following the runaway success of the famous e'gao movie *A Bloody Case Caused by a Steamed Bun* by Hu Ge' (Attardo 2014: 210–11).
12 See, for example, Meme Daily (2015).
13 *Jiefang Daily* (2013).
14 At the 2004 Nation-wide Television Dramas Planning Meeting《2004 年全国电视剧题材规划会议》, Hu Zhanfan 胡占凡 gave a talk in his role as Director of CCTV entitled, 'Seize Hold of Opportunity, Deepen Reform, Strengthen Guidance, and Foster Productivity'《抓住机遇 深化改革 确保导向 促进繁荣》(2004). In his talk, Hu identified a long list of drama categories that should be 'limited' (martial arts drama, courtroom drama, costume drama, and crime-related drama) and 'reduced' (legal thriller and anti-corruption drama), and topics that should be 'straightened' (extra-marital affairs and triangular love affairs). Since then, a whole list of popular genres of television serials disappeared completely in prime time: crime-related, anti-corruption, horror, suspense, Emperor- and dynasty-building, costume, courtroom, time-travel. What remains? 'Super serials'. See Han (2013: 46).
15 In the essay on Sino-Japanese relation in 2001–06, Su-Jeong Kang explains how 'China's domestic political situation during the leadership transition from the early to mid-2000s needs to be considered as an important factor driving the Chinese government's lenient response to public expressions of anti-Japanese sentiment between 2003 and the spring of 2005'. As the Chinese leadership transitioned from the third to the fourth generation, it 'lack[ed] consensus within itself about the country's approach to Sino-Japanese relations'. As a result, Jiang's government had 'a greater incentive to burnish its nationalist credentials', giving not only itself difficulties 'to react promptly to anti-Japanese popular actions' but also the nationalist protesters' 'relative leniency between 2003 and early 2005' for engagement in anti-Japanese protests. See Kang (2013: 172–3).
16 Zhang Li张黎, *The Road*《人间正道是沧桑》(2009), Jiangu Broadcast Media Group, first broadcast by CCTV and Jiangsu TV, June 2009.
17 Kang (2013, at 168). For another analysis of the interaction between domestic anti-Japan protests and the Chinese authorities with a focus on the events in 2005, see Weiss (2014: 127–59).
18 For a discussion of Hengdian as twenty-first-century China's 'new site of resistance' against Japan, see Chen (2013).

References

Attardo, S. (ed.) (2014) *Encyclopedia of Humor Studies*. London: Sage.
CCTV (10.4.2013) Could 'anti-Japan serials' be staged as such?《'抗日剧'可以这么拍？》. Repost in *Sina News*, 'CCTV criticizes anti-Japan *shenju*: the search for excellence in the competition for vulgarity《央视批抗日剧粗制滥造:比着看谁俗争着看谁二》http://news.sina.com.cn/c/2013-04-10/233126788972.shtml.

Chen, Wu陈斌 (2013) Super anti-Japan serials: a distorted artistic sign' 《抗日神剧：一个扭曲的艺术符号》. *Voice and Screen World* 《声屏世界》, 9: 17–19.

Han, Song韩松 (2013) When will the myth of 'anti-Japan *shenju*' end? 《抗日'神剧'的神话何时终结?》. *Broadcast Realm* 《视听界》, 2: 44–7.

Hu, Jubin (2003) Colonial and anti-colonial nationalisms. In *Projecting a Nation: Chinese National Cinema Before 1949*. Hong Kong: Hong Kong University Press, pp. 115–58.

Hu Zhanfan 胡占凡 (2004) Seize hold of opportunity, deepen reform, strengthen guidance, and foster productivity' 《抓住机遇 深化改革 确保导向 促进繁荣》. A talk given at the 2004 Nation-wide Television Dramas Planning Meeting 《2004 年全国电视剧题材规划会议上的讲話》. *Chinese Television* 《中国电视》 12 (8): 10–26.

Jia Jia (2014) Fury and angst – the recent confrontation between state media and social media in China. *China Change: News and Commentary from Those who Work for Change*, February 23. http://chinachange.org/2014/02/23/fury-and-angst-the-recent-confrontation-between-state-media-and-social-media-in-china/.

Jia Ye贾也 (2015) A whole wave of super anti-Japan serials are arriving 《一大波抗日神剧正密集登场》. *Tianya Blog*, August 12. http://bbs.tianya.cn/post-free-5213529-1.shtml.

Jiefang Daily 《解放日报》 (13.4.2013) 'Anti-Japan drama' under attack 《'抗日神剧'遭炮轰》.

Johnson, Ian (2013) Studio city. *The New Yorker*, April 22. http://www.newyorker.com/magazine/2013/04/22/studio-city#.

Kang, Su-Jeong (2013) Anti-Japanese popular nationalism and China's approach towards Japan amid Sino-Japanese political tension, 2001–2006. *East Asia*, 30: 161–81.

Leibold, James (2011) Blogging alone: China, the Internet, and the democratic illusion? *The Journal of Asian Studies* 70(4) (November): 1023–41.

Link, Perry (2012) Beijing's dangerous game. *New York Review of Books*, September 20. http://www.nybooks.com/blogs/nyrblog/2012/sep/20/beijings-dangerous-game/.

Liu Yang刘阳 (2015) Why would anti-Japan super serials be 'endlessly reproduced'? 《抗战雷剧何以'生生不息'》. *People's Daily*, June 19. Repost online in People.cn, http://culture.people.com.cn/n/2015/0619/c87423-27180149.html.

Meme Daily (27.3.2015) 'My grandpa was murdered at nine!' Decoding super dialogues in anti-Japan dramas 《'爷爷9岁被杀害'抗日剧中爆笑雷人台词，真假大破解！》. http://memedaily.com/2864/抗日剧雷人台词真假破解.

Nasr, Alexander (2013) Former China state TV director bemoans anti-Japanese propaganda: 'Where's the creativity?' *Tea Leaf Nation*, January 23. http://www.tealeafnation.com/2013/01/former-china-state-tv-director-bemoans-anti-japanese-propaganda-wheres-the-creativity/.

Shaftesbury, A. (2001) Sensus Communis; an essay on the freedom of wit and humor. In vol. 1 of *Characteristics of Men, Manners, Opinions, Times*, ed. Douglas den Uyl. Indianapolis: Liberty Fund. 3 vols. http://oll.libertyfund.org/titles/811.

Sina News (5.3.2013) Chen Daoming criticizes the trend of staging 'anti-Japan dramas' as amusements: this is horseplay 《政协委员陈道明痛批抗日剧娱乐化：这是在胡闹》. http://news.sina.com.cn/c/2013-03-05/000626425756.shtml.

Tianjin City Post 《城市快報》 (18.5.2015) 'Anti-Japan super serials' put to a stop 《'抗日神剧'被叫停》. Repost in *China Daily*, http://www.chinadaily.com.cn/hqpl/zggc/2013-05-18/content_9069123.html.

Tong, Q. S. and Hung, Ruth Y. Y. (2014) Cultural policy between the state and the market: regulation, creativity, and contradiction. *International Journal of Cultural Policy*, 18(3) (2012): 265–78. Reprinted in *Cultural Policy in East Asia: Contemporary Issues and Trends*, ed. Lorraine Lim. London: Routledge, pp. 5–18.

Weiss, Jessica C. (2014) The 2005 anti-Japan protests and Sino-Japanese relations in the 2000s. In *Powerful Patriots: Nationalist Protest in China's Foreign Relations*. Oxford: Oxford University Press: 127–59.

Xiao Ni 小妮 (2012) Anti-Japan dramas crowd the screen: five novel measures of the theme drama' 《抗战剧扎堆荧屏：主旋律拍出五大新意》. *NetEase*, September 24. http://ent.163.com/special/kangzhanju/.

Zhang Li 张黎, dir. (June 2009) *The Road* 《人间正道是沧桑》. Jiangu Broadcast Media Group.

17

Transformations of state television production, consumption, and regulation in Vietnam

Chi Thong Ma and Catherine Earl

In the Socialist Republic of Vietnam, a single-party communist state that underwent macro-economic reform in the mid-1980s, the television sector continues to be controlled by the government. However, the increasing effects of media globalization since the 1990s have had a profound effect on the Vietnamese television industry. In recent years a rise in viewer demand for particular types of programs has prompted state-owned television stations to take on board new approaches to production. Private media companies have become more directly involved in the production for television of high-rating formats such as drama films and a variety of interactive programs, including game shows, talk shows, and reality shows. Yet, strict monitoring and control of content by the state are posing challenges to private TV producers.

This chapter examines the growing marketization of the Vietnamese television industry and the lessening influence of the ruling Communist Party in the production and consumption of culture. It highlights three aspects of state television transformation. Firstly, it outlines the cooperation between the state television broadcaster and private media companies in producing and distributing entertainment-based programs rather than programs for educational and informational purposes. Secondly, it explores the explosion in popularity of interactive reality television in Vietnam and its challenge to government regulations. Thirdly, it analyzes the changing emphasis of the government and state television stations in regulating television programs in compliance with government viewpoints and values. The discussion focuses on television production practice with regards to the relationship between state television stations and private media companies and their respective responsibilities, from the perspective of producers, including a former talk show producer at HTV, one of Ho Chi Minh City's state-owned stations, and two television directors, the first being a deputy general director of a state-owned television station and the second being the CEO of a private media company.

State television in Vietnam

State television in Vietnam is managed by the government under the National Press Law (1989). The main missions of state-owned television stations are outlined under Article 6 of the amended Press Law number 12/1999/QH10 (Vietnam National Assembly 1999).[1] The Vietnamese government owns and supervises 67 television stations and private television stations are not permitted. Consequently, television programs are produced in accordance with the viewpoint of the ruling Communist Party. Within these parameters, cooperation between private media companies and state-owned television stations is permitted.

The television sector in Vietnam is dynamic. The major revenue source for state television comes from advertising income. Major metropolitan television stations, such as HTV the major broadcaster in Ho Chi Minh City or VTV the national broadcaster in Hanoi, generate annual revenues of more than USD 50 million and so are able to cover their own operating costs without additional government funding. Other smaller regional state television stations rely heavily on government funding; however, the Ministry of Information and Communications draft planning on national press management to 2025 proposes that all state-owned television stations would need to become independent of the state for their funding by 2025 (Bình Minh 2015). This has prompted state television stations to cooperate with private media companies to produce trendy and popular programs that generate revenue and attract audiences. Such partnerships between state television stations and private media companies are growing at a tremendously fast pace. In the Ho Chi Minh City television market, there are approximately 4,000 private media companies, although only 250 of them have entered into production partnerships with HTV. At the same time, new online platforms have diversified the ways audiences engage with television and have generated new ways of viewing television, so that traditional television audiences, especially during the daytime, have continued to fall. It is important to recognize that while these new alternatives have had an impact on numbers of viewers they have not fully displaced traditional broadcast television (Gripsrud 2010: 14–15).

State television production in Vietnam, as in other Communist contexts, has been highly regulated in part due to its role as a vehicle of the ruling Communist Party that disseminates propaganda to the population (Do Anh Duc 2013; Marr 1998; Thomas and Heng 2001). This role of the mass media can be understood as a social institution that, when coupled with other social institutions such as the family, the school and the workplace, exerts a pervasive influence that can reinforce normative individual and group behavior, ideas, and beliefs (Bourdieu 1990). Moreover, the material culture of television has been a central focus of building national culture in Vietnam since national reunification. In 1976 Lê Duẩn, the General Party Secretary of the newly reunified Socialist Republic of Vietnam, promised that within a decade all Vietnamese citizens would have a television (Marr 1988). Yet, in 1980–85 just 0.7 percent of Vietnamese households owned a color television, a figure that grew to 46.7 percent in 1996–99 (Long et al. 2000: 73). Growing private television ownership decreased the symbolic status of a television set and it became a ubiquitous household item in Vietnam's cities from the late 1990s (General Statistics Office 2011; Thomas and Heng 2001).

Television viewing was one of the most popular pastimes among Vietnamese people throughout the 1980s and 1990s, particularly among the youth who watched football and popular entertainment at neighborhood video cafes (Đặng Thanh Trúc 1996) and women, who reported drawing on televized information about skills and public health to improve their household standards of living (Long et al. 2000). Urban television tastes in the 1990s began to transform. Locally produced programs based on globalized formats, such as dramas and soap operas which aimed to socialize as much as entertain, became popular among state television viewers in Vietnam's capital (Drummond 2003; Giang 2014; Nilan 1999). The popularity of locally produced globalized formats has expanded to include interactive programs and a variety of reality show formats, all of which continue to find an audience in the face of challenges from fully online formats.

In today's Vietnam, a post-reform single-party state, television continues to play an important role in socialization and the shaping of morality, but program ratings have also become an important informal mechanism of feedback to state television producers about the alignment of the expectations, interests, and tastes of the population with those of the government. Pettus (2003: 115) describes the post-reform Vietnamese media as playing 'a more genuinely meditative role' in presenting official policy, on the one hand, and the people's interests, on the other. Audience interests are becoming more specialized and television producers, while continuing to meet the requirements of Communist mass communication, are also meeting the desire for market-targeted content (Do Anh Duc 2013).

The highest-rating television programs screened on state television in Vietnam are the interactive shows produced by private media companies. While collaborations between state television stations and private media companies have been developing at a tremendously fast pace, the Vietnamese Communist Party is still debating cooperation policies. Collaboration between the state and private companies is not only specific to the television sector; it also prevails in the broader cultural sector, particularly print and radio media, as well as live music entertainment, theater and dance performances where events may be sponsored by private companies promoting a range of products ranging from household cleaning to cosmetics. The increasing focus of producers on generating advertising revenue has enabled advertisers to begin playing a more prominent role in reshaping the Vietnamese media market.

While sponsorships and collaborations are enabled, the Vietnamese government is not yet pursuing privatization of state-owned media. The collaborations with private media companies in the state television, print, and radio sectors are enabled in order to diversify content and attract larger audiences. Those collaborations occur in accordance with governmental guidelines. The official circular 19/2008/TT- BTTTT of the Ministry of Information and Communications of Vietnam (2009) guides the formal cooperation between state television stations and private media companies. This circular defines the obligations as well as the interests of both organizations in producing programs in line with the perspective of the government. Additionally, the circular outlines the acceptable scope of cooperation, for example stating that producing programs on political events and related topics is prohibited. Thus, television producers in state-owned stations, such as Ho Chi Minh City's HTV, and in private media companies can only cooperate in commissioning, producing, and broadcasting programs successfully if the content is judged by the chief editor of the state television station to be in accordance with the government's viewpoint, as Article 10 of the circular states that the chief editor of the state-owned media organization is responsible for the content of productions produced via collaborations with private media companies (Ministry of Information and Communication of Vietnam 2009). Cooperation with private media companies is the main strategy the state broadcasters use to produce a higher volume of programs that have greater popularity. Such cooperation has been closely scrutinized as claims of unfair competition have emerged with some private media companies being given more favor when selling program ideas and benefiting from securing the lucrative prime-time broadcasting slot.

Interactive-format television programs in Vietnam

Reality shows in Vietnam have been taking up a large amount of broadcasting time on state television since 2000. The majority of the shows are modified versions of franchised foreign programs. These new formats that incorporate web linkages and increased interaction with viewers have helped reality shows attract large audiences. As a result, television stations in

Vietnam have earned substantial income, especially from commercials and SMS voting, which has supported the production of new programs.

There is a growing tendency for local television stations in Vietnam to buy the rights of foreign reality shows. Earlier attempts to create Vietnamese reality shows did not attract sufficient attention from viewers, so state television stations began to spend significantly to obtain the rights of currently popular programs from countries with mature media and entertainment industries. Đinh Thị Xuân Hoà (2012) observes that the Vietnamese state television sector has entered a new phase in which imported reality shows are given priority in scheduling. HTV and other state-owned stations have always scheduled popular programs in prime-time slots in order to attract viewers and grow audiences. The Deputy General Director of HTV Mr Dương Thanh Tùng explains that:

> This is easy to understand. The huge profits from TV commercials and SMS voting for each reality show have always been directly proportional to the attractiveness of the program. We prioritize buying the rights of programs which have been popular around the world.
>
> *(Interview with author)*

Game shows, in particular, have been progressively introduced to Vietnamese audiences by state broadcasters. Modified versions of global franchises, such as *Vietnam's Got Talent*, *Vietnam Idol*, *Dancing with the Stars*, *Perfect Match*, *The Voice*, and *Master Chef*, are currently scheduled in the most important prime-time broadcasting hours each day. Television producers in Vietnam who take on the responsibility of modifying these franchises for a Vietnamese audience can do so to some extent, although they are required to retain the original program format, studio set, selection and arrangement of contestants, and standard games.

The modification of foreign franchised programs presents a challenge to state television producers. On the one hand, copying the foreign program formats and strictly following their rules have limited creativity and imagination in the Vietnamese versions of these shows. On the other hand, state television producers must ensure that the content as well as the dissemination of the productions complies with Article 4 of the Ministry of Information and Communications of Vietnam (2009) circular regarding 'appropriate' cultural content. This involves two interrelated dimensions, as the inclusion of Vietnamese cultural features in foreign program formats that are popular with audiences are not compulsory according to the official circular, but at the same time the appropriateness of the program content 'will be judged and revised according to the government guidelines'. HTV's Deputy General Director Mr Dương Thanh Tùng explains:

> In order to make reality shows become popular with Vietnamese people, it is extremely important to [connect with them and] include traditional cultural features in designing and developing television programs in the future.
>
> *(Interview with author)*

Planned cooperation between HTV and private media companies will produce an ambitious target of over 200 different reality shows, including shows based on foreign formats and original Vietnamese formats, over the next five years to 2020. These programs will necessarily include essential Vietnamese cultural features and will be revised according to the official circular 19/2008/TT- BTTTT of the Ministry of Information and Communications of Vietnam (2009), while also retaining the original format required by the franchise owner.

Finding a suitable balance between meeting requirements of government guidelines and franchise contracts is one aspect of the Vietnamese producers' challenge. Maintaining popularity by catering to audience tastes and therefore generating income is also a concern of the producers. Many foreign format shows initially attract large audiences, but in their second year they lose their novelty and audiences seek something new on another channel. The loss of audience translates to a loss of income for the state television station, which in turn limits their capacity to produce new, more desirable shows.

Prime-time popularity

The prime time period from 8 pm to 9 pm is considered the best time slot. Private media companies compete fiercely to get their programs broadcast from 8 pm because this is the most profitable time for reality shows and game shows which are usually aired live. The private media companies that are the biggest partners of HTV are the ones who secure most of the prime-time slots. HTV's Mr Dương Thanh Tùng explains:

> Though there is no need to mention their names, I can say we now work closely with two partners who are financially strong and have excellent employees. They can quickly obtain rights for different interesting programs.
>
> *(Interview with author)*

However, audiences are becoming saturated with reality shows and producers need to be aware that audiences may change their viewing preferences in the future. Deputy General Director Tùng outlined HTV's strategy to establish new operating mechanisms in the future that create opportunities for more private media companies to collaborate in producing Vietnamese television that focuses on Vietnamese socially significant values (Interview with author).

In order to meet this goal and win business, private media companies must design new versions of reality shows which focus on content deemed educationally and humanistically significant. CEO of MCV Productions, a private media company in Vietnam, Mr Phạm Từ Liêm, reflects that:

> Audiences are getting more interested in the content of each program than the tricks or theatricality of the program, and the television stations always work closely following the viewers' tastes.
>
> *(Interview with author)*

Though HTV did not mention specific mechanisms the station is going to establish to create favorable conditions to work with more private media companies in the future, the private company's response may indicate that the prime-time slots will be intended for programs of moral and traditional cultural significance. Aware of the importance of popularity to successful television production, HTV's Mr Dương Thanh Tùng reiterated that producers of Vietnamese versions of programs might still invite celebrities to participate as well as increase the value of prizes to ensure programs remain appealing to domestic audiences (Interview with author).

In order to attract and retain large audiences Vietnamese television producers use various tricks in reality shows, including arranging the final results and creating scandals. Producers usually hire advertising companies to make comments on forums and social networks to attract public attention, thereby increasing the numbers of viewers and maintaining their participation. Shocking events and scandals are an integral part of reality shows in Vietnam just as they are around the world. It is easy to understand why producers try to attract public attention. HTV's Mr Dương Thanh Tùng reflects that:

> The element of reality has always been doubted by the audiences because there are signs of the results being previously arranged by the producers. ... Because keeping the good quality of the programs is one of the requirements from the foreign partner, it is inevitable that there will be previously arranged results.
>
> *(Interview with author)*

Nevertheless, it would be unacceptable to the government regulators, and therefore to state broadcasters also, if profitable programs challenged traditional Vietnamese cultural and moral values. Such challenges may seem inconsequential in contrast to standards in other countries. For example, in talk shows in other countries political leaders (i.e. the prime minister) might be part of a joke; however, in Vietnamese television it is not possible to mention any leaders' names in a joke. Additionally, swearing or cursing by a guest or a host in some programs in other countries may be acceptable when censored with a 'beep' sound, but in Vietnamese shows it is not acceptable. If moral norms are challenged, the consequences can be serious. For example, in 2016 a Vietnamese artist Trấn Thành was personally fined for breaching moral values when he performed a remixed version of a famous reformed opera (*cải lương*) 'Moonlight Bowl' (*Tô Ánh Nguyệt*) dating from 1936, as the remixed comedy made fun of the original play's serious traditional cultural and moral content. A *Thanh Niên Online* news report listed the fines issued to the artist for Administrative Violations in the Field of Culture and Sports No. 00208/BB-VPHC by the Inspectorate of the Department of Culture and Sports including performing arts abroad without a license (VND 17.5 million), making derivative works without permission of the copyright owner (VND 7.5 million), and distorting the works which are detrimental to the honor and reputation of the author (VND 7.5 million). The total penalty of VND 32.5 million (USD 1,450) is almost ten times the official minimum monthly salary in Vietnam's cities of approximately VND 3.5 million (USD 150). Additionally, the artist was compelled to remove the performance from all online sites and he also apologized to his fans. Later, he was hospitalized for stress-related illness (Mai Ngọc and Ngát Ngọc 2016). Across the cultural sector public events are similarly subjected to moral regulation. For example, in 2012 and 2013 individual female performers in live music concerts and commercially sponsored fashion shows, as well as the event organizers, were fined for breaching moral norms concerning modest appearance and behavior (i.e. wearing skimpy clothing and smoking an e-cigarette) (see Earl 2013).

Broadcasting low-rating morally clean programs

Reality shows which are based on Vietnamese cultural features, that are highly educational and have humanist significance, are currently not broadcast during prime-time slots and they are not sufficiently financed for promotion. These programs can easily be neglected and attract little attention, especially when they are broadcast at midnight. As a result, these programs have low rating indices, indicating their low numbers of viewers. Private media companies that work with HTV on Vietnamese reality shows have often had difficulties improving the quality and expanding the production of their programs. CEO of MCV Productions Mr Phạm Từ Liêm explains:

> The vicious circle is that low ratings leads to no advertising, no advertising leads to no further investments, no further investments lead to difficulties in improving the quality

> and expanding the production of programs, resulting in no money to arrange prime-time slots, and not being broadcast during prime-time slots leads to low ratings.
>
> *(Interview with author)*

Since reality shows of foreign origin have continually been broadcast during prime time, local game show producers must compete for audiences by inviting famous people in different fields in Vietnam. The purpose of using celebrities as judges in one show or as contestants in another is to attract audiences and grab the attention of viewers who expect new elements in programs.

The Vietnamese reality TV program *Gia đình tài tử* (Actors' Families) produced by MCV Productions provides a useful illustration. *Gia đình tài tử* was made in 2011 and it centered on actors' families getting together on screen to practice singing, take part in contests, share happy moments together, and provide a distraction to local Vietnamese families from the difficulties of making a daily living. The program was initially very popular and successful in attracting a wide audience comprising families of different generations who identified with the members of the actors' families (that is older people with the grandparents, younger people with the children, and so on). However, its popularity soon waned. MCV's CEO Mr Phạm Từ Liêm explains:

> The producers did little to improve the program. They did not try to get more attention from audiences using advertising. Also, the program was broadcast at the same time as the [national and local] news bulletins. People tend to watch the news rather than other programs in this time slot. The producer's [poor] level of promotion and the [poor] financing by the sponsors are part of the reason why such a program has not been successful.
>
> *(Interview with author)*

While being inferior to major international reality shows in terms of media promotion and commercials, Vietnamese reality shows which are not broadcast during prime-time slots continue to be broadcast on the basis of their appropriate cultural and moral value for viewers. MCV CEO Mr Phạm Từ Liêm defends the production of low-rating programs. He points out:

> Though our programs are not very popular and can barely attract attention from the public like the major programs do, we still believe in the quality and humanistic significance of our programs. We know that, during hard times like the present time, enterprises want to earn profits immediately, and we must respect it. However, we still expect sponsors to understand the significance and values of our programs as well as the resonance of the enthusiasm of the producers of morally clean programs who work hard to ensure sustainable values of their brands in the long run. We will further improve our promotion activities in the future.
>
> *(Interview with author)*

Morality, culture, and television censorship

Media censorship in Vietnam is a reality that, as outlined by Heng (2001) and Dorsten (2006), has continued consistently under Communist Party rule, although its focus has evolved and has been redirected in response to social and technological change. The major setback for reality shows in Vietnam is that such programs have been judged as creating adverse effects on the national culture and on public viewing habits. Unlike state television in upland areas targeting ethnic minorities (see Messier and Michaud 2012), insufficient priority has been given to developing reality shows that specifically target the urban Vietnamese market with the socialization and cultural messages that the government and state broadcasters consider to be appropriate for the public. A reason for this, obviously, is the focus on ensuring program popularity with audiences in order to generate income that funds state television production.

The popularity of interactive-format television does not mean it becomes immune to government regulation, as the following example illustrates. In 2010, a new-format talk show called *Guest of HTV* that was put forward by Golden Flower, a private media company, was broadcast on HTV, the major state-owned television station in Ho Chi Minh City. This new format featured a panel of guests discussing current affairs and news. Since this was a program produced by cooperation between HTV and a private media company and the content was politically oriented and thus sensitive in nature, the chief editors at HTV were compelled to ensure that the content was created in accordance with the government's viewpoint.

Guest of HTV was broadcast for only three months before an unanticipated incident forced the show off the air. When the comments of one guest that conflicted with the government's viewpoint were broadcast, the talk show was terminated by the chief editor of HTV in line with the responsibility outlined in Article 10 of the official circular 19/2008/TT- BTTTT (Ministry of Information and Communications of Vietnam 2009). This illustrates that, while there has been some liberalization of the media in Vietnam in the post-reform era, the process of producing television programs is complicated by an expectation that producers, and anyone else who takes part in a program, should understand clearly and adhere closely to the viewpoint of the government.

The government's concerns have centered on mitigating the potentially negative effect of various foreign cultural influences, especially materialistic and sexualized content, on Vietnamese culture and morality. Much has been written about the so-called 'social evils' (*tệ nạn xã hội*) of imported popular culture displacing the local culture since the 1990s (e.g. Earl 2014; Nilan 1999). The focus on protecting culture, however, centers narrowly on an essentialized interpretation of Vietnamese national culture. We are not aware of a comparable popular debate in Vietnam about the effect of the mass media's transmission of Kinh (ethnically Vietnamese) cultural influences on ethnic minority cultures in Vietnam, for example.

Television has become pervasive in Vietnamese people's lives after reform. It is worth noting that international cable television is widely viewed in Vietnam's major cities, with one estimate suggesting 80 percent of Ho Chi Minh City residents have cable television at home (Ruwitch and Szep 2011: 5). Cable television provides Vietnamese viewers with direct access to foreign-produced programs, particularly films and serials on HBO, BBC, and other international channels in addition to news commentary and documentaries on BBC, CNN, and other networks such as the now-defunct Australia Network. International cable television programs are subject to censorship by Vietnamese authorities; however, censorship is not always as direct as taking a channel off air. BBC and CNN news channels have not been broadcast on time to Vietnamese audiences for the past three years. This is because these channels are kept on 30-minute delay, to give the state-employed government censors time to cut politically sensitive content. Certain programs are regularly cut. For example, in 2012 the scheduled weekly broadcast of a foreign-produced talk show containing analysis about a foreign country's domestic politics was not aired for a dozen successive weeks. The test pattern that was broadcast during the scheduled time slot announced routine 'satellite maintenance'. This illustrates the scope of government attention directed to media content. Circulars that guide television content are not only applied to state broadcasters concerning programs that focus on political content and thus fall outside the scope of acceptable programming, but also to cable television. Recently authorities in Vietnam have paid increasing attention to online content also, with shows broadcast on YouTube, such as *Những kẻ lắm lời* (Bitches in Town) and *Căn hộ 69* (House 69), being banned by the government due to their lack of relevance to appropriate Vietnamese cultural and moral norms.

Conclusion

Overall, the Vietnamese state television broadcaster is increasingly in competition with local television stations for market share. The desire for ratings and advertising revenue has led to major increases in demand for new television programs that appeal to the domestic audience. It is evident that interactive content and reality shows depend rather heavily on profits and to achieve the popularity that leads to financial success they deliberately generate scandals by going against the Vietnamese traditional cultural and moral values advocated by the government. That is why local television producers are trying to find new approaches through programs that include Vietnamese traditional cultural features while gradually incorporating the compulsory features of the international formats with domestic cultural and moral characteristics. Vietnamese-styled programs may also be broadcast during prime-time slots to widen their exposure in entertaining domestic viewers. How to attract more viewers is a challenge for all television producers, especially those in small private media companies producing less popular local programs. As it is vital to change the structure and organization of the television station to be more modern and professional and improve the quality and popularity of their programs, state television stations have actively developed their awareness and ways of thinking which enables them to adopt new practices of collaboration with private media companies to maximize the results from such partnerships in the market-oriented post-reform media context.

Nevertheless, despite appearing to be a seemingly prosperous industry, state television stations face a shortage of content. Television viewers have been critical of the repetition of shows and also of the growing numbers of foreign media products. It seems likely, therefore, that in the next few years more collaborations between state-owned television stations and private media companies will emerge in order to create more relevant local content that appeals to Vietnamese television audiences. The reality, or the risk, of audience shrinkage will push producers to fight harder to retain desirable time slots for their television programs. To do so, they will require additional investment. Producers will have to spend more money on each program for new equipment installation, self-advertising, and copyright costs. Yet, it is inevitable that the television sector will continue to fall behind the online sector.

Since the online sector, including social media and the Internet, has been growing dramatically in recent years across Vietnam (including outside major urban areas), access to Internet-based content has become convenient and inexpensive. This makes the abundance of relevant, interesting, and popular online content available anywhere and anytime. It seems likely that television audiences will continue to decrease. Moreover, in the face of challenges from the online sector the central regulators will likely lose their power and control over censorship of content.

Note

1 According to Article 6 of the amended Press Law number 12/1999/QH10, the duties and powers of the media are: (1) To inform and update honestly national and international current affairs in accordance with national and civil benefits; (2) To propagate, disseminate, and contribute to the building and protecting of the guidelines and policies of the Party and State laws, the achievements of the country and the world according to the principles and purposes of press agencies; to contribute to political stability, improving people's knowledge, the needs of a healthy culture of the people, protecting and promoting the fine cultural traditions of the nation, building and developing socialist democracy, increasingly strengthening national unity, and building and protecting the socialist country of Vietnam; (3) To reflect and guide public opinion; as a forum to exercise the right to freedom of expression of the people; (4) To detect examples of good people, good deeds, and new factors; to fight against violations of the law and other negative social phenomena; (5) To contribute to preserving the purity of the Vietnamese language and the languages of ethnic minorities of Vietnam; (6) To expand mutual understanding between countries and peoples, to participate in the career of the world's people for peace, national independence, socialist democracy and social progress (Vietnam National Assembly 1999).

References

Bình Minh (2015) Phổ biến nội dung Quy hoạch báo chí đến năm 2025 (Popular content media planning 2025). *Infonet: Report of the Ministry of Information and Communications*, 25 September, <http://infonet.vn/pho-bien-noi-dung-quy-hoach-bao-chi-den-nam-2025-post176697.info>, accessed June 8, 2016.

Bourdieu, P. (1990) *In Other Words: Essays Towards a Reflexive Sociology.* Stanford: Stanford University Press.

Đặng Thanh Trúc (1996) Môi trường đô thị và hành vi phạm pháp của thanh thiếu niên. In Trịnh Duy Luân (ed) *Tìm Hiểu Môn Xã Hội Học Đô Thị,* ('The Urban Environment and Delinquent Behavior of Youth', in *Understanding Urban Sociology*). Hanoi: Social Sciences Publishing House.

Đinh Thị Xuân Hoà. (2012) Vấn đề xã hội hoá sản xuất chương trình truyền hình ở Việt Nam hiện nay (Cooperation problem of producing television programs in Vietnam today.) *Nghề baó*, Ho Chi Minh City.

Do Anh Duc (2013) Television, Urbanisation and Development: A study of Hanoi, the capital city of Vietnam. Unpublished PhD thesis, Macquarie University.

Dorsten, A.-M. (2006) Don't Keep It Private! The Political Economy of Digital Media Innovation in Developing Countries. Unpublished PhD thesis, University of Pittsburgh.

Drummond, L. (2003) Popular television and images of urban life. In Drummond, L. and Thomas, M. (eds.), *Consuming Urban Culture in Contemporary Vietnam.* London: RoutledgeCurzon.

Earl, C. (2013) Saigon style: middle-class culture and transformations of urban lifestyling in post-reform Vietnamese media. *Media Australia International,* 147(1): 85–97.

Earl, C. (2014) *Vietnam's New Middle Classes: Gender, City, Career.* Copenhagen: NIAS Press.

General Statistics Office (2011) *Migration and Urbanization in Vietnam: Patterns, Trends and Differentials.* Hanoi: General Statistics Office of Vietnam.

Giang, N.-T. (2014) Nostalgia for the new oldness: Vietnamese television dramas and national belonging. *Media International Australia*, 153(1): 64–72.

Gripsrud, J. (2010) Television in the digital public sphere. In Gripsrud, J. (ed.), *Relocating Television: Television in the Digital Context.* London: Routledge, pp. 3–26.

Heng, R.H.-K. (2001) Media negotiating the state: in the name of the law in anticipation. *Sojourn: Journal of Social Issues in Southeast Asia*, 16(2): 213–37.

Long, L. D., Le Ngoc Hung, Truitt, A., Le Thi Phuong Mai and Dang Nguyen Anh. (2000) *Changing Gender Relations in Vietnam's Post Doi Moi Era. Policy Research Report on Gender and Development*, Working Paper Series No. 14, Development Research Group/Poverty Reduction and Economic Management Network, World Bank. <http://siteresources.worldbank.org/INTGENDER/Resources/wp14.pdf>, accessed November 25, 2015.

Mai Ngọc and Ngát Ngọc (2016) Trấn Thành bị phạt 32,5 triệu đồng vì 'chế' cải lương Tô Ánh Nguyệt (Tran Thanh fined VND 32.5 million for Moonlight Bowl 'remix'), *Thanh Niên Online*, May 16, <http://thanhnien.vn/van-hoa/tran-thanh-bi-phat-325-trieu-dong-vi-che-cai-luong-to-anh-nguyet-703325.html>, accessed June 8, 2016.

Marr, D. (1988) Tertiary education, research, and the information sciences in Vietnam. In Marr, D. G. and White, C. (eds.), *Postwar Vietnamese Dilemmas in Social Development*. Ithaca, NY: Southeast Asian Program, Cornell University.

Marr, D. (1998) Introduction. In Marr, D. (ed.), *The Mass Media in Vietnam*. Canberra: Department of Political and Social Change, Research School of Pacific and Asian Studies, Australian National University.

Messier, P. and Michaud, J. (2012) 'The nice culture and the good behaviour': state media and ethnic minorities in Lào Cai province, Vietnam. *Identities: Global Studies in Culture and Power*, 19(3): 339–59.

Ministry of Information and Communications of Vietnam (2009) *Quy định về việc liên kết trong họat động sản xuất chương trình phát thanh, truyền hình*, Thông tư số 19/2009/TT- BTTTT ngày 28/5/2009 (Specifying the cooperation policies in production of broadcasting and television programs, Circular number 19/2009/TT- BTTTT). Hanoi.

Nilan, P. (1999) Young people and globalizing trends in Vietnam. *Journal of Youth Studies*, 2(3): 353–70.

Pettus, A. (2003) *Between Sacrifice and Desire: National Identity and the Governing of Femininity in Vietnam*. New York: Routledge.

Ruwitch, J. and Szep, J. (2011) Vietnam's Capitalist Roaders: Special Report. Thomson Reuters, <http://graphics.thomsonreuters.com/AS/pdf/VietCapitalists.pdf>, viewed November 25, 2015.

Thomas, M. and Heng, R.H.-K. (2001) Stars in the shadows: celebrity, media, and the state in Vietnam. In Yao Souchou (ed.), *House of Glass: Culture, Modernity, and the State in Southeast Asia*. Singapore: ISEAS.

Vietnam National Assembly (1999) Luật sửa đổi bổ sung một số điều của luật báo chí Báo chí 1989, luật số 12/1999/QH 10 ngày 12 tháng 6 năm 1999 (Amending and Supplementing a Number of Articles of the Press Law (1989), Law number 12/1999/QU 10 12 June 1999), <http://thuvienphapluat.vn/van-ban/Quyen-dan-su/Luat-Bao-chi-1999-sua-doi-12-1999-QH10-45377.aspx>, accessed June 8, 2016.

18

Four dimensions of regionalization

Japanese popular culture in East Asia

Nissim Otmazgin

Introduction

In the last two decades, East Asia (both Northeast and Southeast) has experienced a massive circulation of popular culture products deriving from multiple sources. Products such as movies, pop music, animation, comics, television programs, and fashion magazines, along with their derivative products such as games, food, toys, and accessories, have been widely disseminated and consumed. While many of the popular cultures found in East Asia originated in the United States and Europe, confluences of Japanese, Chinese, and Korean popular cultures, have also intensified to reach consumers of different national and linguistic boundaries.

Japanese popular culture has been one of the pioneers of the regional circulation of popular culture in East Asia. Starting from the late-1980s, Japanese movies, television programs, pop music, fashion magazines, and more recently manga and anime, have reached consumers throughout this region with an intensity and variety not seen before. Take music, for example. While Japanese popular music reached audiences in the region during the colonial period, especially the *enka* genre (about Korea see Fuhr 2015: 38–40), in the 1990s Japanese pop music, better known as J-pop, was more widely marketed. Japanese music artists frequently appeared in the local music charts and a wide repertoire of Japanese music albums, both legal and pirated, became available in music shops in all major cities in the region – Hong Kong, Bangkok, Singapore, Seoul among others (see JETRO 2006).

These days, however, much of the Japanese popular culture 'wave' has gone, overtaken by Korean and, more recently, Chinese popular cultures, though Japan still remains strong in anime and manga. Nevertheless, looking at the case of Japanese popular culture in East Asia during its peak years is beneficial for this book's investigation as it helps us understand the origins and the processes that brought the emergence of a transnational popular culture market in East Asia. More specifically, it enables us to analyze the cultural, social, and organizational mechanisms that have generated the dense circulation of popular cultures across linguistic and national boundaries. In other words, we can extrapolate from findings in the Japanese context to understand similar developments in popular culture markets in East Asia and possibly beyond.

The Japanese case shows that contemporary cultural flows in East Asia are being generated both 'from above', through the promotion of companies and individuals seeking market expansion opportunities and by the efforts of governments to promote cultural export in order to boost their soft power, as well as 'from below', through the mediation undertaken by local fans utilizing internet technology and social media to access and deliver cultural content. As this chapter shows, the regionalization of Japanese popular culture was driven by the combined efforts of companies and fans, with the government trying to tag along. This experience may not be much different from that of Korean popular culture, whose global spread has been driven by entrepreneurial exploration by Korean companies as well as by the demands of dedicated fans worldwide (see Jin 2016; Otmazgin and Lyan 2013; Shim 2006). The result is a vast dissemination, indigenization, and hybridization of popular culture commodities in the East Asian cultural sphere, together with the adaptation of structural arrangements, technology, and knowledge needed to produce popular culture.

In what follows, this chapter analyzes four dimensions of the regionalization of Japanese popular culture during its peak period, which roughly extended from 1990 to 2005. These include: (1) the circulation of popular culture commodities; (2) the consumption and fandom of Japanese contemporary culture; (3) the normative impact that Japanese popular culture has had on local cultural industries in East Asia; and (4) the Japanese government's response to these processes. This chapter is based on repeated field visits to five East Asian cities (Hong Kong, Singapore, Bangkok, Seoul, and Shanghai) between 2004 and 2011, on interviews with cultural industry personnel in Japan and East Asia, and on my long-term research and publications in this field.[1]

Globalization and regionalization of Japanese popular culture

In the 1990s and early 2000s, Japanese popular culture was regionalized on a massive scale. This process has been documented and analyzed in a large number of academic works, especially in the fields of sociology, anthropology, and cultural studies, though not extensively enough in the fields of political science and economy (recent examples include Otmazgin 2013; Shiraishi 2013; Tsutsui 2010; Yano 2013). The majority of literature in the field usually depicts the transnational reach of Japanese popular culture as part of a wider globalizing process where the domestic market ceases to be the only reference for popular culture production and consumption, where the media industries are constantly searching for new market expansion opportunities in global markets, and where consumers are increasingly aware of new entertainment possibilities coming from other countries.

While cognizant of the region-specific cultural resonance and asymmetry of intra-Asian flow, the literature on popular culture in East Asia was not able to offer adequate theorization of 'region' and continues to focus on the global–local paradigm as the only framework of analysis (Otmazgin 2008). Chua and Iwabuchi (2008), for example, discusses the East Asian region through the lenses of popular culture circulation and consumption, but the notion of the 'region' as a distinct unit of analysis is not developed and regional cultural flows are merely viewed as part of a wider globalization process. This is in spite of the fact that there is a salient regional circulation of Japanese products, evident both in the intensive circulation of products and their variety, only within the cultural geography of East Asia. Thus, for example, while Japanese popular music and television dramas have had a conspicuous regional circulation in East Asia during the 1990s and 2000s, their overseas popularity continued to be described in the literature as part of an overall globalization process and overlooked their specific acceptance in the East Asian context (Berry et al. 2009; Inoue 2010; Iwabuchi 2002, 2004).

To examine the presence of Japanese popular culture in East Asia, in the rest of this chapter I suggest employing a regional framework of analysis. The 'region', as seen from the perspective of popular culture, is not simply a convenient, delimiting marker or a geographical field of inquiry. It cuts across the boundaries that separate 'Northeast Asia' from 'Southeast Asia'. Moreover, as I see it, throughout East Asia, the region as a framework of analysis consists of big cities with a consumption-oriented middle-class population and not a region made up of nation states. In this sense, the regional acceptance of popular culture in East Asia is fragmented: a certain part of the population (overwhelmingly the urban middle classes) are more 'regionalized' than those who live in rural areas because they are more exposed to the transnational flow of popular culture (for an elaborated discussion see Otmazgin 2016b). This definition, however, is far from consensual because this process creates large swathes of excluded populations that are not part of the urban popular culture consumerism. However, for the purpose of investigating contemporary popular culture in East Asia, I suggest that the nation state is no longer a sufficient framework of analysis and that we should rather focus on cultural developments taking place in the vicinity of cities and their middle-class consumers.

The circulation of cultural commodities

The first and most obvious stage in the massive circulation of Japanese popular culture in East Asia has been the production and dissemination of commodities. In the 1990s and early 2000s, Japanese popular culture products were marketed by Japanese companies, entrepreneurs, and other promoters seeking business expansion opportunities outside of Japan. Companies like Avex Trax, Amuse, Rojam, and JET TV, together with various local promoters, duplicated their experience by producing and marketing visual content to the growing consumer markets in places like Hong Kong, Singapore, Malaysia, Indonesia, and Thailand (Otmazgin 2013: 99–104). Japanese television programs (dramas, documentaries, and variety shows) and anime series were broadcast regularly on television channels across the region, satisfying a growing demand for television content that was then accelerated by the expansion of terrestrial and cable TV. Starting in the mid-2000s, the consumption of Japanese popular culture has also been invigorated by internet technology and the advent of social media.

The circulation of Japanese popular culture in East Asian markets has been greatly assisted by piracy, especially during the formative years of the market in the 1990s (ibid.: 181–6). In fact, piracy has played a crucial role in nurturing the awareness of popular culture products and delivering them to consumers. The existence of flourishing markets offering pirated versions of audio-visual products and printed materials, including music, animation, television programs, movies, and comics, have greatly invigorated the transnational transfer and trade in popular culture. As any visitor to East Asia's big cities in the 1990s can testify, foreign popular culture products were ubiquitously available in pirated versions from street vendors and in shops, and were openly offered in places such as Hong Kong's Ho King and Sino Center, Bangkok's Pantip Plaza and night market, Jakarta's Senyan district, Taipei's Shihlin night market, and Seoul's Nandeamon market. These days, online piracy is more important and consumers are able to access cultural content instantly using the internet. In other words, piracy has played a constructive role in the creation of popular culture markets and, in the long term, has helped implant popular culture products, fashions, and influences across East Asia to a degree and intensity, which would probably not have been achieved otherwise.

The result of the above processes is that many Japanese popular culture products have become available in the East Asian markets. Examples include anime series being aired on television stations in many parts of East Asia, as well as being offered for sale on DVD, or downloaded via the internet; Japanese manga being translated into local languages and sold at bookshops and by street vendors in virtually every big city in East Asia, many times illegally; Japanese television variety show formats being bought or duplicated by television production companies across the region; and characters such as Hello Kitty, Doraemon, Pokémon, and others being used to promote a huge variety of popular commodities. Figure 18.1 shows a Vietnamese version of the manga series Doraemon, one of Japan's most famous character. Written and illustrated by Fujiko Fujio, the series has been successfully adapted into anime series and franchises, and has been hugely popular in East Asian societies including Vietnam.

While there is no comprehensive data about the size of Japan's popular culture exports, it is obviously an enormous business. According to Sugiura Tsutomu's calculations (2008), the global export of Japanese popular culture merchandise and related royalties, income, and services deriving from products such as recorded sound and images (music, anime, movies, video games), books, magazines, paintings, art and handicrafts more than tripled from US $8.37 billion in 1996 to approximately $25.4 billion in 2006. The rate of this export growth is outstanding, especially given that during the same period the export of Japan's total merchandise trade (of both culturally and non-culturally related items) grew by only 68 percent, from $447 billion in 1996 to $752 billion in 2006.

According to a survey conducted in 2006, during the heyday of Japanese popular culture, by *Yomiuri Shinbun* (one of Japan's leading daily newspapers), on East Asian markets, while Japanese popular culture has not reached a dominant position, Japanese music, anime, and TV dramas have established footings in a few countries. According to the survey, 25 percent of South Koreans aged 18 or older preferred anime and comics from Japan over American or locally made animation, compared to 30 percent of adults in Indonesia and Malaysia, 18 percent in Thailand, and 12 percent in Vietnam. For movies, the figures were 10 percent in South Korea, 21 percent in Indonesia, 18 percent in Malaysia, 19 percent in Thailand, and 12 percent in Vietnam.[2] Japanese pop music was estimated to occupy between 15 and 20 percent of the

Figure 18.1 Manga in Vietnam

music market in Hong Kong during its peak period from 1996 until 1999, and between 8 and 12 percent in 2003. In Singapore, the share of Japanese music was estimated at 8 to 10 percent of the music market between 1996 and 1998, and about 5 percent in 2003. In Bangkok, estimates for the years 2002 and 2003 were 4 to 6 percent. In Seoul, Japanese music was estimated to have captured between 10 and 12 percent of the music market in the first six months after the market was opened to Japanese cultural products in 2002, and approximately 7 to 9 percent in 2004.[3]

Japanese television dramas were popular in South Korea, before the mounting success of Korean dramas in recent years. According to figures released in 2007 by Japan's Ministry of Internal Affairs and Communication, approximately 60 percent of TV programs exported from Japan in 2005 were broadcast within Asia. According to a 2002 survey conducted by Hakuhodō, Japan's second largest advertising company, 10 percent of the Bangkok residents polled expressed a preference for Japanese television dramas over other types of TV dramas; this was the same percentage that indicated a preference for American television dramas. In the survey, the popularity of Japanese TV dramas outstripped that of American dramas in Hong Kong, Singapore, and three Chinese cities: Beijing, Shanghai, and Guangzhou. Japanese television dramas also ranked second in popularity among youngsters in Hong Kong, with 65 percent watching Chinese dramas, 22 percent watching Japanese dramas, and 8 percent watching American television dramas.[4]

Commercially, much of the Japanese popular culture wave has died out in the past five years because of the rise of alternative popular culture flows, most notably the so-called 'Korean wave', and due to the strategic decision of many Japanese media companies to concentrate on the domestic market, which is better regulated in terms of copyrights and more familiar to them (Daliot-Bul and Otmazgin 2017: 169–72). Nevertheless, there are still successful examples of Japanese products continuing to loom over the markets. Anime-related goods, such as the infamous Hello Kitty, are one example. However, one should remember that popular culture products are not simply consumer commodities as they may have a bigger impact on the life of consumers. Buying a pen, a tablecloth, or a tatami mattress is, after all, different from listening to a music clip, reading a fantasy manga book, or watching an animation series or a movie. The difference is in the way that popular culture products embody cultural messages, narratives, and images that have a huge potential in shaping consumers' everyday lives and identities, an aspect we will explore in the next section.

Japanese popular culture fandom

The second dimension of Japan's popular culture regionalization is the influence it has had on clusters of dedicated fans in East Asia and in other parts of the world. Fans of Japanese popular culture have been overwhelmed by the images it provides, the messages it embodies, and the lifestyle it introduces. For many of these fans, Japanese popular culture serves as a source of inspiration, an example to follow, and a type of primary reporting about Japan. Think, for example, about Japanese television dramas representing the Japanese contemporary lifestyle, anime series depicting children's stories, or a music clip showing Japanese boy bands dressed in the latest Tokyo-designed fashions. For the more dedicated fans, Japanese popular culture fandom constitutes an important part of their identity.

I would like to give two examples. The first is Japan's fashion magazines, which started appearing in virtually every big city in East and Southeast Asia in the 1990s, have served as powerful distributors of contemporary culture and style abroad, and have encouraged many young Asians to learn more about Japan. These days, many of these magazines are translated into the local languages. As Figure 18.2, which was taken in Taipei, shows, in bookshops

Figure 18.2 Fashion magazines in Taipei

and kiosks across East Asia's big cities, it is possible to find translated or original versions of famousJapanese fashion magazines such as *CanCan*, *JJ*, *ViVi*, *COOL*, *Cutie*, *Vita*, *Myojo*, *Brand*, and *nonno*, which keep the youth updated on the latest Tokyo fashions. Although it is difficult to evaluate the exact influence of Japanese fashion magazines on the whole region of East Asia, it is reasonable to say that they have become an integral part of the urban scene in many East Asian cities and help shape the aesthetic and fashion of many young people.

Another example is the practice of 'cosplay', in which fans of Japanese anime and video games wear the costumes of their favorite characters and attend special gatherings where they exchange information and construct a sense of community. Cosplay gatherings take place in every major city in East Asia, as well as in most European countries, North and South America, and even the Middle East. In the US alone, there are over 260 fan gatherings every year, at which Japanese anime plays a central role (see Tsutsui 2010: 45). The largest of these gatherings – Otakon on the US East Coast and Anime Expo on the West Coast – are meticulously organized events, drawing hundreds of thousands of visitors.

In many big cities in East Asia – Bangkok, Seoul, Busan, Hong Kong, Singapore, Kuala Lumpur, Jakarta, etc., cosplay gatherings have been taking place on a monthly basis. Larger commercially driven events are also organized a few times a year in various locations in East Asia. One example is the *Anime Festival Asia*, which started in Singapore in 2008, but also took place later on in Indonesia and Malaysia. Organized by Japanese media conglomerate Dentsu, the anime festival is a celebration of Japanese-inspired popular culture: a large-scale meeting place for anime fans, a stage for amateur animators to show their work, and a chance for anime companies and promoters to gauge and market new products.

In addition to being avid consumers, fans in East Asia also serve as mediators and localizers of Japanese popular culture. They play a decisive role in paving inroads for imported popular cultures to enter the mainstream by spreading the word among circles of acquaintances, and utilizing personal connections as well as the internet and social media. In other words, fans serve as cultural mediators who create necessary bridges between the Japanese cultural industries and local consumers and thus play a decisive role in expanding the reach of Japanese popular culture and bringing it more to the mainstream.

Impact on the local cultural industries

Another dimension, which is relatively overlooked in the available literature, is the normative impact that Japanese popular culture has had on the development of popular culture industries in East Asia. Japanese formats[5] for producing animation, television programs, pop music, and comics have been widely adopted by the local cultural industries in places like Thailand, Taiwan, Hong Kong, and Mainland China, substantively amending the structure of local popular culture markets (Aoyagi 2000; Berndt 2012; Otmazgin 2013: 131–45; Yokota and Hu 2013). This would occur in the United States as well. While in the 1990s and early 2000s the anime market created the so-called 'anime boom', it also had a substantial normative impact on the American animation industry and youth culture (Allison 2006). Anime visual styles and storytelling techniques have been adapted and incorporated into the making of television cartoons and other animated genres in both East Asia and the US over the past 20 years, thus becoming part of the tool kit available to contemporary animation artists (Daliot-Bul and Otmazgin 2017).

In other words, the influence of Japanese popular culture in East Asia goes beyond the immediate sale of products, the anecdotal successes of productions like Miyazaki's animated movies or the hit manga *One Piece*, and the fascination it creates among the communities of fans. Japanese popular culture has also inspired similar productions in many parts of East Asia, where the local cultural industries have come to regard Japanese television, music, anime, and manga productions as a model and an example to emulate (Hu 2010; Otmazgin 2013: 125–60). The impact of Japanese popular culture should thus not be evaluated only by the dissemination of products and the sale records per se, but also by the process they entail, their conspicuous adaptation by local cultural industries, and their overall regional influence.

A good example of the externalization of Japanese popular culture production formats is the girl band AKB48 (short for Akehabara, in Tokyo), commercially Japan's most successful pop music band these days. Created by famous producer Akimoto Yasushi in 2005, approximately 60 fairly average teenage girls, with a meticulously orchestrated line of clothing and accessories, appear in a variety of publicized events, including music concerts, café openings, fashion gatherings, and meetings with fans, as well as in commercials and on television programs. Between one event and another, AKB48's girls also record their own pop music albums, singles, and video clips, which by 2014 had sold more than 30 million records. AKB48's music is offered for sale together with a huge variety of derivative products such as fashion accessories, posters, picture books, T-shirts, toys, magazines, playing cards, and the like. Riding on the wave of success, AKB48's production team created several sister groups in Japan with SKE48, based in the Sakae area of Nagoya; NMB48, based in the Namba district of Osaka; HKT48 in Hakata, Fukuoka; and SDN48 (short for Saturday Night 48). In the past few years, groups have sprung up in Asia as well – an Indonesian version of the band called JKT48 (short for Jakarta) was created in 2011, followed by the establishment of SNH48 in Shanghai a year later. These sister bands have become highly successful and have inspired similar girl band productions.

Another example is the influence of Japanese manga on the development of East Asian comic markets. The Chinese comic industry (*manhua*) initially exerted a huge influence from Japanese manga starting as far back as the 1960s, before developing its own narratives separate from the Japanese model (Berndt 2012). It now caters not only to children but also to teenagers and young adults in their twenties and thirties. In 1993, the first Chinese manga magazine was launched (*manga taisho/manga king*), which included not only manga translated from Japanese but also original stories by young Chinese manga artists (Seno 2007). In the case of Korean manga, known as *manhwa*, Japanese manga books and magazines were illegally translated into Hangul in the 1970s and 1980s when all forms of Japanese culture were banned. In the 1990s, however, Korean manga artists started to develop their own stories, but continued to mimic the storylines, characters, and narratives found in Japanese manga. More recently, Korea has entered a third stage in which Koreans have invented their own manga stories, using the expertise and experience they acquired while translating and developing Japanese manga (Yamanaka 2010).

To conclude, I argue that we need to bring in more of the production perspective to the discussion on the regionalization of Japanese popular culture. This is because its transnational spread may not only reach different consumers and affect their cultural lives but also has an impact on the development of local industries, which have adopted the Japanese aesthetics, production mode, and marketing model. This process involves copying and imitation that inspire the local industries' own innovations.

The reaction of the state

The massive circulation of Japanese popular culture outside of Japan and its enthusiastic acceptance by fans has caught the attention of the Japanese government. In recent years, academics, journalists, politicians, and bureaucrats in Japan have been emphasizing the growing importance of popular culture for the country's future, encouraging the government to intervene, and at times referring to the export of Japan's contemporary culture as a way to spread a new positive image of Japan abroad (Otmazgin 2016a). An integral part of this discourse is the use of the term 'soft power' in relation to the rising importance of popular culture in Japan's economy and diplomacy. This rhetorically invigorating term was initially coined in the early 1990s by Joseph Nye to describe the way states can fascinate other societies through their cultural appeal and not only intimidate them with their military or economic might (Nye 1990, 2004a, 2004b). This theory has been gaining strong ground in Japan, and is seen by many as a way to increase Japan's involvement in world affairs in a non-intimidating way.

This new proactive attitude of the Japanese state is very different from the attitude it took toward the export of Japanese culture to East Asia during most of the post-World War II years (Otmazgin 2012). In the early postwar years, the Japanese government generally refrained from promoting Japanese culture in Asia due to fears that it would resurrect old memories from the time Japan occupied and colonized large parts of East Asia and attempted to inflict its own culture. However, following the success of Japanese popular culture in many East Asian countries and the enthusiastic way it is being accepted by young people in this region, the attitude has gradually changed, and the Japanese government now attempts to utilize its cultural appeal abroad as a way to implant a softer and more positive image of Japan.

Over the past five years, Japan's Ministry of Economy, Trade and Industry (METI) has evolved as an influential player in Japan's popular culture sector. The Research Institute of Economy, Trade and Industry (RIETI) and thinktanks have been examining ways to encourage the development and export of cultural industries, mainly through studying the literature and data on this subject. In July 2011, METI established the Creative Industries Division, better known as the Cool Japan Division. The purpose of this division is to supervise the international promotion of 'cool Japan' and to assist Japanese small and midsize culture-related firms to pursue a global strategy. As part of this move, in October 2011, METI launched the Cool Japan campaign in order to increase the visibility of Japanese products in foreign markets. The overseas campaign, which was engineered by Dentsu Inc., Japan's

Figure 18.3 Cool Japan campaign in Singapore

largest advertisement company, was launched in Singapore and introduced Japanese fashion, food, and anime, which in turn, encouraged tourism to Japan. Cool Japan events were also scheduled in India, China, South Korea, France, Italy, the United States, and Brazil.

The Japanese Ministry of Foreign Affairs (MOFA), for its part, attempts to boost Japan's image abroad through its popular culture. In the past two decades, MOFA has launched a series of campaigns aimed at improving the international image of Japan and increasing the visibility of Japanese products in foreign markets. One such initiative is the appointment of famous anime characters as special ambassadors. Doraemon, a blue robotic cat character from one of Japan's most famous manga and anime series, was appointed by the then Japanese Foreign Minister Komura Masahiko as a special cultural ambassador at an official inauguration ceremony in Tokyo in 2008.

Popular discourse in Japan has largely been supportive of Japan's cultural export and provides a supportive environment for the state to intervene. In recent years, newspapers, magazines, and academic publications have been wielding support for Japan's popular culture export, since it is seen as both an opportunity to upgrade Japan's ailing economy and as a means to establish better relations with people of other countries. One example is the MOFA-supported journal *Gaikō* (Diplomacy), which every few years features a special issue dedicated to Japan's cultural diplomacy and soft power with many of the articles referring to the worldwide popularity of anime and calling on the government to utilize it in Japan's growing international role (see, for example, *Gaikō* 2010). Evidence of Japanese culture's impact abroad is available in a wide range of popular publications, as well as television shows, popular books, and magazine articles dealing extensively with Japan's 'cool exports'.[6]

The result is that the Japanese government, especially METI and MOFA, has become an active player in promoting the export of Japanese popular culture, thus not directly involved in producing it. However, for the purpose of our discussion it is important to note that the government has not initiated the regional circulation of Japanese popular culture and is not the reason for its success in East Asia during its heydays. Company and individual entrepreneurship, market forces, and local fandom have provided much stronger engines for the transfer of Japanese popular culture commodities and practices throughout East Asia. The Japanese state now follows the much more powerful market forces that drive the production and circulation of cultural commodities, and attempts to tap into this process.

Conclusion

Focusing on the regional dissemination of Japanese popular culture in the 1990s and early 2000s, this paper has analyzed the multiple dimensions of the construction of transnational popular culture markets in East Asia. Although these days the commercial success of much Japanese popular culture in East Asia has substantively reduced, we should view the regionalization of Japanese popular culture more comprehensively and pay attention to its different trajectories: the introduction of new products and fashions, the fandom it has created among communities, the regionalization of methods for cultural production, the influence it has had on the development of local cultural industries, and the impact on the state. The increasing involvement of the Japanese state in this process and its support for popular culture export has further placed this sector on the cultural, economic, and diplomatic policy agenda in Japan and later in other East Asian countries as well.

This chapter does not suggest that the operations of Japanese cultural industries ultimately lead to the formation of a Japanese-dominated regional identity in East Asia, to the homogenization of cultural practices, or to the imposition of Japanese norms and values on local societies. As evident from other chapters in this book, the flow of popular culture in East Asia is multidirectional. A variety of cultural flows, both global (American) and regional (Chinese and Korean for example), have rapidly intensified in recent years. It is within this dynamic contest that Japan itself has become an avid importer of popular culture from other parts of East Asia, although there is a conspicuous asymmetry in the import–export ratio, with Japan generally exporting much more popular culture within East Asia than it imports from the region. In other words, the regional circulation of Japanese popular culture and the expansion of Japan's cultural industries within the region are not Tokyo-sponsored operations aimed at constructing a new regional identity, nor do they manifest any Japanese cultural hegemony in the sense of domination or control.

Notes

1 I conducted in-depth semistructured interviews with 68 individuals from major media companies in Japan, Hong Kong, Singapore, Shanghai, Bangkok, and Seoul, as well as government officials, officials from affiliated organizations, academics, media specialists, promoters, and workers from media-related organizations. Next, I conducted a survey of 172 shops selling mostly music, movies, television programs, and animation series in Hong Kong, Singapore, Shanghai, Bangkok, and Seoul, from April 2004 to May 2005. Third, I conducted a survey of primary sources in Japanese, English, and other languages about the export, presence, and consumption of Japanese popular culture in East Asia. These materials included white papers, thinktank reports, advertising companies' estimates, cultural preference surveys of consumers, government statistics and data, and other related publications.

2 Figures for a younger age group would likely be significantly higher, as teenagers appear to be the most enthusiastic consumers of Japan's popular culture (*Yomiuri Shinbun,* September 10, 2006).

3 Estimates were given to the author between April 2004 and May 2005 by 14 promotional managers of Japanese music companies with branches in Hong Kong, Singapore, Thailand, and South Korea. The figures include estimates of pirated music sold in these cities. In reaction to the Japanese occupation of the Korean Peninsula before and during World War II, the sale of Japanese cultural products was banned in South Korea for more than 50 years.

4 The survey was conducted among 15- to 24-year-olds, offering multiple choice answers. See Hakuhōdō News 2003, http://www.hakuhodo.co.jp (accessed October 2005).
5 Here I refer to both format of *production* and format of *product*. The former refers to the technical, artistic, and organizational arrangement and relationships needed to produce, for example, anime series, pop music events, or manga books. The later refers to the imitation or localization of a certain product, for example the 2008 Chinese animation series *Golden Hero* which bears a striking resemblance to Japan's *Ultraman*. There are examples where both Japanese format of production and the product itself were adopted in other markets in East Asia, for example Japan's popular 'trendy dramas' of the 1990s which were remade and broadcasted in Korea (Lee 2004), and more recently the production of AKB48 sister bands in Shanghai, Bangkok, Jakarta, Manilla, and Taipei.
6 See *Sankei Shimbun*, Kuru Japan Kasoku [Speeding Cool Japan], September 26, 2015, p. 2; *Mainichi Shimbun*, February 25, 2015, Available at: http://mainichi.jp/select/news/20150226k0000m040014000c.html

References

Allison, Anne (2006) *Millennial Monsters: Japanese Toys and the Global Imagination*. Berkeley and Los Angeles: University of California Press.

Aoyagi, Hiroshi (2000) Pop Idols and the Asian Identity. In *Japan Pop! Inside the World of Japanese Popular Culture*, ed. Craig J. Timothy, 309–26. New York: M. E. Sharpe.

Berndt, Jaqueline (ed.) (2012) *Mahwa, Manga, Manhua: East Asian Comic Studies*. Leipziger Universitätsverlag.

Berry, Chris, Nicola Liscutin, and Jonathan D. Mackintosh (eds.) (2009) *Cultural Studies and Cultural Industries in Northeast Asia: What a Difference a Region Makes*. Hong Kong: University of Hong Kong Press.

Chua, Beng-Huat, and Koichi Iwabuchi (eds.) (2008) *East Asian Pop Culture: Analyzing the Korean Wave*. Hong Kong: University of Hong Kong Press.

Daliot-Bul, Michal, and Otmazgin, Nissim (2017) *The Anime Boom in the US: Lessons for Global Creative Industries*. Cambridge, MA: Harvard University Asia Center Press.

Fuhr, Michael (2015) *Globalization and Popular Culture in South Korea: Sounding Out K-pop*. London: Routledge.

Gaikō (2010) *Bunkagaikō to Sofutopawa* [*Cultural Diplomacy and Soft Power*], Vol. 3, November.

Hu, G. Tze-Yue (2010) *Frames of Anime: Culture and Image-Building*. Hong Kong: University of Hong Kong Press.

Inoue, Takako (2010) *Ajia no Popyurā Ongaku: Gurōbaru to Rōkaru no Sōkoku* [Asia's Popular Music: Global and Local Conflict]. Tokyo: Keisō Shobō.

Iwabuchi, Kōichi (2002) *Recentering Globalization*. Durham, NC: Duke University Press.

Iwabuchi, Kōichi (ed.) (2004) *Feeling Asian Modernities: Transnational Consumption of Japanese TV Dramas*. Hong Kong: University of Hong Kong Press.

JETRO (Japan External Trade Organization) (2006) *Hakusho* [White Paper].

Jin, Dal-Young (2016) *New Korean Wave: Transnational Cultural Power in the Age of Social Media*. Chicago: University of Illinois Press.

Lee, Dong-Hoo (2004) Cultural Contact with Japanese TV Dramas: Modes of Reception and Narrative Transparency. In *Feeling Asian Modernities: Transnational Consumption of Japanese Television Dramas*, ed. Kōichi Iwabuchi, 251–74. Hong Kong: University of Hong Kong Press.

Nye, Joseph S. Jr (1990) *Bound to Lead: The Changing Nature of American Power*. New York: Basic Books.

Nye, Joseph S. Jr (2004a) *Soft Power: The Means to Success in World Politics*. New York: Public Affairs.

Nye, Joseph S. Jr. (2004b) Nihon no Sofuto Pawā: Sono Genkai to Kanōsei [Japan's Soft Power: Its Limits and Possibilities]. *Gaikō Fōramu* (June).

Otmazgin, Nissim (2008) Japanese Popular Culture in East and Southeast Asia: A Time for a Regional Paradigm? *The Asia Pacific Journal: Japan Focus*, February 8. http://japanfocus.org/-Nissim_Kadosh-Otmazgin/2660.

Otmazgin, Nissim (2012) Geopolitics and Soft Power: Japan's Cultural Policy and Cultural Diplomacy in Asia. *Asia-Pacific Review*, 19(1), 37–61.

Otmazgin, Nissim (2013) *Regionalizing Culture: The Political Economy of Japanese Popular Culture in Asia*. Honolulu: University of Hawai'i Press.

Otmazgin, Nissim (2016a) Soft Powering Popular Culture: Discourse and Policy Making in Japan's Content Industries. In *Social Commentary on State and Society in Modern Japan*, ed. Yoneyuki Sugita, 141–53. Singapore: Springer.

Otmazgin, Nissim (2016b) A New Cultural Geography of East and Southeast Asia: Imagining A 'Region' through Popular Culture. *Japan Focus: The Asia-Pacific Journal*, forthcoming.

Otmazgin, Nissim and Lyan, Irina (2013) Hallyu across the Desert: K-pop Fandom in Israel and Palestine. *Cross Currents: East Asian History and Culture Review*, 9 (December): 68–89.

Seno, Takumasa (2007) Manga kara Kaosu he- Chugokumanga no Henbo [From Manga to Chaos: Change in Chinese Manga]. In *Gendai Chugoku no Popura Karucha* Contemporary Popular Culture), *Ajia Hougaku*, 97 (March), 115–16.

Shim, Doobo (2006) Hybridity and the Rise of Korean Popular Culture in Asia. *Media, Culture & Society*, 28(1): 25–44.

Shiraishi, Saya (2013) *Grōbarukashita Nihon no Manga to Anime* [Globalized Japanese Manga and Anime]. Tokyo: Gakujutsu Shuppankai.

Sugiura, Tsutomu (2008) Japan's Creative Industries: Culture as a Source of Soft Power in the Industrial Sector. In *Soft Power Superpowers: Cultural and National Assets of Japan and the United States*, edited by Yasushi Watanabe and David L. McConnell, 128–53. New York: M. E. Sharpe.

Tsutsui, William (2010) *Japanese Popular Culture and Globalization*. Michigan: Association for Asian Studies, Inc.

Yamanaka Chie (2010) Manga Hyōgen Keishiki no Ekkyō: Kankoku ni okeru Mohō Kaizokuban Manga wo Jirei toshite [Manga Expression Style over the Border: The Case of Manga Imitation in Korea]. In *Comonzu to Bunka: Bunka ha Dare no Monoka* [Commons and Culture: Culture Belongs to Who?], ed. Shōji Yamada. Tokyo: Tokyo dō.

Yano, Christine R (2013) *Pink Globalization: Hello Kitty's Trek Across the Pacific*. Durham, NC: Duke University Press.

Yokota, Masak and Hu, Tze-yue G. (eds.) (2013) *Japanese Animation: East Asian Perspectives*. Jackson MS: University of Mississippi Press.

19

The roles of international art fairs in Hong Kong in facilitating the production and consumption of contemporary art in Asia

Art Hong Kong, Art Basel Hong Kong, and Art Central

Silvia Fok

This chapter traces the impact international art fairs have had in Hong Kong and the Asian region. It focuses in particular on Art Hong Kong, which ran from 2008 until 2012; Art Basel Hong Kong, established in 2013 and still active; and Art Central, also still active and established in 2015. It examines why Hong Kong is ideally suited to be a visual art center within Asia; its role within the global art world and the art market; and how these roles have changed with the advent of these art fairs. This chapter also explores characteristics that are particular to Art Basel Hong Kong, compared to the longer-established Art Basel (est. 1970) or Art Basel Miami Beach (est. 2002) fairs, in featuring contemporary art. Art Basel Hong Kong and Art Central have both influenced the production of and trade in, contemporary art by emerging artists in Asia. Rather than seeing art fairs just as a space to trade artworks, this chapter investigates other roles these fairs have played, their impact on the local art scene, and their impact in enhancing cultural interaction and invigorating the cultural and creative industries in Hong Kong, Macau, and mainland China.

Before the advent of international art fairs, auction houses played a key role in raising interest in art in Hong Kong (Ching, K. et al. 2014: 289). Sotheby's was the first international auction house to open in Asia, and engage with the Asian art market. Established in Hong Kong in 1973, Sotheby's huge annual previews in spring and autumn gave international publicity to art from the region (Ching, K. et al. 2014: 289). Hong Kong had a somewhat developed art world in the 1980s, long-established gallerist Johnson Chang of Hanart TZ Gallery, for instance, worked with artists from Taiwan and mainland China, as well as Hong Kong during that period. In the 1990s, Hong Kong's handover to China became a catalyst for local artists to engage with social and identity issues in their work, while the concurrent establishment of the Hong Kong Arts Development Council in 1995 had its own impact through greater local funding opportunities for the arts. Looking back on this period, art historian Jane Debevoise, Chairperson for the board of the Hong Kong-based Asia Art Archive, remarked that there were several stages in the development of contemporary art in Hong Kong – the development of art galleries; that of the arts funding organization, Hong Kong Arts Development Council; and that of state-run museums such as Hong Kong Museum of Art and M+ (Ching, K. et al. 2014: 286–7). She stressed that contemporary art in Hong Kong had not just appeared in the new millennium with the art market (Ching, K. et al. 2014: 287).

Two decades ago there were only a handful of galleries in Hong Kong (Schoeni, cited in Lau 2013b). In 2004, when auction houses began paying attention to contemporary Chinese art, the big gallery boom began in Hong Kong (Schoeni, cited in Lau 2013b). A growing global interest in contemporary Chinese and Asian art in the 2000s was a key factor in initiating the establishment of the different international art fairs in Hong Kong seen today, especially Art Hong Kong (later Art Basel Hong Kong) founded in 2008. This was more than a decade after Art Asia Hong Kong, one of the first international art fairs in Hong Kong, which closed shop when the market in Hong Kong and Asia could not sustain it. Producers (artists, curators, gallerists, and organizers of art fairs) and consumers (collectors and viewers) of art exist in a symbiotic relationship with each other and there is a clear interdependence between international art fairs in Hong Kong and the contemporary Asian art market, which in recent years has enhanced the production and consumption of art in Hong Kong and Asia as a whole.

Hong Kong: a visual art center to showcase contemporary art

The annual Art Hong Kong fair was co-founded in 2008 by Tim Etchells, Sandy Angus, Will Ramsay, and Charles Ross, who were active in developing key contemporary art fairs in cities in Asia, Europe, and the US (HKAAA 2016). In 2011, Art Basel's parent company, MCH Swiss Exhibition (Basel) Ltd., bought out Art Hong Kong, launching it as Art Basel Hong Kong in 2013, and bringing in 'more big Western art players to mix with the younger, less established, regional contemporary art scene for a week of openings' while maintaining 'the 50–50 split between Asian and Western exhibitors' (Qin 2015a). In 2015, Etchells, Angus, and Ramsay founded Art Central as a new satellite fair to Art Basel Hong Kong. While first Art Hong Kong and then Art Basel Hong Kong were held in the Hong Kong Convention and Exhibition Centre, Art Central was, and still is, staged in a 10,000 square meter tent, a little way along the waterfront from the Hong Kong Convention and Exhibition Centre. Art Central stresses that they are not out to compete with Art Basel Hong Kong, but to offer a younger, funkier art fair that focuses on less established artists (The Works 2015).

In 2013, as an internationally branded art fair, Art Basel Hong Kong plugged into a global, rather than a regional art market, and attracted increased attention from nearby countries such as South Korea (Ching, K. et al. 2014: 295). It was not until 2014 however, that Art Basel realized its success in connecting with the Australian market. Hundreds of Australian collectors came to Hong Kong for the second edition of Art Basel as they began to realize this was their nearest touch-point to the international art world (Ching, K. et al. 2014: 294–5).

Hong Kong has a geographically favorable position, as a central point for people from Asia and the Asia Pacific regions. While its local art scene is considered less established than that of Tokyo's, and less vibrant than Beijing's, Hong Kong is a tax-free port, has few government restrictions on artistic expression, and is an English-speaking financial and commercial center – factors that make it a favorable place to buy and sell art. The tax-free environment has proved particularly important in attracting art fairs to Hong Kong, especially when viewed in the light of collectors having to pay up to 34 percent of the price of the artwork in taxes when buying art on the mainland (Lau 2013a). In comparison with other Chinese cities that are governed by Beijing's law, Hong Kong also has more freedom of expression. Exhibitions on the mainland are bound by censorship, leading to delays as paperwork needs to be approved before a work can be shown (Lau 2013a). Art Basel Hong Kong claims that they have never censored their artists and galleries (The Works 2013) and this freedom of expression, a core value upheld in Hong Kong, has helped attract Art Basel to launch its Asian art fair in this city (The Works 2012). This lack of censorship on art, even in comparison with other cities in Asia, has been particularly attractive for galleries considering participating in Hong Kong's international fairs. Adeline Ooi, Director Asia, Art Basel, and specializing in the Southeast Asian market, states that elsewhere in Asia cultural factors can be an issue with regard to images that deal with nudity and sexuality. Some artworks at the Singapore Biennale art fair in 2011, for example, were forbidden on these grounds. Hong Kong also benefits from wealthy collectors in China, and a combination of all these factors has today positioned Hong Kong as the third largest art market in the world after New York and London. In terms of sales, Hong Kong is the largest art market in Asia (Lau 2015). This development from Art Hong Kong (2008–12) to Art Basel Hong Kong (2013–) and the success of Art Basel Hong Kong, suggests that the city of Hong Kong is particularly suitable for hosting international art fairs.

Influencing collectors and collections: the special role of Art Basel Hong Kong

Hong Kong's proposed state-run M+ Museum in the West Kowloon Cultural District is scheduled to open in 2019 (Lau 2015), and in the absence of a world-class contemporary art Museum, the Art Basel Hong Kong art fair has been a significant force. Its impact has extended well beyond the art market and its ripples have been felt through the contemporary art world of Asia and the Asia Pacific region. In fact it could be argued that the art fairs, rather than the museum infrastructure in the region, have been a key influence on collectors and key local collections. Hong Kong's international art fairs have stepped into a scene with a substantial amount of wealth and limited institutional art infrastructure, and may have been particularly influential.

Art Basel Hong Kong was possibly the biggest art and cultural event in Hong Kong in 2013, the year it launched in the city. Its arrival was a significant indicator that art was taking on a higher profile in Hong Kong. More art auction houses were opening up and more international galleries were coming to Hong Kong (The Works 2013). To promote, to trade in, and to enhance the visibility of art in Hong Kong, the Hong Kong Art Gallery Association, a member-based non-profit organization of over 50 art galleries in Hong Kong, was formed in 2012 and has received funding from the Hong Kong Arts Development Council since 2014.

Since the launch of Art Hong Kong in 2008, the field of contemporary art has expanded in parallel with the gallery boom. Many young private collectors have established their own vast, museum-like, collections (Twigg and Mirandilla 2015; Twigg 2015a, 2015b; Chee 2017). Some of the recently opened private museums in Hong Kong include the Sun Museum in Kwun Tong (est. 2015), F11 Foto Museum in Happy Valley (est. 2014), Liang Yi Museum in Hollywood Road (est. 2013), and The Imperial Museum in Saint John's Building, Central (est. 2013) (Chow 2015). Many private collectors acquire artworks from these fairs for their own collections/museums. Networks such as the Young Collectors Collective (est. 2016) with over 300 members based all over the world, aim at redefining the notion of patronage towards art from Asia and at creating a dialogue around art practices and collections. They come together regularly for social happenings, meeting in venues anywhere from Hong Kong to London, and raising funds for innovative projects. The collective has raised funds for selected local arts organizations in Hong Kong in 2016–17, and in 2017–18 they will focus on Hong Kong's female artists (LinkedIn).

These developments to do with private museums, collectors, and galleries reflect some of the power relations within the contemporary art structure in Hong Kong and the region. The role of international art fairs has become influential in the exhibiting and collecting of contemporary art, and Art Basel's social positioning is akin to that of a taste-maker, with a dominant role in the international contemporary art market system. Artists are not just relying on biennials and triennials, or on major shows held by state-run museums or prestigious galleries around the globe to get international exposure, and art viewers and collectors all over the world can view or collect art through the expanded system of international art fairs.

More than half of the 250-plus galleries showing in Art Basel Hong Kong 2013, were from Asia and the Asia Pacific region (The Works 2013). Not only did galleries have better sales in Art Basel Hong Kong 2013 as compared with previous years, but they were also able to develop a network of collectors in Asia. Ashley Rawlings, Director of Blum & Poe's Tokyo office, states that their sales at Art Basel Hong Kong in 2013 were better than those of previous years (at Art Hong Kong). She further states that there had since been more interest in their artists and program, and that they had built more connections with clients from Hong Kong, Taiwan, and Indonesia (Lau 2013a). Emily Chao of Eslite Gallery, Taiwan has a similar view, and supports the idea that Art Basel Hong Kong should keep its status quo as a fair specific to Asia (*Art Basel Year 45* 2014).

Gallerists noticed a slower pace at Art Basel Hong Kong (2013) than at similar art fairs in Europe and the Americas 'where they are used to bracing themselves for an onslaught of aggressive buying as soon as collectors arrive for the preview' (Lau 2013a). This suggests that both new and experienced collectors might need more time to commit financially to artworks created by emerging young artists in Asia.

The increased acquisition of contemporary Asian art, evident particularly from its vastly increased presence in the many private museums of the region, has been facilitated partly through the international art fairs in Hong Kong, a major site for the sale of artworks. Marc Spiegler, Asia Director of Art Basel, states that they have established Hong Kong as a key location for their fair in Asia. The next challenge is to develop the market to support the fair (Qin 2015a). Art Basel Hong Kong 2015 and its auxiliary events have clearly established an increased interest in art and culture, and a network for collectors to acquire contemporary art in Asia. Melissa Chiu, Director of the Hirshhorn Museum in Washington and previously Director of the Asia Society Museum in New York, states that it is a remarkable time for the development of contemporary art. In the past, there were only a small number of collectors revolving around New York or London but art acquisition has become a global phenomenon brought about by Art Basel Hong Kong and its auxiliary events (Qin 2015b). With its eight years of development, from Art Hong Kong (2008–12) to Art Basel Hong Kong (2013–16), Hong Kong has had a unique role in facilitating the production and consumption of contemporary art in Asia. According to the *Hong Kong Monthly Digest of Statistics* of March 2014 (p. 14) on the cultural and creative industries in Hong Kong, the exports of visual arts and design goods increased from HK $44,926 million to HK $63,450 million from 2005 to 2012 while imports increased from HK $35,187 million to HK $106,054 million from 2005 to 2012.

The international art fair – a window into art practices in the region

The international art fair in Hong Kong has also offered its public more knowledge about the art world and artists, both local and international. It is in the interests of international art fairs to make art more accessible to the public in order to build the market. Tim Marlow, Director of Exhibitions, White Cube Gallery, claims that they put on a museum-quality show for their viewers (The Works 2013). The best commercial galleries, he states, are eager to work with the best artists and these artists would like to have their works shown to as many viewers as possible. This, he says, is the reason why so many artists are keen to work with museums. Although some artists, he believes, might think art fairs are not an ideal platform to show their works, it is a good place to get visibility, expand their market, and reach wider audiences, including museum curators, collectors, art foundations, and critics from cultures further afield. The artist Liu Ye states that there are two sides of the art market: the upside offers the opportunity to make a lot of money, while also promoting artists and making art more accessible; the downside is that the artist's pure creative process may be interfered with by the market (The Works 2010). Liu believes that an artist should have a clear idea in mind: art for the love of making art, and not just for making money.

Marina Schiptjenko, owner and Director of Andréhn-Schiptjenko (Sweden), says that rather than exhibiting at the art fair, she has viewed Art Basel Hong Kong (2013) as an opportunity to gain a better understanding of the art scene in the region and to meet local artists (The Works 2013). Art fair audiences have opportunities to view different genres of art in the region, for example the live performance work *Everything Goes Wrong for the Poor Couple* (2010) by Hong Kong artists Kwan Sheung Chi and Wong Wai Yin Doris, which was presented for five days during the Hong Kong International Art Fair 2010 (The Works 2010). Audiences were also able to engage with critical issues to do with art during the art forums of the same year which included a debate on the idea: 'You don't need great skill to be a great artist' (The Works 2010) and a challenge to the elite role of art, in Art Hong Kong 2012, as one booth styled itself as 'Art Flat,' a typical Hong Kong apartment and sold art at prices from US $10 to US $500. Diana d'Arenberg, Co-curator of Art Flat, says that the idea was born out of the fact that art has become collector-driven, focused on a moneyed elite, and increasingly inaccessible to the majority of the community. Art Flat was born out of a desire to encourage people from a broader demographic to have more interaction with art (The Works 2012).

Yuko Hasegawa, Curator, Art HK Projects, and Chief Curator, Museum of Contemporary Art, Tokyo, stresses that while galleries offer numerous presentations and information, sometimes the art fair audience is confused and needs some mapping, introduction, and contextualization as well as guidelines on how to approach the appreciation of artworks (The Works 2012). As Hong Kong's international art fairs have developed, its visitors have gained an enhanced knowledge of the art showing at these fairs. The fair's collectors, states Adeline Ooi, are sophisticated and their interest in art and knowledge about art has grown tremendously (The Works 2015).

A number of artists share the same view about seeing art fairs as an opportunity to offer the public a better understanding of art. The German artist Gregor Hildbrandt taking part in Art Central 2015 states that he enjoys sharing his work in a solo gallery show (The Works 2015). Hong Kong art collectors have similar views on the educational value of the international art fair. The seasoned Hong Kong collector William Lim thinks Art Basel Hong Kong has become better each year, with interesting artworks worthy of collecting. He points out that many galleries have featured solo exhibitions, which is useful particularly for younger or less experienced viewers to enhance their understanding of a particular artistic practice (The Works 2016). Angelika Li, Director of The Mills Gallery, also believes that the quality of works shown in the international art fairs in Hong Kong is high and that its popularity indicates a growing interest in contemporary art in the region. In her view, Art Basel Hong Kong 2016 made an effort to show museum-quality works, and audiences were fortunate to view these contemporary masterpieces in the fair (The Works 2016).

Hong Kong's international art fairs have also helped connect those interested in art in Asia and located within Asia to those with similar interests in the West. Dealers such as Leng Lin, Regional Partner of Pace Asia, and Neil Wenman, Senior Director of Hauser & Wirth, state that educating and forging links with new collectors in the region is as important as making sales (Qin 2016a, 2016b). Apart from displaying artworks, Art Central 2016 also conducted free workshops for educational purposes (The Works 2016). Dealers have been at pains to highlight their roles in educating collectors and the public alike.

Western galleries have also gained more exposure to artists from Asia through the global art market. Kathryn Erdman, Director of the New York-based 303 Gallery established in 1984, states that while they do not yet have any Asian artists in their program, they may change this strategy (The Works 2013). Observing how Asian collectors respond to the works by their represented artists and given the global market for art, they also feel they need to go beyond New York to exhibit their artists' works. Networking with the rest of the world to gain visibility, she states, is inevitable. Florian Weingrull, an emerging gallerist from Germany, states that gaining greater exposure for its artists is the most important role for a gallery, followed by developing a network of collectors and building trust with them (Money Magazine 2014). Weingrull states that he is now in his fourth year at the art fair in Hong Kong, and it was only in the third year that enough trust was built between his gallery and collectors from Korea and mainland China that they started acquiring works from him.

International art fairs and their impact on Hong Kong's local art world

Similar to Art Dubai (est. 2007), the leading international art fair in the Middle East, Africa, and South Asia, Art Hong Kong (2008–12) was a relatively young fair for relatively young emerging markets. Savita Apte, Director of Art Dubai at the time, stated that the large number of galleries in these fairs showed a regional overview of art in East Asia that people didn't have a chance to see in one place (The Works 2010). Art Hong Kong (2008–12) was positioned with the clear goal of providing opportunities to emerging local artists and regional galleries, giving them more exposure and establishing a market for them. The organizers of Art Hong Kong positioned the fair as one with an Asian flavor and geographical diversity. In Art Hong Kong 2011, the Art Futures section consisted of works by emerging artists from 44 galleries that were less than five years old, while in the Asia One section, galleries presented solo exhibitions by Asian artists (The Works 2011). The Art Futures Award to promote emerging artists went to Hong Kong artist Lee Kit in Art Hong Kong 2012.

While the organizers of international art fairs have made full use of Hong Kong for its strategic location, Hong Kong's own gallerists and artists also appear to have benefited financially from these international art fairs being located in Hong Kong. Lee Kit states that it is useful for local art organizations to promote and present local artists in the fair and that he has also learnt from the fair (The Works 2012). He feels that Hong Kong's own art scene is not as vibrant in terms of the commercial activity seen in international art fairs. Focusing on local artists, Joyce Lau of Exit Gallery says that it is of paramount significance to have an international art market platform in Hong Kong to show work by local artists, even if some of them have already shown their works elsewhere (The Works 2012). However, of the approximately 20 locally based galleries taking part in Art Hong Kong 2012, few featured works solely by Hong Kong artists (The Works 2012).

Given the growing market for art from the Asia Pacific region, Art Central provided a platform for a new generation of regional artists in its 'Rise Sector' in 2015. Sandy Angus of Art Central states that Asian art is developing, that it is at an exciting stage and one of the goals of Art Central is to display more work by Asian artists, in contrast to Art Basel Hong Kong which keeps an even balance between Asian and other artists (The Works 2015). Hong-Kong-based artist Vivian Poon was the winner of the 'Rise Award' in 2015, which she saw as a chance to increase her profile with both local and overseas audiences. Poon is of the view that different events are needed in the world of art and that while Art Basel Hong Kong is a high-end event exhibiting well-established artists' works, other kinds of art fair are needed to fill the gaps (The Works 2015).

Apart from providing an international art market platform for local artists through the mostly local galleries that represent them, international art fairs have also given their local and international audiences opportunities to access and discuss issues relating to local art and cultural history, often through the involvement of independent non-profit organizations. As education partner of the fair since its inception, the Hong Kong-based organization, Asia Art Archive, has organized a series of annual 'Backroom Conversations,' at the art fair. In Art Hong Kong 2012, they featured a case study of the short-lived Artist Village in Oil Street, examining Hong Kong's cultural history and the subjectivity of memory. Claire Hsu, Co-Founder and Executive Director of Asia Art Archive, states their goal as educational partner to the art fair is to provide a different platform within the fair, for a discussion of issues related to the production of art that might otherwise be left out of the fair context (The Works 2012).

Hong Kong's international art fairs have helped increase the representation of local artists internationally (The Works 2013). Local gallerist Henry Au-yeung of Grotto Fine Art states that Art Basel Hong Kong 2013 has been inclusive in presenting art by Hong Kong's artists and has not treated Hong Kong simply as a place to trade artworks (Lau 2013b). Local gallerist Johnson Chang sees a ripple effect of benefit for local artists through greater media exposure. He sees Hong Kong as a salesroom, attracting more buyers to come. But in addition to greater opportunities to trade artworks, he is of the view that more platforms for contemporary art create democratic platforms for free expression (Money Magazine 2014). Out of a total of 245 galleries at Art Basel Hong Kong, having 24 galleries from Hong Kong is a testament to the strength of Hong Kong's local art scene (Money Magazine 2014). Both Henry Au-yeung and Art Consultant Sandra Walters highlight that Art Basel Hong Kong 2013 and 2014 were inclusive in showcasing Hong Kong artists and point to Cat Street Gallery, one of the 19 Hong Kong galleries taking part in Art Central 2015, presenting a group exhibition featuring entirely local artists (Money Magazine 2014).

There are however differing views on the impact that international art fairs have had for local artists. Hong Kong artist Gum Cheng states that there were at least five to eight art fairs in 2013 but he was not sure how local artists benefited from them (The Works 2013). That is, while local artists have taken part in these art fairs and have been able to showcase their works, art practices in Hong Kong have developed slowly. Another local artist Clara Cheung believes that Hong Kong is in danger of ending up with an art market but no art if artistic development in Hong Kong does not grow in its complexity and variety (The Works 2013). Both Cheng and Cheung are concerned with the relatively weak local development in artistic practice in contrast to the vibrant development of the art market, brought about by the art fairs in Hong Kong in recent years.

A variety of local, independently organized artistic and cultural events have accompanied Art Basel Hong Kong 2014 and 2015. Responding to the influx of international art audiences that have accompanied the art fairs, local galleries, private art spaces and artists' studios in Hong Kong have thrown open their doors to show works to these visitors. The auxiliary art activities during Art Basel Hong Kong 2014 for example included the Chai Wan Mei festival of hip bars, where artists, photographers, and designers rented warehouses in Chai Wan – a somewhat disused industrial area – turning them into pop-up studios and even loft homes, against zoning regulations. The two driving forces behind the Chai Wan event were Platform China and 10 Chancery Lane, both local galleries that curated a series of guerrilla art installations in the hallways and elevators of an industrial building (Lau 2014). Adeline Ooi states that visitors would not have expected art exhibitions to take place in the warehouse spaces in Chai Wan, Hong Kong (Lau 2015); and Art Basel Hong Kong 2014 encouraged its visitors to explore the alternative spaces in Chai Wan and in SoHo, Hong Kong's more established art district (Lau 2014). Knowing that international buyers, critics, and art enthusiasts would be in town in large numbers for Art Basel Hong Kong 2015, many galleries, artists, and local art groups moved their open days and events to the same dates as the art fair – notably the Fotanian Open Studios 2015, an art community in the New Territories – in what has been dubbed Hong Kong Art Week (The Works 2015).

Established local artist Wilson Shieh, who also participated in Art Basel Hong Kong 2015 and received visitors in his studio in Fotan, has been witness to developments in the local art scene over the past two decades. He states that many thriving local artists would not have thought of becoming full-time artists when they graduated from art school a couple of decades ago. At that time, Hong Kong was a stop-off point for collectors to carry on to Beijing. He himself would not have anticipated an art scene like the one he witnessed in Hong Kong in 2015 (Lau 2015). Other commentators from outside Hong Kong have made similar observations. Curator Hans Ulrich Obrist for example talks about the influence of the art fair beyond the exhibition hall, which he observes as catalyzing greater creativity and communication as evidenced in the independently organized art-related activities in the city in 2015 (The Works 2015). Local collector William Lim believes that the launch of Art Basel Hong Kong in 2013 has brought the art world's attention to Hong Kong, observing that major international galleries have developed a presence in the city and work with Hong Kong artists (Lim 2014). He points to the fact that curators and museum directors in Hong Kong are planning exhibitions for Hong Kong artists, while museums including the Hong Kong Museum of Art, M+, and the Guggenheim have started collecting works by local artists. Lim anticipates that the Hong Kong art scene will see more growth and relatively small collectors like him will give way to larger museum collections. There are now more budgets for Hong Kong artists to produce large-scale works and even young graduates are approached by galleries, indicating that the price of their artworks may well rise.

Lim implies that Art Basel Hong Kong has had a significant impact on the local art market and practices, and that since 2013 local artists have had more opportunities for sales and to be placed in collections, through both art fairs and acquisitions by museums. With the opening up of the commercial art market, more students of the arts might consider pursuing a career in the creative and cultural industries. On the other hand, some local artists remain outside this system. Debevoise points to seasoned artists such as Tozer Pak, who clearly grew up without an art market and works outside of that reference point (Debevoise 2014).

Conclusion

In summary, Hong Kong's geographical location, English-speaking environment, and favorable institutional and commercial structure has attracted both galleries and collectors from across the world. This has offered networking opportunities not just to local and regional galleries but also to those from elsewhere – all of whom have been able to widen their access to a range of collectors – within Asia, the Asia Pacific region and beyond. The art fairs in Hong Kong have offered international art market platforms for local emerging artists *and* galleries in Asia. Both have had opportunities to showcase their works to an international audience, to meet each other, and to widen their networks. Art fair audiences, both local and those that have flown in from elsewhere, have benefited from the curated exhibitions at the fair and the educational opportunities that have run alongside the fairs, be these workshops, talks, discussion forums, or simply exposure to different types of art. Local audiences have been able to access museum-quality art and have had opportunities to see a far wider range of artistic practice than they would otherwise have access to through the cultural programs in Hong Kong. International audiences meanwhile have been able to gain, under one roof, an insight into artistic practices and associated ideas and issues in the region. All these features combined imply that international art fairs in Hong Kong have fostered more interest and more trade in contemporary art by emerging artists in Asia and greater interest in contemporary Asian art as a whole. Developing from Art Hong Kong (2008–12) to Art Basel Hong Kong (2013–) and Art Central (2015–), an Asian contemporary art network within the global international contemporary art arena is now clearly established. Yet, the overall artistic and cultural development of each of the regions is constrained by its specific artistic institutions and cultural policies in addition to the art market. To which direction they are heading is still too soon to anticipate.

References

Art Basel, Year 45 (2014) Catalog, Eslite Gallery: Interview with Emily Chao. Zurich: JRP/Ringier, p. 261.

Chee, G. (2017) Get to know the 15 biggest art collectors in Hong Kong. *Hong Kong Tatler* (28.3.2017). https://hk.asiatatler.com/life/Get-To-Know-The-15-Biggest-Art-Collectors-In-Hong-Kong [accessed December 27, 2017].

Ching, K., Debevoise, J., Lim, W., McHugh, F., Mong, A., Nittve, L., and Renfrew, M. (2014) Future perfect? In *The No Colors: William Lim, Living Collection. Hong Kong.* Ostfildern: Hatje Cantz Verlag, pp. 286–7, 289, 292, 294–5.

Chow, V. (2015) Hong Kong needs more private museums … say private museum operators. *South China Morning Post* (8.12.2015). http://www.scmp.com/news/hong-kong/education-community/article/1888134/we-need-20-or-30-private-museums [accessed December 25, 2017].

Debevoise, J., Ching, K., Lim, W., McHugh, F., Mong, A., Nittve, L., and Renfrew, M. (2014) Future perfect? In *The No Colors: William Lim, Living Collection. Hong Kong.* Ostfildern: Hatje Cantz Verlag, pp. 286–7.

Hong Kong Arts Administrators Association Website (2016) http://www.hkaaa.org.hk/doc/11428 [accessed May 9, 2016].

Hong Kong Monthly Digest of Statistics: The Cultural and Creative Industries in Hong Kong. March 2014. Hong Kong: Census and Statistics Department, Hong Kong Special Administrative Region, pp. FB1–15.

Lau, J. (2013a) Hong Kong art festival's new look. *The New York Times* (28.5.2016). The Arts/Cultural Desk.

Lau, J. (2013b) Hong Kong welcomes the art world. *The New York Times* (23.5.2013). The Arts/Cultural Desk.

Lau, J. (2014) Hong Kong nourishes local arts scene. *The New York Times* (15.5.2014). http://www.nytimes.com/2014/05/15/arts/international/hong-kong-nourishes-loca-arts-scene.html [accessed April 25, 2016].

Lau, J. (2015) Art Basel shows how far Hong Kong has come. *The New York Times* (13.3.2015). http://www.nytimes.com/2015/03/14/arts/international/art-basel-shows-how-far-hong-kong-has-come.html [accessed April 25, 2016].

Lim, W. (2014) The scholars and the no colors. In *The No Colors: William Lim, Living Collection, Hong Kong*. Ostfildern: Hatje Cantz Verlag, p. 18.

Money Magazine (2014) *Art Basel Hong Kong: A Portrait*, TVB Pearl, 25 May. [TV program]

Qin, A. (2015a) For an art fair, it's all in the timing. *The New York Times* (14.3.2015). https://global.factiva.com/ga/default.aspx [accessed April 25, 2016].

Qin, A. (2015b) Art Basel HK: the reviews are in; collectors from east and west drive sales at 3rd edition of the fair. *International New York Times* (19.3.2015).

Qin, A. (2016a) Art Basel Hong Kong opens to less frenzy. *The New York Times* (24.3.2016). http://www.nytimes.com/2016/03/24/arts/international/art-basel-hong-kong.html [accessed April 25, 2016].

Qin, A. (2016b) Dealers report strong sales at Art Basel Hong Kong. *The New York Times* (28.3.2016), p. C3 (L).

The Works (2010) *Hong Kong International Art Fair 2010*, 1 June, RTHK. [TV program]

The Works (2012) *ARTHK12*, RTHK, 22 May. [TV program]

The Works (2013) *Art Basel Hong Kong 2013,* RTHK 28 May. [TV program]

The Works (2015) *Art Basel Hong Kong and Art Central*, RTHK 24 March. [TV program]

The Works (2016) *Art Basel and Art Central Special,* RTHK 30 March. [TV program]

Twigg, Melissa (2015a) Art talk: the young collectors – Jenny Chau. *Hong Kong Tatler* (26.3.2015). https://hk.asiatatler.com/life/art-talk-the-young-collectors-jenny-chau [accessed December 27, 2017].

Twigg, Melissa (2015b) Art talk: the young collectors – Kevin Poon. *Hong Kong Tatler* (27.3.2015). https://hk.asiatatler.com/life/art-talk-the-young-collectors-kevin-poon [accessed December 27, 2017].

Twigg, Melissa and Leanne Mirandilla (2015) Art talk: the young collectors – Alexandre Errera. *Hong Kong Tatler* (26.3.2015). https://hk.asiatatler.com/life/art-talk-the-young-collectors-alexandre-errera [accessed December 27, 2017].

Part IV

Cultural activism, diversity, and independent culture

20

Indie phenomenon and the creative industries in Thailand

Viriya Sawangchot

Introduction

During the past decades, the creativity of the youth in Thailand has been underrated by the Thai pop music industry. This is by no means surprising as the powerful demands of the market and the commercial logic of music businesses have guided industry expansion to its the farthest corners. However, since the 1990s alternative music movement, Thai youngsters have increasingly accessed music production and cultural space. Therefore, this chapter seeks to understand the roles played by key institutions of the Thai music industry, such as record labels and music programs on radio and TV, and critically consider the broader dynamic in which the rise and development of indie music led by youngsters has been influenced by these institutions and, at the same time, shown potential to stimulate the development of the broader creative industries.

Drawing on research into the music industry in Thailand particularly in Bangkok, I would like to show how the institutions of the music industry have contentiously shaped the contexts of the alternative music movement since the 1990s (Sawangchot 2006, 2013). Focusing on the indie music phenomenon in Thailand, I want to highlight not only how the culture of production informs the institutional context of the music industry (Toynbee 2000) but also how this leads to the rise of new platforms and practices of creative industries (Raunig 2012). In addition, I will also discuss how this process tended to be shaped by the creativities, beliefs, practices, and social relations (Frith 1996) of Bangkok youngsters in the mid-2000s.

In this chapter, I will, firstly, demonstrate how the music industry in Thailand not only generates economic benefits but can also make social contributions and, secondly, how indie music and its creators face a number of constraints in terms of access to the media and the lack of appropriate policy. The following section will introduce readers to the development of the popular music industry and its institutions in Thailand. The second section explores the alternative music movement in the mid-1990s, highlighting the culture of production of new independent record labels and their relationship with major media networks. The chapter then presents case studies of the second wave of alternative music movement, focusing on the creation of new platforms/spaces outside the music industry that eventually helped to boost the industry and the wider creative industries in the country. The final section will consider how we can better understand the practical underpinning of the Thai creative industries, particularly the music industry and its culture.

The era of major labels and the 'star system'

The Thai music industry has enjoyed certain economic liberties that few other Southeast Asian countries can make claim to since the 1980s. The Thai music industry revolves around two music companies RS Promotion and Grammy established in 1982 and 1983 respectively. As of the 1990s, the two companies essentially monopolized the local market. In 2012, Thailand's local music market was worth US $250 million, up from the 2008 revenue of US $238 million, and annual revenue is forecast to grow to reach US $396 million in 2017 (Marketeer 2014). The music industry is one of three important entertainment industries including the animation and film industry according to a report by the Department of International Trade Promotion, Ministry of Commerce (Keawmanee 2016).

Though Thai popular music has been heavily influenced by American rock culture since the mid-1950s, gaining access to the Thai market has been extremely difficult for multinational companies, partly because of complicated Thai laws on foreign investment and partly because of the stranglehold Thai companies have had on music distribution and promotion networks since the 1960s (Siriyuvasak 1992). Thai economic development picked up in the 1980s with the liberalization of trade, the pursuit of a strategy of export-oriented growth, and a tourist industry policy. The fast economic growth of Thailand created a wealthy urban middle class with a strong appetite for mass consumption around Bangkok, the capital city of Thailand (Phongpaichit and Baker 1997).

Although Thai government had a trade protection policy affecting the import of foreign cultural products such as film and recorded music from the early 1980s onwards, Thailand hosted many concerts featuring famous rock singers and musicians from Europe and the USA such as Rod Stewart, Tina Turner, Scorpion, Def Leppard, Hall & Oates, Christopher Cross. These concerts proved not only very successful in gaining large audiences but also brought international music companies coming to establish office in Thailand. From the early 1980s onwards, the local mass media industries expanded enormously with the development of a wide range of entertainment businesses, such as radio, printed media, film, and broadcasting. Undoubtedly, all these factors together fundamentally contributed to the music culture as well as business in Thailand (Eamsa-ard 2006; Wuttipong 2011). The Thai popular music industry started to develop highly manipulative marketing strategies and this was led by Thai major labels at that time. The music industry grew dramatically as each record company was releasing its own artists to compete with those of others through the 'star system' as music industries in other Asian countries did (Shunya 2000). As of the mid-1980s, RS Promotion and Grammy represented a new era in Thai music entertainment. It was the first time in the Thai music business that artists/singers were contractually bound to music companies, receiving percentage payments of the amount of albums sold (mostly in cassette format). In the past, radio played mostly foreign music so there were no national Thai music stars. So when the opportunity finally came for there to be a national music scene with Thai artists invented by the major companies, an 'explosion' of Thai music occurred. Interestingly, what started off as an imitation of American music has deviated into something that is, in a way, inherently Thai. The result was a formula for Thai music that is somewhere in between American rock and pop, C-Pop (Chinese), and J-Pop (Japanese) (Siriyuwasak 1992; Eamsa-ard 2006).

In the major label era, a music career turned out to be a decent work choice that never been available in Thailand before. While talent was valued, it was much more important to find artists who would appeal to the general public. To find talent to feed their entertainment business, schools to train celebrities were established. Wuttipong (2011) mentioned that the first step was to choose and screen artists who had some potential to be label artists or could be matched with a proposed project album by a producer or screening team. Then the music producing team composed songs which the artists then recorded. Once someone completed the music school, their next step was to release their first album. It did not really matter who they signed. The school system allowed the companies to decide who they felt would fit the mold of what they wanted, though most of the music sounded very similar albeit with quite different images. Thai artists usually did not have everlasting fame because of the ways they were treated. Their music was usually constructed by the music companies and there was not much room for artistic autonomy and flexibility. This was the production process for successful national artists such as Thongchai McIntyre (Grammy), Micro (Grammy), Novou (Grammy), Cristina (Grammy), Tao Khemkud (RS), Boy Scout (RS), Idthi' Phalaankuun (RS), etc. Hence, growing stars in this way became standard practice for other major labels founded after Grammy and RS, such as Kita Records, Creatia, Muzer, and Nithithat Promotion.

At the end of the 1980s, RS Promotion, Grammy, and Nithithat started to expand their business into radio and television broadcasting. They also owned radio programs to help promote their artists nationwide and made them by concessions from the military's broadcasting media (Siriyuvasak 1999). This horizontal media integration had a profound effect upon radio and television music charts, as the two major labels had control over a good majority of the music programs broadcast during this period. Moreover, live concerts broadcast on nationwide television such as Channel 7, Channel 5, and Channel 3 were mostly curated and sponsored by major labels and commercial brands. With the advent of cassettes tape (Limpichai 1989) and broadcasting networks of radio and television programs (Siriyuvasak 1992; Eamsa-ard 2006) coupled with the distribution power of the above three companies, Thailand had many national pop music stars in the 1990s. And, therefore, the music companies in Thailand formed the established regime of what Adorno and Horkheimer (2002) term 'the culture industry', where Grammy and RS Promotion essentially monopolized the music market.

It can be seen that from the mid-1980s to the early 1990s Thai major labels had a significant share in the local Thai popular music market dominated by pop rock and dance styles, the two most prevalent forms of popular music in this era (Wuttipong 2011). The role played by major labels in the Thai music industry and entertainment would continue until around the mid-1990s. This was when the alternative music movement and independent labels started to challenge the mainstream business platforms.

'Modern dog effect': the first wave of the alternative movement

During the 1990s, with high national growth rates, the musical and entertainment landscape of Thailand was undergoing a process of dramatic transformation. In the mid-1990s, Bangkok youngsters, who were predominately from middle-class families, started to make their own music, preferring to be in control of the musical work at every stage, from song writing to studio production. This led to many Thai young musicians learning how to write, compose, and play their own songs. The beginnings of the Thai alternative movement began then (Sawangchot 2006). In this section, I will examine the pattern that emerged in the

Thai music industry, focusing on how a change in creative production process as well as the introduction of new music genres from abroad led to the emergence of the Thai alternative music scene.

The interest in British alternative rock known as 'modern rock' in Thailand was started by Wasana Weerachadplee, a famous disc jockey who promoted this genre of British songs on her new independent radio program aired on 107 FM Radioactive in the early 1990s. Her program was filled with 1990s British bands such as Suede, The Stone Roses, The Jesus and Mary Chain, and Manic Street Preachers. Weerachadplee introduced British modern rock music, with her term 'modern rock', and its ethos to her listeners while Thai rock fans favored American grunge bands such as Nirvana, Pearl Jam, and Smashing Pumpkins at that time. Playing all the latest releases from the UK, Weerachadplee was able to acquaint Bangkok youngsters with the songs of the British alternative scene. While the terms 'British alternative' or 'American grunge rock' could be confusing, what is evident about the 'spirit' of British alternative rock was how the musicians were able to control every step of the music production process instead of being controlled by music companies. She noted that 'Good alternative music must change our ideas, and those who want to be in trend but never listen to modern rock cannot call themselves "modern"' (Weerachadplee 1993: 38).

Now some Bangkok youngsters started to search for their music and creative production through British alternative rock. As a result of these practices, Thai alternative rock bands, such as Crub and Modern Dog (coined by Weerachadpree's modern rock) started to emerge, creating a Thai alternative scene with strong influences from British alternative rock (Sawangchot 2007). Crub can be considered the first alternative music band in Thailand. The band members were students at King Mongkut Institute of Technology Ladkrabang, in a suburb of Bangkok. Crub's music was dominated by guitars, bass, and drums and sung in a style reminiscent of British alternative bands such as Charlatans and The Stone Roses. The band's control over the music production process was highlighted by Rungrot Ooppathumpothiwat, the bassist with Crub, who stated 'We recorded our songs in our free time from our jobs. We also did record in our home studio. We used a drum machine in the early stages and then changed to real drummer when we perform live' (Ooppathumpothiwa 1996: 45). Without promotional videos or live shows on television programs like artists from major labels, Crub's songs were not popular among young audiences. They rose to prominence by playing live gigs at universities, mostly in Bangkok, and their performances inspired other university students, particularly in arts and architecture, to form their own bands. It can be seen that Crub was the first Thai alternative band that attempted to blend their creativity and work ethic in the creation of a new Thai pop music aesthetic in the 1990s.

While Crub was never popular, it was Modern Dog, the winner of the Coke Music Award in 1992 when the members of the band were students at Chulalongkorn University, that effectively stirred interest in the alternative music movement in Thailand with their debut album, *Serm Sukaphaph*, released by Bakery Music in 1994. Tanachai Ujjin, Modern Dog's lead singer and song writer, described the 'spirit' of an alternative artist-musician where 'In the past, we used to play cover versions and we didn't know if we could write our own tunes. I feel that we or anyone can make their own music if they have the opportunity. We knew that we could make it and we did. Every musician in Thailand can produce his own album' (Ujjin 1996: 7). In contrast to Crub, Modern Dog's music style was influenced by American grunge bands rather than British alternative, due to the influence of their producer, Sukie Komolsukosol Clapp, who lived in America for a couple of years. This could be seen in the guitar riff in their hit track 'Busaba' echoing Nirvana's 'Smell Like Teen Spirit'.

Modern Dog's debut enjoyed a huge success, selling 500,000 copies. Due to the popularity of 'alternative' music, many Bangkok youngsters picked up their guitars and formed their own bands. While the exact numbers of Thai alternative bands formed at that time are unclear, a journalist reporter has indicated that 300 bands were formed (Ginsak 1999) because of the 'Modern Dog effect' (Sawangchot 2013).

The 'Modern Dog Effect' resulted in a huge market share loss for major labels due to the rise of new independent labels such as Bakery Music, Milestone, Stone Entertainment, Eastern Sky and many artist-run labels. Grammy was the first to strike back immediately. Grammy ventured into the alternative music market with solo artist Ashita Pramoj na Ayudhaya. Ashita was a young model who was educated in England and was completely different from other pop singers with Grammy. However, his album production was exactly the same as for other artists produced by Grammy's star system. As a result, except for the first track, there was nothing else about the other tracks in his debut that were of the alternative rock genre. In addition, Grammy opened a new sub-label for alternative bands, More Music Co., Ltd. led by veteran Thai rocker Asanee Chotikul. More Music released many successful alternative albums.

The growth of the Thai alternative scene can also be attributed to the arrival of international music labels such as Sony Music, EMI, WEA, and BMG (Sawangchot 2007). These companies wanted a share in the Thai music market. A good example is Nakarin Ginsak who released his debut single with Sony Music (Thailand). Nakarin graduated from Chulalongkorn University where he had formed a duo pop band, Hydra, with his friend in the late 1980s. In 1996, he worked as a product manager at Sony Music and was signed as the label's first alternative artist. His 1996 debut, *Kai Pang*, sold over 1 million copies and made him as 'alternative superstar'.

Interestingly, most Bangkok middle-class youngsters formed their bands with the aim of signing with independent and major labels to do the recording. They wanted to be 'studio bands' rather than rely on playing live gigs because of the amount of money to be gained from selling records. Therefore, like the major labels' star system, music producers and business people still played important roles in making the alternative scene fashionable in Thailand in the late 1990s. They possessed an authority in both the creative process and image making (Sawangchot 2006). The role of the media cannot be underestimated as well. While many bands tried to bypass the major label platforms during this time, alternative bands would not have emerged if they have not had the support of mainstream media such as radio stations, music magazines, television programs, and in particular new cable television airing both Thai and Western music. Meanwhile, only a few alternative media emerged at that time. Winit Lertratanachai, the head DJ of Pirate Radio, a new commercial radio channel, commented that 'Our policy is to play songs regardless of labels, underground or mainstream, we play them all' (Letrattanachai 1996: 42).

Most alternative bands emerged between 1994 and 1997 but faded out after the release of one or two albums due to business failure. It can therefore be concluded that the formation of alternative music in the mid-1990s in Thailand was a part of the evolution of the mainstream Thai music industry and, hence, the major labels continued to hold a significant share of the music market. It should be also noted that the alternative music scene was dominated by the well-educated Thai middle class. Arguably, their education backgrounds and understanding of artistic creation contributed not only to their ideas of music production but also their careers. I would like to discuss this issue after talking about the second waves of Thai alternative movement in the next section.

'Panda effect': the second wave of the alternative movement

The 1997 Asian financial crisis radically altered the climate for the Thai economy. The Thai government devalued the country's currency and launched the vastly successful 'Amazing Thailand' tourist campaign, aimed at luring Western tourists and foreign capital. The financial crisis resulted in the Thai government struggling to reconstruct its economy through various means. Surprisingly, media industries such as music, film, and broadcasting were not affected by the crisis. The government encouraged its people to 'buy Thai' in order to help local businesses, and even music fans responded to the campaign by turning to Thai popular music products.

Moreover, following the political uprising in May 1992, the Thai broadcasting media system was heavily pressurized to reform, and this issue was considered when the new 1997 Constitution was being drafted. However, the 1997 Constitution was concerned with the legitimacy of the ownership of broadcasters by government agencies, rather than the possibility of a broader media reform (Siriyuvasak 1999). Due to the delay in decentralizing the centralized broadcasting system of Thailand, particularly radio (re-regulation for state, community, and business sectors) in 1999, Yutthana Bun-Om and his colleagues invented Click Radio Ltd, a new platform of radio programs, launching three new channels: Get 102.5 FM, 103.5 Love FM and 104. 5 Fat Radio. Interestingly, Yutthana had experiences in sales and marketing with A-Time media company, a sub-business sector of Grammy, and was also the coordinator of the Coke Music Award; he then devised new strategies to run the this new platform. He talked about his vision as follows: 'I want to have a private radio station … to have my own studio and to have enough equipment such as CD player, microphone, and transmission device. Importantly, if I have it, I could play music anytime I want to and I could play any kind of music I want. At the present, as a media professional, I can't criticize the songs that I play. Moreover, the audiences don't either. I think pirate radio will become participatory media' (interviewed on May 20, 2004).The advent of Click Radio's 104.5 Fat Radio in particular, including the Fat Music Festival starting in 2001, led to a rise of 'indie communities' that changed not only Thai popular music but also the nation's creative scene broadly. The Fat Festivals were always crowded by university students who came to sell and buy creative products such as CDs, photographs, handmade souvenirs, and so on. In particular, both radio programs and music festivals affected the indie music scene and the power of Bangkok youngsters in the music business significantly in the post-Asian financial crisis years (Sawangchot 2007). Subsequently, as young artists/musicians had their own channels to promote their work and manage their creative endeavors, new platforms of music began to emerge in the early 2000s. In the following paragraphs, I would like to elaborate on two examples of such platforms: SO:ON Dry Flower (SODF) and Panda Records.

In the case of Panda Records, Wannarit Pongprayoon, its owner, is a member of three bands. He is also an organizer of Noise Market Festival and a co-organizer of Stone Free Festival. He is a guest lecturer in music production courses in many universities in Bangkok. He finished his first degree in the Faculty of Engineering at King Mongkut Institute of Technology, Bangkok, where he formed an alternative band, Meow Eui, with his university friends in 1999 and released an album via a new independent record label, Eastern Sky Records. He started Panda Records by chance, when his friends asked him to mix their new album *Pongprayoon*: 'There are lots of music styles out there that might not fit the mainstream but are also good. There are a lot of bands that work really hard to make their albums. They should be supported; otherwise, they might disappear from the scene' (interviewed on August 17, 2013).

Thus, Panda Records was on a mission to encourage and spread music coming from the underground and showing a DIY aesthetic. Redtwenty was the first band that released an album with Panda Records. In 2001, the members of the band came to Pongprayvoon's house with their demo tape recording done in their home studio. Pongprayoon spent a year helping them release their debut album. In the early years, around 20 indie bands signed to release their music with this company. Due to financial issues, Panda Records Ltd, was forced to close in 2006 but returned as a music project. Panda Records changed its business strategies and now organizes monthly music gigs called 'panda showcase', in whatever venues that the bands could play in such as pubs, restaurants, art galleries, sidewalks, etc. Artists working with Panda Records also take part in many annual music festivals in Thailand such as Fat Festival, Big Mountain, Tiger Translate and more.

In 2012, Pongprayoon and his colleagues created the alternative music festival, the Stone Free Festival to help the Thai music indie community. This three-day music festival took place in Saraburi province, 60 kilometers from Bangkok. The festival did not have any sponsors and the entrance fee was cheap (500 baht). It ended up in debt, and one month after the event, fans of Panda Records organized a small music event to raise money to help the festival organizer. This demonstrates the idea of a social community coming together to help an indie music business, which had never happened before within the Thai music industry. From 2013 to the present, Pongprayoon and his colleagues have received funding from Museum Siam, a public organization under the Thai government, to organize an art and music event helping young creative people. The event called 'noise market' has been held at the Museum Siam office in Bangkok. In many aspects, Panda Records serves a new platform of music business in Thailand. Pongprayoon always says, 'Panda Records is not in the music business for profit anymore, but for the fun and fulfilment creative music can bring' (interviewed on August 17, 2013). Panda Records has now become the longest run independent music project in Thailand, supported by college-student-based fans who are interested in post-rock and experimental music.

Another music project that I would like to discuss is SO:ON Dry Flower (SODF), a Japanese-run music project based in Bangkok. It was born from the shared interests and passion of like-minded Japanese musicians and their Thai friends who were looking to change the Thai music scene. The process of creating new cultural spaces for music in Bangkok by SODF is exemplified by the endeavors made by one of its founders Koichi Shimizu who is a Japanese national based in Bangkok. He had experience of New York's underground music scene as he had lived and studied in New York previously. When he first arrived in Thailand, he found it extremely difficult to create new music spaces in Bangkok. This was at the time when there was an upsurge of new musicians in the underground music scene in Bangkok, developing their experimental music with no established music events to showcase their work. So he decided to start his own: 'SODF started from friendship. We don't limit our genre of music. Basically, we accept that all kinds of music inspire us' (interviewed June 13, 2010).

After Koichi interacted with some Thai art and architecture students who were musicians, he found ways to create his own music space by finding new music venues which were not dominated by brands and sponsors. Sompob Pruntrikrak, a lead guitarist in the Thai post-rock band Assajan Jakkawan, describes how he found out about SODF: 'I searched in MySpace to learn about SODF and registered to be their friend. We also have a MySpace page for Assajan Jakawan and one day Napat Snidwong na Ayudhay,a who knew Koichi Shimizu very well, listened to our songs on MySpace and advised us to send our songs to SODF. Then we started to think about recording our music seriously' (interviewed July 17, 2010). In mid-2006, Koichi and Assajan Jakkawanhad held the first live gig under an umbrella of the SODF project at About Café/About Studio, a new art space in Bangkok Old Town.

In 2008, SODF set up their live house called SOL (Soul of Liberty) to produce a series of small venues in the post-rock and experimental scene, both commercial and non-commercial spaces helping to boost music spaces outside the mainstream music business. SODF artists do take part in big music festivals in the country organized by Thai big media and brands such Fat Music Festival and Big Mountain Concert. Being connected to alternative music scenes in Asia, some bands such as Desktop Error and Plot have been invited to play gigs in Hong Kong, Japan, and Singapore. SODF held the first ever international post-rock concerts in Bangkok and invited Asian bands such as Mono, a Japanese post-rock band, in 2010 and Mogwai in 2012 to showcase their works in Thailand. SODF also organized interesting conceptual gigs such as Make Noise Not War in 2011 and 2012. Most artists working with SODF are free to think and create their own works but, ironically, they have other jobs or business to making their living. SODF was closed in 2016 because Koichi wanted to pursue his solo musical work and tour in many countries. Yet, most bands that used to work with SODF are still active in the Bangkok music scene.

Panda Records and SODF show the ways in which the culture of production and the creative processes of indie music are grounded in the development of new musical genres, spaces, and creative milieus, not mainstream businesses. It can be urged, as seen from the history of Thai indie music, that major companies are capable of manipulating the popular music genre/market as well as providing cultural spaces. The new platforms for indie music such as Panda Records and SODF definitely occupy a marginal location, but their importance as a symbol of challenge to the commercial logic of the industry should be duly recognized.

Understanding Thai creative industries: theory and practice

While a number of recent studies have provided important insights into the economic benefits of the creative industries as a whole (Caves 2000; Hartley 2005; Hesmondhalgh 2002; Barrowclough and Kozul-Wright 2008; Flew 2012; Power and Scott 2004), few studies have focused on the music industry (Pratt 2008; Power and Hallencreutz 2004). Similarly, there is a lack of interest in the contribution of youth culture to the creative industries (cf., Frith et al. 2008). In this sense, this chapter provides an alternative view of the creative industries by highlighting the dynamics of Thai youth culture and the culture of music production in and out of the Thai music industry, which is indicative of what is happening in the creative industries in Thailand. The thesis that I want to propose is a simple one: we cannot understand or explain the development of Thai creative industries by merely examining economic indicators; rather, we need to look deeper into the emerging dynamics between youth culture, indie culture making, the influences of new genres and styles coming from abroad, changing platforms as well as the operation of the existing institutions of the industries. I would like to illustrate my case by discussing the first and the second waves of alternative music movement and how these waves have interacted with the institutions of the Thai music industry. A key finding is the capability of mainstream businesses such as Grammy and RS Promotion that are of large scale and well-resourced and their efforts to absorb the first wave of the alternative movement. The platforms of the first wave such as studio bands, radio programs, independent record labels and production processes cannot establish a real advance in creative production in music space; they only define its semi-autonomy through the mainstream of the pop music market dominated by the major labels. The 'indie phenomenon' driven by the second wave, which initially started in the mid-2000s, has created the idea that one should try to avoid working in the field of commercial media production in general and make one's own musical projects/spaces, platforms outside the mainstream music industry dominated by a few recording and broadcasting companies. These new platforms are characterized by no signed contracts, no sponsors, live houses, music festivals and so on. They tend to be project-based, collaborative, and temporary. This is close to what Raunig (2012) calls 'non-institutions'.

This practice of 'non-institutions' involves not only a sense of creativity that everyone in the world can have (McRobbie 2001), but also the social relation of creative production/participation on which creative industries are to be formed (Sawangchot 2013). To understand the social relation of production/participation of these non-institutions, I would like to point out a possible way of making sense of how music production in Thailand has now changed from the 'star system' in the major label era to the semi-autonomy of the alternative movement and then to flexible systems centred around the project-based creative spaces of the indie phenomenon. Contesting the creative industries models, which are generally defined as 'industries' (Moeran and Alcovaska 2012; O'Connor 2010; Flew 2012; Henry 2007; Hesmondhalgh 2002; Garnham 2005; Hesmondhalgh and Pratt 2005), the indie phenomenon in Thailand shows that the grounded spaces of creative industries have developed into a set of 'non-institutions' instead of large-scale clusters or state-funded cultural projects. Here non-institutions must be described as a key factor in the development of the creative industries (Raunig 2012).

The alternative movement of the 1990s, since its very beginnings in the Thai popular music scene, had usually been perceived as being open to a metropolitan, trendy, and sophisticated society. The indie phenomenon of the second wave seems to interact with a culture of experimental music and a new route for Asian music culture. While the first wave has enjoyed its business position as well as the cultural production of the middle class (Sawangchot 2006), the indie phenomenon has been seen by some media and music critics as something creative, ordinary, and anti-establishment (Sawangchot 2013). Moreover, in the Thai music industry, the indie phenomenon provides a clear depiction of the transition from cultural industries to creative industries. This transition is led by a series of changes that progressively affected not only the ways in which youth culture functions but also the way the real economic value of the music industry is produced.

It should be noted that the social relation of production/participation through non-institutions such as Panda Records and SODF is dominated by the practice of middle-class youth, especially in Bangkok, who find that the practices of non-institution provide them with flexible creative spaces regarding identity, work, and leisure. Hence, the study of creative industries in Thailand should be increasingly focused on the issue of the contested space of creativity in everyday life beyond measuring economic impacts such as employment or revenue. Here, the key is to understand the social relation of production/participation in which the implications of a particular process of creative works can be explored from the ground.

Conclusion

Looking at the development of indie music in Thailand in recent decades, this chapter focuses on the alternative and then post-alternative indie movements. The findings help us to look beyond those familiar economic accounts of creative industries and understand complicated social interactions and dynamics where these industries are embedded. While musicians with major labels are limited in how they can express themselves, indie musicians have been freer to experiment and make their own music. Based on the findings above,

I would like to stress that the creative industries, including the music industry, are relationally and situationally constructed and formed by bottom-up networks of creative milieu. This implies that understanding of the formation and operation of various 'non-institutions' of culture-making is essential to enhance our knowledge of the creative industries in their broad sense.

Acknowledgments

This chapter could not have been written without the help of many people. First and foremost, I would like to thank the late Lorraine Lim who gave me invaluable comment on an early version of this chapter. I would like to thank all key creative informants in the Thai music industry. And above all, I would like to thank Professor Swapan Bhattacharrya, Department of Sociology, Calcutta University, India, whose advice and explanations have always been available.

References

Adorno, T. and Horkheimer, M. (2002) The culture industry: enlightenment as mass deception. In Adorno, T. and Horkheimer, M. (2002) *Dialect of Enlightenment.* California: Stanford University Press, pp. 41–72.

Barrowclough, D. and Kozul-Wright, Z. (2008) *Creative Industries and Developing Countries.* London: Routledge.

Caves, R. (2000) *Creative Industries.* Cambridge, MA: Harvard University Press.

Eamsa-ard, L. (2006) Thai popular music: the representation of national identities and ideologies within a culture in transition. Dissertation, Edith Cowan University.

Flew, T. (2012) *Creative Industries.* London: Sage.

Frith, S., Cloonan, M. and Williamson, J. (2008) On music as a creative industry. In A.C. Pratt and P. Jeffcutt (eds.), *Creativity, Innovation and the Cultural Economy.* London: Routledge, pp. 74–88.

Garnham, N. (2005) From cultural to creative industries. *International Journal of Cultural Policy,* 11(1): 15–30.

Ginsak, N. (1996) Thai Alternative. *Bangkok Post Sunday Magazine,* 35(25): 5.

Hartley, J. (2005) *Creative Industries.* London: Blackwell.

Henry, C. (2007) *Entrepreneurship in the Creative Industries.* Massachusetts: Edward Elgar.

Hesmondhalgh, D. (2002) *The Cultural Industries.* London: Sage.

Hesmondhalgh, D. and Pratt, A. C. (2005) Cultural industries and cultural policy. *International Journal of Cultural Policy,* 11(1): 1–15.

Keawmanee, R. (2014) Entertainment industry in the development of creative industries. http://thainews.prd.co.th/ (accessed October 17, 2016).

Letrattanachai, W. (1996) *Nation Junior Magazine,* 14(95): 42.

Limpichai, S. (1989) The Role of Cassette Tape Business in Thai Music Industry. Masters Thesis, Faculty of Communicative Art, Chulalongkorn University.

Marketeer (2014) Segments of Thai music market. http://marketeer.co.th/ (accessed September 20, 2016).

McRobbie, A. (2001) Everyone is creative: artist as new economy pioneer. https://www.opendemocracy.net/node/652/ (accessed June 15, 2016).

Moeran, B. and Alačovska, A. (eds.) (2012) *Creative Industries: Critical Reading.* London: Berg.

O'Connor, J. (2010) The definition of cultural industries. *The European Journal of Arts Education,* 2(3): 5–27.

Ooppathumpothiwat, R. (1996) Thai alternative. *Bangkok Post Sunday Magazine,* 35(25): 14.

Phongpaichit, P. and Baker, C. (1997) *Thailand: Economy and Politics.* London: Oxford University Press.

Power, D. and Hallencreutz, D. (2004) Profiting from creativity? The music industry in Stockholm, Sweden and Kingston, Jamaica. In Power, D. and Scott, A.J. (eds.), *Cultural Industries and the Production of Culture.* London: Routledge, pp. 224–41.

Power, D. and Scott, A. J. (eds.) (2004) *Cultural Industries and the Production of Culture*. London: Routledge.
Pratt, A. (2008) The music industry and its potential role in local economic development: the case of Senegal. In Barrowclough, D. and Kozul-Wright, Z. (eds.), *Creative Industries and Developing Countries*. London: Routledge, pp. 130–44.
Raunig, G. (2012) Creative industries as mass deception. In Ray, G., Raunig, G. and Wuggenig, U. (eds.), *Critique of Creativity*. San Francisco: MayFly, pp. 191–202.
Sawangchot, V. (2006) New labour or new elite: hybridizing Britpop into Thai pop music. *Journal of Communication Art*, 25(4): 63–71.
Sawangchot, V. (2007) Cool media and sub-cultural economy: Bangkokianyouth in the post-economic crisis. Paper presented at Workshop on Asia Pop Music in Transition: New Economy, New Subjectivities and Inter-Asia Perspective, March 3–4, 2007, National University of Singapore.
Sawangchot, V. (2013) *Youth Culture and Bangkok Creative Industries*. Bangkok: Department of Cultural Promotion, Ministry of Culture.
Shunya, Y. (2000) Consuming 'America': from symbol to system. In Ben-Huat, C. (ed.), *Consumption in Asia: Lifestyles and Identities*. London: Routledge, pp. 202–24.
Siriyuvasak, U. (1992) Radio in a Transitional Society: The Case of Modern Thailand. Dissertation, University of Leicester.
Siriyuvasak, U. (1999) *The Political Economy of Thai Broadcasting System and Its Effect to Human Life* (in Thai). Bangkok: Chulalongkon University Press.
Toynbee, J. (2000) *Making Popular Music: Musicians, Creativity and Institutions*. London: Oxford University Press.
Ujjin, T. (1996) Thai alternative. *Bangkok Post Sunday Magazine*, 35(25): 15.
Weerachadplee, W. (1993) Interview. *BunteangKhadi Magazine*, 4(48): 16.
Wuttipong, N. (2011) The Thai Popular Music Industry: Industrial Form and Music Design. Dissertation, University of Nottingham.

Interviews

Bun-Om, Y. Interview by author. Personal interview, Bangkok, May 20, 2004.
Pruntrikrak, S. Interview by author. Personal interview, Bangkok, July 20, 2009.
Pongprayoon, W. Interview by author. Personal interview, Bangkok, August 17, 2013.
Shimizu, K. Interview by author. Personal interview, Bangkok, June 13, 2010.

21

Young, creative, and independent

Cinema Lovers Community (CLC) Purbalingga and its strategies to enliven independent filmmaking in Indonesia

Novi Kurnia

Introduction: independent filmmaking in *Reformasi* Indonesia

From 1998 Indonesia entered a period of transition to democracy after experiencing 32 years of authoritarian government under Suharto's New Order regime. A new political era called *Reformasi* emerged, ushering in social, political, and cultural change. With these changes, a new landscape for Indonesian cinema surfaced and was signified by the flourishing of film communities which have led to the revitalization and redefinition of independent filmmaking in Indonesia.

It was the film *Kuldesak* (Dead End) (1998) that challenged the New Order's bureaucratic and complicated system of filmmaking by offering a new culture of Indonesian independent filmmaking (see Clark 2004; Setiawan 2009; van Heeren 2012; Hughes-Freeland 2011; Kurnia 2014; Yngvesson 2015). *Kuldesak* is a 103-minute omnibus film of four stories about the lives of four young people in Jakarta, each written and directed by four new directors: two women (Mira Lesmana and Nan Achnas) and two men (Riri Riza and Mantovani). *Kuldesak* challenged the authoritarian and patriarchal culture of the New Order in several ways: it symbolized the emergence of a new generation of filmmakers seeking to start a new culture of Indonesian cinema at the turn of twenty-first century; it represented the hybrid identities of young Indonesian consumers of global cultures seen in the characters in the film and in the filmmakers; and it pointed towards gender equity in filmmaking as two of the directors are men and two are women (Kurnia 2014: 152). *Kuldesak* contained a spirit and enthusiasm of 'making-your-own-film' showing that anyone could make a film anywhere in Indonesia, particularly during the period 1999 to mid-2001 of the *Reformasi* era (Ratna 2007: 4; van Heeren 2012: 52).

Reformasi filmmaking clearly does not refer only to the production of mainstream films, but also independent (sidestream) films (Pudjiati and Kusumaryati 2011: 2; Kurnia 2008: 139). Mainstream films are mostly produced by Jakarta-based filmmakers or Jakarta-based film companies in a rigid production process, presented in the Indonesian language, and distributed nationally in movie theater chains. In contrast, independent films are made via a simpler production process. They are produced all over Indonesia and not only in Jakarta, presented in both Indonesian and local languages, and distributed in sidestream channels such as film festivals and limited film screenings.

In addition to the blossoming of both mainstream and independent film production, the Indonesian film landscape has begun to accommodate films not only from its center (Jakarta/Java), but also at its peripheries. Thus, it has opened up a diversity of themes and genres as well as increasing opportunities for women filmmakers.

Such a burgeoning independent filmmaking movement in various cities in Indonesia has been characterized by the emergence of various film communities that conduct a variety of film activities such as film production, film screenings, film discussions, film festivals, film workshops, and film competitions to challenge mainstream film production and its activities. According to Lulu Ratna (2007: 304), a similar movement actually existed during the 1980s when Gotot Prakosa, a filmmaker and academic based at Institute Kesenian Jakarta (IKJ, The Jakarta Arts Institute), developed an alternative way of producing and screening short films outside of the mainstream film production system. However, such filmmaking activities were limited only to the exclusive circle of film students at IKJ at that time, and were different from the culture of filmmaking during the *Reformasi* period that is prevalent across different regions of Indonesia.

Although independent filmmaking has been prospering in cities across Indonesia since 1998, scholarship on this topic remains limited. Among the body of scholarly work is a study that was conducted by Endah Sulistyorini (2004) that focused on independent filmmaking in the early 2000s in Yogyakarta, a city on the island of Java known for its traditional art and heritage. According to Sulistyorini, the films produced in Yogyakarta during this time share key similarities: the filmmakers had the determination to produce films despite the challenges; they were idealistic in seeking to challenge mainstream filmmaking and films; the films were mostly low-budget films; and there was no support from local government in the making of the films. Such findings were also confirmed by my study in 2009 in which the filmmaker informants stated that the prerogative for independent filmmaking in Yogyakarta was to challenge the Jakarta film industry that dominates the Indonesian film industry (Kurnia 2008). Therefore, filmmakers in Yogyakarta tend to present local issues in their films as well as offer different styles of film narrative and aesthetics. Another study conducted by Edwina Primananda (2015) found that the basic core of independent filmmaking in Yogyakarta was the emergence of film communities since 2000. There were about 102 film communities in 2008 (Kurnia 2008) and that has since decreased to 60 film communities in 2013 (Nugroho and Herlina 2013). Problems faced by these communities include funding and sustainability. A number of these communities comprised university students and, thus, it became challenging to maintain activity due to the transient nature of their membership.

Away from Yogyakarta, in Palu, Central Sulawesi, independent filmmaking has a much lower profile. The work of Ade Nuriadin (2015) found that there were ten film communities in Palu that focused on film production and film screenings. Independent filmmaking began in Palu in 2003, a few years behind other cities in Java like Jakarta and Yogyakarta. However, the development of filmmaking in Palu started to increase in 2006 when some filmmakers sent their films to a number of national and international film festivals (Nuriadin 2015). Most of the films produced in Palu can be viewed as a symbol of self-expression among the youth of the region who sought to challenge the dominant representation of mainstream cinema which focuses more on Jakarta- and Java-centric issues (Nuriadin 2015). Thus, independent filmmaking, both in Yogyakarta and in Palu, shares similarities in the motivating factors of the filmmakers to challenge the hegemonic representation and mode of film production of the Jakarta film industry that dominates the national film industry.

Within such a context, it is important to situate the new development of independent filmmaking in Purbalingga, a small city surrounded by hills and paddy fields in Central Java, Indonesia, by looking at the contribution of a particular local film community, Cinema Lovers Community (CLC) Purbalingga.[1] CLC Purbalingga hosts a variety of ongoing film programs to enliven filmmaking in Purbalingga and its neighboring cities Banyumas, Cilacap, and Banjarnegara since its institution in 2006 (Martian 2015; Setiawati 2013). This chapter argues that despite the lack of film facilities, networks, and funding, CLC Purbalingga has employed sound strategies to enliven local independent filmmaking in Purbalingga and its surrounding cities, in turn contributing to the revitalization and the redefinition of local independent filmmaking in Indonesia.

In the absence of a film system: the arrival of CLC Purbalingga in the 2000s

CLC Purbalingga was created on March 4, 2006 in Purbalingga, a city which is located in the southwest of Central Java province on the island of Java in Indonesia. It has an area of about 678 square kilometers and, as of 2014, a population of about 1 million people (Kementerian Dalam Negeri 2015). Besides farming, most Purbalingga residents work in factories which produce products such as eyelashes, wigs, and motorcycle exhaust components (Pemerintah Kabupaten Purbalingga 2015). In the 1980s, Purbalingga had two small, independent movie theatres; Bralink Theatre and Rayuan Theatre (Jemari Gunungwuled 2013). These theatres closed in the 1990s because there was no film production being undertaken in Purbalingga and the films that were screened in the theatres were limited to films from Jakarta that were mostly distributed to large cinema chains in the big cities in Indonesia (see Kurnia 2008; Pasaribu 2011).

Independent filmmaking in Purbalingga started in 2004 with the emergence of new film communities. One of those film communities is Laeli Leksono Film, which was established by Bowo Leksono, a former journalist and filmmaker in Jakarta who returned to his hometown to share his knowledge and experience in filmmaking with the youth, particularly high school students. Leksono's first film, *Orang Buta dan Penuntunnya* (2004, *The Blind Person's Guide)*, was the first Purbalingga film screened widely in schools, universities, and cultural centers in Purbalingga (Nugroho 2010). The film was also screened on national public television on Televisi Republik Indonesia (TVRI) and submitted to Festival Film Indonesia (Indonesian Film Festival) in 2004.

After producing films for about one year, Leksono wanted to share his experience in filmmaking by conducting a number of film workshops in several high schools in Purbalingga in 2005. Leksono funded this program from his own pocket. He invited high school students to express their ideas and opinions through film. He asked them to explore their identity in films, and suggested that the local language, Banyumasan, be used in the film rather than the Indonesian language, in the hope that it would inspire pride in their local identity (Leksono, personal communication, May 2, 2015).

Leksono's efforts to kick-start independent filmmaking by facilitating programs for high school students in 2005 was then supported by other local filmmakers in Purbalingga. They came together to establish Cinema Lovers Community (CLC) Purbalingga in 2006 as a collaboration between several film communities, namely, Laeli Leksono Film, Glovision Production, Beda Studio, and SBH Entertainment (Trianton 2009). As an open film community, CLC Purbalingga's primary goal is to produce as many independent local films as possible. Their other objectives are to facilitate film production and to provide alternative film distribution.

During its early years, CLC Purbalingga produced dozens of local films about local issues, with some of them being screened and winning awards in several film festivals. These films include *Senyum Lasminah* (2005, Lasminah Smile), *Pasukan Kucing Garong* (2006, The 'Kucing Garong' Soldiers), and *Adu Jago* (2006, The Cockfight), all directed by Leksono. *Senyum Lasminah* won second place in Festival Video Edukasi (Educational Video Festival) in 2007. *Pasukan Kucing Garong* won the best fiction film and *Adu Jago* won the best documentary film in the Malang Film Video Festival (Malviefest) in 2007.

In 2006, CLC Purbalingga created an event called *Bioskop Kita* (Our Cinema) to screen the films produced by their filmmakers. The program was well received by the local community because it screened alternative films that were different from mainstream films mostly produced in Jakarta. Unfortunately, the program encountered problems because there was tension with the local government in relation to the use of a government building for film screenings (Ratna 2007). The local government stopped the screening based on the reasoning that the building was not built for such a purpose. In response to this order, CLC Purbalingga held a *Layar Tanjleb* (open-air cinema) event in ten remote villages in Purbalingga to screen local films for villagers who had limited access to movies, especially from local filmmakers. The success of these screenings led to CLC organizing film screenings in Cilacap, a small neighboring city, as a pilot project to build a network with filmmakers from surrounding cities. Spurred on by the success of these events, CLC then developed networks with Sangkanparan Cilacap and Arisan Film Forum (AFF Purwokerto). These three film communities across three cities established Jaringan Kerja Film Banyumas (JKFB), which became a network body for film activities across the Banyumas area (Trianton 2009; CLC 2011). CLC Purbalingga then created an event called Parade Film Purbalingga (PFP) in July 2007 to screen 30 films produced in Purbalingga during 2004 to 2007. This event was an embryo for Festival Film Purbalingga (Purbalingga Film Festival).

During these initial years, it seems that CLC Purbalingga focused its program on film production and distribution as well as establishing a network with other filmmakers in the Banyumas area. However, in more recent years, CLC Purbalingga has shifted focus to develop new and different goals and programs.

Creating a community, creating a new film system: CLC Purbalingga in the 2010s

The CLC Purbalingga official website, launched in 2016 (clcpurbalingga.id), details its new direction which focuses on public education through cinema, especially for the youth demographic. To manage its programs, CLC Purbalingga has been run by a group of ten young filmmakers[2] for the last couple of years. Besides the group, there are also volunteers who contribute in each program area. These volunteers are high school students, young filmmakers, and young villagers. This film community organizes a great variety of film activities to develop filmmaking in Purbalingga, including film production, film distribution, film workshops, film screenings, film festivals, and providing a film database as well as a film library.

Film production remains the primary focus as most of CLC Purbalingga's members are filmmakers and the core objective of this film community is to increase local film production. According to CLC Purbalingga's film database in 2016, about 100 films were produced before 2011, and 85 films were made between 2011 and 2016. The films deal with local issues such as education, environment, politics, corruption, the health system, culture, tourism, and employment. Besides making fictional and documentary films, lately CLC Purbalingga has also been producing campaign videos, event documentation videos, and video blogs.

One example is the making of short videos about the local election in Purbalingga 2015. According to Leksono, the program was not only held during but also prior to the election to encourage youth in Purbalingga to analyze and become actively involved in the local election (Wismo 2015). The latest production is *Balada Bala Sinema* (The Ballad of Cinema's Crews), directed by Yuda Kurniawan to document the journey in organizing Festival Film Purbalingga. This film was still in post-production at the beginning of 2017.

Besides film production, CLC Purbalingga also contributes to distributing films directed by its members and filmmakers in Purbalingga for film screenings, film competitions, and film festivals not only in Purbalingga and the Banyumas area, but also in other cities in Indonesia. Between August and November 2015, for example, CLC Purbalingga sent films to three film festivals, two film awards, two special screenings, two film competitions, and one film exhibition held in various cities across Indonesia including Purbalingga, Jakarta, Yogyakarta, and Surabaya. Using new technology to assist with the dissemination of information which helps to reach the youth audience, CLC also distributes films through social media platforms such as YouTube and Facebook, as well as on its own official website.

To support the work they do in film production and distribution, CLC Purbalingga also organizes various film workshops and training sessions. Since the inception of this focus, these programs have been targeted at junior and senior high school students in Purbalingga and other neighboring cities such as Banyumas, Cilacap, and Banjarnegara, also extending the program into Kebumen in 2016. These programs are usually held for two days over the weekend to work around the schools' teaching schedule. The workshops and training provide the students with the basic skills required for producing films such as film production management, film scriptwriting, using a film camera, and film editing, which augments existing programs around cinematography taught at their schools. The trainers help the students to write a film script as which becomes a deliverable of the workshop to be produced later under their school's name. SMA (Senior High School) Bukateja, Purbalingga, for example, has been inviting CLC Purbalingga to facilitate film workshops since 2012. In this school, film production is a very popular area of study for the students (Hazliansyah 2015b; Sudiaman 2014). Some of the films produced in this school have received awards from several film festivals and competitions (Hazliansyah 2015a). Another school, SMK Muhammadyah Bobotsari, Purbalingga has just started providing film workshops in 2016 (Satelit Post 2015). These examples provide evidence of the enthusiasm of students in Purbalingga for independent filmmaking which is supported by the teachers who invite CLC Purbalingga to conduct the film workshops. Besides conducting film workshops for high school students, CLC Purbalingga also conducts open film workshops targeted to the youth of Purbalingga. One such example is when CLC worked with the Office for Culture, Tourism, Youth and Sport (*Dinas Kebudayaan Pariwisata Pemuda dan Olahraga*), a local government institution, to facilitate film workshops (Dinbudparpora 2015). CLC also contributes as a trainer and assistant for Negeri Awan Cinemamart, a film community based in SMA Karangteja Purbalingga which received the film grant, *Bikin Film Bareng KPK* (Make Films with the Corruption Eradication Commission in 2015) (Sudiaman 2015).

For film screenings, *Layar Tanjleb,* the open-air cinema, has become an important program for CLC Purbalingga that can adapted to various contexts: to celebrate special events (e.g. new year, Independence Day), personal events (e.g. circumcisions, weddings), government and community programs in collaboration with specific institutions (e.g. local general election, intellectual property rights), charity events, and also as general entertainment for villagers. Besides *Layar Tanjleb,* CLC Purbalingga also conducts indoor film screenings and film discussions with filmmakers from other cities in Indonesia. One example is *Program Indonesia*

Raja in September 2015, which screened films produced by filmmakers from Medan, South Sumatra, after which a discussion was held with student filmmakers in Purbalingga. One of CLC's members, Asep Triyatno (in Arif 2015), stated that the aim of the program was to share films and experiences in filmmaking with filmmakers from other cities in Indonesia. This program is part of *Bioskop Rakyat* (People's Cinema) which also invited filmmakers from Semarang, Central Java, to screen and discuss their films in Purbalingga (Arif 2015).

CLC Purbalingga's biggest program is the film festival, Festival Film Purbalingga. The festival launched in 2007, and began to attract both national and international guests in 2015. This festival, which won the Best Festival award in *Apresiasi Film Indonesia* (Indonesian Film Appreciation) 2015, comprises programs such as a film competition for high school students, non-competition film screenings, *Layar Tanjleb,* film discussions, book discussions, networking events for film communities, artistic performances, and an awards night (Martian 2015). The month-long festival has successfully become a public space for its stakeholders with their different interests for various reasons (Kurnia 2015). Firstly, the festival is inclusive as it involves not only CLC members and filmmakers in Purbalingga, but also festival volunteers, judging panels, villagers, film communities, film distributors, local food sellers, high school students, film critics, academics and researchers, and journalists who come from not only Purbalingga and the Banyumas area but from all over Indonesia and also internationally. The festival presents a diversity of issues through the films screened in the festival, and also provides a wide range of programs. Festival Film Purbalingga has a strong identity as a local film festival in Indonesia due to the use of the local language in the films, and is independent both in providing funding and formulating the ideas for its programs. The festival succeeds in facilitating young villagers and other film network activists to work collaboratively with the festival organizers and has created a new film community aligned with *Festival Film Purbalingga* comprising stakeholders representing various interests.

CLC also takes part in the Anti-Corruption Film Festival (ACFFest). In 2015, CLC collaborated with *Komisi Pemberantasan Korupsi* (Corruption Eradication Commission) at the roadshow of ACFest in Purbalingga. The 2015 festival also ran roadshows in other cities such as Sumbawa, Bali, Kendari, and Lhokseumawe (Info Sekitar Kita 2015). This festival aims to support the anti-corruption movement, targeting the youth demographic through a variety of film activities such as a film competition, film screenings, film discussions, and film panel shows.

Alongside its more public activities which aim to engage a variety of participant demographics, CLC Purbalingga also focuses on developing a film database in Purbalingga. The film database collects information mostly about films produced by CLC and films screened in Festival Film Purbalingga. In addition, CLC manages a film library for video, films, books, and other references on film and popular culture. Both the film database and library are open to filmmakers, researchers, academics, and journalists. CLC Purbalingga also organizes non-film activities such as *Kelas Menulis Purbalingga* (Purbalingga Writing Class) which invites youth in Purbalingga to write short fiction, poems, essays, and newspaper articles which resulted in a book published in 2011 (CLC 2012).

The work of CLC via its films, as detailed above, has achieved recognition from film societies at both local and national levels. One example of this acclaim is *Ijolan* (Barter) (2015), directed by Eka Susilawati, which won the best short student film at Apresiasi Film Indonesia (AFI) (Hazliansyah 2015b). Other films directed by Purbalingga filmmakers have received awards in various film festivals and film/video competitions such as the Denpasar Film Festival, Festival Film Puskat, Kampung Halaman Video Diary Competition, Anti Corruption Film Festival, Festival Film Dokumenter, Festival Film Yogyakarta, Competition of

Creative Video from Dompet Dhuafa, Piala Maya, and Kompetisi Plan Indonesia. These filmmakers are either CLC members or Purbalingga student filmmakers facilitated by CLC. Leksono (in TIS 2014) stated that the reason why CLC Purbalingga has received so many awards and acknowledgments is because its members are both exacting and patient as facilitators for young filmmakers in Purbalingga.

The question is then, is creating a great variety of film programs which are mostly aimed at attracting awards and recognition the only strategy for CLC Purbalingga to develop local independent filmmaking in Purbalingga?

Creative and independent: CLC Purbalingga and its strategies

The success of CLC Purbalingga in developing independent filmmaking in Purbalingga and surrounding cities in the last decade can be attributed to several factors: the persistence of its members to achieve the community's goal, its creativity in producing film programs to create a sustainable and comprehensive independent film system, its consistency in maintaining local identity, its capability in building networking with a variety of stakeholders, its development of a support system, its strong publicity presence in various traditional and social media outlets, and its independence in managing the funding and programs.

Since its inception, CLC Purbalingga has been managed by enthusiastic filmmakers and persistent film activists. They have have worked tirelessly to pursue the community's goal, which has become a labour of love. Leksono, for example, demonstrates a strong commitment to producing his own films as well as seeking to facilitate young filmmakers in producing their own local films about local issues in the local language. Leksono left behind a successful career as journalist in Jakarta to live in Purbalingga and develop local filmmaking in the area. Another example is Dimas Jayasrana (Program Director) who, at present, works and lives in Jakarta, but also successfully manages CLC programs from Jakarta and with occasional visits to Purbalingga (Yusuf 2014).

With their work, CLC Purbalingga succeeds in creatively organizing a continuing program of various film and non-film events. Such a process has ensured that local films have their own system which is not only independent but also open to other channels outside Purbalingga and the Banyumas area, with a potential reach to the broader youth demographic throughout Indonesia.

One of the remarkable strategies of CLC Purbalingga, compared with other local filmmaking communities in Indonesia, is their effort to maintain their local identity as their trademark. 'Purbalingga', as an identity, is also linked to the broader identity of 'Banyumas', and this is demonstrated in the films, which represent the geographical area, language, and local issues (Kurnia 2016). In terms of geographical area, CLC Purbalingga specifically targets the involvement of filmmakers, especially youth filmmakers, from Purbalingga and its surrounding cities. In terms of language, all of the films are produced in Banyumasan, a local language, and supported by either Indonesian or English subtitles. In terms of issues represented in the films, CLC Purbalingga always encourages the filmmakers to work with local issues. Based on this local identity, it seems that the films are relevant to the primary audience who are local citizens, though the audience has now broadened to include national and international audiences. Such strong local identity shows that CLC Purbalingga has made a prominent effort to challenge the mainstream Indonesian films predominantly made by filmmakers from Jakarta, produced mostly in Jakarta, presenting issues mostly about Jakarta, and filmed in Indonesian which is sometimes mixed with English. Indonesian films, if they are to represent the nation as a whole, should be not only about Jakarta but also about other cities in Indonesia.

Another key success for CLC Purbalingga is how the members have developed networks starting in Purbalingga, then expanding to the wider Banyumas area and recently to a national context, Indonesia. In the initial years, CLC Purbalingga focused on building networks with filmmakers and high school students in the Purbalingga and Banyumas area. During its development, CLC Purbalingga also established networks not only with filmmakers from other cities in Indonesia (for instance, Jakarta, Medan, Aceh, Jepara, Cilacap, Bali) but also with government institutions, universities, libraries, high schools, youth organizations, and other cultural or art communities and institutions. Because a number of their programs are run in collaboration with government agencies, including local government, the tension between local government officials and CLC Purbalingga is sometimes problematic. In addition, CLC Purbalingga also maintains networks with journalists from various media both at local and national level.

Besides maintaining networks with various communities and institutions, CLC Purbalingga places priority on its presence on various social media platforms in order to manage its relationship with the youth of Purbalingga and the Banyumas area as well as other cities in Indonesia. Various platforms are chosen to disseminate information about the programs as well as to publish films produced or facilitated by CLC Purbalingga. No-cost blog sites, both for CLC Purbalingga (clc-purbalingga.blogspot.com) and Festival Film Purbalingga (festivalfilmpurbalingga.blogspot), were their primary platforms until 2015. CLC Purbalingga also maintained a blog in Kompasiana as part of Kompas, one of the leading national newspapers in Indonesia, from 2011 until 2015. Besides its blogs and website, CLC Purbalingga also uses YouTube, Facebook, Twitter, and Instagram. There are two YouTube accounts (CLC Purbalingga and Festival Film Purbalingga) which are used for uploading documentation videos (for example, press conferences, behind-the-scenes shorts, film discussions), films, and video blogs. The use of two accounts to provide distinction between general information about CLC Purbalingga and specific information about Festival Film Purbalingga is also applied to other social media platforms such as Facebook, Instagram, and Twitter. The dynamic activities of CLC Purbalingga are not only seen in a real and physical context, but also in the virtual realm, which is important to their objective of engaging the youth demographic as well as the stakeholders who are not able to attend or participate in the programs. In addition, an open access database that is also supported by a library provides comprehensive data for journalists, film critics, academics, and researchers to write about CLC Purbalingga and its programs.

Another important strategy is CLC Purbalingga's decision to maintain its independence in determining and developing its programs although the opportunity to work collaboratively with, and receive funding from, other communities and institutions is also present. To manage its independence, Leksono explained that although Festival Film Purbalingga has several times been funded partially by government and private institutions, CLC Purbalingga maintains autonomy over the main programs and ensures that this content is not influenced by the interests of donors (Leksono, personal communication, June 2, 2017). However, to accommodate the interests of funding organizations, the festival sometimes incorporates additional programs so long as they align with the festival's objectives. According to Jayasrana, CLC Purbalingga has attempted to source financial support via crowdfunding but has yet to be successful in this (Jayasrana, personal communication, June 2, 2017). There are also plans to secure international funding so that CLC Purbalingga can attain financial security into the future, not only for the festival but also other programs (Leksono, personal communication, June 2, 2017). Leksono stated that CLC Purbalingga has no specific target for external funding as the facilitation of the programs takes priority over seeking funding

(Leksono, personal communication, June 2, 2015). However, Jayasrana mentioned that this external funding usually comprises about 25 percent of the total budget though this figure can vary (Jayasrana, personal communication, June 2, 2015).

From the strategies above, it can be said that CLC Purbalingga is independent, creative, and persistent in not only developing independent filmmaking but also in creating a 'new' film system in Purbalingga and surrounding cities. In addition, it also promotes local identity which, in turn, challenges mainstream (Jakarta-based) filmmaking. However, borrowing an argument by film critic Windu W. Yusuf (2014), while CLC Purbalingga is a film community determined to develop local independent filmmaking in Indonesia, it is at the same time facing challenges in funding its programs and managing its relationship with local government.

Conclusion: the future of CLC, the future of filmmaking in Indonesia

Within the dynamics of independent filmmaking in Indonesia, CLC Purbalingga is an example of a film community that contributes to the revitalization and redefinition of independent filmmaking in Indonesia. In terms of revitalization, CLC Purbalingga is the main player in supporting the film system in Purbalingga and its surrounding cities, which has continued to expand over the course of a decade. Various programs such as film workshops and training, film production, film screenings and discussions, as well as a library and a film database are parts of a film system that supports independent local filmmaking. This system does not depend on Jakarta as the center of mainstream film production. CLC Purbalingga offers pride in the promotion of local identity in producing the films so that local filmmaking in Indonesia, which tends to be based on the geographical area of the film production or origin of the filmmakers, is redefined by adding local language and local issues to the films. Purbalingga films have become unique and distinct to other local films in Indonesia.

CLC Purbalingga applies cultural strategies in motivating youth in filmmaking; for instance, teaching filmmaking as a subject in local high schools, organizing film festivals where local films are screened and compete for awards, and presenting *Layar Tanjleb* events in remote villages in the area to present these local films to the villagers, especially the youth. These strategies cultivate a spirit of independent filmmaking among the youth in the area who treat film as a medium to express their ideas about social, cultural, and political issues in their environment. The strategy of combining conventional and emerging platforms to reach its stakeholders brings young people and the wider community together to enjoy local films. As a local film community, CLC Purbalingga proves its significant contribution in creating local films with local identities, which challenges existing independent filmmaking in Indonesia which is dominated by big cities such as Jakarta and Yogyakarta.

With these strategies, CLC Purbalingga has proven its position as a successful film community not only in independent filmmaking, but also in creating an alternative film production system that places priority on local films and local filmmakers. Such efforts are important in challenging the domination of mainstream films both from the national film industry and international film industry so as to be able to develop a thriving local film system in Indonesia which showcases various local cultures.

Along with its many successes, CLC Purbalingga also faces challenges from various aspects in local independent filmmaking in Indonesia. In terms of funding, CLC Purbalingga needs to consider applying new strategies to secure external funding to accommodate the expansion of the programs and stakeholder groups into the future. The question of independence in running programs should be negotiated between its primary objective to educate youth and the interests of funding institutions. In terms of community, CLC Purbalingga should involve more young people in order to prepare the next generation of filmmakers and film consumers as the programs are now being conducted in more cities. These challenges should become key considerations for CLC Purbalingga in the future.

With such successes and challenges, the case of CLC Purbalingga is an example of the role of film communities in local, independent filmmaking in Indonesia during the *Reformasi* era. Therefore, it is important to elaborate on other film communities to assess the landscape of independent film in Indonesia more comprehensively.

Notes

1 The term 'local' here refers to a specific district or geographical area in Indonesia, for example, Purbalingga. Therefore, the term 'local' when relating to films within the Purbalingga context means films produced in Purbalingga by filmmakers who live in Purbalingga, which are screened and distributed mostly locally in sidestream film distribution. This term can be compared to the term 'national' which describes films produced in Jakarta, the capital city of Indonesia and the center of film production, made by filmmakers who live in Jakarta. However, these 'national' films are screened and distributed nationally in mainstream film distribution. One of the most important characteristics of Purbalingga films is their local identity which is highlighted in the films and provides a point of difference from other local films in Indonesia. All of these films use the local language, Banyumasan, rather than the national language of Indonesian. Besides the difference in language, Purbalingga films consistently represent local issues, local settings, local talents, and local filmmakers.

2 The group of ten are the aforementioned Bowo Leksono as Founder and Director; Dimas Djayasrana as Program Director; Canggih Setyawan as Program Manager; Nanki Nirmanto as Film Festival Manager; Cahyo Prihantono as Operational Coordinator; Mochammad Zacky NS and Reza Haryanto as Assistants to the Program and Operational Manager; Nur Muhammad Iskand and Asep Triyatno as Publicists; and Astri Rahma D. as Administration and Financial Officer.

References

Arif, A. (2015) Pelajar Purbalingga Diskusikan Film Pendek dari Medan. *Tribun Jateng Online*, July 5, 2015. Available at http://jateng.tribunnews.com/2015/07/05/pelajar-purbalingga-diskusikan-film-pendek-dari-medan/ [accessed December 17, 2017].

Cinema Lovers Community (2011) *Cinema Lovers Community dalam Sejarah*, November 18, 2011, updated June 25, 2015. Available at http://www.kompasiana.com/clcpurbalingga/cinema-lovers-community-dalam-sejarah_5509aa42813311eb01b1e24a [accessed December 10, 2017].

Cinema Lovers Community (2012) *Kelas Menulis Purbalingga Buka Angkatan Kedua, Kompasiana*, January 22, 2012. Available at http://www.kompasiana.com/clcpurbalingga/kelas-menulis-purbalingga-buka-angkatan-kedua_550d7867a33311091b2e3c5d [accessed December 14, 2017].

Clark, M. (2004) Men, masculinities, and symbolic violence in recent Indonesian cinema. *Journal of Southeast Asian Studies*, 35(1): 113–31.

Dinbudparpora (2015) Workshop Pemutaran Film, Dinas Kebudayaan Pariwisata Pemuda dan Olahraga (Dinbudparpora), September 16, 2015. Available at http://dinbudparpora.purbalinggakab.go.id/?p=125029 [accessed December 15, 2017].

Hazliansyah (2015a) Festival Film Purbalingga Raih Penghargaan AFI 2015. *Republika Online*, October 27, 2015. Available at http://www.republika.co.id/berita/komunitas/aksi-komunitas/15/10/27/nwv11d280-festival-film-purbalingga-raih-penghargaan-afi-2015 [accessed December 10, 2017].

Hazliansyah (2015b) Workshop Produksi Film SMA Bukateja Purbalingga 2015. *Republika Online*, November 23, 2015. Available at http://republika.co.id/berita/komunitas/aksi-komunitas/15/11/23/ny8x66280-workshop-produksi-film-sma-bukateja-purbalingga-2015 [accessed December 17, 2017].

Hughes-Freeland, F. (2011) Women's creativity in Indonesian cinema. *Indonesia and the Malay World*, 39(115): 417–44.

Info Sekitar Kita (2015) *KPK Gelar Anti Corruption Festival (ACFFest di Purbalingga),* Info Sekitar Kita, June 18, 2015. Available at http://isknews.com/kpk-gelar-anti-coruption-film-festifal-acffest-di-purbalingga/ [accessed December 10, 2017].

Jemari Gunungwuled (2013) *Riwayat Dua Bioskop di Kota Purbalingga,* Jemari Gunungwuled. Available at http://www.jemarigunungwuled.or.id/2013/04/riwayat-dua-bioskop-di-kota-purbalingga.html [accessed December 18, 2017].

Van Heeren, K. (2012) *Contemporary Indonesian Film: Spirit of Reform and Ghosts from the Past.* Leiden: KILTV Press.

Kementerian Dalam Negeri (2015) *Kabupaten Purbalingga,* Kementerian Dalam Negeri. Available at http://www.kemendagri.go.id/pages/profil-daerah/kabupaten/id/33/name/jawa-tengah/detail/3303/purbalingga [accessed December 5, 2017].

Kurnia, N. (2008) (Komunitas) Perfilman Yogyakarta dalam Perfilman Indonesia': Ironi Ketersisihan dan Keterbukaan. Paper presented in *Workshop on 10 Years Reformasi in Indonesia,* Flinders University, Adelaide, Australia, April 14–15.

Kurnia, N. (2014) Women Directors in Post-New Order Indonesia: Making Film, Making Difference. PhD Thesis, Flinders University, Adelaide, Australia.

Kurnia, N. (2015) Ruang Publik dan Lokalitas: Studi Kasus tentang Festival Film Purbalingga. Paper presented in Research Days FISIPOL 2015, Faculty of Social and Political Sciences, Universitas Gadjah Mada, Yogyakarta, December 15–18, 2015.

Kurnia, N. (2016) Understanding the Public Sphere: The Views and Contribution of the Stakeholders of Local Film Festival in Indonesia. Paper presented at Indonesian International Alumni Symposiun 2016, Flinders University – Jembatan, Yogyakarta, November 5, 2016.

Martian, A. D. (2015) Konsumsi Film Penonton Festival Lokal: Studi Etnografi Praktik Konsumsi Film Penonton Festival Film Purbalingga 201., Undergraduate Thesis, Department of Communication Science, Faculty of Social and Political Sciences, Universitas Gadjah Mada, Yogyakarta.

Nugroho, G. and Herlina, D. (2013) *Krisis dan paradoks film Indonesia.* Jakarta: FFTV IKJ Press.

Nugroho, I. D. (2010) Bowo Leksono: Better Than Sinetron. *The Jakarta Post.* Available at http://www.thejakartapost.com/news/2010/02/12/bowo-leksono-better-sinetron.html [accessed December 18, 2017].

Nuriadin, A. (2015) Sutradara lokal indie pendek antara author dan pelaku Komunikasi: Studi Etnografi terhadap tiga filmmaker indie pendek di kota Palu. Masters Thesis, Department of Communication Science, Faculty of Social and Political Sciences, Universitas Gadjah Mada, Yogyakarta.

Pasaribu, A. J. (2011) Bioskop Jawa Tengah, Riwayatmu Kini. *Film Indonesia.* Available at http://filmindonesia.or.id/article/bioskop-jawa-tengah-riwayatmu-kini#.WTDRzROGOi4 [accessed June 1, 2017].

Pemerintah Kabupaten Purbalingga (2015) *Tentang Purbalingga.* Pemerintah Kabupaten Purbalingga. Available at http://www.purbalinggakab.go.id/index.php/selayang-pandang/tentang-purbalingga.html [accessed December 16, 2017].

Primananda, E. P. (2015) Distribusi film independen di Yogyakarta: Studi Kasus Distribusi film di komunitas Pabrik Film. Undergraduate Thesis, Department of Communication Science, Faculty of Social and Political Sciences, Universitas Gadjah Mada, Yogyakarta.

Pudjiati, K. and Kusumaryati, V. (2011). 'Industry or not? Rethinking Contemporary Indonesian Film Production', presented at *the AAS-ICAS Conference on Asian Studies*, Honolulu, Hawaii, 31 March – 3 April.

Ratna, L. (2007) Indonesian short films after Reformasi 1998. *Inter-Asia Cultural Studies*, 8(2): 304–7.

Satelit Post (2015) Beradu Akting dan Otak-atik Kamera: Workshop Produksi Film Pendek, November 9, 2015. Available at http://satelitnews.co/berita-workshop-produksi-film-pendek-.html#.VkB7HRjZK9Y.facebook#ixzz3sLGPairk [accessed December 16, 2017].

Setiawan, D. (2009) *Kuldesak:* popular culture, urban youth identity, and social change in late-20th century Indonesia. In Michalick, Y. and Coppens, L. (eds.), *Asian Hotshots: Indonesian Cinema.* Schuren: Marburg, pp. 98–112.

Setiawati, I. (2013) Indie film festivals, an alternative forum of entertainment. *Jakarta Post,* January 20, 2013. Available at http://www.thejakartapost.com/news/2013/01/20/indie-film-festivals-alternative-form-entertainment.html [accessed April 15, 2017].

Sudiaman, M. (2014) Workshop Produksi Film SMA Bukateja Purbalingga. *Republika Online.* Available at http://www.republika.co.id/berita/komunitas/aksi-komunitas/14/09/21/nc8x1i-workshop-produksi-film-sma-bukateja-purbalingga [accessed June 1, 2017].

Sudiaman, M. (2015) Pelajar Purbalingga Produksi Film Hibah KPK. *Republika Online*, August 24, 2015. Available at http://www.republika.co.id/berita/komunitas/aksi-komunitas/15/08/23/ntjika319-pelajar-purbalingga-produksi-film-hibah-kpk [accessed December 28, 2017].

Sulistyorini, E. (2004) Perkembangan komunitas film independen Indonesia: studi kasus komunitas film independen di DIY Rentang waktu 2000–2002. Undergraduate Thesis, Department of Communication Science, Faculty of Social and Political Sciences, Universitas Gadjah Mada, Yogyakarta.

TIS (2014) Bowo Leksono raih award 'Insan Penggerak Komunitas Film' dari ACFFest, Tabloid Kabar Film, December 16, 2014. Available at http://www.tabloidkabarfilm.com/profilm/eksklusif/589/589.html [accessed December 10, 2017].

Trianton, T. (2009) Regenerasi Sinematografi Purbalingga. *Suara Merdeka*, March 10, 2009. Available at http://suaramerdeka.com/v1/index.php/read/cetak/2009/03/10/55202/Regenerasi.Sinematografi.Purbalingga [accessed January 5, 2017].

Wismo, B. (2015) CLC Purbalingga Kembali Luncurkan Video Kritisi Pilkada Purbalingga 2015, Braling.Com, 2 November 2015. Available at http://braling.com/2015/11/clc-purbalingga-kembali-luncurkan-video-kritisi-pilkada-purbalingga-2015/ [accessed December 17, 2016].

Yngvesson, D. (2015) *Kuldesak* and the inexorable pulp fiction of Indonesian film history. *Indonesia and the Malay World*, 43(127): 345–77.

Yusuf, W. (2014) CLC Purbalingga: Edukasi Film, Edukasi Politik, Film Indonesia, 26 May 2014. Available at http://filmindonesia.or.id/article/clc-purbalingga-edukasi-film-edukasi-politik#.VUCJGPmUdtg [accessed April 26, 2017].

22

The collaborative DIY approach to creativepreneurship

Taking charge of (own) future

Dina Dellyana and Sonny Rustiadi

Introduction

Up to 2007, the concept of 'creative industries' had not received the specific attention of Indonesian policy makers who were in charge of developing the industrial sector in macroeconomic policy. However, the country's creative industries began to grow as the market increasingly demanded creative products and services. Realizing their potential, the Ministry of Trade then developed a road map in 2008 (Departemen Perdagangan 2009). This was the starting point for the Indonesian government's policy in this area, which is concerned with facilitating the nation's creative businesses and activities.

This chapter argues that one of the main avenues for the formation of creative businesses is the DIY (Do-It-Yourself) approach, which is little discussed by the existing literature (but see Flew 2005; O'Connor 2009; Oliver and Green 2009). Kuznetsov and Paulos (2010) coined a noteworthy definition for DIY that will be used throughout this chapter. The definition captures an important 'feel' of the spirit of DIY, which is not driven by materialistic motives but rather by the fortitude to pursue one's personal interest. This is the feel that the authors get from interviewing various DIY creative workers in Bandung. The definition is as follow:

> any creation, modification or repair of objects without the aid of paid professionals. We use the term 'amateur' not as a reflection on a hobbyist's skills, which are often quite advanced, but rather, to emphasize that most of DIY culture is not motivated by commercial purposes.
>
> *(Kuznetsov and Paulos 2010: 1)*

DIY is a manner directly related to the mode of mass production and generally taken as a reaction to it. Many creative entrepreneurs in Bandung are 'independent' in the sense that they are responsible for all the activities necessary to design, manufacture, market, sell, and provide after-sales services to their customers without relying on established channels – thus practicing the so-called DIY approach. This gives the entrepreneurs much more scope for experimentation and artistic freedom without sacrificing financial sustainability.

Bandung is widely recognized by Indonesians as a creative city. Its environment is very dynamic, where local communities, universities, and small businesses thrive. Youngsters in the city are easily inspired by such a broader environment: for example, they see their friends and families succeeding by developing their own creative products. Grahadea, a professional working in the music industry in Bandung, highlights:

> The success stories of their seniors inspire them so much that they even become the major driving force while pushing them to become bigger and better at creative business than their seniors. I think the #killyouridol attitude plays an important role here. The newer breed of creators learned much from their seniors (through partnership, employment, or friendship), so they absorbed the same level of idealism but with a higher level of competition that forces them to scale bigger while having a stronger foundation in terms of corporation values and best practices.
>
> *(Grahadea, HMGNC band[1] and CEO of Kuassa,[2] Bandung, September 2017)*

In the city, there is a wide range of interesting exhibitions that are held either by private companies, communities, or government bodies mainly on a monthly basis. There are also various creative communities in Bandung which are keen on interactions and working together with each other: the Bandung Creative City Forum (BCCF) and Common Room are two good examples of such collaboration. In addition, many creative places and co-working spaces have been established so that artists, musicians, and other creatives can exchange their ideas and easily hang out, for example Co'nCo working space, Spasial, Eduplex, Freenovation, and Taman Tengah Joint Space. Each of them has routine activities which include sharing sessions, gatherings, and workshops – either free or with a minimum charge as sponsored events. The value of these places is aptly pointed out by the owner of a local shop:

> People in Bandung are very creative and the creative spirit is contagious here. We meet creative youngsters every day, we share with each other different stories every day, who knows what remains in their thoughts and unintentionally inspires them ... The structure of the city and the environment in the city are very supportive. DIY businesses are fostered by the policy environment in which the government supports and encourages youngsters to be creative and become entrepreneurs.
>
> *(Marine, Owner of Loubelle shop[3] and FFWD records,[4] Bandung, September 2017)*

Importantly, creatives can easily find resources in Bandung; from raw material, workers, production space, and access to distribution channels. To find raw material, they have many options with reasonable price in two famous markets in Cigondewah and Pasar Baru. Even creatives from neighboring countries such as Malaysia regularly come to buy good-quality materials there. Production centers range from micro-scale places to mass production centers. If designers want to have their own production house, it is easy to find crafters and workers. Cheap labor can be found easily with supply from surrounding smaller cities such as Cimahi, Garut, and Tasikmalaya. To sell their products, creatives can either put them in consignment stores or sell them online through Instagram or websites. Adit Yara, a bag designer points out that:

> People in Bandung can make anything by themselves since it is relatively easy to get the material and find production vendors here. The material and labor are cheap compared to other cities hence the growth of DIY fashion in Bandung is faster than other cities all over Indonesia.
>
> *(Adit Yara, owner of Niion,[5] Bandung, August 2017)*

The rise of the DIY movement in the city's fashion industry has also coincided with an increase in the number of independent music labels that lead with new musical works from various music genres. These music businesses share the same DIY spirit as their fashion counterparts. It should be also noted that the DIY movement has spread to other cities in Indonesia such as Semarang, Surabaya, Jogjakarta, Bali, and Makassar. This chapter will look at the development of two of the biggest creative industries in Bandung – music and fashion – to learn lessons from the city's experience and contemplate the future development of these industries.

A qualitative approach was chosen in this research, as the research aimed to explore and explain the DIY culture of Bandung's music and fashion industries. The data were collected by in-depth interview with those who were actively involved in these industries to gain a holistic view of the phenomenon and cross-check findings (Morse et al. 2002). It was started by selecting five companies that conduct DIY practices in their business and had been operating for more than two years and interviewing their owners or CEOs. These included Grahadea Kusuf (HMGNC, CEO Kuassa), Marine Ramdhani (Owner of Loubelle shop and FFWD records), Aditya Rahman (Owner of Niion Indonesia), Anggung Suherman (Bottlesmoker), and Aninda Nazmi (Owner of Nazmi Indonesia). All interviews were conducted in Bandung from August to September 2017.

Initial development of the music and fashion industries

In Bandung and Indonesia, it can be observed that the music and fashion sectors share similar ideals and values in terms of their social engagement. In the 1990s, there was a social struggle against the oppressive dictatorship government of President Soeharto and many artists in these sectors actively responded to the nation's social and political conditions through their work. For example, indie music resisted the regime through lyrics (which were often political and anti-establishment) and fashion designers expressed their views through the design of garments and visual graphics. Today, these sectors form a space where young people can find creative tools and ideas to respond to their social issues – from the issues pertaining to local neighborhoods to the current conditions of the nation. After all, youth have always served as an important social force in Indonesia and are keen to address problems specific to their generation. The social movement relies on cooperation, collective action, and complex interdependencies between different creative disciplines, organizations, and practitioners. After the victory of the reformation era in Indonesia in late 1998 and early 1999, the spirit of the youth evolved into a form of artistic counterculture in which creative and artistic works were produced to run counter to the prevailing cultural tastes and social values of the time. This spirit continues to be the fuel of the creative industries in Bandung.

Importantly, many creative workers in the music and fashion sectors distribute their products through informal channels. They also routinely collaborate with one another. Furthermore, there is notable intersection between these sectors, although each sector has its own networks and specific mode of production. The networks, relationships, and interactions with other organizations play very key roles in helping the survival and development of creative organizations and businesses, which make Bandung the creative capital of the nation.

The intersection between indie music and fashion is encompassing. This occurs because it is often the case that creative workers in indie music also work in fashion, or at least they are colleagues in the same community. Therefore, there is constant collaboration between the two sectors. For example, the fashion industry assists indie musicians in terms of manufacturing band t-shirts, accessories, and merchandising items. The strength of such collaborative relationships depends on the genre of music and the orientation of the fashion business in question.

As defined by the Indonesian Ministry of Trade (Departemen Perdagangan 2009), the music industry can be any kind of business and creative activity relating to education, creation/composition, recording, promotion, distribution, sales, and performance of works of musical art. The ecosystem of the music industry in Indonesia includes activities that occur at every stage of creation, reproduction, distribution, and consumption. The main roles in this creative process are played by producers, composers, lyricists, songwriters, sound engineers, and music directors. In addition, there are creative people from other areas of service industries which include recording studio providers and CMOs (Collective Management Organizations).[6] Meanwhile, reproductive process is the process of placing the music in certain media, be it physical or digital, using the master track for later use. The process of distribution refers to the activity involving the delivery of music both physically and digitally to the hands of consumers through conventional and non-conventional channels. In the consumption process, consumers engage themselves with digital products, physical products, or live performances (musicians' tours and concerts).

In early 2000, there was a new phenomenon in the music scene in Bandung. At that time, many independent record labels that utilized the DIY approach such as Fast Forward Records, Literacy Records, Sinjitos, Demajors, and Ivy League Music among others were emerging. This was happening because major labels were lacking interest in accommodating the full scope of Indonesian music because some of the music was not considered 'pop' enough to enter the mainstream market. Therefore, many musicians and artists did not receive attention from the major labels and turned to independent record labels to publish their work.

Today, DIY musicians still have high ideals for their music, wanting to produce the music they like without being scared of not reaching the Top 10 Best Songs list. They also think they can manage their music by themselves with help from various platforms such as TuneCore for digital music publishing. With help from their managers, these musicians still have income from their live shows so that they can manage their time and schedule as they want. As the CEO of Kuassa, a company that works with musician states:

> The biggest turn-off from becoming part of the mainstream is to sacrifice your idealism and passion. It [doing DIY] makes them somehow feel like they stand above the crowd, makes them a stronger character which can inspire many others. It's like your music having a strong differentiation. They are not afraid to be part of the niche, or even create their own particular market. They organically grow, scaling-up while preserving the very same idealism when they started.
>
> *(Grahadea, HMGNC band amnd CEO of Kuassa. Bandung, September 2017)*

We find that something similar has happened in the fashion industry in Bandung. Looking at its initial development demonstrates that most fashion brands developed from hobby-based activities and sports activities such as skateboarding and surfing. The first fashion company in Bandung can be traced back to 1994. At that time there was a famous music studio in Bandung called *Reverse Studio*. This studio signed and nurtured some of the most popular bands at that time such as *Pas Band* and *Puppen*. The unique thing about *Reverse Studio* is that in addition to operating as a music studio, they were also selling special products relating to rock music and skateboarding. It sold CDs and music-related items (such as t-shirts, bags, and posters) of other famous bands, which at that time were very difficult to obtain because they were all imported. For several years, *Reverse* grew rapidly and successfully harnessed the enthusiasm of Bandung's young people.

However, the Asian financial crisis in 1997 meant that imported products became very expensive and out of reach of local consumers, leading to serious obstacles in its business. Yet *Reverse* owners Helvi, Marin, and Dxxxt did not give up. Knowing that the market was ready to accept local products, they began to establish their own fashion brand. At the same time, there was another store, *347-fashion* established by Dendy Darman, which produced goods related to skateboarding, BMX biking, and surfing. It turns out that the items worn by *Reverse* and *347-fashion* owners themselves attracted the attention of young audiences at the time. Furthermore, the purchasing power of the youth in Bandung could afford local products only because of the high exchange rate. This created a golden opportunity for the creative entrepreneurs (frequently shortened as creativepreneurs[7]) to continue to grow their business. The success of *Reverse* and *347-fashion* began to inspire other people to try their luck in the fashion business. For example, *Ouval Research* fashion was established in 1998 with a link to the skateboarding and hardcore music scene and *Riotic*, another fashion brand, was popular with the punk scene. Through the efforts of the founders, these creative businesses began designing, manufacturing, and selling their own goods because of their hobby – be that in skateboarding, surfing, or BMX biking, or a particular interest in a specific music genre (punk or rock).

The practice of DIY in the music and fashion sectors

DIY music grew at the same time with the development of digital music production and online music platforms. Most of the musicians in Bandung could record or produce their own music. Although they used free music software (or even pirated software, which is easily found in the city), they could maximize the minimal features of the software to create and produce good-quality music. They sold their music online by using content aggregator services like TuneCore. The development of digital music production and online music platforms could help a musician or rights holder to distribute and sell/stream their music through online retailers such as iTunes, Spotify, Amazon Music, and Google Play. The payment system was cheap and easy and they did not need to have a large amount of capital to start selling their music online. This opportunity was not lost on Grahadea, who points out that 'economically, the vast growth of the internet enabled them to reach a wider audience, even allowing them to tap into the global /international market'.

To promote their music, DIY musicians in Bandung have utilized social media such as SoundCloud, Instagram, Twitter, Bandcamp, Reverbnation, and Facebook. Sometimes they give away their songs for free, but downloaders need to follow their social media account as a trade-off. Mostly sponsored by cigarette companies, music gigs are held almost every weekend. From cafés and bars to proper music venues, the musicians can take to the stage to promote their music or gain inspirations from other musicians. The fan base of each music genre is tight and fans' support for their chosen artists is strong. The musicians obtain an income from the gigs or sponsorship/endorsements from local or other bigger fashion brands. Anggung, a musician from the band Bottlesmoker, feels that the relationship with fans and fashion brands is possible because 'Bandung's youngsters always want to be different and they don't want to consume (and create) something similar to the items available in the mainstream market. And that's Bandung's culture' (Bandung, September 2017).

In the city, music studios for practice and recording are easy to find and are very cheap. For practice, the average music studio charges around IDR 50.000–100.000 (around USD 10) per hour and for recording about IDR 300.000–700.000 (around USD 27–70) per session. For music production, many freelance sound engineers can help musicians shape their music and they sometimes collaborate for free. To produce a music CD is also easy and cheap. It usually cost around IDR 5 million (around USD 470) per 1,000 CDs which includes simple packaging. Design for the CDs is often free or very inexpensive since Bandung has a lot of graphic designers who are open to collaboration. Some bands or musicians also create or design their own packaging to minimize the budget. Bandung also has a number of analog and digital music instrument producers. In addition, other facilities include Virtual Studio Technology, provided by the aforementioned company Kuassa. Very often, these companies support each other to develop their brands.

The following diagram depicts the business model of DIY music in the city. A conventional music store's primary function is to sell music products and their derivatives such as music-themed merchandising items. These stores are commonly found in shopping malls or their own buildings. However, they are decreasing in number nowadays as many of the big chain music stores are closing their physical branches and moving toward online platforms. On the other hand, there has been a growth of non-conventional music stores. Their main function is not selling music albums. These are fashion shops, convenience stores, and even fast-food chains. Examples of non-conventional music stores which are commonly used by DIY musicians in Bandung are fashion stores. Such collaboration between the two industries allows for effective distribution of music as directly as possible to consumers as the fashion stores already have a captive market of people who visits their premises.

As such, in Bandung these processes are mostly accomplished by DIY approaches. Known as 'self-release', this is an attempt by musicians to act as a record label to produce, distribute, and sell their own musical works. The DIY approaches are applied in the production

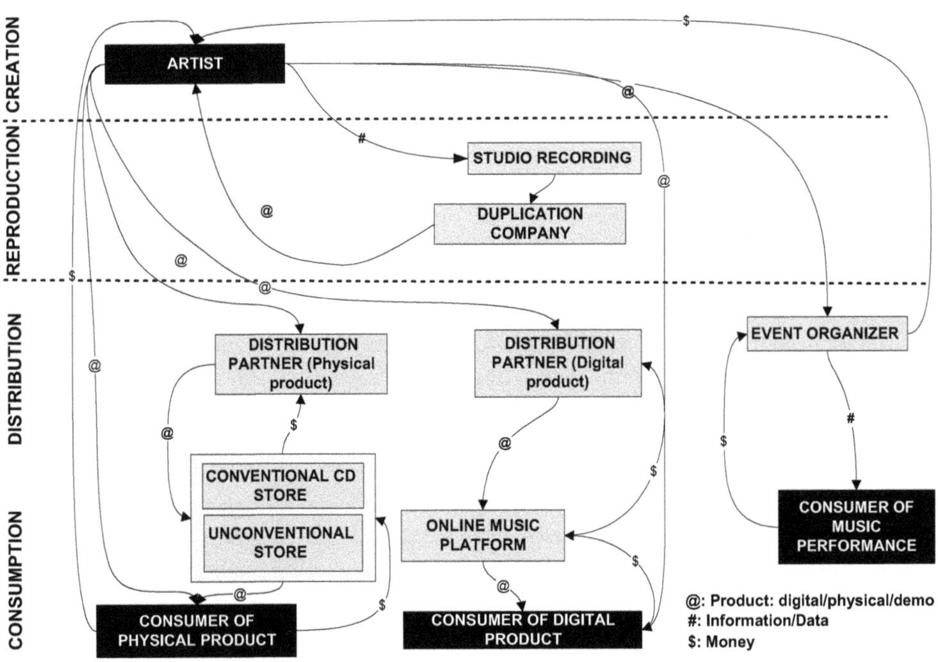

Figure 22.1 The business module of DIY music-making in Bandung

process which consists of song writing, song arrangement, tracking, mixing, and mastering. During the process of distribution, these musicians work in cooperation with independent distributors. There are two types of DIY here. The first is DIY in the production process in which the artist uses their own funds (often called bootstrapping DIY[8]), but the process is still carried out by a third party. The second is full DIY in which the whole process of production is done by the musician themselves (commonly known as the 'bedroom musician'). Bootstrapping DIY production processes has been done by various independent artists in Bandung since 1997. Bedroom musicians' DIY was mostly started by electronic musicians during the same period.

From the artist's point of view, after the music has been created the three processes of reproduction, distribution, and consumption follow. For reproduction, most artists work with a third party to manufacture their product (cassette/CD/vinyl) in small quantities of 100–500 pieces. The album covers are usually designed by themselves or by their friends to lower the cost. The finished album in the form of cassette/CD/vinyl is commonly distributed through fashion stores or distributed by exclusive music distribution partners. It is not uncommon for the musician to also sell their album on their website or through social media accounts. This approach enables the artist to obtain a bigger margin compared to selling CDs through conventional channels as it cuts distribution costs.

At the same time as the music sector grows, the presence of fashion businesses also continues to grow. This is the main reason the 'distro' business (short for 'distribution' outlet) began to emerge. Distro is a store that displays and stocks a variety of brands of independent fashion – a sort of one-stop shop for independent brands. The exponential growth of distro and fashion businesses in Bandung began to inspire other cities such as Semarang, Surabaya, Yogyakarta, and Makassar in starting their own distro and fashion sector. The many creative communities, often from different cities throughout Indonesia, support each other and even started to hold events together to strengthen their engagement with one another. These have included creating music concerts, skateboarding competitions, BMX competitions, and many other youth activities.

Young creatives prefer not to be part of a bigger distribution channel since they can make more money by producing and distributing themselves. Social media such as Instagram and Facebook really help them grow as they can promote and sell their products without being charged and they still get 100 percent of the profit from the sales. They also can hold on to their idealism to produce what they want; they can quit or progress anytime they want. They can also determine their promotion and marketing activity as they desire. The other reason for relying on distro shops is that it can cost a lot to have bigger distribution channels.

However, since Instagram and Facebook changed their algorithm, small brand owners have found it hard to increase viewers and followers on their social media. This has caused sales decline and meant that immediate action was required. Thus, most local brand owners started to use Instagram ads and Facebook ads to increase awareness. Apparently, this does not need a high budget since they can do it for (almost) free. Some of the small brand owners started to change their sales strategy, and moved to their own channel such as their own ecommerce website while others started to shift their sales focus to partner stores at the fashion marketplaces like www.berrybenka.com or www.zalora.com. Instagram and Facebook then can be utilized just to spread their marketing campaigns and other promotional activities.

> We no longer can rely ourselves fully on Instagram. They have changed its algorithm to push us to advertise. We need to change our strategy to sell our product.
>
> *(Aninda Nazmi, Owner Nazmi Indonesia, Bandung, August 2017)*

Bigger retailers or distribution channels often require a deposit and prefer to have brands which are already well known. Further, committing to join a big distribution channel means that indie cultural producers need to increase production capacity and scale up their businesses. This requires additional investment and increases the risk of under-sales. Most local brands are not ready for taking such risks, as pointed out by Yara, the owner of a local shop: 'If I join a large distribution channel such as a department store, the first investment would be very big so I would rather open my own store.' She continues, 'A brand needs to deposit almost IDR 100 million (around USD 9,000) and the consignment fee is nearly 45 percent from the revenue of every purchase' (Bandung, August 2017).

The evolution of DIY approaches in the music and fashion sectors

A notable trend today is that most artists are offering free downloads via music platforms such as SoundCloud. This is done to attract attention from the audience. There are also musicians who have started to use third-party services such as TuneCore to distribute their songs on online music platforms such as iTunes, Deezer, and Spotify. Having said that, there are still many local artists who struggle to utilize digital channels due to a lack of knowledge, skills, and financial tools such as a credit card. Another DIY approach is that many artists finance their own concerts and tours. Their livelihood comes from the proceeds of concert performances as well as support from sponsors. Although this usually does not happen on a large scale, these concerts are preferred by their fans as they feel more intimate and always demand them.

There are, however, factors both internal and external that serve as challenges to a creator. Internally, the biggest challenge is consistency and teamwork. Most of the independent musicians in Bandung are amateurs. Some of them have already succeeded in that they can make a living from music. They potentially expand their income by launching businesses related to music, such as becoming a producer, software maker, publisher, artist manager, or small indie label producer. Clearly, being a musician is now beyond creating music. Musicians need to think about including business management aspects to their core activity to survive. The main problem is getting the best talent for a particular task – for instance finding a social media manager at a time when not many people are interested in this type of professions which is deemed unpopular. Another problem is that even if the right person is found, it is hard to keep them in the business. People come and go as they look to find a better job with a stable income. This is a challenge that is familiar to Grahadea who witnessed human resource issues arising when businesses were scaled up because 'Most of the management practices are based on friendship/fellowship values rather than a proper corporate/professional principle, thus, making them vulnerable to mismanagement and business fraud' (Bandung, September 2017). He also highlights that many indie musicians have difficulties in building a strong management team, resulting in them micro-managing their business rather than developing their music.

From the external perspective, the challenge is in the changing media landscape. Before the arrival of digital technology, promoting an artist meant putting a video clip on MTV and the radio and that was the length of any promotion activity. Nowadays, fewer people watch TV. The consumer has many other choices of media – from YouTube, radio streaming, and various social media platforms. Artist management needs to attract and direct the consumer to many channels; from internet marketing to below-the-line activities such as fan gatherings, mini gigs, and much more. The artist management also needs to be very creative in designing the promotion strategy. This is a challenge that Rico, a musician from the band

Mocca, highlights. In an interview (Bandung, August 2017), he discusses how bands need to be professional with different members being responsible for different roles unrelated to the music such as social media management, but the biggest challenge he felt was 'environmental changes'. He states, '[p]reviously, if you hit TV to promote the band, it [the marketing activity] is done, since the choice of media is limited. Now consumers have choices, and you need to be visible and consistent in all media'.

In the fashion sector, the booming growth of distributions and fashion started to decline as early as 2005. This was because many new businesses were flooding the market and sales of products declined as competition was really high with the increased number of fashion brands. Everyone has the same access to materials, production, and distribution channels. As many brands became established, it became hard to differentiate one from another. Consequently, many fashion companies started to close their business. But the big players such as *unkle347* (which was the new brand of *347-fashion*) and *Ouval* still survive to this day.

Bandung fashion brands also suffer from limited opportunities for branding. They cannot launch their brand internationally as they cannot manage their branding in the same way more established designers do. Also, their budget for branding and marketing activities is limited. Thus, they only focus on local markets with the hope that their efforts will spread organically as happened in 1990 when Bandung became the pioneer of indie and distro fashion in Indonesia. Furthermore, they have trouble scaling up their production capacity. With little operating capital, it is hard for them produce good-quality products in high quantities. This is an aspect that is of concern to Marine, the owner of a local fashion shop:

> Thinking globally is a major undertaking. In addition, government policy and support need to be streamlined, although it will take time ...They [creative entrepreneurs] actually want to have a broader distribution, but do not have capital. Moreover, social media and websites already satisfy them [in term of sales]. Joining bigger distribution channels means an increase in production scale and, of course, capital.

A new trend is happening where many new young designers do not actually want to market their product with fashion companies such as *unkl347*, *ouval*, and *airplane*. Interviews with the new generation of designers have found they think that fashion companies tend to make mass products and get in the way of the uniqueness that these designers want to be known for. This new generation of designers prefers to design and produce their own products in limited quantities. With their own capital, which is also limited, they price their product above the price range of fashion brand and distro stores. Quality and design become their main concerns with each independent designer having their own distinctiveness and identity. It is hard to find similarities of design in each product of these designer-makers.

Not all designers have sufficient capital to have their own shop. But thanks to the rise of social media, they have begun to implement multichannel strategies for distribution by exploring both offline and online distribution channels. They actively utilize their presence in social media on Instagram, Twitter, and Facebook for their online distribution channels. On the other hand, their offline distribution channel is helped by the emergence of 'concept stores'. Similar to distro stores, concept stores only accept consignments for brands that they think are of high quality. There is a curation process with which products are displayed in accordance with the theme of the concept store. One of the pioneers of Bandung's concept stores is *Happy Go Lucky* (HGL). Continuously working on its own identity as a concept store by heavily relying on a robust product curation process, HGL has successfully developed as a platform for young designers, labels, and brands to help to leverage them into the fashion industry. Although concept stores are growing rapidly, they still try to remain lean and conduct all activities of design, production, marketing, and distribution by themselves. Another trend is that, in recent years, pop-up markets and various fashion markets have started to emerge, which bring great opportunities for designers to market their products.

Fashion brands need to make unique products or create interesting marketing or promotion activities. Collaborations with others that have different product focuses, collaborations with artists or social media celebrities, or collaborations with concept stores have become their solutions. Our fieldwork has revealed that currently Bandung's indie brands are pursuing co-branding strategies to gain access to new markets, creating a useful brand association and gaining extra financial benefit using momentum in the fashion industry such as Indonesia Fashion Week or a curated market. Moreover, the process of co-branding focuses heavily on the preparation and sales marketing phase. However, there are challenges that the brands must overcome. For instance, internal challenges include communication issues and the battle of egos among indie producers. Meanwhile, external challenges include how they adapt their design and creative ambition to the available technology and material limitations.

The increasing activities of co-branding within the local fashion brands seem influenced by international fashion brands' co-branding strategies such as the collaboration between high-fashion brands and mass-market fashion brands, for instance Louis Vuitton and H&M. Other forms of co-branding, such as collaboration between brands and fashion retail stores are also prevalent, for example Commes Des Garcons with Dover Street Market. Lastly, there is also a trend in celebrity co-branding, such as Adidas with Stella McCartney. For the local brands, the motivation in conducting a co-branding strategy varies. Most of them aim to gain access to new markets. Therefore, local indie brands prefer to choose collaborators who have different customer segments. Another motivation is to gain advantage from value transfer and brand association through working with collaborators who are widely known in the society. In Indonesia, co-branding activities are mostly conducted for indie producers to enter a big fashion event since they could serve as an effective promotion strategy. The final motivation is to gain more revenue from the spillover of co-branding and the arrangement with retailer, while cutting costs (Setio and Dellyana 2016).

Conclusion

DIY culture is often associated with anti-consumerist, creative, and even militant aspects of experimental work practice. The DIY scenes in Bandung's cultural industries are hard to delineate as they are quite fluid and free flowing, and are not exclusively tied to any typical organizations. DIY artists also function in a completely different way. Our interviews with local DIY designers show that they are self-motivated, carrying on with creative ideas and projects themselves rather than depending on others who may not understand them. They are driven by passion rather than the desire for fame or fortune. Furthermore, one of the key qualities of the DIY scene is its effect on talent cultivation and nuturing creativity as well as the combination of fun and work. Few artists in this scene have huge aspirations and they even avoid signing contracts with big companies as declared by a number of interviewees. Instead, they choose to do their crafts for themselves with a somewhat naive target of being self-sufficient as a way of sustaining their passion. Furthermore, the DIY culture is greatly helped by the development and global distribution of technologies and devices such as digital technologies, the internet, and personal computers – these diminish reproduction and distribution costs while increasing the producer's own technical skills and knowledge to produce their arts.

The experience in Bandung is arguably unique but it also may illustrate the typical journey of a creative business in Indonesia. The creative workers develop their own businesses by actually doing it, learning from their friends, and collaborating with like-minded people. As such, the DIY approach is an exciting and effective strategy of cultural production and distribution in Bandung and may prove valuable in other contexts.

Notes

1 HMGNC is a contemporary indie electronic music group. Homogenic was founded in 2002 and has since produced four albums.
2 Kuassa is a software company specializing in digital guitar amplification and audio processing.
3 Among the most well-known fashion stores in Bandung.
4 One of the earliest and most influential recording companies in Bandung
5 Bag design and manufacturer brand from Bandung.
6 Collective Management Organization (CMO) is organizations which exercise copyright and related rights acting in the interest and on behalf of the owners of rights (WIPO n.d.). CMO manages rights licensing, royalties collecting, and rights enforcing on behalf of the copyright holders.
7 In this research creative entrepreneurs are defined as the people working in all sectors of the creative industries. This term is not limited to fashion designers.
8 The term is popular in Bandung's creative scene. It originated from the term 'bootstrapping' in entrepreneurship discourse, where an entrepreneur financed all activities of his/her venture from their own money without the help of third parties. The combination of the words 'bootstrapping' and 'DIY' reflects the spirit of being independent.

References

Departemen Perdagangan Republik Indonesia (2009) *Studi Industri Kreatif Indonesia 2009: Update* [Creative Industry Study 2009: Update]. Jakarta: Ministry of Trade Republic of Indonesia.

Flew, Terry (2005) Creative Commons and the creative industries. *Media and Arts Law Review*, 10(4), pp. 257-264. Available at https://eprints.qut.edu.au/39367/1/c39367.pdf [accessed September 2019].

Kuznetsov, S. and Paulos, E. (2010) Rise of the expert amateur: DIY projects, communities, and cultures. Available at http://www.staceyk.org/hci/KuznetsovDIY.pdf [accessed January 2018].

Morse, J. M., Hupcey, J. E., Penrod, J., and Mitcham, C. (2002) Integrating concepts for the development of qualitatively-derived theory. *Research and Theory for Nursing Practice*, 16(1): 5–18.

O'Connor, J. (2009) Creative industries: a new direction? *International Journal of Cultural Policy*, 15(4): 387–402.

Oliver, P. and Green, G. (2009) Adopting new technologies: self-sufficiency and the DIY artist. *UK Academy for Information Systems Conference Proceedings 2009.* https://aisel.aisnet.org/cgi/viewcontent.cgi?article=1046&context=ukais2009 [accessed September 2019].

Setio, W. A. and Dellyana, D. (2016) A managerial perspective of co-branding strategy in Indonesian fashion industry. *Asia Pacific Journal of Advanced Business and Social Studies*, 2(2): 206–16.

WIPO (n.d.) *Collective Management of Copyright and Related Rights.* Available at http://www.ipr.gov.ba/upload/documents/dokumenti_podstranice/brosure_i_publikacije/engleski/collective%20management%20of%20copyright%20and%20related%20rights%20wipo_pub.pdf [accessed May 2018].

23

Creative industries as tool for cultural resistance in Indonesia

Sonny Rustiadi, D.A.E. Savitri Sastrawan, and Salfitrie Roos Maryunani

Introduction

A major part of the creative industries literature is on the discourse of how these industries contribute to the economy (Howkins 2007), positively affecting business climate (Florida 2002), enhancing the urban image and identity of a city/nation (Landry 2008), and increasing the spirit of innovation and creativity (Hartley et al., 2013). Meanwhile, what is less discussed is their potential cultural and social impacts (but see Said, 1993). In addressing this gap in the existing discourse of creative industries, this chapter explores how creative workers can spur alternative movements and mobilize resistance to social problems by utilizing their particular skills and tools.

Identity formation is a communal activity carried out by all communities (Said, 1993). However, in a close-knit[1] group, important issues can magnify with remarkable speed. Sense of community also drives passion and obsession. Many times in Indonesia, people have fought against the oppression imposed by revolutionizing the way the society thinks. There are two particular examples that illustrate this point. The first was the independence of Indonesia in 1945. The proclamation of the independence of the nation by Soekarno may not have happened had the student activists led by Soekarni Kartodiwirjo and Chaerul Saleh not 'kidnapped' Soekarno and the future Vice President Hatta to call for independence. The event is known as 'The Rengasdengklok Affair'.[2] The other example was the series of events that led to the infamous 'May 1998 Affair'. The central event of the May 1998 Affair was the fall of Soeharto regime, the second President of Indonesia, which would not have happened without pressure from the multitude of students who marched and stormed the House of Representatives in Jakarta for days. In linking such historical and social dynamics in the country to what is happening in the creative industries, this chapter aims at investigating the progressive social functions of the country's creative sector.

The chapter focuses on cases from two prominent regions in Indonesia. The first is from Bandung where a creative movement has a formal presence in the city's government as one of the local creative entrepreneurs and community leaders was successfully elected as Mayor through a campaign supported by creative workers. The campaign began because the city government had been deemed helpless in developing the city's creative potential and leaving this task in the hands of rigid and corrupt politicians and bureaucrats. The second is an ongoing case that is happening in Bali at the time of writing this chapter, where creative activism has become an important tool in raising an important environmental issue. The 'Bali Rejects Reclamation Masking as Revitalization' movement, magnified by the works of local musicians and bands like Superman Is Dead and Navicula, has declared the Balinese rejection of its latest governmentally driven development initiative. These two case studies demonstrate how creatives and their projects generate major cultural and social effects, be that on movements inside or outside the bureaucratic system of government.

Bandung city governance: the fight within the system

The city of Bandung, Indonesia, is the third largest city in the country, with a population of 2.6 million. It is the capital city of West Java Province and it is comparable to Yogyakarta and Bali. Yogyakarta is the capital city of the Special Region of Yogyakarta, which has the same authoritative level as a province. Bali is actually an island and a province on its own, with Denpasar as the capital city, but people tend to think of Bali as a single place. Bali is renowned as a tourist destination, however as a province it also has several other fascinating towns and cities apart from Kuta and Ubud which tourists always visit. Bandung's close proximity to the country's capital, Jakarta, and cool climate make it the get-away destination from people all over the country. Historically, when Indonesia was under Dutch colonial rule, Bandung was always seen as the city of retreat, as opposed to Jakarta as a military base. Rahardjo (2002) states that Bandung has two main assets: the first is science and technology and the other is human resources. Science and technology has something to do with the large number of higher educational institutions in the city. As for human resources, Bandung is located in the mountains and does not have plentiful natural resources so its people have always relied on their own human capital in order to survive.

In July 2007, the UK–East Asia Creative Cities Forum was held in Yokohama, Japan, in partnership with the British Council. This event was a conference conceived to explore the theme of the 'Creative City', namely, how cities can fully actualize their potential in the era of globalization, exploring arts, culture, industries, and other resources distinctive to specific regions. The forum promoted debate on arts and cultural policies and related subjects from creative perspectives; it also concerned exchanges and interactions between local artists and creators. At this event, Bandung was chosen for the pilot project of the East Asia Creative Cities programme by the British Council. Creative Cities, a three-year programme developed by the Council with a budget of £2 million, aimed to support the development of creative and open cities with a successful knowledge economy in East Asia and the UK. The programme focused on four broad themes: working with artists and designers to reimagine cities; promoting accessibility and participation; transforming public spaces; and supporting creative entrepreneurs (British Council 2008).

One of the outcomes from the programme was Bandung Creative City Forum (BCCF), a non-profit organization and a forum for creative communities in the city. It was established in January 2008, and since then has become an independent association with the objective of advocating the development of creative activities for Bandung in general and its creative communities in particular. In its every activity, BCCF uses three approaches, which are creativity-based education, planning and improvement of the city infrastructure as a means for developing creative economy, and nurturing individuals and communities into creative entrepreneurs. In the long run, this forum aims to participate in creative city branding and develop an extensive network through collective efforts to facilitate collaboration between creatives and make them ready for global competition (BCCF 2012)

Creative culture in Bandung has always been considered as the 'people culture', perhaps due to the fact that the city is also known as a city of education, which results in a young population (about 70 per cent of the inhabitants are aged 40 or younger). According to Soemardi (2006), when compared with other cities in Indonesia, Bandung relies more on human capital as the fundamental and reliable resource for the city's economic development and cultural vibrancy. Whereas Yogyakarta is best known for 'traditional' culture, Bali for 'religion-based' culture and Jakarta for 'commercial' culture and media, Bandung can be described as a city of 'creativity'. The city's creative vision is clearly noted by Pearson (1998, cited by Soemardi, 2006: VI–162) writing in *Indonesia: Design and Culture:*

> the city of Bandung is the intellectual heart of the country. Home to nearly fifty universities ... it is part college town, part colonial hill station, and part industrial center. Higher, drier and cooler than Jakarta ... Bandung is also an arts center. Some of the country's top artists are based here, supplementing their incomes with teaching jobs at local institutions and enjoying a less frantic pace than their colleagues in Jakarta.

Dwinita Larasati, the general secretary of BCCF, stated in our interview that prior to the establishment of the forum, there was awareness among communities of the city's creative potential being based on its history, culture, and social context, and even geographical nature. In addition, the city's strong education sector and the existence of abundant young people who are always open to novel things, are also seen as a driving force of the city's creativity (interview, July 2013). The city is also a chic and fashionable shopping destination, popular not only among local Indonesians, but also among neighbouring Malaysians and Singaporeans and many other foreigners in the region.

Bandung is arguably the most popular destination in Indonesia for people to obtain an excellent education. The city has many public and private schools. Hundreds of universities — four of which are state-owned universities — and more than 90 vocational schools are located all over the city (see Table 23.1). Numerous branches of education institutions specializing in various disciplines from social sciences, technology, to tourism can be found in the city.

The climate of Bandung is cool and the size of the city is not so big so getting around is not a problem. In addition, the attitude of the urban society is open and tolerant, encouraging people to be more dynamic in adapting to change. Further, the younger generation in the city is quick to adapt to global and regional trends and tech-savvy. This generation is spearheaded by young musicians, artists, and designers in the city. These creative youngsters produce brilliant creative products and help the city to be connected to global trends of creative industries.

Table 23.1 Number of schools in Bandung in 2014

Formal education	*Elementary schools and equivalent**	*Junior high schools and equivalent**	*High schools and equivalent**	*Vocational high schools*	*Universities and colleges*
Quantity	1,023	250	209	96	130

Notes: Quantity includes both public and private institutions

* The number includes both conventional curriculum-based school system and Islamic curriculum-based school system

Source: Data compiled from various sources.

Dwinita Larasati then explained further that this awareness of Bandung's creative potential led to the foundation of BCCF, when a group of people from different communities recognized the potential in creative workers in the city, and how the notion of the creative economy could be implemented in Bandung. Originally, one of the objectives of the forum was to foster inclusive communication between the creative agents and communities in the city so that the development of the creative economy would not be merely guided by discussion among elites; rather it hoped to be able to accommodate the various needs of every stakeholder.

The long-term vision of the forum was to generate significant impacts for the society, particularly in terms of job creation and economic opportunities – not only for the people in Bandung but also for neighbouring regions in general. However, there were hindrances to achieving this – for example, the insufficiency of public spaces as well as the bureaucratic approach taken by a city government that was susceptible to corruption. The forum was created to build a bridge between the city's stakeholders and parties of interest, including the city government, creative workers, and the youth.

Muhammad Ridwan Kamil, an award-winning architect and a lecturer by profession, was elected as the first chairman of BCCF in 2008. As the winner of the British Council Creative Entrepreneur of the Year in 2006, he was invited to the UK where he was made aware of the power of creative industries and the creative city movement from the British perspective. As he reflected on the conditions in Bandung, he began to see very strong potential for the creative industries in the city. However, the term 'creative economy' was still new for Indonesians and he was disappointed by the fact that the government took time to respond to the demand for suitable public policy to boost these industries. Eventually, he came to realize that if he wanted to change the city, he had to take the lead on various initiatives with a hope that people would start to follow. Nevertheless, he stressed a key point to be noted, 'Basically, you have to be contextually aware and [be] creative. You cannot just cut and paste what you have experienced in London' (Rowntree et al. 2011).

Recalling its inception, Dwinita 'Tita' Larasati who is also an artist, said that BCCF did not have a smooth start. Together with the team, she and Kamil strived to build trust among creative communities in Bandung as they saw distrust as an issue obstructing the development of creative industries within the city. As for the role of government, the general opinion shared by interviewees for this research[3] was that the government had not utilized its authority wisely and lacked the willingness to communicate with other stakeholders, especially those in the creative industries. This was a serious issue. One of the respondents, Fiki Satari (interviewed August 2013),[4] told of a damaging experience in dealing with government that destroyed his trust in the West Java Provincial Government (WJPG), as follows:

> After much persuasion, the government finally provided initial financial support to KickFest.[5] In the end, however, due to the lack of government support they managed to organize the event by themselves on their own effort. But then during a ministerial visit at the opening of KickFest, the officials reported to the Minister of Trade that KickFest was a government-initiated program, when in fact it was our (the local clothing community's) original idea and effort. They (the government) only helped with the initial funding and the amount was not that significant … Because the truth is that they (the government) did not initiate or have any program at all (to help the clothing industry) … Another example is during the exhibition there was a visit of

> high-ranking officials from a particular ministry who said, 'Oh, these are under the care of Mr. X … under the care of Z agency …' – names of city government officials that we, as the organizer, had never heard of. That's when we knew that our event (KickFest) was sold on behalf of 'certain' officials … That was when we lost trust (toward the city government).

It took the Head and Secretary General of BCCF (Kamil and Larasati) two years going door to door, discussing with and convincing stakeholders in the creative sector. 'The approach was if we want to make a change we have to do it ourselves and strengthen civil society', Kamil stated in the Cultural Leadership Programme interview (Rowntree et al. 2011: 17). After some time, they finally succeeded in gathering more than 20 communities that were ready to get involved.

One of BCCF's initial programmes was Helar Festival (Helarfest), a month-long city festival in 2008 showcasing 30 parallel series of events ranging from arts, culture, fashion, music, design, architecture as well as an automotive and academic conference. It was created to promote the design and economic aspects of the city's creative enterprises. When the BCCF tried to contact the city council, they received negative replies as the council decided not to play a part in the implementation. For the second Helarfest in 2009, the council started giving support after seeing the success of the first event. Larasati (in a 2013 interview) added: 'Gradually we change the idea of the city, suddenly the city is a bit more excited, particularly because we have gone from the idea [of Helarfest] to implementation by ourselves.'

This was the main reason why he decided to take part in the Bandung mayoral election in 2013 as an independent candidate. With five years experiences being involved in creative and social activities with BCCF and also his decades of professional background as an architect, urban planner and lecturer, he succeeded in winning the mayoral election in 2013 for the period ending in 2018.

In his interview with us (2013), creativepreneur Nazar Noe'man, who has more than 30 years of experience in the media industry, observed that Bandung in the past had never had leaders capable of combining the creativity of its people with good town planning; at least such a case had not been yet seen or felt by the general public. Noe'man added that the industry hoped that the government had a wide vision and creativity to make the city comfortable enough to live in. He also stressed that this would increase people's productivity and creativity, and eventually lead to good governance.

In *The Rise of the Creative Class*, Florida (2002) states that people's creativity is closely related to the city where they live. The quality of the city in which a person lives really affects the creativity of the person. Florida says that there are three dimensions of a place's quality; the first is *what's there*, that is the combination of the built environment and the natural environment; a proper setting for pursuit of a creative life. Secondly, is what he describes as *who's there*, the diverse kinds of people, interacting and providing cues that anyone can plug into and make a life in that community. The third part of a good-quality place is related to *what's going on* in that place, which means the vibrancy of street life, cafe culture, arts, music, and people engaging in outdoor activities. Florida's creative capital theory argues that the holders of creative capital – creative people – choose places that are diverse, tolerant, and open to new ideas for their settlements, which will eventually drive its regional economic growth. This is what Ridwan Kamil in his mayoral work is trying to achieve in Bandung; to create a comfortable place for people to live and provide as many opportunities as possible for people to utilize their creative potential and to increase their role in the creative industries.

Within several months of Kamil's incumbency, many initiatives were implemented to increase the quality of life in the city. For example, he came up with the initiation of '*kampung kreatif*' (creative village) in the city. He stated that in the next five years, every *kecamatan* (borough) in Bandung would have its own '*kampung kreatif*', with particular capabilities in art, culture, and creativity. These kampungs are developed as a means to encourage cultural activities of the people, and in the long run, stimulate the region's economic growth (Redaksi 2013). None of these had happened in previous mayoral tenures. In contrast, the previous mayor and some of his associates are currently on trial on charges of bribery after they were accused of misappropriating funds that were meant to help the city's poorest residents (Bland 2014).

One of Kamil's missions was raising the happiness index in Bandung, as a top-down campaign led by the city government (British Council 2014). The mission was supported by in an initiative called 'Bandung Fun Days' that continues today. This is a social programme with the goal of increasing the level of happiness of the city's inhabitants. It starts with a free bus-ride for students on Mondays, no-smoking Tuesdays, and promoting the use of the Sundanese language (a traditional language of West Java Province) on Wednesdays and English on Thursdays in daily activities, respectively. On Fridays, he introduced biking Friday to promote health awareness and traffic reduction. Another observation of the effort made by Ridwan Kamil as creative leader came from the British Council (as quoted in British Council Creative Economy Blog, 2014).

> [E]very Saturday, the historical area of Braga is closed to traffic and turns into a vibrant food festival, bringing thousands of people from Bandung and beyond together. Bandung has a proud reputation as a top culinary destination and the food festival creates a space where people can take ownership of the streets and come together in a communal experience. It's one of many ways this young Mayor is transforming this city, and fulfilling his mission to make 'Bandung the happiest city in Asia'.

These initiatives are widely popular with the general public as they are believed to raise the quality of life in the city. With this, it is hoped that the increased creative potential of the city in terms of its lively young population, good education, and open society will lead to more production of creative activities and products. The initiatives are quintessential examples of how the city of Bandung, with strong support from the government, was able to reveal itself as creative, vibrant, and inhabitable city for both residents and visitors. On top of that, in order to maintain government transparency, the mayor set up www.bandungjuara.com, a Bandung-focused news portal aimed at providing information and a platform for Bandung citizens in particular to monitor the performance of the city's governing body, including the progress of its programmes.

'Little Bandung' is another creative programme initiated by the city government to strengthen the competitiveness of Bandung products. This involves establishing outlets in various cities abroad to promote and brand Bandung's creative products to global value chains and eventually contribute to the national economy. Little Bandung shops have been opened in Seoul, Paris, and Kuala Lumpur. Kamil also focuses on renovating and opening various public spaces and parks in Bandung. Other initiatives implemented include Movie Nights, in which movies are screened publicly for free on a big screen set up under a flyover that has been renovated; pedestrian-only streets to promote retail and street life; and building a micro library made of recycled materials above a public building. Within the community, the Mayor also initiated various programmes to meet the different interests of community groups: the programmes include the Smart City Council, Architecture Advisory Board, One Village One Architect programme (where architects assist local villages in micro-architecture projects), as well as anti-corruption and cultural advisory groups. One of the most popular policies is 'If I Were A Mayor' programme in which citizens are invited to submit ideas to improve the city. This initiative has resulted in more than 1,000 ideas implemented in and around the city (Za 2016). In budgetary policy, Kamil believes and practises a transparent management policy so that citizens can see how government money is spent on various public projects through the e-government website.

According to Leadbeater (2008) there are two accounts of a creative city. The first is what he calls a 'narrow' account, where creativity is confined to a narrow group that works in particular areas of the city, and their creativity is mainly applied to a range of cultural activities. Yet this core creative class has a huge multiplier effect on the atmosphere and economy of the city. He argues that cities are increasingly managing how they make people feel as much as how they manage their roads and buildings. Leadbeater also argues for a broader understanding of creativity whereby a city has to be creative about all aspects of city life – not just culture. The density and scale of cities poses significant challenges in terms of housing, transport, health, utilities, waste disposal, education and so on. This means that cities require continual social and political creativity to address the problems that are caused as they grow.

However, the strategy for this 'broader' social creativity in cities is far less clear. Three essential key aspects arise. First, we need a more social, cumulative, and collaborative account of creativity, in contrast to the traditional idea that creativity comes from a spark of individual genius. Second, social creativity has to apply to things that are not widely seen as worthy of creativity: for example, waste disposal, health provision, housing and transport. Third, the ingredients for 'broader' social creativity are very different in different cities depending on their governance, history, and the strength of civil society organizations (Redaksi 2014).

To a certain extent, Kamil's idea to infuse seeds of creativity among the residents of Bandung was one way to keep the city's creativity energized so it could eventually lead to a growing sense of love from the inhabitants towards their city. Larasati[6] (interviewed in 2013) argues that a city becomes less enjoyable to live in because of the stress and frustration experienced by its inhabitants. The role of the residents in enlivening the city is key; nevertheless, it should begin with each and every individual, who must develop a positive suggestion so that the city grows an enjoyable dynamic in order to change effectively.

Bali rejects reclamation: a struggle outside the system

Bali Tolak Reklamasi Berkedok Revitalisasi Teluk Benoa (known as Bali Tolak Reklamasi), which means 'Bali Rejects Reclamation Masking as Revitalization at Benoa Bay' is a movement by ForBALI, the Bali Society Rejects Benoa Bay Reclamation Forum, 'an alliance of the people of Bali, made up of both organizations such as NGOs and individuals including students, artists, the youth and those who are concerned with conserving Bali's environment and believe that the Reclamation of Benoa Bay is a step towards the destruction of Bali' (ForBALI 2015). This movement has shown itself as a social movement outside the bureaucratic system and also as an expression of Bali citizens' aspiration towards creative strategies to deal with the problematic governance of the city that is potentially damaging the existing culture and environment in the region. To date, it has become an example of cultural resistance in Bali and Indonesia.

Figure 23.1 Public digital advertisement for 'Benoa Bay Revitalization' on a digital screen in Jl, Raya Kuta, Bali (private documentation 2016). (The complete website advertisement states: Introducing Benoa Bay revitalization from Bali for Indonesia. Development of a new custom and culture-based destination prioritizing environment conservation and also business development with the people of Benoa Bay and Benoa Cape.)

ForBALI was formed on 26 June 2013 after the announcement of 'a massive new project' set to take place 'in Bali's overcrowded south' (Langenhaim 2014). Benoa Bay would be reclaimed and smaller islands would be created by a mega project that promised to generate more jobs, a better economy, and a better environment for the people of Bali. The *Jakarta Post* newspaper supplement, *Bali Daily*, revealed that the reclamation planned by the development firm PT. Tirta Wahana Bali International (TWBI) would create 'luxury tourist facilities, including a Disneyland-like theme park, apartments, hotels, villas, an international hospital, and entertainment [centres]' (Erviani 2013).

Before this project, a proposal to the Bali Governor to form a nature tourism company, PT. Tirta Rahmat Bahari, had been rejected. This proposal was about managing the Ngurah Rai mangrove forest park (Tahura) within the Benoa Bay area in 2012. However, the Benoa Bay reclamation, which will affect the same mangroves, was accepted. Because of this, the Bali Tolak Reklamasi (BTR) movement emerged involving organizations dealing with mangrove forest park (Tahura) such as student alliances, musicians, WALHI Bali, and KEKAL Bali (both are environmental advocacy committees/NGOs). The cultural resistance grew when KEKAL Bali's response to the Benoa Bay reclamation encouraged further involvement of members of the public, other NGOs, and musicians.

Figure 23.2 Anti-reclamation movement banner, banners at Benoa Bay (private documentation 2015). (Translation: Head of Benoa Cape Village absolutely and consistently rejects Benoa Bay reclamation revoke presidential decree No. 51 Year 2014)

To trace the emergence of this cultural resistance, it is important to look back at the cultural imaginations of Bali. Bali's survival as an island located in Indonesia, Southeast Asia, is excruciating. Bali is known to be the 'paradise island', a cultural imaginary of the island. Southeast Asian cultural historian, Adrian Vickers (2012), explained,

> Bali is the "enchanted isle," "the last paradise," one of the world's great romantic dreams ... More than any other tropical island, Bali has become the most exotic of exotic locations, a fantasy of all the [splendours] of the Orient and the beauties of the Pacific. Over three centuries the West has constructed a complex and gorgeous image of the island that has come to take over even Balinese thought[s].

The sea surrounding Bali has become a part of its tropical island beautification. This argument coincided with Australian anthropologist Michael Taussig's (2000: 252) statement that the sea is 'a new structure of feeling'. Thus, to Taussig the 'reconfiguration of money and the sea began and has been completed' in his lifetime – such as the Aboriginal lands claimed by the British government 'as without owners' in the late eighteenth century – which 'was achieved freely by the anonymous force of the market instead, the market of fantasy' (257). The beach has been the 'geography of the human soul', however, intriguingly the tendency of Marx's 'primitive accumulation'[7] and structure of feeling obtained have led towards a fetishism of it: the fantasy of the beach (Taussig 2000: 274). Hence, fetishizing the need to use the beach – an important environmental geographical area – as capitalistic venture is problematic.

On the other hand, another kind of fetishism has started 'in the history of images of Bali', especially in anthropology – including Margaret Mead, one of the twentieth century's best-known anthropologists, who put Bali on the map of international scholarship (Vickers 2012: 21). She and Gregory Bateson wrote *Balinese Character: A Photographic Analysis* in the 1930s, when Bali was still under Dutch control. The anthropological approach of Mead and Bateson created through photographic analysis has become an aesthetic that people consume. Thus, anthropologizing could be a form of aestheticizing and fetishizing, used to revive Bali as pursuers wished. Therefore, this statement seems to be its result: 'Bali's role as a paradise has been vital for the development of the Indonesian national economy' (Vickers 2012: 25) – which is echoed in TWBI's statement of 'from Bali for Indonesia'.

Despite the main concept of that economy being 'cultural tourism', it felt like 'mass tourism' instead, and has been found problematic by the people of Bali, as indicated by the interviews with those who have been involved in Bali Tolak Reklamasi, which took place during this research. As *a fantasy of all splendours*, Taussig's argument of the beach as object of commodity fetishism and related structure of feeling, combined with the effects of anthropological fetishism/aestheticism on Balinese culture, has engendered Benoa Bay as a 'spatial product', through changing a presidential decree.

The Indonesian Presidential Decree No. 45 (2011) clearly stated that Benoa Bay is a conservation area and it is protected. During 2012 and 2013, the Bali regional government had its laws changed again and again suggesting that Benoa Bay was the target of a development program (or 'exploitation' from Bali Tolak Reklamasi's point of view). However, the regional government and the current Governor of Bali, Made Mangku Pastika, refuse to acknowledge that the laws were changed. This is the reason why the people involved in the movement distrust the provincial government. Then comes along the Indonesian Presidential Decree No. 51 (2014), signed by Indonesia's sixth president, Susilo Bambang Yudhoyono. This allowed 700 hectares of sea in Benoa Bay, South Bali, to be reclaimed in order to revitalize the area but this 'revitalization' project is kept vague with no further details of the advantages and disadvantages and what the processes and developments entailed. The current president, Joko Widodo (Jokowi), has promised to revive Indonesia as a maritime nation state. However, Bali society[8] and particularly the Bali Tolak Reklamasi community report that the reclamation project, which contradicts his promise, is still ongoing as the decree has not yet been revoked at the writing of this chapter. For many years, Bali society was quiet about this kind of exploitation. This time, however, Bali Tolak Reklamasi has become a rare social movement that raises these issues 'through the arts'.

Music band Navicula, musicians Man Angga, poet and performer Cok Sawitri, and visual artist and performer Made 'Bayak' Muliana are artists who have been involved in BTR events. Though they are professional artists, they acknowledge that this is not why they are involved. They admit to having been affected by the changes in Bali, pushed through 'in the name of mass tourism' instead of cultural tourism: 'the reclamation despises and underestimates the sea' which the Hindu religion sees as sacred (interview with Navicula Angga, Sawitri and Muliana, 2015). Also, as 'our own reflection of our era … our own history', they feel moved to do something 'with whatever we can do' as musicians and artists. They do not have to be activists to be involved (interview with Angga and Muliana, 2015).

Benoa Bay is well known as a water sport and fishing area where many Benoa locals are employed in related businesses. To many of them, a revitalization did not appear an urgent necessity. Muliana pointed out that a 'miscommunicated understanding of Bali's tourism concept' has become the access to let the reclamation plan go through (interview with Muliana, 2015). Benoa Bay is South Bali's golden triangle or golden point – the sunrise and sunset can be seen from this area with no hills or mountains blocking the view. It is close to the airport (especially with the toll way that has been built) as well as famous tourist places such as Kuta, Nusa Dua, and Uluwatu. Thus, 'it has a high economy value' for the property investor, yet 'none of this is based on Bali society's priorities and necessities' and that is why it is being rejected by Bali society, particularly the Bali Tolak Reklamasi community (interview with Navicula, Muliana and Venusia, 2015).

Their first small demonstration took place on 1 August 2013 in the waters of Benoa Bay involving almost 100 local people from different walks of life including university students, academicians, environmental activists, urban activists, musicians, and members of a local journalist association. This was followed the next day with another bigger demonstration, involving hundreds of people, at Renon public square with musicians and NGO organizations. The response through the demonstration resulted in the formation of ForBALI.

ForBALI Coordinator, Wayan 'Gendo' Suardana, stated that Serangan Island, which was created via 300 hectares of sea reclamation in 1994, becomes the one example that Bali Tolak Reklamasi did not want to see happening again. It was 'aimed to be a tourism centre with the same concept of marine tourism' yet 'today there are only empty lands and the Bali Turtle Island Development master plan was never seen'. It has damaged the mangroves, washing up hundreds of hectares of corals and turtle habitats, also causing erosion throughout the Sanur shores up to the east shores of Karangasem (interview with Suardana, 2015).

Suardana mentioned how 'there is no compensation and no recovery effort' and that is 'very ironic', while the government keeps continuing with their 'logic and common sense' that is 'neoliberal'. This 'goes hand in hand' with the mass tourism practice that they are applying instead of the cultural tourism they have promised – like 'mining', where 'there is a potential place to be exploited by the tourism industry', thus it is allowed to 'fully dredge it and sell (it) cheaply' and so 'they will be given a project permit' – and not surprisingly, this practice seemed to be part of 'the liberal MP3EI (Indonesia Masterplan of Economic Development Acceleration and Expansion) [formed by former President Yudhoyono]' (interview with Suardana, 2015).

Suardana recounted that 'the expansion of this movement is a reflection of the people's exhaustion towards the political elites who prioritise greedy investors' interests'. This is reflected by the fact that more than 200 organizations are involved in this movement at different levels, from Bali, nationally, and internationally, which has led to the group winning a Rolling Stones Indonesia Editor's Choice Award for the People Power category. 'ForBALI is known as a people power representation that fights cheerfully and happily' having 'youths to be critical towards government policy that is seen as not in favour of the environment' and 'artists to be brave (about) using their skill and power to voice the earth ... also demonstrations don't have to be a scary activity' as 'criticizing the government is not a taboo' (interview with Suardana, 2016).

For three years, the movement has produced different kinds of activities: demonstrations in the form of cultural parades (*parade budaya*); media campaigning on mainstream, online and social media (website, Twitter, Instagram, Facebook, YouTube) where artworks and photographs are shared; published campaigns (posters, bulletins, leaflets, banners); public campaigns; cultural campaigns (big and small music concerts); online petitions; and also political efforts (sending letters and facilitating discussion) targeting the regional and central government, which has resulted in a mass demonstration at the Governor's office, Denpasar

House of Representatives, and the Indonesian President's Residency in Jakarta (interview with Suardana, 2015).

Bali Tolak Reklamasi interestingly juxtaposes Bali's mass/cultural tourism and its plan for land reclamation of 700 hectares. The former is a tool used to revive Bali's traditional status through tourism started by the colonial Dutch. Now, 'an environmentally and culturally friendly revitalization plan' that 'should' be good for the people is underway. Either way, these notions are imposed on and do not come from the people of Bali themselves. The key word of the reclamation project is *revitalization*. Remarkably, this word is also what TWBI uses as their slogan.

The Benoa Bay reclamation – as an example of the continuing tendency of 'revitalization fantasy' in Bali – has been 'interrogated' by a cultural movement that utilizes artistic and creative inputs to effectively problematize political and social issues. In this way, Bali Tolak Reklamasi 'de-anthropologizes' Bali as the 'evidence' of the 'revitalization fantasy' has been revealed through the artistic practices of the participants of Bali Tolak Reklamasi. Beyond an artistic movement, it is also a resistance towards further commodification of space and society in Bali.

Conclusion

Culture can be manifested in an intangible idea, action, or form of material objects. It relates to human interaction and develops through a process of learning. Human beings are creative and this enables them to endure life challenges and to improve quality of life. Thus, culture always reflects the soul, the spirit, and the struggle of people at a given time. This means that each generation has its own cultural expression as it has different challenges. The two case studies from Bandung and Bali can be understood from this perspective.

The experience of the people of Bandung and Bali in making their voice heard conveys a certain optimistic spirit. It gives the feeling that the people can take back a sense of hope and power; the idea that what has existed does not have to continue to exist; and that people coming together are able to better their condition if they make the effort. From Bandung, people have learned that the use of organized movement by winning leadership within the bureaucratic system can be a way to settle social problems. Whereas from Bali, the lesson is that a mobilizing social movement requires not only political consideration and action but also creative expression and alternative imagination. Both cases highlight the potential social and political power of creatives and their activities, which have rarely been discussed in the existing literature on creative industries.

Notes

1 Closely bound together by intimate social or cultural ties or by close economic or political ties.
2 For a more detailed information on the Rengasdengklok Affairs and the part that the youth has played in the moments culminating in Indonesia's independence please see for example Anderson (2005).
3 We interviewed five creative workers, social activists, and academicians. Creative practitioners include business owners in various creative industries, such as design, fashion, media, music, and culinary. Social organizations like Bandung Creative City Forum act as not-for-profit intermediaries in which members work in a voluntary manner. For example, its general manager and Dwinita Larasati and Fiki Satari are university lecturers at the Institute of Technology Bandung and University of Padjadjaran, Bandung, respectively, but voluntarily donate their time and effort to the activities of BCCF. In regard to the academic sector, our interviewees included experts in creative industries development, such as Professor Togar Simatupang at of the School of Business

and Management as well as Dr Budi Rahardjo from the School of Electrical Engineering and Informatics. Both schools are under the Institute of Technology Bandung, Indonesia.

4 Fiki Chikara Satari, a fashion designer and owner of Airplane Systm Clothing (ASC). Fiki started his business in 1998 by selling his products through several established stores. This was done because he did not yet have enough capital to open his own shop. But slowly his efforts paid off. In September 2001, he opened his own shop and the business began growing rapidly. His products reached dozens of cities in Indonesia, and in 2010 ASC opened a branch in Kuala Lumpur, Malaysia. ASC has even penetrated the European market by opening a store in Bordeaux, France. Fiki was the Head of Bandung Creative City Forum before being succeeded by Dwinita Larasati.

5 KickFest is one of the biggest annual clothing expos in Indonesia initiated by the clothing community in Bandung. The event was started in 2007. The festival gets bigger each year and the number of participating companies has risen to more than 200, attracting thousands of visitors. Recently the festival was also held in other cities in Indonesia.

6 Another informant, Dwinita Larasati, was the Head of the Masters Programme at the Faculty of Arts and Design, Institute of Technology Bandung, Indonesia. As a graphic artist, she was also involved in the foundation of Bandung Creative City Forum (BCCF) in 2008, and currently acts as the chairman of BCCF.

7 Which Taussig interpreted as 'the argument that control over the trick of truth' and how '"labour", meaning human beings at work, is flip-flopped between its market-value and its use-value so as to create profit' became relevant. He crucially argued that 'the secret of the expansion in value' is a 'trick' – 'deface the commodity of [labour] … allowing its mimetic or use-value component to surge forth' and enabling 'modern capitalist magic' to function well. Therefore, 'fetishism is not a consequence but the magical precondition for the commodity'; the capitalism we are facing today.

8 'Society of Bali' or 'Bali society' is used instead of Balinese as Balinese usually refers to real Balinese, while in Bali there are many citizens from other parts of Indonesia who have lived there a long time, and would not call themselves Balinese.

References

Anderson, B. R. (2005) *Java in a Time of Revolution: Occupation and Resistance, 1944–1946.* Jakarta: PT. Equinox Publishing Indonesia.

Bandung Creative City Forum (BCCF) Official Website (2012) [online]. Available at http://www.bccf-bdg.com/webs/contact/about-us.html [accessed January 2014].

Bland, B. (2014) Top architect uses role as mayor to transform Indonesian city. *Financial Times*, Urban Resilience [online]. Available at http://www.ft.com/cms/s/0/0820c7c4-b358-11e3-b09d-00144feabdc0.html#axzz3q77eIu9H [accessed October 2015].

British Council (2008) *Annual Report 2007–08* [online]. Available at http://www.britishcouncil.org/annual-report/ea1.htm [accessed March 2016].

British Council (2014) Cable cars, free wifi and streetfood: Ridwan Kamil's ingredients for a happy city. British Council Creative Economy Blog, [blog]. Available at http://creativeeconomy.britishcouncil.org/blog/14/09/26/cable-cars-free-wifi-and-streetfood-ingredients-ha/ [accessed October 2015].

Erviani, N. K. (2013) Green light for Benoa Bay development. *Bali Daily* [online]. Available at http://www.thebalidaily.com/2013-07-09/green-light-benoa-bay-development.html [accessed May 2015].

ForBALI. (2015) About Us [online]. Available at http://www.forbali.org/en/about-us/ [accessed May 2015].

Florida, R. (2002) *The Rise of the Creative Class.* New York: Basic Books.

Hartley, J., Potts, J., Flew, T., Cunningham, S., Keane, M., and Banks, J. (eds.) (2012) *Key Concepts in Creative Industries.* London: Sage.

Howkins, J. (2002) *The Creative Economy.* London: Penguin.

Landry, C. (2008) *The Creative City: A Toolkit for Urban Innovators,* 2nd edn. London: Earthscan.

Langenhaim, J. (2014) Battle for Bali: Campaigners fight back against unchecked development. The *Guardian* [online]. Available at http://www.theguardian.com/environment/the-coral-triangle/2014/oct/22/battle-for-bali-campaigners-fight-back-against-unchecked-development [accessed May 2015].

Leadbeater, C. (2008) *What Makes Cities Creative?* British Council Creative Cities Workshop, Warsaw, March 16/18, 2008 [online]. Available at http://creativecities.britishcouncil.org/files/data/kb/cc_-_charlie_leadbeater_think_piece.pdf [accessed February 2016].

Pearson, C. A. (1998) *Indonesia: Design and Culture*. New York: The Monacelli Press.
Presidential Decree No. 45 Year 2011 in the document: Peraturan Presiden Republik Indonesia Nomor 45 Tahun 2011 Tentang Rencana Tata Ruang Kawasan Perkotaan Denpasar, Badung, Gianyar, dan Tabanan [online]. Available at www.bpkp.go.id/uu/filedownload/5/3/1885.bpkp [accessed January 2015].
Presidential Decree No. 51 Year 2014 in the document: Perpres No 051 Tahun 2014 Perubahan atas Peraturan Presiden Nomor 45 Tahun 2011 tentang Rencana Tata Ruang Kawasan Perkotaan Denpasar, Badung, Gianyar, dan Tabanan, Inaugurated : 30/05/2014, Published by Sea and Fishery Ministry Law Information [online]. Available at infohukum.kkp.go.id/index.php/hukum/download/367/?type_id=1 [accessed January 2015].
Rahardjo, B. (2002) A Story of Bandung High-Technology Valley. Paper presented at the National Seminar on Telecommunications and Information Technology-Based Industries, 11 May 2002. Bandung: Institute of Technology, Bandung.
Redaksi (2013) *5 Tahun ke Depan, Bakal Ada 30 Kampung Kreatif di Kota Bandung* [online]. Available at: http://bandungjuara.com/program/5-tahun-ke-depan-bakal-ada-30-kampung-kreatif-di-kota-bandung.html [accessed July 2016].
Redaksi (2014) *Kontak Kami* [online]. Available at: http://bandungjuara.com/kontak-kami [accessed November 2016].
Rowntree, J., Neal, L., and Fenton, R. (2011) *International Cultural Leadership: Reflections, Competencies and Interviews*. London: Cultural Leadership Programme, Arts Council, England.
Rustiadi, S. 2015. *Connecting the Unconnected: Unlocking the Potential for the Development of Creative Industries in the city of Bandung, West Java Province, Indonesia*. Doctoral thesis, Goldsmiths, University of London [Thesis]
Said, E. W. (1993) *Culture and Imperialism*. New York: Vintage Books.
Soemardi, A. R. (2006) Bandung as a Creative City: Visions on Creative Culture and the Making of Place. Paper for International Seminar on Urban Culture – Arte-Polis: Creative Culture and the Making of Place – Bandung, 21–22 July 2006.
Taussig, M. (2000) The beach (a fantasy). *Critical Inquiry*, 26(2), 248–78.
Vickers, A. (2012) *Bali: A Paradise Created*. Singapore: Tuttle Publishing.
Za, Wong Li (2016) The Mayor who transformed Bandung into a livable and lovable city. Available at https://www.star2.com/culture/design/2016/08/10/the-major-who-transformed-bandung-into-a-livable-and-lovable-city/#zL8WQehIsO1CDzHG.99 [accessed May 2018].

24

Culture, digitalization, and diversity

Asian perspectives

Hye-Kyung Lee and Lorraine Lim

Digitalization has transformed cultural ecologies at national, regional, and global levels. As it de-materializes cultural products and transforms them to intangible digital data, the existing distinction between goods and services loses its efficacy. De-materialization potentially lowers costs for cultural distribution and broadens public access. It makes cultural content easy to store, reproduce, and archive, often fuelling tensions around ownership and control of digitalized content and its online dissemination. Digitalization leads to easier, cheaper, and immediate online connections between producer–producer, producer–consumer and consumer–consumer. This comes with an increased cross-national/regional connectivity that overcomes time, geographical boundaries, and linguistic barriers. At the same time, previously separate areas of activities are increasingly integrated, blurring the boundary between cultural production, distribution, and consumption, facilitating consumer creativity, and encouraging the merger between the existing cultural forms and new media. All these phenomena are observed in the cultural and creative industries in Asia. Along with promising new opportunities such as lowered costs and easier access, challenges are also emerging, such as digital divides within society (and in the region) and the increasing power of a small number of global online platforms (CEIM 2015: 9). This chapter intends to demonstrate how cultural sectors and cultural policies in China, South Korea, Singapore, and Thailand are responding to digitalization in diverse ways, and how the agenda of cultural diversity can be newly addressed and affirmed based on the political, social, and cultural contexts in these countries.

Arts, creativity, and the limits of digitalization

De-materialization, connectivity and convergence indicate the possibilities of new methodologies and processes within art-making, which result in new forms of creative expression and innovative ways of communicating with an audience. In the five Asian countries, there are painters, sculptors, and architects who actively use digital technologies such as sampling, simulation, and 3D printing as part of their production of existing art forms.[1] Furthermore, an increasing number of artists use digital technologies and online engagement in order to create new aesthetic expressions, defining their work as 'new media art', 'digital art' or 'social media art' (Korean Economic Daily 2012). These cultural expressions rely on the convergence between art, computing, coding, media, social networks, and virtual reality and seek interactive modes of exhibition and performance. They are recognized as new genres of art-making of which require an advancement of relevant knowledge and skills on the side of artists. At the same time, these types of artworks are convenient to share via social networks and online platforms and have potential to easily relate to young people whose everyday cultural life is shaped heavily by media consumption and online connectivity.

In addition to broadening the creation process and boosting new types of creativity, digital technologies have brought about substantial changes to how we record, preserve, and archive existing cultural expressions. Although the surveyed countries do not have a coherent policy framework on the digitalization of culture, policy makers and cultural institutions are keen to digitalize, catalogue, and archive arts and cultural heritage. For instance, the last two decades have seen South Korea continuously develop a number of digital cultural archives such as the Digital Archive of Performing Arts, the Arts Council Korea Arts Archive (which includes a digital archive), the Gugak (traditional Korean music) Archive (which include digital resources), and the Korean Film Archive (incorporating a digital cinema archive). Similarly, China has made a large investment in digitalizing its folk culture and cultural heritage, and key institutions such as the Gugong Museum (Forbidden City) and Dunhuang Research Center have made significant advances in digitalizing their collections with support from the government. Viet Nam is also developing cultural archives such as the National Center of Cultural Heritage Archive which includes digitally recorded cultural content. In Singapore, the National Heritage Board is currently aiming to digitize every object in its collection so as to set up an online collection and portal where the general public, students, educators, and researchers would be able to download images for use in the future. Similarly, Centre 42, an organization that supports writers and artists to create work for the Singaporean stage, has sought to create a digital archive of Singaporean theater through digitizing information and audio and visual artefacts from theater productions.

Going digital and online allows cultural organizations a new means of communicating and disseminating their work. They have begun showing their collections, exhibitions, and video clips of performances and talks via their website and engaging with these audiences via social media networks and messenger services. What is notable, however, is that the products of these organizations cannot be completely digitalized and their online space is rather secondary to physical space, tangible collection, and human interaction. The focus of most organizations is on using online platforms to promote their offline products rather than creating new content specifically designed for online platforms, clearly manifesting 'the limit of digitalization' of those art forms and content that necessitate a physical medium, activity, and space. When it comes to most small, less-resourced organizations, their online space is used primarily for information dissemination as developing an interactive digital interface would often need capital investment. The interviewed policy makers and practitioners indicate that online services can offer an 'augmented' experience rather than a replacement to physical attendance. Another barrier is copyright: online streaming or screening requires copyright clearance, which would be a complicated and time-consuming process.

For non-mainstream, minority, and independent artists who are excluded from dominant and official distribution channels, the digital space and online connectivity play key roles in reaching out to audiences, sometimes beyond national borders. Artists can promote their works and make their voices heard via alternative, online routes, not confining their work to the parameters set by mainstream views and strict censorship. For example, Shivaji Das in Singapore has used Facebook as well as the mobile phone communication app, WhatsApp, to reach out to the Bangladesh migrant worker community in the country to encourage them to take part in the first ever Migrant Workers Poetry Competition. In Viet Nam, Nha San Collective and San Arts, two independent art studios, are active in promoting their work domestically and internationally via their website and social networks. In Thailand, digital technologies have enabled an independent arts practitioner to run workshops with people in the south of the country to enable them to make their own short films so as to be able to start telling their stories. Digital technologies are also helping non-governmental organizations such as the People's Empowerment Foundation to devise new business models to enable minority communities in the north of Thailand to sell cultural products derived from their lands in an attempt to create a self-sustaining economy in order to rely less on aid.

However, it might be over-optimistic to conclude that digitalization will automatically guarantee a greater level of diversity in artistic expressions. The 'attention economy', where the gigantic quantity of digital content and services on online platforms fiercely compete for audience's attention (Webster 2014), is not a friendly environment for minority, independent, and non-mainstream artists. Attracting an audience, keeping their attention, and broadening their perspective is not an easy task, and the audience base for these artists could remain small. Unsurprisingly, online content of traditional culture, heritage, and non-mainstream arts is heavily shadowed by that of popular content such as film, TV, pop music, and games. Digital and new media arts could be more easily connected to popular culture and have a strong relevance to today's media environment. Yet, there is a long way to go for these converged art forms to gain more recognition in the surveyed Asian countries.

Cultural industries' digital transformation

Asian cultural policy makers, industry practitioners, and experts agree that, unlike the arts and cultural heritage, cultural industries have been fundamentally impacted by digitalization. They think the existing distinction between physical goods and intangible services is no longer sustainable, and digital/online products are now substituting analogue/offline products. Although cultural audiences, for example music consumers in Japan and China, are still willing to buy CDs to support their chosen artists (New York Times 2014; also Chinese interviewees), the rise of digital music in the form of downloading and streaming is an irreversible tide and this transformation also applies to other parts of the cultural industries albeit to varying extents (IFPI 2015).[2] Overall, Asian cultural industries are becoming 'weightless' notwithstanding the gaps and differences between countries.

Digital technologies and online connectivity now seem to be a key part of the audiovisual production process. Yet, industry practitioners note that while there are some areas in which costs have been lowered (e.g., distribution), such a change does not necessarily mean a noticeable reduction of production costs as there is still a need to invest in digital equipment (e.g., for 3D film production), new technologies, and skills development (e.g., special effects). Cultural producers – especially mainstream, commercial producers who compete for audience share – will have an increasing need for talents who are equipped with skills that match new technologies. A key issue to consider here is the cultural industries' inherent reliance on human skills and talents that cannot be substituted by mechanical processes (Baumol and Bowen 1965). As many experts comment, this is the fundamental feature of the cultural industries and the wider 'creative industries'; this implies that, in spite of digitalization, the cost and efforts for generating creative and innovative ideas/contents would not reduce significantly in many sectors of the industries. For instance, major broadcasters in Thailand are recognizing the talent and creativity of independent TV producers and have started to hire them to produce content to fill air time on their programming schedules. In addition, interviewed experts note that promotional activities on popular online spaces could incur substantial expenses, counteracting the cost reduction effect of digitalization.

Meanwhile, digitalization has triggered the emergence of new forms of popular culture such as online comics (webtoon), web serials (or webdrama), and web-based entertainment shows (also see Yecies and Shim 2018, this volume). These are seen as adaptations of existing forms of comics, dramas, and TV shows for the online environment, and are beginning to serve successfully as original stories for other media products. In the case of web-based serials and entertainment shows, the shorter running time (a few to 15 minutes per episode) and quick online releases imply a relatively smaller scale of investment and low entry barriers, in comparison with existing TV and film production, and thus a new testing ground for creative ideas and new trends. The rapidly surging popularity of web serials is indicated by the launch of Asia's first web serial festival, KWeb Fest, in Seoul in July 2015 (Yonhap News 2015).

Yet, the impact of the digitalization is felt more strongly in distribution and consumption rather than production. Firstly, de-materialization means that a substantial part of physical distribution channels have become obsolete and redundant. Secondly, while existing companies such as terrestrial broadcasters struggle to keep up, a range of internet-based companies and independent 'creatives' have risen up and are now offering cultural content on new media platforms on varying devices – increasingly on mobile phones. This is accompanied with new business models: mainly commercial broadcasting models (free content funded by advertising income), freemium models (free content + subscription) and subscription models. And yet, the popularity of YouTube as well as China's online video sites such as Youku Tudou and Sohu shows that the 'free' provision of cultural content is at the heart of the new business model.

It has been found that YouTube is the most popular online video distribution platform in all surveyed countries except China where it is banned. A media expert in Korea points out that although paid film and TV services online are being gradually established, typical Asians prefer YouTube as it provides a wide range of free content. In the meantime, China has witnessed an extremely rapid expansion of domestic online video sites such as Youku Tudou, Sohu, and iQiyi. These companies are powerhouses in the Chinese new media economy, and have already developed substantial capacity to create original content such as web serials, film and TV drama, both competing and collaborating with existing TV and film companies. The rise of these online-based companies in China can be explained by the term 'internet plus': these internet-based companies are leading the convergence between the internet and traditional cultural industries, proactively seeking, acquiring, and even producing cultural content themselves.

Other countries, too, have witnessed the growth of new media companies as major players in the cultural industries, e.g., Viet Nam's online-based video producers such as Zing TV, Hayhay TV, and Soha TV, South Korea's Gom TV, TVing, Naver TVcast, and IPTVs such as Ole TV, Thailand's Guchill TV, and Singapore's Toggle TV. Witnessing such developments, Asian TV broadcasters are becoming new media themselves, offering services via various online platforms. Yet, they are facing fierce competition with online video sites and IPTV providers for audience share and advertising income (e.g., Chinese advertisers now prefer putting advertisements on online platforms). Therefore, for public service broadcasters, producing high-quality and reliable current affairs, educational and cultural programs would be an effective way to maintain their legitimacy and visibility. Amidst the fast development and expansion of online content platforms in the five surveyed countries, there has emerged a trend of concentration. Network effects are strong and the platforms' attractiveness is hugely dependent on their capacity to offer fast speeds, manage traffic and provide convenient user interfaces, which require huge capital investment. Clearly, the concentration tendency that used to define audiovisual distribution offline[3] applies to online distribution too.

The popular online platforms operate commercially and without public responsibilities that used to be imposed on traditional terrestrial TV (various quotas for news, current affairs, and education programs) and physical screens (screen quota). Cultural distribution online is very much market-driven with the platforms investing primarily in popular content. Although small, non-mainstream and indie content is available on commercial platforms, it is often too 'deeply' located (difficult to be found among numerous layers of content) and the issue of cultural diversity is hardly considered. In theory, independent producers can make their content available on major platforms to reach out to a wide audience. The reality is that the majority of such content struggles to achieve popularity. There are indie content platforms (e.g., Korean indie film sites IndiePlug and Youefo) but they tend to be much smaller than mainstream platforms and the opportunities for growth are limited. This is because, as mentioned before, the successful operation of an online platform needs capital investment with regard to servers, traffic management, and interface design on one hand, and audience attention on the other.

Still, digital space and online communications are crucial means for minority and non-mainstream groups to gather together, collaborate, and engage with their existing and potential audience. For instance, LGBT communities in Asia feel the online space is a sphere where they can express their identity openly, communicate with those who are interested in their issues, and organize events such as LGBT gatherings. The PinkDot Movement in Singapore has used the internet to organize themselves, inspiring similar PinkDot gatherings internationally as well. A local academic highlights an online forum for LGBT Muslim women that connects them to each other, providing a network and information source and ultimately holding meetings offline. Importantly, digital space can work as an alternative media where young people can make their voices heard. One such example is Trang, an independent group of Vietnamese youth who share a passion in producing high-quality entertainment shows of relevance to young people's ways of life and thinking. The group started a YouTube channel in November 2014 with the name Trang TV (in English 'White TV'), focusing on representing young people's emotions and issues. Similarly, innovative uses of new media and social networks seem to be very important for independent musicians in China who used to be tied to where they live and found it difficult to engage with a wider audience. The musicians now can collaborate easily beyond geographical barriers via social networks and also actively showcase their work online. These platforms are also used by overseas musicians and artists who hope to introduce their work to Chinese audiences.

Access, sharing, and convergence

The surveyed countries have seen the increasing penetration of the internet and mobile communications infrastructure. Singapore and South Korea's broadband and mobile infrastructure is mature and the internet penetration rate is very high; 98.5 percent of Korean population had access to the internet (including mobile access) in 2014 (MSFP and KISA 2014). In Singapore, the number of broadband connections exceeds that of households (106.6 percent, 2015) and similarly the number of mobile phones exceeds that of its citizens (148 percent, 2014) (Singapore Statistics 2015). As of 2015, China's current internet penetration rate is only 48.8 percent[4] but the actual size of the internet-using population explains the impressive growth of online companies and services that make up one of the biggest digital economies in the globe. The size of China's digital economy is expected to increase rapidly in the near future as 94.5% percent of Chinese people now use a mobile phone,[5] potentially accessing the internet via their phones. In the case of countries where the internet infrastructure is yet to be expanded, the impact of digitalization on cultural consumption might be relatively less significant. Still, they are very likely to see a constant rise of mobile access to the internet as mobile phones are now an essential part of everyday life. In 2014, Thailand's broadband penetration rate was only 8.50 percent but there are 144.9 mobile phones per 100 people.[6] The internet penetration rate in Viet Nam is 42.9 percent and, yet, there are 145 mobile phones per 100 people (though the smartphone penetration rate is 36 percent).

The internet and the new media environment facilitate an alternative mode of cultural economy, based on voluntary production and sharing. In the analogue age, the provision of free content was possible mainly via commercial broadcasters relying on advertising income and the public's collective support for non-profit cultural institutions. The rise of the internet expanded this model of business to almost all areas of cultural consumption, leading to the powerful regime of 'free culture' (Lessig 2004). The other side of the coin is that cultural content providers find it more and more difficult to distinguish their paid services from the abundant free content and collective knowledge. Thus it is not surprising that the existing framework on copyright is heavily challenged. Although the surveyed countries have seen the emergence of paid film, music and TV content providers working on various platforms, copying and sharing is an essential feature of the digital and online age.

While acknowledging that copyright protection is still a contested area, where different views and positions prevail, this report points out the double-sided effects of unauthorized online sharing of cultural contents – such as music, TV shows, and film, particularly those originated in Asia – across national and linguistic borders. Such sharing can expand the cultural repertoire of society and facilitate cultural flows between societies. One example is the free sharing of foreign-language films and TV shows: avid members of the audience themselves translate the original language into the local one, provide subtitles, and share the translated versions online. The negative side of this activity would be potential copyright infringement and a decrease in audiences for domestic products, e.g., popular South Korean drama and film and Japanese manga can overshadow Vietnamese domestic products (Ministry of Culture, Sports and Tourism of Viet Nam 2013); but the positive effect would include grass-root, non-commercial cultural flows and exchanges as well as the enhancement of mutual understanding between societies, beyond national and linguistic borders (Lee 2011). The boom of amateur translation of foreign cultural products as well as file sharing in general indicates that cultural consumers in the digital age are difficult to manage and control, and the industries' business model should find a way to reconcile this with the 'economy of sharing'.

At the center of the booming economy of sharing, there is the abundance of UGC as a new type of entertainment and popular culture. UGC not only brings more diversity to society's audiovisual content but also influences professional cultural producers by giving them fresh and innovative ideas. For this reason, major TV companies such as CCTV (China) and VTV (Viet Nam) are keen to interact with an audience – especially online opinion leaders – and engage them in program making. This means a significant change to professional TV producers' relationship with their audience from a hierarchical to a horizontal one, or from government control to market consideration. The strengthened online connectivity and proliferation of self-expression indicates a potential transformation of the relationship between cultural policy makers and ordinary cultural consumers to a more direct and equal one. This could also widen the scope for cultural policy discussion involving relevant stakeholders including government policy makers, public cultural institutions, civil groups, and cultural consumer communities. In some countries such as South Korea and Singapore, noticeable efforts have been made to engage civil society in policy discussion and the management of cultural organizations. Digital and online tools are key features of this progress. Policy documents and information are available online via the ministry and key agencies' websites and some countries have created a dedicated online policy zone where members of the public can view key statistics and policy documents related to culture: Korean cultural ministry's Cultural Statistics Portal[7] is a very good example. In Singapore, REACH is an online website that allows citizens to participate and provide feedback on various government initiatives.[8] The Chinese government and public organizations are expanding their online communications with members of the public, especially via active use of social network platforms such as WeChat. Yet, this is mainly for disseminating and promoting government policy and related information rather than revolutionizing citizens' participation.

Meanwhile, there are groups and communities whose access to digitalized content and opportunities for self-expression are limited due to the lack of internet infrastructure (e.g., rural residents in Thailand, Viet Nam, and China), lifestyles that are not in accord with online communications (e.g., elderly people in Korea and in Singapore), the lack of skills and knowledge (e.g., immigrants and migrants in Korea, Thailand, and Singapore[9]) and the lack of financial resources (those who live in poverty, including less-resourced ethnic minorities). Importantly, for most Asians today, their mobile phone is a crucial device as it allows them to be connected to and potentially access internet-based cultural provision. Therefore, strengthening mobile infrastructure and providing relevant training would be a key to widening the benefits of the digitalization and reducing geographical, generational, and sociocultural divides.

Another tendency is that ethnic minority language users are increasingly marginalized as popular mainstream-language products are widely shared and consumed online. Policy makers and cultural practitioners indicate that ethnic minority cultures are regarded as something to be preserved digitally rather than something that can be positively promoted as part of contemporary digital culture in the region. The low visibility of ethnic minority cultures online, for example in China and Viet Nam, might be because of the minority groups' lack of resources and skills. Another problem faced by minority ethnic groups is that their culture is often perceived as traditional, sometimes old-fashioned, by the general public. Even if they are able to highlight their cultures using digital technologies, the groups may find it very hard to challenge the public's existing opinion and promote their contemporary creations.

Cooperation in the region and beyond

Collaboration has been actively taking place between cultural industries across countries: from audiovisual coproduction, format transfer, cross-Asian investment in cinema chains and entertainment agencies to the creation of multi-national pop music bands. Performing and visual artists' regional collaboration, too, has expanded at various levels, from coproduction, forums, artist residences to archives such as the Singapore-based Asia Shakespeare Intercultural Archive, a digital archive of all performances of Shakespeare that take place within the region. Another initiative is the Hong Kong-based Asia Art Archive that showcases the digitalized version of artworks from China, Taiwan, South Korea, Japan, Viet Nam, India and many others. The proliferation of digital tools has improved the ease of communication and sharing beyond national boundaries, and this has meant that regional cultural cooperation is now much more convenient. This can greatly benefit smaller arts companies by helping them overcome financial and linguistic barriers. For instance, Singapore's The Necessary Stage used online communications as a way to work with their Japanese counterparts in developing a new work: the script was co-written and developed via emails, the meetings took place over Skype, and videos were made and shared via Facebook, radically reducing the costs involved.

At the governmental level, there are various international cultural cooperation and exchange initiatives. For instance, Viet Nam has signed 42 bilateral agreements and treaties on cultural cooperation.[10] Meanwhile, China has signed intergovernmental accords on cultural cooperation with 145 countries and numerous implementation agreements on cultural exchanges in addition to actively implementing international cultural assistance.[11] South Korea's case is not different in terms of having signed numerous international agreements and treaties and having increased cultural assistance projects with African and Southeast Asian countries.[12] Yet, it is not fully certain if there are collaborative and exchange schemes that are specific to 'digital' production, distribution, and consumption of culture and the arts. While the digital and online have constituted an environment where cultural activities in Asia are increasingly embedded, it appears that there is no focused policy collaboration or discussion on this area. For policy makers in the surveyed East Asian countries, the working definition of cultural diversity appears to be rather narrow, focusing on protecting and preserving traditional culture, cultural heritage, and ethnic minority cultures.

It should be noted that there are noticeable 'digital gaps' among the surveyed countries. If we took the broader Asia (and Asia-Pacific) region into account, the gaps would increase enormously. More proactive initiatives of regional sharing of skills and know-how would be helpful to reduce the gaps and increase digitalization's benefits for the region. From this perspective, overseas cultural assistance schemes could more proactively consider potential ways of sharing and transfer of knowledge and experience in this area. There are non-governmental regional initiatives – such as ICHCAP (International Information and Networking Center for Intangible Cultural Heritage in the Asia-Pacific Region, UNESCO category 2 organization)[13] and the non-profit Asia Art Archive[14] – that explore varying ways of regional collaboration towards establishing regional art and cultural resources. C-Asean is a newly established social enterprise that seeks to develop regional collaborations for cultural entrepreneurs.[15] These initiatives have the potential to provide a regional forum where the roles and impacts of digitalization on the region's culture could be discussed and regional sharing of related know-how could be encouraged. It would be also crucial to identify and encourage various grassroot initiatives by minority groups, non-mainstream cultural producers, and civil societies. Knowing and sharing of the experiences of minority cultural groups' creative uses of digital technologies and online spaces would be crucial for a better and more balanced understanding of the implications and effects of digitalization.

Digitalization helps Asian cultural producers to showcase their work to an international audience and seek potential partners and collaborators. This takes place at varying levels, from grassroot to government-sponsored initiatives, and often in partnership with global online platforms. As mentioned before, Viet Nam-based Nha San Collective and San Arts are proactively communicating with a global audience via both offline and online initiatives. The founder and director of the Museum of Contemporary Art Bangkok is currently in discussion with Google to digitalize the artworks in their collection offering Thai contemporary artists an international platform that would not have been possible before. In South Korea, the Korean Artist Project is an example of an online project linking the country's visual artists to global audiences and partners.[16] The project, which provides holistic information of the chosen artists and their works including digital exhibitions and video clips, is funded by the government and hosted by the Korean Art Museums (an association of private art museums) and has recently entered a partnership with Google Art Project. Similarly, the Korean Film Archive has launched the Korean Classic Film Theater on YouTube to allow global audiences to learn about and appreciate the country's classic films including those that have been digitally restored.[17] The country's National Gugak (traditional music) Center recently launched a YouTube channel and began providing recordings of all in-house productions. Interestingly, all of these examples highlight the central position of Google and YouTube in online showcasing and sharing of Asian culture and the arts at domestic, regional, and global levels (except China).

Opportunities

The digitalization and the active use of online space can bring a wide range of noticeable opportunities for the diversity of cultural expressions in Asia. Firstly, in addition to helping generate new types of creative ideas and cultural forms, it brings changes to the production process of existing cultural forms. Some of these new digital cultural forms (such as web serials and comics) are on the way to becoming established as part of the ecology of cultural industries. There are increasing opportunities for collaboration and co-creation of cultural producers, overcoming geographical, national, and linguistic barriers. Online interaction can help to reduce communication and transaction costs although organizations find that digitalization per se does not automatically reduce production and promotion costs. Secondly, in the traditional cultural sector such as performing and visual arts which require physical artworks, performers, and space, the effects of digitalization are felt strongly in the area of archiving, showcasing, promotion, and information delivery. Meanwhile, the effects are more significant in the cultural industries as physical products are giving way to intangible services. This has accompanied the diversification of business models and the popularization of businesses that capitalize on the prevailing 'free culture'. The third area is consumption, where digital distribution allows for greater consumer choice, immediacy between consumers and producers, more width and depth of distribution, and increasingly 'mobile' cultural consumption.

Cultural consumers can easily transform into producers, generating their own creative expressions online and sharing them widely. Their creation constitutes a core part of free content, promoting the free culture movement online and even manifesting the possibility of an economy of sharing and volunteering. Finally, the rise of online as an alternative space is another opportunity we are identifying. For culturally and socially marginalized groups and producers, online spaces can play key roles in promoting their identities and agendas, sometimes with much of their work taking place beyond national and linguistic borders. Often, going online can be a way to find freedom of expression when there is strong content regulation for offline cultural activities.

Key challenges

The effect of digitalization on the cultural sector in the surveyed five countries is complicated as this process is driven, encouraged, governed, and regulated by multiple actors including governments, public cultural institutions, private media businesses, non-profit arts organizations, civil groups, and cultural consumers. In addition, we have noticed that the effect is shaped by the current political, economic, and technological contexts of the given society. As the UNESCO Convention for the Protection and Promotion of the Diversity in Cultural Expressions (2005, Article 2) asserts, cultural diversity benefits from freer expression of ideas and from the government acting as a facilitator rather than regulator; in turn, socially responsible expressions could be encouraged by more open debate about the existence of dissimilar viewpoints. In some of the surveyed countries, there is tight control in music, TV, film, and arts, for example, requiring artists to submit their script/lyrics beforehand to acquire a license, or monitoring live performances. The similarly tight approach is extended to the online space, making politically and socially challenging content very difficult to be staged or released. Considering that a lot of innovative work is being created at grassroots levels, policy makers should consider how they can engender freer environments for creative thinking, expression, and experimentation, which often push the existing social, religious, and political norms.

The cultural ecology in the digital age is composed of a complex web of creators, platforms, networks, and devices. There is a consensus among the interviewed cultural policy makers and practitioners that digital and online means help to diversify the profile of creators and enhance diversity in cultural expressions. Yet, they also acknowledge that the trend of concentration is becoming more visible in platforms, communications networks, and devices. Although there are newcomers and start-ups, the above areas tend to be defined by concentration rather than diversity: there is a noticeable domination by a few global and several large-scale domestic companies (Kulesz 2014: 8–10). In this context, it is interesting to witness the dual roles of global platforms such as Google, YouTube, and Facebook that are playing in the digital economy in Asian countries. On one hand, these companies are powerful engines of US-led cultural globalization and disseminators of dominant values and ideas. On the other hand, they offer space where varying ideas are sought, presented, and shared beyond national and linguistic borders, often assisting grassroot creativity, knowledge transfer, and multi-directional cultural flows. For non-mainstream and minority producers and creators, these platforms work as a useful means of advocating their work and going around society's conservative political and social parameters. For example, YouTube serves as not only a site of popular entertainment but an outlet for alternative ideas and lifestyles. Nevertheless, those platforms commercially operate and have privileged access to global big data. They are sites where forces of US cultural hegemony and those of local expression converge and where commercialism and voluntarism work together. The popularity of these platforms requires us to shift our conceptualization of global cultural distribution, from cultural trade to cultural flow, which is difficult for policy makers to regulate.

The next issue is the digital divide across different Asian countries, and also across different groups of people with a country. The most excluded are the elderly, ethnic minorities, rural residents, and people with less economic and educational resources in societies with a low level of digital and online infrastructure. Meanwhile, in societies where internet access is ubiquitous, a new question is beginning to rise: if and how the inclusion of and access to digital culture can compensate for the exclusion from offline cultural activities and physical cultural facilities. In South Korea, it is reported that, for the younger generation who live in poverty and suffer from unemployment and low income, consuming digitalized culture online (such as film, TV, and animation) is perhaps the only and cheapest way to live their cultural life (Chosun Ilbo 2015). Here, it would be worth asking in what way and under what conditions 'digital abundance' helps to address the problem of 'cultural paucity' (for example, a lack of access to physical cultural facilities, goods, and services). Or, could the former be a manifestation of the latter? Another related question is if the expansion of online access to digitalized culture would result in the decline of physical cultural activities and venues. For arts and cultural organizations where funding is linked to their quantitative figures of audience attendance, this would impact upon policies on cultural funding.

Commercially operating online platforms are relatively free from the existing regulation on offline and analogue media in relation to public service provision. For example, popular internet portals are not obliged to provide high-quality educational and informative content in the same way public TV (and commercial terrestrial TV) is bounded by a range of public responsibilities. In addition, it is not clear if the surveyed countries have a coherent policy framework that concerns how the online space of public cultural institutions can address the issue of public interest and cultural diversity. Even for some public institutions such as the Korean Broadcasting System, online services on its website and other new media platforms, in comparison to its services on traditional TV, are seen as a more deregulated and marketized area, where commercialism prevails (Lee 2015). In the case of cultural industries in the countries where a socialist economy is giving way to market mechanisms, the decline of government control is likely to mean market control, rather than the development of public cultural services. Among the surveyed countries, however, the regulation of new media raises complicated issues: while policy makers are encouraged to consider potential ways to secure more public interest on new media platforms and services, applying the existing regulation for the old media to the new ones would be problematic, especially when the old media has been under the government's strict censorship.[18]

Finally, we want to point out the huge gap in availability of data on the arts and cultural sector and their digitalization. In some countries, the government is not active in gathering and publishing data in this area, leaving this job to the private sector. Only well-resourced private companies are capable of carrying out this research and the findings are likely to remain their property. One of the implications would be that investments in infrastructure and audience development based on the research data are driven by economic interests. As a policy maker in Thailand highlights, private telecommunications companies tend to invest heavily in cities due to the potential of high returns which results in duplication while in rural areas there is minimum ICT infrastructure. Data that is used for market optimization can also result in ignoring the needs of minority groups where there is low or little return of investment. To ensure parity in access to digital opportunities, there needs to be an investment by governments and public agencies to generate their own data to be able to determine areas of investment and allow for parity of access across the whole country. More nuanced data can also enable governments to create more targeted approaches in engaging with groups that have limited or no access to digital tools.

Conclusion

Without an adequate understanding of the nature of cultural digitalization, it is now difficult to comprehend the contour and shape of diversity in cultural expressions in the contemporary world. While being conscious of the danger of overgeneralization and overexaggeration of digitalization's effects, we believe that there is a strong case for incorporating a digital agenda to national and international discussion on cultural diversity. Often, policy makers rather narrowly interpret cultural diversity from the perspective of the promotion of traditional and ethnic minority cultures, as their periodic reports on the implementation of the UNESCO 2005 convention demonstrate (e.g., Chinese and Vietnamese governments' periodic reports). We recommend that the meaning of diversity be broadened, in which the current and potential roles of digital technologies and online connectivity are considered and relevant policy options are discussed in a more focused manner. Governments' active intervention is in demand to tackle the digital divide within society and to provide a structure that can help the potential of digital technologies to be maximized for the preservation of cultural heritage as well as creation of new cultural knowledge and artistic expressions. Under what conditions digital technologies and online communications can effectively assist independent, less commercial and minority cultures reach broader audiences, should be part of the cultural diversity agenda. We also propose that Asian policy makers should encourage more open cultural environments where cultural creativity and innovations of bottom-up, unfamiliar, and challenging natures are encouraged and enrich cultural repertories of the given society. At the same time, the roles played by national and international online media platforms in both promoting and limiting diversity in cultural expressions need to be carefully examined.

Acknowledgments

This chapter is a shortened version of 'Challenges and opportunities for the diversity of cultural expressions in the digital era in East Asia' (2015), commissioned from the authors by UNESCO Bangkok office. This research involved field trips to Bangkok, Beijing, Seoul, and Singapore in August 2015 and 66 interviews with policy makers, practitioners, and researchers in China, South Korea, Singapore, Thailand, and Viet Nam from July to September 2015. The authors thank the interviewees and their research assistants (Zeo Huyhn Linh, Xinyu Su, and Nitchakan Hongkarnjanapong).

Notes

1 '3D-printed artwork reaches viewers' http://vietnamnews.vn/life-style/264041/3d-printed-artwork-reaches-for-viewers.html (accessed September 24, 2015) and 'The Today Art Museum show features augmented reality display' http://www.ecns.cn/cns-wire/2015/08-28/179038.shtml (accessed September 24, 2015).

2 As for the replacement of CD sales with digital music in South Korea, see 'CD, its bitter disappearance' http://news.kmib.co.kr/article/view.asp?arcid=0923242653&code=13110000&sid1=cul (accessed September 24, 2015).

3 For example the concentration of offline film distribution and exhibition is clearly dominated by a few major companies in each country, with some cross-national investment: South Korea's three majors CGV, Lotte, and Megabox, Viet Nams's Galaxy Cinema and CGV Cinema, China's Wanda Cinemas, China Film Stellar Theater Chain, and Shanghai United Circuit, Thailand's GTH and Singapore's Mediacorp and Golden Village.

4 According to the 36th (the latest one) Statistical Report on Internet Development in China published by China Internet Network Information Centre, up to June 2015, the internet penetration rate is 48.8 percent (488 internet users among 1,000 people). http://www.cnnic.net.cn/hlwfzyj/hlwxzbg/hlwtjbg/201507/P020150723549500667087.pdf (accessed August 31, 2015).

5 According to the data shown on the official website of National Bureau of Statistics of China, mobile phone penetration rate as of 2014 is 94.50 percent (945 mobile phone users among 1,000 people). http://data.stats.gov.cn/easyquery.htm?cn=C01&zb=A0G0X&sj=2014 (August 31, 2015).

6 http://www.nbtc.go.th/TTID/ (accessed August 31, 2015).

7 http://www.culture.go.kr/index.do (accessed August 1, 2015).

8 https://www.reach.gov.sg/ (accessed October 4, 2015).

9 The Silver Arts Initiative by the National Arts Council of Singapore is one such initiative where programs within this initiative include funding workshops that allow senior citizens in Singapore (those aged 60 and above) to take part in digital film-making classes.

10 Ministry of Culture, Sports and Tourism of Viet Nam (2013) *Periodic Report on the Implementation of the UNESCO Convention on the Protection and Promotion of the Diversity of Cultural Expressions*. https://en.unesco.org/creativity/mr/periodic-reports-available-reports (accessed August 1, 2015), p. 7.

11 Ministry of Culture of the People's Republic of China (2012) *Quadrennial Report on the Implementation of the UNESCO Convention on the Protection and Promotion of the Diversity of Cultural Expressions.* https://en.unesco.org/creativity/mr/periodic-reports-available-reports (accessed August 1, 2015).
12 Korea Culture and Tourism Institute (2014) *Study on Periodic Report on the Implementation of the UNESCO Convention on the Protection and Promotion of the Diversity of Cultural Expressions* (including a draft periodic report). Chapter 2. Seoul: KCTI.
13 http://www.ichcap.org/eng/index/index.php._(accessed August 31, 2015).
14 http://www.aaa.org.hk/ (accessed August 31, 2015).
15 http://www.c-asean.org/ (accessed October 4, 2015).
16 http://www.koreanartistproject.com/ (accessed August 31, 2015).
17 https://www.youtube.com/user/KoreanFilm (accessed August 31, 2015).
18 In Singapore, there has been a drive to regulate new media via the *Media Convergence Report* in 2012. This has been deemed to be problematic by interviewees as the basic premise of this regulation is to apply rules based on 'old media' such as newspapers and television broadcasting to 'new media' without taking into consideration how differently both forms of media operate and function.

References

Baumol W. and Bowen, W. (1965) On the performing arts: the anatomy of their economic problems. *The American Economic Review*, 55(1/2): 495–502.

CEIM (2015) For a diversified networked culture: bringing the Convention on the Protection and Promotion of the Diversity of Cultural Expressions (CPPDCE) in the digital age. http://www.ieim.uqam.ca/IMG/pdf/rapportcdec-court-en-vfinale.pdf (accessed August 1, 2015).

Chosun Ilbo (2015, February 24) Dalgwansedaega saneun beop (How the generation of dalgwan).

IFPI (2015) IFPI digital music report. http://www.ifpi.org/downloads/Digital-Music-Report-2015.pdf (accessed September 24, 2015).

Korean Economic Daily (2012, April 1) Teuwiteo daetgeuldo misul sojaettSNS sidae sosyeorateuga tteunda (Twitter and online replies become material for art making: social art is rising in the age of SNS).

Kulesz, O. (2014) UNESCO Convention on the Protection and Promotion of the Diversity of Cultural Expressions: analysis of parties' periodic reports and contemporary digital trends. Paris: UNESCO.

Lee, H.-K. (2011) Participatory media fandom: a case study of anime fansubbing. *Media, Culture and Society*, 33(8): 1131–47.

Lee, H.-K. (2015) Public broadcasting, the Korean Broadcasting System (KBS), and its online services. In Hjorth, L. and Khoo, O. (eds.), *Routledge Handbook of New Media in Asia.* London: Routledge:

Lessig, L. (2004) *Free Culture: The Nature and Future of Creativity.* London: Penguin Books.

Ministry of Culture, Sports and Tourism of Viet Nam (2013) *Periodic Report on the Implementation of the UNESCO Convention on the Protection and Promotion of the Diversity of Cultural Expressions.* https://en.unesco.org/creativity/mr/periodic-reports-available-reports (accessed May 13, 2016).

Ministry of Science and Future Planning (MSFP) and Korean Internet and Safety Agency (KISA) (2014) *Internet Use Survey Summary Report.* Seoul: MSFP and KISA.

New York Times (2014, September 16) CD-loving Japan resists move to online music sales in Japan resisting. http://www.nytimes.com/2014/09/17/business/media/cd-loving-japan-resists-move-to-digital-music-.html?_r=0 (accessed August 31, 2015).

Singapore Statistics (2015) *Singapore in Figures.* Singapore: Singstat.

Webster, J. G. (2014) *The Marketplace of Attention: How Audiences Take Shape in a Digital Age.* Cambridge, MA: MIT Press.

Yonhap News (2015, July 14) Asia's first web series to open in Seoul.

Part V

Heritage and the cultural market

25

Consuming Indian-ness

Anxieties about the nation, handicrafts, and artisans in contemporary India

Sowparnika Balaswaminathan and Thomas Evan Levy

Although its origins could be traced back to the fifteenth century, it was in the early twentieth century that France began to crystallize laws that would regulate the production of wine by associating the quality of wines to the *terroir* (the natural environment) of their production. Known as 'appellations of control' (AOC), these laws eventually became Geographical Indications (GI) and were internationalized through the World Trade Organizations to be used by other countries. In Europe, GIs are used to index food materials and agricultural products to particular territories or towns. When India came to know of GIs, the logic of anchoring a food and its unique qualities to the land that produced it was transplanted to handicrafts. For scholars of Indian art, crafting communities, the handicraft industry and its consumers, handicrafts from India are believed to carry Indian history and culture, its very essence. This notion of Indian-ness in handicrafts has had a long and complicated history, and it is often accompanied by anxieties surrounding the state of handicrafts and the status of artisans, both of which, this chapter argues, are proxies for anxieties around the national identity of India. This chapter examines how Indian handicrafts and artisans have been historically constructed as the repositories of tradition from the colonial period until today. Furthermore, it explores the forms taken by the anxieties of present-day Indians who express their association with the country and its values through consuming crafts. When Indians consume handicrafts, they are also producing themselves, and thus, the health and character of these consumables become significant. This paper enquires into the act of consumption as an act of identity affirmation, and untangles the intersections between Indian nationalism, art and handicrafts, and the contemporary Indian subject.

Handicrafts, nationalism, and the market

Operating in cycles of protective and contemptuous reactions, the British discourse on South Asian art during the colonial period followed patterns of support and censure. Although initial British attitudes towards South Asian art had been of benign interest, the intensifying colonial project and conservative religious developments in England during the early ninettenth century resulted in the emergence of a supercilious perception of these same arts, which discouraged patronage. The precolonial forms of artistic patronage had started to wane, and the colonial scholars were not interested in South Asian art, decrying it either as monstrous (Sundar 1996: 22) or a pale imitation of Greek forms (Guha-Thakurta 1992: 121). However, the tides turned once more and the mid-nineteenth century saw the defense of South Asian art and craft gathering steam. During this period, Sir George Birdwood identified the deterioration of vernacular arts practices in India as a result of negligent governmental policy, and William Morris led the Arts and Crafts movement to encourage the British public to perceive Indian art as having design applications such as in home furnishings and furniture (Sundar 1996: 27). The idea that Indian art and craft had value, aesthetically and economically, was in vogue again, although these early British activists still did not think Indian art was equal to that from the West.

Pushpa Sundar (1996: 131) asserts that an increasing entrepreneurial interest in Indian craft from the British colonial government resulted in high-quality, traditional products and replicas of antiques being made to be sold as 'Indian' craft objects. During this same period, Indian-ness also becomes reified as Hindu and Buddhist. As Rajendralal Mitra's 1880 book *The Antiquities of Orissa* exemplifies, authenticity was being equated to pre-Islamic South Asian traditions (Guha-Thakurta 1992: 120). This is in line with the discourse of the Orientalist Indologists whose influence was strong and intensifying during this period. E. B. Havell (1861–34), a colonial arts administrator who became an art historian and critic, not only considered handicrafts and decorative arts as the only artistic tradition still 'alive' in India, he also wrote of Indian art as having a spiritual core that was central to understanding it, over any technical knowledge (Guha-Thakurta 1992: 159). These ideas were further elaborated upon by Ananda Kentish Coomaraswamy, an art historian and scholar, whose initial work in Ceylon advocated for bringing back the artisan guild of the precolonial, and especially medieval period, resonating with the ideals of the earlier Arts and Crafts movement, which valorized artisans, craftsmanship, and in India specifically, 'the pre-industrial village community' (Guha-Thakurta 1992: 149). For Coomaraswamy (1977: 5), art could be 'constant and normal', or 'variable and individualistic', and Asiatic arts were of the former category. Not only were physical and spiritual values intertwined in such arts, their practice was founded on the ideal of 'vocation', where knowledge and skill was passed on hereditarily. Furthermore, historical Indian society is described based on Hindu texts on social order, and aesthetic principles are assumed to be Hindu. The work of these Orientalists to protect, defend, and promote Indian art did three things that are relevant to the post-independent history of India, and the argument of this chapter: they constructed art and craft as Indian; they reified Indian as spiritual at the least, but also arguably Hindu; and they strongly articulated the economic value of arts and crafts as historical and organic.

The Indian nationalist movement that was gaining momentum in the nineteenth century was thus able to appropriate these arguments as they stood in opposition to the British who promoted Western-influenced art education, while supporting Indian art and craft only to exploit the labor of local artisans and fill the coffers of the regime (Sundar 1996: 135). In many respects, both the British regime and the nationalists recognized the economic and political power of arts and crafts, but the latter also endorsed them as synonymous with the national identity of a nation that deserved to be independent. Tapati Guha-Thakurta traces the infusion of the Japanese nationalism model from Kakuzo Okakura (1882–1913), an arts scholar who was a proponent of pan-Asianism, as well as the politico-spiritual discourses of the Scots-Irish supporter of the Indian nationalist movement, Sister Nivedita (1867–1911), who proclaimed that art was 'the most important vehicle of nationality' (Guha-Thakurta 1992: 168, 173). The discourse of 'khadi', or hand-spun, hand-woven cotton fabric, popularized by Mahatma Gandhi, resonated with colonial subjects not only because it made a rational economic argument against purchasing inflated British textile imports, but also because it was built upon the premise of resuscitating an 'Indian' tradition.

It is in this context that after India's independence in 1947, the conservation and revival of handicrafts was one of the most important dictates for the new government, which saw artisans living in deplorable conditions and traditional craft dying quietly. Commingled with the developmental projects to energize the local industries, several governmental projects were initiated to promote production and employment. Spearheaded by Kamaladevi Chattopadhyay, the handicrafts and handloom revival projects in the 1950s were facilitated by a series of institutions that were established for this very purpose. From the All India Handicrafts Board to the Central Cottage Industries Emporium, as well as several craft museums, Chattopadhyay had a strong vision for the position and trajectory of traditional arts and crafts. Associating crafts with the rural, Chattopadhyay championed the notion of the master craftsman, who had an affective and spiritual relationship with the craft that is supposed to be born out of divine inspiration (Chattopadhyay 2000: 2, 4, 13, 16). Her establishment of the National Award for Craftsmen in 1965, which continues today, facilitates this discourse. The installation of the National Craft Museum in New Delhi, and the various craft promotion organizations set up during this period, were to assist in the commercial viability of handicrafts. Thus, this chapter argues that in India, crafts occupy a position of symbolic and economic significance endorsing an Indian nationalism rooted in a nostalgic past dominated by Hindu and Buddhist spirituality. In this construction, artisans are not only the repositories of this tradition, but also the vehicle for an economically hopeful future in which crafts are a viable livelihood and a profitable export for the nation.

Identity, consumerism, and anxiety/global market

The association of handicrafts with Indian-ness continues in today's India, as does their pecuniary nature. In an article entitled 'Crafts aren't just our heritage, they are India's global comparative advantage', the author, Rana Kapoor, opens with a quote from the book *Handicrafts of India* by M. N. Upadhyay: 'To write about Indian handicrafts is almost like writing about the country itself' (Kapoor 2016). The article itself proclaims the global market as an accessible opportunity since the present Indian share is only 2 percent. Craft-promoting NGOs such as Dastkar (meaning 'hand work') and Dastkari Haat Samiti conduct exhibitions in several major cities around India, inviting artisans to display and sell their wares. In an interview, Jaya Jaitly, the founder and head of Dastkari Haat Samhiti, and the creator of Dilli Haat, an artisan-centric market operated by the Government of India in New Delhi, differentiates between 'ethnic' and 'Indian-ness', stating that the former has colonial vestiges, while the latter is about 'delving into India's craft skills and resources' (Dhareshwar 2016). Furthermore, Indian-ness continues to be narrated through a pre-Muslim South Asian history. In its sales pamphlet *Crafts of Tamil Nadu*, Poompuhar, the Tamilnadu Handicrafts Development Corporation Limited, a government run for-profit institution that promotes handicraft training and sells crafts from all over the state in its many national outlets, recounts the history of art in India starting from the Indus Valley civilization of the Bronze Age, the 'Vedic age' from 1500 BCE, the Hellenistic Gandhara period of the third century BCE, the Mathura school which was Buddhism influenced, and the various Hindu and Buddhist kingdoms in the third century CE, stopping short of the period of Islamic art and architecture of the seventh century (Poompuhar 2000: 2–3).

It is in this context that the labor of consumption is explored in this article. The literature on consumption theory forges a link between value-laden objects and the people who consume them. While explicating human consciousness, G. W. F. Hegel (1977) enumerated a two-stage process that starts with objectification, which is the act of reaching out to the world to make contact with an object that is not the self (externalization), resulting in the realization that there is an other and a self. This is followed by the act of sublation in which the external is internalized through an appropriation of the knowledge and qualities of the contacted object. Sublation causes the self to gain further understanding of the self and the world, which changes the self itself. Daniel Miller (1997: 35) uses Hegel's notion of objectification but following Marx, makes it material by rooting it in practice, specifically consumption. As the title of his book *Material Culture and Mass Consumption* suggests, Miller is interested in how people's consumption of objects can be analyzed to reveal how they understand themselves. Production, Miller (1997: 3) argues, is not ideal for studying society if the scholar is interested in the work that the objects perform, because Marxist theory attends to labor, not the objects. Furthermore, for Marx and labor theory, the act of objectification is not completed because the alienation of the worker from their labor makes sublation impossible (40). In the case of Indian handicraft, a Marxist theory of production would put the focus merely on the matter of alienation of the artisan-turned-worker from their handicraft, and thus the focus would be on their incapacity to serve as true artisans. In the media debates, changes in artistic production, and craft fairs that are described below, to focus only on production would be to miss what people seem to see as being at stake.

With regard to Miller's preference for consumption, focusing on production gives the impression that the producer might be the source of the object's meaning and value when it might very well be a consumer-driven market. Miller (1997: 140) provides the example of William Morris who championed Indian art and craft during the colonial period by encouraging indigenous craft production through the Arts and Crafts movement. His socialist logic was that such an elevation would also raise the status of the craftsmen who had been ignored as producers of utilitarian objects by the British art world. His efforts were successful in popularizing Indian crafts, but unfortunately, they also missed the mark and reproduced class distinctions, because the consumption of crafts became an elite preoccupation. Craft objects produced during this time acquired a 'conspicuous handmade image' and were 'immediately recognized as a quality and luxury product' resulting in them being used by the new elite to index their social status (Miller 1997: 140). Thus it is consumption that becomes the fount of value for crafts. What developed later with Indian handicrafts is that the Orientalist values and their adoption by the independence movement as laid out in the previous section made these objects about 'Indian-ness', often with a spiritual connotation. By consuming these objects then, people consume 'Indian-ness', whatever that might be. Since handicrafts are a stand-in for the character and status of the nation, any change in the conditions of artisans and nature of handicrafts is equated with similar changes in the nation itself. Although the revival of handicrafts in India started in the 1950s after the country's independence, and multifarious organizations, governmental, non-governmental, non-profit, and for-profit, have been involved in efforts to engender it, it is striking that even now, there are anxieties about the status of handicrafts and artisans. This chapter argues that a lot of recent debates around handicrafts and traditional arts and crafts in India come from the anxieties Indians have about their nation and themselves. Considering the long historical link between handicrafts and Indian-ness, and especially considering the effort that has been put into constructing this link, these parallel anxieties make sense.

Tradition in a neoliberal India

The Bharatiya Janata Party (BJP), which is the present ruling political party in the Central Government of India, and its leader Narendra Modi, the current Prime Minister of India, ran their election campaigns on promises of neoliberal progress (Gopalakrishnan 2006; Kaur 2015). Various scholars (Chopra 2014; Pal 2015; Srivastava 2015) have analyzed the planning and strategy of these campaigns, and how they found success especially among the young and middle class, whose urban ambition towards upward mobility found expression through social media and its associated neoliberal values, while confirming their identity as citizens of a country that itself valued tradition. As Maureen Liebl and Tirthankar Roy (2003: 5372) found in their detailed study of the Indian craft industry in a project commissioned by Policy Sciences Center, Inc. and funded by the World Bank, there has been a change in the consumption patterns of handicrafts in the domestic Indian market. While historically, handicrafts were either priceless objects patronized by elites or everyday objects made for and by rural persons, the current demand for handicrafts comes from the urban middle class who have a burgeoning disposable income, a taste that straddles the traditional and modern, and purchasing habits shaped by media and online social media trends.

Nowhere is this better illustrated than the social media group called *Kai Thari*, meaning handloom in Tamil, in which members post photographs of themselves in (usually) saris[1] that show varying degrees of connection to hand craft. Combining the performative politics of selfies (Kuntsman 2017) with a sincere interest in learning about and promoting Indian textiles, the over-12,000 members of *Kai Thari* appear to be mostly middle class and affluent women who identify as Indian or with Indian culture, living all over the world. Among its members is the handicraft activist, Laila Tyabji, founder and head of Dastkar, a non-profit for promoting and reviving Indian crafts, who decided to post a sari-clad selfie a day for a month in an effort to promote handloom saris as everyday wear. In an interview about the exercise, she is quoted, 'I deliberately avoided the fancy, festive and heirloom sari in favour of the cottons one wears to work, and that usually get discarded and forgotten once they fade or tear' (Nayar 2016). Although aiming to promote saris generally, her choice of handloom textiles valorizes the handcrafted saris particularly. This is an association that is replicated in the posts of many members who declare the sari to be very comfortable, elegant and eye-catching, and detailing the particular type of handloom they are sporting. Often, this creates a discussion of the various handlooms, the history of the tradition, and where 'authentic' pieces can be sourced. Posters share childhood stories, often of their regional background, and connect it to the handloom sari tradition they wear. Sometimes, there is also policing of the images and the information provided, especially when it comes to the authenticity of the loom. Another such noteworthy effort to promote handicrafts through social media was by Smriti Irani, the current Textiles Minister in the Government of India, who began a Twitter campaign with the hashtag #IWearHandloom (Neelakantan 2016). She tweeted, 'Indian handlooms symbolise India's heritage & culture. Wear it to carry on our rich tradition and support 43 lakh weavers & their families.' Several government officials followed suit, tweeting photographs of themselves in handloom textiles. The #100SareePact is another social media driven movement in which women swear to wear saris at least 100 times in a year, and share a selfie of themselves each of those days on Instagram, Facebook, or Twitter (Hebbar 2015). This also branched out into a handloom variation where traditional weaves were exclusively or predominantly worn.

The case of *Kai Thari* highlights intricate linkages between the consumption of handicrafts, Indian-ness, and presentation of oneself as an Indian in the current political and social climate. Class is clearly an important element in the consumption of handicrafts since many of these saris are expensive and sourcing them requires a knowledge of the handicraft market as well as connections with local artisans and dealers. These communities favor consumption, which is celebrated both for its work in promoting craft and artisans, as well as the status of the individuals. Performing the sari and highlighting its handcrafted nature also indexes a connection to India, and the large number of posters who place themselves in international locations demonstrates a globalized and urban Indian populace that is comfortable being marked as traditional in Western environments. In fact, these can even be perceived as efforts to normalize saris as everyday wear for professional and casual settings by these women of varied age and class. Minister Irani's explicit linking of handlooms with Indian-ness and use of Twitter to promote such performative Indian-ness exemplifies the tightrope-walking between a neoliberal modernity and tradition. Lastly, the debates over authenticity express a concern about representation, knowledge, and Indian-ness.

The push to globalize handicrafts has been especially noticeable recently with large corporations noted for diverse products and enormous international audiences incorporating handicrafts into their product lines. Amazon India has added Handicrafts and Handlooms as one of the product categories in its online commercial portal, in which artisans can sell their wares to customers directly. To encourage artisans to go online, Amazon has been conducting on-the-ground workshops to teach artisans about email, assuage fears about e-commerce, and educate them about how commission and tax works when selling online (Shah 2018). It has recruited artisans who were already using its services to speak to new audiences about their experience. Through the Kala Haat initiative, Amazon has also formed partnerships with non-profits and governmental organizations such as the Cottage Industries Emporium, a central government organization promoting crafts, to bring their products on board (Amazon India 2018). While Amazon India focuses on the Indian market, there are also corporations like IKEA, which through its Social Entrepreneurs initiative is working with craft collectives in India to source products for its international market (Dasey 2016; Morris 2018). There are also online portals such as Jaypore and Gaatha which feature arts and crafts from named artisans for a limited period and reach an elite audience both within India and outside.

What kind of Indian-ness are handicrafts symbolizing in today's economy? And what kind of Indian-ness will be consumed by the patrons of handicrafts? A recent debate on the position of the sari in the Indian psyche that played out online and through journalists is especially indicative of the kind of anxieties Indians have about their identity and how it is negotiated around consumption. A *New York Times* article called 'In India, fashion has become a nationalist cause' by Asgar Qadri was published on November 12, 2017. In it, Qadri claims that the Hindu nationalist aspirations of the ruling BJP party government has curtailed any growth in international trade and especially in the fashion industry because of its efforts to promote 'traditional attire and bypass Western styles'. Linking a series of contentious moves by members of the BJP party, including the public lynching of a Muslim man who had been accused of eating beef, to the Prime Minister Narendra Modi's fashion choices, which have been predominantly handloom textiles and traditional styles, Qadri claimed that the promotion of indigenous fashion was part of the larger drive to portray and make India Hindu. Confusingly, Qadri also situates PM Modi's 'effort to restore Indian-ness in Indian fashion' in the 'Make in India' campaign, which was started in 2014 to encourage investment in local industries, including from foreign sources (Qadri 2017). Although acknowledging the history of fashion in the political circle, Qadri claims that this current push from the government is much larger in scale than ever before, associating the promotion of handloom textiles and indigenous fabrics such as Banarasi silk and embroidery with that of promoting 'traditional Indian clothing styles'. That this particular handloom is from the city Banaras (or Varanasi) is also striking to Qadri is demonstrated by his descriptions of the city's centrality in Hinduism as the holiest city, not to mention it being PM Modi's constituency when he ran for the position of Prime Minister. Although Qadri does not explicitly state that the support for Banarasi weaves is really about supporting Hinduism, he implies the same by highlighting the plight of the weavers of Banarasi saris, who are Muslims still living in poverty. PM Modi's schemes have only helped the middlemen who intervene in the distribution of these saris, especially the high-end weaves. Qadri also remarks on the role of the Minister for Textiles, Smriti Irani (quoted earlier), in 'Indianizing popular fashion', and her beginnings as a soap actress who played a 'traditional Indian daughter-in-law' (Qadri 2017). The journalist ends his article, 'The government's aim certainly has been to produce a popular fashion aesthetic that matches the broader political program of Hindu nationalism', and ponders if only time will tell if these efforts will be successful.

A flurry of angry responses soon emerged from *New York Times* readers as well as public figures including journalists, handicraft activists, and fashion designers. Barkha Dutt, a renowned television journalist, responded in the Opinion section of the *Washington Post*, taking the *New York Times* and its editorial team to task for simplifying the complexities of the political and cultural reality in India and relying on 'lazy tropes', 'broad clichés' and 'forced narratives' (Dutt 2017). Many of the reactions drew memories from childhood or of mothers to construct the sari as personal instead of political. Dutt's essay begins with her memories of her mother sporting various handlooms and textiles, while Smita Barooah reminisces about the saris worn by her grandmother and the regional handloom saris that were part of her wedding trousseau (Barooah et al. 2017). Amrita Bhinder, writing in the same article, identifies herself as a 'north-Indian Sikh woman married to an Andhraite' who would not be generally associated with the sari since the salwar khameez is the traditional clothing of choice for Sikh women. Many others connect the sari to their own personal efforts to recognize their own culture or significant cultural moments from their lives and the role that saris played in them. In each of these accounts, the rebuttal not only personalizes the sari as a reaction to the perceived politicization by Qadri in the *NYT* article, it also highlights the significance of handlooms, especially in their diversity. The sari, especially the handloom sari, is constructed as Indian through personal memories and regional identity. Dutt goes so far as to call the sari 'the most democratic clothing' in India, where social stratification is ubiquitous. She further associates Mahatma Gandhi's use of the hand-spun and woven fabric *khadi* during the Indian independence movement with protest, and extrapolates that certain traditions continue to be preserved by Indians as a continued resistance to globalization, which she characterizes as Westernization. 'Are jeans from Gap, shirts from Zara and dresses from Banana Republic supposed to be the inane index of our progressiveness?' asks Dutt. It is interesting that while decrying the communal politics of the *NYT* article, Dutt herself politicizes the sari by indexing it to the democratic, nationalist ideals popularized by the Indian freedom movement.

In further support for handlooms, several critics of the *NYT* article cite the economic significance of the handicraft and handloom market. Laila Tyabji, the craft revivalist and activist introduced earlier, published a public post on her Facebook page explaining how Qadri had communicated with her for the article but had chosen not to include any of her comments, because it went counter to his thesis. Tyabji explains that firstly, while the BJP government has been pushing Hinduism-based lifestyles and products such as yoga and Ayurveda, it has not promoted traditional clothing. In fact, she cites PM Modi as being an anomaly in that he wears Western clothes while traveling abroad while every past Prime Minister wore only Indian clothes. More importantly, Tyabji notes that the efforts to promote Indian handicrafts and handlooms have been targeted at international markets, and not domestic ones. The Symphony of Weaves showcase cited as evidence of the government pushing traditional clothes by the *NYT* article was in fact to foster international business and attract foreign investors in Indian markets (Vasudev 2017). Thus, critics pointed out that Qadri was confusing not only Indian traditional clothing with Indian handicrafts and handlooms, but he was also ignoring the economic significance of the industry and assuming a greater religious and cultural importance. Promotion of saris could be considered nationalistic, but only from the perspective of increasing the country's Gross Domestic Product.

However, criticism of the article also became quite personal, targeting the author, Asgar Qadri. A tweet claimed to have googled Qadri and found that he claimed to be from 'Indian-controlled Kashmir' and researches 'nationalism in South Asia', concluding 'Enough said' (Times Now digital 2017). This was picked up by journalists who identified Qadri as Kashmiri, with one article being titled 'New York Times publishes saree-shaming article by Kashmiri man'. Shefali Vaidya, writing in the right-wing *Swarajya* magazine, accuses the article of 'Hinduphobia and racism' (Barooah et al. 2017). Another tweet asks if the sari can be equated to nationalism, whether the burqa symbolizes women's empowerment, clearly a targeted question to Qadri who has been marked as Muslim. The author's identity as not only a Muslim but as Kashmiri became significant for his critics, even though there has been no verified confirmation of the details. Kashmir has been a contested region between Hindu-majority India and the Islamic state of Pakistan since their respective independence from the British colonial regime. In 1949, an armed struggle between both countries for control over Kashmir resulted in an arbitrary border called the 'line of control' which separated the state into two, each belonging to the two countries. The Indian government calls the area under Pakistan's administration Pakistan-occupied Kashmir, and the Government of Pakistan calls the Indian state as India-occupied Kashmir. Muslims from Kashmir are generally regarded with suspicion by Hindu Indians for being inclined to support Pakistan's sovereignty over the state instead of India's. Thus, Qadri's supposed reference to his home as 'India-occupied Kashmir' seemingly exposes his affiliation with Pakistan against India. The critics who bring up his identity as Kashmiri are explicitly and implicitly questioning his agenda in writing an article that accuses the current Indian government of promoting Hindu values as Indian values.

To an extent, it is understandable why the push for handicrafts and handlooms might have made Qadri think of Indian-ness as Hinduism. As explained in the previous section, there has been a long, effortful history of infusing traditional arts and crafts in India with an Indian-ness that has also been defined by a Hindu-Buddhist spirit. The work of Orientalists, freedom fighters, and post-independence craft revivalists has been making these associations explicitly and implicitly. Thus, Qadri's correlation of Indian-ness with Hinduism is understandable. In fact, the personal attacks against Qadri, on his Muslim identity and the doubts about his loyalty to India, are also fueled within the same frame; it is because handicrafts and handlooms are so closely identified with Indian-ness that Qadri's criticism of what he perceived as the forceful actions of the current Indian government to promote Hinduism was in turn recognized as an attack on Indian values and the current state of the nation. Defenders of the sari used their own personal histories about their culture, their memories growing up in India, their consumption of indigenous textiles, and the economic importance of the handicraft sector – all of which defend Indian culture. What is significant is that these debates over the sari are in fact debates over what India is supposed to be, what work tradition is supposed to perform, and how much modernity is too much modernity. The international character of the *New York Times* might have also added to the concerns of Indians who saw their nation being framed as parochial on a global platform. To defend the sari and handicrafts then becomes a performance of political and personal identity. The tight-rope walking between preserving traditions while working towards a progressive future presents challenges because many Indians prefer one over the other, or have differing conceptions of what they mean. Handicrafts, and in the above instance, the sari, become the carrier of these anxieties because of their intrinsic value of Indian-ness.

One striking aspect of the sari controversy was what everyone did agree on, and it was the poor condition of artisans in India. Alongside anxieties about the state of craft itself are also anxieties about the persons who produce them. This is also linked to who the artisan is supposed to be in the grand narrative of the construct of India.

The dilemma of the Indian artisan

It is necessary to go back a little in time to recognize why artisans and their plight is important to the Indian nation. As explained earlier, both the Arts and Crafts movement of the eighteenth century and the Orientalist thinkers and art historians who derived some inspiration from it centered the artistic heritage of South Asia in the body of the artisan. Coomaraswamy (1909: 1, 7) had described artisans as 'organic elements in the national life' of Indian society, and typifies three forms artisanship takes: as a village artisan who fulfils a particular duty but also has the privilege of a perennial contract with the village; an urban guild member where the guild operated as a proto-trade union; and as a 'feudal servant of the king, or a chieftain of a temple'. This formed the basis of the craft revival movement after the independence of the country, where artisans were considered to be the repositories of Indian tradition. The evidence of their position was in the products that they made, as they were material remnants of the artistry and ideology passed on through dozens of generations from thousands of years ago. So what happens to artisans when craft changes? What happens to Indian-ness? And alternatively, how can the framing of artisans be used to preserve a traditional culture?

Artisans were and continue to be perceived as the repositories of tradition, and thus it follows that if artisans are threatened, tradition also appears to be threatened. There is a preponderance of class in the art and craft industry, or more specifically, the binary of elite-consumer to not-elite producer, and this feed into the tropes of the suffering artisan and the patron-consumer. Artisans are often perceived as based in rural areas, which falls within the first of the three categories propounded as historical by Coomaraswamy. Both the royal and urban artisans have disappeared in India, with the changing of times, and while temples might have a particular artisan they resort to, the process has become more professional and less vocational. This makes the rural artisan the most visible, and partly explains why that perception continues. It is also a fact that many artisans produce art that they themselves cannot afford, or practically use, as Jaya Jaitly (2001) notes in her book detailing the biographies of diverse artisans. Asgar Qadri, the author of the polarizing *NYT* article, dedicates a section to write about the plight of the weavers of Benaras, who are Muslim, and the lack of assistance from the Government of India, even though the latter made promises to support the handicraft and handloom market. PM Modi, who won the national election, was running his candidacy out of Benaras, and made particular promises to enliven the industries of the city and bring it the neoliberal progress he promised the nation. Yet, not much has been done and the weavers are still struggling. Any efforts of the government to promote Benaras textiles have benefited the middlemen and resellers rather than the weavers. Even Qadri's critics agree with this point and bring it up in their responses. Laila Tyabji notes that, 'In fact many of us in the sector feel that not enough is being done, given the double blow demonitisation and GST [Goods and Services Tax] has dealt to small weaver communities' (Tyabji 2017). Here, she is referring to a series of disastrous financial measures taken by the BJP government to reduce corruption in the economy. While the effectiveness of the schemes in terms of corruption are still debated, one definite impact has been the slowdown of the informal economy, which is the sector in which most artisans operate.

Artisans in India do have a difficult time, especially because as an unorganized sector, any attempt to research, plan, and implement schemes at national or even state levels never reaches them all. A newsletter of the Craft Council of India, a governmental non-profit organization dedicated to improving the lives of artisans, promoting handicrafts, and facilitating training for artisanal skills describes artisans as 'in the millions … still delegated to the humiliating category of "informal, unorganized sectors"' (Chatterjee 2018). The Census of India, which periodically takes measure of the status of industry, clumps handicrafts along with several other professions in the 'Unorganized Sector' and, most startlingly, there is no universally accepted definition for handicrafts and artisans across craft-oriented Indian institutions, governmental and non-governmental (Liebl and Roy 2003: 5366). The fact that artisans are actually suffering is not in question, but it also makes sense that casting artisans as in need of patronage emplots artisans into their historical position, as traditional and rural, and cyphers for the Indian-ness promoted since the independence movement. Thus, it follows that individuals, especially women, and organizations continue to take up handicrafts revival as a developmental, nationalistic project toward crafts. The act of revival not only performs as an effort to support Indian artisans, it also reconstructs the contemporary Indian consumer as a patron, mimicking the form of patronage economy of yesteryears, and fixates the artisan as the repository of Indian-ness. In this framework, the artisan cannot become an urban middle-class individual, an equal to the current Indian consumer. *Kai Thari*, the Facebook group introduced earlier has a smaller collective that focuses on reviving *kunbi* saris from Goa and *spandana* saris from Karnataka by organizing their sales through the Facebook group. Both are handlooms saris that have nearly become extinct. Having contacted weavers directly, the leaders of this initiative make bulk purchases from them based on pre-orders they receive from the group members and handle the shipping to each buyer themselves. As a non-profit and informal initiative, no profit or commission is made, and all proceeds go directly to the weavers (minus shipping). But revival also changes the nature of the craft since it is a strategic effort to sell a product to a neoliberal market. Herein lies the conundrum of revival, which while striving to turn back time, actively changes its subject.

Madhubhani paintings which are merchandized today on all kinds of consumer products started off as ritualistic fertility paintings drawn on walls by women in the town of Mithila in Bihar (Jain 1989). Now they feature as illustrations in books, as framed paintings to be hung on a wall, on bags, t-shirts, and even on shoes. Several Madhubhani artists who are successful now also happen to be men. Clearly, Madhubhani is not the same as it used to be and changes have occurred in order to make the craft sustainable in the current economy. However, this raises questions about authenticity and the nature of revival. Recently, designers such as Sanjay Garg of label Raw Mango and independent designer Pradeep Pillai, who make contemporary versions of traditional textiles, have consciously problematized the term 'revival', asking if the term makes sense when the art they are creating is not quite the same as the source (Mahalakshmi 2018).

What has happened in many cases of revival is that design has become the compromise necessary for the continued sustenance of traditional arts and crafts. This was clearly illustrated in the developments between two exhibitions conducted by the same organization in Chennai a year apart. Dastkari Haat Samiti (DHS), a New-Delhi-based NGO led by Jaya Jaitly, conducted a craft and textile exhibition, inviting over 100 artisans from all over the country, in Chennai in February 2015. Dastkari Haat Samiti has the byline, 'A National Association of Indian Crafts People', and describes its composition on its website as 'a large membership of crafts persons as individuals, family units, Co-ops, Associations and Societies'(Dastkari Haat Samiti 2013). They 'believe in sustaining traditional skills and livelihoods and in ensuring the continuity of India's cultural heritage through crafts, arts and textiles by according respect and dignity to practitioners of handwork'. Having conducted such exhibitions in other parts of the country, including one in Chennai, the organization had a system in place to ensure the smooth execution of the event and that enough publicity would be created to attract visitors. An enormous hit, Chennai residents thronged the exhibition, several returning on multiple days during the ten-day period, and purchasing diverse products ranging from several hundred rupees to several hundred thousand rupees. The artisans were ecstatic, and some had to call their families back home to send more products since they had sold everything within a few days. When DHS came again the next year at the same location in Chennai with many returning artisans, things did not turn out so well. There were hardly any visitors, and a disastrous storm ruined several of the artisans' wares. Searching for reasons, the artisans concluded it must be wrong timing – instead of early in the year, the DHS exhibition was at the end of the year, and there had already been a couple of other exhibitions a few months earlier which might have drawn the larger crowds. An employee of the organization wondered if perhaps it was because of the sameness of the products. If artisans were making the same old products, and if the same old artisans were being brought out again and again, perhaps consumers were getting understandably bored. There needs to be more design, the employee claimed, more innovativeness. What is interesting in this case is a subtle contradiction that illustrates the complexity of authenticity: on the one hand, it was felt that if craft remains the same it could lose its attractiveness, because market principles dictate that innovation is necessary to constantly attract consumers. On the other hand, how much authenticity could the craft and its makers claim if design took precedence over whatever was considered the substance of the art?

Conclusion

Conspicuous consumption of crafts reflects on one's own values and what one supports, and this is why there is contestation over these objects. Not only are crafts merchandise in the neoliberal market produced to increase India's exports and value-laden visual representations of an individual's aspirational class, they are also a symbol of Indian-ness, which could be a different thing for every person in contemporary India. This association between crafts and India has been effortfully constructed by Orientalist thinkers, Indian freedom fighters, the Government of India, as well as craft revivalists and entrepreneurs, stretching from colonial to postcolonial times. Thus, crafts are a stand-in for Indian-ness and the problematized position of craft and craft producers in present-day India highlights the complexity of identity and status present among Indians today. Indians wrangle with the in-between-ness of their identity concerning the nature of their past and the promise of the future, between idealistic arts and profit-driven commodities, authenticity and sustainability, and between

Indian-ness, secularism, and Hindu-ness. This paper contends that it is anxieties about these questions that fuel discussions about producing and consuming handicrafts, as well as the position of artisans themselves.

Note

1 Saris are considered the traditional attire of South Asian women.

References

Amazon India (2018) Amazon India launches Central Cottage Industries Emporium (CCIE) online @ Amazon.in. Retrieved April 19, 2018, from https://www.amazon.in/b?ie=UTF8&node=14696952031

Barooah, S., Vaidya, S., Bhinder, A., and Mehrishi, S. (2017) Sari clad and proudly so. *Swarajya*. Retrieved November 22, 2017, from https://swarajyamag.com/culture/sari-clad-and-proudly-so

Chatterjee, A. (2018) An exhibition in Calcutta 1922: Moorings of Indian craft and design. *The Crafts Council of India Newsletter*, pp. 1–3.

Chattopadhyay, K. (2000) *India's Craft Tradition*. New Delhi: Publications Division, Ministry of Information and Broadcasting, Government of India.

Chopra, S. (2014) *The Big Connect: Politics in the Age of Social Media*. Noida, UP: Random House India.

Coomaraswamy, A. K. (1909) *The Indian Craftsman*. New Delhi: Munshiram Manoharlal Pub Pvt Ltd.

Coomaraswamy, A. K. (1977) *Traditional Doctrine of Art*. Ipswich: Golgonooza Press.

Dasey, D. (2016) Weaving a brighter future for women. *IKEA/US/EN*. Retrieved April 19, 2018, from https://www.ikea.com/ms/en_US/this-is-ikea/ikea-highlights/A-story-about-Dipti/index.html

Dastkari Haat Samiti. (2013) Dastkari Haat Samiti: Identity. Retrieved April 12, 2018, from http://www.dastkarihaat.org/identity.php

Dhareshwar, A. (2016) Interview with Jaya Jaitley. *One India One People Foundation*. Retrieved April 17, 2018, from http://oneindiaonepeople.com/funnily-enough-despite-the-success-of-dilli-haat-and-everyone-knowing-it-was-my-concept-and-effort-that-made-it-happen-no-one-has-come-and-asked-me-to-guide-them-on-how-to-set-up-a-haat-and/

Dutt, B. (2017) The New York Times tried to explain sari fashion – and became the laughingstock of India. *Washington Post*. Retrieved November 18, 2017, from https://www.washingtonpost.com/news/global-opinions/wp/2017/11/17/the-new-york-times-tried-to-explain-sari-fashion-and-became-the-laughingstock-of-india/

Gopalakrishnan, S. (2006) Defining, Constructing and policing a "New India": Relationship between neoliberalism and Hindutva. *Economic and Political Weekly*, 41(26), 2803–13.

Guha-Thakurta, T. (1992) *The Making of a New "Indian" Art: Artists, Aesthetics and Nationalism in Bengal, c. 1850–1920*. Cambridge, UK: Cambridge University Press.

Hebbar, P. (2015) How 2 Indian women made A #100SareePact to revive six yards of memories. *HuffPost India*. Retrieved February 12, 2018, from https://www.huffingtonpost.in/2015/03/26/100-saree-pact_n_6945050.html

Hegel, G. W. F. (1977) *Phenomenology of Spirit* (A. V. Miller, tran.). Oxford: Oxford University Press.

Jain, J. (1989) Ganga Devi: Tradition and expression in Madhubani painting. *Third Text*, *3*(6), 43–50.

Jaitly, J. (2001) *Vishvakarma's Children: Stories of India's Craftspeople*. New Delhi: Concept Publishing Co.

Kapoor, R. (2016) Crafts aren't just our heritage, they are India's global comparative advantage. *HuffPost India*. Retrieved February 18, 2018, from https://www.huffingtonpost.in/rana-kapoor/collaborate-to-contempori_b_10043634.html

Kaur, R. (2015) Good times, brought to you by Brand Modi. *Television & New Media*, 16(4), 323–30.

Kuntsman, A. (2017) *Selfie Citizenship*. Berlin: Springer Nature.

Liebl, M. and Roy, T. (2003) Handmade in India: Preliminary analysis of crafts producers and crafts production. *Economic and Political Weekly*, 38(51/52), 5366–76.

Miller, D. (1997) *Material Culture and Mass Consumption*. Oxford: Wiley-Blackwell.

Morris, A. (2018) IKEA supports marginalised women in India with handmade homeware collection. *Dezeen*. Retrieved February 19, 2018, from https://www.dezeen.com/2018/03/30/ikea-supports-marginalised-women-india-handmade-homeware-collection/

Nayar, A. (2016) PHOTOS: Laila Tyabji wears cotton saris for a month, shows how fabulous they are. *HuffPost India*. Retrieved April 18, 2018, from https://www.huffingtonpost.in/2016/07/08/laila-tyabji-sari-_n_10829016.html

Neelakantan, S. (2016) Smriti Irani goes to bat again, this time for handloom saris – Times of India. *The Times of India*. Retrieved February 18, 2018, from https://timesofindia.indiatimes.com/india/Smriti-Irani-goes-to-bat-again-this-time-for-handloom-saris/articleshow/53493656.cms

Mahalakshmi, P. (2018) New yarn for old weaves - Times of India. *The Times of India*. Retrieved April 12, 2018, from https://timesofindia.indiatimes.com/city/bengaluru/new-yarn-for-old-weaves/articleshow/63660378.cms

Pal, J. (2015) Banalities turned viral: Narendra Modi and the political tweet. *Television & New Media*, 16(4), 378–87.

Poompuhar (2000) *Crafts of Tamilnadu*. Chennai: The Tamilnadu Handicrafts Development Corporation Ltd.

Qadri, A. (2017) In India, fashion has become a nationalist cause. *The New York Times*. Retrieved from https://www.nytimes.com/2017/11/12/fashion/india-nationalism-sari.html

Shah, B. (2018) Six amazing strategies Amazon India is using to bring every local artisan online. *YourStory.com*. Retrieved April 6, 2018, from https://yourstory.com/2018/04/six-amazing-strategies-amazon-india-using-bring-every-local-artisan-online/

Srivastava, S. (2015) Modi-masculinity: Media, Manhood, and "traditions" in a time of consumerism. *Television & New Media*, 16(4), 331–8.

Sundar, P. (1996) *Patrons and Philistines: Arts and the State in British India, 1773–1947*. New York: Oxford University Press. Retrieved August 12, 2013, from http://www.barnesandnoble.com/w/patrons-and-philistines-pushpa-sundar/1111444886

Times Now digital (2017) New York Times publishes saree-shaming article by Kashmiri man, here's how twitter reacted. *Times Now News*. Retrieved November 22, 2017, from http://www.timesnownews.com/india/article/new-york-times-publishes-saree-shaming-article-by-kashmiri-man-heres-how-twitter-reacted/125479

Tyabji, L. (2017) Laila Tyabji facebook post. *Facebook*. Retrieved November 15, 2017, from https://www.facebook.com/laila.tyabji/posts/10207774128350729

Vasudev, S. (2017) Sari, they're so wrong. *The Indian Express*. Retrieved November 23, 2017, from http://indianexpress.com/article/opinion/columns/sari-theyre-so-wrong-new-york-times-article-laila-tyabji-asgar-qadri-4940893/

26

Negotiating cultural industries

A case study from Cambodia

Frances Rudgard and Phloeun Prim

A Brief History of Cambodian Living Arts (CLA)

Cambodian Living Arts is a US-registered organization, currently operating solely in Cambodia, but with a strong institutional connection to the USA. This connection is largely thanks to the organization's founder, Arn Chorn-Pond. Arn is Cambodian born, from a family of artists. He grew up in Battambang, Cambodia until the Khmer Rouge regime took over the country. According to the Yale University Genocide Studies Program (2018), during the period 1975–9, up to 2 million people (approximately 21 percent of the population at that time) died from starvation, torture, and execution. During the Khmer Rouge period, Arn was a child soldier. He spent time in the band of a prison camp, which he believes saved his life, before escaping and eventually finding his way to a refugee camp in Thailand. There he met an American reverend, Peter Pond, who adopted Arn and a number of other Cambodian children, and took them to America. At that time, Arn was approximately 16 years old. He went on to complete his high school and college education in the US, before becoming an international advocate for human rights. Arn continues to tell his personal story and perform his music around the world, to communicate a message of peace and love.

After several years, Arn decided to return to Cambodia, and find a space where he could contribute to the re-building of his country. Arn could have chosen to turn his attention to education, to healthcare, to infrastructure. However, he chose to focus on culture. This motivation came partly from his family connection with the arts, and partly from the role that the arts, particularly music, had played in his own experience of survival during and post the Khmer Rouge regime. Another reason was the observation that arts and culture already had a significant role to play in the post-conflict development context, especially in terms of healing and resilience.

The urgent need for preservation

It is estimated that during the Khmer Rouge regime, 90 percent of the country's artists died (Sam 1990). Educated people, intellectuals, and artists were deliberately targeted by the Khmer Rouge. In Cambodia, as with much of Asia, arts and other cultural practices have typically been passed from one generation to another orally, and via a master-teacher model. When such a significant proportion of artists lost their lives during the Khmer Rouge regime, art and culture itself was put in grave danger of extinction due to the loss of knowledge and skill that went along with the artists themselves.

As such, in 1998, with strong support from some close friends in America, Arn founded what was to eventually become known as CLA, but at that time was called the Cambodian Masters Performing Project. The project was grassroots-based, and simple in its approach; it focused on finding master artists who had survived the Khmer Rouge regime, and equipping them with the tools and resources they needed in order to start passing their skills and knowledge to young people. Typically this included instruments, a financial contribution to allow them to dedicate their time to the project, and support to recruit and manage students. It was also necessary to provide a small stipend to students in order to make it viable that they take time out from work or study to participate in studying arts. The model at that time was that of a 'school without walls'; classes took place in teachers' homes, or in community spaces such as pagodas around the country.

Although simple in execution, Arn and his co-founders had already identified the larger significance of these efforts to revive and preserve endangered performing arts and culture. On the one hand, the preservation of the culture was an end in itself. On the other they all saw the greater meaning of the work in relation to healing, and to restoring positive associations with the meaning of Cambodian identity, which had been greatly impacted by the events of modern history.

A changing Cambodia

In 2000, the CLA Board of Directors set a vision for 2020, by which time they wanted to see a cultural renaissance across Cambodia, with a vibrant and dynamic cultural sector throughout the country, and the arts as its national and international signature. This vision spurred the evolution and expansion of CLA's work over the following decade, which saw the organization growing in size and breadth of activities: from audience development by initiating festivals and new commissions, to audio-visual archiving of endangered forms and expanding partnerships and support to other actors in the arts community

By 2010, the context was very different. Children that CLA had begun working with ten years earlier had become young adults, many of whom wanted to continue their involvement in the arts, and needed jobs and a market for them to be able to do so. At that time, there were few performances, even ad hoc, in the country, and only one semi-regular production, run by puppet-theatre company *Sovanna Phum*.

In addition to wanting to develop the viability of the troupe and sustainability of the artists' careers, CLA also wanted to enhance the artistic vitality of the city. So that same year, in partnership with a dance troupe that CLA had been working with for the past ten years, CLA launched a pilot project to test the market for cultural performance in Phnom Penh.

The troupe, *Children of Bassac*, performed once a week for five to six months during the high season of the tourist industry. They danced on the steps of the National Museum of Cambodia, in Phnom Penh, and the audience sat on rented chairs, set up each week on the museum grounds. The target audience at that time was primarily tourists. In Cambodia, the tourism industry follows a high and low season, with 65–70 percent of tourists visiting during the high season (October–April), with the average stay of tourists in Phnom Penh being just one night.

During the pilot seasons, CLA subsidized both the direct and indirect costs of the production, with some costs being recouped through ticket sales. But from the beginning, the long-term view was that the production must generate enough revenue from ticket sales and sponsorship to become at minimum self-sustaining, and ideally to generate a profit. In general, the private sector needed to be a driving force in establishing public arts programming as the Ministry of Culture was unable to take on such initiatives at that time. Therefore, with no public subsidy (other than a preferential rate secured for renting the museum venue) taking an entrepreneurial approach to funding was essential.

Fruit and flowers: creating a market for a new generation of artists

After two pilot seasons (October 2010–March 2011; and October 2011–March 2012), the CLA team conducted a review of the project to date. This coincided with the launch of CLA's first five-year strategic plan. This meant that the review was taking place in the context of the long-term goals of CLA, and within a broader review of program goals and staff structures. At this point, the performance project developed into a program, meaning it became a long-term feature of CLA's portfolio of activities as part of a subset of a newly formed 'Creative Industries' program.

At that time, CLA made the following decisions:

- To run the program all year round, with shows taking place six nights per week in high season (October–March) and three to four nights during low season (April–September)
- Rather than featuring only one troupe, and one art form, the shows would present three troupes and a diverse set of art forms
- To target both local and tourist audiences.

The first decision was taken primarily for practical reasons, and with economic motivations. In the two pilot seasons it had taken time to build up momentum in terms of sales. Each time the season took a break, the fruits of the labors were lost. Secondly, in order to meet the financial goals of the project a key target audience was the tourist market. Feedback gathered from the tourism industry, including local travel agents, international tour companies (programming itineraries for tourists), and hotels was that they were unable to easily include activities in their itineraries or promote activities to their guests, unless there was a simple and regular schedule.

Making this decision led CLA to develop a more long-term-oriented business model, which resulted in decisions that had both economic and cultural impacts. For example, related to seating, as mentioned above, the pilot productions with *Children of Bassac* were performed on the steps of the National Museum entrance, with the audience seated on rented chairs, set up and taken down each time the show was performed. Moving to a near daily performance, it made neither financial nor logistical sense to continue renting chairs. First, the team explored buying chairs, but then realized for the same budget a simple raked seating structure could be built, with capacity for 120. Step-by-step decisions were made, and by the end of the project (thanks to seed funding from AirAsia Foundation and the support of the Cambodian Ministry of Culture and Fine Arts), CLA had built an outdoor theater on the grounds of the National Museum. For the economic model of the production, this was hugely beneficial; the fixed costs were low and the National Museum is one of the leading tourist attractions in Phnom Penh, thereby offering access to footfall from an audience already identified as having some interest in culture.

The second decision, to promote a diverse range of forms, came from artistic, cultural, and social motivations rather than financial. From the artistic angle, CLA had spent nearly 15 years investing in reviving and developing more than 15 art forms, as well as commissioning original creations and presenting festivals of both traditional and contemporary arts. At the same time as launching the production in Phnom Penh, CLA was gearing up for the *Season of Cambodia* festival. This USD 2.6 million project, initiated by CLA, who was also the Executive Producer, saw 125 of Cambodia's best artists go to New York City for a six-week festival program. The festival was presented across 34 venues, from the Metropolitan Museum of Modern Art, to the Guggenheim, Brooklyn Academy of Music, and the Lincoln Centre. It featured dance, music, film, theatre, humanities, and visual art, and aimed to present a contemporary perspective on Cambodia, highlighting the artistic diversity and creativity of the country three decades after the Khmer Rouge.

Although the Phnom Penh performance project was on a much smaller scale, and working with emerging artists and a different audience, CLA wanted to apply the same philosophy to the programming. That is to say, CLA's goal was to present to audiences the diversity of Cambodian arts and the creativity of a new generation of young artists. Although knowing that for the financial viability of the program it was necessary to attract a tourist audience, CLA wanted to differentiate its production from a tourist 'dinner and dance' show, such as might be found easily in Cambodia's tourist capital, Siem Reap, and focused first on independent cultural tourists rather than a mass market. In addition to the dance program, CLA chose to present:

- *Mak Therng*: a *Yike* (opera) piece, named after the lead character, about power and justice told through a tragic love story. The piece comes from the established *Yike* repertory but had been workshopped by the artists and given a revised ending that they felt was more suited for the contemporary context.
- *Passage of Life*: this piece was commissioned by CLA in order to provide a platform to present the various musical forms that had been preserved through the organization's work. CLA collaborated with two leading artists from the Ministry of Culture, a music specialist and a theatre teacher from the government's secondary school of fine arts, to create a show. The end product was a one-hour piece that moved through life, from birth to death, highlighting rituals and music on the way. For tourists it was an insight into Cambodia's culture; for a local audience it was access to rare forms of cultural heritage.

Considering the local audience was important from the start. Marketing materials were produced both in Khmer and in English, and work was done through local press and media to promote the shows to a local audience. CLA implemented a two-tier pricing system (USD 5 for Cambodian adults, USD 10 for non-Cambodian adults), in order to enable local audience attendance while still giving a value to the production (also an important part of developing a sustainable arts sector). The goal at the start of the program was that within three years the audience would be 50 percent Cambodian and 50 percent international (to date it has achieved 20 percent Cambodian/ 80 percent international). In the longer term CLA also hoped to be able to rotate the shows on an on-going basis, perhaps with each troupe being featured for a two- to three-year period, during which time they would present more than one work, and eventually graduating out of the platform on to new ventures.

From the social angle, CLA wanted to be able to impact a greater number of young artists. Still today, many artists, or arts students, abandon their practice because they are unable to afford to continue. At that time, CLA started the project offering each artist a $10 fee per show. That meant an artist performing two evenings per week in high season could make $80 per month for a reliable part-time job. At that time, the average monthly salary for a full-time (six days per week) entry-level garment worker in Phnom Penh was less than $100 (International Labour Organization 2014), including benefits, so relatively this was a fair wage. By employing three troupes CLA was able to support more than 90 artists, in addition to approximately 30 staff through box office, marketing, and production teams; so the project had a meaningful social impact in terms of job creation.

With these founding decisions and principles, CLA launched the program in October 2012. The three elements of economic impact, cultural/artistic impact, and social impact comprised the desired return on investment from the program. The production was branded *Plae Pakaa*, a Khmer expression literally translating as fruit and flowers, and meaning fruitful or coming to fruition.

Reflections and tensions

This case study was written in late 2015, after three years of implementation of the *Plae Pakaa* program. It explores the design and implementation of a creative industries program, and the dynamics of balancing the 'triple bottom line' of economic, social, and cultural return. The following section will focus on some successes and challenges CLA has experienced during the three and a half years of running the program to date, highlighting some key decisions that were made on that journey.

Social impact versus economic impact: professionalizing the artists

At the beginning of the project, CLA was working with three different groups of artists. Two of them were troupes that had formed from classes CLA had supported during the first decade of its work. One of them, *The Children of Bassac*, was an experienced troupe with a strong leader, Master Ieng Sithul; they already received regular bookings for performances at private events, and had experience of performing overseas. The second, *Yike Amatak*, was a more newly formed troupe coming out of a community-based class that had been running for several years and although able to perform several pieces of the Yike repertoire, was not yet undertaking many professional and paid performances.

The third group could not be considered a troupe in the same sense as the other two. Rather it was a group of artists recruited to perform in the show. While the show had an Artistic Director, who took on a leadership and management role with the artists, there was a noticeable difference in the dynamic of working with this group versus the other troupes and there was higher attrition among the members, and eventually, despite a handful of committed and passionate artists, the group could not sustain its membership beyond the third year of the program. This perhaps indicates something around the importance of the troupe organizational structure within the Cambodian context.

For the three groups and CLA, it was the first time that all parties had entered into a relationship where they were committed to a sustained, high-volume regular performance schedule. From CLA's perspective, trying to support the dual goals of creating a fair and professional working environment for the artists, and trying to manage an economically viable production, raised some interesting tensions. Simultaneously occupying the role of capacity builder and employer, it was sometimes challenging to balance priorities.

For example, in the early stages of setting up the production, the negotiations with the troupes around the number of artists that could be supported in each show were challenging.

At that time, the fee was based on a rate per person, with an additional fee being paid to the directors and trainers of the troupes. In order to maintain a fair rate for each performer and achieve a break-even operating model, CLA had budgeted based on a certain number of performers per show, according to information provided by the troupes. During rehearsals and even once the first high season was underway, all troupes tried to increase the number of performers and were resistant to CLA's concerns that this was not manageable from a production and financial standpoint. In some cases their motivation for adding extra performers was artistic, for example in a case where the Director wanted to realize a new artistic vision and felt additional artists were required. In other cases it was more socially driven, in that the troupe leader wanted to ensure a job for a troupe member.

CLA could have made a greater financial return by dictating artist quotas to the troupes. But the organization took the position that the program was to be a business with a social impact; part of this social impact was working with artists and arts managers new to a professionalizing arts sector, and this learning curve was an important element of that journey. There is also a symbiosis between the presenter and the troupe; as much as the troupes were relying on CLA to create a sustainable platform via which they could perform, CLA needed the troupes and the artists in order to make the venture successful.

Working in a more commercial context, while challenging, also provided important opportunities for professionalization and development of the artists. For example, at the outset of the project the artists did not see their work as a business, but at the same time had high expectations regarding compensation and other employment conditions. During the course of the program to date, they have become more interested in understanding the overall finances of the production. CLA has been able to work with the artists to apply some of the more business-like approaches to management, finances, and budgeting to their independent activities. For example, since being engaged in the project, *Children of Bassac* has now developed a formal internal management structure with troupe members having designated authority for specific tasks, they keep simple accounts, and have financial policies.

Cultural impact versus economic impact: audience demand

An important note for this section is that CLA's financial model for the production relied on revenues from the tourist market; their higher ticket price would cover the costs and subsidize the lower rate offered to local audience. As stated above, one of CLA's underlying goals in launching the shows was to present a diverse view on Cambodian arts and culture. Without realizing it at the time, this came with an underlying assumption that a tourist audience buying tickets would be equally interested to see any form that CLA was to present, and would appreciate seeing a quality show presented by a reputable arts organization that would give them a deeper insight into Cambodian culture. Right from the beginning, however, there was a marked difference in audience figures for the three shows (dance, opera, and music theatre), with consistently higher sales for dance.

Remaining committed to its original goal, CLA tried various strategies over the three years in order to increase the sales of the opera and music theatre shows. These included:

- *Changing the day of the week:* thinking that perhaps sales were higher due to audience/tourist flows.
- *Changing the translation of* Yike: at the start of the project, *Yike* was translated as 'opera' on all the English-language marketing materials and by the sales and marketing staff when talking about the show in English. Even during the first high season, CLA began

to be concerned that the use of the word 'opera' might be discouraging customers due to inbuilt preconceptions about the form and its audience in a Western context. CLA tried various alternative translations including music-theater and folk opera.

- *Changing the marketing materials:* the design team changed the photographs on the flyers and advertisements in order to give higher prominence to the non-dance shows, thinking that this might generate more interest.
- *Assessing the quality of the shows:* the reviews of those who saw *Yike* were consistently very high, as were reviews of the dance. Audiences found *Passage of Life* less compelling, so CLA commissioned French-Cambodian director Jean-Baptiste Phou to work with the artists to reframe, rewrite, and develop the production. Following that investment, the production had a more positive response from those who did see it, but sales still remained low. In the low season of 2015, CLA tested a new production of shadow puppets in collaboration with artists from the Department of Performing Arts, an arm of the Ministry of Culture and Fine Arts. Although it received a positive response, sales still remained low compared to the dance show.

The net effect of the lesser interest in the *Yike* and the music theatre shows among tourists, combined with a low ticket price for the local audience with no scope to significantly increase it in the short to medium term, was that the overall program was struggling to break even on direct costs after two and a half years. This meant that the cultural goal of presenting a diverse range of Cambodian artistic and cultural expression was compromising the economic viability of not only the program, but the other, non-revenue-generating activities of CLA.

CLA assessed the data and calculated that even with no improvements to marketing or sales success, simply changing the program to be only a dance program would result in a 35 percent increase in sales, thus allowing the program to begin moving into making profit. Although this meant that the program itself would not be making a significant contribution to promoting the diverse arts of Cambodia, it would allow CLA to generate income that could be reinvested into developing new work targeting primarily a local audience. The difficult decision was made that from October 2015, the regular show would only feature dance. It would also be rebranded from *Plae Pakaa* to *Traditional Dance Show.*

To mitigate the negative impact of this decision from a cultural context, CLA would work towards a goal of using the theater for other work, targeting a local audience, when the dance show was not on. As the space had already been used for several successful festivals and one-off performances, it was clear that there was a local audience, interested in engaging with diverse forms of arts and culture. In that way, the financial bottom line could enable an artistic and cultural impact through generating profit to be invested in creation and production, and by covering the costs of running a small venue.

Cultural versus social: impacts of tourism on the culture

CLA's program of shows in Phnom Penh is in some ways a social enterprise, bringing as it does sustainable and socially responsible tourism to the city, and creating dignified and fairly paid employment and economic return through doing so. It is also a creative/cultural enterprise, inasmuch as it is adopting a commercial approach to financial sustainability of the production and using the proceeds to support other artistic and cultural projects.

However, there is also a tension between these two impacts. In presenting the show, CLA is contributing to the construction of the conceptualization of Cambodian arts and culture for a tourist audience, particularly because of the dual influences of CLA's own reputation as a long-standing and experienced arts organization and the positioning of the theater and the show within the National Museum grounds. The choices that will lead to economic viability of the show, that is, to limit the diversity of what is presented and to highlight 'tradition' in the marketing, can often be at odds with the choices that would demonstrate the contemporary cultural vitality of Cambodia. In performing the shows on the purpose-built stage in the city in front of an urban and tourist audience, the meanings and the symbols engrained in the arts, which have been so painstakingly revived and transmitted to this new generation, risk being commoditized and in the process losing their context and value.

The current challenge for CLA is balancing the positive social and economic impacts of the project with these cultural and artistic risks. Managing those risks is not easy, and requires complex negotiation of perspectives and expectations from diverse stakeholders, from artists to audiences to policy makers and peers in the arts community. However, one thing remains clear: in order to build a vibrant and dynamic arts sector in Cambodia, institutions cannot rely on donations or subsidies but must explore sustainable financing models, complicated though they may be.

Future challenges and opportunities

At the time of writing in mid-2016, as Cambodia continues to develop there will be new challenges and opportunities associated with the creative and cultural industries.

In July 2014, the Royal Government of Cambodia approved a National Policy for Culture. In broad terms the policy provides a supportive environment in which CLA and other arts organizations can implement activities in the creative and cultural industries. Of the three policy goals, one is 'to contribute to socio-economic development'. Of seven strategies, four explicitly relate to creative and cultural industries with actions ranging from 'promoting Cambodia to become a center for performing arts, cultural products and a location for foreign film productions' to 'cooperating with relevant ministries and institutions to coordinate measures concerning cultural products and related issues' and 'providing incentive and supporting the establishment of creative industries'.

In actuality, the Ministry of Culture and Fine Arts currently has limited financial and human resources to implement the strategies and actions outlined within the policy. Therefore actions will need to be prioritized, and it is likely that key focus areas will be reform and human resource development within the Ministry itself, and on the key roles in the Ministry regarding heritage and preservation. Therefore, CLA expects that, at least within the next three to five years, there will be little change to the current situation as regards funding and other support mechanisms for the independent arts sector and creative and cultural industries. However, there are still many areas where CLA sees the Ministry and the National Policy for Culture able to take actions that will help CLA, and partners, to develop its work in creative industries. Three examples follow below.

a) Inter-ministerial collaboration

An important objective for CLA is to increase advance bookings from tourists, that is when they are still planning their trips. This objective is shared with other arts organizations with similar programs. CLA has been working with partner *Phare the Cambodian Circus* to explore creation of a shared marketing platform to promote multiple performing and visual arts activities that tourists (both international and domestic) can enjoy in Cambodia.

CLA hopes to see inter-ministerial cooperation between the Ministries of Culture and Tourism in order to promote Cambodia as a cultural tourism destination, and has raised this at a forum organized by the Ministry of Culture. The Ministry of Culture has the subject matter expertise and arts networks; while the Ministry of Tourism has the funding and the mechanisms by which to implement international outreach. This public sector support will greatly benefit the private sector and the cultural industries in general.

b) *Public–private partnerships on arts spaces*
The existing theater that CLA has built at the National Museum is a good example of effective public–private collaboration. The space was provided by the government, and the theater was built and is operated by CLA. There is a pressing need for space for both rehearsal/creation and professional performance/exhibition. In the past six to twelve months, CLA has seen increasing demand from other artists and producers wanting to use its theater space at the National Museum. Aside from being one of the only performing arts venues available in central Phnom Penh, it is also an affordable space thanks to the CLA and National Museum collaboration, which maintains low costs.

However, it is likely within the next couple of years that the season of the dance show will extend and the number of performances increase. This will limit the availability of the theater for other programming. If CLA and other partners wish to present more regular work in an affordable and welcoming setting, new spaces must be developed. CLA intends to explore further public–private partnerships with the Ministry of Culture, whereby CLA is able to rent space in government-owned property at a preferential rate while finding funds and resources to manage that space privately. Possible sites might include the National Library building.

c) *National Fund for Creativity*
CLA understands that the Ministry of Culture will launch a National Fund for culture within the next six to eighteen months. It remains to be determined how this fund will be used, but it is understood from the open forums regarding cultural policy development and implementation, that the fund will support creativity. This would be a very positive move from the government. It would also benefit projects like CLA's dance show, allowing CLA to dedicate more resources and focus to audience development and marketing, thereby increasing the social and economic impact of this cultural industries activity.

In conclusion, there remains a very good opportunity for Cambodia and Cambodian artists through the creative industries. This is essential in a context where access to subsidies for the arts is very limited, and artists and arts organization are looking to earned income in order to remain viable. Fundamentally, at this stage of the revival and development of Cambodian culture and arts after the Khmer Rouge regime, the arts community and the government have shared goals, that is they wish to see increased vitality and viability of Cambodian arts. Therefore, the policy environment is conducive to creating and launching cultural industries activities. However, as seen above, this comes with risks and challenges, therefore experience such as CLA's in negotiating the cultural industries is a valuable resource and CLA must make sure to continue to reflect and share lessons learned with the wider community.

NOTE: This case study has been written by staff of Cambodian Living Arts. Therefore the authors had full access to CLA's planning and reporting data, and intimate knowledge of the decision making and strategy of the organization. CLA has also participated in consultation on the development of the National Policy for Culture, and various other forums organized by the Ministry of Culture and Fine Arts and UNESCO Phnom Penh. Information on policy matters and future plans has largely been taken from these sessions. The case study represents the interpretations and experiences of the authors.

References

International Labour Organization (2014) *Wages and Working Hours in the Textiles, Clothing, Leather and Footwear Industries*. Issues paper for discussion at the Global Dialogue Forum on Wages and Working Hours in the Textiles, Clothing, Leather and Footwear Industries (Geneva, September 23–25, 2014). Geneva: ILO.

Sam, S.-A. (1990) Preserving a cultural tradition. Ten years after the Khmer Rouge. *Cultural Survival*, 14(3).

Yale University Genocide Studies Program (2018) *Cambodian Genocide Program. The CGP, 1994–2018*. Available at: http://gsp.yale.edu/case-studies/cambodian-genocide-program (accessed April 12, 2018).

27

Safeguarding intangible cultural heritage in the Philippines

Jason Vitorillo and Maria Sharon Mapa Arriola

Arts funding policy in the Philippines: the role of the National Commission for Culture and the Arts

The Philippines is a culturally diverse country having more than a hundred ethnolinguistic groups. The number of indigenous people in the Philippines is estimated to be 17 million (UNDP 2010). Thirty-one percent of this population is concentrated in Northern Luzon (Cordillera Administrative Region) and 61 percent in Mindanao, Southern Philippines. Intangible cultural heritage in the Philippines is shaped significantly by the country's environment as an archipelago, as well as by elements both 'human' and 'natural' including the 171 living languages from the various ethnicities (Flores 2010). Republic Act 8371, commonly known as the Indigenous Peoples Rights Acts (IPRA), of 1997 recognizes the rights of indigenous people to manage their own ancestral domain, and mandates the government to recognize, protect, promote, and fulfil the rights of indigenous people.

However, in spite of the IPRA, most indigenous communities in the Philippines still suffer from poverty, historical discrimination, and marginalization. And with these come the loss of their traditional ways of life, culture, and identity. Amid globalization, modernization, and armed conflicts, especially in Mindanao, the needs and rights of indigenous people are lost in the formulation of policies and relevant decision-making.

Intangible cultural heritage conservation projects are not new in the Philippines. In May 2001, the National Commission for Culture and the Arts (NCCA), the *de facto* cultural ministry and mandated to administer public funding for the preservation, conservation, and promotion of Philippine culture and arts, was informed that the Hudhud – an Ifugao non-ritual chanting practice – was proclaimed by UNESCO as a 'Masterpiece of the Oral and Intangible Heritage for Humanity'. In response, the NCCA-Intangible Heritage Committee (NCCA-IHC) was created to safeguard, revitalize, and enhance the oral and intangible heritage, as well as coordinate and monitor the implementation of action plans. In order to do this, the NCCA together with the local government and non-government units, the provincial Department of Education, and the Ifugao community built the Hudhud Schools for Living Traditions (HSLT).

Articulated in Republic Act 7356 (RA 7356), an Act creating the National Commission for Culture and the Arts (NCCA) and establishing the National Endowment Fund for Culture and the Arts (NEFCA), the NCCA is governed by several principles. Section four of this Act defines culture being independent; free of any political and economic structures which inhibit cultural sovereignty. Culture, both tangible and intangible, is always an essential component of a community's identity. Stated in section two, the NCCA defines culture as a manifestation of the freedom of belief and of expression, and is a human right to be accorded due respect and allowed to flourish. These beliefs and expressions emulate the aspirations of the people's cultural wisdom, thereby shaping their lives and defining who they are as a community. Furthermore, as explicitly stated in Section 14.5 and 14.6 of said Act, in order for the NCCA to conserve, protect, and promote the nation's historical and cultural heritage, it should encourage the private sector to establish and maintain museums, libraries, learning centers, and archives, as well as support scholarly research into, and documentation of, Philippine cultural traditions, arts and crafts, and significant cultural movements, achievements, and personalities especially in literary, visual, and performing arts, and in mass media, as well as the various aspects of Filipino culture. All these programs and initiatives must be done in cooperation with the Departments of Education, Tourism, Interior and Local Government, Foreign Affairs, and all other concerned agencies both public and private.

According to Fairclough in the 'Council of Europe Framework Convention on the Value of Cultural Heritage for Society' (Faro Convention 2015), the conservation of culture and heritage has a reciprocal relationship with the quality of life of the community (Fairclough 2009: 32). The Faro Convention defines cultural heritage in the broadest sense, considering both intangible and tangible, perceptual and physical, action performance, custom and behavior, as well as objects and buildings. The Faro Convention takes a people-centered approach in which heritage is central to the everyday, ordinary 'real' life of people, those who construct and use heritage. It therefore sees heritage as a continuing process of creating, constructing, using, and modifying heritage rather than as an object or product. It is along these lines that the NCCA safeguards the culture of the people, and develops means for communities to grow and for their culture to develop amid societal and economic changes.

Since its creation in 1992, the NCCA, using funds from NEFCA and other sources, has been giving financial support to the preservation and development of projects for indigenous culture and arts. The NEFCA was established exclusively for the use of Philippine cultural and art programs, projects, and activities all over the country. This fund was established through the seed capital of 100 million pesos (2.5 million USD) given by the Philippine Amusement and Gaming Corporation (PAGCOR) in 1992. From the year 2005 to 2010, the NCCA through its NEFCA Division annually proposes a budget ranging from 200 to 500 million pesos (5 to 12.5 million USD). However, the average NEFCA Project Fund released by the Department of Budget and Management (DBM) is only between 150 to 170 million pesos (3.7 to 4.3 million USD). Moreover, the NEFCA Project Fund is not only allocated to the projects that the NCCA is supporting. This fund is shared by all seven affiliated cultural agencies; thus, making the budget of the NCCA much smaller. The NCCA's share of the budget is further divided among its four subcommissions.[1]

The main problem here is that the budget allocated for projects on culture and the arts is very small in comparison with the entire budget of the government, and yet the government demands that culture and arts must improve the quality of life of Filipinos towards national development. There is a huge discrepancy between how the national government says that it uses culture and arts as drivers for national progress and the amount of public funding it allocates to realize projects for this goal. The NCCA envisions a Filipino people and a nation united, empowered, and sustained by its cultural and artistic life and heritage. But how can the nation realize this vision if it lacks the means to materialize it? Even though the NCCA budget, of which 70 percent goes to funding projects and programs, is equitably distributed to the four subcommissions, the SCCTA (Subcommission on Cultural Communities and Traditional Arts) only received 24,716,918 pesos (500,000 USD) from 2005 to 2007 based on the NCCA Terminal Report for said period. Putting it in perspective, the SCCTA's budget for three years is only but a 5 percent share of the total pie; and yet it serves a huge sector of more than a hundred indigenous cultural communities all over the country.

A plethora of intangible cultural heritage (ICH) conservation projects have been implemented in the Philippines in the last 15 years. In 2014, the Medium Term Philippine Development Plan for Culture and the Arts (MTPDPCA) was formulated to create policies and initiatives to address certain needs in the cultural sector. In this chapter, we will discuss the various programs for the conservation of intangible cultural heritage supported by the National Commission for Culture and the Arts (NCCA), and will look specifically into the rationale and value behind such support. We will also investigate how the NCCA evaluates its intangible cultural heritage conservation efforts through the Hudhud Schools of Living Traditions (HSLT) of the Ifugao indigenous community. Does the NCCA use an 'integrated approach' to ICH conservation as proposed by the UNESCO Convention for the Safeguarding of the Intangible Cultural Heritage in 2003? What impact is expected from these programs?

The cultural policy model in the Philippines

Overseeing the administration of state support for indigenous culture and arts is the Subcommission on Cultural Communities and Traditional Arts (SCCTA). It is mandated to preserve and integrate culture and its various creative expressions as a dynamic part of the national cultural mechanism. Based on this, the NCCA acts as an *architect*[2] who sets the agenda, guides the communities in their projects, and nourishes the culture and arts sector through grants as part of its social democratic policies framed by its societal goals, which are to improve the quality of life towards national development.

Section five of RA 7356 pushes for the active involvement of the people in a climate of freedom and responsibility to evolve and develop their culture and identity; and thereby nurture a Filipino national culture and identity. A foremost prerequisite to this pluralistic goal is to instill respect for the cultural identity of each locality, region, or ethno-linguistic community, as well as elements assimilated from other cultures through the natural process of acculturation. In the process, the NCCA adopts the *patron* model where an arm's-length mechanism of arts funding allows the communities to present their agenda and plans for their communities' cultural development. Through evaluations and recommendations from peers and other cultural practitioners, as well as from a panel of experts, the NCCA then decides on who gets to be funded. This model places part of the responsibility in the conservation, preservation, and promotion of culture and identity on the communities. Moreover, the NCCA follows an entity-relationship model, which is a common approach to 'mapping' government cultural administrations whereby entities such as agencies are actors in the cultural policy system, where the relationships are linkages between them.

The duality of being an *architect* and a *patron* promotes a consultative approach to arts funding that generates ideas from both the national government through the NCCA, and from grassroot organizations and other stakeholders. The NCCA is very keen on and takes much pride in this approach. The NCCA is unique in this regard because it is unlike cultural agencies or ministries in other Southeast Asian countries who solely create the agenda and make decisions for culture and arts. This consultative approach encourages and empowers the communities to identify and propose which aspect of their culture will be conserved and supported. According to Dr. Jesus Peralta, the Director of the UNESCO project in safeguarding the Hudhud of the Ifugao, the NCCA does not really intervene with what the communities want, but it creates the platforms and environment for the community to make the right decisions on the conservation of its intangible cultural heritage (Peralta 2010). Through dialogues, studies and evaluations by a panel of experts, the NCCA is able to collaborate with the communities on their own capacity-building.

The NCCA provides five major types of grants that follows the core priorities or directions set by the Office of the President in consultation with the Executive Director of the NCCA. These priorities or directions revolve around the seven needs defined in the Medium Term Philippine Development Plan for Culture and Arts (MTPDPCA), namely: culture and development, culture and education, promotion of culture and arts, continued support for artistic excellence, conservation of cultural heritage, culture and peace, and culture and diplomacy.

The grant with the widest appeal is the competitive grant which is divided according to the focus of the National Committees, and given directly to the individual or group who is the proponent of the project. Second, institutional grants provide financial resources for institutionalized programs such as the Philippine International Arts Festival, National Indigenous People's Month, Filipino Heritage Month, National Artists Award, and the *Gawad Manlilikha ng Bayan* (National Living Treasures) *Award* (GAMABA). Third are grants for outreach programs, which are geared towards providing projects for marginalized communities. Fourth are grants for the Speakers Bureau Program, which provides the honoraria, transportation, and accommodation for experts who give training and workshops in response to the NCCA's mandates. Lastly, the NCCA also provides automatic financial assistance to affiliated agencies as governmental inter-agency support to promote synergy of efforts.

In its hybrid model, the NCCA identifies the themes, objectives, design, and activities of the institutionalized programs. On the other hand, groups or communities propose projects to the NCCA for the competitive grants, which goes through a series of evaluation by a panel of experts. However, the proponents of these projects have to make sure that their projects align with the agenda and fall under the categories set by the NCCA. This is to ensure that proposed and eventually funded projects are anchored on what the NCCA deems as its focus or goals, and that they follow bureaucratic rules, regulations, and procedures to ensure progression and development.

Examining the Hudhud Schools for Living Traditions

The project of safeguarding and transmitting the Hudhud chant of the Ifugao has six main components and was done over a span of three years. This project had several number of simultaneous major thrusts. The first thrust is geared towards the development of pride in the practice of the Hudhud. Through an intensified publicity campaign, the HSLT program works to teach, inspire, and nurture new generations of Ifugao chanters in key areas in the province. This new generation of Hudhud chanters are then encouraged to practice and perform through various opportunities and competitions, which in turn arouse interest and participation among the Ifugao communities both young and old. By giving awards to recognize and honor these practitioners of the Hudhud, especially the lead chanters and teachers of the Hudhud (*munhaw-e*), as well as key individuals in the community, the HSLT is able to further community participation and encourage the indigenous communities to take on more active roles in sustaining the conservation efforts. To achieve this thrust, the NCCA-Intangible Heritage Committee (NCCA-IHC), in consultation with members of the community, first identified cultural bearers among the Ifugaos, and mapped and recorded the oral traditions of the community. Once this was established, the NCCA-IHC proceeded to create the HSLTs, which is an informal education system wherein the culture bearers teach the practice to the younger generation enabling them to gain deeper insights and understanding of their traditions within their proper context.

The second major thrust of the NCCA on the HSLT is to ensure its sustainability by engaging provincial and other local government offices in the programs. Doing so allows continued research into the Ifugao culture, and in the process documents other versions of the Hudhud. One such engagement is with the provincial Department of Education that is eyed to develop a curriculum where the teaching of the chant becomes a permanent feature in schools outside the HSLT.

Lastly, to elevate the chanting of the Hudhud into a continuing social practice instead of a mere performance for competitions and demonstrations, the NCCA created the Hudhud Perpetual Award and established the Perpetual Hudhud Trophy, in effect, creating an aspiration among new generations of chanters, and again building a sense of pride on the practice of their culture. The creation of the Hudhud Perpetual Award was also a step towards moving away from merely popularizing the Hudhud in the communities, but to recognize the practice in its cultural and social context.

The proclamation of the Hudhud as a 'Masterpiece of the Oral and Intangible Heritage for Humanity' necessitated the NCCA to form a permanent body to organize and execute an action plan for the Hudhud conservation. An ad hoc committee, the Ifugao Intangible Heritage Subcommittee (IIHSC), was organized in Kiangan, Ifugao soon after to assist the NCCA in the preservation and propagation of the Hudhud. The safeguarding and transmission of the Hudhud was a three-phase program. In its first year, which is the Assessment Stage, policies and programs were analyzed and formulated; libraries for archiving were identified; a local research base was organized; cultural bearers and practitioners were contacted; a methodology in recording, archiving, and publishing was established; and meetings to train field specialists were organized. In the same year, the Department of Education (DepEd) – Division of Ifugao assisted the IIHSC in selecting five sites for the HSLT.

In its second year, which is the Collection Stage, the IIHSC held several consultative meetings with field specialists, organized field operations to research on and document the Hudhud practice, and did overall coordination of the project. This was highlighted by a two-day seminar workshop conducted by the HSLT Coordinator to teach the HSLT lead teachers in the operations of the HSLT and test the learning guides, which are articulated in the *Hudhud Teaching Guides*. This culminated in the organization of the first Hudhud Festival where each HSLT performed an episode of the Hudhud.

In the last year of the project, which was the Policy and Development Stage, aside from an on-going implementation of all intangible heritage conservation efforts including the HSLT, the NCCA worked on the institutionalization of the program in the provincial government structure. One of the critical steps initiated by the NCCA-IHC in this regard was to replace the Ifugao Intangible Heritage Subcommittee with the creation of the Ifugao Intangible Heritage Executive Committee (IIHEC) composed of the representatives of the Office of the Governor, Department of Education–Division of Ifugao, Ifugao Central Heritage Office, National Museum, and the private sector. Through the IIHEC, policies, local ordinances, and other legal instruments were formulated to support such institutionalization of the HSLT. As a result, the Ifugao Research Center was established with technical assistance from the National Museum to look into the research and documentation of all the intangible heritage of the Ifugao.

According to Jesus Peralta and Cecilia Picache, the Director and Planning Officer respectively of the project for safeguarding and transmitting the Hudhud chant of the Ifugao, in retrospect the project was a success because it was able to address the immediate and long-term cultural needs of the Ifugao, and raised awareness and transmitted the Hudhud among the communities. Specifically, it was able to integrate the Hudhud Schools for Living Tradition in the curriculum of the Department of Education–Division of Ifugao, and was able to institutionalize the Hudhud Festival. It was also able to institutionalize the Hudhud Perpetual Award into the cultural program of Ifugao. It published and distributed two children's books on the practice to libraries, cultural institutions, and research centers. And most importantly, the NCCA-IHC and IIHSC were able to turn over the project to the Department of Education–Division of Ifugao for continued implementation of the HSLT and Annual Hudhud Festival, thus ensuring its sustainability.

The benefits and challenges of the NCCA's consultative approach

The Hudhud Schools for Living Traditions (HSLT) is just one of many ways to conserve intangible cultural heritage. When a program or project provides a platform for cultural transmission or exchange from one generation to another, one can argue that a community is continuously being built and in the process this community defines who it is. Furthermore, as mentioned earlier, the HSLT has been integrated into the provincial curricula of the Department of Education–Division of Ifugao. This integration allows for a collective undertaking in building the Ifugao community, and reinforces the grassroots aspects of the approach taken by the NCCA – that it is the community that decides on what aspects of and how it will conserve and develop its culture and practices within its socio-cultural context. This emphasizes the importance of intangible cultural heritage enabling different groups to assert their cultural identities, thereby allowing humanity to maintain its diversity (Kurin 2004). The integrated approach is very important in the efforts on community building and identity construction because it puts people at the center of cultural activity and conservation efforts. It protects the environment and circumstances on which the community recreates its cultural expressions. Although the difficulty of defining and keeping what is authentic is always present, the integrated approach nevertheless helps the community to recognize and respond to this issue. Therefore, the HSLT is a concrete example that highlights the very mandate and models of cultural funding of the NCCA, that unlike the other subcommissions, the SCCTA focuses on cultural preservation rather than on the economic gains from cultural tourism. The indigenous community is the core value of the program.

However, in spite of the achievements and success of the HSLT, and evidences of a consultative approach taken by the NCCA-IHC in the process of identifying cultural bearers, mapping the Ifugao intangible heritage, and creating the HSLT, one can still question whether the integrated approach used in the Hudhud HSLT project ensures that the voice and sentiments of the community are indeed heard. In the midst of institutionalizing the HSLT, where can we hear the voice of the Ifugao community, and is it this voice that dictates the direction of the conservation efforts?

This then puts into question the dual approach in the model of arts funding of the NCCA. Because of its duality as an architect and a patron, the NCCA needs to balance on one hand a top-down approach where certain themes, directives, or agenda are set in place, and such become the guiding framework in which projects are considered for support; and on the other hand a grassroots approach where it allows the communities to propose an idea or concept of a project or program that will benefit them. As Dr. Peralta argued, the NCCA does not intervene with what the communities want, but in the process of creating the platforms and environment for the community to voice their thoughts, these are funneled into a framework set by the NCCA; and thus, must abide by the political and bureaucratic purposes of such framework. Such a situation, it can be argued, is even more marked in the process of institutionalization where the different governmental agencies are the ones setting the agenda as they see fit. One only needs to look at the composition of the IIHEC to see this issue, and ask if there is any value in institutionalization for the communities.

According to Mark Dela Cruz of the Program Monitoring and Evaluation Division of NCCA, to address this issue the NCCA requires from field monitors regular reports, both verbal and written, with photo documentations and at times video recordings, to document the voice and sentiments of the community (Dela Cruz 2016). On top of this, the NCCA appoints community cluster representatives who are elected by the members of their respective clusters to officially represent them within the structure of the NCCA. These representatives hold an important role in this cultural engagement. They hold the responsibility as well as the power to voice the issues and concerns of their respective communities, bring them to the attention of the NCCA, and propose resolutions together with their fellow representatives.

Furthermore, Dela Cruz shares that field monitors who are assigned to the HSLT conduct their own monitoring and reports in written and video formats, and present these during the committee meetings of the NCCA. They then cascade agreed resolutions to the communities where the communities then discuss the details of the resolution with the lead of their community cluster representatives. The NCCA also holds special gatherings for indigenous people such as the Dayaw Cultural Festival and School for Living Traditions Summit for the purpose of bringing the communities to discuss pertinent issues.

However, there is a problem here with regards to the dual approach in the hybrid model of the NCCA. As Madden (2009) correctly notes, it is not necessarily the set-up of an additional institution but the actual degree of independence from the government that makes for effective civil society participation, and thus good governance in cultural policy. Thus, when we look into the factors that impact arts funding, the complexity in intangible heritage conservation, cultural policy, and cultural governance of institutionalized initiatives such as the Hudhud Schools for Living Traditions, Holden's ecology concept (2016) seems most appropriate. This is because it recognizes the multi-dimensionality of culture within a society and state apparatus become increasingly important in many low-income countries or those emerging in conflict (Brennert 2016) – which parallels the situation of indigenous people in the Philippines. The ecology lens is a viable tool to analyze cultural governance, and is appropriate to apply in the context of the Philippines, because the ecological approach argues for the need of cultural policy to concern itself with a broad set of concerns from a national to a regional or local scale. This approach asks questions about relationships and connections, causes, and effects (Holden 2016). The ecology concept highlights interdependencies where governance looks at how interdependencies are managed, and culture defines the terms of such management.

The problem with cultural governance, as summed up by Holden (2006), is that cultural policy is a closed conversation among experts. Politics has struggled to understand culture, and failed to engage with it effectively. This issue stems from the fact that cultural governance is still a concept that defies precise definition. Baltà, Copic and Srakar (2014) argued that if the term is defined as 'governance of culture' then it is composed of two sub-areas: the new approaches to the formulation and implementation of sectorial cultural policy that are inspired by the interaction of the state, the civil society, and the market; and the improvements in the steering and supervision of cultural organizations that lead to efficiently, expertly, independently, and transparently-operating cultural organizations.

On one side of the wide concept of cultural governance is a narrow sense of a sectoral concept of governance that points to cultural policy based on the relationship of culture and administration. This also concerns the governance of cultural institutions, which entails the direct and indirect involvement of government (Baltà et al. 2014). Mercer (2012: 4) argues that even in the narrow sense cultural governance should be put in a broader political context referring to the burning issues of the modern world: the shift from government to governance as 'our joint and uneven terms of engagement with the complex field of economic, social, political, and cultural power relations in which we are all "stakeholders"'. The focus then is not how cultural policy empowers civil society, or in the context of the Ifugao, how the government through the Hudhud Schools for Living Traditions empower the communities. The focus should be shifted to how the communities, in a collaborative manner, work with the government in shaping and articulating cultural policy.

Moreover, the duality approach – not necessarily the consultative approach – can create confusion that may lead to various problems, misinterpretations, or misrepresentations of communities. Although the implementation of the Hudhud Schools for Living Traditions goes through several evaluation and assessment processes, and representations and conversations with various stakeholders, there still is the concern as to whether what is presented at the discussion table truly represents the needs and concerns of the communities. Bernan Joseph Corpuz (2010), the head of the Planning and Policy Office of the NCCA, explains that the vision of the committees is aligned to the vision of the government. Both visions are married and weaved in this duality approach, which is framed and guided by the main thrust of the government on development of communities and their cultural practices. Corpuz (2010) further explains that if programs proposed by the communities through the committees do not align to this governmental thrust, then the NCCA cannot and will not give funding or technical support. Fortunately, what the culture and arts sector often, if not always, identifies aligns with the government's goals specifically on the development of the Filipino national culture and identity.

But this clearly shows the assumption of the NCCA that the culture and arts sector will identify initiatives that align to the government's goals. What happens if the indigenous communities wish to push for something different and not aligned to the government's goal, then will public funding and support stop?

It is precisely this kind of mindset – that community initiatives or projects should align to the national agenda in order for them to be funded or supported – that is a cause of concern, and in effect takes away the democratic process of cultural governance. It also seems to leave the planning for culture and the arts to chance, hoping that it aligns with the government's goals so that it will receive funding, or that the culture and arts sector deliberately aligns its projects to secure funding regardless of their actual value to the community – basically playing the funding game. This brings into question if the communities seek to make their projects aligned with government interests to gain funding rather than working out what they actually need or want.

What if the community's definition of Filipino culture and identity is different to that of which the government subscribes to or identifies, then will such a definition be set aside? This is very problematic given the Philippine's geographical nature and ethno-linguistic composition. There is potential here for the culture and arts sector to go against the very mandate and purpose of the NCCA, and this raises the questions of whose value is actually being valued.

Landry and Matarasso, in the British context, defined democratization of culture as a perspective that focuses on the 'civilizing value of the arts' and prioritizes the general public's access to mainly European forms of high culture (Landry and Matarasso 1999). With this perspective, the government funds projects, programs, or platforms that give audiences access to arts and culture experiences that otherwise they would not have access to due to lack of income or resources. In the case of the Hudhud Schools for Living Traditions, this perspective pushes for the funding of such programs to invigorate the community and give them the means to transmit the cultural practice for the greater community to learn and experience. The success of this policy and efforts is measured by the socio-economic and demographic attendance to major cultural works. Thus, the NCCA looks into: (1) the increasing number of Schools for Living Traditions in the region or province; (2) the increasing number of students who attended and are attending the HSLTs; (3) the increasing participation of adults and children to the annual Hudhud Festival and chanting competitions; (4) the growing number of cultural bearers or *munhaw-es*; and (5) the creation and institutionalization of the Perpetual Award Trophy for the practice to perpetuate.

This is not to say that these should not be the indicators of success of an intangible cultural heritage conservation project. Instead it raises questions about how true and relevant these numbers are to the communities, and about the preservation of its cultural practices and identity. This is still a top-down approach to culture, and in some ways the authorities are imposing or dictating the success of the initiative on the community. The NCCA's consultative approach is in question if such is the case of monitoring the development and evaluating the success of the HSLTs and other intangible cultural heritage conservation projects. Success is therefore argued as not simply about providing the public audience or members of the community an access to arts and cultural works and practices, but more importantly it recognizes the role and voice of various cultures and communities, and includes this in the decision-making processes in policy making.

Gattinger (2011) opens three main ideas for debate and discussion on these perspectives. First, democratization of culture and cultural democracy can be most effectively pursued by public arts funders if they do so through the lens of governance and multi-level governance. In this context, governance means encompassing, non-hierarchical, decentralized, and collaborative policy-making approaches between interdependent public, private, and civic actors (2011: 4). This perspective pushes the NCCA to engage in more long-term collaborations with local government units, cultural agencies and institutions, the Department of Education, non-government organizations, private corporations, and most importantly the communities. It takes this ecosystem of stakeholders to plan on what intangible cultural heritage will be conserved, and whether it is of interest and relevance to the community – not necessarily to set aside its economic value, but more for its intrinsic value. Such policy will also somehow unburden the Philippine government through the NCCA to shoulder the financial and technical needs of the HSLT. Because otherwise it may be difficult for the NCCA to sustain the operations of the HSLT, and in this debate may be counterproductive because cultural change works at a faster pace, actors change, and resources remain scarce or limited.

Second, public arts funders should carefully analyze the possible repercussions for democratization of culture and cultural democracy of making fundamental changes to existing governance arrangements between business, government, and society (Gattinger 2011: 4). Third, public arts funders would do well to identify the multi-level governance arrangements best suited to pursuing democratization of culture and cultural democracy. This involves identifying the most supportive coordination arrangements for democratization of culture and cultural democracy and identifying which aspects of democratization of culture and cultural democracy should be pursued by which level of government (Gattinger 2011: 5). Thus, there is a need for the NCCA and other stakeholders to develop a more comprehensive, robust, and comparable methodologies and a more critical evaluation framework for evaluating the HSLT, which will acknowledge the complex issues associated with intangible cultural heritage conservation, and ensure that the voice of the community is always heard.

The NCCA is now in a conundrum. There are two potential approaches which the NCCA can pursue in the future. On the one hand, the NCCA can adopt a democratization of culture perspective and on the other it can be open to a more pluralistic approach to intangible cultural heritage conservation. Given the duality of its approach, and the strengths and weakness of its funding model, it remains to be seen how the NCCA will balance both perspectives.

Conclusion

This paper has argued that more often than not cultural practitioners and creators focus on satisfying the policy demands of the NCCA to gain its support. But the reality is, the NCCA will not be able to truly support communities until it has a broader and clearer articulation of what a 'democratic' consensus is. Using the argument of Holden (2006), publicly funded programs for culture and the arts generate three types of value: intrinsic value, instrumental value, and institutional value. But politics, in this case the NCCA, cares more about the social outcomes – Peralta (2016) argues that the NCCA does not look at the economic implications and viability of the HSLT – but the communities may have a completely different set of concerns, which may result in a misalignment of programs to the concerns they are designed to address; thus resulting in a dysfunctional system.

Holden (2006) argues that the 'cultural system' has become a closed conversation between professionals and politicians, with too much emphasis placed on satisfying funders, rather than on achieving the self-generated purposes of the cultural organizations themselves, or on engaging the public. The solution therefore is a better understanding of the different types of value that culture creates, and understanding what is important to the communities and the NCCA. The community and other stakeholders, both private and public, have to be accountable.

In all its efforts in forming national committees to safeguard and transmit intangible cultural heritage, specifically the Hudhud chant through education and research, documentation and awareness, and capacity-building, one can definitely argue that the HSLT program is a resounding success. The NCCA's consultative approach as a mechanism for cultural democracy and governance allowed the voice of the Ifugao community to be heard. There is a clear recognition of this voice and an alleviation of the cultural value without the pressure to compare to other values nor for justification. There is a clear pattern that fosters participation in different levels by the community. The approach taken by the NCCA through the HSLT allowed democratic participation that generated a sense of belonging in the conservation efforts. But more evaluative study needs to be done on a long-term basis because the articulated success is from the lens of the NCCA, using its own evaluation tools and methods. We would be curious to know if such success holds true in the eyes of the indigenous communities.

The Faro Convention promotes a broader, living heritage aligned with a sense of place, landscape, sustainability and comprehensiveness, and context, but which might not allow us to 'keep' everything physically (Fairclough 2009: 34–5). This now is an approach that the NCCA, together with the other stakeholders of the HSLT, needs to critically consider if it wishes for the sustainability of the HSLT and the SLT program. Moreover, the language of cultural policy must be scrutinized. The NCCA needs to further its mean to understand the communities' needs and desires to create value for themselves. Although its consultative approach and 'hybrid' model addresses these, such an approach and model need to be reviewed, evaluated, and developed to be more responsive to the communities. What are the other means for the communities to generate their preferences and ideas, and contribute to the creation of cultural value? The NCCA therefore needs to realize that solutions to intangible cultural heritage conservation issues are best generated by people who are closest to the issues because they deal with the dynamic relationships and changes on the ground, rather than from a national office in Manila.

Notes

1 The NCCA has four subcommissions made up of 19 national committees composed of artists and cultural workers from both the public and private sector, representing different cultural and non-government organizations. The four subcommissions are: Subcommission on the Arts (SCA), Subcommission on Cultural Heritage (SCH), Subcommission on Cultural Dissemination (SCD), and Subcommission on Cultural Communities and Traditional Arts (SCCTA). The SCCTA is further divided into national committees on Northern Cultural Communities, Central Cultural Communities, and Southern Cultural Communities.

2 Models of cultural policy. Adapted from Harry Hillman-Chartrand and Claire McCaughey (1989) 'The arm's length principle and the arts: an international perspective – past, present and future,' in Cumming, M. and Schuster, M. (eds.), *Who's to Pay for the Arts? The International Search for Models of Support.*

References

Balta, J., Copic, V., and Srakar, A. (2014) Literature review on cultural governance and cities. Kult-ur. *Revista interdisciplinària sobre la cultura de la ciutat,* 1(1): 183–200.

Brennert, K. T. (2016) *The Arts Council Formula: Exploring Cultural Governance Solutions in Cambodia.* International Conference on Cultural Policy Research, 2016.

Corpuz, B. (2010) Interviewed by author, August 31.

Dela Cruz, M. (2016) Interviewed by author, April 29.

Fairclough, G. (2009) New heritage frontiers. In: Therond, D. and Trigona, A. (eds.), *Heritage and Beyond.* Strasbourg, France: Council of Europe Publishing, pp. 29–42.

Flores, A. (2010) Interviewed by author, August 23.

Gattinger, M. (2011) *Democratization of Culture, Cultural Democracy and Governance.* Whitehorse, Yukon: Canadian Public Arts Funders.

Holden, J. (2006) Cultural policy is a closed conversation among experts. What culture needs is a democratic mandate from the public… *Cultural Value and the Crisis of Legitimacy: Why Culture Needs a Democratic Mandate.* London: Demos.

Holden, J. (2016) *The Elephant and the Flea. Ensuring the Future of the Arts in London Depends on Understanding Culture as an Ecosystem.* London Essays, No.4.

Kurin, R. (2004) Safeguarding intangible cultural heritage in the 2003 UNESCO Convention: a critical appraisal. *Museum International,* 56(1–2): 66–77.

Landry, C. and Matarasso, F. (1999). Balancing act: twenty-one strategic dilemmas in cultural policy (Note no. 4 on Cultural Policies Research and Development Unit Policy). Strasbourg, France: Council of Europe Publishing.

Madden, C. (2009) The independence of government arts funding: a review. *D'Art Topics in Arts Policy,* No. 9: 16, International Federation of Arts Councils and Culture Agencies, Sydney.

Mercer, C. (2012) *From Data to Wisdom: Building the Knowledge Base For Cultural Policy.* 11th Annual Experts Assembly of the Council of Europe. http://www.culturalpolicies.net/web/files243/en/Mercer_Helsinki.pdf.

Peralta, J. (2010) Interviewed by author, September 7.

Peralta, J. (2016) Interviewed by author, April 14.

UNDP (2010) *Indigenous Peoples in the Philippines. Fast Facts.* United Nations Development Programme, Philippines.

Index

Taylor & Francis Group
an informa business

Taylor & Francis eBooks

www.taylorfrancis.com

A single destination for eBooks from Taylor & Francis with increased functionality and an improved user experience to meet the needs of our customers.

90,000+ eBooks of award-winning academic content in Humanities, Social Science, Science, Technology, Engineering, and Medical written by a global network of editors and authors.

TAYLOR & FRANCIS EBOOKS OFFERS:

- A streamlined experience for our library customers
- A single point of discovery for all of our eBook content
- Improved search and discovery of content at both book and chapter level

REQUEST A FREE TRIAL

support@taylorfrancis.com

Routledge
Taylor & Francis Group

CRC Press
Taylor & Francis Group

For Product Safety Concerns and Information please contact our EU
representative GPSR@taylorandfrancis.com
Taylor & Francis Verlag GmbH, Kaufingerstraße 24, 80331 München, Germany

www.ingramcontent.com/pod-product-compliance
Ingram Content Group UK Ltd.
Pitfield, Milton Keynes, MK11 3LW, UK
UKHW050051200926
475702UK00019B/2787

* 9 7 8 0 3 6 7 6 5 9 6 5 3 *